mdeltree

```
mdeltree msdosdirectory [msdosdirectory ...]
```
The mdeltree command deletes one or more MS-DOS directories. It is similar to the DOS DELTREE command.

mkdir

```
mkdir [-p] [-m mode] [--parents] [--mode=mode]
➥ [--help] [--version] directory ...
```
The mkdir command creates one or more directories.

more

```
more [-dlfs] [--number] [+number] [file ...]
```
The more command displays one or more files, screen-by-screen, and allows for searching and jumping to an arbitrary location in the file.

mount

```
mount -a [-rvw] [-t vfstype]
mount [-rvw] [-o options [,...]] device | dir
mount [-rvw] [-t vfstype] [-o options] device dir
```
The mount command mounts a file system to a specified directory.

nslookup

```
nslookup [host | - [server]]
```
The nslookup command queries a DNS nameserver. It can be run in interactive mode. If no hostname is provided, then the program enters interactive mode. By default, the DNS server, as specified in /etc/resolv.conf, is used unless otherwise specified. If you want to specify a server but not look up a specified host, you must provide a - in place of the host.

passwd

```
passwd [-S] [-d delim-list] [file...]
```
The passwd command changes a user's password. When run by the root user, it can be used to change a specific user's password by providing the username as an argument.

ping

```
ping [-fR] [-c number] [-i seconds]
➥ [-s packetsize] host
```
The ping command sends echo request packets to a network host to see if it is accessible on the network.

ps

```
ps [lumaxwr] [txx] [pid ...]
```
The ps command displays status reports for currently running processes. Given a specific process ID as an argument, ps displays information about that particular process. Without options or arguments, ps displays the current user's processes.

pwd

```
pwd
```
The pwd command displays the name of the current directory.

rm

```
rm [-firR] [--force] [--interactive] [--recursive]
➥ file | directory ...
```
The rm command deletes one or more files or directories.

rmdir

```
rmdir [-p] [--parents] directory ...
```
The rmdir command deletes empty directories.

rsh

```
rsh [-Knx] [-l username] host [command]
```
The rsh command opens a shell on a remote system. If a command is provided, the command is executed on the remote host, the results are returned, and the connection is terminated.

su

```
su [-flmp] [-c command] [-s shell] [--login] [--fast]
➥ [--preserve-environment] [--command=command]
➥ [--shell=shell] [-] [user]
```
The su command runs a new shell under different user and group IDs. If no user is specified, the new shell will run as the root user.

tar

```
tar [-crtuxz] [-f file] [--file file] [--create]
➥ [--delete] [--preserve] [--append] [--same-owner]
➥ [--list] [--update] [--extract] [--get] [--gzip]
➥ [--ungzip] [file | directory ...]
```
The tar command creates an archive file of one or more files or directories.

top

```
top [d delay] [q] [c] [S] [s]
```
The top command displays a regularly updated report of processes running on the system.

unzip

```
unzip [-cflptuz] file[.zip]
```
The unzip command manipulates and extracts ZIP archives.

zcat

```
zcat [-f] [file ...]
```
The zcat command uncompresses one or more compressed files and displays the results to the standard output. If no files are specified, then the standard input is uncompressed and displayed.

zip

```
zip [-efFgmrSu@] [ zipfile [ file1 file2 ...]]
```
The zip command creates a Zip archive from one or more files and directories.

zmore

```
zmore [file ...]
```
The zmore command displays the contents of compressed text files, one screen at a time, allowing searching in much the same way as the more command. If no files are specified, the standard input will be used.

Mastering Red Hat Linux 7.1

Mastering™ Red Hat® Linux 7.1

Arman Danesh

SYBEX®

San Francisco • Paris • Düsseldorf • Soest • London

Associate Publisher: Richard J. Staron
Acquisitions and Developmental Editor: Ellen L. Dendy
Editor: Linda Recktenwald
Production Editor: Leslie E.H. Light
Technical Editor: Elizabeth Zinkann
Book Designer: Kris Warrenburg
Graphic Illustrator: Tony Jonick
Electronic Publishing Specialist: Judy Fung
Proofreaders: Nanette Duffy, Amey Garber, Emily Hsuan, David Nash, Laurie O'Connell, Yariv Rabinovich, Nancy Riddiough
Indexer: Ted Laux
Cover Designer: Design Site
Cover Photographer: Jack D. Myers, Design Site

Library of Congress Card Number: 2001091747

ISBN: 0-7821-2927-7

Screen reproductions produced with either The GIMP (a graphics package included with Red Hat Linux 7.1) or Capture Express 2000.

Capture Express 2000 is a trademark of Insight Software Solutions Inc.

SYBEX is a registered trademark of SYBEX Inc.

Mastering is a trademark of SYBEX Inc.

Netscape Communications, the Netscape Communications logo, Netscape, and Netscape Navigator are trademarks of Netscape Communications Corporation.

Netscape Communications Corporation has not authorized, sponsored, endorsed, or approved this publication and is not responsible for its content. Netscape and the Netscape Communications Corporate Logos are trademarks and trade names of Netscape Communications Corporation. All other product names and/or logos are trademarks of their respective owners.

TRADEMARKS: SYBEX has attempted throughout this book to distinguish proprietary trademarks from descriptive terms by following the capitalization style used by the manufacturer.

The author and publisher have made their best efforts to prepare this book, and the content is based upon final-release software whenever possible. Portions of the manuscript may be based upon pre-release versions supplied by software manufacturer(s). The author and the publisher make no representation or warranties of any kind with regard to the completeness or accuracy of the contents herein and accept no liability of any kind including but not limited to performance, merchantability, fitness for any particular purpose, or any losses or damages of any kind caused or alleged to be caused directly or indirectly from this book.

Photographs and illustrations used in this book have been downloaded from publicly accessible file archives and are used in this book for news reportage purposes only to demonstrate the variety of graphics resources available via electronic access. Text and images available over the Internet may be subject to copyright and other rights owned by third parties. Online availability of text and images does not imply that they may be reused without the permission of rights holders, although the Copyright Act does permit certain unauthorized reuse as fair use under 17 U.S.C. Section 107.

Manufactured in the United States of America

10 9 8 7 6 5 4 3 2 1

To the people who are using GNU and Linux to help bridge the Digital Divide. For more information, navigate to www.digitaldividenetwork.org.

ACKNOWLEDGMENTS

Computer books, even revisions, are a group effort. As an author, I am only a small part of this. First, let me thank the original author, Arman Danesh, for listening to my input during the development of this revision. The people whom Sybex brought together on this book are a well-oiled team. Leslie Light made sure that the project stayed on track in every detail. Linda Recktenwald brought diverse inputs together and added her own common sense to the final product. Elizabeth Zinkann brought a unique perspective, which makes this book useful for the widest possible audience. The book could not go to press without the gracious efforts of the other members of the team, including Dick Staron, Kristine O'Callaghan, Judy Fung, Nanette Duffy, Emily Hsuan, Laurie O'Connell, Yariv Rabinovich, Nancy Riddiough, and Ted Laux.

Thanks especially goes to Ellen Dendy, for bringing us together on this venture, making sure that everything went smoothly with the rest of the team.

On the home front, thank you, Nancy, for your constant love and support.

—*Michael Jang*

CONTENTS AT A GLANCE

CONTENTS

Appendices

INTRODUCTION

Thank you for buying this book, and welcome to the world of Linux. As one of the few alternatives to Microsoft operating systems on affordable desktop-class personal computers, Linux has gained notoriety and, more recently, acclaim as an example of what can be done by a group of motivated people without any fiscal incentive.

Linux is a freely distributable, efficient, fast operating system that offers the power of Unix—once the domain of expensive servers and workstations—on hardware affordable to the budget-conscious home computer user. This has sparked a mini-revolution in the computer world leading to acceptance of free software for a wide range of tasks—from mission-critical Web sites to corporate information systems infrastructure to education applications.

This book is designed as an introduction to the installation and use of Linux based on Red Hat Linux 7.1. Red Hat Linux 7.1 is a widely used version of Linux that is well suited to use on server systems, as well as Linux workstations and desktop computers. Any operating system with the breadth of features and capabilities offered by Linux cannot be covered completely in a single book. Still, this book provides the sound knowledge of Linux, and Red Hat in particular, needed for users to move on and learn more on their own as they use Linux in their everyday work.

Who Should Read This Book?

This book is really designed for anyone who uses a PC. Although Linux may not yet have all the ease-of-use refinements found in commercial desktop operating systems such as Windows 95/98/Me and the Mac OS, Linux can be used by almost anyone and mastered by anyone who can master Windows.

Having said that, learning to use any operating system is always easier if you already possess some basic computer knowledge, including an understanding of the difference between a hard disk and RAM, an understanding of the basic configuration (in Windows) of peripherals such as video cards and sound cards, and a sense of how data is organized and stored by computers (for instance, the difference between directories, subdirectories, and files).

This book aims to open the world of Linux to the average computer user. In doing so, a passing familiarity with Windows (or the Mac OS) and basic PC hardware is assumed. Without this assumption, this book would be a primer on basic computing concepts rather than a robust introduction to the Linux operating system.

If you are already comfortable using a Windows or Macintosh system and you haven't experimented with the DOS prompt, it would be helpful to do so before diving into the world of Linux, where the command line is more powerful, and therefore more heavily used, than in the Windows arena.

If you are already a power user of Windows, then you are more than ready to become a power user of Linux. Just as this book will make the everyday computer user proficient at getting their work done using Linux, it will help you become an advanced Linux user.

This book also has something to offer for the SOHO (Small Office/Home Office) user or manager of a small network. You will learn how to use Linux in many situations in your office environment, in roles that include file server, intranet Web server, and router.

What You Need to Use This Book

To use this book, you will need access to a personal computer with the following minimum specifications:

- A Pentium CPU or higher (In theory, you can run Linux on a 386 system, but the performance will likely be poor enough that it isn't worthwhile for most users.)

- 32MB of RAM or more (You will notice a significant performance gain if Linux has 64MB or more of memory.)

- A hard disk with at least 1GB of free disk space; 1.5GB for the Workstation or Laptop configurations (If you can afford 3GB or more, this will greatly enhance your freedom to experiment with Linux and Linux applications.)

- A CD-ROM drive (preferably an ATAPI/IDE CD-ROM or SCSI CD-ROM drive)

- A backup of your current system in case you need to recover existing data or applications

- A video card and VGA or better monitor

- A keyboard and mouse

You may also want to have the following options:

- A printer (Opt for a PCL or PostScript printer if you have a choice.)

- A sound card and speakers

- A telephone modem, ISDN modem, or other high-speed connection

How This Book Is Organized

This book is divided into seven sections:

Welcome to Linux   This section introduces you to Linux as an operating system and as the foundation of the GNU General Public License software model. It looks at the most popular distributions (versions) of Linux and helps you make preparations to install Linux on your system.

Installing Red Hat Linux 7.1   This section covers the installation of a stand-alone Linux system. It includes a discussion of how to prepare to install Linux and special installations (such as on systems with no CD-ROM drive).

Using Desktop Environments in Red Hat Linux 7.1   This section looks at the use of X Windows with the GNOME desktop manager (the standard Red Hat Linux GUI). This discussion includes an overview of some common X Windows applications.

Mastering the Essentials   This section describes a range of essential skills needed to truly master Linux. Topics covered include file management, system configuration, and printers and peripherals.

Basic Connectivity   This section explains how to connect a Linux system to the Internet using a dial-up connection. Topics covered include accessing the World Wide Web and working with e-mail.

Using Linux in the Small Office/Home Office (SOHO)   As an inexpensive but powerful computing environment, Linux is well-suited to many small or home office tasks. This section looks at the installation of Red Hat Linux 7.1 in a networked office environment and the use of Linux as a file or print server for Unix and Windows networks and will give you an awareness of basic security issues when using Linux in a networked environment. Finally, this section examines DOS and Windows compatibility and integration in Linux, which allows many organizations to migrate from their current Windows environments to Linux without sacrificing their current investment in software and applications.

Using Red Hat Linux 7.1 As a Web and E-Mail Server   In addition to being an ideal file and print server for the SOHO, Linux can be used to create robust enterprise Web and mail servers. This section describes how to set up Linux-based Web and mail servers.

If you already have some experience with Linux, you probably can skip straight to the second section of the book, "Installing Red Hat Linux 7.1," and begin installing a Linux system. If you have never used Linux before, start at the beginning with "Welcome to Linux" to get your feet wet and become comfortable with the world of Linux and its dynamic nature. Whatever your background, though, always remember that computers are tools that bring added power to your work, and Linux is a great way to enhance that role.

PART I

Welcome to Linux

CHAPTER

ONE

What Is Linux?

■ Linux History

■ Linux As an Operating System

■ Linux As Free Software

■ Commercial Applications for Linux

If you have made it this far—buying this book, wading through the front-matter, and looking at the table of contents—then you probably have some idea of what Linux and the Linux phenomenon are all about. If you don't, read on.

Linux is a truly amazing development in the computer industry. It shows that quality software isn't necessarily dependent on the financial blessing of the commercial software industry. The history of Linux illustrates how free software can evolve, grow, and become an attractive alternative to the commercial software packages with which most of you are familiar.

In addition, the technical excellence of Linux shows why it is a serious contender against rival operating systems from Microsoft, Apple, Novell, and IBM. As it is also handling more demanding applications, it is also a serious contender against rival Unix-derivative operating systems such as Solaris, HP-UX, and SCO-Unix for larger businesses.

This chapter paints a quick picture of the history of Linux and then looks at the key features that make Linux a powerful alternative operating system for a variety of technical applications. Finally, this chapter looks at the free software model used in Linux and examines its implications for the whole software industry.

Linux History

The emergence of Linux onto the computing scene grew out of the Unix culture. As an operating system (really a variety of different operating systems with similar features), Unix long predates the era of desktop computers; Unix was first developed in 1969 when minicomputers and mainframe computers were the norm in the corporate world. Unix continues to be widely used in this corporate environment, as well as in the educational world, although it is also often found running on today's client-server intranet networks.

The problem with Unix, historically, has been its inaccessibility to programmers and developers who want to work with it outside the context of corporate or university computing centers. While versions of Unix have long been available for PCs, they never had the grace or power of the operating systems available for minicomputers, mainframes, and today's servers. In addition, the early commercial versions of Unix were costly, sometimes costing more than the PC hardware they were destined to run on.

This lack of accessibility ultimately gave birth to Linux as a means to make a Unix-like operating system available on a widespread basis.

Richard Stallman and the Free Software Foundation (FSF) began work on this alternative operating system in the mid-1980s. By the end of that decade, they had developed functional alternatives to every major Unix component except the *kernel*. Linus Torvalds at the University of Helsinki in Finland developed the original Linux kernel in 1991. The combined work became the Linux you know today.

Torvalds originally intended to develop Linux as a hobby. Early versions of Linux didn't have consumers in mind; instead, they provided the barest bones of functionality to allow Unix programmers the apparent joy of programming the kernel. As the core of the operating system, the kernel keeps everything running smoothly—without a stable, powerful kernel, you don't *have* an operating system.

But as programmers integrated the work of the FSF with the Torvalds kernel, the base software for a complete operating system emerged. It became clear to those involved that Linux was evolving to the state where it could respectably be called an operating system. In March 1992, version 1.0 of the kernel came into being, marking the first official release of Linux. At this point, Linux ran most of the common Unix tools from compilers to networking software to X Windows.

Linux continues to evolve as the preeminent Unix-clone operating system for PCs. Hardware support is now broad, including the most popular and common peripherals; performance is strong, giving many PCs power comparable to that of mid-range workstations such as Sun Microsystems' SPARC systems. Linux is even now ported to the PowerPC and Compaq Alpha platforms, among others. Although technically today's Linux is not Unix because it fails to qualify for the brand name, Linux is functionally equivalent to Unix in almost every important way.

Linux As an Operating System

The term "Linux" is actually somewhat vague. "Linux" is used in two ways: specifically to refer to the kernel itself—the heart of any version of Linux—and more generally to refer to any collection of applications that run on the kernel, usually referred to as a *distribution*. The kernel's job is to provide the basic environment in which applications can run, including the basic interfaces with hardware and the systems for managing tasks and currently running programs.

In the specific sense, there is only one current version of Linux at any one time: the current revision of the kernel. Torvalds keeps the kernel as his domain in the world of Linux development, leaving all the applications and services that sit on top of the kernel to any of the thousands of other Linux developers in the world.

In the general meaning of the term "Linux," referring to cohesive collections of applications that run on top of the Linux kernel, there are numerous versions of Linux. Each distribution has its own unique characteristics, including different installation methods, different collections of features, and different upgrade paths. But since all distributions are fundamentally Linux, in almost every case an application that works with a current version of one distribution will work with a current version of another distribution.

NOTE Chapter 2, "Choosing a Distribution," contains a complete discussion of Linux distributions.

The interesting thing about this dichotomous use of the term "Linux" is that it exactly parallels the same confused usage of the term "operating system." For consumers, an operating system has come to mean a large collection of applications centered around a kernel. This is what Windows 95, 98, Me, NT, and 2000 are. This is what the Macintosh OS is.

In a purist, technical sense, an operating system is a much smaller core kernel that provides those basic system functions needed to develop any application.

In both ways, Linux is an operating system. One of the features of the Linux kernel that sets it apart from other consumer operating systems designed to run on desktop PCs is that it is both multitasking and multiuser.

A Multitasking Operating System

You are probably familiar with the term "multitasking," even if you are not really sure what it means.

When desktop computing graduated from Windows 3.1 to Windows 95, the multitasking capabilities of the then-new Windows 95 were among its biggest claims to fame.

To say that a system can multitask is to say that it can appear to be running more than one application, or process, at a time. For example, the system can print a document, copy a file, and dial into the Internet while the user is comfortably typing in a word processing program. Even with these background tasks happening, the foreground word processor should not freeze up or be unusable.

This is the wonder of multitasking: It allows a computer with a single processor to appear to be performing multiple tasks simultaneously. Of course, a single CPU can execute only a single instruction at a time—that is, only one action can be taking place at any one time. Multitasking creates the appearance of simultaneous activity by switching rapidly between tasks as the demands of those processes dictate.

When multitasking works well, a user running a word processor while several other things happen will not be aware of the extra work the computer is doing. All processes will seem to be running smoothly and the computer will be responsive.

Historically, Unix systems have been much better than Windows at multitasking; Unix is able to run large numbers of simultaneous applications in a way that made it an ideal fit for large corporate servers and high-powered workstations. Today, only Windows 2000, and its predecessor Windows NT 4.0, can really claim to offer a similarly robust multitasking implementation. Even Windows 95/98/Me, despite all of its fanfare, has trouble effectively handling large numbers of simultaneous processes.

To take things further, Linux, like Windows NT and Windows 2000, offers support for computers with multiple processors, such as dual-Pentium III systems. These systems can in fact perform two actions at exactly the same time. Combining multitasking with multiple processors greatly increases the number of simultaneous applications a computer can run smoothly.

A Multiuser Operating System

Even more important than being a multitasking operating system, Linux—like all versions of Unix and Unix clones—is a multiuser operating system.

All consumer versions of Windows and the Mac OS are single-user systems. In other words, only one user can be logged in and running applications at any one time in these operating systems. By comparison, Linux allows multiple simultaneous users, fully leveraging the multitasking capabilities of the operating system. The great advantage of this is that Linux can be deployed as an applications server. From their desktop computers or terminals, users can log into a Linux server across a LAN and actually run applications on the server instead of on their desktop PCs.

Linux Applications

As an operating system, Linux can be used to develop almost any type of application. Among the applications available for Linux are the following:

Text and word processing applications   In addition to commercial word processing software such as WordPerfect, StarOffice, and Applixware, Linux offers powerful tools for editing text files and processing text in an automated fashion.

Programming languages   A wide variety of programming and scripting languages and tools are available for Linux and all Unix operating systems. This abundance of programming tools makes it easy to develop new applications that can run not only on Linux but also on most Unix and Unix-like operating systems.

X Windows   X Windows is Unix's answer to the graphical user interface (GUI). X Windows is a highly flexible and configurable GUI environment that runs on Linux as well as on most Unix systems. Numerous applications that run in X Windows help to make Linux an easy-to-use operating system.

> **NOTE**   Chapters 6 through 12 provide complete coverage of X Windows.

Internet tools   In addition to supporting well-known software such as Netscape and Mosaic, Linux provides a wide range of Internet software, including character-based and graphical mail-reading applications, the full range of software needed to create Internet servers (Web servers, mail servers, and news servers), plus complete network support to connect to the Internet via a local network or modem.

Databases   Like all Unix platforms, Linux provides a robust platform for running client-server database applications. From its earliest days, powerful, free databases such as mSQL and PostgreSQL have been available for Linux. As Linux has grown in popularity, especially in corporate information systems, the number of commercial relational database servers for Linux has grown. Today, Oracle, Sybase, and Informix all offer relational database products for Linux.

DOS and Windows compatibility software   As you will see in Chapter 30, "Red Hat Linux 7.1 and DOS/Windows," Linux can be made to run DOS software with a high degree of stability and compatibility and offers several approaches to running Windows software. In fact, the entire text of this book was written using Microsoft Word for Windows on a computer running Linux. This provides strong evidence of Linux's ability to work well in a Windows environment. In addition, emulators are available for other popular computer systems, including the Macintosh and Atari ST computer lines.

This list touches only the tip of the iceberg. Many more applications exist for Linux. A good source for finding Linux software is the Linux Software Map, which can be found on the World Wide Web at `http://www.execpc.com/lsm/`.

Linux As Free Software

Given all the capabilities promised by Linux, you might think that the operating system is expensive. On the contrary, the Linux kernel and most of the applications written for Linux are available for free on the Internet, often with no restriction on the copying and redistribution of the software.

To begin with, the Linux kernel is distributed under the GNU General Public License (GPL). This special software license, developed by Stallman's Free Software Foundation, promotes the open distribution and, more importantly, open development of software. Unlike the software licenses common with most commercial software, the GNU license allows anyone to redistribute software, even for a fee, so long as in the redistribution, the terms of the GNU license are still in force. In other words, anyone can take GNU software, alter it if they wish, and redistribute it, but they can't stop someone who buys GNU-licensed software from them from turning around and redistributing it again.

Most of Linux is available under the GNU General Public License. This makes it possible for many different vendors to produce both free and commercially available Linux distributions.

This approach to free software is not the same as public domain software. With GNU products, the software developers retain the copyright to the software and may choose in the future to stop distributing that software under the GNU license. What is special about the GNU license is that it encourages iterative development of applications by many people, each making changes that they consider important or necessary and then redistributing the software.

This process is enabled by the fact that all GNU-licensed software must be distributed with its complete source code. Unlike commercial software, where the original code is unavailable and hence unalterable, GNU software not only makes it possible to alter and customize software but actually encourages interested and capable users to do so.

In fact, this model has been so successful in the development of Linux and applications for Linux that Netscape has adopted it for its Web browser product lines. Using basic GNU principles, Netscape makes its Web browsers freely available and allows anyone to license the source code for its Web browsers or to redistribute them.

Commercial Applications for Linux

As you will see later in this book, there are commercial applications for Linux as well as commercial distributions of Linux. In these cases, most products are licensed under terms more restrictive than the GNU standards of the Linux world.

But even if a distribution of Linux includes commercial components that cannot be redistributed freely, this doesn't change the underlying GNU license that applies to the Linux kernel and those core applications found in all Linux distributions. If the original license of an application is the GNU General Public License, then the license of the redistributed copy of the software is likewise the GNU General Public License.

Looking Ahead

In this chapter, you have taken the first step into the world of Linux. You now know what the basic components and philosophy of Linux are, and you have become acquainted with the features that make it an excellent choice for many applications.

Chapter 2 examines the Linux distribution philosophy and the many distributions, or flavors, of Linux that are available.

Chapter 3 describes the practical steps of preparing to install Linux on a PC. Chapters 4 and 5 walk you through various installations and associated issues and potential pitfalls. Then you will be ready to look at Linux desktop environments, described in Chapters 6 through 12.

Chapters 4 and 5 describe how to install Linux on a stand-alone PC; they also address any special installation issues, such as PCs with no CD-ROM drive. From that point, the book is divided into five sections dealing with using Linux; these sections cover X Windows and GNOME, essential Linux skills, connecting Linux to the Internet, and using Linux in a small or home office (the so-called SOHO environment).

CHAPTER

TWO

2

Choosing a Distribution

- What Is a Distribution?

- An Overview of Major Distributions

- Red Hat Linux

As you saw in Chapter 1, "What Is Linux?," the entire approach to the development of Linux breaks with traditional commercial software development. Most of the components that go into making a complete Linux system—including the kernel (the heart of the operating system), modules for devices, and all the applications and utilities that make the system do useful things—are developed by loosely knit groups of developers scattered around the globe.

To top it all off, most of these components are distributed under licenses allowing free redistribution, such as the GNU General Public License. (Appendix D contains a copy of this license.)

All this leaves the potential users of Linux at a bit of a loss as to how to put together a working Linux system and what components to include in that system.

The answer to this quandary has emerged in the form of Linux *distributions*. Distributions are prepackaged Linux systems that are ready to install. They come in numerous flavors from the freely available to the fully commercial, and they all offer different core sets of applications, utilities, and management tools to ease the use of Linux.

This chapter takes a broad look at some of the major and better-known distributions and then takes a somewhat closer look at the latest release of Red Hat Linux 7.1, the distribution included on the CD-ROM with this book.

What Is a Distribution?

The concept of a distribution can be a little hard to understand in a world of commercial operating systems such as Windows 98 and 2000, Mac OS, and even commercial Unix systems such as Solaris and HP-UX.

After all, in all these cases, the name of the operating system denotes a very specific product. For instance, Windows 98 defines the complete set of Windows utilities, applications, and drivers that Microsoft ships. There is no room for variation. Any application, driver, or utility that users add to their systems is not considered part of Windows 98, and Windows 98 doesn't technically exist as a product with less than its complete set of software and tools.

In the Linux world, however, this definition becomes blurred. While strictly speaking, "Linux" is just the kernel (the heart of the operating system), the term "Linux" can refer to everything from the kernel to any collection of Linux-based applications put together with a kernel to produce a functioning system running Linux.

This lack of a clear set of applications, utilities, drivers, and a kernel that together can clearly be identified exists because Linux has opened the door to different flavors of Linux that meet different needs. These flavors are the distributions.

Distributions can be built on different versions of the kernel, can include different sets of applications, utilities, tools, and driver modules, and can offer different installation and upgrade programs to ease management of the system.

It might seem that with this type of flexibility would come chaos. This is a logical deduction. After all, how is it possible to have potentially infinite varieties of Linux and yet have some level of reasonable assurance that Linux applications can be installed and run on any of these systems?

Luckily, this system tends to work: In all the diversity that is Linux is an underlying thread of similarity that provides the compatibility needed to develop applications that can be used on most Linux systems.

At the heart of most Linux distributions is a common set of basic programs, utilities, and libraries that application developers can reasonably expect to find on any Linux system. In addition, most Linux distributions now adhere to such standards as the Linux File System Hierarchy Standard (FHS).

Therefore, large-scale commercial applications such as Netscape or Corel WordPerfect can be developed for Linux and be expected to work on the majority of Linux systems. Even if a component, such as a program or library, upon which an application depends is missing, it can be downloaded from one of the large Linux software repositories on the Internet to enable the application to work.

An Overview of Major Distributions

The majority of Linux distributions are freely available. They can be downloaded from the Internet from Linux software archives such as the Metalab FTP site or the TSX-11 Linux Repository at MIT.

TIP See Appendix B, "Sources of Linux Information," for a complete list of Linux sites offering distributions and for a list of CD-ROM vendors.

Of course, the average Linux distribution can be quite large, ranging from a few dozen megabytes to several gigabytes in size, and most users will not want to spend valuable online time and bandwidth downloading a complete Linux distribution. To alleviate this situation, numerous Linux distributions are available on CD-ROM from the organizations that produce the distributions or from third-party sources that bundle one or more distributions into CD-ROM sets that include additional Linux software and documentation.

For instance, Edition 27 of CheapBytes' MONDO Pack (`www.cheapbytes.com`) is a set of 11 CD-ROMs, which contains the latest Red Hat, Slackware, Mandrake, and StormLinux distributions. Alternatively, LinuxMall (`www.linuxmall.com`) offers Linux MegaPak 2.0, which is a set of 16 CD-ROMs that contains the same distributions included in the MONDO Pack as well as the latest Debian, Storm, S.u.S.E., FreeBSD, and Turbolinux distributions.

NOTE FreeBSD, like the different Linux distributions, is a clone of Unix.

Generally, CD-ROM copies of free Linux distributions range in price from $2 to $50, with more popular sets such as the Linux MegaPak costing less than $30.

The Major Distributions

There are numerous Linux distributions. In recent years, though, six distributions have emerged as the most common: Red Hat, Slackware, Caldera, S.u.S.E., Debian, and Corel. Generally, these distributions have some of the longest histories in the Linux community, and together they control the lion's share of the market. In addition, all six distributions are freely available, which has made them the basis for other distributions and for commercial packages that include a Linux distribution.

After these six, there is a second tier of Linux distributions that includes some long-standing distributions such as Yggdrasil and newer distributions such as Turbolinux and easyLinux.

Red Hat

By most counts, Red Hat Linux from Red Hat Software (www.redhat.com) has emerged as the favorite Linux distribution for most users. This distribution is the target, or base, distribution for many commercial Linux software developers and is the benchmark against which many Linux distributions are measured.

Red Hat has gained fame particularly for its tools for installing and upgrading the operating system and for its well-designed system for installing, uninstalling, and tracking software application packages.

Red Hat Linux has also won numerous awards, including *Network Magazine*'s Product of the Year award in 2000. In 1998, Red Hat Linux came in first in a survey of *InfoWorld*'s Web site visitors that asked readers to indicate their choice for Product of the Year (receiving 27 percent of the vote, well ahead of the number-two package, OS/2 Warp 4, which had just over 8 percent). Red Hat Linux has also been used in projects that have proven the commercial viability of Linux, including animation work for the movie *Titanic*.

Red Hat Linux is available in a free version that can be downloaded from popular Linux archives on the Internet and in a reasonably priced $40 commercial version that includes a manual, a CD-ROM, and several commercial applications to supplement its collection of free software. Red Hat Linux 7.1 is also available in Deluxe Workstation and Professional Server editions.

Red Hat Linux 7.1 is the current version of the distribution and is the distribution included with this book. This chapter will take a deeper look at Red Hat.

> **NOTE**
>
> In addition to the Red Hat Linux 7.1 distribution included on the CD-ROM, you can always download the latest version from the Red Hat FTP server at ftp.redhat.com or from the Ibiblio Linux Archive at ibiblio.org/pub/Linux/distributions/redhat. If neither of these sites is easily accessible, there are a number of "mirror" sites with a copy of the distribution listed at http://www.redhat.com/download/mirror.html.

Slackware

Before Red Hat Linux came to fame, Slackware was the distribution to beat. Slackware is still a popular distribution; but as of this writing, its future is in some doubt due to some recent industry consolidation. Patrick Volkerding, the head of the Slackware project, is currently looking for another sponsor for his developers. For the latest developments on Slackware and for more information, including download sites and sales, refer to their home page (www.slackware.com).

The version of Slackware available at the time of this writing is Slackware 7.1. The distribution offers the full range of expected utilities, tools, and applications, including X Windows, development tools such as the GNU C Compiler, PPP support, full Java support, and the Java SDK (Developer's Kit) for Linux. Like most Linux distributions, Slackware offers the Apache Web server for using Linux to set up an intranet or Internet Web site, as well as several freely available Web browsers.

As of this writing, Slackware can be downloaded from a number of different FTP and HTTP sites as listed on http://www.slackware.com/getslack/.

Caldera OpenLinux

Caldera caused a stir in both the Linux and the broader computer markets by trumpeting the call of supportable commercial Linux. Now the call has been roundly taken up by other Linux vendors, most notably Red Hat. The idea is to offer tested, stable, and supported versions of Linux that appeal to the corporate market and to application developers who want a secure target distribution of Linux to develop for.

To some extent, this strategy has worked. Corel's WordPerfect 6 for Linux was initially targeted for Caldera's Network Desktop distribution. Previous versions of StarOffice for Linux were aimed at Caldera distributions, and the Linux version of Netscape's FastTrack Web server package has been ported by Caldera and is available as part of the eDesktop and eServer packages.

Currently, the Caldera OpenLinux distribution comes in two editions: eDesktop 2.4 for workstations and eServer 2.3 for servers. It can be purchased or downloaded from the Web. Both distributions include the following features:

- The K Desktop Environment (which you will learn about in Chapter 11, "Using KDE")

- A non-commercial license of StarOffice for Linux

- NetWare support

- A license of DR-DOS for DOS compatibility

- Webmin, a powerful, customizable Linux administration system that opens up in a Web browser

- An integrated version of Partition Magic to help users configure their hard drives before installing Linux

Caldera's eDesktop 2.4 won the *CNet* Editor's Choice Award in October 2000. In awarding eDesktop this honor, *CNet*'s editors noted the added value in its Internet-based administration tools. Caldera's eDesktop and eServer can be downloaded at no cost from Caldera's Web site at www.caldera.com.

S.u.S.E. Linux

S.u.S.E. Linux is a popular Linux distribution available primarily in Europe and is offered in both English and German versions.

The version of S.u.S.E. available at the time of this writing, 7.1, is unique in several ways when compared against the other major distributions. S.u.S.E. offers the following:

- KDE 2.0, the latest version of the XFree86 X Windows server (some distributions are one version behind)

- System administration tools called YaST and YaST2, which are useful for configuring everything from dial-up Internet connections to scanners and network cards

- SaX2, a custom utility for configuring X Windows

- A copy of the latest version of StarOffice

Like Caldera and Red Hat, there are two editions of S.u.S.E. 7.1 that are currently available. The boxed version of S.u.S.E. Linux 7.1 Personal Edition includes over 700 programs and separate application and configuration manuals. The boxed version of S.u.S.E. Linux 7.1 Professional Edition includes over 2500 applications on seven CD-ROMs and one DVD, which may make this the most comprehensive Linux distribution available today.

S.u.S.E. Linux supports versions for non-Intel platforms as well, including Digital Alpha, the PowerPC, and the IBM S/390 Enterprise Server.

Debian/GNU

As one of the six major Linux players, Debian/GNU (www.debian.org) is the odd man out, because it is not "owned" by any specific company. Red Hat is developed by Red Hat Software and Slackware has a home at Walnut Creek; however, Debian/GNU Linux is produced by a team of volunteers in much the same way that Linux development itself takes place.

Debian offers more than 3950 software packages using its own package-management system, which is designed to offer similar functionality to that offered by the Red Hat distribution. As of this writing, the current version of Debian/GNU Linux is 2.2.r3.

The Debian distribution is unique in some ways. Their Web site highlights a commitment to giving back any code they generate to the free software world. They publicize their bugs, making bug reports easy to find, and they won't include applications in their distribution that don't match Debian's definition of free software (which includes free redistribution rights, available source code, and allowances for modifications and derived work).

Corel

The newest major distribution is Corel Linux. It was developed as the first Linux distribution explicitly targeted as a replacement for Microsoft Windows on the desktop. Corel Linux Second Edition includes these features:

- The Corel Control Center, a system administration tool based on the KDE Control Center

- A four-step installation process

- Tools such as User Manager and Print Wizard that are explicitly based on equivalent Microsoft Windows tools

- SmartMove, which allows you to import profiles and settings from existing Microsoft Windows computers

Corel Linux is built on the Debian distribution. In other words, they add features to Debian Linux and sell it as their own distribution. This is explicitly allowed under the terms of the General Public License, as shown in Appendix D.

Other Distributions

Other English-language distributions of Linux that are worth noting include LinuxPro, LinuxWare, Turbolinux, and Yggdrasil, among others. In addition, there are several non-English distributions, particularly in French and German, which are covered in Appendix A, "Linux around the World."

You can learn more about other distributions and find links to the relevant Web sites from Linux Online's English-language distributions page at `www.linux.org/dist/english.html`.

Red Hat Linux

The distribution of Linux used in this book is Red Hat Linux 7.1. As mentioned earlier, Red Hat Linux is currently one of the most well-known and widely used Linux distributions.

The feature that launched Red Hat Linux into popularity was its package-management system, known as the Red Hat Package Manager (`rpm`). This system allows software applications to be tested, configured, and provided in a ready-to-run state for Red Hat Linux. It has been adapted by a number of other distributions, including S.u.S.E. and Caldera. Using simple package-management tools, you can download, install, and run new packages without the sometimes-tortuous configuration required with other packages—such as software that is distributed with its own special installation program or that doesn't use the Red Hat (or the similar Debian) package-management system.

Of course, package management alone is not enough to explain the success of Red Hat Linux. After all, the key software needed to implement the Red Hat package-management system is made freely available by Red Hat, and other distributions also use the system.

One benefit provided by package management is upgradability. It is possible to upgrade versions of Red Hat without having to reinstall Linux from scratch. This problem plagued earlier distributions by Slackware, when it was the leading distribution, and still plagues some distributions today.

Another major feature of the Red Hat distribution is that it is available not only on the Intel PC platform but also on the Compaq Alpha-based computer platform. While the Compaq Alpha platform offers higher performance hardware than the typical Intel PC, it generally requires expensive commercial versions of Unix. Red Hat makes it possible to use Linux on both these systems, and because the distributions are fundamentally the same, management and configuration of systems running Red Hat Linux for either platform are simplified, as is the porting of software.

What's New about Red Hat Linux 7.1

Version 7.1 of Red Hat Linux offers several new features not found in earlier versions and still not found in all distributions of Linux. These features include the following:

- The 2.4 Linux kernel

- New configuration tools for printers and firewalls

- Updated X Window systems, including XFree86 version 4.0.3, KDE 2.1, and GNOME 1.2

The Linux 2.4 Kernel

The evolution of the Linux kernel over the past year is impressive. While every revision to the Linux kernel is small, the development of the kernel over the past year has resulted in new features for the desktop, for servers, and for smaller devices such as handheld computers. These new features include the following:

Integrated PC hardware support   While USB support is growing, version 2.4 also promises improved performance for PCMCIA (PC Card) and Plug-and-Play ISA devices, by integrating their drivers directly into the kernel.

A diversity of platforms   With the new kernel, you can now run Linux on a wide variety of non-Intel platforms, including Alpha, Sparc, MIPS, PowerPC, and ARM-based computers. The new kernel even supports the IBM S/390 mainframe computer.

Support for smaller devices   The new kernel is designed for use in compact devices such as handheld computers and other portable network devices.

Few limits   The new kernel now supports a large amount of RAM (64GB), virtually unlimited multitasking, and the ability to create a single volume over multiple disks for very large files.

New Configuration Tools

Linux has always had a strong set of both command-line and graphical tools for configuring and administering a Red Hat Linux-based system. Starting with Version 5, these were expanded to include a user information tool to set user information such as name and phone number, a user password tool that makes it easy to change users' passwords, and a file system tool that allows the mounting and unmounting of file systems from a graphical interface.

Red Hat Linux also offers a tool for configuring the free version of X Windows, XFree86, called Xconfigurator. Xconfigurator has always been easier to use than the configuration program included with XFree86. In Red Hat Linux, Xconfigurator offers additional improvements such as automatic detection of video cards and their features.

Red Hat Linux now includes new tools for configuring printers and firewalls, known as `printconf` and `gnome-lokkit`. `Printconf` allows you to set up printers locally or remotely through a standard graphical user interface. `Gnome-lokkit` allows you to configure a firewall to protect your computer and network from intruders, configuring firewall rules based on simple questions that determine your communication needs.

Altogether, these improvements make Red Hat Linux easy to manage for most users and help bring to the Linux world the types of graphical management tools found in rival systems such as Windows 2000.

Improved X Window Systems

Red Hat Linux 7.1 includes XFree86 Version 4.0.3, the latest version of the Linux X Window System. This creates a more stable platform and improved 3-D graphics for the two major desktop environments, GNOME and KDE, both of which are also included in Red Hat Linux 7.1.

GNOME and KDE are desktop environments for X Windows designed to make application development easier and to provide a more consistent, professional-quality desktop environment for Linux users. GNOME 1.2 and its companion Sawfish window manager are discussed in detail in Chapter 10, "Advanced GNOME Configuration." KDE 2.1 is discussed in detail in Chapter 11, "Using KDE."

Improved Performance Features

Red Hat Linux 7.1 offers several new or improved features that can be used to leverage high-end hardware to improve the performance and stability of Red Hat Linux systems. These features include better implementation of symmetric multiprocessing (SMP), which allows Red Hat Linux to leverage the performance gain offered by multiprocessor systems. In addition, Red Hat Linux 7.1 includes an improved version of Disk Druid, which detects errors as you set up partitions during installation.

Looking Ahead

Now that you have a firm sense of what Linux is all about and what the options are in terms of the various distributions, you are ready to focus on actually working with Linux (the Publisher's Edition of Red Hat Linux 7.1 is on the enclosed CD-ROM).

Chapter 3, "Getting Ready to Install Red Hat Linux 7.1," will cover the preparation that is needed to ensure that installing Linux will go smoothly. This includes understanding some of the hardware issues involved in getting a Linux system up and running with minimum fuss and also making sure you have all the necessary information on hand to provide the installation program the data it needs to do its job.

In Chapter 4, "Installing Red Hat Linux 7.1," you will walk through the actual steps involved in installing a Red Hat Linux system. While the specific steps vary, you can learn about installing any Linux distribution from the installation of Red Hat Linux.

PART II

Installing Red Hat Linux 7.1

CHAPTER

THREE

3

Getting Ready to Install Red Hat Linux 7.1

- What You Need

- Checking Your Hardware for Compatibility

- Recording Your Hardware Information

- Choosing an Installation Method

- Arranging Your Hard Disk

In this chapter, you finally get down to the business of installing Red Hat Linux 7.1. Most of this chapter is concerned with decisions that affect the installation process, rather than with the actual installation process itself, but this decision-making is an essential step to ensure that your Linux installation goes smoothly and that you end up with a well-configured system.

This chapter starts with a brief discussion of the minimum Linux system. What hardware is necessary to run a useful Linux system? It is possible to boot Linux from a single floppy disk, but the resulting system will be so limited that it will be useless for most purposes. This chapter describes what equipment you need in order to make Linux a useful tool in your computing arsenal.

From there, this chapter discusses a crucial issue: hardware compatibility. Even in the Windows world where vendors quickly provide drivers for almost every conceivable piece of hardware, things go wrong, and hardware incompatibility can be the cause of long, sleepless nights trying to get the Windows operating system to work. In Linux, there is equal potential for problems, especially if you try to use hardware for which there is currently limited or no support.

What You Need

Before you can install Linux, it is important to step back and consider exactly what type of computer you need. Linux can be installed on a wide range of hardware, including the following:

- ARM processors
- Motorola 68000 series processors
- 8086 CPUs
- Alpha processors
- SPARC processors
- MIPS systems
- PowerPC-based systems
- S/390-based servers
- Acorn computers

- Power Macintoshes

- Intel and Intel-compatible PCs

By far, though, Intel-compatible PC hardware is the most common Linux platform. It generally provides the lowest cost-performance ratio for Linux and is the primary development platform for most Linux tools. Intel Linux offers the best selection of device drivers for peripheral hardware, the largest body of available applications (both commercial and free), and the strongest user community on the Internet to turn to for support and assistance.

For these reasons, this book focuses on Linux for Intel-compatible *x*86-based computers; the companion CD-ROM for this book contains Red Hat Linux 7.1 for the Intel platform.

The Minimum PC for Linux

As an operating system, Linux has amazingly modest requirements for computer resources. It is possible to get Linux up and running on a 386-based computer with only 4MB of RAM. Such a machine will, of course, be limited in the following ways:

- It can't run X Windows (so, no GUI).

- The number of simultaneous programs it can run is limited by the amount of physical RAM.

- Its performance will be slow enough to prevent its use in most mission-critical applications (for instance, as a mail server or Web server).

Given these limitations, a system like this can still play a role in an organization as:

- A terminal to another Linux or Unix server where applications are running

- A low-end server for services such as DNS (Domain Name Service, which helps computers translate hostnames such as www.yahoo.com into actual numeric [IP] addresses) or as an authentication server for a small network

In fact, Linux can provide a better way to leverage this type of old hardware than DOS can. DOS has limited networking capabilities and cannot handle the server duties described above.

If you want to try to run this type of minimalist Linux system, turn to the Small Memory Mini-HOWTO at http://www.linuxdoc.org/HOWTO/mini/Small-Memory for some basic tips to help you get Linux up and running in a system with limited memory.

A Good PC for Linux

This book's main focus is on running Linux on a personal workstation or as a small intranet server. Needless to say, just as you wouldn't want to run Windows on the type of machine described in the previous section, you need a more robust PC to fully enjoy the features and benefits of Linux.

Linux actually requires far fewer resources to perform far more functions than the average Windows 98 or Windows NT/2000 system. For instance, a functional workstation can be put together with a 486-100MHz processor and 16MB of RAM. This system will be able to run X Windows (for a graphical interface), access the Internet, run a graphical Web browser, and, all the while, perform as a low-end server on a network.

Still, the average user will want a somewhat more powerful Linux system. A respectable Linux workstation needs the following specifications:

A Pentium-class CPU   Even a Pentium 133 will do just fine for most users. It is wise to avoid certain clone chips, such as the Cyrix 686 line, because of some reported difficulties people have had running these chips. Generally, though, most Pentium-class systems work just fine. Of course, if you are buying a new PC today, you won't be able to find a standard Pentium, so choose a Pentium IV, Celeron, Athlon, Duron, or Itanium-class system.

32MB of RAM   Linux is exceptionally good at taking advantage of any extra memory you throw at it. 32MB is enough for the average workstation, but you will notice the difference if you can afford 64MB or more of RAM.

A 3GB hard disk   You can get away with a 1GB (or even smaller) hard disk, but a roomier disk is preferable. Larger disks tend to perform better than the older, smaller ones. In a number of cases, you won't be able to install all of the features associated with Red Hat Linux 7.1 unless you have at least 3GB of hard disk space.

A supported video card   See the section on hardware compatibility later in this chapter.

With a system like this, you will have more than sufficient resources to run Linux as a desktop operating system. You don't need to go out and buy the latest 1.7GHz Pentium IV system with all the bells and whistles to get Linux up and running at a respectable speed. In fact, you may want to avoid the latest hardware, especially if it was just released in the past few weeks. For more information, see the discussion on hardware compatibility later in this chapter.

Added Bonuses

Of course, in today's computing environment, you will probably want to extend your PC's capabilities into areas such as multimedia and the Internet. There are a few add-ons that greatly enhance any Linux system, and you should consider them as a way to round out your workstation:

A CD-ROM drive   If you are going to install one, consider an IDE/ATAPI CD-ROM drive or, if you can afford it, a SCSI CD-ROM drive. Generally, it is best to avoid proprietary CD-ROM drives that work with their own interface cards or connect directly to special interfaces on sound cards. These CD-ROM drives are usually poor performers and difficult to configure in Linux.

A sound card   Most Sound Blaster®-compatible cards are supported in Linux; check the hardware compatibility section of this chapter.

A modem   In terms of speed, the same rules apply here as with Windows: It is generally best to get the fastest modem you can that will be able to connect at its top speed to your Internet service provider (ISP). (If your ISP can't offer 56Kbps connections, then you may not want a 56Kbps modem at this time.) Two caveats, though: First, it is generally wise to opt for external modems in Linux. This is especially true for ISDN modems, because there is limited support in Linux for internal ISDN modems. The advantage of external modems (ISDN or analog) is that they are easier to configure and they offer external indicators so you can more easily debug configuration problems. Second, it is generally wise to avoid "winmodems," which are modems that use Microsoft Windows driver library files. Linux supports only a few winmodems without difficulty.

While a CD-ROM, sound card, and modem are fairly standard equipment on newer PCs, if you plan to use Linux as a small server on your intranet, you should consider the following add-ons:

A SCSI card   SCSI offers much better performance for hard drives than the IDE interface and has better support for multiple devices. If you plan to run any type of multiuser system (for instance, file server, Web server, or applications server), you really need to use a SCSI card. Make sure to consult the hardware compatibility section before selecting a SCSI card and, if possible, choose a card with Ultra-Wide SCSI support.

SCSI hard drive(s) One function of the SCSI card is to be able to use the faster SCSI hard drives. If possible, use Ultra-Wide SCSI drives for the best performance. You may want to consider multiple disk drives. For instance, if you estimate that you need 8GB of space for your users' data as well as the operating system and all installed applications, you may want to consider two 4GB drives (one for the user data and the other for the system and software). By splitting the software and the data, you will probably find that performance improves because the same disk is not being accessed for both.

A tape drive If you plan to run a server, you will want to do backups to ensure that your data is safe from system failure and other disasters. While it is possible to use some tape drives that connect through the floppy disk bus, you will find that life is a lot easier if you opt for a SCSI tape drive, if you can afford one. They are faster and better supported by Linux.

Checking Your Hardware for Compatibility

As with a Windows (especially Windows NT/2000) system, it is important to check that hardware you intend to buy will work with your Linux operating system and with the rest of the hardware in your computer before committing the money to purchase it. Hardware incompatibility with the operating system and other hardware can be the source of endless difficulty and time spent trying to debug and reconfigure a computer.

This issue is especially important in the Linux community. Although support for Linux is growing among hardware vendors, many vendors still do not provide Linux drivers for their hardware, and their support staff may be unable or unwilling to work with users to debug hardware conflicts and problems in a Linux environment. This means that the hardware needs to be supported by drivers included in the user's Linux distribution or by add-on software that provides drivers for the hardware in question. In addition, users must rely on the Linux community for help when problems arise.

While a vast majority of hardware is supported in some way by Linux, it is wise to do some research before installing Linux or before purchasing new hardware for a Linux-based system. Here's what you can do:

- Try consulting the Red Hat Hardware Compatibility List at `hardware.redhat .com`. This contains a searchable database of compatible hardware for the most current Red Hat distributions.

- Consult the Linux Hardware Compatibility HOWTO. This document, authored by Patrick Reijnen, contains extensive lists of hardware known to work with Linux, hardware known not to work with Linux, and issues related to both types of hardware. If you purchase hardware that has the stamp of approval from this HOWTO guide, your life will be easier. You can find the latest version of this guide at `http://www.linuxdoc.org/HOWTO/ Hardware-HOWTO.html`.

- Consult the `comp.os.linux.hardware` newsgroup. This is a good source of information about hardware issues as they relate to Linux. If you are unsure whether your intended hardware purchase is wise, post a question to the group asking if anyone has had any experience with the hardware in question. You will usually find that others have tried what you are considering, and their collective wisdom is an invaluable resource in making informed purchase decisions. Alternatively, search through newsgroup archives at `http://groups.google.com`.

- Try to evaluate the hardware before purchasing it. If you are considering making a corporate purchase of hardware from a vendor you use regularly, it may be possible to borrow the hardware to test it with Linux before actually purchasing it. This, of course, is the only way to be certain that the hardware will work the way you want it to.

Recording Your Hardware Information

Once you have put together your target Linux PC, you need to collect the hardware-related information necessary to get your hardware working. This section briefly looks at the information you should be aware of in order to get your hardware working quickly with Linux.

Video Cards

If you install Linux without X Windows (the graphical user interface for Unix systems), you will probably have no difficulties with any video card. However, with X Windows, you need to take care and pay attention to detail to get your card working. Record the following information about your video card before installing Linux:

- Vendor and model of the card

- Video chipset used on the card (Sometimes X Windows may not provide explicit support for a particular card but will offer general support for the chipset used in the card.)

- Amount of video memory on the card

- Type of clock chip on the card (If there is one; many common cards do not have clock chips.)

- Type of RAMDAC on the card (If there is one; many common cards do not have RAMDACs.)

All of this information should be available in the documentation that came with your card or in Linux-related archives, HOWTOs, or the card manufacturer's Web site if you no longer have the documentation.

Sound Cards

Sound cards require that you supply very specific information in order to get them working. The following information is critical to configuring most sound cards:

- Vendor and model of the card

- IRQ(s) of the card

- I/O address(es) of the card

- DMA address(es) of the card

You may have to set the IRQ, I/O address, and DMA address manually, using jumpers or DIP switches. Depending on your card, not all of this information may be required. Refer to the card's documentation for instructions.

Monitors

As with your video card, it is important to record the technical specifications of your monitor in order to get it working optimally with X Windows. If you don't have this information, or use the wrong information, there is a risk that your monitor could be damaged. Record the following specifications after consulting your monitor's documentation:

- Vendor and model of the monitor

- Top resolution of the monitor

- Top refresh rate of the monitor when running at its top resolution

- Horizontal sync range of your monitor

- Vertical sync range of your monitor

Consult Chapter 7, "Installing and Configuring X Windows," for a discussion of horizontal and vertical sync ranges as they apply to the configuration of X Windows.

Mice

In order to get your mouse working, both in Linux's character-based console mode and in X Windows, you need to note the following information:

- Vendor and model of the mouse

- Number of mouse buttons

- Protocol of the mouse (Consult the mouse's documentation for this; common protocols include the Microsoft protocol, USB, the Mouse Systems protocol, and the PS/2 protocol.)

- Port where your mouse is connected to your computer (In DOS terms, this is generally COM1:, COM2:, or the PS/2 mouse port.)

Hard Drives

If you plan to use Linux to repartition your hard drive during installation (see the section later in this chapter about arranging your hard disk's partitions), you may need the following information:

- Total storage capacity of the hard disk

- Number of cylinders
- Number of heads
- Number of sectors per track

Generally, you will not need to provide this information because Linux will successfully auto-detect it when the system is booted.

Modems

If you have a modem, you should record the following information:

- Vendor and model of the modem
- Speed of the modem
- Port that your external modem is connected to or that you have configured your internal modem to use (In DOS terms, this is generally COM1: or COM2:.) or with internal modems, the IRQ, I/O address, as well as the port

Network Cards

If you have a network card, you should record the following information:

- Vendor and model of the network card
- IRQ(s) of the card
- I/O address(es) of the card
- Specialized drivers, if available
- Compatibility with Novell 1000 or 2000 network card drivers

Some network cards include driver disks with Linux drivers. Alternatively, if your card is compatible with Novell 1000 or 2000 network card drivers, you may be able to use these drivers to install your network card on Linux. Consult your network card's documentation for more information.

USB

Several Linux distributions include partial USB support, primarily for keyboards and mice. These distributions include S.u.S.E. 6.4, Red Hat 7.0, Mandrake 7.1, and Corel Linux Second Edition (and above). As of this writing, Linux support for USB hardware within the 2.2.*x* kernel is limited to static configuration.

However, Red Hat 7.1 is based on the 2.4.*x* kernel, which allows nearly the full available range of USB support. As shown in the Linux-USB device database at `http://www.qbik.ch/usb/devices`, Linux USB support is available at some level for just about every type of USB device, from modems to Web cameras.

If you're interested in "hotplugging," where you can install a USB device while your computer is in operation, refer to the Linux Hotplugging Web site at `http://linux-hotplug.sourceforge.net`. This site includes downloadable scripts in `rpm` format that are designed to work with Red Hat Linux.

Considerable work on USB for Linux is in progress. If you can't install your USB hardware on your distribution, you can review the Linux USB project at `http://www.linux-usb.org` for additional drivers and utilities.

Other Peripherals

Many other peripherals have specific requirements for configuration. The number and type of possible peripherals are too varied to list here; the details needed to configure these peripherals are left to those sections of this book where the hardware types are discussed. Generally, additional hardware such as specialized serial cards, specialized PCMCIA or PC Cards, and tape drives are not configured and installed at the time Linux is installed but rather after you have a running Linux system.

If you are planning to install your Linux system on a local area network, consult Chapter 27, "Installing Red Hat Linux 7.1 for the SOHO," for information pertaining to network cards and Linux installation.

Choosing an Installation Method

Generally, Linux is distributed on CD-ROMs because of its sheer size. While Linux can be downloaded from the Internet, it is too large for most people to download unless they have access to a high-speed, dedicated Internet connection.

A CD-ROM, then, is usually at the core of installing Linux, as it is in the case of the Red Hat Linux 7.1 distribution included with this book. While it is theoretically possible to install Linux directly off the Internet, this method is too time-consuming or too expensive to be practical for most Linux users.

This section will consider different approaches to installing Linux from the CD-ROM included with this book. The procedures will be similar to most other Linux distributions that are available on CD-ROM; consult the documentation for those distributions to determine the differences.

From CD-ROM

If you have an IDE/ATAPI CD-ROM drive and a computer with a fairly recent BIOS, it is possible to boot your computer from the Linux CD-ROM to start the installation process.

To check this, consult your computer's or main board's manual, or enter the BIOS setup of your computer while it is booting and see if you can switch the default boot device to your CD-ROM drive. If you can boot from the CD-ROM drive, insert the Red Hat Linux 7.1 Installation CD-ROM and attempt to boot your system. You should see an Installation menu and a boot prompt that says boot:.

NOTE   Even though an installation CD may be designed to boot from the CD-ROM, it still may not boot in all PCs that support bootable CD-ROMs. If you experience difficulty booting the copy of Linux that comes with this book or your own copy of Linux, then try installing from a floppy disk and CD-ROM as described in the "From Floppy Disk and CD-ROM" section in this chapter.

From Floppy Disk and CD-ROM

If you have a CD-ROM drive but can't boot from it, the next best thing is to install Linux from a combination of floppy disk and CD-ROM. In this scenario, you boot from one or more floppy disks to start the installation process and then proceed to install the actual Linux software from the CD-ROM.

Some preparation is necessary to do this. For most distributions of Linux, you need to prepare a boot floppy disk and, possibly, one or more supplementary disks. Everything you need to do this should be included on the CD-ROM containing your Linux distribution.

If you need a boot disk and any supplementary disks, you can build them off most Linux installation CD-ROMs from DOS or the Windows DOS prompt.

On the Red Hat 7.1 CD-ROM, the Images subdirectory contains two files, boot.img and bootnet.img, that are disk images of the floppy disks used for installing Red Hat Linux 7.1 from files on the local computer or through a network. It also includes various driver disks for PCMCIA cards (pcmcia.img and pcmciadd.img), drivers for older CD-ROMs (oldcdrom.img), and other drivers (drivers.img). Each of these images requires a blank, formatted, high-density 1.44MB floppy and the rawrite.exe utility.

For instance, assuming that your CD-ROM drive is drive D, you use rawrite.exe as follows to create the Red Hat boot install disk:

```
C:\>d:\dosutils\rawrite.exe
Enter disk image source file name: d:\images\boot.img
Enter target diskette drive: a
Please insert a formatted diskette into drive A: and press -ENTER- :
```

Similarly, you enter **d:\images\bootnet.img** as the source filename to create the network boot installation disk.

Once this is done, you can boot from the boot install disk to start the installation process.

From Hard Disk

If you have plenty of disk space, you may want to copy the entire contents of the CD-ROM to your hard disk and install from the hard disk. Starting with Red Hat Linux 7.1, hard disk-based installation requires the use of ISO images, which is a single file that contains all of the files in a Red Hat Installation CD-ROM.

There are two basic ways to get the right ISO images. First, you can download them directly from the Internet, from a source such as ftp.redhat.com. The ISO file for each Red Hat Linux 7.1 CD-ROM is as large as the CD-ROM itself; in other words, about 650MB. Alternatively, you can create an ISO image from a Red Hat Linux 7.1 Installation CD-ROM, using the mkisofs command. More information on this process is available in Chapter 5, "Special Installations."

Of course, if you have access to a CD-ROM drive to create an ISO image, then you don't need to install from a hard disk. The only time this should really become necessary is if the Linux installation software won't recognize your CD-ROM drive. And with the drivers available on the previously mentioned oldcdrom.img file, this should rarely be necessary.

Arranging Your Hard Disk

When it comes time to install Linux, you are going to have to make some fundamental decisions regarding where to place the operating system on your hard disk(s). If you are extremely lucky, then one of the following two situations applies to you:

- You have a blank hard disk, or one you can reformat, available on which to install Linux.

- You have a blank partition, or one you can reformat, available on which to install Linux.

Unfortunately, most users who are looking at installing Linux for the first time want Linux to coexist with their current Windows and DOS installations and do not want to reformat an existing partition or hard disk to do this.

Partitioning Concepts

In order to install Linux into an existing system with no free partitions or hard disks, you need to find sufficient disk space and then carefully adjust your system's partitioning to free up a partition to work with during the Linux installation. Generally, if you want to install a fairly complete Linux system, you should free up at least 2GB of disk space. The space you free up should be on a single partition. (In Windows, each partition appears as a separate drive letter such as C, D, or E, so you need to find a drive with 2GB or more of free space.)

A Sample Partition Scheme for a Windows 98 System

Let's look at a simple example. You have a computer with a single 12GB hard disk divided into two 6GB partitions as drives C and D under DOS. You are able to free up 3GB of disk space on drive D and want to use this to install Linux.

There are two steps to be taken before you are ready to install Linux:

1. Defragment the drive to ensure that you have a large, continuous area of free space at the end of the partition.

2. Repartition the drive to make the space available for the Linux installation.

Defragmenting a Drive

Defragmenting a drive under Windows 98 is fairly simple. Just follow these steps:

1. Back up the data on your drive.

2. In My Computer or Windows Explorer, right-click the Drives icon.

3. Select Properties from the drop-down menu.

4. Choose the Tools tab at the top of the Properties window.

5. Click the Defragment Now button. Wait until defragmentation is complete and then proceed to the next section.

Partitioning Your Disk

Once you have defragmented a drive with sufficient space to install Linux, you need to create a new partition out of the free space. Most Linux distributions, including Red Hat Linux 7.1, come with a free DOS tool called `fips.exe`, which is in the `dosutils` subdirectory or in a subdirectory of this directory. In the Red Hat version included with this book, you can find the program in the `\dosutils\fips20` subdirectory.

WARNING   Red Hat does not support `fips`. It is covered under the General Public License, which means that the people behind `fips` have no liability even if you use it correctly and it destroys your data. While I've used `fips` a number of times and have never had a problem, be warned: Use it at your own risk. There are alternative commercial partition-splitting programs, including System Commander (`www.v-com.com`) and Partition Magic (`www.powerquest.com`).

This tool allows you to adjust the size of an existing partition, making it smaller by removing empty space at the end of the partition. This empty space is then converted into another partition.

To use `fips.exe`, you first need to be in MS-DOS mode. To do this, select Shut Down from the Start menu and choose Restart In MS-DOS Mode. Windows 98 should shut down and switch to a full-screen DOS environment.

WARNING   This is a critical step. You shouldn't use a program like `fips.exe` inside a DOS window or full-screen DOS environment while Windows 98 is running. Unlike DOS, Windows 95 and above allow multiple programs to run simultaneously, so it is possible for other programs to try to access the partition being worked with by `fips.exe`. If this happens, your data may be corrupted and irretrievable.

Once in DOS mode, run `fips.exe` from your CD-ROM. If your CD-ROM drive is drive E, use the command

`c:\>e:\dosutils\fips20\fips.exe`

The program first presents your partition table. In the previous example of a two-partition drive, this will look something like the following:

```
Partition table:

      |         | Start     |        |      End       | Start  |Number of |
Part. |Bootable |Head Cyl. Sector|System|Head Cyl. Sector| Sector |Sectors   | MB
------+---------+----------------+------+----------------+--------+----------+-----
1     | yes     |  1   0   1 | 06h | 254 222  63 |      63| 3582432 |1749
2     | no      |  0 223   1 | 05h | 254 286  63 | 3582495| 1028160 | 502
```

On most systems, identifying your partitions is easy since drive C is partition 1, drive D is partition 2, and so on. If you have trouble, use the size of the partition in megabytes in the last column to help.

You are then prompted to choose a partition. In this case, choose 2, since you want drive D to be adjusted. Once you choose, the partition will be scanned and summary information about the partition, similar to the following, will be presented:

```
Bytes per sector: 512
Sectors per cluster: 8
Reserved sectors: 1
Number of FATs: 2
Number of rootdirectory entries: 512
Number of sectors (short): 0
Media descriptor byte: f8h
Sectors per FAT: 145
Sectors per track: 63
Drive heads: 16
Hidden sectors: 63
```

```
Number of sectors (long): 141057
Physical drive number: 80h
Signature: 29h
```

Assuming you have free space at the end of the partition you have chosen, you are asked which disk cylinder to use as the line where the partition is cut and split. You can use your arrow keys to change the selected cylinder. As you do this, the size of the partitions in megabytes is shown so that you can make sure that the new partition is large enough. The fips.exe program handles the job of making sure that you can't choose a cylinder to split that would leave some of the data from your current partition on the new partition.

Finally, a revised partition table appears, and you are asked to confirm that everything looks okay. In this example, you should now have three partitions, with the third being your new partition and the second being smaller in size than it was originally.

TIP   To protect against mistakes, copy fips.exe, restorrb.exe, and errors.txt from your Linux Installation CD-ROM to a bootable floppy disk. These files are usually located in a subdirectory such as dosutils. When asked if you want to write backup copies of your boot and root sectors to a floppy disk, answer **Yes**. Then, if you need to recover from a mistake, you can boot from the floppy and run restorrb.exe to restore your original boot and root sectors.

Looking Ahead

In this chapter, you conducted the basic preparation needed to install Linux. Now you are ready for the actual installation.

In Chapter 4, "Installing Red Hat Linux 7.1," you will run through a basic installation of Linux, discussing each screen of the installation program and how to decide what choices to make.

In Chapter 5, "Special Installations," you will look at special cases, such as how to install Linux on multiple hard drives and how to install Linux onto an existing DOS partition.

CHAPTER

FOUR

Installing Red Hat Linux 7.1

- ■ Starting the Installation

- ■ Configuring Your System for Installation

- ■ The Installation Process

You're finally here: You are going to install Linux. By now you should be able to boot the Linux Installation CD-ROM or should have produced a set of Linux boot floppy disks. You should also have determined where you will be installing Linux and made the space available.

Now you can begin. While the installation program may ask questions unfamiliar to you if you have not used a Linux-like operating system before, in reality the whole process is quite simple, and many of the tough decisions are made for you by the installation software.

In fact, for the average user who is installing Linux as a second operating system in a Windows 95/98/Me system, the process is generally straightforward, with a few odd turns required. While this chapter is based on installing Red Hat Linux 7.1, the principles are the same for the latest version of most Linux distributions.

Starting the Installation

This chapter looks at a straightforward installation: installing Linux from the CD-ROM onto a non-networked, stand-alone PC.

In order to do this, you need to have selected which media to boot from to start the installation. As outlined in the last chapter, your two options are as follows:

- Booting directly from the Linux Installation CD-ROM. This requires that your computer's BIOS supports booting from your CD-ROM drive.

- Booting from a set of boot floppy disks and then installing from the CD-ROM.

In either case, insert your boot disk (floppy or CD-ROM) and boot your computer. When the computer starts booting from a Red Hat Linux 7.1 floppy disk or CD-ROM, you will be presented with an initial welcome screen, as shown in Figure 4.1.

FIGURE 4.1:

The Red Hat Linux 7.1
installation boot screen

FIGURE 4.1:

The Red Hat Linux 7.1
installation boot screen

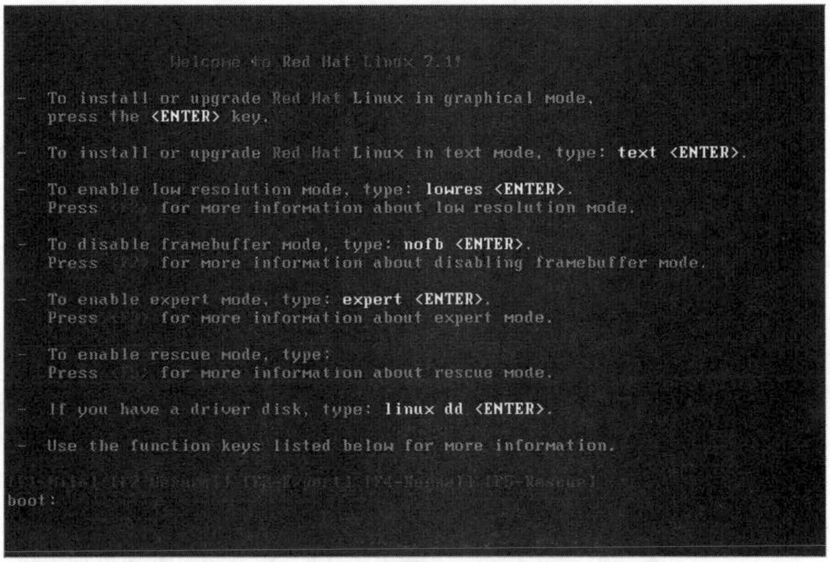

Here you have seven main installation options:

- Press Enter to start the normal graphical installation process.

- While this item is not explicitly shown on the menu, you can type in boot parameters that allow the installation software to detect some types of obscure hardware, and then press Enter to start the normal installation process. (Most hardware is detected automatically during installation.)

- Type **text** and press Enter to boot in text mode. (In text mode, installation starts in a less-graphically-demanding screen. If Linux is having trouble detecting your video card, text mode may be a viable option. Some of you may recognize the text-mode screen graphics from Red Hat Linux 6.0 and below.)

NOTE   Compared to the text mode of installation just described, the next two installation modes I describe are closer to the normal graphical installation process.

- Type **lowres** and press Enter to boot in low resolution mode. In this mode, graphical installation starts in a 640 × 400 screen, instead of the standard installation 800 × 600 screen. If you have a video card that does not have enough memory to support 800 × 600 graphics, low resolution may be a viable option.

- Type **nofb** and press Enter to boot in no frame buffer mode. In this mode, graphical installation starts without the frame buffer associated with accelerated graphics cards. If your graphics card does not support 2-D or 3-D accelerated graphics, then no frame buffer mode may be a viable option.

- Type **expert** and press Enter to boot in expert mode. (In expert mode, hardware detection is not performed, and you will need to provide configuration parameters for all your hardware during the installation. You should revert to this option only if your hardware is not being detected properly and you are fairly confident of the parameters to enter.)

- Type **linux rescue** and press Enter to boot a generic Linux rescue disk. This can help you recover from some system failures. It allows you to access your computer as the root user with basic editors and tools that let you reconfigure damaged or lost configuration files. Generally, you should create a dedicated rescue floppy with critical configuration files; rescue mode may be an option if you lose that floppy.

- The linux dd option is not a separate option but an alternate way to start the normal graphical installation process. If you type **linux dd**, the installation program prompts you to insert a driver disk for special equipment. A typical driver disk can be created from the drivers.img file on the images directory on the installation CD-ROM.

NOTE
Generally, most users will find that all of their hardware will be successfully detected if they choose the first option, so simply press Enter to start the boot process. If you fail to press any key within 60 seconds, the installation automatically starts as if you had pressed Enter without providing any options. To disable this timer, press one of the help keys (F1–F5). Then you will have all the time you need to decide how to start the installation program.

Configuring Your System for Installation

The installation process has several steps, which we will consider in turn. However, before we do that, you should learn how to use the keyboard to work in the installation program.

Keyboard Controls

As shown in Figure 4.2, there are several elements to the average installation screen. These elements include text input fields, check boxes, and buttons.

FIGURE 4.2:

A typical Red Hat Linux 7.1 installation screen

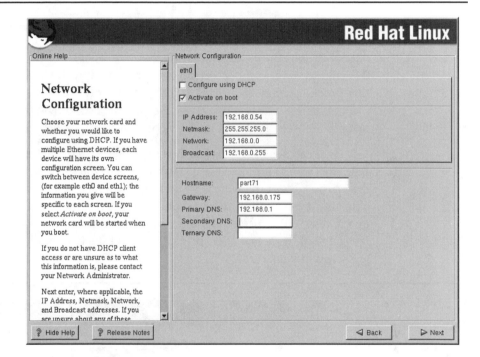

This screen contains the following elements:

- Text input fields (IP Address, Netmask, etc.)
- Check boxes (Configure Using DHCP and Activate On Boot)
- Buttons (Hide Help, Back, and Next)

You can move between these elements using the Tab key (or the Shift+Tab combination to move backward), or you can use your mouse. The arrow keys can also be used to move between fields.

To toggle the state of a check box, move to the check box and press the spacebar. To press a button, move the cursor to the button using the Tab or arrow keys and then press the spacebar or the Enter key. With a Next button, the F12 key generally works the same as pressing Enter or the spacebar. Of course, if the installation program detects your mouse, you can left-click your selections as well. Just in case, the remaining descriptions in this chapter assume that your mouse doesn't work in the Linux installation program.

Choosing a Language

After you start the installation program at the boot screen as described earlier in this chapter, a welcome screen appears, followed by the first screen of the installation process: Language Selection. This affects only the language that you see during the installation process. To change the language shown on Red Hat Linux 7.1 after installation, see the "Language Support Selection" section later in this chapter.

As you can see in Figure 4.3, the Language Selection screen has a selection list field and a Next button. When the cursor is in the selection list field, you can use the arrow keys or the Page Up and Page Down keys to move through the available languages until the desired one is selected. This selection determines the language that will be used during the installation process. (This is distinct from the language of the actual operating system and the keyboard layout, both of which are selected later.)

FIGURE 4.3:

Choosing a language

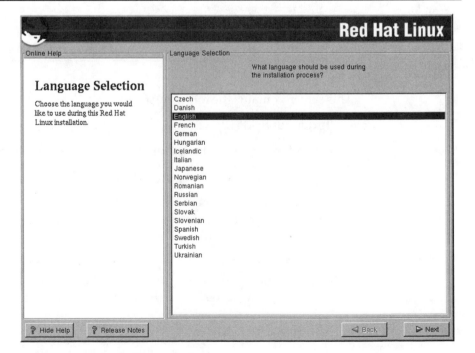

Choosing a Keyboard Type

The next screen presents selection list fields for choosing a keyboard model and layout. If you don't see your keyboard in the model list, the default is Generic 104-key PC. The layout generally corresponds to different languages or dialects (e.g., French or Swiss French). In the United States, the correct layout will almost always be US English. Other common models and layouts include those listed in Tables 4.1 and 4.2.

TABLE 4.1: Typical Keyboard Models

Model	Description
Dell 101-key PC	For certain Dell PC keyboards
Japanese 106-key	With Japanese characters
Microsoft Natural	Microsoft Natural (split) keyboard
Winbook Model XP5	Winbook Special Model XP5 keyboard

TABLE 4.2: Typical Keyboard Layouts

Layout	Description
Brazilian	Brazilian Portuguese keyboard
Canadian	Canadian English keyboard
German	German keyboard
Swiss German	Swiss German keyboard

You can test your selection at the bottom of the screen, in the Test Your Selection Here text box. You should test your selection especially if you have doubts about your choice of keyboard.

> **NOTE**   If you have a special keyboard and don't see it in the standard mode of the Red Hat Linux 7.1 Installation program, start the installation program again in text mode. Red Hat Linux 7.1 includes nearly 80 different keyboard types in this mode.

Configuring Your Mouse

After you configure your keyboard, the next step is to configure your mouse. First, the installation software attempts to detect your mouse. Then, you are presented with a list of possible mouse types from which to select (if automatic detection was successful, then the appropriate mouse type is preselected). If you cannot find your specific brand of mouse on the list, choose a generic mouse most similar to yours. Consult your mouse's documentation to determine the type of mouse you have.

If yours is a two-button mouse, make sure that you check the box for three-button mouse emulation. Linux expects a three-button mouse, as do all Unix operating systems. This emulation allows you to click the left and right mouse buttons together to simulate clicking the middle mouse button. This feature, while not absolutely necessary, will enhance X Windows functionality.

> **NOTE**   If you have a mouse with a center wheel, press it. If you hear a click, Linux may be able to recognize it as a three-button mouse. In this case, you may not need to select three-button mouse emulation.

You also need to set up the mouse port, which is typically PS/2 (with a round connector), serial (trapezoidal connector with nine holes), or USB (small rectangular connector). If you have a serial mouse, you also need to set up or confirm the mouse port, usually COM1: or COM2:.

Installing or Upgrading?

Once you have selected and configured your mouse, the next menu allows you to install Red Hat Linux in four different ways. Alternatively, if you already have Linux on your computer, you can just select the Upgrade option. If you want to upgrade without overwriting your configuration files, you generally need to upgrade with the same branded distribution. Most Linux distributions allow you the same options, but the organization of the install screens can differ.

If you are installing Red Hat Linux 7.1 for the first time on your computer, there are four possible ways to install it:

Workstation   Performs a default installation for a Linux workstation. This option automatically erases all existing Linux partitions on your system, and it requires at least 1.2GB of free space on your hard drive.

Server   Performs a default installation for a Linux server. This option automatically erases all existing partitions on your system, including any other non-Linux operating systems and data on your computer. It requires at least 650GB of free space on your hard drive.

Laptop   Similar to a Workstation installation, this option performs a default installation for Linux on a laptop computer. It includes packages typically required by a laptop computer, such as PCMCIA drivers. This option automatically erases all existing Linux partitions on your system. It requires at least 1.2GB of free space on your hard drive.

Custom   Provides complete control over all aspects of the installation process. The default Custom installation requires just over 700MB of free space on your hard drive.

In order to learn the details of installing Red Hat Linux 7.1, you will work with the fourth option, Custom, throughout this chapter and in Chapter 5, "Special Installations," in Chapter 27, "Installing Red Hat Linux 7.1 for the SOHO," and in Chapter 31, "Security and Red Hat Linux 7.1 As an Inexpensive Router."

Setting Up Your Disk Partitions

After you select an installation class, you face a decision about how to allocate disk space for your Linux installation. This is a crucial step in the process because a mistake can erase existing data on your system that you want to keep.

Let's assume that you have a single hard drive in your system, that—as directed in Chapter 3, "Getting Ready to Install Red Hat Linux 7.1"—you created an area of free space (preferably larger than 1GB) using the techniques described there, and that the space is now ready to be used.

The first question you are asked is which tool you want to use to set up your partitions. The two choices in Red Hat Linux are Disk Druid and fdisk.

Fdisk is the standard Linux tool for configuring disk partitions and is available for every Linux distribution. However, it is difficult to use and can be especially daunting for first-time Linux or Unix users.

WARNING	If you don't know what you're doing, **fdisk** can cause you to lose all of your data. Also, the Linux **fdisk** tool is quite different from the MS-DOS **fdisk** tool, in that Linux **fdisk** includes a large number of options, as discussed in Chapter 5.

To help ease this process, Red Hat Linux 7.1 provides its own tool for disk partition management called Disk Druid. This section focuses on using Disk Druid because it eases the initial installation process for users new to the Linux environment. If you select the Disk Druid button, the main Disk Druid screen appears, as shown in Figure 4.4.

FIGURE 4.4:

The main Disk Druid screen

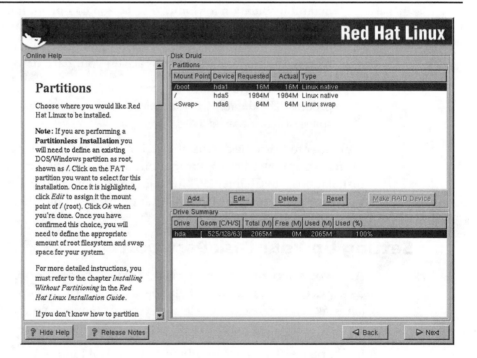

This screen has three main sections: the Partitions section, the button row, and the Drive Summary section.

In the Partitions section, a single row is displayed for each existing disk partition on your system. The following information is presented about each partition:

Mount Point   This indicates where the partition appears in your Linux directory structure. Linux directories all appear as subdirectories of the root directory. The root directory is / and all subdirectories start with /, such as /home, /opt, and /usr/X11R6. At a minimum, you need to have a partition mounted as / and a swap partition. If you choose to mount additional partitions as subdirectories, this will spread your Linux distribution across additional directories. For instance, if you mount a partition as /usr, then any content stored under this subdirectory is stored on the /usr partition, while all other data is on the root-mounted (/) partition. If you want to limit or dedicate a certain amount of space to a directory, you can mount that directory in a limited amount of space. The primary roles of the standard top-level Red Hat Linux directories are as follows:

/bin   Standard system utilities are stored here.

/boot   The kernel, boot loader, memory maps, and module details are stored here. Commonly set up in a separate partition.

/dev   Device files are stored here.

/home   Users' home directories are stored here.

/mnt   Temporarily mounted filesystems, such as /mnt/cdrom and /mnt/floppy, are normally stored here.

/opt   Optionally installed software is stored here.

/root   The home directory of the root user. Do not confuse this with the root-mounted (/) partition.

/sbin   Standard system administration files are stored here. Typically, these files should be accessible only to the root user.

/usr   Additional system software and administration tools are stored here.

/var   Log files and print spools are stored here. This is commonly mounted separately in limited space on Web servers, as the log files from a Web site can otherwise easily crowd out any other information on that Linux computer.

/etc   Administrative files and configuration files are contained here. Other commands formerly in this directory should be moved to /bin or /sbin.

Device   This indicates the Linux device name for each partition. For IDE disks, the drives are labeled hdx, where x is a letter designating a drive (a for the primary master drive, b for the primary slave, c for the secondary master, and d for the secondary slave). Thus, if you have a single IDE hard disk, it is disk hda. SCSI disks are labeled sdx with *x* again designating a drive. Partitions on the disk are then numbered consecutively starting with hda1 and moving up. Generally, partitions 1 through 4 are primary partitions, and 5 and above represent the logical partitions common on many DOS systems. In Figure 4.4, you see Linux partitions associated with the boot directory (hda1), the root directory (hda5), and the swap partition (hda6).

Requested   This indicates the minimum size of the partition in megabytes.

Actual   This indicates the actual space allocated for a partition. Disk Druid allows the creation of growable Linux partitions, which increase in size as free space is available on the hard disk and space runs out in the partition. DOS partitions should have matching actual and requested values.

Type   This field indicates the type of partition that you can create with Disk Druid. Possible values include Linux native, Linux swap, Linux RAID, DOS 16-bit<32M, and DOS 16-bit>=32M. (While you can't create FAT32 or NTFS partitions here, Disk Druid now recognizes these common Microsoft Windows partitions.)

The next main section of the screen is the set of five task buttons. Use the Add button to create the necessary Linux partitions for your installation and the Edit button to make sure your existing DOS and Windows data is accessible in Linux or to change previous settings. You can delete an individual partition with the Delete button. If you want to start over, use the Reset button. If you need more speed and security with your data, the Make RAID Device button lets you distribute files over a series of independent partitions.

Finally, there is the Drive Summary section. This presents one line for each hard disk on your system and includes the following information about the drives:

Drive   This is the device name for the hard drive, discussed previously.

Geometry   This indicates the number of cylinders, heads, and sectors (in that order) for the drive.

Total   This indicates the total available space on the drive, in megabytes.

Free   This shows how much of the drive is available, in megabytes, for additional partitions.

Used   This indicates the total used space on the drive, in megabytes. This number actually reflects how much is used in the sense of how much has been allocated to partitions. These partitions may not be full, but the space is no longer available to be allocated to other partitions. The number associated with the main Linux native partitions must be more than zero and should be more than 1GB before proceeding, because you need to use this space to install Linux in. If you don't have any free space, consult the discussion in Chapter 3, which describes how to allocate space for your Linux installation.

Used (%)   This indicates the percentage of space on the drive allocated to partitions. If this number is less than 100%, you can add more partitions.

Finally, the button bar across the bottom of the screen has Hide Help, Back, and Next buttons. You can use the Hide Help button to hide the explanation screen on the left-hand side of the page. You can use the Back button to return to the previous menu. Use the Next button when you want to continue to the next menu. The Next button will be available only after partitions are configured correctly for Linux to be installed.

Adding New Partitions

To add a new partition, you simply press the Add button on the main Disk Druid screen. A screen appears asking for the following main information:

- Mount point
- Size in megabytes
- Whether the drive can grow to use unallocated disk space as needed (through the Use Remaining Space check box)
- Partition type (from a selection list field)
- Which drives the partition can be created on. If more than one drive is indicated as allowed and all allowed drives have sufficient space to create the partition, then Disk Druid will decide which disk to use. If you want to create the partition on a specific disk, make sure that only that disk is checked.

You should use the Add button to create at least the following partitions:

A swap partition   Linux needs a separate partition to use for swapping. This is necessary when you use up all your physical RAM and the operating system must draw on virtual memory (disk space masquerading as RAM) to keep functioning. Subject to the limitations in the following note, you generally should at least match the amount of physical RAM you have on your system; if you have plenty of free disk space, make the size of the swap partition as much as double that of your physical RAM. So, on a 32MB system, create a swap partition of between 32 and 64MB. The partition type should be set to Linux swap, and no mount point should be indicated. To save room for other partitions, the Use Remaining Space check box should be unselected.

NOTE
In Red Hat Linux 7.1, swap partitions need to be at least 32MB. If you selected a Workstation or a Laptop-class installation, the Red Hat 7.1 installation program allocates 64MB for your swap partition. Alternatively, if you chose a Server-class installation, you'll get a 256MB swap partition.

A root partition   In this chapter, you are going to install Linux in two partitions. (The next chapter discusses the use of multiple partitions or drives for the installation of Linux.) To do this, you need to add another partition. You will probably want the partition to be at least 1GB to give you room to work once Linux is installed. This partition should be type Linux Native, should have a mount point of /, and can be marked with the Use Remaining Space option if there is unallocated free space on your drive that you want to use if the partition grows larger than its initial size.

A boot partition   When you let Red Hat Linux 7.1 partition your drive automatically, it sets up a boot partition by default. Boot partitions include the key components required to boot Linux: the kernel, system map, and hardware module locations. On most Linux systems, a boot partition has to be located below the 1024th cylinder on a hard drive. However, if you've set up your partitions with fdisk, Red Hat Linux 7.1 allows you to bypass this limitation by adding lba32 as a kernel parameter when you set up LILO later.

Editing a Partition

You can edit existing partitions by selecting them from the list of current partitions and then clicking the Edit button. This brings up a window like the one you used when adding a new partition, except that here all the fields are filled in to match the settings of the partition you are editing.

If you have pre-existing DOS partitions, you can make them available to Linux by specifying a mount point for them. To do this, select the partition you wish to make accessible in Linux, press the Edit button, and then fill in a mount point for the partition.

If you have a single DOS partition, you could mount it as /dos, for instance. If you have two DOS partitions, which are drives C and D in DOS and Windows, you could choose /dosc and /dosd (or /c and /d), respectively, as the mount points.

Deleting a Partition

If, in the process of creating your Linux swap and root partitions, you make a mistake (maybe the swap partition is too large or your root partition too small), you can delete the partitions and then re-add them. To do this, select the partition in the list of current partitions and then press the Delete button.

WARNING   Take care when deleting a partition. Don't accidentally delete any partitions that already existed before you started installing Linux and that contain important data or software you want to keep.

Reset

If, in the process of creating your Linux partitions, you feel the need to start again, click the Reset button. This restores the partition table to the state before you started Disk Druid.

Make RAID Device

If you are setting up Linux as a server, you are setting up a computer for multiple users. The programs and data on that server become even more important. You can protect the data by spreading it out among multiple hard drives, known as a Redundant Array of Independent Disks (RAID). If you set up a series of RAID partitions, you can then configure them together with the Make RAID Device option.

Moving On

Once you have finished creating and configuring your partitions, you are ready to move on. You can do this by pressing the Next button.

Formatting Your Linux Partitions

The next step is to format your Linux partitions in preparation for installing Linux. A list of partitions of type Linux Native appears with indications of the mount points they have. Any newly created partitions should be marked for formatting by selecting the check box next to the drive.

If you have additional partitions of type Linux Native, they should be formatted if they are new partitions. If they already existed (this is unlikely for new Red Hat users) and you want to retain the data they hold, don't mark them for formatting.

You can also indicate that a bad block check should be performed during formatting. This is a good idea, especially for new hard drives.

Setting Up LILO

LILO is the Linux boot loader. In order for your system to boot properly, you need to configure and install LILO. LILO also provides the dual-boot features that can allow you to choose which operating system to launch at boot time, providing you with access to your existing Windows or DOS system as well as Linux.

There are four parts to this process, as shown in Figure 4.5. First, you need to decide where to install LILO: on your hard drive and or on a boot disk.

Next, if you choose to install LILO on your hard drive (as you should), there are two viable locations: on the Master Boot Record (MBR) or on the first sector of the boot partition. You should install LILO on your MBR unless you are running an operating system with a boot loader such as OS/2 or Windows NT/2000 or have set up another boot loader such as Partition Magic or System Commander. If you already have one of these other boot loaders, you don't need LILO in the way; you should therefore install LILO on the Linux boot partition.

WARNING   You need to either install LILO or create a boot disk during this step in order to boot your Linux system. It is highly recommended that you install LILO during this initial installation.

FIGURE 4.5:

Configuring the Linux boot loader

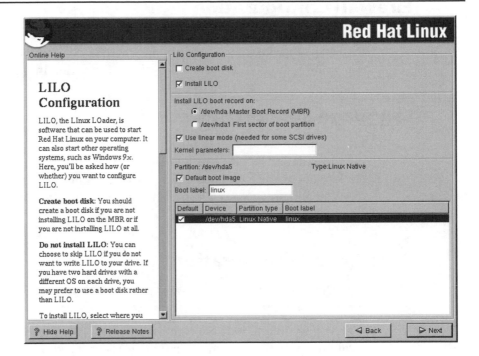

Most hard drives can be accessed in linear mode. Unless your hard drive does not use logical block addressing (LBA) mode (check your BIOS), keep the Use Linear Mode option selected.

In the next part of the screen, you can see all partitions with operating systems. When you set a Default Boot Image, you set the operating system (usually Linux or Microsoft Windows) that starts by default when you boot your computer. The Boot Label is the name you use (linux in Figure 4.5) to select which operating system will boot when you start your computer.

Network Configuration

The next item to be configured is your network. Because you are installing a stand-alone system in this chapter, choose not to configure your network. Chapter 27 discusses network configuration in more detail.

Firewall Configuration

Your firewall is the next item to be configured. But again, because you are installing a stand-alone system in this chapter, choose not to configure your firewall. Chapter 31 discusses firewall configuration in more detail.

Language Support Selection

Here, you can set up the language that you see on your Red Hat Linux system after installation is complete. Red Hat Linux 7.1 gives you a choice of 104 different languages and/or dialects. If disk space is scarce, choose only the language(s) that you will use; if you choose all 104 options, then that would require an additional 135MB of disk space.

Time Zone Configuration

The next step is to configure your computer's clock and time zone. You need to make two decisions.

First, you need to indicate whether you want your system's clock set to your local time or to Greenwich mean time (GMT), also known as Coordinated Universal Time, which is known by its French acronym, UTC. If you run only Linux on your computer, set the clock to UTC. Linux then converts it to the current time for your time zone. But if you also run other operating systems on your PC, don't select this option.

Second, you need to choose the actual time zone from the list of available time zones.

Account Configuration

As a multiuser operating system, Linux needs at least one user to exist in order for it to be used. On all systems, you have to have a root user, so you are prompted to provide a root password (twice, for confirmation). The root user is the all-powerful system administrator. When logged in as the root user, you can view all users' files, perform all system administration tasks, and, if you want to, delete all files on your system. This is a powerful account, so you need to keep this password secure if other people are going to have access to your system.

You can then set up individual accounts, based on a desired account name and password. Enter a descriptive name in the Full Name text box.

Authentication Configuration

Next, you are prompted to make authentication configuration selections. There are five options on this screen and each can be selected individually. They are not mutually exclusive. The options are shown here:

Enable MD5 Passwords   Typically, Unix systems have used a relatively weak encryption scheme for storing passwords. This option makes Linux use a more rigorous encryption scheme for storage of user passwords. By default, this option is selected.

Use Shadow Passwords   Using shadow passwords is a technique designed to make it harder for an attacker or a regular system user to steal the user database and then attempt to crack the system administration password at their own leisure. By default, this option is selected.

Enable NIS   This is a type of network authentication common in many Unix networks, especially those with Sun Solaris-based servers. You can specify the domain name of the group of computers on this network or specify a specific server where NIS usernames and passwords are stored. By default, this option is not selected.

Enable LDAP   The Lightweight Directory Access Protocol is set up for special directories of users. If you know the name of an LDAP server on your network, you can enable LDAP. By default, this option is not selected.

Enable Kerberos   Kerberos is a secure means of encrypting passwords that are transmitted across a network. Kerberos requires access to a server that grants Kerberos tickets, which includes the encryption scheme. Do not enable Kerberos unless you plan to set up all Linux services to use this protocol. By default, this option is not selected.

Unless you are familiar with these options and have compelling reasons to alter them, leave the default selections the way they are and move on.

Chapter 4 • Installing Red Hat Linux 7.1

Selecting Packages

Now that your hard disks are configured and your Linux partitions are formatted, you are ready to begin installing the actual software. The default installation includes all the necessary core software, but several optional components are also available, including those shown in Figure 4.6.

FIGURE 4.6:

Selecting additional components

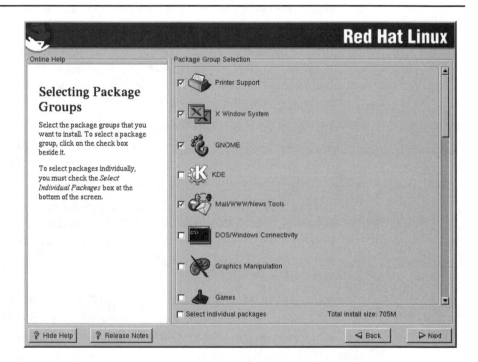

Each component is a collection of related packages for specific tasks such as dial-up connections, Web surfing, and others. You can choose the packages individually by marking their respective check boxes or you can choose the Everything option, which is the last entry in the list.

The Select Individual Packages option that appears below the list field indicates that you want to select individual packages within each component. However, if you are a first-time Linux user, it will be hard to choose the packages. Leaving this option unselected means that each component is installed in its entirety.

If you have plenty of disk space (more than 3GB; 4GB is preferable), then select everything so that you have a complete Linux installation. Note the Total Install Size shown at the bottom of Figure 4.6. If your space is in more limited supply, consider installing the following components at a minimum:

- Printer Support (If you don't have a printer, then this is unnecessary.)
- X Window System
- GNOME
- Mail/WWW/News Tools
- DOS/Windows Connectivity
- Multimedia Support

If you have sufficient room, install KDE as well as GNOME to help you follow Chapter 11, "Using KDE." If you choose to install X Windows, you next get to configure your video card and monitor. Otherwise, you are taken directly to installation, as described at the end of the next section.

NOTE   If you're installing more than the minimum components shown, you may need both Red Hat Linux 7.1 Installation CD-ROMs. Since the second installation CD-ROM is not included with this book, you would either need to purchase the official CD-ROMs from www.redhat.com or just the CD-ROMs themselves from an alternate supplier such as www.cheapbytes.com or www.linuxmall.com.

Configuring X Windows

X Windows is Linux's graphical user interface (GUI). Chapter 7, "Installing and Configuring X Windows," discusses configuring X Windows in detail. For now, let's quickly run through the configuration process. Configuration can be quite complex and a whole chapter is devoted to it, so any problems will be left to that chapter for resolution.

First, a list of monitor types appears. If you find an exact match for your monitor, choose it; otherwise, select Unprobed Monitor or hold off until you read Chapter 7. An incorrect configuration can cause damage to the monitor. The match should be exact.

Next, an attempt is made to determine what type of video card you have. If this fails, a list of available video cards appears. Select the one that most closely matches your card (if none match, select Generic Standard VGA or leave the configuration of X Windows until Chapter 7). Select the amount of video memory available on your video card. Consult your video card's documentation for this information. Once you've made your selections, you can click Test This Configuration to make sure that the chosen settings work for your system.

If you see and choose a Customize X Configuration option, you can customize the resolution of X Windows on your monitor (aka Video Modes). With the Use Graphical Login option, you can set up a graphical login screen. If you want to configure graphics after installing Linux, select the Skip X Configuration option. You can then leave graphical configuration to Chapter 7.

NOTE In some distributions, including older versions of Red Hat, a list of clock chips appears. If your card doesn't have a clock chip or you don't know whether it does, choose No Clockchip. Do not guess on this question. If you don't know about your card's clock chip, leave this until Chapter 7.

Now you've completed the basic configuration requirements. When you click Next, you're warned that the actual installation is about to begin. Most distributions create a log of your installation process. Red Hat Linux 7.1 saves this as the file /tmp/install.log. Several other distributions create their installation logs in the same file. Click Next, and then installation begins.

The Installation Process

The installation proceeds automatically, and no input is required during this process. On the screen, you'll see a timer that indicates how long you need to wait before the installation is finished. During the installation of the software, the screen also displays the current status of the installation, indicating which package is currently being installed, how many packages and how many megabytes remain, and the overall progress of the installation.

Creating a Boot Disk

Once the Linux software has been successfully installed, the installation proceeds to the final step: creating a boot disk. Creating a boot disk is wise because it allows you to boot your system in case of an emergency. You can then attempt to resurrect a sick system. Insert a blank (formatted) floppy disk as directed in Figure 4.7, then click Next.

FIGURE 4.7:

Creating a boot disk

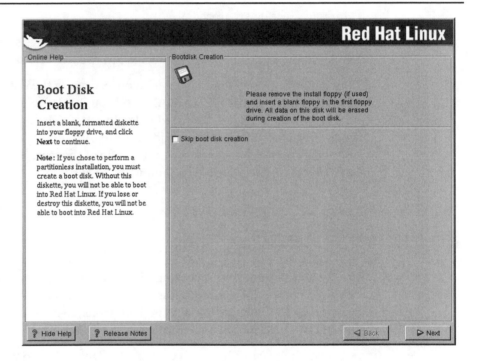

The Red Hat Linux 7.1 Installation program copies the boot files to your floppy disk. After this process is complete, the installation program is finished.

Rebooting Your System

Finally, you are prompted to remove any floppy disks from the computer and reboot. Some Linux distributions eject the CD-ROM automatically. If this doesn't happen, remove the CD-ROM before you reboot. If you left Linux as the default operating system, the system boots into Linux, giving you five seconds at the graphical prompt during start-up to select an alternate operating system.

In Red Hat Linux 7.1, if you have more than one operating system on your computer, use the up and down arrow keys to choose an operating system. If you choose Linux and all goes well, a Red Hat Linux login prompt appears. You can log in here as the root user using the username root and the password you provided earlier. A command prompt appears similar to the following:

```
[armand@localhost armand]$
```

You will learn about commands later, but the premise is simple: Type the command and press the Enter key to execute it. Type **exit** and press Enter to log out.

Linux allows you to log in more than once, even in the initial character-based mode. Using the combinations of Alt+F1 through Alt+F6, you can switch between up to six virtual consoles. You need to log in separately in each virtual console. You can log in as different users and perform different tasks or log in to different virtual consoles as the same user—this is one of the features of Unix and Linux that make them such flexible environments to work in.

Looking Ahead

By now you should have a working Linux system. If you are one of the few readers who have special circumstances that made it impossible to get your Linux system running by following the steps in this chapter, then take a look at the Chapter 5, "Special Installations," which discusses some special-case installations:

- Installing from a hard drive partition. (This is important if, for some reason, you cannot get Linux to install from your CD-ROM drive.)

- Installing to multiple partitions or hard disks. (This is useful if you have lots of disk space spread over multiple disks or need the performance gain from splitting Linux in this way.)

- Using fdisk instead of Disk Druid to configure your partitions. (Disk Druid is useful but not standard for Linux; using fdisk allows you to learn the workings of this standard tool and provides access to the more powerful tools desired by the expert user.)

If any of these special installations are useful, turn to Chapter 5. If your system booted correctly, though, you are ready to move on and learn about X Windows. Skip to Chapter 6, "An Overview of X Windows," and continue from there.

CHAPTER
FIVE

Special Installations

- Installing from a Hard Disk Partition

- Installing Linux on Multiple Partitions

- Using *fdisk* instead of Disk Druid

In Chapter 4, "Installing Red Hat Linux 7.1," you learned how to take the straightforward approach to installing Linux: from a local CD-ROM to a single hard disk partition.

This chapter looks at a few installation variations that are not uncommon. First among these is installing from a hard disk partition. There are cases where installing from the local CD-ROM drive is not practical. For instance, you may have one of the few CD-ROM drives that the Red Hat installation software can't recognize, or you may have only temporary access to a CD-ROM drive. In these cases, one option is to copy the contents of the Red Hat CD-ROM to blank space on a hard drive and then install from the hard drive.

In addition, with the lower cost of hard drives today, you may have available multiple partitions or hard drives that you can use for your Linux installation. In these cases, you can maximize the performance of your system by spreading your Linux system across multiple partitions and drives.

Finally, this chapter looks at how to use the fdisk program instead of Disk Druid for configuring your hard disk partitions. Fdisk is standard with all distributions of Linux; Disk Druid is available only with Red Hat Linux.

Installing from a Hard Disk Partition

For some users, there are compelling reasons to install Linux from a different hard disk partition than the one they plan to run Linux from. Possible reasons include the following:

- A CD-ROM drive that the Linux installation program fails to recognize

- Lack of a permanent CD-ROM drive, but access to a CD-ROM drive to copy the CD-ROM to a hard disk

- A notebook computer with a switchable floppy drive and a CD-ROM drive that cannot be booted from the CD-ROM drive

In all these cases, the process of installing from a hard disk partition is basically the same:

1. Create an ISO disk image from the Red Hat CD-ROM on a dedicated hard disk partition. If you copy both Red Hat CD-ROMs, be sure to copy them to the same directory.

2. Make sure you have the correct installation floppy disks ready.

3. Start the installation process by booting from an installation floppy disk created from the boot.img file.

NOTE

If you want to install extra packages such as Linuxconf, you'll need both Red Hat Installation CDs. You can purchase the full Red Hat Linux 7.1 package from many major computer stores or online from www.redhat.com, or you can download the CDs online. You can also purchase downloaded CD-ROMs from vendors such as Cheap Bytes (www.cheapbytes.com) or Linux Mall (www.linuxmall.com).

Copying the CD-ROM to a Hard Disk Partition

In order to install from a hard disk partition, you need a dedicated partition available to store the contents of the Linux Installation CD-ROM. This partition should contain at least 650MB of free space in order to accommodate the complete contents of the standard Red Hat Linux 7.1 Installation CD-ROM. If you're installing more than the standard packages, this partition needs twice that amount of space.

To create ISO image files from the Red Hat Linux CD-ROM, you need to create a package from the contents of the CD-ROM in a file such as cd1.iso. One way to do this is with the following commands in root user mode, which first mount the CD-ROM and then create the ISO image:

```
# mount -t iso9660 /dev/cdrom /mnt/cdrom
# mkisofs -J -r -T -o /tmp/cd1.iso /mnt/cdrom
```

NOTE

Place the CD ISO image file in a subdirectory such as /tmp or /home/mj. This makes it easier for the installation program to identify the location of the image. If you're making ISO images for both installation CD-ROMs, place them in the same directory.

If your CD-ROM device is different, substitute accordingly for /dev/cdrom. In the mkisofs command, the -o switch comes before the filename of the ISO image that you want to create. The -T switch adds a TRANS.TBL file in each directory to preserve long filename information for operating systems that can't handle them, such as MS-DOS. The -r switch uses "Rock Ridge" extensions to allow long filenames, and the -J switch uses "Joliet" records to make this ISO usable on Microsoft Windows computers.

If you have the second Red Hat Linux 7.1 Installation CD-ROM, you'll want to create a second ISO image in the same directory.

NOTE　　The publisher's edition of Red Hat Linux 7.1 included with this book has only one installation CD-ROM.

Because of its size, it can take several minutes to create an ISO. To check the result on a `cd1.iso` file, you can mount it in a similar fashion to mounting a regular CD-ROM:

```
# mount -t iso9660 -r -o loop /tmp/RedHat/cd1.iso /mnt/cdrom
```

The result should be just like mounting a regular CD-ROM. You can then compare the files on the ISO against the Red Hat Linux 7.1 Installation CD-ROM.

Preparing the Installation Floppies

Chapter 3, "Getting Ready to Install Red Hat Linux 7.1," discusses how to create the necessary installation floppy disks. Refer to the section "From Floppy Disk and CD-ROM" in that chapter for all the details.

In order to install from a hard disk partition in some distributions, you may need both the primary boot installation floppy disk and a driver or supplementary floppy disk, so it is best to have the appropriate disks prepared before starting the installation process.

The Actual Installation Process

To begin the installation, boot from the boot floppy. Follow the steps used for a normal installation from CD-ROM (set out in Chapter 4, "Installing Red Hat Linux 7.1"). The boot disk takes you to a text mode screen, which is really a graphical screen that is less demanding than the standard installation screens shown in Chapter 4. After selecting an installation language and keyboard, you are taken to an installation method screen. In this screen, select Hard Drive instead of Local CD-ROM.

After selecting Hard Drive, you are prompted to indicate the partition and directory with your Linux hard disk images, as shown in Figure 5.1. Based on the example shown earlier, you would type **/tmp** in the Directory Holding Images text box.

WARNING   As of this writing, these instructions are slightly different from those shown in the documentation for Red Hat Linux 7.1. What you're reading here was tested against a downloaded version of this operating system.

NOTE   Refer back to Chapter 4 for a discussion of Linux device names for disk partitions. If you aren't sure which partition contains the Linux installation image, try each partition in turn. If you make the wrong choice, the prompts bring you back to the screen in Figure 5.1, where you can try again.

FIGURE 5.1:

Selecting a partition and directory

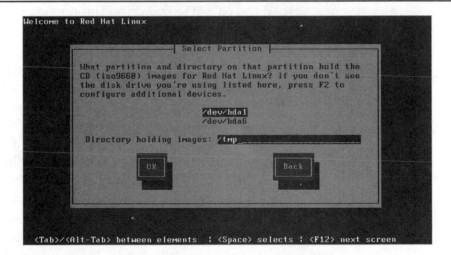

The rest of your installation should proceed in much the same way as outlined in Chapter 4.

Installing Linux on Multiple Partitions

The title of this section is something of a misnomer. After all, for the typical Red Hat Linux 7.1 installation, you are using at least three partitions: one for your boot files, one for storing the rest of your operating system, and one for your swap space. There can be compelling reasons to use more than one partition for storing Linux.

One obvious reason for this would be if you have a disk that has two available partitions that are not physically contiguous. It is difficult to create one contiguous volume from two different physical partitions. In this case, it is often better to divide your Linux installation across the two partitions. For example, installing Linux on multiple partitions can increase speed and data flexibility. There are several ways to take advantage of having more than one disk for your Linux installation.

Putting Swap on a Separate Physical Drive

If you have a large partition on one drive and a smaller partition (of anywhere from 32 to 200MB) on a second physical drive, you may want to consider putting your swap partition on that second drive. This can noticeably improve performance if you find yourself swapping frequently.

Consider this scenario: Your Linux installation and your swap partition are on the same physical drive. You are running many applications and your system has already been swapping a lot. You attempt to launch a new application, but in order for it to be launched, it needs to be loaded from disk into memory—and at the same time, existing data in memory needs to be swapped out to disk. Since the drive can perform only one operation at once, your one physical drive suddenly becomes a bottleneck as the operating system tries to perform both actions at nearly the same time.

But if your swap partition is on a separate physical drive, there is less of a bottleneck: One disk can be reading data from the disk into memory while the other is finishing the process of moving data from memory onto the disk. Even though the computer can't perform two instructions at the same time, the fact that the slow disk operations are spread over two disks helps minimize the time the CPU is left waiting for the disks to finish their work.

NOTE   When you have two physically separate disk drives, they can both send data to the rest of your computer simultaneously. You can reduce data bottlenecks further by physically connecting each drive to its own disk controller.

Splitting Linux across Multiple Partitions

Another way to use two or more partitions for your Linux software is to split the storage of your Linux software across the partitions in a logical manner. This can provide two benefits:

- Expanding the disk space available in critical Linux directory trees such as the /home directory tree

- Improving performance by splitting disk accesses across multiple hard disks if the available partitions are on more than one disk

Let's consider how you might want to split your Linux distribution across two partitions. As mentioned in Chapter 4, in the discussion of how to specify the mount point for an existing DOS partition, you use your additional disks by specifying their mount points.

For example, if you want to store all users' home directories on a separate partition, then you would make the mount point for that partition /home while leaving the mount point for your main Linux partition as /. Then, when you write to or read from any subdirectory under /home, you are actually accessing a different partition than when you access other directory trees outside /home.

There are several other popular ways to split your Linux installation across two partitions:

- If you plan to install a lot of your own software (including commercial software such as word processors, Web browsers, and Windows emulation software), you will find that much of it is installed in the /opt directory tree. If your main Linux partition has plenty of room for the operating system plus user data, then consider mounting your additional partition as /opt. This will give you a separate area for all of your applications, and when you launch applications, the main system disk will still be free for accessing data or running the system utilities and background tasks that Linux is always performing.

- If you expect to have many users or plan to store a large amount of data in users' home directories, then consider mounting your additional partition as /home. This way, you can separately monitor user disk usage, and you will get a performance gain when many users are accessing their data while other users are trying to launch applications, because these two actions will require access to separate disk partitions.

- If you find that neither partition on its own can contain your complete Linux installation, you may want to choose a fairly large directory tree such as /usr/X11R6 (the X Windows directory tree) and install that to a separate partition so that you can install your complete Linux system.

- While many new packages are installed in /opt, if you install much software you will find that /usr may also fill up quickly, making it a good candidate for a separate partition.

- If you are using Linux as a busy mail server or a heavily used, multiuser server, consider giving /var its own partition, since mail spool queues and system logs sit in this directory and can grow quickly in these types of servers.

Using *fdisk* instead of Disk Druid

In Chapter 4, you used Disk Druid to configure your disk partitions when installing Red Hat Linux 7.1. Disk Druid, however, is a program that is available only in the Red Hat installation process. Normally, Linux users use fdisk to configure their disk partitions, both during the installation process and later when they need to adjust their disk geographies.

In fact, fdisk is so familiar to power Linux users that Red Hat acknowledges its predominance as a tool for configuring disk partitions by offering it as an alternative to Disk Druid.

While fdisk is an extremely complex and powerful tool (and a potentially dangerous and destructive one if misused), the job of performing basic tasks such as displaying a partition table, creating a new partition from free space, and assigning types to partitions is fairly simple.

When you select fdisk instead of Disk Druid during the installation process, first a screen appears and asks you which disk you want to work with. Unlike Disk Druid, fdisk works with only one physical disk at a time. Once you select a disk to work with, you temporarily leave the now-familiar Red Hat installation program and are presented with the initial fdisk screen shown in Figure 5.2.

FIGURE 5.2:

The *fdisk* welcome screen

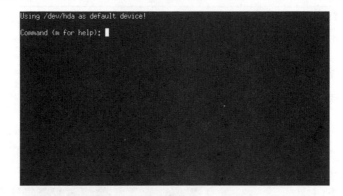

```
Using /dev/hda as default device!

Command (m for help):
```

NOTE   The **fdisk** figures in this chapter are based on starting the installation with the **boot.img** installation floppy, as discussed in this chapter. If you enter **fdisk** from the regular graphical Red Hat Linux installation screen, you'll see the exact same content, except within the graphics of the standard Red Hat installation program.

Fdisk operates using simple commands, each a single character long. To issue a command, simply type the command and press the Enter key. If the command needs additional information to perform its task, it prompts you for the missing information.

The simplest command is m or ?. Either of these characters causes fdisk to display the help screen shown in Figure 5.3. This screen lists all the common fdisk commands, including all the commands described in this section.

FIGURE 5.3:

The *fdisk* help screen

```
Using /dev/hda as default device!

Command (m for help): m
Command action
   a   toggle a bootable flag
   b   edit bsd disklabel
   c   toggle the dos compatibility flag
   d   delete a partition
   l   list known partition types
   m   print this menu
   n   add a new partition
   p   print the partition table
   q   quit without saving changes
   t   change a partition's system id
   u   change display/entry units
   v   verify the partition table
   w   write table to disk and exit
   x   extra functionality (experts only)

Command (m for help):
```

> **NOTE**
> You can start the Linux **fdisk** utility after installation with the **/sbin/fdisk** command. Some users find the alternative **/usr/sbin/cfdisk** utility easier to use.

Displaying the Partition Table

One of the most useful **fdisk** commands, p, displays the current partition table for the active disk being worked with. This looks like the table in Figure 5.4.

FIGURE 5.4:

The partition table

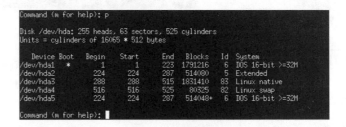

For each partition on the current disk, the device name, start and end blocks, partition size in blocks, and system type are displayed.

Adding a Partition Using Free Space

To add a new partition using existing free space on your hard disk, use the n command. As shown in Figure 5.5, you are prompted for a partition type. Generally, you should choose Primary as the type.

> **NOTE**
> With Linux **fdisk**, you can create four primary partitions as compared to DOS's single primary partition.

Once the partition type is selected, you assign the partition number and finally the start and end disk cylinders. To use all remaining space (assuming all available space is at the end of the drive), take the default first and last cylinders for your partition.

FIGURE 5.5:

Adding a new partition

```
Command (m for help): n
Command action
   e   extended
   p   primary partition (1-4)
p
Partition number (1-4): 2
First cylinder (224-525): ▮
```

Changing the Partition Type

By default, all new partitions created with fdisk are assigned the type Linux Native (type number 83). To change the type of a partition, use the t command.

You are prompted for a partition to work with, which you can select numerically, as shown in Figure 5.6, and then you are prompted for the type ID. To view a list of type IDs, use the L command at this point to see the list shown in Figure 5.6.

FIGURE 5.6:

Changing the partition type
ID in *fdisk*

```
Command (m for help): l

 0  Empty           17  Hidden HPFS/NTF 5c  Priam Edisk     a5  BSD/386
 1  FAT12           18  AST Windows swa 61  SpeedStor       a6  OpenBSD
 2  XENIX root      1b  Hidden Win95 FA 63  GNU HURD or Sys a7  NeXTSTEP
 3  XENIX usr       1c  Hidden Win95 FA 64  Novell Netware  b7  BSDI fs
 4  FAT16 <32M      1e  Hidden Win95 FA 65  Novell Netware  b8  BSDI swap
 5  Extended        24  NEC DOS         70  DiskSecure Mult c1  DRDOS/sec (FAT-
 6  FAT16           3c  PartitionMagic  75  PC/IX           c4  DRDOS/sec (FAT-
 7  HPFS/NTFS       40  Venix 80286     80  Old Minix       c6  DRDOS/sec (FAT-
 8  AIX             41  PPC PReP Boot   81  Minix / old Lin c7  Syrinx
 9  AIX bootable    42  SFS             82  Linux swap      db  CP/M / CTOS / .
 a  OS/2 Boot Manag 4d  QNX4.x          83  Linux           e1  DOS access
 b  Win95 FAT32     4e  QNX4.x 2nd part 84  OS/2 hidden C:  e3  DOS R/O
 c  Win95 FAT32 (LB 4f  QNX4.x 3rd part 85  Linux extended  e4  SpeedStor
 e  Win95 FAT16 (LB 50  OnTrack DM      86  NTFS volume set eb  BeOS fs
 f  Win95 Ext'd (LB 51  OnTrack DM6 Aux 87  NTFS volume set f1  SpeedStor
10  OPUS            52  CP/M            8e  Linux LVM       f4  SpeedStor
11  Hidden FAT12    53  OnTrack DM6 Aux 93  Amoeba          f2  DOS secondary
12  Compaq diagnost 54  OnTrackDM6      94  Amoeba BBT      fd  Linux raid auto
14  Hidden FAT16 <3 55  EZ-Drive       9f  BSD/OS          fe  LANstep
16  Hidden FAT16    56  Golden Bow      a0  IBM Thinkpad hi ff  BBT

Command (m for help): _
```

The most commonly used partition types are shown in Table 5.1.

TABLE 5.1:   Commonly Used Partition Types

ID	Type
5	Extended
6	DOS 16-bit (larger than 32MB)
7	OS/2 HPFS
b	Windows 95 FAT32
c	Windows 95 FAT32 with Logical Block Addressing (LBA)
82	Linux Swap
83	Linux Native

Deleting a Partition

Sometimes you want to delete an existing partition to create one or more new partitions for your Linux installation. To do this, simply use the d command and, when prompted, enter the partition number you wish to delete.

Committing Your Changes

While you are working with fdisk, none of the changes you make are actually made to the physical disk. This is a safety precaution so that if you accidentally delete a partition with important data, you will be able to revert to your previous configuration before permanently deleting the partition containing the data.

For that reason, the changes you make are not actually processed until you explicitly ask fdisk to do so at the time of quitting. Therefore, before you quit from fdisk, take care to view the partition table to be sure you have done exactly what you want. If you exit and commit the changes, they are permanent, and going back is not really an option. (In theory, you can save the partition table of your disk to a floppy disk before working with fdisk and then recover from a serious mistake by replacing the new partition table with the saved one; however, this is a complicated procedure and not foolproof. You are better off taking care and making sure that the changes you make to your partition table are exactly the way you want them before committing the changes.)

The two alternative commands for quitting from fdisk are shown in Table 5.2.

TABLE 5.2: Alternative Commands for Quitting from *fdisk*

Command	Effect
q	Quits from fdisk without processing or saving any of your changes.
w	Processes and saves all your changes and then exits from fdisk. This is a permanent action, so take care.

Looking Ahead

Finally, you are ready to get into the business of actually using Linux. As your first step on that path, you will look at the X Windows environment. X Windows gives all Unix operating systems, including Linux, a highly flexible, mouse-driven graphical user interface.

Many Linux books start with the command line because this is really the heart of Linux. But X Windows enables new users to quickly start using Linux before they have a thorough grasp of the Linux command line.

Chapter 6, "An Overview of X Windows," shows you what X Windows offers and how it compares with the Microsoft Windows environment. Then it will move on to the configuration and use of X Windows and take a look at some common X Windows applications.

PART III

Using Desktop Environments in Linux

CHAPTER
SIX

An Overview of X Windows

6

- ■ What Is X Windows?

- ■ Microsoft Windows vs. X Windows

- ■ X Servers, Window Managers, and Desktop
  Environments

- ■ What Is Motif?

Now that you have succeeded in installing Linux, you will start your learning process by diving straight into the X Windows environment. Many Linux diehards will shudder at our considering X Windows before mastering the intricate details of the Linux command line and the Linux configuration. But it is X Windows that makes Linux an acceptable alternative to Windows and to the Mac OS as a productive operating system for everyday tasks such as word processing, desktop publishing, and browsing the World Wide Web.

This chapter starts by describing exactly what X Windows is. X Windows offers a graphical user interface (GUI) to the Unix world. X Windows provides a way to deliver all the now-commonplace user interface paradigms such as windows, dialog boxes, buttons, and menus. It is X Windows that enables the creation of the sophisticated graphics that make Unix-based workstations the systems of choice for many engineering and design applications, and it is X Windows that has made it possible for Linux to emerge as a strong contender in the PC operating system market.

To fully understand what X Windows is all about, this chapter provides a detailed comparison of Microsoft Windows and X Windows, including changes based on X Windows 4. Having done that, the chapter wraps up by looking at some key components of X Windows such as X servers, window managers, desktop environments, and Motif.

What Is X Windows?

Put in its simplest terms, X Windows is a complete graphics interface for Unix—and by extension, for Linux. But this doesn't say it all. X Windows is a highly configurable environment that provides a broad range of flexible options for both the user and the application developers producing software to run under X Windows.

The core X Windows concept is the client-server framework. What this means in practical terms is that X Windows provides an environment that is not bound to a single processor. Applications can run on different servers and machines on a network, and applications can display to X Windows terminals and workstations elsewhere on the network.

This separation between where an application runs and where it is displayed is a concept missing in the Windows and Macintosh environments, which tie the application to the display. The benefit of this separation is that in a networking environment, it is possible to have sophisticated graphics desktops displaying applications that are running on well-maintained, powerful, and easy-to-manage central application servers. In fact, this very capability is what gives Unix/Linux and X Windows such a good reputation among professional system administrators of large networks.

Another concept introduced in the X Windows environment is the separation of windowing from the interface. On an X Windows system, two applications must run to provide a complete GUI. The first is the X server, which sets up the graphics display (i.e., resolution, refresh rate, and color depth), displays the windows, and tracks mouse movements, keystrokes, and multiple windows. But an X server does not provide menus, window borders, or mechanisms for moving, switching, minimizing, or maximizing windows. If you look at Figure 6.1, you can see how an X server screen appears without a window manager.

FIGURE 6.1:

An X server display with no window manager

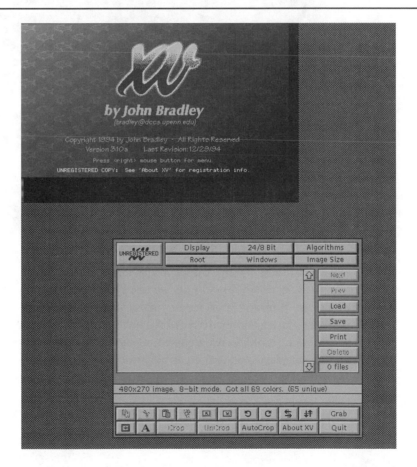

Notice the bare simplicity in Figure 6.1. There is no fancy color background, no sophisticated window borders or menu controls, and no other features that make a complete GUI. All these features are provided by a second application called a *window manager.* Figure 6.2 shows a complete X Windows desktop running the fvwm95 window manager. Notice the features of the window frames, the control buttons, and the control menus, as well as a Taskbar and a virtual desktop system. The window manager provides all of these.

FIGURE 6.2:

An X Windows display running a window manager

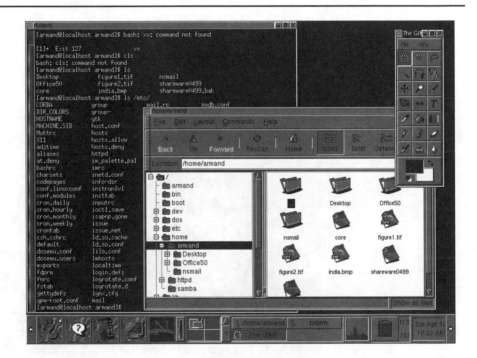

The window manager talks to the X server in a standard, predefined way, as does the X server to the X applications. This means that different window managers with different interface features can all talk in this standard way to the X server. Likewise, the variety of X servers that are available, which offer support for different graphics cards, monitors, and other performance features, can also talk in a standardized way to applications.

Microsoft Windows vs. X Windows

Given some of the descriptions of X Windows you've seen, it would be natural to assume that Microsoft Windows and X Windows are pretty much the same thing. The reality, though, is that they are fundamentally different beasts.

For example, Microsoft Windows is a complete operating system, with everything from a kernel to a shell to a windowing environment and more. X Windows is just one piece of that operating system puzzle: the windowing environment. Another contrast is in the interface: The Microsoft Windows interface is fairly rigid while the X Windows interface has an amazingly flexible and customizable design.

Similarities

So, what is similar about X Windows and Microsoft's current operating system? The main similarities are that they both provide graphical interfaces and make it possible to work with multiple windows. On top of this, they allow the user to interact with information using more than a keyboard and plain characters. Users can utilize a mouse as well as a keyboard and can create interfaces that combine menus, forms, windows, and dialog boxes.

Differences

There are numerous differences between the two windowing systems. The main differences are in the following areas:

- Flexibility of the interface
- Fine-tuned control over the interface configuration
- Client-server technology

Flexible Interface

The flexibility of the X Windows interface is one of the joys of this environment for many users. As discussed already, the separation of the user interface layer from the basic windowing layer makes it possible to create multiple interfaces for X Windows through the creation of different window managers.

Multiple interfaces don't simply provide subtle differences in appearance, as some customization tools for the Microsoft Windows interface offer; rather, they allow complete redesigns of the user interface from window manager to window manager.

By way of example, Figure 6.3 shows a sample window interface running a window manager that resembles the user interface of the NeXT operating system. Compare that to Figure 6.4, running on the same system and displaying the same applications, which shows a user interface that resembles none of the popular PC or Macintosh operating systems.

FIGURE 6.3:

The Afterstep window manager

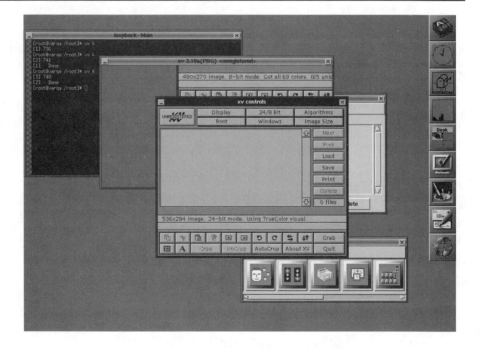

FIGURE 6.4:

The Lesstif window manager

These examples represent just two of the many look-and-feel designs offered by X Windows window managers. The better-known window managers are discussed briefly later in this chapter.

Fine-Tuned Control

Another advantage of the X Windows environment is that it offers fine-tuned control over all aspects of the windowing environment and the interface. By setting any of dozens of settings, it is possible to control all aspects of the environment, from the background and foreground window colors to cursor color, default font, and default window size. Users can also define modes of interaction. For instance, it is possible to use the mouse pointer to make a window automatically jump to the foreground or to change cursor focus to a background window.

In addition, these and other features can be defined on a per-application basis, creating different settings for each application so that each application launches in the most convenient way possible.

It is also possible to define which windows and applications open each time the X environment starts, as well as to have the system make logical choices about which window manager to use when starting X Windows.

Chapter 7, "Installing and Configuring X Windows," discusses the basic X Windows configuration options.

Client-Server Environment

As mentioned previously, the X Windows world works on a client-server model in which applications are clients to an X server that drives the physical display. This has made X Windows well adapted to network environments, allowing applications to run on one machine on the network while displaying their output on another.

Microsoft Windows lacked this ability until very recently and now has it only in a limited and expensive fashion through its Terminal Server services on high-end multiuser Windows NT and 2000 systems. In the Linux, Unix, and X worlds, even the lowliest system is capable of playing either the client role or the server role in this X Windows client-server model.

X Servers, Window Managers, and Desktop Environments

Now that you have a sense of where X Windows fits into things, you need to understand the fundamental components of X Windows: X servers, window managers, and desktop environments. It is these components and the modularity that they represent that provide the power and flexibility of X Windows.

X Servers

As you have already seen, the core of the X Windows system is the X server. The X server handles several tasks:

- Support for a variety of video cards and monitor types
- Resolution, refresh rate, and color depth of the X Windows display
- Basic window management: displaying and closing windows, tracking mouse movements and keystrokes

Multiple X servers with these basic capabilities have sprung up. In the Linux world, there are three main choices: XFree86, Metro-X, and Accelerated-X.

XFree86

XFree86 is the default X server with almost every noncommercial Linux distribution because it is available for free under the same sort of terms as Linux. Full source code is available, users are free to change the code to meet their own needs, and anyone can redistribute it. Red Hat Linux 7.1 ships with XFree86 4.0.3. Minor updates are released every few months and can be downloaded from the XFree86 Web site at `http://www.xfree86.org`.

The XFree86 Web server is designed to provide broad support for common hardware in the Intel-compatible x86 PC, as well as computers with the Compaq Alpha, PowerPC, Sparc, and MIPS processors. While its performance is not always stellar, XFree86 is the norm for X servers in Linux and other Intel-based Unix variants and therefore is the X server that most people are familiar with.

TIP While MIPS support is not complete at the time of this writing, according to the XFree86 Project Web site, considerable documentation is available with the MIPS HOWTO at `http://oss.sgi.com/mips/mips-howto.html`.

Among the popular graphics card chipsets supported by XFree86 are Tseng's ET3000, 4000, and 6000, the full range of Trident chips, most of the Cirrus Logic line, Chips and Technologies graphics chips, and many others. You can find a full list of supported hardware on the Driver status page of the XFree86 project at `http://www.xfree86.org/4.0.3/Status.html`. If you are using a later version, substitute accordingly for 4.0.3.

While the XFree86 4 X server goes a long way toward making Linux a complete, free, Unix-like operating system, it does suffer from some drawbacks that make it less than attractive for corporate or mission-critical environments. XFree86 sometimes requires painstakingly difficult configuration and installation, has less-than-stable or imperfect support for some graphics cards and monitors, and often will not take advantage of the accelerated features of a graphics card.

Luckily, Red Hat Linux 7.1 ships with an excellent utility called Xconfigurator, which greatly eases the job of configuring XFree86, even to the point of auto-detecting some hardware and suggesting the best options for that hardware. Other distributions ship with utilities of similar quality. This works great unless you present the tool with one of those rare problematic hardware combinations, in which case you will be right back to configuring XFree86 manually.

What's New about XFree86 4?

Version 4 of XFree86 includes a number of new features not found in earlier versions. Some of these new features borrow functionality from the commercial X servers. These features include the following:

- One unified X server Modular Architectural Design

- Support for multiple graphics cards

- Independence from the operating system

- 3-D rendering

- FreeType support

With one unified X server, XFree86 4 allows the use of different types of graphics cards without reconfiguration. With a runtime loader donated by Metro Link, XFree86 4 no longer depends on the driver libraries of Linux (or any other Unix-based operating system). With GLX extensions, XFree86 now supports 3-D rendering through Silicon Graphics' OpenGL 3-D graphics language. With FreeType support, XFree86 can now manage TrueType fonts.

XFree86 now enhances and adds support for more platforms, including computers based on the Alpha, MIPS, and PowerPC processors. It is expected to be ready for the Intel Itanium IA 64-bit platform when that is released.

> **NOTE**   As of this writing, XFree86 version 4 does not support the older XF86Setup tool. Alternate utilities such as Xconfigurator and xf86config are more than adequate alternatives.

Commercial X Servers

In addition to the XFree86 project, which is a vital part of making Linux a complete and free solution, there are two leading commercial X servers for the Linux world: Metro-X and Accelerated-X.

These products offer the advantage of broader support for various graphics chips and cards and generally take full advantage of the accelerated features of those chips and cards. In addition, Metro-X and Accelerated-X offer more intelligent configuration and can usually be installed and working in a matter of minutes.

Metro-X Metro-X from Metro Link is a high-performance X server option. Among the many benefits of Metro-X are a well-designed graphical configuration interface like the one in Figure 6.5, support for multi-headed displays (the standard configuration supports four different monitors), support for some brands of touch screens, and more.

FIGURE 6.5:

Metro-X's Configuration window

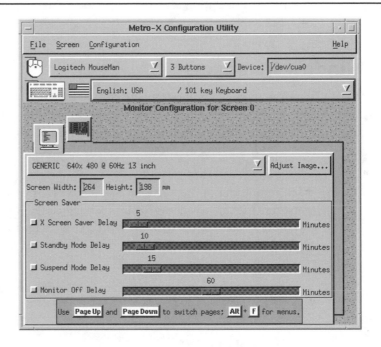

Complete information about the Metro-X server, including supported graphics cards, is available on the Metro Link home page at http://www.metrolink.com/. Metro-X costs U.S.$39 for Linux.

Accelerated-X X-Inside actually offers a range of X servers for Linux. These include the Accelerated-X server for Linux, a 3-D Accelerated-X server, a Multi-head Accelerated-X server, and a specialized Laptop Accelerated-X server. The Laptop Accelerated-X server is significant because the chipsets found on laptops are different than those in desktop graphics cards and because LCD screens have their own set of requirements that are ignored by desktop drivers.

In fact, support for laptop displays is quite limited in XFree86, and a small mistake can mean that your LCD will be damaged. If you plan to use a notebook full-time as a Linux system, look at the list of systems supported by the Laptop Accelerated-X server to see if yours is there.

Accelerated-X offers support for more than 400 graphics cards from over 60 manufacturers. The Multi-head Accelerated-X server supports up to 16 screens and offers all the features of Accelerated-X on each screen.

Overall, X-Inside's servers are competitively priced. Accelerated-X costs U.S.$99.95, the Laptop server is $149.95, and the Multi-head server is $199.95. Complete information is available on the X-Inside Web site at `http://www` `.xinside.com/`.

Window Managers

Window managers fill out the niceties of the GUI not provided by X servers. Among other features, window managers include window decorations (which provide the means to resize, move, close, and minimize windows) and mechanisms for launching applications (such as desktop menus, control panels, and button bars).

The remainder of this section takes a brief look at some of the main window managers that are available for Linux, including FVWM, fvwm95, twm, olvwm, and others. The default window manager with Red Hat Linux 7.1 is Sawfish, but any reasonably complete installation will include FVWM and other alternative window managers.

An overview of window managers for X Windows is available online at `http://www.plig.org/xwinman/`.

FVWM and fvwm95

During the mid-1990s, the most common window manager for Linux was FVWM or some variation on this package. The name FVWM is a strange one because no one is sure what the "F" stands for in the name. Some say it stands for "Feeble" Virtual Window Manager; others argue that it is "Fine" Virtual Window Manager; still others argue that the meaning of the "F" has long been forgotten and isn't important anyway. (I tend to agree with the latter.)

FVWM is a lightweight window manager that provides a flexible, customizable windowing environment designed to look a bit like the Motif Window Manager (MWM, a commercial product). FVWM provides multiple virtual desktops and a module system for extending the window manager and, in the more recent version 2.2.5, allows on-the-fly configuration changes and window-specific feature customization. The FVWM home page is at `http://www.fvwm.org/`. Figure 6.6 contains a sample FVWM desktop.

FIGURE 6.6:

A sample FVWM desktop

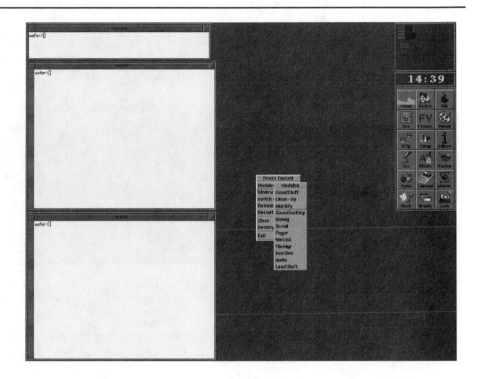

FVWM ships with almost every Linux distribution and is known for its usefulness as the basis for newer window managers with their own look and feel, including the following:

fvwm95   Designed to look like Windows 95

Afterstep   Designed to look like the NeXT environment

SCWM (Scheme Configurable Window Manager)   Configurable using the Scheme language

Figure 6.7 contains a screen of fvwm95 in action.

FIGURE 6.7:

Fvwm95 provides a Windows 95-like environment.

Fvwm95 is based on version 2 of FVWM and retains the flexible, easy configuration of that release. It continues to support FVWM modules but adds the modules needed to implement Windows 95-style features such as the Taskbar. Fvwm95 information is available on the Web at http://www.plig.org/xwinman/fvwm95.html.

> **NOTE**   The FVWM2 package is available on the second Red Hat Linux 7.1 Installation CD-ROM (not included with this book).

twm

The Tab Window Manager (twm), often called Tom's Window Manager after the name of its primary developer, is a basic, functional environment that is included with Red Hat Linux 7.1 as an alternative window manager. Figure 6.8 shows a typical twm desktop.

FIGURE 6.8:

The twm desktop

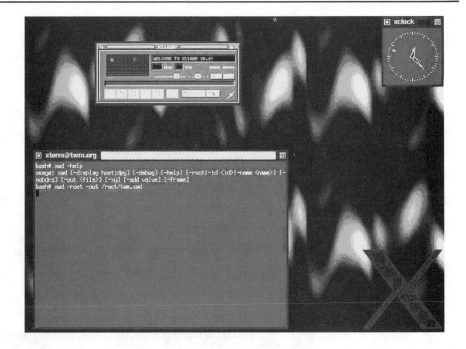

The twm window manager offers many key features that users expect in an X Windows window manager, including click-to-type or pointer-driven keyboard focus and user-defined key and button bindings. However, the interface is visually simple and some would see it as limited. Vtwm, a version of twm that includes a virtual desktop, is also available and can be downloaded from ftp://ftp.x.org/R5contrib/vtwm-5.3.tar.gz.

olvwm

Olvwm, the OpenLook Virtual Window Manager, is an extension of the Open-Look Window Manager (olwm), which was the standard window manager on Sun systems for many years. While Sun systems now sport Motif and the Common Desktop Environment (discussed later in this chapter), the unique Open-Look interface is still popular among many users. Olvwm adds support for virtual desktops to the OpenLook package. Figure 6.9 shows a sample olvwm desktop.

The interface used in olvwm will feel awkward to many users, especially in terms of the way in which menus and windows respond to mouse buttons. This is one reason why OpenLook didn't gain huge popularity outside the Sun world. Olvwm can be downloaded from ftp://ftp.x.org/R5contrib/olvwm4.tar.Z.

FIGURE 6.9:

The olvwm interface

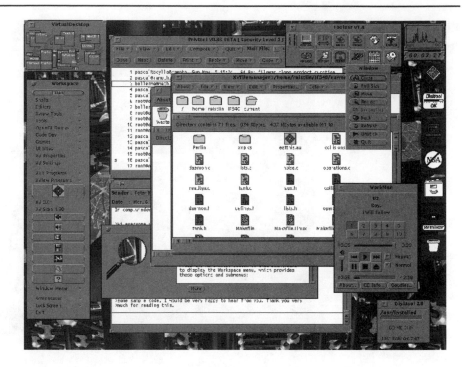

Afterstep

Afterstep is another variant on the original FVWM code. This product is based on an earlier window manager called Bowman and is designed to provide the look and feel of the NeXTSTEP window manager from the NeXT platform. Figure 6.10 shows a sample Afterstep desktop.

Major features drawn from NeXTSTEP are the look of title bars, buttons, and borders, the appearance of the style menu, and the NeXTSTEP-like icons and button bar. Since it is based on FVWM version 1 code, any modules from that version of FVWM should continue to work with Afterstep. Unlike some window managers, such as fvwm95 and olvwm, organized development work on Afterstep continues today.

The Afterstep home page is at http://www.afterstep.org/.

FIGURE 6.10:

The Afterstep desktop

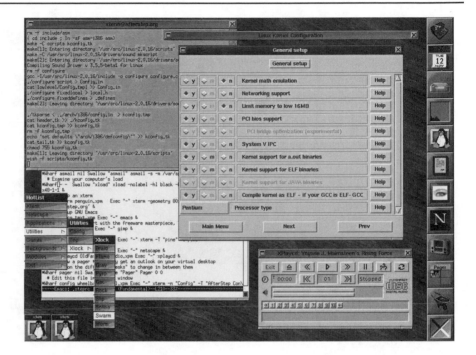

AmiWm

If you are a former user of the Amiga computer and fell in love with its interface, then AmiWm may be the window manager for you. AmiWm emulates the Amiga workbench, as shown in Figure 6.11. With support for multiple screens such as that found on the Amiga, AmiWm can ease the move to X Windows for former Amiga users.

You can learn about AmiWm and download the software from the AmiWm home page at http://www.lysator.liu.se/~marcus/amiwm.html.

FIGURE 6.11:

The AmiWm window manager

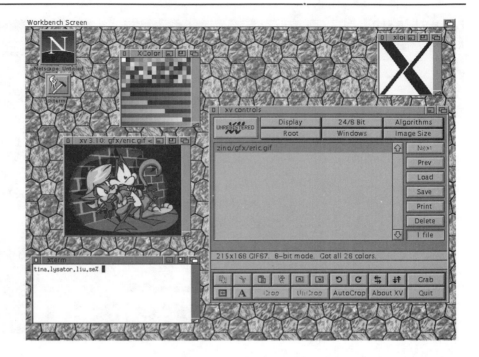

Enlightenment

Enlightenment is a grand project, attempting to develop a window manager that goes beyond the conventional. It provides a useful but also visually attractive environment and allows the user to define everything from functionality to the appearance of the window manager. Figures 6.12 and 6.13 show just two possible configurations of the Enlightenment environment. Among the many features that help Enlightenment stand out are the abilities it gives users to handcraft the look and feel and to embed new features easily.

While Enlightenment is an ambitious project and offers visually stunning interfaces, installation can be a bit of a challenge for the novice user, often requiring the user to compile and install new libraries. The Enlightenment home page is at http://www.enlightenment.org/. Note also that the authors consider Enlightenment to be in an early pre-release stage (the current version as of this writing is 0.16) and therefore warn of bugs and the potential for crashes. Still, this is an interesting project and a unique concept among window managers.

FIGURE 6.12:

The Enlightenment window manager

FIGURE 6.13:

Users can fully customize the Enlightenment environment.

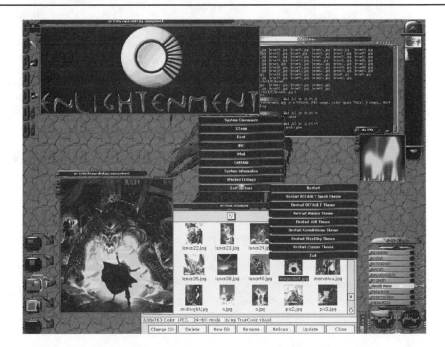

Sawfish

The Sawfish window manager is the new default with the GNOME desktop environment. Like Enlightenment, Sawfish maximizes the ability to configure each window, in this case, through tools that use the LISP programming language. As part of the GNOME desktop, Sawfish controls are integrated with the GNOME Control Center, as shown in Figure 6.14. Chapter 10, "Advanced GNOME Configuration," covers the GNOME Control Center and Sawfish in detail.

FIGURE 6.14:

Users can fully customize the Sawfish environment.

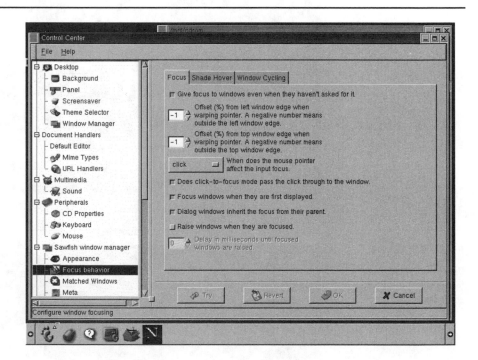

Like Enlightenment, Sawfish is also a work in progress. The current version as of this writing is 0.38. For more information, go to the Sawfish home page at www.sawfish.org.

Desktop Environments

Desktop environments are more than just window managers. Desktop environments aim to provide a complete, cohesive GUI. With simple window managers, there is no guarantee of consistency of look and feel between applications and features found in other operating systems, such as drag-and-drop between applications and cross-application data embedding.

There are different desktop environments for Linux that provide robust, integrated GUIs and provide a target platform for application developers to build software with a common look and feel and include integration features such as drag-and-drop.

Two of these desktop environments, the K Desktop Environment and GNOME, are freely available and have emerged as competitors for the de facto standard Linux desktop environment.

The K Desktop Environment

The K Desktop Environment (KDE) is an attempt to provide a free alternative to the Common Desktop Environment (discussed later in this section). In this effort, KDE combines a set of applications, such as a file manager, terminal emulator, and display configuration system, with a window manager to create a consistent look and feel for X applications. Figure 6.15 shows a typical KDE desktop.

FIGURE 6.15:

A KDE desktop

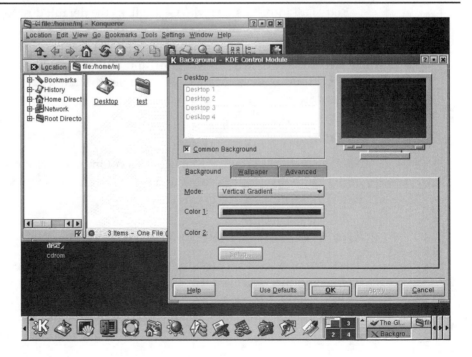

KDE is the default desktop environment for a number of Linux distributions, including Caldera, S.u.S.E., and Corel. It is an alternative desktop environment for most of the other distributions.

Part of the planning behind KDE is that standards be specified and the development environment be such that developers can create applications that are consistent in features as well as appearance. KDE provides an attractive, professional-looking environment in which to work, and if the necessary applications are developed for KDE, it will become a likely prospect for the business desktop. The KDE Web site is http://www.kde.org/. Chapter 11, "Using KDE," covers KDE 2.1.1, included with Red Hat Linux 7.1, in detail.

GNOME: The GNU Network Object Model Environment

GNOME is the result of an alternative effort to develop a comprehensive, free desktop environment for Linux. Unlike KDE, which includes a built-in window manager, GNOME is window manager-independent. It provides a programming interface that allows window manager developers to integrate full support for GNOME in their window manager.

Red Hat Linux 7.1 ships with GNOME as the default desktop environment using the Sawfish window manager. Other window managers and KDE are included with this distribution, but since the default installation uses GNOME and Enlightenment, this book will use GNOME and Enlightenment as the target desktop. For an introduction to using GNOME, refer to Chapter 8, "Using GNOME and X Windows."

MWM

MWM, the Motif Window Manager, is a commercial window manager that is part of the Motif distribution. Motif as a complete environment is discussed in more detail in the next section of this chapter.

The Common Desktop Environment

The Common Desktop Environment (CDE) is an ambitious project to standardize the graphical environment and development arena on various Unix platforms, including AIX, Compaq Unix, HP/UX, and Solaris. Now CDE is also available for Linux as the DeXtop Graphical Interface from X-Inside (http://www.xinside.com/). This commercial application, which costs U.S.$49, requires X-Inside's Accelerated-X server.

In addition to a consistent graphical environment based on Motif, CDE offers a set of cohesive tools and applications to standardize administrative procedures and ease the configuration and management of a user's graphical work environment. Among the enhancements brought to the X environment by CDE are drag-and-drop capabilities and the types of folders and icons found in other GUI operating systems.

What Is Motif?

If you begin to look around the Web for X Windows applications to install on your Linux system, you will inevitably come across applications that refer to the fact that they use the Motif library or the Motif toolkit.

Motif is a development environment for X Windows that was introduced by the Open Software Foundation (OSF) in the late 1980s to provide a consistent policy for X Windows applications. Motif provides a toolkit of widgets that developers can use in developing their applications. By using these widget libraries, Motif developers produce applications that adhere to Motif policies for a consistent look and feel.

Motif was recently re-released under an "open" license, which means that developers who want to build and distribute applications based on the Motif libraries no longer need to pay for the privilege. However, the Open Group, the organization behind the new Open Motif, still sells the documentation behind this language and set of libraries. And many Linux developers read the Motif license to mean that it cannot be used to develop software for free operating systems such as Linux.

NOTE   The Open Group is an industry organization dedicated to software standards. They are not related to the sponsors of the Open Source license. In fact, they admit that their Motif license does not meet Open Source requirements.

In addition to the toolkit and libraries, the Motif distribution includes its own window manager, MWM, after which the original FVWM look and feel was patterned. Figure 6.16 shows a sample MWM desktop.

FIGURE 6.16:

An MWM desktop

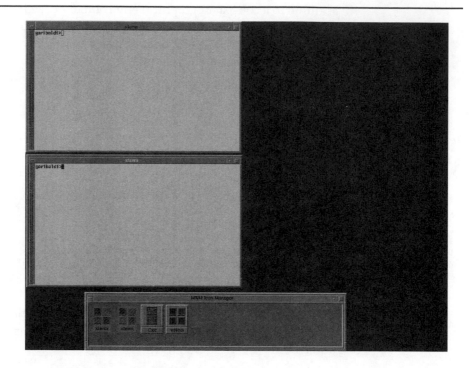

Do I Need Motif?

For most Linux users, there is probably no need to use Motif. Users who should consider Motif include the following:

- Developers who want to develop applications using the Motif toolkit.

- Users who want to run applications that require the presence of the Motif libraries. Most commercial applications that use the Motif libraries either embed the necessary Motif code in the application (so it is not necessary for the user to own the license) or include a complete version of the runtime Motif libraries.

You can download Open Motif from the Open Group Web site at http://www .opengroup.org/. Metro Link currently sells a package with several different versions of Motif tools starting at $99.

An Alternative to Motif

Like so many things in the Linux world, efforts are under way to produce a freely available alternative to Motif so that Linux developers and users don't have to purchase Motif. The Lesstif Project has developed a product that is compatible with Motif version 1.2 and available under the GNU Public License.

Lesstif hasn't reached full maturity yet (the version at the time of this writing is 0.92.26), but Lesstif can already be used to develop some applications and run some software. The Lesstif FAQ on the Lesstif home page (`http://www.lesstif.org/`) is quick to point out that Lesstif is still not complete. Even so, some of the applications that use Motif can work with Lesstif 0.92.26, including Mosaic 2.7 and the GNUCash personal finance manager.

> **NOTE**
>
> You can download Motif for free. Thus the question "Why use Lesstif now that Motif is free?" The Free Software Foundation believes that the new Motif license prohibits its use on most current Linux distributions and that therefore Motif isn't really free. Thus, there is still a need for Lesstif as an alternative to Motif.

Looking Ahead

This discussion of X Windows is your first step toward hands-on use of the Linux operating system.

In the next two chapters, you will master the basics of the X Windows interface using the default desktop environment for Red Hat Linux 7.1: GNOME. You will learn to install X Windows and begin to experiment with using some of the most common X Windows and GNOME applications.

Chapter 7, "Installing and Configuring X Windows," serves as a step-by-step guide to installing and configuring X Windows.

CHAPTER
SEVEN

7

Installing and Configuring X Windows

- Obtaining X Windows

- Preparing to Configure X Windows

- Configuring XFree86 with Xconfigurator

- Configuring XFree86 with Xf86config

- Testing Your Configuration

Now that you have a sense of what X Windows is all about, it is time to install and configure the software so that you have a system up and running X Windows as quickly as possible.

This chapter discusses where to obtain X Windows for your system if you don't or can't install the version of X Windows that shipped with your distribution of Linux. Following that, it describes how to configure XFree86 so that it works optimally on your computer.

Obtaining X Windows

If you are using the copy of Red Hat Linux 7.1 that came with this book and you chose to install all of the key X Windows components suggested in Chapter 4, "Installing Red Hat Linux 7.1," then you don't need to read this section because you already have obtained and installed the X Windows files. You can skip ahead to the section entitled "Preparing to Configure X Windows."

Installing from the Red Hat Linux 7.1 CD-ROM

If you are using Red Hat Linux 7.1 but didn't install X Windows when you installed Linux, then installing X Windows is a fairly easy process. The procedure outlined here relies on techniques described in Chapter 14, "Working with Files," for accessing your CD-ROM drive.

Using *rpm*

In this section, you will be using **rpm** (The Red Hat Package Manager), a tool that is shipped with Red Hat Linux and several other distributions for managing Red Hat-style packages.

Rpm allows you to install new packages, uninstall installed packages, and look at information about packages, such as what files they include.

To install a package, use the following command:

```
$ rpm -i package-file-name
```

To view a list of all installed packages, use this command:

```
$ rpm -qa | more
```

Continued on next page

This command presents the list of installed packages one screen at a time; you can scroll down to the next screen by pressing the spacebar. The package names shown on the list are not the filenames originally used when installing the packages. They are used, however, in uninstalling a package with the following command:

```
$ rpm -e package-file-name
```

In order to install X Windows from your Red Hat 7.1 CD-ROM, the first step is to mount your CD-ROM drive so that Linux can access it. This process is not as straightforward as it seems, because it will vary depending on the type of CD-ROM drive you have (IDE/ATAPI, SCSI, or proprietary) and on how the drive is installed. An extensive discussion of CD-ROM options is found in Chapter 19, "Linux Multimedia."

The directions that follow assume that you have an IDE CD-ROM drive, since these are extremely common in today's multimedia PCs. These directions also assume that the CD-ROM drive is installed as the secondary IDE slave device, since most off-the-shelf computers sold today contain only one hard drive.

Given these assumptions, your CD-ROM drive will be device /dev/hdb. For other drive types and configurations, refer to the discussion in Chapter 19 to determine what device your drive is.

Insert the Red Hat Linux 7.1 CD-ROM into your drive and type the command

```
$ mount /dev/hdb /mnt/cdrom
```

to mount the disk and make it accessible to Linux. You can use the following command to look at the contents of the CD-ROM and make sure it is accessible:

```
$ ls /mnt/cdrom
```

The results should look like those shown here:

```
autorun   dosutils  RedHat            RELEASE-NOTES.es RELEASE-NOTES.ja
boot.cat  images    RELEASE-NOTES     RELEASE-NOTES.fr RPM-GPG-KEY
COPYING   README    RELEASE-NOTES.de  RELEASE-NOTES.it TRANS.TBL
```

NOTE If you don't know what your CD-ROM device is, the
`mount /dev/cdrom /mnt/cdrom`
command usually works fine. If you run the
`ls -l /dev/cdrom`
command, you'll probably see that it's linked to the actual device used by your CD-ROM.

The next step is to change into the directory on the CD-ROM that contains all the packages that make up Red Hat Linux 7.1. This directory is the RedHat/RPMS subdirectory. Use the following command:

```
$ cd /mnt/cdrom/RedHat/RPMS
```

If you type the command

```
$ ls
```

you should see a long list of files scroll by, and all of them should end in the extension .rpm, indicating that they are Red Hat Package Manager files.

Now you are ready to install the X Windows packages. In order to do this, you need to determine which packages to install. To start with, you need the general XFree86 files that are in the XFree86-4.0.3-5.i386.rpm package. Next, you need all the X Windows fonts, which are in the following files:

```
XFree86-100dpi-fonts-4.0.3-5.i386.rpm
XFree86-75dpi-fonts-4.0.3-5.i386.rpm
```

In addition, you need the shared XFree86 libraries and the X Windows font server:

```
XFree86-libs-4.0.3-5.i386.rpm
XFree86-xfs-4.0.3-5.i386.rpm
```

You also need the XFree86 configuration utility provided by Red Hat, which is in the file Xconfigurator-4.9.27-1.i386.rpm, and you want the collection of X Windows programs that can be found in XFree86-tools-4.0.3-5.i386.rpm.

XFree86 4 no longer requires a separate X server package. However, the version available at the time of this writing does not support all of the monitors and graphics cards supported in version 3.3.x. Review the release notes for your XFree86 package. The release notes for version 4.0.3 can be found at http://www.xfree86 .org/4.0.3/RELNOTES.html. If you have a different version of the XFree86 4 package, substitute for 4.0.3 accordingly.

NOTE   With XFree86 4, separate packages for graphics card-specific X servers are no longer required.

Now that you have built a list of the files that you need to install, you can use the command rpm -i to install the following files:

```
$ rpm -i XFree86-4.0.3-5.i386.rpm
$ rpm -i XFree86-100dpi-fonts-4.0.3-5.i386.rpm
$ rpm -i XFree86-75dpi-fonts-4.0.3-5.i386.rpm
$ rpm -i XFree86-libs-4.0.3-5.i386.rpm
$ rpm -i XFree86-xfs-4.0.3-5.i386.rpm
$ rpm -i Xconfigurator-4.9.27-1.i386.rpm
$ rpm -i XFree86-tools-4.0.3-5.i386.rpm
```

Once you've done this, all the necessary X Windows files should be installed on your system.

NOTE   One alternative is to download XFree86 RPM files from the Internet. A comprehensive source for RPMs is the rpm "search engine" at http://www.rpmfind.net. The drawback is that there is usually a delay between the release of a new Linux application and its release in RPM format. The next section shows how to download and install the latest version of XFree86.

Installing from the Internet

If you want to install a newer version of XFree86 than is available with your Linux distribution, you can download the necessary files from the Internet and then install them. For XFree86 version 4.0.3, installation is a two-stage process: First you install version 4.0.2; then you can install version 4.0.3 as an "update." If you want to install a more advanced version of XFree86 and it is available, the process will be similar.

NOTE   Chapter 22, "Connecting Linux to the Internet," discusses connecting to the Internet, and Chapter 23, "Using the World Wide Web," discusses using Netscape. If you aren't ready to take on these tasks in Linux and you kept your old Windows or DOS installation on your system, you can use the Windows or DOS Internet connection to download the files and then access your Windows or DOS partition from Linux to install the files.

XFree86 is developed by the XFree86 Project, which is on the Web at `http://www`
`.xfree86.org`. Figure 7.1 shows the XFree86 Web page.

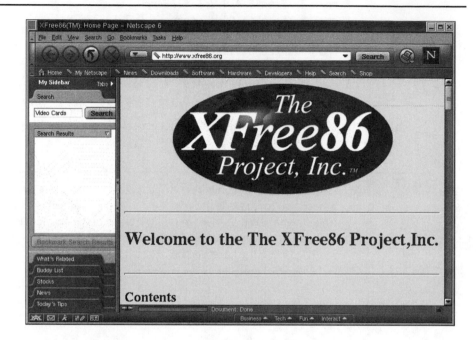

From this Web site, you can access the directory containing the files for the
latest version of XFree86 from a number of sites, including `http://ftp-stud`
`.fht-esslingen.de/pub/Mirrors/ftp.xfree86.org/XFree86/`. Here you will find
libraries available for many versions of Linux, including the following:

Linux-alpha-glibc21   Linux for Compaq's Alpha processors.

Darwin   Linux for the Darwin operating system, developed by Apple for
the PowerPC and Intel type computers.

Linux-ix86-libc5   Linux for Intel x86 processors, usually for older Linux
distributions.

Linux-ix86-glibc2x   Linux versions for Intel *x*86 processors that use the
newer `Glibc` libraries. Most newer distributions use these GNU C language
libraries. Red Hat 7.1 uses the `Glibc 2.2` libraries.

Installing XFree86 Version 4.0.2

To repeat, the first step of the process is to install the base package, in this case, version 4.0.2. From the download site, access the version 4.0.2 directory. Next, choose the library that applies for your version of Linux. If in doubt, download the Xinstall.sh script, then run the sh Xinstall.sh -check command. The output tells which library to download for your distribution. Once you have chosen the library for your version of Linux, download the following files:

Xinstall.sh	extract	Xetc.tgz
Xbin.tgz	Xdoc.tgz	Xfnts.tgz
Xlib.tgz	Xman.tgz	Xfenc.tgz
Xvar.tgz	Xxservtgz	Xmod.tgz

In most cases, you can use the installer script, Xinstall.sh, to install XFree86 on your computer. Go to the directory with your downloaded files, in this case /dos/tmp, and run the script with the following commands:

```
$ cd /dos/tmp
$ sh Xinstall.sh
```

You should now go through a series of prompts. If this does not work, you can still install XFree86 with several commands. First, create the necessary directories for the installation. You do this with the mkdir command, which is discussed in detail in Chapter 14:

```
$ mkdir /usr/X11R6
$ mkdir /etc/X11
```

Next, you need to run the installation programs provided in the files you have downloaded. Let's assume that you downloaded them to the tmp directory of your Windows partition and that in the installation process in Chapter 4, you chose to mount this partition as /dos. If this is the case, issue the following command to get into the X Windows directory:

```
$ cd /usr/X11R6
```

The next step is to prepare and extract the files from the archives you downloaded. You do this with the following commands (some of these commands are discussed later in the book; just use them for now to get X Windows running and you will learn what they all mean later):

```
$ chmod +x /dos/tmp/extract

$ /dos/tmp/extract -C /usr/X11R6 X[a-df-uw-z]*.tgz
$ /dos/tmp/extract -C /etc/X11 Xetc.tgz
$ /dos/tmp/extract -C /var Xvar.tgz$
$ ln -s /etc/X11/app-defaults /usr/X11R6/lib/X11
$ ln -s /etc/X11/fs /usr/X11R6/lib/X11
$ ln -s /etc/X11/lbxproxy /usr/X11R6/lib/X11
$ ln -s /etc/X11/proxymngr /usr/X11R6/lib/X11
$ ln -s /etc/X11/rstart /usr/X11R6/lib/X11
$ ln -s /etc/X11/twm /usr/X11R6/lib/X11
$ ln -s /etc/X11/xdm /usr/X11R6/lib/X11
$ ln -s /etc/X11/xinit /usr/X11R6/lib/X11
$ ln -s /etc/X11/xsm /usr/X11R6/lib/X11
$ ln -s /etc/X11/xserver /usr/X11R6/lib/X11
$ /sbin/ldconfig /usr/X11R6/lib
$ /usr/X11R6/bin/mkfontdir /usr/X11R6/lib/X11/fonts/misc
```

As cryptic as it all may seem at this point, the end result of all this typing is that the necessary files for X Windows will be installed on your Linux system.

Installing XFree86 Version 4.0.3

Now you're ready for the second stage of the process, installing XFree86 version 4.0.3 as an update to version 4.0.2. Return to the download site listed earlier, and navigate to the version 4.0.3 directory. Use the same library category that you used before, then download the following files:

```
Xinstall.sh          extract          Xupdate.tgz

Xdocupd.tgz          Xdrivers.tgz
```

In most cases, you can use the installer script that you downloaded for version 4.0.3, Xinstall.sh, to install XFree86 on your computer. Go to the directory containing your downloaded files, in this case /dos/tmp, and run the script with the following commands:

```
$ cd /dos/tmp
$ sh Xinstall.sh
```

This works only if you've already installed XFree86 version 4.0.2. You should now go through a series of prompts. After the installation is complete, configure X Windows using Xconfigurator or xf86config. Both of these utilities are discussed in following sections.

Preparing to Configure X Windows

Before you can actually configure X Windows, you must gather some critical information about your hardware to ensure that you do not damage your monitor in the process of trying to optimize X Windows. You need the following information:

- The make and model of your video card

- The make and model of your monitor

- The video memory on your video card

- The type of mouse you are using

- The horizontal sync range for your monitor

- The vertical sync range for your monitor

Without this information, it is possible to make mistakes in configuring XFree86 that could potentially damage your monitor. Let's take this information one piece at a time.

Make and Model of Your Video Card

These specifications shouldn't be too difficult to obtain. Generally, if you check your card's manual, you can glean this information.

If you have purchased a non-name-brand video card, then the make isn't relevant. In this case, check the documentation for the video card to see which chipset is being used on the card. Common chipsets include those from Cirrus Logic, S3, and Chips and Technologies, among others. In all cases, be sure to record the model number of the chipset as well as the maker of the chips.

If you have a computer with video support built into the motherboard, check the documentation for your computer or motherboard to determine the chipset maker and model number.

If you do not have your documentation, there is an XFree86 utility known as SuperProbe that can help detect your video hardware. If successful, this command can detect the X server, chipset, and RAMDAC associated with your hardware. To run the program, use the command

```
$ SuperProbe
```

Make and Model of Your Monitor

Check the manual of your monitor for its make and model. This information may be useful in configuring XFree86 if your monitor is a type that the configuration software knows about.

Video Memory on Your Video Card

Check the manual for your video card for the amount of memory on the card. In modern computers, this is generally no less than 4MB, and on some PCs it may be 8MB or as much as 32MB. On older computers or video cards, you may find as little as 256KB of video memory.

If you can't determine the amount of memory on your card from the manual, try powering on your PC and restarting it. The first screen to appear, usually very quickly, after you power on your computer is often generated by your video card and will display the make, model number, and possibly the amount of video memory on the card.

Type of Mouse You Are Using

This information is necessary in order to get your mouse working under X Windows. If you configured your mouse when installing Linux in Chapter 4, then you need the same information on hand to configure X Windows.

If you didn't configure your mouse then, you need to check the type of mouse you have. Possible types include the following:

- Microsoft-compatible serial mouse (usually with two buttons)
- Mouse Systems-compatible serial mouse (usually with three buttons)
- Bus Mouse
- PS/2 Mouse
- Logitech serial mouse

- Logitech MouseMan (Microsoft-compatible)

- Microsoft IntelliMouse

Most mice should be compatible with one of these types.

NOTE As of this writing, neither Xconfigurator nor xf86config can configure USB mice. The `/usr/sbin/mouseconfig` utility in Red Hat Linux 7.1 can serve this purpose.

NOTE If you have a mouse with a wheel, you may need to do some post-installation configuration. In some cases, the wheel is set up like a middle button. If you see a commented `ZAxisMapping` variable in your `/etc/X11/XF86Config` or `/etc/X11/XF86Config-4` file, you may be able to activate scrolling with your mouse wheel by deleting the # at the front of that line. Otherwise, review Mouse Support in the XFree86 document at `http://www.xfree86.org/4.0.3/mouse.html` for more information.

Horizontal Sync Range for Your Monitor

This information is crucial, especially if your monitor is not explicitly supported by the configuration software. Without this number (and the vertical sync range discussed in the next section), you risk damaging your monitor by asking your video card to provide a signal to your monitor that is outside its display capability.

You will find the information for the horizontal sync range (sometimes referred to as *horizontal scanning range*) in your manual, either under the monitor specifications or in the section discussing video modes. This information will be presented as a range of values in kilohertz, such as 30–70kHz. Generally, this range starts somewhere around 30kHz. You should also make note of the maximum possible value and choose a setting that is slightly less than the maximum.

Vertical Sync Range for Your Monitor

Like the horizontal sync range, the vertical sync range (sometimes called the *vertical scanning range*) is essential to preventing damage to your monitor. You should find the information in the same location as the horizontal sync range. It should appear as a range of values in hertz (not kilohertz like the horizontal value), such as 50–160Hz. (Generally, the larger number should exceed 75Hz unless you have an extremely low-end or old monitor. Monitors that cannot produce vertical scanning speeds higher than 72Hz suffer from flicker problems that can lead to eyestrain and headaches during even short-duration use.) Be sure also to note the maximum possible value for the vertical sync range.

Configuring XFree86 with Xconfigurator

Red Hat Linux comes with Xconfigurator, a configuration program for XFree86 that is much easier to use than the one that comes with XFree86. Let's look first at using Xconfigurator to configure X Windows and then at configuring XFree86 on systems that do not have Xconfigurator available.

Xconfigurator is a simple, menu-driven tool that greatly simplifies the process of configuring XFree86. To run the program, use the command

```
$ Xconfigurator
```

which should run the program and display a welcome screen like the one in Figure 7.2.

FIGURE 7.2:

The Xconfigurator welcome screen

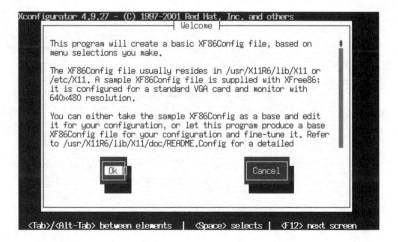

TIP

You need to be the root user to successfully complete all the steps involved in configuring X Windows.

To start using the program, press Enter to move past the welcome screen. Xconfigurator first tries to detect your graphics card. If it succeeds, you can see the result, like the one shown in Figure 7.3.

FIGURE 7.3:

PCI graphics card probe results

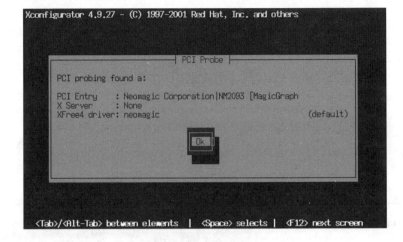

If this is what you see, you need not identify the graphics card and associated X server. Otherwise, the first menu you see is shown in Figure 7.4.

FIGURE 7.4:

The video card menu

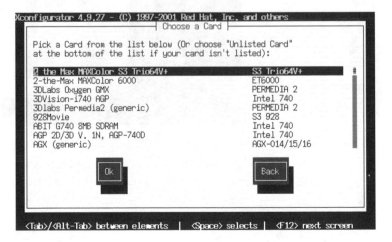

Here you choose the type of video card or chipset your system is running. Use the up and down arrows (or the PgDn and PgUp keys) to scroll through the long list of video cards and chipsets, which are presented alphabetically.

It is important to make sure that you have an exact match for your card or chipset. If you don't, it is unwise to guess and choose something that seems similar—a "similar" card can in fact be distinctly different from yours. In this case, select Generic VGA Compatible in the middle of the list or Unlisted Card at the bottom of the list. Once you have made your selection, press Enter to move to the next screen.

If you select Unlisted Card, a second menu appears, where you can choose the appropriate server for your card, as shown in Figure 7.5. If you are uncertain about which server to choose, use the generic server you selected earlier in the section on installing X Windows. For most modern multimedia computers, this will be the SVGA server.

FIGURE 7.5:

The X server menu

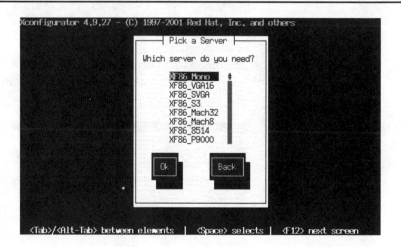

Once you have selected your card and possibly specified a server, the next step is to indicate your monitor on the monitor selection menu, shown in Figure 7.6.

FIGURE 7.6:

The monitor selection menu

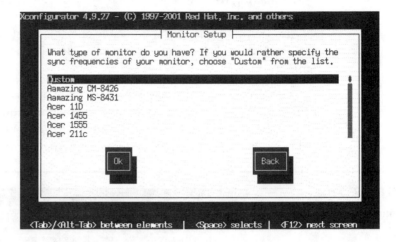

```
Xconfigurator 4.9.27 - (C) 1997-2001 Red Hat, Inc. and others
                    ┤ Monitor Setup ├
    What type of monitor do you have? If you would rather specify the
    sync frequencies of your monitor, choose "Custom" from the list.

    Custom                                                          #
    Aamazing CM-8426
    Aamazing MS-8431
    Acer 11D
    Acer 1455
    Acer 1555
    Acer 211c

            Ok                              Back



    <Tab>/<Alt-Tab> between elements  |  <Space> selects  |  <F12> next screen
```

If you can't find your specific monitor on the list, then you have three choices:

- Select Custom and then specify the horizontal and vertical sync ranges for your system (as explained previously).

- If you have a general idea of the maximum resolution and/or sync range for your monitor, select one of the generic monitors. Different generic monitors are available for the major resolutions (640 × 480 through 1600 × 1200). Other generic monitor options are available for LCD screens, which correspond to *most* laptop computers (see Warning).

WARNING   Be especially careful when configuring an LCD monitor or laptop computer, as maximum resolution and sync range vary. The wrong setting could permanently damage your LCD screen. Consult the documentation that shipped with your LCD or laptop, or check with the manufacturer before selecting a maximum resolution and/or sync range.

- If you don't have the sync ranges available for your monitor and you don't know whether your monitor is a multisync monitor, then select Generic LCD Panel or Generic Standard VGA with the lowest available vertical sync rate (these are lowest common denominators and should be your selection of last resort).

After making your selection, you may be offered a chance to probe your hardware for the correct resolution and color depth of your video card. Many modern PCI cards support this, and if you have one, it is worth trying to probe. If you have an older card or if probing fails, you can still configure the relevant settings manually.

If you select Custom in the monitor selection menu and you choose not to probe or the probing fails, a warning screen appears reminding you that entering the correct ranges is critical to avoiding damage to your monitor. Press Enter to proceed to the horizontal sync range menu shown in Figure 7.7.

FIGURE 7.7:

The horizontal sync range menu

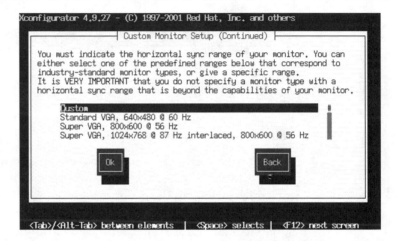

Scan the list and see if you find an entry that matches your monitor precisely. If you do, press Enter with that entry selected. In Xconfigurator, the choices are not by range, but by maximum possible value. This information is provided in the same place as the sync ranges in your monitor manual. Try to match the entry with the highest resolution and sync rate possible. Never choose an entry that offers a value beyond that listed in your monitor's manual.

Alternatively, if you have specific sync ranges from your monitor's manual, choose Custom. In the next menu, you can specify the exact horizontal and vertical sync ranges of your monitor. Once you make that selection, a menu of vertical sync ranges appears, as shown in Figure 7.8.

FIGURE 7.8:

The vertical sync
range menu

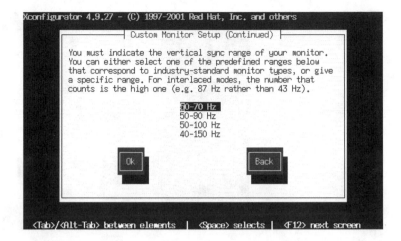

Choose a value from this menu where the larger number doesn't exceed the larger number in the vertical sync range for your monitor and the smaller number is not smaller than the smaller number in the vertical sync range for your monitor.

If Xconfigurator detected your card at the beginning of the process, the next screen offered by Xconfigurator is the choice of whether or not to probe your video card for possible video modes. Generally, most new cards can be probed successfully, although attempting this with old cards and certain recent cards can cause problems.

The best bet here is to try probing. If there is an error, you are notified and you have to proceed with manual configuration as outlined here. If probing succeeds, then you save yourself several steps.

If you choose not to probe or if probing fails, the next screen you see will be the video memory menu shown in Figure 7.9. Choose the value that matches your video card, as discussed earlier in the section on preparing for configuration.

FIGURE 7.9:

The video memory menu

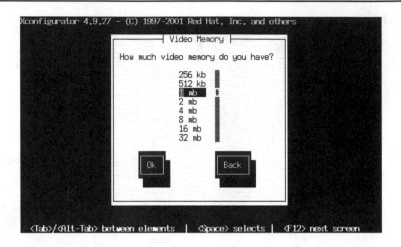

The next screen offers a selection of clock chip settings. Unless you are certain that your card has a clock chip and you know the exact type of clock chip, you are better off selecting the default No Clockchip Setting, as shown in Figure 7.10.

FIGURE 7.10:

The clock chip menu

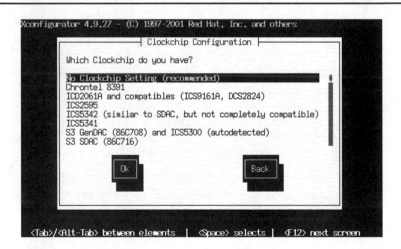

Unless Xconfigurator detected your card at the beginning of the process, you are asked if Xconfigurator should try running X -probeonly. This command attempts to detect the clock information that is needed when a clock chip is unavailable. Not all cards can be probed successfully, however. If you have selected a card that does not support probing, probing will fail. If you attempt to probe your hardware and get a failure notice or Xconfigurator crashes, then you know your card can't be probed.

After choosing a clock chip, a screen like the one in Figure 7.11 appears, where you can choose your preferred video modes.

FIGURE 7.11:

The video modes screen

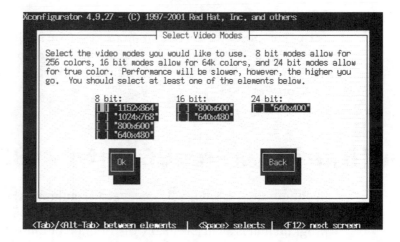

The higher bit depth you choose, the more colors will be displayed, but the slower your video performance will be. Similarly, the higher your resolution, the more desktop real estate you will have, but at the price of the size of letters and icons on the screen. You will probably want to experiment with these settings to find the best one for your system, but generally the best resolutions are 640×480 for a 14-inch monitor, 800×600 for a 15-inch monitor, and 1024×768 for a 17-inch monitor. If you have sufficient graphics card memory, 16-bit or 24-bit color is worthwhile, especially for color-intensive applications such as Netscape or The GIMP.

To make your selection, use the Tab key to move between bit depths and the arrow keys to move between resolutions. Use the spacebar to select a mode. When you have selected a mode, use the Tab key to select the OK button, and press Enter.

NOTE   If you choose more than one video mode, you can switch between modes in the X Window with the Ctrl+Alt+Keypad Plus and Ctrl+Alt+Keypad Minus commands.

Finally, Xconfigurator tests the configuration. After a number of seconds, the screen flashes. If the configuration is successful, you are taken to a screen with the following prompt:

```
Can you see this message? Automatic timeout in 10 seconds.
```

If you can see the message, click Yes. Next, Xconfigurator gives you the option of starting the X server when you reboot. When you do reboot, Linux takes you to a graphical logon screen.

This completes the configuration process. You are informed that a configuration file has been created, and then you can press Enter to exit Xconfigurator. In Red Hat Linux 7.1, the file that is created is called XF86Config and is placed in the directory /etc/X11.

Configuring XFree86 with Xf86config

Xconfigurator provides only one way to configure XFree86, and this method is available only with Red Hat Linux. XFree86 itself comes with a configuration program that is available in any distribution of Linux that includes XFree86: xf86config.

Xf86config is also menu-driven, but it does less of the work for you and is somewhat more cumbersome to use than Xconfigurator. However, xf86config also allows you to configure mice and keyboards. To run xf86config, use the following command:

```
$ xf86config
```

A welcome screen like the one in Figure 7.12 appears.

FIGURE 7.12:

The xf86config welcome screen

```
This program will create a basic XF86Config file, based on menu selections you
make.

The XF86Config file usually resides in /usr/X11R6/etc/X11 or /etc/X11. A sample
XF86Config file is supplied with XFree86; it is configured for a standard
VGA card and monitor with 640x480 resolution. This program will ask for a
pathname when it is ready to write the file.

You can either take the sample XF86Config as a base and edit it for your
configuration, or let this program produce a base XF86Config file for your
configuration and fine-tune it.

Before continuing with this program, make sure you know what video card
you have, and preferably also the chipset it uses and the amount of video
memory on your video card. SuperProbe may be able to help with this.

Press enter to continue, or ctrl-c to abort.▯
```

TIP

You need to be the root user to successfully complete all the steps involved in configuring X Windows with xf86config.

NOTE

Xf86config presents a lot of dense text on the screen during the configuration process. The welcome screen is just the first example of this. It is a good idea to read everything thoroughly if you are not familiar with xf86config so that you are fully aware of the significance of the choices you make. Once you make a choice, even if it is blank, you cannot go back; you would need to restart xf86config.

The first menu presented is the mouse protocol menu shown in Figure 7.13. Select the correct option by typing the associated number and pressing Enter. You will then be presented with a series of mouse-related questions, which may include the following:

- "Do you want to enable ChordMiddle?" If you have a three-button Microsoft-compatible mouse made by Logitech, you can select ChordMiddle to make the middle button work. Otherwise, only the left and right mouse buttons will work.

- "Do you want to enable Emulate3Buttons?" This option should be enabled when you are using a two-button mouse and a two-button mouse protocol such as the Microsoft-compatible protocol. This allows you to emulate a middle button, which is necessary in some X Windows applications, by clicking the left and right mouse buttons together.

FIGURE 7.13:

The mouse protocol menu

```
First specify a mouse protocol type. Choose one from the following list:

1.  Microsoft compatible (2-button protocol)
2.  Mouse Systems (3-button protocol)
3.  Bus Mouse
4.  PS/2 Mouse
5.  Logitech Mouse (serial, old type, Logitech protocol)
6.  Logitech MouseMan (Microsoft compatible)
7.  MM Series
8.  MM HitTablet
9.  Microsoft IntelliMouse

If you have a two-button mouse, it is most likely of type 1, and if you have
a three-button mouse, it can probably support both protocol 1 and 2. There are
two main varieties of the latter type: mice with a switch to select the
protocol, and mice that default to 1 and require a button to be held at
boot-time to select protocol 2. Some mice can be convinced to do 2 by sending
a special sequence to the serial port (see the ClearDTR/ClearRTS options).

Enter a protocol number: []
```

- The final question related to your mouse will be a request to enter the mouse device. If you are using the same mouse you used when you installed Red Hat Linux and you configured the mouse during installation in Chapter 4, then you should enter **/dev/mouse**. Because this is the default, you can just press Enter here.

> **NOTE** The version of xf86config included with Red Hat Linux 7.1 does not recognize USB equipment. If you have a USB mouse and Red Hat Linux 7.1, use the `/usr/sbin/mouseconfig` utility.

The next major section involves configuring your keyboard. The first screen is a menu of possible keyboard types, as shown in Figure 7.14.

FIGURE 7.14:

The keyboard menu

```
Please select one of the following keyboard types that is the better
description of your keyboard. If nothing really matches,
choose 1 (Generic 101-key PC)

  1  Generic 101-key PC
  2  Generic 102-key (Intl) PC
  3  Generic 104-key PC
  4  Generic 105-key (Intl) PC
  5  Dell 101-key PC
  6  Everex STEPnote
  7  Keytronic FlexPro
  8  Microsoft Natural
  9  Northgate OmniKey 101
 10  Winbook Model XP5
 11  Japanese 106-key
 12  PC-98xx Series
 13  Brazilian ABNT2
 14  HP Internet
 15  Logitech iTouch
 16  Logitech Cordless Desktop Pro
 17  Compaq Internet
 18  Microsoft Natural Pro

Enter a number to choose the keyboard.

[]
```

Choose the keyboard that most closely matches yours. The Generic 101-key or 104-key PC keyboards are the likeliest candidates for most North American English-language computers. The next menu shows a series of different languages or dialects. The list of countries extends beyond one screen, and you can use the Enter key to cycle to the next screen of countries.

> **NOTE** Non-English keyboards and non-standard keyboards, however, will require manual configuration, which is discussed in Chapter 12, "Advanced X Windows Configuration."

Next, you can configure your keyboard further. If you type **y** to the "Do you want to select additional XKB options?" prompt, you can set different keyboard groups, which is useful if you're using multilanguage keyboards.

After configuring your keyboard, the next step is to specify the horizontal and vertical sync ranges for your monitor. The first menu presented is the horizontal sync range menu shown in Figure 7.15.

FIGURE 7.15:

The horizontal sync range menu

```
You must indicate the horizontal sync range of your monitor. You can either
select one of the predefined ranges below that correspond to industry-
standard monitor types, or give a specific range.

It is VERY IMPORTANT that you do not specify a monitor type with a horizontal
sync range that is beyond the capabilities of your monitor. If in doubt,
choose a conservative setting.

    hsync in kHz; monitor type with characteristic modes
 1  31.5; Standard VGA, 640x480 @ 60 Hz
 2  31.5 - 35.1; Super VGA, 800x600 @ 56 Hz
 3  31.5, 35.5; 8514 Compatible, 1024x768 @ 87 Hz interlaced (no 800x600)
 4  31.5, 35.15, 35.5; Super VGA, 1024x768 @ 87 Hz interlaced, 800x600 @ 56 Hz
 5  31.5 - 37.9; Extended Super VGA, 800x600 @ 60 Hz, 640x480 @ 72 Hz
 6  31.5 - 48.5; Non-Interlaced SVGA, 1024x768 @ 60 Hz, 800x600 @ 72 Hz
 7  31.5 - 57.0; High Frequency SVGA, 1024x768 @ 70 Hz
 8  31.5 - 64.3; Monitor that can do 1280x1024 @ 60 Hz
 9  31.5 - 79.0; Monitor that can do 1280x1024 @ 74 Hz
10  31.5 - 82.0; Monitor that can do 1280x1024 @ 76 Hz
11  Enter your own horizontal sync range

Enter your choice (1-11): []
```

If you don't find an exact match for your horizontal sync range and you have the range for your monitor on hand, select Enter Your Own Horizontal Sync Range and provide the correct range. If you don't have access to this information, choose a conservative value. For an average 15-inch multisync monitor, try the Super VGA or Extended Super VGA setting. For a low-end 14-inch monitor, it is probably safest to select Standard VGA.

Next, you need to specify the vertical sync range for your monitor. Xf86config presents a small number of options, but you can select Enter Your Own Vertical Sync Range to specify the range for your monitor. If you don't know the range for your monitor, it is probably safest to choose the lowest and smallest range, generally 50–70 in most versions of XFree86.

Once you have specified this monitor data, xf86config asks you to specify a freeform definition for your monitor (e.g., My Linux Monitor). This definition does not actually affect the configuration or performance of XFree86, but it provides an easy way to identify the monitor definition in your XFree86 configuration file if you need to refer to it in the future.

Once you have all your monitor information entered, you need to specify your video card or chipset. The first screen asks if you want to look at a database of known cards and chips to make your selection. If you choose to do this, a menu of known cards appears, similar to that shown in Figure 7.16.

FIGURE 7.16:

The video card menu

```
 0  2 the Max MAXColor S3 Trio64V+          S3 Trio64V+
 1  2-the-Max MAXColor 6000                 ET6000
 2  3DLabs Oxygen GMX                       PERMEDIA 2
 3  3DVision-i740 AGP                       Intel 740
 4  3Dlabs Permedia2 (generic)             PERMEDIA 2
 5  928Movie                               S3 928
 6  ABIT G740 8MB SDRAM                    Intel 740
 7  AGP 2D/3D V. 1N, AGP-740D              Intel 740
 8  AGX (generic)                         AGX-014/15/16
 9  ALG-5434(E)                           CL-GD5434
10  AOpen AGP 2X 3D Navigator PA740        Intel 740
11  AOpen PA2010                           Voodoo Banshee
12  AOpen PA45                             SiS6326
13  AOpen PA50D                            SiS6326
14  AOpen PA50E                            SiS6326
15  AOpen PA50V                            SiS6326
16  AOpen PA80/DVD                         SiS6326
17  AOpen PG128                            S3 Trio3D

Enter a number to choose the corresponding card definition.
Press enter for the next page, q to continue configuration.

[]
```

You can press Enter to page forward through the menus, and at any time you can type the number of a specific card and press Enter to select it. If you find that there isn't a match for your card, simply enter **q** to skip this phase.

After you select a video card, a menu screen appears like the one in Figure 7.17. Here you have to select the amount of video memory on your video card.

FIGURE 7.17:

The video memory menu

```
Now you must give information about your video card. This will be used for
the "Device" section of your video card in XF86Config.

You must indicate how much video memory you have. It is probably a good
idea to use the same approximate amount as that detected by the server you
intend to use. If you encounter problems that are due to the used server
not supporting the amount memory you have (e.g. ATI Mach64 is limited to
1024K with the SVGA server), specify the maximum amount supported by the
server.

How much video memory do you have on your video card:

1   256K
2   512K
3   1024K
4   2048K
5   4096K
6   Other

Enter your choice: []
```

Once you have selected an amount of video memory, you are asked to provide a freeform definition for your video card. As with your monitor, these entries have nothing to do with the proper functioning of your X Windows system, so you should enter something that you will recognize later if you ever need to manually edit your XFree86 configuration file.

The next menu, shown in Figure 7.18, allows you to select a color depth, which is the number of colors that can be shown on each pixel. More color depth bits provide truer color. The number of bits that you can practically use depends on the amount of memory in your graphics card and the resolution you are running at. For example, if you have a graphics card with 512KB of video memory, you probably can't support 24-bit color.

FIGURE 7.18:

The color depth menu

```
Please specify which color depth you want to use by default:

1  1 bit (monochrome)
2  4 bits (16 colors)
3  8 bits (256 colors)
4  16 bits (65536 colors)
5  24 bits (16 million colors)

Enter a number to choose the default depth.

[]
```

The final set of questions asks you where to write the XF86Config file. First, it asks if you should write the file to /etc/X11/XF86Config, the normal location. You are asked this so you can make sure you don't overwrite an old, working copy of your configuration file with a new one that might not work. If you have been using X Windows successfully and are trying to reconfigure it to slightly different settings, you may want to keep a copy of your old configuration file before you allow xf86config to write the new one.

If you answer **n** to the question, xf86config provides a series of alternate locations to write the file, as described in the following paragraphs.

First, you are asked if you want to write the file to the "default" location (/usr/X11R6/lib/X11/XF86Config). If you want to specify your own location for the file, answer **n**.

Next, you are asked if you want the file to be written in the current directory. If the current directory is a logical location (such as the root user's home directory or /tmp), then you can answer **y**. If you answer **n**, then you are finally prompted to supply the complete path and filename where you want the new configuration to be saved.

In order to use this configuration (once it is working to your satisfaction), you need to copy the file you have just saved to the correct location for the XFree86 configuration file, which for most versions of Linux is either /etc/XF86Config or /etc/X11/XF86Config. For Red Hat 7.1, the file should be /etc/X11/XF86Config.

Another approach is to copy your current configuration file to a backup location before running xf86config; then, when you are asked if you want to overwrite the current configuration, you simply answer **y**. You will learn how to copy files in Chapter 14, but a simple way to make a backup copy of the Red Hat 7.1 XFree86 configuration file is with the following command:

```
$ cp /etc/X11/XF86Config /etc/X11/XF86Config.keep
```

This command creates a copy of your existing configuration named /etc/X11/XF86Config.keep.

Testing Your Configuration

Now that you have finished configuring X Windows, it is time to see if the configuration you created actually works. To do this, you need to try running X Windows. Red Hat Linux 7.1 comes with X Windows set up to run a default window manager and some default initial applications, so you should be ready to go once XFree86 is configured.

To start X Windows, use the following command:

```
$ startx
```

This starts X Windows running. If all goes well, a number of lines of information flash by on the screen, and then the screen switches to graphical mode and you see your default X Windows environment. This will probably look like the one in Figure 7.19.

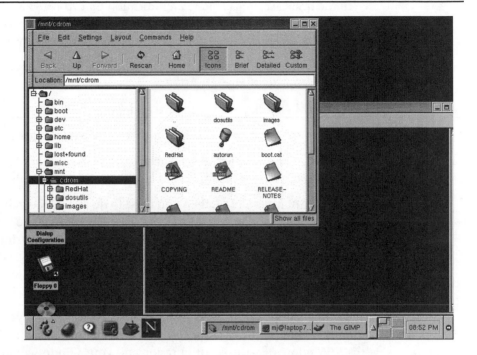

FIGURE 7.19:

A typical desktop in Red Hat Linux 7.1

You can run X Windows as a regular user or as the root user for the purpose of verifying that it is working properly. But it is generally wise to run X Windows as a non-root user so that you minimize the chance of using X Windows applications to accidentally damage, erase, or change critical system files that only the root user has permission to modify.

The real problems begin if things don't work. Failure is usually indicated in one of three ways:

- You get an error message and are returned to the command prompt without your computer ever switching to graphical mode.

- You are switched to graphical mode but are left with a blank gray desktop, no window manager, and no functioning windows.

- You are switched to graphical mode, but this is quickly exited and you are returned to the command prompt.

In the first case, this is likely an indication that XFree86 is not configured correctly. Unfortunately, the number of possible reasons for configuration failure is probably as large as the number of different hardware combinations that exist.

Before you rerun Xconfigurator or xf86config, here are a few tips that may help you get things working:

- Double-check your video card and monitor data.

- Try using smaller horizontal and vertical sync ranges.

- Try using a simpler server, such as the VGA16 rather than the SVGA server, or the SVGA server instead of a card-specific accelerated server.

If these attempts all fail, then you need to do some research into your specific problem. The best place to start is the XFree86 HOWTO file. You may already have this on your system if you have a fairly complete distribution. You can read the HOWTO on the Web at `http://www.linuxdoc.org/HOWTO/XFree86-HOWTO/index.html`. Alternatively, read the documentation for your version of XFree86. For version 4.0.3, this is located at `http://www.xfree86.org/4.0.3/index.html`.

If you experience one of the other two problems (where your system switches to graphical mode but things don't quite work out), then the first step is to check the X Windows start-up configuration and your window manager configuration. Chapter 12 discusses these configurations in detail.

Looking Ahead

Now that you should have X Windows working, it is time to actually try your hand at using the X Windows environment for practical tasks. To do this, let's start with a look at GNOME, the GNU Object Model Environment.

GNOME is one of two competing standards emerging for the future of Linux graphical desktops. GNOME offers a fully integrated desktop environment for developing and running applications. GNOME is the default desktop in Red Hat Linux 7.1.

Chapter 8, "Using GNOME and X Windows," looks at the basics of using X Windows with the GNOME desktop. Chapter 9, "Using Applications with GNOME and X Windows," discusses running GNOME and X Windows applications, including terminal emulators, file managers, graphics applications, and more. By the end of these two chapters, you should have enough experience and confidence to experiment with other available X Windows applications.

CHAPTER

EIGHT

Using GNOME and X Windows

- Starting X Windows and GNOME

- The GNOME Panel

- The GNOME Interface

- Managing Files with GNOME

Now that you have X Windows set up and running on your system, you will learn how to make use of the X Windows environment as it is designed for Linux.

This chapter provides an overview on using the GNOME desktop. The GNOME desktop is sophisticated enough that it could easily warrant a book of its own. Instead of providing a complete guide to using GNOME, the goal here is to provide you with enough familiarity that you will feel confident to experiment with GNOME. For those who have used Windows 9*x*, Me, NT, or 2000, the basics of using GNOME should be quite straightforward.

Starting X Windows and GNOME

Because Red Hat comes preconfigured for GNOME, starting the desktop manager is as simple as starting the X Windows environment. As you learned in Chapter 7, "Installing and Configuring X Windows," you begin by logging in as a user and then issue the command

```
$ startx
```

This command starts X Windows and launches the GNOME desktop manager. Initially, this results in a screen similar to the one in Figure 8.1. It includes two types of icons: launchers that start applications and folders that open through the GNOME file manager, known as the GNU Midnight Commander.

> **NOTE**   Depending on how your Red Hat installation is configured, Red Hat may launch X Windows when you start your system and present a graphical login prompt. If this is the case, then GNOME automatically starts as soon as you log in and you don't need to use the `startx` command.

Manually Installing GNOME

By default, Red Hat Linux 7.1 will install the GNOME desktop environment. If, for some reason, you chose not to install GNOME or GNOME was not automatically installed, you will need to install GNOME manually.

Continued on next page

To do this, you need to install the following packages from the **RedHat/RPMS** directory of the Red Hat Installation CD-ROM:

- gnome-applets-1.2.4-3.i386.rpm
- gnome-audio-1.0.0-12.noarch.rpm
- gnome-audio-extra-1.0.0-12.noarch.rpm
- gnome-core-1.2.4-16.i386.rpm
- gnome-core-devel-1.2.4-16.i386.rpm
- gnome-games-1.2.0-10.i386.rpm
- gnome-games-devel-1.2.0-10.i386.rpm
- gnome-kerberos-0.2.2-2.i386.rpm
- gnome-libs-1.2.8-11.i386.rpm
- gnome-libs-devel-1.2.8-11.i386.rpm
- gnome-linuxconf-0.64-1.i386.rpm
- gnome-lokkit-0.43-6.i386.rpm
- gnome-media-1.2.0-12.i386.rpm
- gnome-objc-1.0.2-11.i386.rpm
- gnome-objc-devel-1.0.2-11.i386.rpm
- gnome-pim-1.2.0-9.i386.rpm
- gnome-pim-devel-1.2.0-9.i386.rpm
- gnome-print-0.25-9.i386.rpm
- gnome-users-guide-1.2-3.noarch.rpm
- gnome-utils-1.2.1-5.i386.rpm

Some of these packages are found on the second Red Hat Linux 7.1 Installation CD-ROM. If you have only the publisher's edition of Red Hat Linux 7.1 included with this book, do not be concerned about missing packages, as they are not essential to the basic operation of GNOME. To install each of these packages, use the **rpm** command:

```
# rpm -i filename
```

FIGURE 8.1:

A typical GNOME desktop in Red Hat Linux 7.1

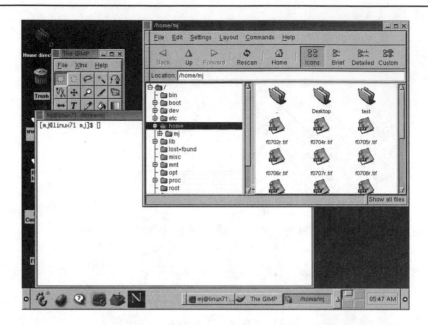

The GNOME Panel

The GNOME Panel, shown in Figure 8.2, is displayed across the bottom of the screen. It includes a System menu button (the button with the stylized footprint at the far left), a small Panel displaying the time and date at the far right, and a pager and other buttons for default actions.

FIGURE 8.2:

The GNOME Panel

In this Panel, there are five buttons that serve as launchers to specific programs:

- The lock starts a password-protected screensaver.

- The question mark opens the GNOME help system.

- The monitor starts the GNOME command-line terminal.

- The toolbox starts the GNOME control center.

- The stylized *N* is the now-familiar symbol for Netscape.

Using the System Menu

The System menu works in the same way as the Start menu in Windows 98 and Windows 2000. Clicking the System menu button pops up a menu like the one in Figure 8.3.

FIGURE 8.3:

The GNOME System menu

| Programs |
| Favorites |
| Applets |
| KDE menus |
| Run... |
| Panel |
| Lock screen |
| Log out |

NOTE   Although the figures shown in this chapter may not have the same "look and feel" as the standard installation of GNOME on Red Hat Linux 7.1, the content is identical.

The System menu contains several items:

Programs   This submenu provides access to most of the applications and utilities available on GNOME.

Favorites   This option provides access to any favorites that you may have created, including Web sites.

Applets   This submenu provides access to standard GNOME applets, including load monitors, clocks, and CD players. GNOME places any applet that you choose on the Panel.

KDE Menus   This submenu provides access to the standard KDE menus if you have installed KDE as an alternate desktop manager on your system.

Run   Use this option to run any program or application installed on your Linux system. Selecting this option opens the dialog box shown in Figure 8.4. Enter the path and name of the program, and click the Run button to launch the application. Or you can click the Browse button to choose the program to run from the file-selection window shown in Figure 8.5.

FIGURE 8.4:

Running a program

FIGURE 8.5:

Choosing a program to run

Panel   This submenu provides tools for configuring your GNOME Panel. Chapter 10, "Advanced GNOME Configuration," describes these tools in more detail.

Lock Screen   This option lets you activate the screen saver with a password.

Log Out   This option allows you to log out and exit GNOME. If you start GNOME by logging in from a graphical login screen, then this option causes

GNOME to exit and return to the login screen. If you start GNOME from a command-line console, you are returned to the command line.

Programs Submenu   There are several additional submenus you can access from the Programs submenu, each with a right arrow to the right of the submenu name. Each of these options opens a submenu containing programs that can be launched. The standard submenus are as follows:

Applications   This submenu offers standard GNOME applications such as the GNOME calendar tool and the GNOME spreadsheet, Gnumeric.

Utilities   This submenu provides access to commonly used GNOME and X Windows utilities, including the rvxt terminal, a calculator, and a file-search tool.

Development   This submenu includes a development utility called GLADE, the GTK+ user interface builder.

Games   This submenu offers a set of X Windows and GNOME games.

Graphics   This submenu provides a handful of graphics tools for GNOME, including the acclaimed image-editing software, The GIMP.

Internet   This submenu provides quick access to standard Internet tools, including Netscape, the new Mozilla browser, and the GNOME FTP tool, gFTP.

Multimedia   This submenu offers a selection of multimedia tools, including a CD player and volume control tools.

Settings   This submenu provides a collection of tools for configuring GNOME. Chapter 10 looks at these tools in more detail.

System   This submenu offers access to a few system tools, including a GNOME-based package management system for Red Hat rpm packages, GnoRPM.

File Manager   Selecting this menu entry launches the GNOME file manager, like the one shown in Figure 8.6. The GNOME file manager is discussed in more detail later in this chapter.

Help System   This option can be used to launch the GNOME help system. The help system is an HTML system using a built-in HTML browser, as shown in Figure 8.7. The GNOME help system provides comprehensive documentation on using GNOME, and you should refer to it for detailed guidance on using GNOME.

FIGURE 8.6:

The GNOME file manager

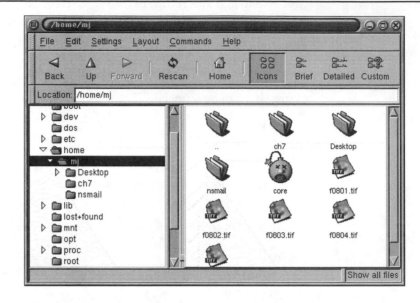

FIGURE 8.7:

The GNOME help system

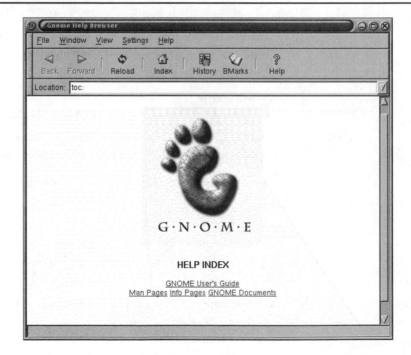

Manipulating the GNOME Panel

One drawback of the GNOME Panel is that it takes up considerable screen space for users with small screens, such as those using notebooks or those with smaller 14- and 15-inch monitors. Luckily, there are several ways to alleviate this problem.

One option is to roll up the Panel into a small rectangle. The standard Panel sits horizontally across the bottom of the screen. You can roll up the Panel into a small rectangle at the bottom-left corner of the screen by clicking the small left-arrow button at the left end of the panel. The Panel disappears and only a small rectangle containing a right arrow remains. Clicking the right arrow unrolls the Panel to fill the bottom of the screen.

Similarly, clicking the right arrow at the far-right side of the Panel rolls up the Panel to the bottom-right corner of the screen with only a left-arrow button visible. Clicking the left arrow unrolls the Panel.

If this isn't sufficient and you find that the arrows take up too much space, you can shrink the desktop real estate consumed by a rolled-up Panel to almost nothing by eliminating the arrows from the buttons. To do this, right-click the background of the Panel. In the menu that appears, choose Panel ➢ Properties ➢ All Properties. This opens the Panel Properties dialog box for the Panel, shown in Figure 8.8.

Here, you can deselect the Show Arrows On Hide Button option and click the Apply button to remove the left and right arrows from the buttons at each end of the Panel and make the button as narrow as possible.

Another useful option for reclaiming desktop space is to select the Enable Auto-hide option in the Panel Properties dialog box and click the Apply button. This hides the Panel, leaving visible only a narrow strip across the bottom of the screen. You need only move the mouse over this narrow strip for the entire Panel to be made visible. As soon as you move the mouse pointer out of the Panel, it automatically hides again, leaving only the small strip visible.

Another useful feature of the Panel Properties dialog box is that it gives you the ability to place the Panel on a different edge of the screen than the default bottom edge. For instance, some users prefer to place the Panel along the top, left, or right of the screen. You can do this by selecting the appropriate side in the Panel Position section of the dialog box and clicking Apply.

FIGURE 8.8:

The GNOME Panel Proper-
ties dialog box

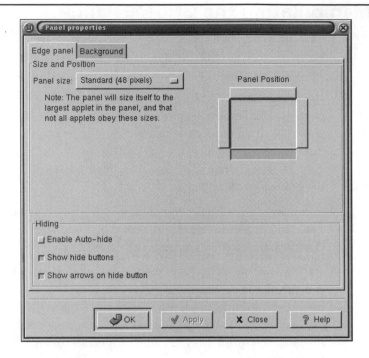

Panel Applets

The GNOME Panel is a highly customizable tool. One of its most powerful capabilities is to run small applets inside the Panel.

GNOME includes numerous applets and provides an interface by which programmers can develop their own applets. Some of the applets included with
GNOME on Red Hat Linux 7.1 are these:

- A small scrambled-tile game

- Monitor applets to track battery usage, CPU load, and disk space

- A CD player applet

- An applet to check your inbox for new messages

- A clock applet

- A printer control applet

- A desk guide applet for providing virtual desktops

By default, the clock and desk guide applets are displayed on the GNOME Panel.

There are several types of actions you need to take with respect to Panel applets:

- Adding applets to the Panel
- Moving applets on the Panel
- Changing applet properties
- Removing applets from the Panel

Adding Applets to the Panel

Adding applets to the Panel is fairly easy. To add the Desk Guide applet, right-click the background of the Panel. This causes a menu to appear. On this menu, choose Panel ➢ Add To Panel ➢ Applet ➢ Utility ➢ Desk Guide. A series of four blocks appears on the Panel.

Another way to add an applet is from the main System menu. To add the Tasklist applet, click the main System menu and choose Applets ➢ Utility ➢ Tasklist. A tasklist of currently running applications appears on the Panel.

Moving Applets on the Panel

Once an applet is on the Panel, you may find that you want to move it to a different location on the Panel as dictated by the way that you use the Panel. To move an applet, right-click the applet itself and choose Move from the menu that appears. Then, use your mouse to drag the applet to a new location on the Panel, and click the mouse to make the move permanent.

Changing Applet Properties

Most applets have properties that you can configure to customize their behavior. These properties are controlled from a Properties dialog box that can be opened by right-clicking the applet and selecting Properties from the menu that appears.

Removing Applets from the Panel

The ability to remove applets from the Panel once they are placed there is important. This makes it easy to experiment with the many applets included with GNOME and allows you to clean up your Panel as it gets too cluttered. To remove an applet, right-click the applet and select Remove From Panel from the menu that appears.

Using the Desk Guide and Tasklist Applets

This section shows how to use applets by discussing the Desk Guide and Tasklist applets that you added earlier. The Desk Guide applet, shown in Figure 8.9, provides virtual desktops.

NOTE   The Desk Guide and Tasklist applets together were known as the Pager in previous versions of GNOME.

FIGURE 8.9:

The Desk Guide and Tasklist applets

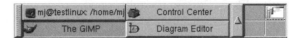

The concept of virtual desktops is simple. Let's start with a basic example. If you have two virtual desktops, this is like having two monitors but only one power cable for those monitors. You could have two different sets of applications open, running, and displayed on the monitors and switch between these environments by switching the power cable between the monitors.

Virtual desktops provide similar functionality but without the delay, difficulty, and frustration of switching your power cable between two monitors. Each desktop in a virtual desktop system is like a brand-new work environment in which you can open windows and run applications. At the same time, these applications, regardless of which desktop they appear in, are running in the same X Windows session, which means you can cut and paste between them as if they were visually displayed on the same desktop.

You can switch desktops by clicking the left mouse button on any of the four squares on the Desk Guide. This immediately switches the displayed desktop to the one selected.

In contrast, the Tasklist applet includes space to display buttons for all open windows on the current desktop. You can bring any window to the foreground by clicking its button. If the window is already in the foreground, you can minimize it by clicking its Tasklist button.

Between the virtual desktop and the applications buttons in Figure 8.9 is a small button with an up arrow. Clicking this button displays a menu of all open windows on all virtual desktops. You can click any application to switch to the desktop where that window is located and bring the window to the foreground.

The GNOME Interface

GNOME has many critical user interface elements. This section discusses the features of GNOME that allow you to manipulate windows and to work with the desktop.

Manipulating Windows

The windows in GNOME look a lot like their counterparts in Windows 98 and behave in much the same way. This is advantageous for Windows users, since it makes moving from a Microsoft Windows operating system to X Windows a simple process in terms of interacting with windows.

Let's take a look at the main window components: the title bar, window action icons, the Window Operations menu, and the window border.

Title Bar

The title bar is displayed across the top of the window. It contains the name of the window, which in most cases is the name of the application that is displaying the window. In the case of an xterm window, the title is xterm by default (although it is possible to change it, as you will see later).

The title bar area serves several functional purposes in GNOME. As you might expect, you can click once with the left mouse button in the title bar to bring a window to the front of other open windows. Clicking and dragging with the left mouse button allows you to move the window. When you release the left mouse button, the window remains in the new location.

Double-clicking the title bar minimizes the window to just the title bar, hiding the contents of the window but leaving the title bar visible. The title bar can continue to be used in the same way as when the window contents are visible, and double-clicking the title bar again redisplays the window contents. In GNOME terminology, this is known as *shading* and *unshading* the window.

Window Action Icons

The window action icons appear as a group of three icons in the top-right corner of most windows.

From left to right, these icons perform the following actions when single-clicked:

Minimize the Window   This icon hides the window, leaving a button for it in the Tasklist applet on the GNOME Panel.

Maximize/Reset the Window   This icon acts as a toggle, switching the window between full screen (Maximize) and its original size before being maximized (Reset).

Close the Window   This icon closes the window. In the case of multiwindow applications, this does not act as a kill operation but leaves other windows in the application open.

Window Operations Menu

To the left of the title, in the top-left corner of the window, there's an icon that, when clicked, displays the Window Operations menu from the Start menu. This menu offers several options for controlling your windows. The first three options are Minimize, Maximize, and Close, which correspond to the aforementioned action icons. The other options are in submenus in the following categories:

Toggle   Various submenus under this option allow you to keep the window with you when you change desktops (Sticky), to minimize the current window (Minimize), and hide everything but the title bar (Shaded).

In Group   The In Group submenus associate the current window with another window.

Send Window To   You can use this submenu to move the current window to another desktop by specifying the direction in which to move the window (for instance, the window to the right of the current window).

Stacking   The submenus here govern where the current window is "stacked" relative to other open windows.

Frame Type   The Frame Type submenus govern where the frame is located around the title and/or border of the window.

Frame Style   The submenus under Frame Style govern the look and feel of the frame.

History   These submenus change the default position, dimensions, and attributes of the subject window.

Window Borders

Most windows have a border that is five pixels wide. This border is used to visually indicate the edge of the window as well as to allow users to resize a window.

It is possible to resize a window horizontally, vertically, or both. Simply click and drag anywhere on the border except the edges immediately adjacent to the title bar. As you drag outside the existing window border, the window resizes based on the location of the mouse pointer. Clicking the left or right side allows you to resize horizontally; clicking the bottom edge allows vertical resizing; and clicking the bottom corners allows resizing vertically and horizontally in one action.

The GNOME Desktop

You probably noticed that the GNOME desktop contains a single folder icon when you first start GNOME. This icon is a folder with the name Home Directory. Double-clicking this icon opens the GNOME file manager and displays the current user's home directory in the file manager, as shown in Figure 8.10.

FIGURE 8.10:

The GNOME file manager

Right-clicking the GNOME desktop displays a menu that you can use for several purposes, including the following:

- Opening a new GNOME file manager window
- Arranging the icons on the desktop
- Opening new terminal windows

For instance, choosing Arrange Icons rearranges the icons on your desktop into a clean grid pattern. This is useful if you keep a large number of icons on your desktop and they become disorganized and cluttered. The Create New Window option opens a new file manager window (in the same way as double-clicking the Home Directory folder icon on the desktop does).

Managing Files with GNOME

Windows 3.1 users have File Manager, Windows 95/98 users have Windows Explorer, and Mac OS users have Finder. All of these programs provide facilities for managing files (including copying, moving, renaming, and deleting) as well as for launching applications.

In the X Windows world, there has traditionally been no standard tool to provide these features. Numerous applications that call themselves file managers or desktop managers attempt to provide this functionality. You can find a selected list of file managers at `http://www.xnet.com/~blatura/linapp2.html#file`.

However, with the emergence of GNOME and KDE as alternative standards for the Linux desktop environment, the situation is stabilizing. Both GNOME and KDE offer standard file managers. The GNOME file manager, also known as the GNU Midnight Commander, provides a flexible, high-quality file management and browsing tool. This section will look at the GNOME file manager.

Launching the GNOME File Manager

The GNOME file manager can be launched by selecting File Manager from the default GNOME Programs submenu. Alternatively, you can issue the command

```
$ gmc &
```

from the command line of an xterm window or, if you need to specify the complete path,

```
$ /usr/bin/gmc &
```

in a Red Hat Linux 7.1 installation; gmc stands for GNU Midnight Commander.

The File Manager Window

As shown back in Figure 8.10, the GNOME file manager window displays the contents of a single directory on your computer. By default, the directory displayed is the home directory of the user running the program. In that figure, user mj has run the file manager so the directory displayed is his home directory: /home/mj.

The window is divided into three main sections:

- Directory tree (left side)

- Display pane (right side)

- Toolbar (across the top)

The Directory Tree

On the left side of the GNOME file manager window is an expandable and collapsible directory of your Linux system. This directory tree is reminiscent of the one used in Windows Explorer in Windows 95, 98, and 2000. The tree works in the same way as its Windows counterpart:

- Clicking a right-facing triangle next to a directory name expands the segment of the tree to display the next level of subdirectories below the particular directory.

- Clicking a down triangle next to a directory name collapses the segment of the tree and hides all children of the particular directory.

- Clicking the name of the directory displays the contents of the directory in the pane on the right side of the file manager window.

NOTE   In some versions of GNOME, including the version that comes with the default Red Hat Linux 7.1 installation, there are plus signs in place of right-facing triangles and minus signs in place of the down triangles shown in Figure 8.10.

The Display Pane

On the right side of the GNOME file manager window is the display pane, where the contents of the directory currently selected in the directory tree are displayed. In this pane, the default display shows each file as a full-sized icon. There are several types of icons that represent different types of files and other elements such as directories. The most important icons to familiarize yourself with are those representing directories, generic documents, packages and archives, and HTML files.

NOTE   A full discussion of file types and the directory structure of Linux is provided in Chapter 14, "Working with Files." You already have a basic understanding of the Linux directory structure from the discussion provided in Chapter 4, "Installing Red Hat Linux 7.1."

 The folder icon represents a directory and should be familiar to users of both Macintosh and Windows systems.

 A blank piece of paper represents a generic document file such as a text file or a Microsoft Word file.

 A piece of paper with the word HTML floating above it represents an HTML file.

 Finally, the press icon represents packages and archives such as Zip files.

The Toolbar

Across the top of the file manager window is a toolbar, which contains nine buttons:

Back   Returns the previously displayed directory.

Up   Changes to the parent directory of the current directory.

Forward   Returns to the next directory in the history list (you have to have moved back using the Back button to be able to move forward).

Rescan   Rescans the currently displayed directory and synchronizes the displayed files to those actually stored on disk. The display doesn't automatically update when other programs make changes to the contents of the currently displayed directory; you must use Rescan to reflect these changes in the file manager window.

Home   Changes to the user's home directory.

Icons   Switches the current display mode to large icons (this is the default mode when you first open the GNOME file manager).

Brief   Switches the current display mode to a list of file and directory names with a small folder icon next to each directory name (as shown in Figure 8.11).

FIGURE 8.11:

Displaying a directory in Brief mode

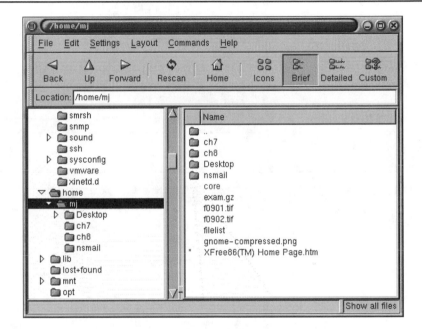

Detailed   Switches the current display mode to a detailed list including the name, size, and modification time of the files or directories (as shown in Figure 8.12).

Custom   Switches the current display mode to a detailed list displaying customized statistical information specified by the user (as shown in Figure 8.13).

FIGURE 8.12:

Displaying a directory in
Detailed mode

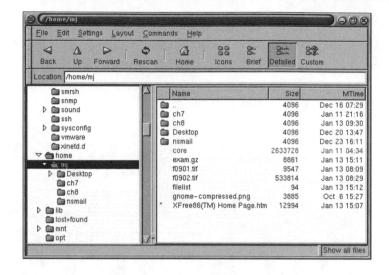

FIGURE 8.13:

Displaying a directory in
Custom mode

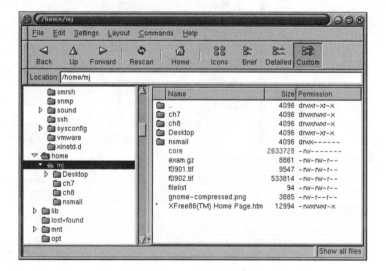

Important Menu Options

The GNOME file manager has five menus offering several commands and options.
Let's take a quick look at some of the more commonly used menu options in the file
manager. Other, less-important options are available under the GNOME control

panel but are not covered in this book. For complete documentation on the GNOME file manager, refer to the GNOME help system by selecting Help System from the main GNOME System menu.

File ≻ Create New Window

The GNOME file manager allows you to have multiple windows open, each displaying a different directory. You can move files between open directories by dragging and dropping them between two GNOME file manager windows.

File ≻ Copy

To copy a file to a new location, select the file in the display pane and then choose File ≻ Copy. A Copy dialog box like the one in Figure 8.14 appears. Click the Browse button to choose a destination directory or enter the destination path in the text field.

FIGURE 8.14:

Copying a file

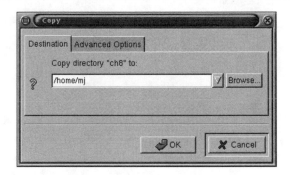

Another way to access the Copy dialog box is to right-click the file in the display pane and then choose Copy from the resulting pop-up menu.

File ≻ Delete

To delete a file, select the file in the display pane and then choose File ≻ Delete. A confirmation dialog box appears in which you can confirm the deletion of the file or cancel it. Once confirmed, the action is not reversible. An alternate way to delete a file is to right-click the file in the display pane and choose Delete from the resulting pop-up menu.

File > Move

To move a file to a new location, select the file in the display pane and then choose File > Move. A Move dialog box appears, similar to the Copy dialog box shown in Figure 8.14. Here you can specify the destination. Another way to access the Move dialog box is to right-click the file in the display pane and choose Move from the resulting pop-up menu.

Layout > Sort By

To change the order in which files and directories are displayed in the display pane, select Layout > Sort By. A dialog box like the one shown in Figure 8.15 appears. In this dialog box, you can choose to sort files and directories by name, file type, size, or time of access, change, or modification. In addition, you can specify if the sorting should be case-insensitive and reverse the normal sort order by using the two check boxes in the lower part of the dialog box.

FIGURE 8.15:

Changing the sort order

Commands > Find File

To find files on your computer, you can use the Commands > Find File option in the GNOME file manager. The Find File dialog box shown in Figure 8.16 appears.

FIGURE 8.16:

Searching for a file

In this dialog box, you can specify three possible parameters:

- Where to start your search using the Start At field

- The filenames to search for using the Filename field

- The text to search for inside a file using the Content field

When specifying filenames, you can use wildcards. For instance, indicate gi* to search for all files starting with gi and *gi for all files ending in gi. When specifying the directory from which to start your search, you can specify an entire directory path (such as /home/username), a slash (/) for the top-level directory of your Linux system, or a dot (.) for the currently selected directory. Search results are displayed as they are found in a window like the one in Figure 8.17.

FIGURE 8.17:

The results of a file search

Looking Ahead

By now, you should be feeling fairly comfortable navigating your chosen X Windows environment. You can control basic options of GNOME, you can launch applications, and you can manipulate windows.

In Chapter 9, "Using Applications with GNOME and X Windows," you will learn how to use some actual applications in GNOME. These applications include everything from simple applications such as gedit, the GNOME text editor, to utilities such as terminal windows, to high-end software such as The GIMP, a professional-quality image-editing package.

CHAPTER
NINE

Using Applications with GNOME and X Windows

- Using *xterm*

- Customizing *xterm*

- X Windows Applications

- X Windows Utilities

This chapter looks at some X Windows and GNOME applications and how they can be run and used within the GNOME desktop. These applications include xterm, the GNOME file manager (called Midnight Commander), a graphics program known as The GIMP, and several X Windows utilities.

These applications have been selected based on one of two criteria: They are useful in everyday Linux operations, or they are representative of the power or range of many Linux applications.

This chapter should give you the confidence to begin experimenting with other X Windows applications.

Using *xterm*

While X Windows puts a nice-looking and user-friendly face on Linux and allows the creation of fully graphical applications, the fact remains that as a Unix clone, Linux is a command-line-oriented operating system.

Although it is possible to use Linux for everyday work without ever using the command prompt, to take advantage of the real power and flexibility of a Unix-like operating system, you need to make at least occasional forays into the world of the command line.

Fortunately, this doesn't mean abandoning the ease of X Windows. The xterm program provides a command prompt window that is fully integrated into the X Windows environment, with a scroll bar, a resizable window, and the ability to copy and paste with other X Windows applications—all features that a standard Linux console lacks.

NOTE   You can launch an xterm window in Red Hat Linux 7.1 by selecting Regular XTerm from the System submenu of the Programs menu. GNOME includes a clone of xterm, known as GNOME terminal. Nevertheless, this chapter describes xterm in detail, because it is available in other Linux graphical environments, including KDE. Many of the same commands work for GNOME terminal; some require slight changes such as an extra dash. Only significant functional differences between these two types of terminals are noted in this chapter.

If you want to launch additional xterm windows, you can also do so from the command line of another xterm window using the command

```
$ xterm &
```

or, if you find that for some reason xterm isn't on your path, use the command

```
$ /usr/X11R6/bin/xterm &
```

> **TIP**
>
> You can locate most files easily with the `locate` command. If you want to find the directory where xterm is located, run the `locate xterm` command. Unfortunately, `locate` doesn't work with recently created or moved files; in that case, use the `find` command as described in Chapter 13, "Introducing Linux Commands."

Alternatively, you can launch additional GNOME terminal windows from the command line of another xterm window using the command

```
$ gnome-terminal &
```

or you can just click the terminal icon on the default GNOME panel.

By default, this opens a window that is 80 characters wide and 24 lines deep with a scroll bar. The window can be resized to provide more space for viewing information and working. As shown in Figure 9.1, the default color scheme for new xterm windows in Red Hat Linux 7.1 is black characters on a white background. The default title of the window specifies the current user and directory.

FIGURE 9.1:

An *xterm* window

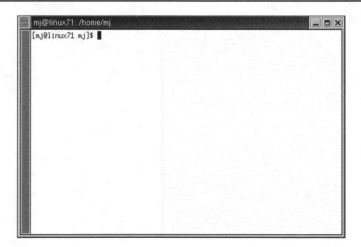

Customizing *xterm*

The xterm program is highly customizable. Among other things, you can change the following characteristics:

- The window's font
- The color scheme
- The default window size
- The placement of new windows on the screen

This section will look at these options and describe how to use them when launching new xterm windows.

At first it might seem that this flexibility has no real value, but in reality it does. On different monitors, different color combinations produce the most readable text, so being able to change the color scheme is a valuable feature.

Flags and Arguments: A Quick Unix Primer

Before going forward, you need a quick tutorial about how Unix commands work. A complete introduction to Unix and Unix commands as used in Linux comes in Chapters 13 and 14.

To execute a program (or command), you simply need to type the name of the program (and possibly the complete location of the program) and press the Enter key.

For instance, to launch xterm, you can use the command

```
$ xterm
```

or, if the directory where xterm is located is not on your path, use the command

```
$ /usr/X11R6/bin/xterm
```

The path is where Linux searches for commands. You can find the path with this command:

```
$ echo $PATH
```

Most programs either require or can accept information that alters the way they behave or provides information to be processed. Two types of information can be provided to a command: flags and arguments.

Continued on next page

Arguments are information provided to the program to be processed; they can be anything from filenames to text to search for.

Flags are options that alter the behavior of a program. They appear after the command, separated by one or more spaces and preceded by a dash. For instance, the flag `-help` causes `xterm` to print out a help message:

```
$ xterm -help
usage:
        xterm -options ... -e command args
```

where *options* include:

```
        -help                       print out this message
        -display display_name       X server to contact
        -geometry geom              size (in characters) and position
        -/+rv                       turn on/off reverse video
        -bg color                   background color
        -fg color                   foreground color
        -bd color                   border color
        -bw number                  border width in pixels
        -fn fontname                normal text font
        -iconic                     start minimized
        -name string                client instance, icon, and title
                                    strings
        -title string               title string
        -xrm resourcestring         additional resource
                                    specifications
        -/+132                      turn on/off column switch
                                    inhibiting
        -/+ah                       turn on/off always highlight
        -/+ai                       turn on/off active icon
```

Complex flags can also be created to provide information that the flag needs to function correctly. For instance, to set `xterm` colors, you use the `-fg` and `-bg` flags, but you also need to provide the colors that you want to appear in the foreground and background. The command

```
$ xterm -fg white -bg black
```

creates an `xterm` window with white text on a black background. On the other hand, one simple flag is the ampersand (&). For example, the command

```
$ xterm &
```

Continued on next page

opens another `xterm` window and returns the current `xterm` window to the command-line interface.

Arguments, on the other hand, are not configuration options but information provided to a program to be processed. Arguments are not preceded by a dash as are flags. Arguments are often the names of files to be opened, processed, or edited—as in the following example, which indicates that the file `testfile` should be opened for editing with the editor `emacs`:

```
$ emacs testfile
```

Setting the Color Scheme

Using a variety of flags, it is possible to set almost all aspects of an `xterm` window's color scheme from border color to the color of the cursor. This section examines the main elements of the color scheme: foreground color, background color, and cursor color.

Understanding X Windows Colors

Before looking at the specific flags used to set colors of an `xterm` window, you need to look at how colors are referred to in X Windows.

Colors in X Windows are specified in *RGB (red-green-blue)* format. RGB format consists of ordered triplets of numbers, with each number having a value from 0 to 255. The numbers represent the value of the red, green, and blue channels, respectively, with 0 representing no color and 255 representing the highest possible value of the color.

Luckily, you don't need to figure out the color channel combinations to get your desired color. The work has already been done and is stored in a file that X Windows uses to map color names to their numerical triplets. This file, normally called `rgb.txt`, is usually found in the directory `/usr/X11R6/lib/X11/`.

A selected list of values in the Red Hat Linux 7.1 `rgb.txt` file appears here to make it easy to experiment with colors as you work through this section:

snow	GhostWhite	PapayaWhip	LemonChiffon
AliceBlue	LavenderBlush	MistyRose	white

DarkSlateGray	DimGray	gray	MidnightBlue
NavyBlue	SlateBlue	blue	SteelBlue
turquoise	cyan	DarkGreen	SeaGreen
LawnGreen	green	GreenYellow	DarkKhaki
LightYellow	yellow	gold	RosyBrown
IndianRed	sienna	beige	wheat
tan	chocolate	DarkSalmon	orange
tomato	red	DeepPink	pink
maroon	magenta	violet	orchid
purple	DarkCyan	DarkRed	LightGreen

NOTE Depending on the color depth of your video display and the applications you are running, you may find that the colors you use don't appear quite the way you expect. This is due to video card limitations and differences between systems.

Background and Foreground Colors

Setting background and foreground colors allows you to control the appearance of the text on your screen. Text appears in the foreground color while the background color, logically, is assigned to the background of the window.

The usual default xterm window is black text on a white background. Use the -fg and -bg flags to set the foreground and background colors:

```
$ xterm -fg white -bg black &
```

This command provides exactly the reverse color scheme of the default xterm window, causing the background to be set to black and the foreground to white. The result looks like Figure 9.2.

NOTE The -bg and -fg flags are not specific to xterm. In fact, they are standard X Windows flags that can be used to change the color schemes of most X Windows applications. However, these flags do not work for the gnome-terminal command. To find the right switches for GNOME terminal, run the gnome-terminal -help command.

Cursor Color

If you tried the last example for setting colors, you probably noticed that the cursor stayed the same color as the default xterm color scheme. You can change this color as well, using the -cr flag. For instance, if you want a dark blue cursor, you might use the command

```
$ xterm -bg white -fg black -cr MidnightBlue &
```

Setting the Window Size and Location

When you open an xterm window (or any other application's window, for that matter), the size of the window is set to a default size and the location of the window is determined by the configuration of your window manager (you will see xterm commands in key files when you read Chapter 12, "Advanced X Windows Configuration").

However, you can specify the exact size and placement of windows in X Windows using the -geometry flag. This flag is a standard X Windows flag (like -bg and -fg) and works with most X Windows programs.

The basic syntax of the flag is -geometry *widthxheight+x+y*. The variables in this command are shown below:

- *width* specifies the width of the window in pixels.

- *height* specifies the height of the window in pixels.

- *x* specifies the horizontal placement of the window as an offset in pixels from the left side of the display.

- *y* specifies the vertical placement of the window as an offset in pixels from the top of the display.

Xterm accepts the use of the -geometry flag but handles the information in a somewhat nonstandard way. When you think about it, specifying the height and width of a terminal window in pixels doesn't make a lot of sense. Instead, xterm interprets *width* and *height* as the number of columns and rows of characters to display and sizes the window according to the font being used.

The default window size is 80 columns by 24 lines of characters. But what if you want a small 10-character by 10-character window to be placed 200 pixels from the left side of the screen and 300 pixels down from the top of the screen? You could use the command

```
$ xterm –geometry 10x10+200+300 &
```

to get a window like the one in Figure 9.3. Note the position of the window relative to the left edge and the top of the screen.

FIGURE 9.3:

Using the *-geometry* flag

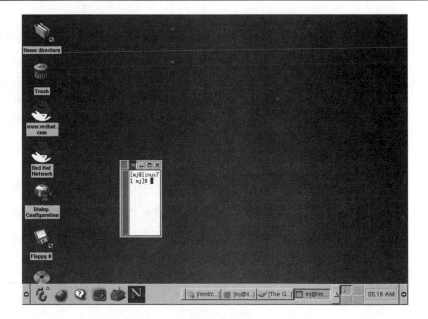

The corresponding command for the GNOME terminal is `gnome-terminal –geometry=10x10+200+300 &`. However, the effect of this command is limited since GNOME terminals have a minimum width of 25 columns.

By adding the -fg and -bg flags, you can also change the default color scheme at the same time you define the size of the window when it opens:

```
$ xterm -geometry 10x10+200+300 -fg DarkRed -bg cyan &
```

The result looks like Figure 9.4.

FIGURE 9.4:

Combining the -*geometry* flag with the color flags

Running an Application in an *xterm* Window

While the purpose of an xterm window is to use the command line to execute commands, you may want certain character-mode programs to run by default when you launch the xterm window. For instance, if you always keep top running inside an xterm window while you work, you might want to have top launch when you open its xterm. This is done with the -e flag:

```
$ xterm -e top &
```

This command opens a window like the one in Figure 9.5.

When the program running inside the window quits, the xterm window closes.

It is important to note that the default window title when you use the -e flag in xterm is the name of the program launched with the -e flag.

While the -e flag works for the `gnome-terminal` command, it does not set the default window title.

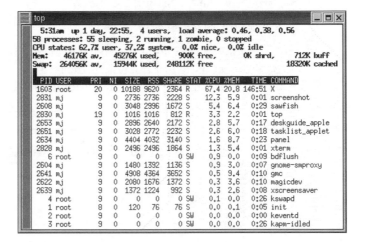

Setting the Font

The default font used by xterm is usually quite readable and suited to the average monitor. But if you have a particularly large or small monitor or use an unusually low or high resolution, you may find it wise to change the font you use in your xterm windows.

In order to do this, use the -fn flag. But how do you refer to fonts? Fonts are referred to by names that can be as simple as 7×13, which indicates 7 pixels wide and 13 pixels deep, or as complex as -sony-fixed-medium-r-normal–24-230-75 -75-c-120-iso8859-1, which indicates the 24-point Latin character set, medium weight, Roman-style font named fixed from the Sony font foundry.

X Windows offers a program, xlsfonts, that provides a list of available fonts on your X Windows system. To see a list of available fonts on your system, use the following command in an xterm window:

```
$ xlsfonts | more
```

The | more part of the command allows you to page through the long list of fonts by hitting the spacebar to move forward a page.

So, to choose the 10×20 font, use the command

```
$ xterm -fn 10x20 &
```

to get a window with a large font like the one in Figure 9.6. When you compare this to Figure 9.1, note that not only is the font bigger, but the xterm window is also bigger to accommodate the bigger font with the same number of rows and columns.

FIGURE 9.6:

The 10×20 font

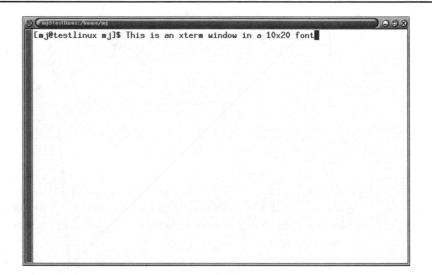

In theory, any of these fonts can be used with the -fn flag and the xterm command. In practice, though, this doesn't work. The nature of xterm is that it needs fixed-width fonts—that is, fonts in which all characters occupy the same amount of space regardless of their comparative sizes. In the world of Microsoft Windows, an example of a fixed-width font is Courier.

By contrast, many fonts are proportionally spaced. This means that a letter "i" takes up less space than a "w" because the latter is a wider letter. Xterm doesn't do a good job of handling these proportionally spaced fonts, as you can see in Figure 9.7, where the selected font is from the Times family.

FIGURE 9.7:

Using a proportionally spaced font

Listed below are some of the common (and easy-to-type) fixed-width fonts that are available in the X Windows distribution included with Red Hat Linux 7.1:

5×7	6×13bold	7×14bold	9×15bold
5×8	6×9	8×13	10×20
6×10	7×13	8×13bold	12×24
6×12	7×13bold	8×16	
6×13	7×14	9×15	

If you want to experiment with other fonts, use xlsfonts to see a list of fonts, select a font, and then use the xfd command to display the font in a window. For instance, to display the Sony font -sony-fixed-medium-r-normal–24-230-75-75-c -120-iso8859-1 that you saw earlier, use the command

```
$ xfd -fn -sony-fixed-medium-r-normal–24-230-75-75-c-120-iso8859-1
```

Notice the use of the -fn flag to specify the font name. The font will be displayed in a window like the one in Figure 9.8. Click the Quit button to close the window.

FIGURE 9.8:

Displaying fonts with the
xfd command

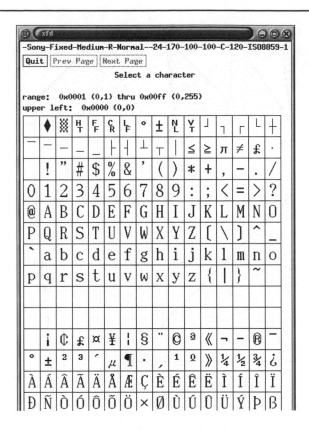

Other Features

Xterm offers many more features than the ones listed here. You can find out
about them in the xterm man page. A man (short for manual) page provides information about how to use a specific program. To access the xterm man page, use
the command

```
$ man xterm
```

in an xterm window. This command displays a man page like the one shown in
Figure 9.9. Use the arrow keys to scroll through the man page. To exit the man
page, type **q**.

FIGURE 9.9:

The *xterm* man page

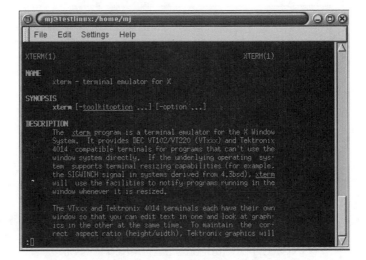

NOTE　As of this writing, there is no man page available for GNOME terminal. For more information about this program, open up a GNOME terminal window, then choose Help ➢ GNOME Terminal Users Guide.

X Windows Applications

So far, you have seen two of the most basic of X Windows applications in action: xterm and the GNOME file manager. If there were nothing more than this, it would reinforce the views of the naysayers who complain that X Windows doesn't have any applications and that Windows and the Mac OS are where the action is.

The reality, though, is that powerful, effective applications do exist for the X Windows environment. Even among the free tools out there are those that rival the features of commercial applications.

This section looks at two of the components of the GNOME Office Suite: The GIMP graphical utility and the Gnumeric spreadsheet. Because these are both large programs with extensive feature sets, this section just provides an overview of the applications and what they do and then points to where complete information on the applications is available. Mastering an application like The GIMP or Gnumeric, after all, would require a book in itself.

NOTE Other components of the GNOME Office Suite include the AbiWord word processor, the Dia program for Visio-style diagrams and flowcharts, and the GNOME-PIM personal information manager.

The GIMP

The GIMP (GNU Image Manipulation Program) is an attempt to offer the Linux community a freely available, full-featured image-editing package to rival the likes of Adobe Photoshop or Corel PhotoPaint. Figure 9.10 shows The GIMP running with several of its dialog boxes and tools open. The GIMP is designed to integrate tightly into GNOME and is considered the standard image-editing application for GNOME and a showcase of a high-powered GNOME application. GNOME is included as part of Red Hat Linux 7.1.

FIGURE 9.10:

The GIMP

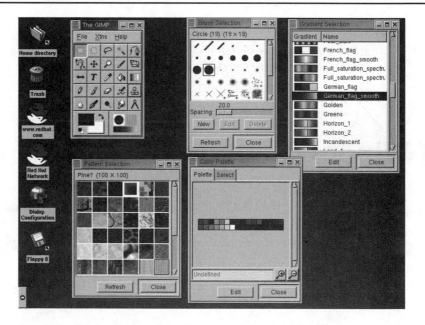

Offered under the General Public License, The GIMP is under constant development by Spencer Kimball and Peter Mattis at the University of California–Berkeley.

The GIMP includes all the tools expected of a full-featured image-editing package, including numerous brush types, special-effects filters, intelligent scissors, Bezier selection, layers, transparencies, and 24-bit image support.

The GIMP also provides a plug-in mechanism. Numerous plug-ins are freely available on the Internet to perform a variety of tasks, including despeckling, mapping to a sphere, creating mosaics, generating lens flares, and more.

In addition, the version included with Red Hat Linux 7.1 (The GIMP 1.2.1) includes a downloadable manual that provides the in-depth instruction and documentation often lacking in free software. This is all available from The GIMP Web site at `manual.gimp.org`.

You can run The GIMP from an `xterm` window with the command

```
$ gimp &
```

or

```
$ /usr/bin/gimp &
```

Alternatively, from the main GNOME system menu, choose Programs ➢ Graphics ➢ The GIMP to start The GIMP.

The GIMP starts up by displaying its toolbar and a number of other design screens shown in Figure 9.10. For the purpose of this section, the only important window is the toolbar. This window, shown in Figure 9.11, offers access to a wide range of tools plus the main File menu.

FIGURE 9.11:

The GIMP toolbar

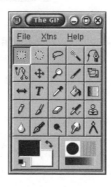

Let's take a quick look at some of the main tasks in The GIMP: opening and saving images, cropping an image, and capturing a window to an image file. To learn the full set of The GIMP features, refer to the manual for the software that is on The GIMP's Web site, mentioned earlier.

Opening Images

To open an image, choose File ≻ Open. A dialog box like the one in Figure 9.12 appears.

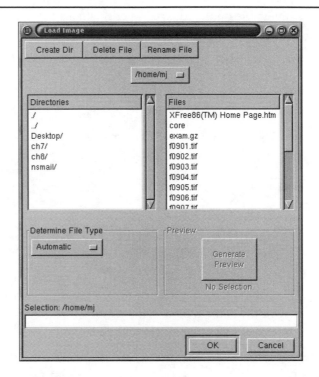

This dialog box works in a vaguely Mac-like fashion. Above the list of files, you see the name of the current directory. You can click the directory name to get a list of its parent directories and, by selecting one of these, quickly change to that directory.

Select the filename of your choice. If you are not sure which file you need, you can preview a thumbnail by clicking the Generate Preview button in the Preview section of the Load Image window. When you see the file that you need, click the OK button. The file appears in the viewer window and the dialog box closes.

Saving Images

If you want to save an image, you need The GIMP main menu. While working on an actual image, right-clicking anywhere in the image brings up the complete menu for The GIMP, like the one shown in Figure 9.13.

FIGURE 9.13:

The GIMP main menu

To open the Save Image dialog box, choose File ➤ Save As from The GIMP main menu. The result shown in Figure 9.14 is similar to the Load Image dialog box. Directory navigation works in the same fashion; you select existing filenames by clicking them in the file list, and clicking OK saves the current file to the name displayed in the Selection field.

FIGURE 9.14:

The GIMP Save Image window

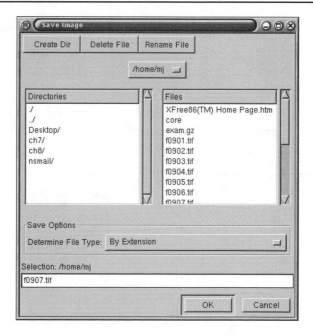

If you want to save the image to a new filename, simply type the name you want in the Selection field.

When saving an image, you also want to specify the type of image. In the middle of the dialog box is the Determine File Type button. By clicking this button, you can view a list of available file types. Select the file type you desire from the list. Once you are ready to save your file, click OK.

Cropping an Image

Cropping an image is a simple process: Turn on cropping, select the area you want to crop, and press the Crop button in the Crop & Resize Information window.

To turn on cropping, right-click an image. In the menu that opens, select Tools ➢ Transform Tools ➢ Crop & Resize. To select an area for cropping, drag out a rectangle with the left mouse button in the viewer window. Figure 9.15 shows an image displayed in the viewer window with a rectangle indicating where the user has dragged the mouse.

FIGURE 9.15:

Selecting a crop area

Once you have selected an area to crop, simply click the Crop button in the Crop & Resize Information window. The result would be something like Figure 9.16 for the previous example.

FIGURE 9.16:

The result of cropping

If you don't like the results of your cropping, right-click the image. In the menu that opens, select File ➢ Revert to return to the original image.

Capturing a Window

One of the popular uses of The GIMP is to create screen shots. If you want to capture an open window to an image file, you can do this using the Acquire Screen Shot feature. When you have a window that you want to capture, choose File ≻ Acquire ≻ Screen Shot, which opens a Screen Shot dialog box like the one in Figure 9.17.

FIGURE 9.17:

The Screen Shot window

You can grab an individual window or the entire contents of your desktop. To grab an individual window, select Single Window. Click OK, and then click the window of your choice.

If you don't want to show the window frame or title, deselect With Decorations. For example, if you were to grab an xterm window of the top utility, with background and foreground colors reversed, the result would look almost as if you were not using the X Window, as shown in Figure 9.18.

FIGURE 9.18:

A screen shot of *top*

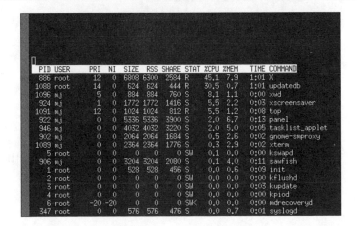

Alternatively, you can grab the entire contents of your desktop in the Screen Shot window by selecting Whole Screen. Set the Seconds Delay box to give you time to close or open other windows before The GIMP makes a screen shot of your desktop.

Once you have grabbed a window, the image of that window appears in the viewer window, and you can save it like any other image in The GIMP.

Gnumeric

Gnumeric is another component of the GNOME desktop environment, designed to manage numeric data through spreadsheets. This program offers Linux users a freely available full-featured spreadsheet program that can exchange data with other spreadsheet programs such as Microsoft Excel. It is installed by default on Red Hat Linux 7.1.

Offered under the General Public License, Gnumeric is under constant development by a number of independent developers, most prominently Miguel de Icaza and Jody Goldberg. The version included with Red Hat Linux 7.1 is 0.61; in other words, it is not "officially" ready for release. However, support as of this writing can be purchased from Ximian at `http://www.ximian.com`.

Gnumeric includes most of the tools of normal spreadsheets. You can find more information about Gnumeric at `http://www.gnome.org/gnumeric`, including a public list of "pending tasks." If you are interested, you can contribute to the development of this spreadsheet.

Using Gnumeric

Let's take just a quick look at using Gnumeric. This spreadsheet is part of a number of standard Linux distributions, including Red Hat Linux 7.1. You can run it from an `xterm` window with the command

```
$ gnumeric &
```

or with the command

```
$ /usr/bin/gnumeric &
```

Alternatively, you can run Gnumeric by clicking the Main Menu button and choosing Programs ➤ Applications ➤ Gnumeric.

Gnumeric starts with a blank spreadsheet, as shown in Figure 9.19. Like other spreadsheet programs, Gnumeric includes a number of icons that serve as shortcuts to various tools for editing and creating formulas.

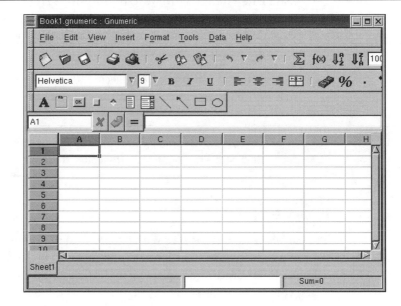

Now you can open up a Gnumeric file when you choose the File ➤ Open command. This takes you to a Load File dialog box where you can navigate to the file that you need, in Gnumeric XML file format.

Importing Files

From the File menu, you can import Gnumeric data from a number of other file formats. When you choose File ➤ Import and then select a file, Gnumeric prompts you to place the file in one of the following five categories:

HTML File Made By Gnumeric   If you saved a spreadsheet as an HTML file from Gnumeric, you can re-import data from the HTML file.

Text File Import   One common way to distribute data is in a text file, where commas separate each data point. This is sometimes known as comma-delimited format. The Text File Import option allows Gnumeric to use each comma to assign data to different cells.

SC/xspread File Import   Gnumeric can import data from other spreadsheet formats, including those based on Microsoft Excel, IBM (Lotus) 1-2-3, and Applixware spreadsheets.

Data Interchange Format (DIF) Import   The Data Interchange Format is a common way to exchange data between databases and spreadsheets. It is also used as a common translation medium between spreadsheets when there are no other compatible file formats.

Experimental Gnumeric   This category is used for "importing" from a file that is already in Gnumeric format, with a .gnumeric extension.

NOTE   In later releases of Gnumeric, you can also import text files as simple text. Each line in the text file is assigned to consecutive cells.

Exporting Files

You can share Gnumeric files with people who use other spreadsheets. Gnumeric supports exporting to 14 different file formats. To set up this process, choose File ➤ Save As. Enter the desired filename in the Selection box. Click the File Format button to see your options, as shown in Figure 9.20. Select a file format, then click OK.

FIGURE 9.20:

The Save Workbook As window

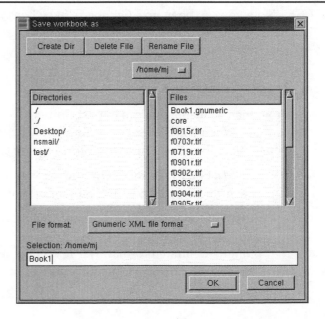

> **NOTE**
>
> The ability to exchange files between different applications is typically less than perfect. This premise holds true for Excel and Gnumeric. Some users have successfully imported Excel 2000 files into Gnumeric; however, not all functions of these two programs are compatible.

Formulas

The heart of any spreadsheet application is its formulas. By definition, formulas are defined and embedded in specific cells in a spreadsheet. Formulas include functions such as SUM, which totals the cells in a specified range. When Gnumeric converts files from other spreadsheets, it converts these functions as well. If you do not recognize a Gnumeric function, get help by choosing Help ➢ Gnumeric Function Reference.

X Windows Utilities

Before closing this chapter, let's look at a few handy X Windows utilities and how to use them. These utilities are as follows:

- gedit
- xclock
- xcalc

Using *gedit*

Gedit is a GNOME application that provides functionality similar to Windows Notepad. You can use it to open and change the contents of plain text files, search and replace text, and create new files.

Admittedly, as Figure 9.21 shows, the gedit interface is a bit spartan, but for quick editing of simple text files, it does the trick.

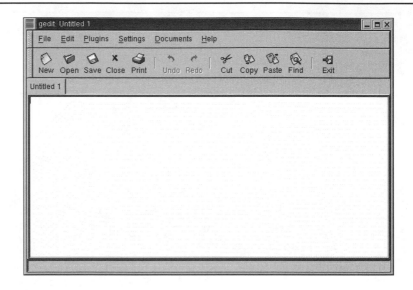

You can launch gedit with the command

$ **gedit &**

or, if gedit is not on your path, with the command

$ **/usr/bin/gedit &**

or you can click the main GNOME System menu and choose Programs ➢ Applications ➢ Gedit.

The interface is simple. Across the top is the toolbar with self-explanatory buttons for loading and saving files, cutting, copying, pasting, and searching for text.

To load an existing file, click the Open button or choose File ➢ Open. A dialog box appears, where you can browse for and select a file to open. When a file is opened, it appears as shown in Figure 9.22.

You can save a file you have opened by clicking the Save button on the toolbar or by choosing File ➢ Save.

The Find button on the toolbar brings up the Find dialog box shown in Figure 9.23. You can also open this dialog box by choosing Edit ➢ Find.

FIGURE 9.22:

The results of loading a file

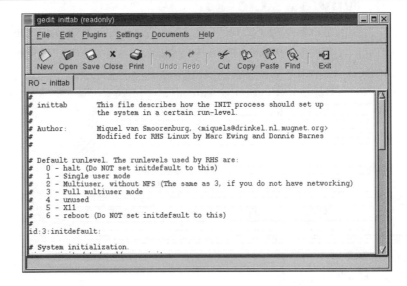

FIGURE 9.23:

The Find dialog box

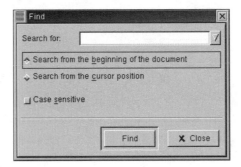

Using this dialog box is relatively simple: Fill in the text to search for and click the Find button. You can also indicate if you prefer to start your search at the beginning of the document or the current cursor position and whether or not the search should be considered case-sensitive.

Replace takes things one step further. You can open the Replace dialog box by selecting Edit ➤ Replace. This dialog box looks like the Find dialog box except that it has an additional field for indicating the text with which to replace each found item. In addition, you can use the Replace button to indicate that you want to be prompted before replacing any text.

X Windows Clocks

You have probably noticed the clock that appears in the GNOME panel. Some users, though, like to see a larger digital or analog clock on their desktop.

This can be achieved using the xclock program. Xclock is a basic clock program that allows you to create an analog or digital clock. By default, xclock displays an analog clock, so the command

```
$ xclock &
```

or

```
$ /usr/X11R6/bin/xclock &
```

creates a window like the one in Figure 9.24.

FIGURE 9.24:

The default *xclock* style

The -digital flag causes xclock to display a digital clock like the one shown in Figure 9.25.

FIGURE 9.25:

A digital *xclock* window

Mon Jan 15 11:29:31 2001

The -digital flag is not the only flag accepted by xclock. The -hd and -hl flags help create a more interesting visual display for an analog clock. The -hd flag is used to specify a color for the hands of the clock, and the -hl flag specifies the color for the outline of the hands of the clock. (Remember the discussion of RGB colors earlier? This is one instance where you would use RGB colors.)

For example, the command

```
$ xclock -hd yellow -hl green &
```

creates a clock that has yellow hands with green outlines as in Figure 9.26 (of course, this is hard to see in the black-and-white reproduction you are looking at).

FIGURE 9.26:

FIGURE 9.26:

Setting the color of the
clock's hands

Notice the lack of contrast between the hands and the white face of the clock. This can be rectified with a standard X Windows flag: the -bg flag that you saw earlier in the discussion of xterm. By specifying a background color of black with

```
$ xclock -hd yellow -hl green -bg black &
```

you end up with something like Figure 9.27.

FIGURE 9.27:

Setting the background
color

While the hands are now clearly visible, a new problem has arisen: The marks that indicate the points of the clock are now invisible, since they are black and they are drawn against a black background. These marks are considered part of the foreground, and their color can be changed with the standard X Windows -fg flag. The command

```
$ xclock -hd yellow -hl green -bg black -fg cyan &
```

gives a result like Figure 9.28.

FIGURE 9.28:

Setting the foreground
color

Using the GNOME Calculator

Finally, let's take a quick look at the GNOME Calculator, the default GNOME calculator tool that should be available in every distribution of Linux that includes GNOME.

As you might expect by this point, you can run the GNOME Calculator with the command

```
$ gcalc &
```

or with the command

```
$ /usr/bin/gcalc &
```

The GNOME Calculator can also be opened by selecting Simple Calculator from the Utilities submenu of the main GNOME System menu.

The GNOME Calculator window looks like Figure 9.29.

FIGURE 9.29:

The GNOME Calculator window

The Calculator operates much as any standard scientific calculator does. It provides all the expected scientific functions, including trigonometric and logarithmic functions, plus a memory. The actual use of such a calculator and its functions is not really the subject of this chapter, and a full description of the meaning of these functions is best left to a mathematics text.

Looking Ahead

By now, you should be feeling fairly comfortable navigating your GNOME environment. You can control basic options of GNOME, you can launch applications, and you can manipulate windows.

As mentioned earlier, though, the power of both X Windows and GNOME comes from their flexibility and configurability.

Chapter 10, "Advanced GNOME Configuration," looks at how to go about configuring GNOME to meet your personal needs. This includes customizing the main GNOME panel, changing your desktop appearance and themes, and performing other common GNOME configuration tasks.

CHAPTER

TEN

Advanced GNOME Configuration

- ■ Using the GNOME Control Center

- ■ Configuring GNOME Panels

Now that you have learned to use GNOME and to run applications in the GNOME desktop environment, let's look at the advanced configuration options available in GNOME. At the center of GNOME configuration is the GNOME Control Center. From the GNOME Control Center, you can do the following:

- Use a graphical interface to configure your desktop's background and theme.

- Define multimedia properties for your system.

- Fine-tune dialogs and other interface items.

- Configure the Sawfish window manager.

GNOME Panels are the center of the user interface. GNOME Panels have a separate configuration procedure that allows you to control the position, size, behavior, and other settings of the main GNOME Panel as well as any additional Panels you create.

This chapter will consider both aspects of GNOME configuration.

Using the GNOME Control Center

The GNOME Control Center can be accessed in two main ways:

- Click the Toolbox button on the main GNOME Control Panel.

- Select the Programs ➤ Settings ➤ GNOME Control Center option from the main GNOME System menu.

When you first launch the Control Center, a window like the one in Figure 10.1 appears.

This window contains two main parts:

- The left side displays a hierarchical tree of configuration options organized in seven main categories: Desktop, Document Handlers, Multimedia, Peripherals, Sawfish Window Manager, Session, and User Interface.

- The right side displays the controls for the particular section of the configuration tree that you have selected. For instance, in Figure 10.2, the Desktop Background section is displayed.

FIGURE 10.1:

The initial GNOME Control Center window

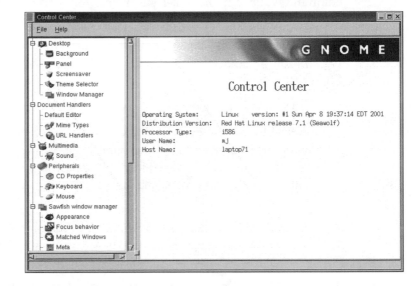

FIGURE 10.2:

The Desktop Background section

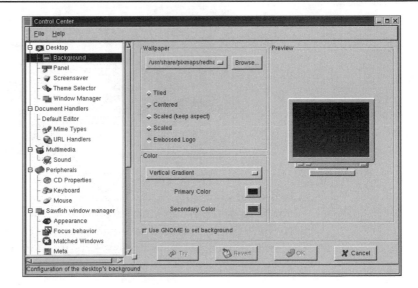

Desktop

The Desktop section of the Control Center makes it possible to control several aspects of your desktop's appearance and behavior, including the background color and wallpaper, the screen saver, and your choice of desktop themes.

To control your background properties, choose the Background entry in the Desktop section in the left side of the Control Center window. In the right side of the window, the Desktop Background applet appears, as shown previously in Figure 10.2.

In this window, you can create three possible desktop backgrounds:

A desktop wallpaper   Click the Browse button and choose an image from your hard disk to use as background wallpaper. You can choose to center this on the desktop, tile it repeatedly on the desktop, or scale it to fill the desktop. Alternatively, you can use the Embossed Logo option to add a Red Hat logo to your background.

A single solid color   Select Solid from the Color drop-down list and then select Primary Color to open the Pick A Color window shown in Figure 10.3.

FIGURE 10.3:

The Pick A Color window

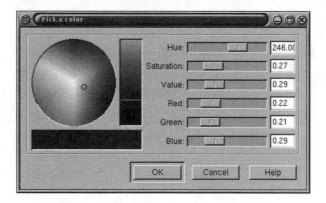

A two-color gradient   Select Vertical or Horizontal Gradient from the Color drop-down list and then choose colors for both Primary Color and Secondary Color. This creates a gradient effect from the top to the bottom (or from left to right) of the screen changing from Primary Color to Secondary Color.

When you have finished changing your background settings, click the OK button to commit the changes.

To control your Panel settings, select the Panel entry in the Desktop section of the GNOME Control Center. In the right side of the GNOME Control Center window, the Panel configuration applet shown in Figure 10.4 appears.

FIGURE 10.4:

Configuring your Panel

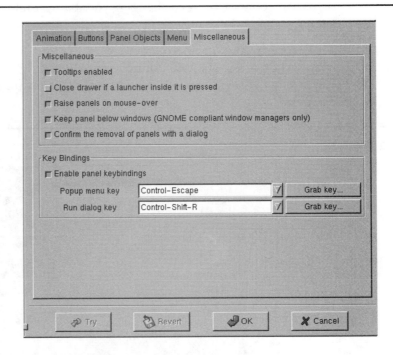

There are five tabs associated with configuring your Panel. These settings allow you to configure the look, feel, and behavior of each icon and menu on the Panel.

- The Animation tab lets you control the motion of menus and drawers from the GNOME Panel.

- The Buttons tab allows you to manage the look and feel of each program launcher button on the Panel. You can adjust the depth, border, and relative location of each button. When you choose Tiles Enabled, you can select Normal Tile or Clicked Tile to change the color and pattern behind the tiles.

- The Panel Objects tab regulates what happens when you move objects on the GNOME Panel.

- The Menu tab regulates the size of icons and menus, as well as their location relative to the main menu.

- The Miscellaneous tab includes settings such as Tooltips Enabled, which provides a brief description of a program when you move your mouse over a specific button.

When you have finished changing your background settings, click the OK button to commit the changes.

To control your screen saver settings, select the Screensaver entry in the Desktop section of the GNOME Control Center. In the right side of the GNOME Control Center window, the screen saver configuration applet shown in Figure 10.5 appears.

FIGURE 10.5:

Configuring your screen saver

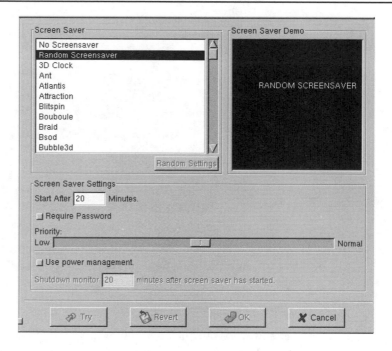

In the top-left corner is a list of screen savers available on your system. To the right of this list, a small demonstration of your currently selected screen saver is displayed. Below the list, you can indicate how many minutes of inactivity should pass before starting the screen saver and whether a password is required.

The Priority setting indicates how much of your computer's resources should be devoted to the screen saver. When the Priority is set to Normal, then any background process is denied access to computer resources in favor of smooth screen saver animations. By contrast, choosing a Low priority means that your background processes get priority in accessing system resources; the cost of this may be choppy screen saver graphics.

Finally, you can specify whether to allow power management to power down your monitor while the screen saver is active and how many minutes to wait after starting the screen saver before powering down the monitor.

Again, once you have finished with your settings, click the OK button to save them.

Another useful feature of the Desktop section of the Control Center is the Theme Selector shown in Figure 10.6.

FIGURE 10.6:

The Theme Selector

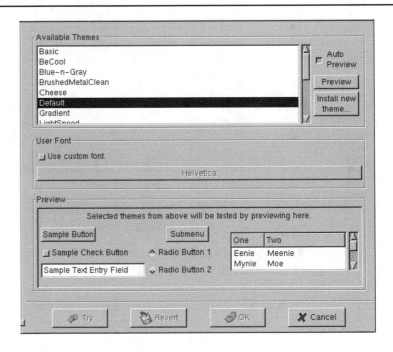

In this section, you can choose from a list of desktop themes in the upper part of the window. These desktop themes define cohesive sets of window backgrounds, button styles, window styles, and color schemes. You can adjust a theme by selecting Use Custom Font. When you then click the font shown (in the case shown in Figure 10.6, it's Helvetica), the Pick A Font window opens, which gives you a choice of fonts, styles, and sizes. When you select a theme, a sample of the theme is displayed in the lower half of the applet, as shown in Figure 10.7, where the Quiet theme is selected.

FIGURE 10.7:

Selecting the Quiet theme

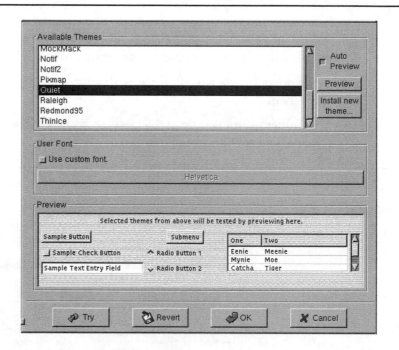

The final feature of the Desktop section of the Control Center is the Window Manager selector shown in Figure 10.8.

This section includes all available window managers. You can switch between window managers in this menu. The Run Configuration Tool For Sawfish option opens another window where you can configure the same options as shown in the Sawfish window manager section of the GNOME Control Center. These options will be discussed later in this chapter.

FIGURE 10.8:

The Window Manager
selector

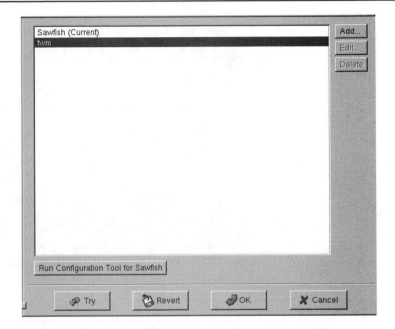

Document Handlers

The Document Handlers section manages the applications associated with various types of files, including default text editors, mime types for other applications, and URL handlers for Web addresses. In other words, this section sets the application when you open a data file in the GNOME file manager.

To define the editor associated with text files, select the Default Editor entry. This displays the configuration applet shown in Figure 10.9.

Click the Gnome Editor drop-down box to select the default editor of your choice. Emacs is the default Gnome editor. If you stay with the default and emacs is not installed on your computer, you get an error message when you try to open a text file from the GNOME file manager.

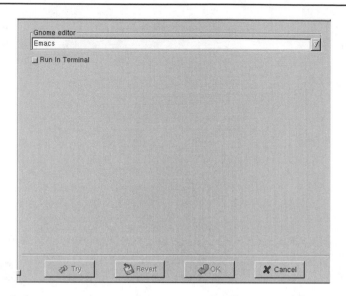

To define the type of application associated with a document extension, select the Mime Types entry. The Mime Types entry displays the configuration applet shown in Figure 10.10.

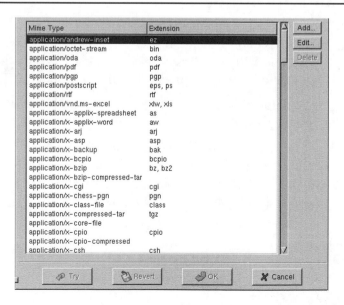

Even though extensions are not required for Linux files, they are a convenience that can help classify different types of files. Click the mime type of your choice, and then click Edit. In the Set Actions For ... window that opens, you can set the icon, extension(s), and applications associated with that mime type.

To define the type of application associated with a Web page or any file that uses Universal Resource Locators (URLs), select the URL Handlers entry. This entry displays the configuration applet shown in Figure 10.11.

FIGURE 10.11:

URL handlers

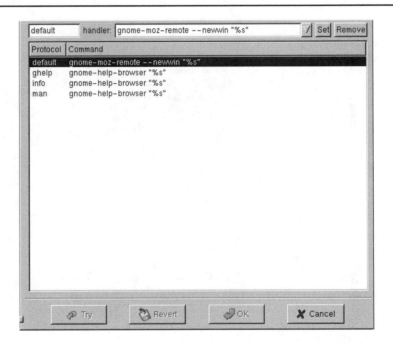

As shown in Figure 10.11, there are four different types of files, or protocols, that are set up as URLs. Although URLs are most often associated with Web pages, GNOME also indexes help files, info pages, and man pages as URLs.

By default, you have a choice of two different browsers: Netscape and the GNOME help browser. You can open either in the current browser or a new window. Highlight the protocol you want to change. Click the drop-down arrow in the Handler box to examine the choices. Make your selection, and then click Set.

Multimedia

The Multimedia section allows you to control two aspects of sound on your GNOME-based system: whether the sound system starts when you start GNOME and the actions that create a "sound event."

To define the sound start-up sequence, select Sound under Multimedia in the left-hand Panel. By default, the General tab opens, as shown in Figure 10.12.

FIGURE 10.12:

Configuring the sound start-up sequence

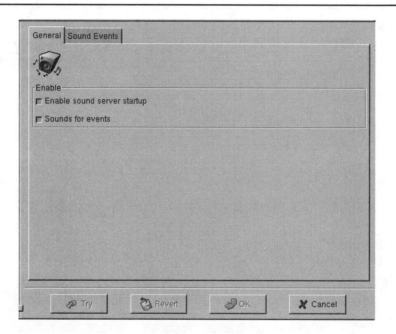

To get sound service in the GNOME window, the Enable Sound Server Startup option must be selected. To enable sound events under this tab, the Sounds For Events option must also be selected. To define sounds when events occur, click the Sound Events tab, shown in Figure 10.13.

You can use the Sound Events tab to specify individual sound files (in WAV format, which is common on Windows systems) to play for a wide range of sound events. Each listed event is associated with a specific WAV file. If you select an event, you can test the current sound by clicking the Play button. Alternatively, you can select a new sound by clicking the Browse button and finding a different WAV file to use.

The Sound Events tab

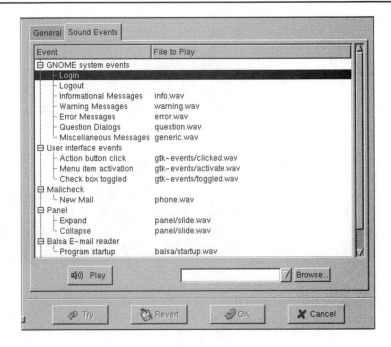

Peripherals

The Peripherals section allows you to control basic aspects of compact disc, keyboard, and mouse behavior using the CD Properties, Keyboard, and Mouse entries.

The CD Properties entry shown in Figure 10.14 configures Linux actions when a compact disc is inserted into a properly configured CD drive.

If you insert a CD containing data, this section allows you to configure any or all of three options: automatically mounting the CD's files onto the default drive (/mnt/cdrom in Red Hat Linux 7.1), the auto-running programs on the main directory of that drive, and opening the GNOME file manager to that directory.

If you insert an audio CD, you can set up Linux to run a specific command when Linux recognizes the CD. By default, the GNOME Control Center is set up to use the GNOME CD Player to play whatever music is on that medium. For more information on GNOME CD Player command options, open up xterm and run the gtcd –help command.

FIGURE 10.14:

Configuring your CD drive

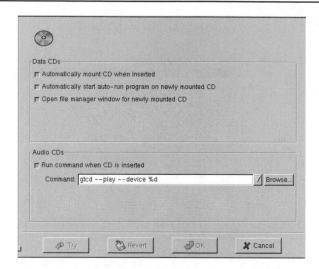

The Keyboard entry, shown in Figure 10.15, allows you to indicate if you want keyboard auto-repeat enabled and, if you do, to specify the delay before repeating starts and how quickly characters should repeat. In addition, you can choose to enable a click sound to be played each time a key is pressed. If you enable keyboard clicks, you can control the volume of the click. You can also specify the volume, pitch, and duration of the keyboard bell, which rings when there is a keyboard message or error.

FIGURE 10.15:

Configuring your keyboard

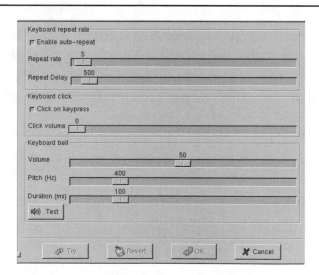

The Mouse entry, shown in Figure 10.16, allows you to indicate whether the mouse user is left- or right-handed, effectively swapping the default behavior of the left and right mouse buttons, and to specify the mouse speed and responsiveness.

FIGURE 10.16:

Setting your mouse's behavior

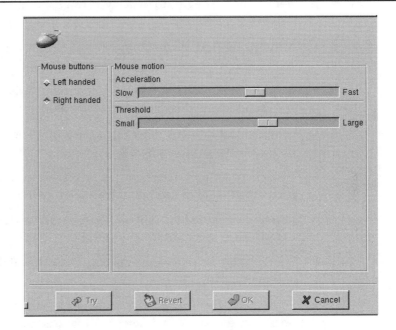

Sawfish Window Manager

Assuming that the Red Hat Linux 7.1 default Sawfish window manager is installed, this section allows you to control its configuration, which provides the "look and feel" of the graphical user interface within the GNOME desktop. As you browse through different options, four buttons are available: Try, Revert, OK, and Cancel. If you make a change, you can click Try to test its effect. You can then click Revert to restore the original configuration.

There are 11 categories where you can configure Sawfish:

- Appearance, through the default frame style. The GNOME default frame style for Red Hat Linux 7.1 is known as CoolClean. Fonts, dialog windows, and animations can be customized for the frame style of your choice.

- Focus Behavior determines the behavior of a window when you point to it.

- Matched Windows allows you to link the behavior of different types of windows.

- Meta includes three options—Novice, Intermediate, and Expert—which determine the degree to which you can configure Sawfish in the GNOME Control Center.

- Minimizing And Maximizing controls virtual window locations when minimized and window behavior when maximized.

- Miscellaneous settings determine the characteristics of other windows when one is raised and the available tooltips associated with each window.

- Moving And Resizing determines the animation and positioning of windows when moved or resized.

- Placement settings determine the position of a window when opened, including that of dialog windows related to a specific program.

- Shortcuts include key combinations that are associated with specific commands, such as logout from GNOME.

- Sound settings drive sound effects for window events such as minimizing and maximizing.

- Workspaces determine the number of virtual desktops, as well as the actions necessary to move to a different virtual desktop.

As Sawfish is unusually configurable, the options you see in this section are quite likely to be different from the options shown on your computer. You can also get to the same configuration options directly with the Sawfish user interface, which you can start from the command line as

```
$ sawfish-ui &
```

Or, if you find that for some reason sawfish isn't on your path, use the command

```
$ /usr/bin/sawfish-ui &
```

This calls up the Sawfish window manager user interface shown in Figure 10.17. Note that the Meta options for novice, intermediate, or expert users are shown in the first Sawfish configuration window.

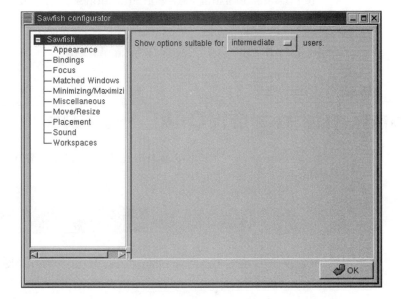

FIGURE 10.17:

Configuring the Sawfish
window manager

Session

The Session section allows you to control what happens when you start
GNOME. The Startup Hint option configures the hints or messages that you
see when you log in. The Startup Programs option configures the programs
that start when you log in to this desktop manager, as well as how they
behave.

User Interface Options

The User Interface Options section allows you to control various aspects of your
user interface, including the following:

- The default appearance of windows elements, such as menus and toolbars,
  for GNOME applications

- The way in which dialog box elements are displayed

- How multiple windows from the same application are handled

For details on using these configuration settings, along with other settings in the Control Center that haven't been discussed in detail in this chapter, consult the GNOME help system. You can access the GNOME help system by selecting Help System from the main GNOME System menu.

Configuring GNOME Panels

The center of the GNOME user interface is GNOME Panels. GNOME creates a default Panel when it first starts.

Users can create their own Panels. From the main GNOME menu, select Panel ➢ Create Panel to open a choice of five different Panels:

- The Menu Panel includes drop-down menus from the top of the GUI window; only one Menu Panel can be added.

- An Edge Panel adds a Panel along a different edge of the GUI window.

- An Aligned Panel is like an Edge Panel, except it is only as long as needed for the buttons that have been added.

- A Sliding Panel is like an Aligned Panel, except it does not have to be placed in a corner or the center of a window.

- A Floating Panel is the freest of the Panels, in that it can be placed anywhere on the screen.

The properties of any Panel, once created, can be changed. Right-click the Panel. In the pop-up menu that appears, choose Panel ➢ Properties ➢ All Properties. In the Properties window that appears, you can then adjust the location, colors, etc. of any Panel except the Menu Panel.

You can also configure GNOME Panels in other ways. For the purposes of this section, you will work with the default GNOME Panel.

The main configuration tasks you want to perform with a Panel are these:

- Adding a drawer
- Adding a logout button
- Adding a launcher
- Controlling Panel properties

Adding a Drawer to a Panel

You add a drawer to a Panel by right-clicking the background of the Panel and choosing Panel ➤ Add To Panel ➤ Drawer from the menu that appears.

To open or close a drawer, click it. An open drawer can display and contain other icons, such as those for launching applications. When the drawer is closed, the icons are hidden. You can move icons and applets from a Panel to the drawer by right-clicking the item you want to move to an open drawer. Then select Move from the menu that appears, and use your cursor to drag the item in question to the desired location. Finally, click that location to complete the move.

Adding a Logout Button to a Panel

Normally, you log out of GNOME by choosing Logout from the main GNOME menu. You can add a button to a Panel, though, to allow for single-click logouts. To do this, right-click the background of the Panel, then click Panel ➤ Add To Panel ➤ Log Out Button. A logout button is added to the Panel.

Adding a New Launcher

The default GNOME Panel contains several buttons that launch applications such as Netscape and a terminal window. These are *launcher buttons*. You can create your own launcher button by right-clicking the background of the Panel and then selecting Panel ➤ Add To Panel ➤ Launcher from the menu that appears. This opens a dialog box like the one in Figure 10.18 for defining which application to launch.

FIGURE 10.18:

Defining a new application launcher

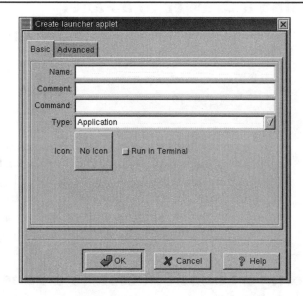

You need to provide at least a name for the launcher and the path and name of a GNOME or X Windows application as the command. You can also choose an icon for the launcher by clicking the button labeled No Icon to display a collection of icons to choose from.

If you want the launcher to start a console application (one that needs to run at the command line and inside a terminal window), select the Run In Terminal check box.

Controlling Panel Properties

If you right-click a Panel's background and select Panel ➤ Properties ➤ All Properties, the Panel Properties dialog box shown in Figure 10.19 appears.

This dialog box contains two tabs. The Edge Panel tab controls the Panel's position on the screen, the size of the Panel (and associated icons), the activation of the auto-hide features, and the state of the hide buttons at both ends of the Panel. These features are described in Chapter 8, "Using GNOME and X Windows."

FIGURE 10.19:

The Panel Properties dialog box, Edge Panel tab

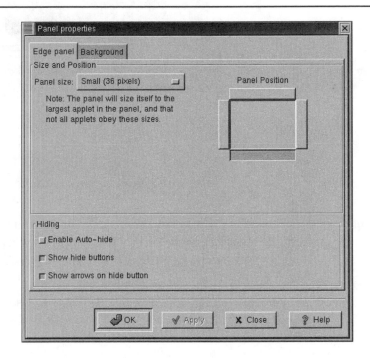

The Background tab is shown in Figure 10.20. This screen allows you to define a background image or color for a Panel. At the top of the screen, you can choose between a Standard, Pixmap, or Color background. A Standard background follows the theme or color scheme you have defined for GNOME, Pixmap uses a bitmap image as a background, and Color allows you to define a solid color for the background.

FIGURE 10.20:

The Panel Properties dialog box, Background tab

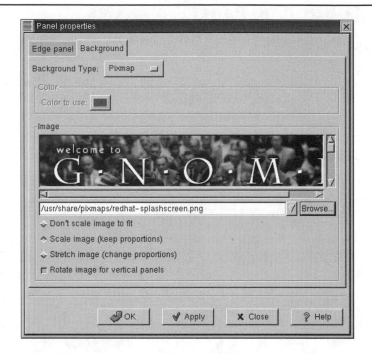

If you select Pixmap, you can click the Browse button and choose an image file from the file-selection dialog box that appears. By default, the image is tiled. Alternatively, you can choose to have the image stretched, scaled to fit, or rotated (if the Edge Panel is vertical).

If you select Color, you can click the Color To Use button to open a Pick A Color window where you can choose a color for the background of the Panel.

Looking Ahead

By now, you should feel fairly comfortable with GNOME and X Windows. In Chapter 11, "Using KDE," you will explore an alternate graphical user interface called KDE. You will learn the history of KDE and then move on to installing it.

Once you have the KDE desktop up and running, you will explore its features and browse its file system. After you understand the basics of navigation, you will learn to configure KDE to suit your needs. By the end of the chapter, you will be able to use KDE to view text and graphics, manage your time, and administer your Linux system.

CHAPTER
ELEVEN

Using KDE

- A History of the KDE Project

- KDE and Red Hat Linux 7.1

- Exploring the KDE Desktop

- Browsing the File System

- Configuring KDE

- Using the KDE Utilities

One of the most promising developments in the user interface of Linux has been the K Desktop Environment (KDE). KDE is a complete graphical desktop environment developed from scratch. KDE is also the default desktop environment on most major Linux distributions. Although Red Hat Linux 7.1, which is included in this book, installs the GNOME desktop by default, it also includes the files need for KDE version 2.1.1.

A History of the KDE Project

As with most components of a complete Linux distribution, KDE was developed by a group of dedicated programmers who wanted to create something new and useful. Matthias Ettrich founded the KDE Project in October 1996 in Germany. Its original purpose was to create a powerful desktop environment for Linux and other Unix systems similar to the commercially available Common Desktop Environment (CDE) available for commercial Unix platforms such as Solaris. The end result has been a project much wider in scope than simply emulating CDE.

Contributors to the KDE Project include hundreds of developers around the world who communicate via e-mail and the occasional in-person conference. Individuals who want to participate in the development of KDE can work on the core components such as the window manager, the desktop Panel, and other components, or they can create their own application for KDE, using the KDE-defined Application Programming Interfaces (APIs).

Among the contributors to the KDE Project are translators, writers, user-interface designers, and multimedia specialists, in addition to systems and application programmers.

KDE doesn't replace the X Windows system on your Linux computer. Instead, KDE uses the X Windows system as a graphical base on which to build the desktop.

If you've used other X window managers, such as Sawfish, AfterStep, or even CDE, you may recognize that KDE includes its own window manager, called kwin. Part of the window manager functionality includes the ability to place icons on the desktop background.

In addition to the kwin window manager, which provides core functionality for creating and managing on-screen windows, KDE includes a few key components such as a Taskbar and a main menu that enable you to easily access applications.

Finally, a KDE distribution includes a large collection of applications such as standard utilities, system administration tools, and entertainment packages. It even includes an integrated office suite similar to GNOME Office and Microsoft Office 2000.

Reviewing a KDE Distribution

As with Linux, KDE uses the term *distribution* to describe a complete collection of desktop components and the default set of applications that accompany them.

A KDE distribution includes the following components:

- The graphical libraries used by all KDE applications

- The core KDE libraries, also used by all KDE applications

- A collection of support functions, used by most applications

- The base applications that define KDE, such as the window manager and the Panel/Taskbar programs

- Optional applications that can be installed on a running KDE system

As with most Linux-related projects, the source code to KDE is available for download and review. The KDE code is licensed under the GNU General Public License (GPL).

Writing KDE Applications

KDE was developed from ground zero into a full-featured desktop in about two years. This was possible only by using a pre-built commercial graphical toolkit called Qt, from Troll Tech in Oslo, Norway.

NOTE   By using Qt, KDE developers were able to focus on design issues for the desktop and immediately begin coding, rather than spending additional months or years creating a toolkit to standardize the interface.

Qt is a cross-platform graphical toolkit that forms the basis of the KDE API. Any application written for KDE can use the Qt functionality. The result is that a complete KDE application can be created in only a few days.

> **NOTE**   Since Qt was recently re-released by Troll Tech under the GNU General Public License, KDE is gaining increasing acceptance in the Linux community.

Both Qt and KDE itself are written in C++, an object-oriented programming language. You can also write KDE applications in Python, a high-level object-oriented scripting language, or in Perl.

There are number of robust development tools available for KDE, including KDevelop and KDbg. Check the KDE Developer Web site for more information (`http://developer.kde.org`).

KDE and Red Hat Linux 7.1

For Red Hat Linux 7.1, the files needed to run KDE version 2.1.1 are available with the distribution. If you installed KDE during the Red Hat installation process, then you already have KDE on your system. If not, you can find the RPM files you will need to use in the next section on one of the Red Hat Linux 7.1 Installation CD-ROMs at /mnt/cdrom/RedHat/RPMS (assuming you mounted the CD-ROM at /mnt/cdrom).

The KDE files on the Red Hat Linux 7.1 CD-ROMs are as follows:

- kdeadmin-2.1.1-3.i386.rpm
- kdebase-2.1.1-8.i386.rpm
- kdebindings-2.1.1-1.i386.rpm *
- kdebindings-devel-2.1.1-1.i386.rpm *
- kdebindings-kmozilla-2.1.1-1.i386.rpm *
- kdegames-1.1.2-6.i386.rpm *
- kdegraphics-1.1.2-6.i386.rpm *
- kdelibs-2.1.1-5.i386.rpm

- kdelibs-devel-2.1.1-5.i386.rpm *

- kdelibs-sound-2.1.1-5.i386.rpm

- kdelibs-sound-devel-2.1.1-5.i386.rpm *

- kdemultimedia-2.1.1-1.i386.rpm

- kdenetwork-2.1.1-1.i386.rpm

- kdenetwork-ppp-2.1.1-1.i386.rpm

- kdepim-2.1.1-1.i386.rpm

- kdesdk-2.1.1-1.i386.rpm *

- kdesdk-devel-2.1.1-1.i386.rpm *

- kdesupport-2.1.-3.i386.rpm

- kdesupport-devel-2.1.-3.i386.rpm *

- kdetoys-2.1.1-2.i386.rpm *

- kdeutils-2.1.1-1.i386.rpm

- kdevelop-1.4.1-2.i386.rpm *

- kdoc-2.1.1-1.noarch.rpm *

- koffice-2.0.1-2.i386.rpm

- kpppload-1.04-23.i386.rpm

The packages marked with an asterisk (*) are on the second Red Hat 7.1 Installation CD-ROM, not included with this book. You can download them from the KDE home page at http://www.kde.org or the RPM database site at http://www.rpmfind.net.

Updating KDE

As of this writing, Red Hat Linux 7.1 includes the most up-to-date version of KDE. However, KDE upgrades the features on its desktop every few months, so you may want to update your system. You can upgrade the KDE available in any version of Linux based on files from the KDE home page at http://www.kde.org. The latest KDE files are also available in RPM format for a number of distributions at http://www.rpmfind.net.

When you download the latest packages, look for the latest versions of the files named in the previous list, as well as their "base" packages, which include various packages that start with htdig, libmng, and qt. As described in earlier chapters, once you have the necessary packages, you can install them with one of the following commands, depending on whether you're installing (-i) a package for the first time or upgrading (-U) to a later version of a package:

```
# rpm -i filename
# rpm -U filename
```

> **TIP**   Alternatively, you can use the Kpackage or GnoRPM utility to manage RPM packages in the X Window. If installed, Kpackage is available through the KDE main menu under System ➢ Package Manager, and GnoRPM is available from the KDE main menu under GNOME Programs ➢ System ➢ GnoRPM.

Starting KDE

In Red Hat Linux 7.1, the default desktop environment is GNOME. Once you've installed KDE from the Installation CDs or from downloads, you can start KDE from the default GNOME graphical login window. To do this, follow these steps:

1. Choose the Session menu.

2. Select KDE from the list of possible desktops.

3. Log in using your username and password.

When KDE starts, an initial screen appears, like the one in Figure 11.1.

If you normally start X Windows by logging in at the console login prompt and then using the startx command, then you need to configure your system so that KDE launches when you issue the startx command.

In this regard, you have three options:

- If you want to change the default desktop for every user, edit the global Xclients file, which you can find at /etc/X11/xinit/Xclients.

- If you want to change only your default desktop user, copy the global Xclients file to your home directory, name the file .Xclients, and then edit the file in your home directory. You can copy the file with the command

```
$ cp /etc/X11/xinit/Xclients ~/.Xclients
```

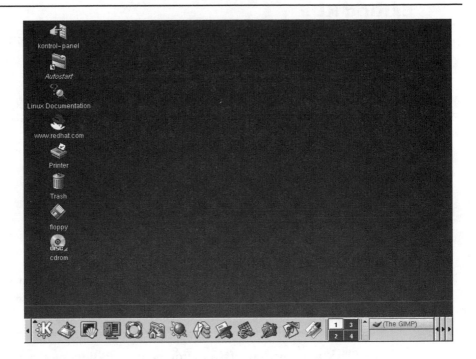

In either of the first two cases, you need to make only one change to the file. The fifth line should initially read

```
PREFERRED=
```

Change this line so that it reads

```
PREFERRED=startkde
```

Once you make this change and save it, X Windows should start with KDE as your desktop when you use the startx command. If you make this change to the global Xclients file, then every user will have KDE as their default desktop.

- If you want to change only your default desktop user, use the Red Hat Linux 7.1 switchdesk command. This opens the Desktop Switcher dialog box, where you can select your preferred desktop environment. For example, if you select KDE, this modifies the .Xclients file in your home directory to look to a .Xclients-default file, with a single line:

```
exec startkde
```

Exiting KDE

When you're ready to exit KDE, select Logout from the main menu. The screen is grayed and the End KDE Session confirmation window appears. Choose Logout to exit KDE.

If you have any windows open when you choose Logout, and you want to restore these windows the next time you start KDE, select the Restore Session When Logging In Next Time check box. The next time you start KDE, it attempts to reopen those windows, launching KDE or other graphical applications that you were running to reestablish the same desktop that you had when you selected Logout. Not all applications may be successfully restarted, but KDE will attempt to do so.

NOTE You can always exit KDE using the default keyboard method of exiting the X Windows system: Hold down Ctrl+Alt and then press the Backspace key. However, this method should be used only for emergencies (such as if the graphics lock up), because it doesn't allow KDE to exit gracefully—you may lose some data if you use this keyboard method to exit KDE.

The status of your KDE environment, including information about the windows that you had open when you selected Logout, is all saved in one or more hidden files in your home directory, which may include `.kderc`, `.gtkrc-kde`, and files in the `.kde/share/config` subdirectory. You can review these files if you'd like, but be careful about changing them, since you may confuse KDE the next time it launches.

NOTE Information about the state of specific applications, such as the file manager or a networking utility, is saved in the application's configuration file, normally located in your home directory under `.kde/share/config`.

Using *kdm* for Graphical Login

If you're accustomed to using xdm or the GNOME display manager (gdm) for a graphical login to your Linux system, you may want to try the kdm graphical login application provided with KDE.

The functionality of gdm and kdm is very similar; kdm can be graphically configured using the KDE Control Center (described later in this chapter in the section "Exploring the KDE Desktop").

Configuring Graphical Logins

To enable a Red Hat Linux 7.1 graphical login, first make sure that the X Windows system is working, then change the /etc/inittab file to use run level 5 instead of 3 by changing the following line from

```
id:3:initdefault
```

to

```
id:5:initdefault
```

Changing from xdm or gdm to kdm is easy once you have KDE installed. Just open the /etc/inittab file in a text editor and locate the following line, which indicates what program should be launched to use the graphical (x) login:

```
x:5:respawn:/etc/X11/prefdm -nodaemon
```

You may see a different desktop manager in place of /etc/X11/prefdm -nodaemon. Change this line to read as follows:

```
x:5:respawn:/usr/bin/kdm -nodaemon
```

Now when you restart your system, the kdm graphical login is used.

Configuring *kdm*

By using kdm, you can configure many features of the graphical login, including the greeting string, the icon in the dialog box, and the background color or wallpaper graphic displayed.

Assuming you made the changes to /etc/inittab noted in previous sections, you can configure kdm with the following steps:

1. Log in to your Linux system using the graphical login dialog box.

2. Open the main menu by clicking the K icon in the lower-left corner of the KDE screen.

3. Choose Preferences ➢ System ➢ Login Manager.

The kdm configuration dialog box appears, as shown in Figure 11.2.

FIGURE 11.2:

Use the Login Manager dialog box to configure features of the *kdm* graphical login screen.

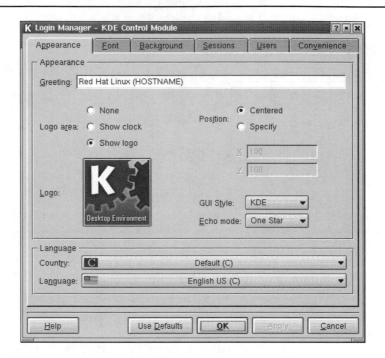

> **NOTE**   If you did not log in to KDE as the root user, you will be prompted for the root password.

On the Appearance tab (shown in Figure 11.2) you can select the following items:

- The greeting used at the top of the graphical login window.

- The logo used within the login window, which can be a real logo or a clock. If you select Show Logo, you can browse available logos when you click the KDE logo button.

- The GUI style, such as KDE, Motif, SGI, or Windows.

- The language and national dialect used for messages in the graphical login window.

The Font tab lets you define the text font used for the Greeting, Fail, and Standard messages. To change a font, choose which font you want to alter from the drop-down list and click the Change Font button. A Select Font dialog box appears, where you can select the font that you want.

The Background tab (shown in Figure 11.3) enables you to select a background color pattern or a background graphic image for the login screen.

If you prefer a colored background, you have several choices when you click the Mode drop-down box, including the following:

- Flat for a single color (the first of the two color bars)

- Horizontal Gradient for two colors blended side to side

- Vertical Gradient (the default) for two colors blended top to bottom

To select a color, click Color 1 or Color 2. A Select Color dialog box (shown in Figure 11.4) appears, where you can select the color that you want to use.

FIGURE 11.3:

From the Background tab, you select the colors or wallpaper graphics to use behind the *kdm* login window.

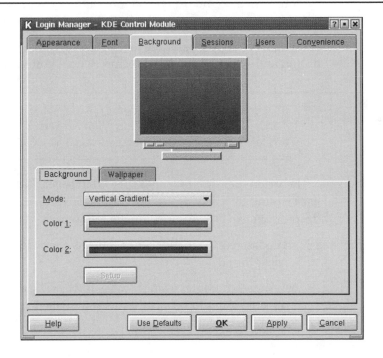

FIGURE 11.4:

The standard KDE Select Color dialog box lets you define the color that you want to use for the *kdm* background.

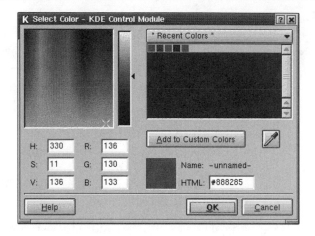

If you prefer to have a wallpaper graphic in the background of the login screen, select the Wallpaper tab under the picture of the monitor.

More than 25 standard wallpaper graphics are provided with KDE 2.1.1. You can select any of these from the Wallpaper drop-down list.

If you have another graphic that you want to use as wallpaper, click the Browse button and select it from the directory where you have the graphic file stored.

> **TIP**
>
> It's a good idea to copy the graphic file that you want to use as wallpaper to the standard KDE wallpaper directory, `/usr/share/wallpapers`, so that you don't accidentally delete the file after specifying it as a KDE wallpaper.

The wallpaper graphic can be placed in several different locations on your background by selecting among the buttons shown below the Mode selection drop-down list. Options include the following:

- Tiled to use the wallpaper graphic as a repeating pattern across the entire background.

- Centered to center a single copy of the wallpaper in the middle of the kdm screen—it might be mostly covered by the kdm login window in this case.

- Scaled to expand the wallpaper to the edges of your screen.

NOTE
If you use a wallpaper option such as Tiled or Scaled, none of the background colors that you select will be visible. If you want to use only a background color without a wallpaper graphic, be sure to choose the No Wallpaper option in the Wallpaper drop-down list.

The Sessions tab lets you specify how login sessions are defined. For example, you can add other window managers that you've installed, such as CDE. The Users tab lets you configure which users are shown as icons within the login window. Finally, the Convenience tab allows you to set up situations where KDE does not require passwords for logons.

When you have defined the kdm options you want, click OK to close the dialog box and save your settings. You'll see them the next time you see the KDE login screen.

Adding Other KDE Applications

When you install KDE, you have at your disposal a comprehensive set of utilities and entertainment programs, as described later in this chapter. However, many other KDE applications are available to meet the unique needs of your specific installation.

In particular, you may want to update to a newer version of a favorite KDE application or download an application that wasn't included in the default KDE distribution.

The main source for KDE applications is the KDE Applications Web site at http://apps.kde.com. The KDE Applications Web site is regularly updated, and it includes over 800 KDE applications, each with a short description and a link directly to the FTP download directory.

Examples of what you can find on this applications page include the following:

- The KDE Office Suite
- Utility to configure BIND (DNS)
- Additional sets of icons and color schemes (KDE themes)
- Video file player
- KDE-aware Telnet application

- ISDN line-management tool

- Laptop power-management utility

- User administration tool

- Dozens more games

Remember, these are in addition to the many KDE applications that you probably already have installed on your KDE system. Fortunately, most of these applications are available as regular RPM packages, which you can install as described in this and previous chapters.

Unfortunately for new KDE users, some additional KDE applications are distributed as source code. In order to use them, you'll need to install the development packages and compile the source code on your Linux system.

This actually isn't very difficult. The problems arise for users who are not familiar with the development tools. In that case, resolving any error or warning messages that appear can be quite time-consuming.

Once you have the development libraries installed for KDE, Qt, and the X Windows system, you can prepare a source code tree that you have downloaded and unarchived using these simple commands:

```
# configure
# make all
# make install
```

With these commands, the new application is compiled and placed in your KDE menus or binary directories so that you can immediately execute it. Some applications may require more complicated steps to compile and install them. In these cases, consult the README file and installation files that are included with most applications to provide detailed instructions to get you started.

NOTE   For detailed instructions on compiling the latest version of KDE from its source code, navigate to http://www.kde.org/install-source.html.

Exploring the KDE Desktop

Once you have KDE installed and running, you can start learning how to use it. The elements on the KDE desktop are probably familiar to you. Figure 11.5 shows a blank KDE desktop with the main menu open. Only The GIMP has been opened (see Taskbar) in order to provide a screenshot of this desktop.

The elements you see on the desktop are as follows:

- The background, which shows icons for programs and files that you want to have easily accessible (eight icons are shown by default).

- The Panel, which is a bar of icons across the bottom of the screen (you can reconfigure the location of the Panel, as well as the icons on the Panel). Clicking an icon launches a commonly used program.

- The Taskbar, which shows a button for each main application window that you have opened in KDE. Clicking a button brings that application's window forward.

- The main menu, which you view by clicking the K icon on the Panel. All of KDE's major functions are available from the main menu and its submenus.

FIGURE 11.5:

The initial KDE desktop, with the main menu opened, the Panel below, and one of the initial desktop icons visible

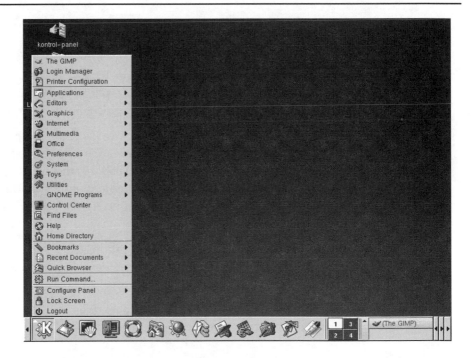

You can explore many of KDE's applications by choosing items from the main menu or by clicking buttons on the Panel.

Launching KDE Applications

Start a couple of KDE applications to experiment with as you learn about the KDE graphical environment. The KDE text editor and a terminal emulator window provide a good starting point. Choose System ➤ Terminal on the main menu to open a command-line window. Next, choose Editors ➤ Text Editor to open a graphical KDE text editor.

TIP   Once you have a terminal emulator window open, you can enter the name of any KDE program instead of selecting it from a menu or clicking a Panel icon. For example, you can launch the text editor by entering **kedit & or /usr/bin/kedit &** at the command line.

Now try launching another terminal window from the Panel by clicking the Terminal Shell button, shown below.

When you are running the KDE desktop, KDE applications are special compared to most other X Windows system graphical applications because they can interact with each other, use common graphical libraries to save system resources, and have the same look and feel.

Other graphical or text-based applications can also be used in KDE, of course. Some of the more popular graphical applications, including GNOME-based applications, may be included in the KDE main menu under a Non-KDE Applications submenu. In Red Hat Linux 7.1, you can find most GNOME applications under the GNOME Programs submenu.

You can also launch your favorite applications from a command-line terminal window in KDE, just as you would in any other window manager such as GNOME or CDE.

To try this, enter a command like **xv** or **gimp** or **gs** in a KDE terminal emulator window. (The program name you choose will depend on what you have installed.)

TIP One quick way to enter a command to start a program is through the pop-up command window in KDE. To use this, press Alt+F2 and enter the command in the small pop-up window that appears.

Using Multiple Desktops

If you're familiar with other Linux window managers, you might have used the Pager to manage multiple virtual desktops, each containing many open windows. In one virtual desktop, you might have your browser; in another, your word processor; in another, terminal windows where you edit code.

KDE uses the same idea to provide you with multiple visual workspaces. By default, KDE includes four virtual desktops, which you can switch between by clicking the desktop name or number in the Panel or by pressing Ctrl+F1 for Desktop One, Ctrl+F2 for Desktop Two, and so forth.

TIP You can change the number of desktops and rename them to fit how you use each one. From the KDE main menu, choose Preferences ➤ Look & Feel ➤ Desktop. In the dialog box that appears, click the Number Of Desktops tab. The slider atop this window allows you to configure anywhere from one to 16 virtual desktops. Each text box associated with a virtual desktop allows you to rename that desktop.

You can rotate between desktops by holding down the Ctrl key and pressing Tab or Shift+Tab repeatedly.

Working with Application Windows

Working with application windows in KDE is similar to working with other graphical environments you may have used. The same methods of moving, resizing, and closing windows can be used in KDE.

When you have multiple windows open on your KDE desktop, you can activate any window by clicking anywhere in the window.

TIP   The KDE *focus policy* determines which window is the active window in KDE. If you're accustomed to a particular type of focus, such as being able to type in whichever window your mouse pointer is in, you can alter the focus policy of KDE by choosing Preferences ➤ Look & Feel ➤ Window Behavior. In the dialog box that appears, click the Actions tab and select the focus policy of your choice.

KDE's multiple virtual desktops can make it easy to work with many open windows at the same time, but you also have available other methods for switching between open application windows:

- The Taskbar displays a button for each open window. You can click a Taskbar button to activate that window and bring it to the front.

- You can hold the Alt key and press Tab or Shift+Tab repeatedly to rotate between the open windows, much as you would in Microsoft Windows.

- You can press the middle mouse button to open a list of windows and desktops in the current KDE session. From this list you can select any window to activate it and bring it to the front.

NOTE   If you have a two-button mouse, you may have configured middle mouse button emulation while reading Chapter 4, "Installing Red Hat Linux 7.1." Click the left and right buttons together to emulate clicking the middle button. You can change the "button" that calls up the Window List. You can set up the middle mouse button in Red Hat Linux 7.1 with the `/usr/sbin/mouseconfig` utility.

Browsing the File System

A big part of using any graphical system is accessing the files on your computer. Linux provides a completely integrated file manager to do this. In addition, you can directly access the file system from the KDE main menu using the Quick Browser, though this method doesn't provide the interaction of a file manager window.

This section describes how to work with KDE file manager windows and the Quick Browser menus.

Using Konqueror Windows

The file manager in KDE is called Konqueror, which also doubles as a Web browser. You can start Konqueror by clicking its icon, shown below, on the Panel.

This starts Konqueror as a Web browser, as shown in Figure 11.6.

FIGURE 11.6:

Konqueror

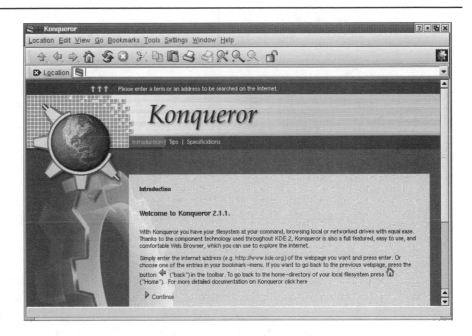

Alternatively, you can open your home directory in Konqueror by clicking the Home Directory icon, shown below, on the Panel.

A Konqueror window appears, as shown in Figure 11.7.

FIGURE 11.7:

Konqueror lets you view the contents of your home directory and browse to other directories.

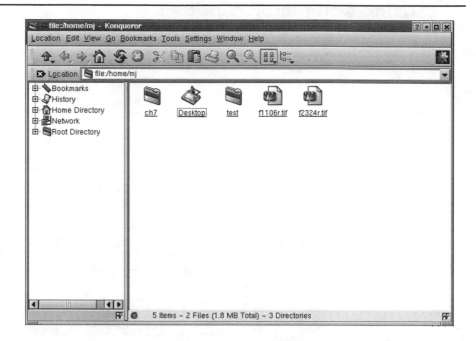

The default view of your file system uses medium-sized icons in the right-hand pane (assigned by KDE according to file type). You can see a toolbar and Location line in the top of the Konqueror window. There is also a directory tree in the left-hand pane, equivalent to the Folders pane in Microsoft Windows Explorer.

Changing the view of these files to see more information is easy: From the Konqueror toolbar, choose another display option from View ➢ View Mode, such as MultiColumn or Text View. You can also select Show Hidden Files on the View menu to see all the files in your home directory.

Clicking the up-arrow icon on the left end of the toolbar changes to the parent directory; clicking any directory opens that directory and displays its contents within the same Konqueror window. To open a new Konqueror window at the current location, choose Location ➢ New Window or press Ctrl+N.

To move or copy a file or directory, click and drag any icon, dropping it in the directory where you want to move or copy it. (A pop-up menu lets you choose Move, Link, or Copy.)

Any time you left-click an icon in Konqueror, KDE attempts to launch that item. If it's a text file, for example, KDE opens it in the KDE text editor; graphics files appear in the graphics viewer. When possible, the application opens the file in Konqueror's right-hand pane.

If KDE can't figure out what to do with the file, an Open With dialog box appears, where you can specify a program to use for launching the icon you clicked, as shown in Figure 11.8. This dialog box includes a Known Applications menu from the main KDE menu.

FIGURE 11.8:

Selecting an application to use to open a file

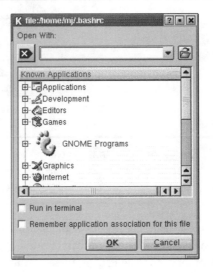

Changing File Properties

Within Konqueror, you can alter any file or directory properties that you have access to. To view the file or directory properties, right-click any file or directory icon. From the pop-up menu that appears, choose Properties. A Properties dialog box, as shown in Figure 11.9, appears with tabs that you can use to change at least the name and permissions associated with that file or directory.

The Properties dialog box lets you view and change information about objects in Konqueror windows.

NOTE   The specific tabs that appear in the Properties dialog box depend on the type of object that you are viewing. For example, the properties associated with KDE Link files (described later in this section) include associated utilities and applications.

You can also create new objects by using the Edit ➤ Create New submenu. From this submenu, you can create a new folder (subdirectory) or new information objects such as HTML files, application links, or removable drive devices that KDE can use to access your system resources.

Browsing with Konqueror

Konqueror resembles Web browser windows and, in fact, can be used to access any Web page. If you browse your local file system to a directory that contains an index.html file, that file will be displayed rather than icons for the contents of the directory.

TIP   Deselect View ➤ Use Index.html to see the files in a directory instead of the HTML index of the directory.

While viewing any directory, you can click in the Location field and enter a full Web URL, such as

```
http://www.sybex.com
```
or
```
ftp://ftp.kde.org
```

If you're currently connected to the Internet, the appropriate Internet page will be downloaded and displayed in Konqueror.

Configuring Konqueror

You can configure the actions and behavior of Konqueror as a file manager as well as a Web browser. On the Konqueror toolbar, choose Settings ➢ Configure Konqueror. As shown in Figure 11.10, you can configure Konqueror in nine different categories.

FIGURE 11.10:

The Konqueror configuration window

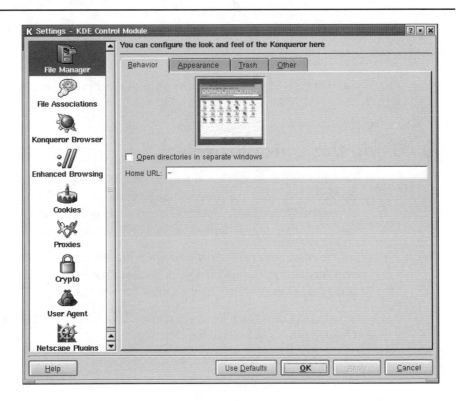

- File Manager allows you to set up the behavior and appearance of file manager windows.

- File Associations lets you associate file types such as XLS files to a specific application such as KSpread.

- Konqueror Browser settings manage rules for links, text sizes, Java, and plug-ins.

- Enhanced Browsing allows you to configure various keywords for different Web sites; this applies only to Konqueror as a browser.

- Cookies allows you to configure the configuration messages that you will accept from different Web sites. You can customize this by domain.

- Proxies allows you to connect to the Internet or other Web networks through a proxy server computer.

- Crypto settings allow you to set up the encryption/decryption schemes to be used.

- User Agent lets you control how your browser is seen by the Web servers you use.

- Netscape Plugins lists the plug-in modules associated with various file types.

Using the Quick Browser

Konqueror provides a great way to graphically manage files, but if you want to immediately launch a program or access a data file, Konqueror can seem a little slow. The Quick Browser enables you to access any part of your file system using the KDE main menu, without ever opening Konqueror.

Of course, you can't drag-and-drop files between directories or open Properties windows for items via the Quick Browser menus, but for launching an application or opening a data file, the Quick Browser is the perfect tool.

To access the Quick Browser, choose Quick Browser on the main menu. The Quick Browser submenu has three options:

- The Home Directory option accesses files and directories starting with your home directory.

- The Root Directory option accesses files and directories starting with the root (/) directory, the top-level directory in Linux.

- The System Configuration option accesses configuration files and directories under the /etc directory.

To see how the Quick Browser can be used to view your file system, choose Quick Browser ➢ Root on the main menu and spend a moment browsing through the submenus that appear, as illustrated in Figure 11.11. Note the following features:

- Whenever you move to a directory, the contents of that directory are displayed.

- Whenever you click a file, KDE attempts to launch or open that file.

- In any submenu, when you click the name of the directory, you can then select Open In File Manager or Open In Terminal to open Konqueror or the command-line window in that directory.

FIGURE 11.11:

You can use the Quick Browser submenus to browse through your file system without opening a file manager window.

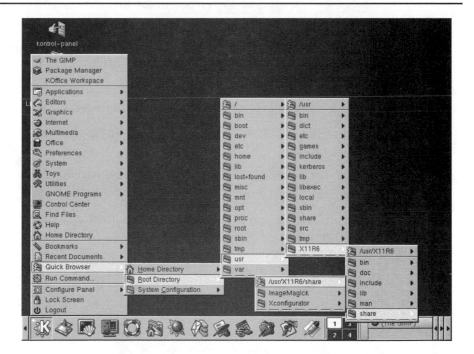

For example, browse in the Quick Browser menus to Home Directory. Click the file of your choice from your home directory. KDE opens the file in the associated application.

Creating KDE Link Files

You've read a lot by now about KDE Link files. These files are small informational text files that describe a system resource so that KDE can use it.

For example, a KDE file that refers to your CD-ROM drive is part of the default KDE desktop. This KDE Link file (and the icon associated with it) enables you to access the file system on your CD-ROM drive without ever using a command line. You can mount, unmount, and view the CD-ROM contents directly from the desktop. Fortunately, KDE lets you create these KDE Link files graphically.

If you want to see what a KDE Link file really looks like, go to the Desktop subdirectory of your home directory. If your home directory is /home/mj, go to /home/mj/Desktop and open one of the files that correspond to the icons on your desktop in your text editor.

To create a new KDE Link file that refers to a graphical application such as the graphics viewer The GIMP, follow these steps:

1. Open a file manager (Konqueror) window to view your home directory, then navigate to the local Desktop subdirectory.

2. Choose Edit ➤ Create New ➤ Link To Application. A Properties dialog box appears.

3. Change the first part of the name shown to match your application, in this case, The Gimp.

4. Click the icon to bring up a menu with other available icons. Select the icon of your choice, and then click OK.

5. Choose the Execute tab (see Figure 11.12).

6. In the Command field of the Execute tab, enter the command used to launch the program that you want to access using this KDE Link file.

7. Click OK to close the Properties dialog box.

TIP You can store additional information about this application as well. For example, under the General tab, click the default icon to select a new icon, or choose the Application tab to define which data types this application can work with.

FIGURE 11.12:

On the Execute tab of the Properties dialog box of a KDE Link file, you define how to launch an application.

You've now created a KDE Link file. The next time you log in to KDE, the icon for this file should appear on your desktop. You can use various Link files to extend the KDE menus, add icons to your desktop, auto-start applications, and add icons to your KDE Panel. The next section, "Configuring KDE," describes how to complete some of these tasks with a KDE Link file.

Configuring KDE

You've already seen many of the KDE configuration options as you've learned about the kdm graphical login program and some of the windowing options provided by KDE. These and many other settings can be configured using the KDE Control Center. Some of the most useful configuration options are described in this section.

Using the KDE Control Center

To start the KDE Control Center, choose KDE Control Center from the main menu or click the Control Center icon on the default Panel, shown below. The Control Center opens with a list of areas on the left side of the window. You can click any of these areas to open a list of configuration topics. When you click a topic, the right half of the screen changes to display those configuration options.

TIP

The items in the Control Center match the Preferences submenus on the main menu. Depending on how much configuration you want to do, using the Control Center can be more convenient.

NOTE

Choosing Apply in the Control Center activates your configuration changes but doesn't close the Control Center window. To do that, choose File ➤ Quit or click the close button on the title bar.

Several dozen configuration options are included in the Control Center, divided into 11 sections, as shown in Figure 11.13. The sections that follow describe how to work with a few of the most useful options for the average KDE user.

FIGURE 11.13:

The KDE Control Center

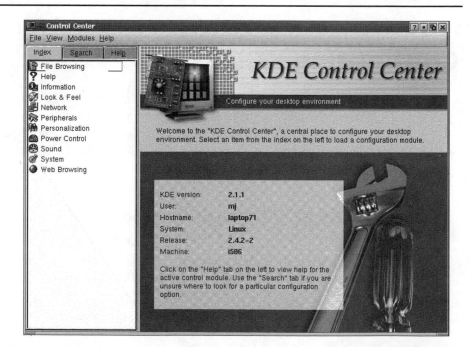

One of the major changes with the release of KDE 2.*x* is with the Index, Search, and Help tabs in the upper-left part of the Control Center, just under the menu bar. The Index tab includes the various configuration items. The Search tab allows you to look for the right configuration item based on keywords. The Help tab provides a brief overview of the currently highlighted item.

KDE File Management

The File Browsing section of the KDE Control Center sets up the way files are linked and organized within the graphical user interface. The File Associations subsection takes file extensions such as .txt and .jpg and associates them with specific applications. When you click a file in the KDE file manager, Konqueror, it is opened with the associated application. When you select a specific type of file, you can change the associated application.

The File Manager subsection configures the behavior of Konqueror for opening new directories in appearance, in actions when moving files to the Trash, and in the associated command-line terminal program.

The Help System

The KDE Control Center has three layers of help. In the upper-right corner of the window, along with the sticky, minimize, and maximize buttons, is a question mark button. When you click the question mark and then click an item, the KDE Control Center gives you a brief pop-up description of that item.

There is a Help tab just below the menu bar in the upper-left section of the Control Center. When you highlight an item under the Index tab, you can then click the Help tab for more information on that item. Clicking the Help button near the bottom of the window is another way to select the Help tab for a specific item, as shown in Figure 11.14.

Finally, at the bottom of the Help information is the following statement: "To read the full manual click <u>here</u>." When you click the word "<u>here</u>," Konquerer opens up, usually to the relevant part of the KDE Control Center manual.

FIGURE 11.14:

The Help tab provides
some information about
the purpose of a specific
KDE Control Center item.

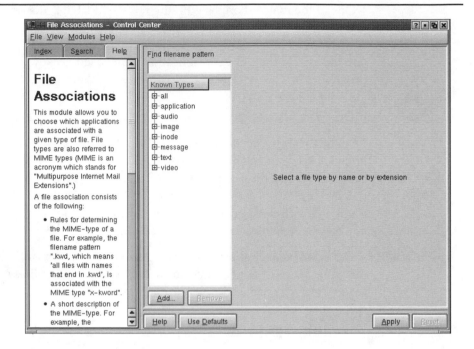

Gathering System Information

The Information section of the Control Center provides detailed statistics and technical information about your Linux system. The information in these tabs cannot be changed; it is provided for your review so that you can learn about your system settings and status. The available subsections are as follows:

Block Devices   Lists configured and mounted block devices, such as the root (/) directory, a CD-ROM (/mnt/cdrom), and connected network drives.

DMA-Channels   Lists the DMA memory access channels and associated hardware active on your system.

Devices   Lists the device types that Linux recognizes (not individual devices, however).

IO-Ports   Shows the IO port addresses used on your system.

Interrupts   Shows the interrupts, also known as IRQ channels, defined on your system (not all of them, however, so this may be of marginal value at this point).

KDE IOSlaves   Displays a list of protocol-specific small programs such as `nfs`, `pop3`, and `telnet`.

Memory   Displays a live memory usage screen, with second-by-second graphical updates of your virtual and actual system memory usage.

PCI   Provides a report of the status of all PCI devices.

PCMCIA   Lists the PCMCIA slots on your computer, including the type of PC Card installed in each slot.

Partitions   Lists available partitions on your system, as defined in the `/etc/fstab` configuration file.

Processor   Displays an information screen about your processor, with processor type, speed, and other information.

SCSI   Lists any information about your SCSI devices.

Samba Status   If the Samba server is configured and running, shows all users who are currently logged in and which Linux shares they are using.

Sound   Shows the status of your Linux sound system.

X-Server   Displays the version, server, color depth, and resolution used by your X server.

Changing the Look and Feel of KDE

Many of the Control Center pages are used to define the appearance and interface options of KDE. You've already seen a few of these, such as the Login Manager configuration, in previous sections of this chapter. The most interesting interface configuration options are provided in the Look & Feel section.

The Background subsection allows you to set up a different background for each desktop. It includes three configuration tabs, as shown in Figure 11.15. The Background and Wallpaper tabs enable you to define a background color and wallpaper, much as you can for the `kdm` login manager. More than 100 wallpaper graphics are included with KDE. Each desktop can have a separate wallpaper and background color scheme. The Advanced tab allows you to limit the memory cache for the background and set up blending of different wallpaper patterns.

In the Colors subsection, you can define the appearance of all the windows opened in KDE. In this section, you can select a color scheme (see Figure 11.16). This subsection is similar to the Display Properties, Appearance tab in Microsoft

Windows. In KDE, you can also easily create additional color schemes or modify each window component (called a *widget*) individually.

FIGURE 11.15:

The Background subsection enables you to define background colors and wallpaper for each desktop.

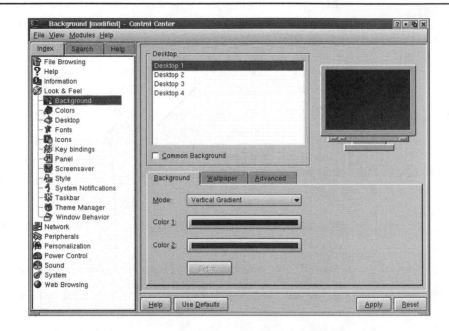

FIGURE 11.16:

The Colors subsection defines a color scheme for all KDE windows.

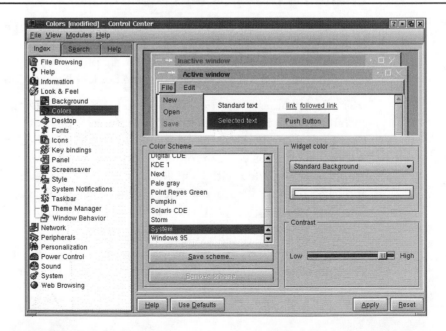

In the Desktop subsection, you can specify the font and icons on your desktop, the activity around desktop borders, the actions associated with each mouse button, and the number of virtual desktops.

In the Panel subsection, you can update how the Panel and Taskbar are arranged. From the five tabs in this section, you can configure items such as the following:

- The screen location of the Panel and Taskbar

- The animation of Panel and Taskbar items

- Special items on the main menu

- The color behind different categories of shortcut buttons

- Applets loaded on KDE start-up

In the Screensaver subsection (see Figure 11.17), you define a screen saver program that KDE will use when your system is inactive for a few minutes. KDE includes 21 screen saver applications to choose from. Most of them can be precisely configured by choosing the Setup button.

FIGURE 11.17:

Use the Screensaver subsection to define and configure one of the KDE screen saver programs for use on your system.

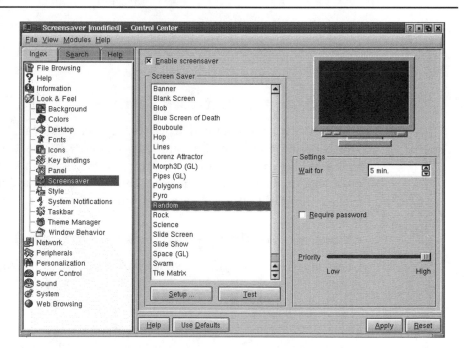

TIP   The KDE main menu includes a Lock Screen option that requires your Linux password to restore the screen. To use this option when you step away from your computer, choose Lock Screen from the main menu.

Many additional interface settings can be configured using the dialog boxes in the Windows section of the Control Center. These options are more advanced and will be of interest to only a few users. They include the following:

- Setting fonts for different categories of desktop items, titles, and menus

- Selecting between different types of desktop icons

- Altering keyboard shortcuts for various functions on the desktop and within individual windows

- Configuring the type and styles of icons and menus

- Adjusting notification events for various actions within the KDE system, for the KDE window manager, as well as for instant messages

- Locating the Taskbar of active applications

- Setting the baseline theme for everything on your desktop

- Adjusting the focus behavior of your windows based on different mouse actions

Understanding Network Settings

The Network section of the KDE Control Center includes LAN Browsing and Talk configuration. LAN Browsing uses the new KDE LAN Information Server tool, also known as LISa, to set up Samba connections. Talk configuration settings are related to the Unix talk daemon, which is a command-line-based predecessor to the current instant-messaging programs.

Choosing Hardware Settings (Peripherals)

Generally, you can't configure your hardware through the KDE Control Center. However, there are a few exceptions related to some basic hardware.

In the Peripherals section, you can set up information about your keyboard and mouse:

- The Keyboard subsection defines the auto-repeat setting and the volume of keyboard clicking (this depends on your hardware itself, of course).

- The Mouse subsection defines whether you're using your mouse with your right or left hand and how quickly you like to have the mouse pointer move around the screen.

Personalization Settings

In the Personalization section, there are a number of ways to configure KDE 2.1.1 for your personal needs, including more keyboard and mouse behavioral characteristics, language and dialect, e-mail defaults, encryption, and passwords:

- Accessibility allows you to change the system bell to a visible flash, to adjust keyboard settings, and to set up the keyboard to move the cursor.

- Country & Language settings allow you to set up the language and dialect used by KDE for local numbering systems, currency, and time.

NOTE If you want to set up a language other than U.S. English and did not install that language during installation of Red Hat Linux 7.1, you can install the appropriate RPM from the Publisher's Edition Installation CD-ROM included with this book. For example, before you can set up Ukranian, you need to install the `kde-i18n-Ukrainian-2.1.1-2.noarch.rpm` package using the previously discussed `rpm -i` command.

- Crypto settings allow you to set up the encryption/decryption schemes to be used.

- Email settings allow you to set up ID, server, and e-mail client information.

- Keyboard Layout allows customization of a large number of national keyboards available and supported by the X Windows system, including languages such as Brazilian Portuguese and Russian.

- News Ticker is a new feature for KDE 2.1. It allows you to customize sites to search periodically for headlines. The current list of news sites that may be able to work with News Ticker is located at `http://www.webreference.com/services/news/`.

- Passwords lets you set up how passwords are shown on your display. If you select the Remember Password option, KDE stores the superuser password for KDE utilities that require the root password for a specified amount of time.

Laptop Power Control

Running Linux on laptop computers requires power control to maximize the battery life. The Power Control section includes utilities to manage power consumption and measure power or battery supply levels. Specifically, it includes the following subsections:

- The Battery Monitor subsection allows you to add icons to the Panel that measure remaining power levels for any batteries currently installed on your computer. It assumes that the advanced power-management daemon is currently installed.

- The Energy subsection configures timers that can place your monitor in Standby, Suspend, or Off mode.

- The Laptop Power Control subsection can put your laptop computer (not just the monitor) into a Standby or Suspend state. The actual effect depends on the specific laptop in question.

NOTE   Before you can set Laptop Power Control settings, you need to modify the permissions on Advanced Power Management. As the root user, run the `chmod u+s /usr/bin/apm` command.

- Low Battery Critical and Low Battery Warning send messages as configured, based on a specified number of remaining minutes of battery power. This is most accurate with Lithium-ion batteries, which discharge power at a steadier rate than other types of computer batteries.

Sound Control

There are several ways to configure sound in KDE. The Sound section in the KDE Control Center contains four subsections:

- Midi allows you to configure the instrument device drivers used, such as various versions of Sound Blaster, to create sound on your computer, assuming more than one are available.

- Mixer lets you increase the detected sophistication of your sound card(s). If your sound cards have special capabilities, increase the number of probed mixers and devices per mixer.

- Sound Server drives the resources given to your sound card. For example, full duplex operation allows sound to travel through your microphone and speaker(s) simultaneously.

- The System Bell settings drive the volume, pitch, and duration of the bell that rings when you have a system bell event.

System Events

The System section allows you to configure or review a number of basic parameters in the following five subsections:

- Boot Manager provides a graphical front end to configure the Linux Loader (LILO), which allows you to set up the different operating systems and kernels that have been installed on your computer. When you reboot, LILO allows you to select and boot the operating system of your choice.

- Date & Time allows you to modify the date, time, or time zone specified for your computer.

- KDE System Control allows you to review some of the settings associated with your computer's hardware.

- Login Manager works with settings previously described for changing the KDE login screen.

- Session Manager sets defaults for requiring confirmation when you log out and restoring previous sessions when you log in.

Web Browsing

The Web Browsing section allows you to configure Web communications through cookies, proxies, and different types of browsers. Specifically, you can configure items in the following subsections:

- Cookies allows you to configure the information exchanged between your browser and different Web sites. You can customize this by domain.

- Enhanced Browsing allows you to configure various keywords for different Web sites; this applies only to Konqueror as a browser.

- Konqueror settings let you control the appearance of Web pages, including the use of Java.

- Netscape Plugins lists the plug-in modules associated with various file types.

- Proxies allows you to connect to the Internet or other Web networks through a proxy server computer.

- User Agent lets you control how your browser is seen by the Web servers you use.

- Windows Shares allows you to set up the local computer as a Samba client in a Microsoft Windows network.

Updating Menus and the Desktop

In addition to the configuration options provided by the Control Center, you can update your KDE environment by changing the menus, the desktop icons, and the Panel.

In order to update any of these items, you first need to create a KDE Link file to describe the item that you want to add to KDE. The section "Creating KDE Link Files" in this chapter describes how to graphically create a KDE Link file.

Once you have a KDE Link file that represents a device or application, you can drag the icon for that file from the directory where you created it and drop it in several places to configure KDE:

- Drop the KDE Link file icon on the Panel to add the icon for that application or device to the Panel. (Right-click any Panel icon to rearrange or delete it from the Panel.)

- Drop the KDE Link file icon on the Autostart folder on your desktop to make that application launch automatically each time you start KDE.

- Drop the KDE Link file icon on your KDE desktop to have instant access to that device or application by clicking the icon at any time.

TIP   When you drop an icon on another folder, notice a small menu that allows you to copy, move, or link the file into the location. For KDE Link files, Copy is often the best choice so that you still have a copy of the file in the original location should you wish to place it somewhere else as well.

- Finally, you can drag-and-drop a KDE Link file to one of the directories that define the KDE menus. The application defined by the KDE Link file will then be part of the KDE menus. Log in as root, and then you can place a new KDE Link file in the directory /usr/share/applnk to change the main KDE menu for all users. Alternatively, you can drop the file into one of the /usr/share/applnk subdirectories to place the item in a submenu.

Using the KDE Utilities

KDE includes a number of standard utilities that you can use to view text and graphics, manage your projects, and administer your Linux system. This section describes just a few of the most popular utilities.

Viewing Text and Graphics

KDE includes text editors, image viewers, and an image-editing tool (similar to a paintbrush program). You can access the standard text editor, KEdit, by choosing Editors ➢ Text Editor on the main menu. You can also access the advanced text editor, KWrite, by choosing Editors ➢ Advanced Editor on the main menu.

Similarly, you can access several image viewers, including the KView graphics viewer (aka Image Viewer), KDE Pixmap2Bitmap, and Xpaint, from the Graphics submenu. Likewise, you can access The GIMP as an image-editing tool from the same Graphics submenu.

When you right-click an appropriate file in Konqueror, you can use these applications to open the file. For example, when you right-click a text file, click Open With from the pop-up menu. You can then choose from all applications configured to open text files, as shown in Figure 11.18.

If you want another choice, click Other. This opens the Open With dialog box, which allows you to choose an application from those shown in the KDE main menu.

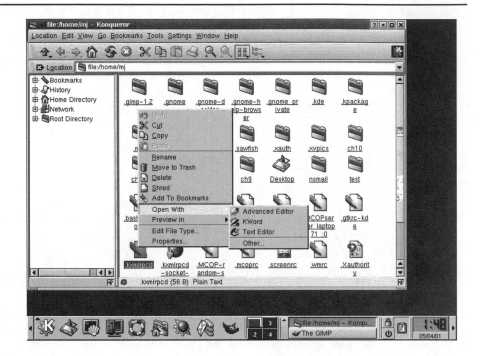

Managing Your Time

Linux doesn't have a native copy of Microsoft Outlook or Project, but KDE does
include a few tools to manage your time as you work.

KDE includes a time manager called KOrganizer, which includes an event calendar, prioritized to-do lists, scheduling, and so forth. You can access this tool by
choosing Applications ➤ Organizer on the main menu.

Figure 11.19 contains the main KOrganizer screen. From this screen, you can
move to different days, add to your to-do list, and schedule events based on different priorities.

In addition to KOrganizer, KDE includes a time tracker, which enables you to
start and stop a clock to track how much time you spend on various projects that
you work on. This tool is available by choosing Utilities ➤ Personal Time Tracker.

FIGURE 11.19:

The KOrganizer program includes a calendar, a to-do list, and various scheduling tools.

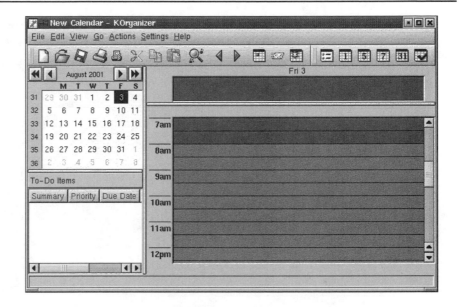

KDE also includes a simple Address Book utility. Use this program to record contact information and notes about friends or colleagues whom you need to reach while working at your computer. The Address Book records several phone numbers, fax numbers, and numerous e-mail addresses for each person. To start the Address Book, choose Utilities ➢ Address Book.

KDE Office Suite

With the release of KDE 2.0 came the first official release of the KOffice suite, which includes a number of sophisticated applications, similar to Microsoft Office, Sun Star Office, or the Applix AnywareOffice suites. KOffice includes five basic tools that you can access by choosing Office from the KDE main menu:

- KWord is a FrameMaker-style word processor that can also import Microsoft Word files.

- KSpread, shown in Figure 11.20, is the KOffice spreadsheet application that can import Microsoft Excel files as well as data files in comma-separated format (CSV).

- KPresenter is the KOffice presentation application that can import Microsoft PowerPoint files.

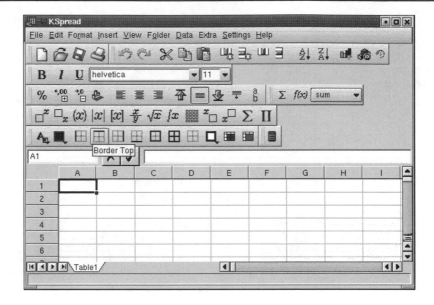

- KChart allows you to create charts and graphs.

- KIllustrator is a vector-drawing program suitable for computer-aided design.

You can integrate these applications together in the KOffice Workspace, which allows you to start any of these applications in one program window. Having all of your KOffice applications in one place also makes it easier to share data between applications.

Other available tools include Krayon, the KOffice image-manipulation program; Kugar, the report generator; Katabase, the associated database program; KFormula for formula manipulation; and Kivio for flow charts. As of this writing, Krayon and Kugar will be released with the next version of KOffice sometime in 2001.

Administering Your Linux System

KDE continues to add new system-administration tools at a furious pace. Some of the most useful at this point allow you to manage your RPM packages, users and groups on your system, processes running on your system, and the System V initialization scripts of Linux.

Many of these utilities are available on the Utilities and System sections of the main menu.

You'll still need to work with some text-configuration files for most Linux administration tasks, but using tools like KPackage makes it much easier to complete most tasks. To start KPackage, choose System ➤ Package Manager. The main KPackage window appears and reads all the RPM package information for your system (see Figure 11.21).

FIGURE 11.21:

The main KPackage window lists all your installed RPM packages by category.

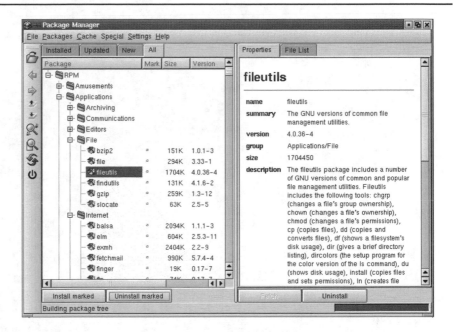

From this window, you can review installed packages, search for individual packages and files on your system, or install new RPM packages.

Looking Ahead

Now that you are more familiar with the variety of graphical Linux desktops, it's time to move on to more complex configurations of the X Windows environment.

Chapter 12, "Advanced X Windows Configuration," takes a look at how to go about configuring X Windows and the window or desktop manager of your choice to meet your personal needs and tastes. These tasks will include configuring the XFree86 server for special situations as well as the X Windows start-up sequence.

CHAPTER

TWELVE

12

Advanced X Windows Configuration

■ The *XF86Config* File

■ The X Windows Start-Up Sequence

■ X Resources

As you have already seen in this part of the book, the X Windows environment provides a degree of flexibility and customizability not commonly found in many GUI-based operating systems. Of course, with this degree of flexibility comes some degree of complexity: To fully utilize the X Windows flexibility, you must use sometimes-complex configuration methods.

This chapter describes in detail the main components of X Windows and how they can be customized. It starts with an XFree86 version 4 XF86Config file, which tells the X server how to behave. This file specifies everything from the type of video card and monitor in use (including the desired resolution and color depth) to the input devices (mouse and keyboard) being used.

Once the X server is fully configured the way you like it, you will probably want to control how X Windows starts: what programs launch at start-up, what actions take place before X Windows loads, and how the window manager gets launched. In addition, the X resources database provides a mechanism through which it is possible to control settings such as the colors and fonts used in windows and the behavior of windows in response to certain actions. These settings (and others) can be specified either globally or on a per-application basis.

The *XF86Config* File

The configuration of XFree86 is in the file XF86Config. This file usually can be found at /etc/XF86Config or /etc/X11/XF86Config, depending on your distribution. Red Hat Linux 7.1 places the file in /etc/X11. Alternatively, you can start with a generic configuration file, such as the /usr/X11R6/lib/X11/XF86Config.eg file.

If you don't know where your installation of XFree86 has placed this file, use the locate command to find it:

```
# locate XF86Config
```

The XF86Config file contains information pertinent to the operation of the X server, including keyboard definitions, mouse specifications, and monitor information. This file is generated by XFree86 configuration applications such as Xconfigurator and xf86config.

Sometimes though, fine-tuning your X Windows environment can be achieved only by directly editing the XF86Config file with your favorite text editor.

NOTE   As of this writing, the XFree86 version 4 server does not include drivers for as many graphics cards as XFree86 version 3. Therefore, many configurations include both an XF86Config and an XF86Config-4 file. If you have both files in your /etc/X11 directory, the following instructions apply to your /etc/X11/XF86Config-4 file.

The XF86Config file is broken down into several sections. Not all of these sections are required for a working GUI. And with the release of XFree86 version 4, the order of these sections is no longer important.

Files   This section specifies where XFree86 can find its supplementary files, such as fonts, loadable modules, and the color table.

ServerFlags   This section is used to enable and disable X server features, such as how to handle certain key sequences.

Module   This section specifies run-time loadable modules loaded during X server startup. These include font rasterizer modules. In most cases, you already have a working X server and the standard fonts are sufficient, so you may not even have a Module section in your XF86Config file.

InputDevice   This section specifies input devices, including keyboards and mice. Not required if there are Keyboard and Pointer sections.

Keyboard   This section specifies the keyboard protocol that controls how the key map is defined and other keyboard features, such as the repeat rate. Not required if there is an InputDevice section for the keyboard. Can work with XFree86 version 4.

Pointer   This section indicates the type of mouse being used, the device port occupied by the mouse, and the button behavior of the mouse. Not required if there is an InputDevice section for the keyboard. Can work with XFree86 version 4.

VideoAdaptor   This section is supposed to support video as a "primitive," in other words, a video adapter that is a component of some larger system. Not used as of this writing.

Monitor   This section defines the specifications of your monitor. May incorporate information in the Modes section.

Device   This section defines available graphic devices (display adapters).

Modes   This section defines the refresh rate and the resolution capabilities of your monitor. May be incorporated into the Monitor section.

Screen   This section links monitors to video adapters. It also defines the behavior of available X servers, such as the generic SVGA server, vendor-specific servers, and the monochrome server. May include multiple Display subsections, which correspond to alternate resolutions and color depths.

ServerLayout   This section links screens to specific input devices, namely keyboards and mice.

DRI   This section addresses any special settings you might have for the Direct Rendering Interface (DRI), which is more common for graphics-intensive workstations. DRI configuration is beyond the scope of this book. For more information, refer to the following Web site: http://www.xfree86 .org/current/DRI.html.

Vendor   This section will be used for vendor-specific settings. Not used as of this writing.

Files

The Files section is used to specify where certain critical files are located on your system. The following is a sample Files section without the comments:

NOTE   In the XF86Config file, comments start with a hash mark (#) and continue to the end of the line. XFree86 ignores all the content contained in comments.

```
Section "Files"

    RgbPath  "/usr/X11R6/lib/X11/rgb"

    FontPath "/usr/X11R6/lib/X11/fonts/local/"
    FontPath "/usr/X11R6/lib/X11/fonts/misc/"
    FontPath "/usr/X11R6/lib/X11/fonts/75dpi/:unscaled"
    FontPath "/usr/X11R6/lib/X11/fonts/100dpi/:unscaled"
```

```
FontPath "/usr/X11R6/lib/X11/fonts/Type1/"
FontPath "/usr/X11R6/lib/X11/fonts/Speedo/"
FontPath "/usr/X11R6/lib/X11/fonts/75dpi/"
FontPath "/usr/X11R6/lib/X11/fonts/100dpi/"

#  ModulePath     "/usr/X11R6/lib/modules"

EndSection
```

There are several basic rules to note here that apply to the other six sections as well:

- Each section starts with a Section line.

- Each section ends with an EndSection line.

- On the Section line, the name of the section is specified in double quotes (in this case, Section "Files").

There are three commonly used directives in this section, described in Table 12.1.

TABLE 12.1: *Files* Directives

Directive	Effect
RgbPath	This directive specifies the name of the RGB (red-green-blue) database without the .txt or .db extension. The RGB file specifies the amount of red, green, and blue associated with other named colors. Generally, the default value can be left untouched unless you move or change the name of your RGB database (which is not a good idea, anyway, because several applications make use of the database and expect to find it in its normal location).
FontPath	This directive is used as many times as needed to specify where X Windows can find the installed X fonts on your system. Both scalable fonts and bitmap fonts can be indicated (the bitmap fonts, which can't be scaled, have :unscaled appended to the end of the directory). If you add new font directories to your system, you should add a FontPath directive for them here.
ModulePath	This directive is used on operating systems, such as Linux, that support dynamically loaded modules. This directive indicates where to look for modules. With most versions of XFree86, this directive won't appear or will be commented out as in our example. The default path for modules is /usr/X11R6/lib/modules, and you need to use this directive only if you need to change this value.

Other font modules are available in the /usr/X11R6/lib/modules/fonts directory.

ServerFlags

The ServerFlags section allows you to enable and disable some features of your X server. An example ServerFlags section, without comments, appears as follows:

```
Section "ServerFlags"

#  Option   "NoTrapSignals"

#  Option   "DontZap"

#  Option   "DontZoom"

#  Option   "DisableVidModeExtension"

#  Option   "AllowNonLocalXvidtune"

#  Option   "DisableModInDev"

#  Option   "AllowNonLocalModInDev"

#  Option   "AllowMouseOpenFail"

#  Option   "blank time"     "10"
#  Option   "standby time"   "20"
#  Option   "suspend time"   "30"
#  Option   "off time"       "60"

#  Option   "EstimateSizesAggresively"  "0"

#  Option   "NoPM" "false"

#  Option   "Xinerama" "true"

EndSection
```

Uncomment any of these directives that you want to activate; leave them commented (the usual default state) if you don't want them activated. Any options specified here are superseded by options in the ServerLayout section.

The directives in this example have the effects described in Table 12.2.

TABLE 12.2:   *ServerFlags* Directives

Directive	Effect
NoTrapSignals	This directive is used for debugging. When a signal indicating an error is received, the server performs a core dump that dumps the contents of its section of memory to a file on the disk. This can cause instability in your system but is invaluable when debugging problems, particularly with beta and test versions of different X servers. Unless you are troubleshooting or testing an X server, you are best advised to leave this directive commented.
DontZap	Normally, the key combination Ctrl+Alt+Backspace causes X Windows to abort and returns you to the console. With this directive enabled, Ctrl+Alt+Backspace will be ignored and the key combination will be passed on to the current application for processing. You should uncomment this line only in those rare instances when you are running an application that needs to use this key combination to function properly.
DontZoom	Normally, the key combination Ctrl+Alt+Keypad Plus cycles through available configured screen resolutions for your X server, increasing the resolution each time. Ctrl+Alt+Keypad Minus is similarly used to decrease the resolution. If these key combinations are needed for other purposes by an application, uncomment this line to have X Windows ignore these key combinations and pass them on to your application.
DisableVidModeExtension	This directive prevents tuning of your video display with the xvidtune client. (Xvidtune isn't discussed in this book; documentation for this program can be found by typing the command **man xvidtune** in an open **xterm** window.) There is no need to uncomment this entry, and you can leave it commented out by default.
AllowNonLocalXvidtune	Related to the previous directive, this directive allows non-local (in other words, out on the network somewhere) xvidtune clients to access your X Windows system. For security reasons, it is best to leave this directive disabled.
DisableModInDev	By enabling this directive, it becomes impossible to change keyboard and mouse settings dynamically while X Windows is running.

Continued on next page

TABLE 12.2 CONTINUED: *ServerFlags* Directives

Directive	Effect
`AllowNonLocalModInDev`	Uncommenting this directive allows nonlocal computers to alter your keyboard and mouse settings. It is unwise to enable this directive unless you need to.
`AllowMouseOpenFail`	Allows the X server to start even if you don't have a working `Pointer` (mouse).
`"blank time"  "10"`	If there is no activity on your computer for the specified period (10 minutes, in this case), a screen saver is activated. The exact action depends on the specifications of your monitor.
`"standby time"  "20"`	If there is no activity on your computer for the specified period (20 minutes, in this case), your monitor goes into standby mode. The exact action depends on the specifications of your monitor.
`"suspend time"  "30"`	If there is no activity on your computer for the specified period (30 minutes, in this case), your monitor goes into suspend mode. The exact action depends on the specifications of your monitor.
`"off time"  "60"`	If there is no activity on your computer for the specified period (60 minutes, in this case), your monitor goes into off mode. The exact action depends on the specifications of your monitor.
`EstimateSizesAggresively`	If you have BIOS problems detecting second video adapters, setting this variable to *2* may help. As of this writing, documentation is sketchy on this variable.
`NoPM "false"`	Disables Power Management.
`Xinerama "true"`	Precursor for multiple monitors, each with a separate graphics card.

Module

The `Module` section specifies server and font extensions over and above basic parameters. No modules are required for a working graphical user interface. An example `Module` section, without comments, appears as follows:

```
Section "Module"
```

```
#  Load "dbe"

#  SubSection "extmod"

#    Option "omit XFree86-DGA"

#  EndSubSection

#  Load "type1"

#  Load "freetype"

EndSection
```

Uncomment any of these directives that you want to activate; leave them commented (the usual default state) if you don't want them activated. The directives in this example have the effects described in Table 12.3.

TABLE 12.3: *Module* Directives

Directive	Effect
Load "dbe"	Loads Double Buffer Extensions, which allows consecutive images to be loaded into different buffers.
Option "omit XFree86-DGA"	Disables the Direct Graphics Access extension.
Load "type1"	Loads the PostScript type1 font module.
Load "freetype"	Loads the named TrueType clone.

Other extension modules are available in the /usr/X11R6/lib/modules /extensions directory.

InputDevice — Keyboard

The InputDevice sections specify pointers (mice) and keyboards. While InputDevice is the default for XFree86 version 4, the legacy Keyboard and Pointer modules can still be used as well. Normally, there are two InputDevice sections: one each for a keyboard and a pointing device.

As you might expect, one InputDevice section specifies information pertinent to the functioning of your keyboard, including the keyboard type and protocol. While this section is no longer used by default, it is still recognized by XFree86 version 4. Even though Red Hat Linux 7.1 uses XFree86 version 4, the Keyboard and Pointer sections (not InputDevice) are part of the default Red Hat Linux 7.1 XF86Config configuration file. A typical InputDevice section, without comments, is shown here:

```
Section "InputDevice"
#  Option   "Protocol"     "Xqueue"

#  Identifier   "Keyboard1"
#  Driver       "keyboard"

#  Option   "AutoRepeat"   "500 5"

#  Option   "XkbDisable"

#  Option   "Xleds"        "1 2 3"

#  Option   "LeftAlt"      "Meta"
#  Option   "RightAlt"     "ModeShift"
#  Option   "RightCtl"     "Control"
#  Option   "ScrollLock"   "Compose"
#  Option   "XkbDisable"
#  Option   "XkbModel"     "pc101"
#  Option   "XkbModel"     "pc102"
#  Option   "XkbModel"     "pc104"
#  Option   "XkbModel"     "pc105"
#  Option   "XkbModel"     "pc106"
#  Option   "XkbModel"     "microsoft"

#  Option   "XkbLayout"    "us"
#  Option   "XkbLayout"    "de"
#  Option   "XkbVariant"   "nodeadkeys"
#  Option   "XkbOptions"   "ctrl:swapcaps"

#  Option   "XkbRules"     "xfree86"
#  Option   "XkbKeymap"    "xfree86(us)"

EndSection
```

This looks like a complicated section, but, as Table 12.4 describes, it is actually quite simple.

TABLE 12.4: *Keyboard* Directives

Directive	Effect
"Protocol" "Xqueue"	The Xqueue protocol is used for various Sun Solaris servers (SRV3, SRV4). If this line is missing, XFree86 defaults to Standard, which works for almost all other systems.
Identifier, Driver	Names assigned by the administrator to the keyboard and keyboard driver.
AutoRepeat	This directive is used to specify how long to wait while a key is pressed down before auto-repeat should start and how often the key should be repeated. All values are in milliseconds. In the previous example, AutoRepeat 500 5 indicates that auto-repeat should start after a key has been held down for 500 milliseconds (half a second) and then the key should repeat every 5 milliseconds.
Xleds	This directive specifies which keyboard LEDs, such as Num Lock and Caps Lock, can be controlled by the user using the xset command.
LeftAlt, RightAlt, RightCtl, and ScrollLock	X Windows originally ran on Unix workstations that had keyboards distinctly different from the standard PC keyboard. These keyboards included special keys such as Meta, ModeShift, Compose, and ModeLock. If you find that you need these keys for Unix or other applications, then uncomment these directives.
XkbDisable	If this line is uncommented, then an extension to X Windows called XKB is disabled. When XKB is enabled (the directive is commented out), XKB determines the keyboard mapping using a series of directives, generally for older X servers.
XkbModel	This directive is used when XKB is enabled to specify the keyboard model. Standard U.S. keyboards are pc101. The U.S. "Windows" keyboard is pc104. The Microsoft Natural keyboard is microsoft. Most European keyboards are pc102 or pc105. The standard Japanese keyboard is pc106.
XkbLayout	This directive is used when XKB is enabled to specify which keyboard layout to use. It's most common when there is more than one language for a keyboard model; for example, de, for deutsch, corresponds to a German-language keyboard.

Continued on next page

TABLE 12.4 CONTINUED: *Keyboard* Directives

Directive	Effect
XkbOptions	This directive can be used when XKB is enabled to swap the position of your Caps Lock and Ctrl keys. To do this, set the directive to the value `ctrl:swapcaps`.
XkbRules	Basic ruleset for keyboard layout. Required to use the XFree86 server.
XkbKeymap	This directive is used when XKB is enabled to load a keyboard mapping definition.

> **TIP**
>
> If you are setting up a non-English keyboard, help is available in the HOWTO documents at `http://www.linuxdoc.org`. There are a number of language-specific HOWTOs that can help you configure keyboards for the specified languages.

InputDevice — Pointer

The second InputDevice section deals with mouse-related configuration. As discussed earlier, you can set up an InputDevice or a Pointer section for mouse-related configuration under XFree86 version 4. The default Red Hat Linux 7.1 XF86Config file includes a Pointer section to configure a mouse. In this section, you set such information as the type of mouse you have, the port the mouse is connected to, and the behavior associated with different mouse buttons.

```
Section "InputDevice"

#  Identifier  "Mouse1"
#  Driver      "mouse"

#  Option  "Protocol"  "PS/2"
#  Option  "Protocol"  "Xqueue"
#  Option  "Device"    "/dev/mouse"
```

```
#  Option   "BaudRate"     "9600"
#  Option   "SampleRate"   "150"

#  Option   "Emulate3Buttons"
#  Option   "Emulate3Timeout"      "50"

#  Option   "ChordMiddle"

EndSection
```

Let's take these entries line by line in Table 12.5.

TABLE 12.5: *Pointer* Directives

Directive	Effect
Identifier, Driver	Names assigned by the administrator to the mouse and pointing device driver.
Protocol	This directive specifies the protocol used by your mouse. Typical options include **Microsoft**, **Logitech**, **MouseSystems**, **Bus-Mouse**, **PS/2**, and **Auto** (for certain Plug-and-Play mice that Linux can recognize).
Device	This directive is used to specify which device port your mouse is connected to. If you configured your mouse correctly when you installed your distribution, the device **/dev/mouse** is linked to your mouse and you can use this. Otherwise, specify **/dev/psaux** for the PS/2 mouse port, **Xqueue** for Solaris systems, **/dev/ttyS0** for COM1 in DOS and Windows, and **/dev/ttyS1** for COM2 in DOS and Windows. Other options are available for pointing devices such as trackballs and touchscreens.
BaudRate	This directive is used for only a few older Logitech-brand mice. Check your mouse's documentation.
SampleRate	This directive is used for only a few older Logitech-brand mice. Check your mouse's documentation.
Emulate3Buttons	This directive should be used for a two-button mouse. When uncommented, clicking the left and right mouse buttons at the same time will emulate the middle mouse button on a three-button mouse. Because X Windows relies on the presence of three mouse buttons, it is a good idea to enable this for a two-button mouse.

Continued on next page

TABLE 12.5 CONTINUED: *Pointer* Directives

Directive	Effect
Emulate3Timeout	This directive is used to specify how close in time the two mouse buttons must be clicked to be considered a simultaneous click; this value is relevant only when **Emulate3Buttons** is enabled. By default, the time is set to 50ms. If you find it hard to get the mouse buttons to click together, lengthen the time by assigning a higher value. This directive assumes that the units are in milliseconds, and you should specify only the numeric value, not the units. In other words, **Emulate3Timeout 100** is valid while **Emulate3Timeout 100 ms** is not.
ChordMiddle	This directive is used to enable the middle button on some three-button Logitech mice. If you have a Logitech mouse and your middle button is not working, try enabling this directive.

For more information on configuring other types of mice, including USB and scroll or wheel mice, see Chapter 7, "Installing and Configuring X Windows."

Monitor

So far, the configuration directives you have seen have mostly been self-explanatory and not difficult to use. For every monitor that you attach to your computer, you need a separate Monitor section. Consider the following sample Monitor section:

```
Section "Monitor"

Identifier   "monitor"
VendorName   "LG"
ModelName    "StudioWorks"

HorizSync    30-70
VertRefresh  50-160

End Section
```

Table 12.6 describes the various directives for the Monitor section.

TABLE 12.6: *Monitor* Directives

Directive	Explanation
Identifier	This directive identifies with a user-assigned name the specifications for the monitor; this is used in other parts of the **XF86Config** file to refer to the monitor.
VendorName	This directive identifies the vendor of the monitor being defined. This value has no effect on the operation of XFree86, so it is best to assign a meaningful value that will help you identify the definition at a later date.
ModelName	This directive identifies the model of the monitor being defined. This value has no effect on the operation of XFree86, so it is best to assign a meaningful value that will help you identify the definition at a later date.
HorizSync	This directive specifies the horizontal sync range in kHz for your monitor. You may either specify a range as shown in the example or provide discrete values in a list with ranges of values separated by commas (e.g., 15-25, 30-50). It is essential that you consult your monitor's documentation and provide the correct values for your monitor. If you enter the incorrect values here, you have the potential to destroy or damage your monitor.
VertRefresh	This directive specifies the vertical refresh rates in Hz supported by your monitor. You may either specify a range as shown in the example or provide discrete values in a list with values separated by commas (e.g., 40-50, 80-100). It is essential that you consult your monitor's documentation and provide the correct values for your monitor. If you enter the incorrect values here, you have the potential to destroy or damage your monitor.

Modes

For every monitor that you attach to your computer, you need a separate Modes section. Consider the following sample Modes section:

```
Section "Modes"

Identifier "Modes[0]"
Modeline "640x480" 46.02 640 656 760 832 480 490 498 522
Modeline "800x600" 71.91 800 808 928 1000 600 612 622 632
Modeline "1024x768" 117.53 1024 1088 1208 1360 768 783 796 829
Modeline "1600x1200" 200 1600 1616 1968 2080 1200 1200 1212 1253

EndSection
```

These Modelines specify possible modes for your monitor. Modes combine a resolution with a refresh, a dot clock, and timings to determine how to display to the monitor. The X server deletes any incompatible modes found in the XF86Config file when it tries to load them. However, getting the information correct for these lines is difficult. Generally, it is best to let your XFree86 configuration software create these lines for you and not to alter them.

TIP

If you have multiple monitors, it is best to incorporate **Modes** information into the corresponding **Monitor** sections, to avoid confusion.

Table 12.7 describes the function of each number in the first Modeline, from left to right.

TABLE 12.7: Modeline Items

Item	Explanation
640x480	Screen resolution in pixels
.46.02	Pixel clock, in mHz
640	Horizontal pixels displayed
656	Horizontal Sync start
760	Horizontal Sync end
832	Horizontal Sync total
480	Vertical pixels displayed
490	Vertical Sync start
498	Vertical Sync end
522	Vertical Sync total

Another way to express the first Modeline

```
Modeline "640x480" 46.02 640 656 760 832 480 490 498 522
```

is as follows:

```
Mode "640x480"
    DotClock     46.02
    HTimings     640 656 760 832
    VTimings     480 490 498 522
EndMode
```

Device

The XF86Config file generally can contain multiple Device sections, to allow for multiple graphics adapters or video cards. The Device sections describe the video cards that can be used by the X server. Usually the server can fill in most of this information, but it is wise to check the result in your XF86Config file. Because this information includes some highly technical specifications about your video hardware, you should let your XFree86 configuration software handle this section unless you really need to make these changes yourself.

A Device section is active only if referenced by a Screen section.

Let's look at two example Device sections:

```
Section "Device"
    Identifier   "Generic VGA"

    VendorName   "Unknown"
    BoardName    "Unknown"
    Chipset      "generic"

#   VideoRam     256

#   Clocks       25.2 28.3
#   BusID        "PCI:1:0:0"
EndSection

Section "Device"

    Identifier   "MGA Millennium I"
    Driver       "mga"
    Option       "hw cursor" "off"
    BusID        "PCI:0:10:0"

EndSection
```

Table 12.8 describes the basic directives used in the Device section.

TABLE 12.8: *Device* Directives

Directive	Effect
Identifier	As in the Monitor section, this directive provides a name that can be used elsewhere in the XF86Config file to identify the video card.
VendorName	This directive doesn't affect the operation of the X server but helps you identify the hardware later.
BoardName	This directive also doesn't affect operation but is an aid in identifying the device definition.
Chipset	This directive identifies your video chipset. If XFree86 doesn't support your hardware, then the generic chipset will be used.
VideoRam	This directive specifies the amount of video memory available, in kilobytes. If you don't provide this information, the server will attempt to ascertain it directly from the video card.
Clocks	This directive specifies the clock settings for your video hardware. Don't edit this line by hand, but rather let your configuration software set it.
ClockChip	This directive specifies the clock chip being used by your video hardware, if it has one. If it does, there is no need to specify a Clocks line, since the clock chip will provide all the information.
Driver	This directive identifies the name of the driver for this particular device.
Option	Some drivers can be further configured. In the example shown, "hw cursor" "off" addresses a particular problem of some graphics cards with cursor placement in the X Window.
BusID	Specifies the location of a PCI or AGP graphics card. Significant when there is more than one graphics card in use.

Screen

The Screen section is used to bring together the information contained in your Monitor and Device sections. You can have multiple Screen sections.

The following is an example section for one Screen:

```
Section "Screen"
    Identifier "Screen L"
    Device     "MGA Millenium I"
    Monitor    "monitor"
    Subsection "Display"
        Depth       24
        Modes       "1024x768"
        ViewPort    0 0
    EndSubsection
    Subsection "Display"
        Depth       32
        Modes       "800x600"
        ViewPort    0 0
    EndSubsection
EndSection
```

The Screen section connects a chosen X server with a device and a monitor and then defines the accessible display modes (combinations of resolution and color depth). Table 12.9 describes the four main directives used in the Screen section:

TABLE 12.9: *Screen* Directives

Directive	Effect
Identifier	This directive specifies a unique name for the given **Screen**. If you need a **ServerLayout** section, you'll need to use this **Identifier**.
Device	This directive specifies the name of a **Device** identifier. Make sure this corresponds to the appropriate identifier in your **Device** section.
Monitor	This directive specifies the name of a **Monitor** identifier. Make sure this corresponds to the appropriate identifier in your **Monitor** section.
DefaultDepth	This directive specifies the color depth used when a **Depth** directive in the **Display** section is not specified.

Display

In addition to these directives, a subsection called Display is also used in the Screen section. You can use multiple Display subsections to specify available video modes.

Let's analyze the first subsection from the previous example:

```
Subsection "Display"
    Depth        24
    Modes        "1024x768"
    ViewPort 0 0
EndSubsection
```

This `Display` subsection specifies four directives, as described in Table 12.10.

TABLE 12.10:   *Display* Subsection Directives

Directive	Effect
Depth	This directive specifies the color depth of the display in the number of bits per pixel. For instance, 8-bit allows 2^8 or 256 colors, 16-bit allows 2^{16} or 65,536 colors, and 24-bit allows 2^{24} or 16.7 million colors.
Modes	This directive specifies the resolution of the display. Common resolutions are 1024×768, 800×600, and 640×480.
ViewPort	This directive specifies the size of a possible virtual desktop. For instance, your 640×480 screen may be a window in a larger 1024×768 virtual display. As your mouse reaches the edge of the screen, the display will scroll to the edge of the virtual display. The **ViewPort** directive specifies the horizontal and vertical dimensions of the vertical desktop in pixels, but the values are separated by a space rather than by an *x*. The entry here, **ViewPort 0 0**, indicates that there is no virtual desktop.
Virtual	This directive specifies a screen size larger than the **Modes** directive, or the resolution of the display. If you have this directive, you can use your mouse or pointing device to move around this larger virtual area.

ServerLayout

A `ServerLayout` section completes your configuration by binding the `Screen` and `InputDevice` sections. As discussed earlier, the `Screen` section already brings together information from the `Monitor` and `Device` sections. A `ServerLayout` section is not required for a "standard" configuration; if it isn't a part of your `XF86Config` file, the active `Screen` and the keyboard and mouse `InputDevice`(s) are used.

The following is an example ServerLayout section:

```
Section "ServerLayout"
#  Identifier  "Configuration 1"

#  Screen       "Sony Setup"
#  Screen       "Samsung Setup" RightOf "Sony Setup"

#  InputDevice  "Mouse1"     "CorePointer"
#  InputDevice  "Keyboard1"  "CoreKeyboard"

EndSection
```

This ServerLayout section specifies three directives, as described in Table 12.11.

TABLE 12.11: *ServerLayout* Section Directives

Directive	Effect
Identifier	Specifies a unique name for this **ServerLayout**.
Screen	Identifies the **Screen** sections that you want to use. In this case, there should be two **Screen** sections, and their **Identifier** directives should be "**Sony Setup**" and "**Samsung Setup**".
InputDevice	Identifies the **InputDevice** sections that you want to use. In this case, there should be two **InputDevice** sections, and their **Identifier** directives are "**Mouse1**" and "**Keyboard1**".

The X Windows Start-Up Sequence

In addition to configuring your XFree86 server to provide the optimal display quality, you may want to configure the way in which your X Windows environment starts up. The two main files that allow each user to control their X Windows start-up sequence are .xinitrc and .Xclients. Both of these files sit in the user's home directory. When installed, they override system default files, which in Red Hat Linux 7.1 are /etc/X11/xinit/xinitrc and /etc/X11/xinit/Xclients.

The *.xinitrc* File

Xinit is a special program that is used to start the X server and an initial client program, usually a window manager. By default, startx first checks for the existence of the .xinitrc file in the user's home directory and runs xinit based on this file. If the user's .xinitrc file is not found, the system-wide xinitrc file (/etc/X11/xinit/xinitrc in Red Hat Linux 7.1) is used by xinit. If neither of these is found, xinit will open a single xterm window after launching the X server.

The xinitrc or .xinitrc file is an executable shell script. You will learn about shells in Chapter 16, "Understanding the Shell." Accordingly, this chapter doesn't go into the details of the shell or shell scripts; rather, it will quickly look at the default xinitrc file from Red Hat Linux 7.1 to see what it does. (The lines are numbered to help make the discussion easier. The line numbers are not part of the actual file.)

```
1:      #!/bin/sh
2:      # (c) 1999, 2000 Red Hat, Inc.

3:      userresources=$HOME/.Xresources
4:      usermodmap=$HOME/.Xmodmap
5:      userxkbmap=$HOME/.Xkbmap

6:      sysresources=/etc/X11/Xresources
7:      sysmodmap=/etc/X11/Xmodmap
8:      sysxkbmap=/etc/X11/Xkbmap

9:      # merge in defaults
10:     if [ -f "$sysresources" ]; then
11:         xrdb -merge "$sysresources"
12:     fi

13:     if [ -f "$userresources" ]; then
14:         xrdb -merge "$userresources"
15:     fi

16:     # merge in keymaps
17:     if [ -f "$sysxkbmap" ]; then
18:         setxkbmap `cat "$sysxkbmap"`
19:         XKB_IN_USE=yes
20:     fi
```

```
21:    if [ -f "$userxkbmap" ]; then
22:        setxkbmap `cat "$userxkbmap"`
23:        XKB_IN_USE=yes
24:    fi

25:    if [ -z "$XKB_IN_USE" -a ! -L /etc/X11/X ]; then
26:        if grep '^exec.*/Xsun' /etc/X11/X > /dev/null 2>&1 && [ -f
                /etc/X11/XF86Config ]; then
27:        xkbsymbols=`sed -n -e 's/^[      ]*XkbSymbols
                ]*"\(.*\)".*$/\1/p' /etc/X11/XF86Config`
28:        if [ -n "$xkbsymbols" ]; then
29:            setxkbmap -symbols "$xkbsymbols"
30:            XKB_IN_USE=yes
31:        fi
32:        fi
33:    fi

34:    # xkb and xmodmap don't play nice together
35:    if [ -z "$XKB_IN_USE" ]; then
36:        if [ -f "$sysmodmap" ]; then
37:            xmodmap "$sysmodmap"
38:        fi

39:        if [ -f "$usermodmap" ]; then
40:            xmodmap "$usermodmap"
41:        fi
42:    fi

43:    unset XKB_IN_USE

44:    # The user may have their own clients they want to run. If they
45:    # don't, fall back to system defaults.

46:    # run all system xinitrc shell scripts.
47:    for i in /etc/X11/xinit/xinitrc.d/* ; do
48:        if [ -x "$I" ]; then
49:    . "$i"
50:        fi
51:    done

52:    if [ -f $HOME/.Xclients ]; then
53:        exec $HOME/.Xclients
```

```
54:   elif [ -f /etc/X11/xinit/Xclients ]; then
55:       exec /etc/X11/xinit/Xclients
56:   else
57:           # failsafe settings. Although we should never get here
58:           # (we provide fallbacks in Xclients as well) it can't
                 hurt.
59:           xclock -geometry 100x100-5+5 &
60:           xterm -geometry 80x50-50+150 &
61:           if [ -f /usr/bin/netscape -a -f /usr/doc/HTML/index.html
      ]; then
62:                   netscape /usr/doc/HTML/index.html &
63:           fi
64:           if [ -f /usr/X11R6/bin/fvwm2 ]; then
65:                   exec fvwm2
66:           else
67:                   exec twm
68:           fi
69:   fi
```

The following steps take place:

1. Lines 3 to 8: The locations of files needed throughout the script are set. Note that these are variables that are used in following lines.

NOTE The System X Resources file, shown in line 6 as `sysresources`, is located in the /etc/X11/xdm/Xresources file in Red Hat Linux 7.1. If you want to set this file as common default X Windows preferences, as discussed later, change line 6 to reflect the actual location of file.

2. Lines 10 to 12: If a global Xresources file exists, apply it. (See the next section for a discussion of X resources.)

3. Lines 13 to 15: If the user has a .Xresources file in their home directory, apply it by merging it together with current settings.

4. Lines 17 to 20: If a global X Window keyboard map file exists, apply the rules in the file.

5. Lines 21 to 24: If the user has an X Window keyboard map file in their home directory, apply it.

6. Lines 25 to 33: These lines probably don't apply to you unless you are using a Sun X server for your system.

7. Lines 34 to 43: If there are conflicts between the user- or system-defined X Window keyboard map file, set the keyboard definition to that file.

8. Lines 47 to 51: These lines execute all shell scripts located in the /etc/X11/ xinit/xinitrc.d/ directory.

9. Lines 52 to 69: This is where you actually start running the first clients after the X server starts. First, the script checks whether the user has a .Xclients file. If this file exists, this file is executed to launch any clients specified in the file. If this file doesn't exist, the script checks for the existence of the global Xclients file and, if it exists, executes it. Finally, if neither file exists, some default programs are launched, including xclock, an xterm window, a Web browser, and, if available, either the fvwm2 or twm window manager.

The *.Xclients* File

As you noticed in the discussion of the xinitrc file, the user can override the global Xclients file with a .Xclients file in their home directory. In either case, in the Red Hat environment, xinit ends up calling one of these files to launch the initial clients after the X server has started.

Like xinitrc, this file is a shell script and follows all the pertinent rules for shell scripts. To understand the types of functions that Xclients can be used for, this section will look at the default Xclients file that shipped with Red Hat Linux 7.1 (line numbers have again been added):

```
1:  #!/bin/bash
2:  # (c) 1999, 2000 Red Hat, Inc.

3:  # check to see if the user has a preferred desktop
4:  PREFERRED=
5:  if [ -f /etc/sysconfig/desktop ]; then
6:      if [ -n "`grep -i GNOME /etc/sysconfig/desktop`" ]; then
7:    PREFERRED=gnome-session
8:      elif [ -n "`grep -i KDE /etc/sysconfig/desktop`" ]; then
9:    PREFERRED=startkde
10:      elif [ -n "`grep -i AnotherLevel /etc/sysconfig/desktop`" ];
    then
11:    PREFERRED=AnotherLevel
12:      fi
13:  fi
```

```
14:  if [ -n "$PREFERRED" -a "$PREFERRED" != "AnotherLevel" ] && \
15:    which $PREFERRED >/dev/null 2>&1; then
16:      PREFERRED=`which $PREFERRED`
17:      exec $PREFERRED
18:  fi

19:  # now if we can reach here, either they want AnotherLevel or there
20:  # was no desktop file present and the PREFERRED variable is not
     set.

21:  if [ -z "$PREFERRED" ]; then

22:      GSESSION=gnome-session
23:      STARTKDE=startkde

24:      # by default, we run GNOME.
25:      if which $GSESSION >/dev/null 2>&1; then
26:        exec `which $GSESSION`
27:      fi

28:      # if GNOME isn't installed, try KDE.
29:      if which $STARTKDE >/dev/null 2>&1; then
30:        exec `which $STARTKDE`
31:      fi
32:  fi

33:  # Last, try AnotherLevel

34:  # these files are left sitting around by TheNextLevel.
35:  rm -f $HOME/Xrootenv.0
36:  rm -f /tmp/fvwmrc* 2>/dev/null

37:  # First thing - check the user preferences
38:  if [ -f $HOME/.wm_style ] ; then
39:      WMSTYLE=`cat $HOME/.wm_style |tr A-Z a-z`
40:      case "$WMSTYLE" in
41:    afterstep)
42:    exec /usr/X11R6/bin/RunWM -AfterStep
43:      ;;
44:    windowmaker|wmaker)
45:    exec /usr/X11R6/bin/RunWM -WindowMaker
46:      ;;
```

```
47:    fvwm95|fvwm|fvwm2)
48:    exec /usr/X11R6/bin/RunWM -Fvwm95
49:    ;;
50:    mwm|lesstif)
51:    exec /usr/X11R6/bin/RunWM -FvwmMWM
52:    ;;
53:      esac
54:  fi

55:  # Argh! Nothing good is installed. Fall back to fvwm2 (win95-
     style) or twm
56:  /usr/X11R6/bin/RunWM -Fvwm95 || {
57:      # gosh, neither fvwm95 nor fvwm2 is available;
58:      # fall back to failsafe settings
59:      xclock -geometry 100x100-5+5 &
60:      xterm -geometry 80x50-50+150 &
61:      if [ -f /usr/bin/netscape -a -f /usr/share/doc/HTML/index.html ];
     then
62:    netscape /usr/share/doc/HTML/index.html &
63:      fi
64:      if [ -f /usr/X11R6/bin/fvwm ]; then
65:    exec fvwm
66:      else
67:    exec twm
68:      fi
69:  }
```

Let's break down the steps of the Xclients file:

1. Lines 4 to 13: Set a preferred desktop. As discussed in Chapter 11, "Using KDE," you can set your preferred desktop using the PREFERRED variable in line 4. If PREFERRED is not set to any desktop, lines 5–12 check the default desktop shown in the /etc/sysconfig/desktop file against GNOME, KDE, and AnotherLevel.

2. Lines 14 to 18: Make sure the PREFERRED desktop is not AnotherLevel.

3. Lines 21 to 32: If there is no PREFERRED desktop, try GNOME. If GNOME is not installed, then try KDE.

4. Lines 35 to 36: Perform some cleanup by removing temporary files that may have been left behind the last time X Windows was run.

5. Lines 38 to 54: Check for a style for the AnotherLevel window manager, and launch AnotherLevel with that style and exit the script.

6. Lines 56 to 69: Attempt to launch AnotherLevel with the Fvwm95 style. If that fails, launch xclock, xterm, and Netscape and then attempt to launch fvwm if it exists. If it doesn't exist, launch twm instead.

If you want to add your own clients to be run every time X Windows is started, you can copy the global Xclients file to your own .Xclients file in your home directory (Chapter 14, "Working with Files," describes file copying) and then edit it. The key to this process is to add the commands for the programs you want to run before the sections where the different window managers might be launched. The reason for this is that the exec keyword used to launch the different window managers causes the script to stop running as soon as the window manager is launched.

X Resources

The X resources database provides applications with preferences information that controls such attributes as colors and fonts, among others. X resources can be used by most X Windows applications to control almost every aspect of behavior that is controlled by command-line flags. With the X resources database, you can specify more suitable defaults than those that are standard for the application.

How X Resources Work

Every time you start the X Window, different settings are loaded into the X resources database. Default settings are taken from various files listed earlier in the discussion on xinitrc. They are modified by any .Xdefaults file in your home directory. But these settings are detailed and complex.

In order for this all to work, application-related information needs to be categorized so that only the appropriate applications are affected by X resources entries. This is done by grouping applications into classes. Most applications have their own classes; the documentation for the application specifies the class name. For example, xload belongs to the XLoad class and xterm belongs to the XTerm class. Where a number of similar applications exist, they often are part of the same class (oclock and xclock belong to the Clock class).

NOTE

Observe how capital letters are used to differentiate between applications and classes. For example, `xterm` is the standard X Window terminal application, and `XTerm` is the class to which it belongs.

For each class, a standard set of resources allows you to specify such features as foreground and background colors (`foreground` and `background`), window size and placement (`geometry`), and default font (`font`). In addition, there are resource classes that group related resources. For instance, the `Foreground` class includes the `foreground` resource plus any additional foreground-related resources the application may have. Generally, though, you will not need to pay attention to individual resources and will work only with resource classes.

Setting X Resources with *.Xdefaults*

Setting X resources involves loading entries into the X resources database. These entries take the form

```
<ApplicationClass>|<applicationName>*<ResourceClass>|<resourceName> :
<value>
```

In Linux man pages and other documentation, the vertical bar (or pipe character: |) is often used to represent "or." Therefore, in the example above, you can use either `<ApplicationClass>` or `<applicationName>` for the first entry, and `<ResourceClass>` or `<resourceName>` for the second entry.

These values are generally placed into the `.Xdefaults` file for user-specific resources. Let's look at a sample `.Xdefaults` file:

```
XTerm*background: Black
XTerm*foreground: Wheat
XTerm*cursorColor: Orchid
XTerm*reverseVideo: false
XTerm*scrollBar: true
XTerm*reverseWrap: true
XTerm*font: fixed
XTerm*fullCursor: true
XTerm*scrollTtyOutput: off
XTerm*scrollKey: on
XTerm*titleBar: false
```

```
xclock*Geometry: 100x100+100+100
xclock*Foreground: purple
xclock*Background: mauve
```

This `.Xdefaults` file sets X resources for both the `XTerm` class of applications and for the `xclock` application. For the `XTerm` class, you find resources setting the colors, the window properties (such as the presence of a scroll bar), and more. For `xclock`, you see color and geometry being set. The values being taken by these resources match the values that would have been provided to command-line flags such as `-fg` and `-geometry` where applicable.

The Database of X Resources

The sources for X resources are the `app-defaults` files. There are `app-defaults` files for most X and KDE applications. You can look up these files for settings that you can use in your own `.Xdefaults` file. In Red Hat Linux 7.1, these files are located in the `/usr/X11R6/lib/X11/app-defaults/` directory. KDE applications have their own special `app-defaults` files in the `/usr/share/apps/kdisplay/app-defaults/` directory.

Using the *xrdb* Command to Load X Resources

Normally, the `.Xdefaults` file is loaded when X Windows starts in the `.xinitrc` file. However, new values can be loaded into the database while X Windows is running by using the `xrdb` command. This is particularly useful for experimenting with values until you find just the combination you want.

If you've set up experimental settings in a file named `experiment`, you can load these settings temporarily into the database with the command

```
$ xrdb -merge experiment
```

Once you're satisfied with any changes, you can incorporate them into future X Window sessions by adding the settings from your `experiment` file to `.Xdefaults`.

Looking Ahead

This chapter wrapped up the focus on X Windows. You will now move on to an area that is essential to gaining complete mastery of Linux: the command-line environment.

Chapter 13, "Introducing Linux Commands," and Chapter 14, "Working with Files," describe the basics of Linux commands. They discuss basic commands as well as how to work with files and directories on your disk drive(s). In later chapters, you will learn about the shell, which provides a powerful command-line environment in which to work, and you will learn how to use graphical Red Hat control tools to ease some of the more obscure aspects of Linux system configuration.

PART IV

Mastering the Essentials

CHAPTER
THIRTEEN

13

Introducing Linux Commands

- What Is a Linux Command?

- Executing a Linux Command

- Common Linux Commands

In this chapter, you start your exploration of the Unix command-line environment. The command-line environment is where the heart and power of Linux lies. You have seen that X Windows provides quick and easy access to graphical applications that can make most users productive immediately. What is missing, though, is the ability to fully manipulate and work with your Linux system. This ability emerges when you begin to experiment with commands.

Here you'll learn to use some of the more common commands such as ls, find, and grep. Since these commands are found in most distributions, Unix users should immediately know what these and similar commands can do and what power they can provide in the hands of a knowledgeable user.

NOTE   For this chapter, you need to be using a Linux command line. You can get a command line in two ways: When your system boots, log in to one of the Linux virtual consoles, or, from X Windows, launch a terminal window such as **xterm**, the GNOME terminal, or KDE's Konsole.

What Is a Linux Command?

Before looking at specific commands, you need to understand exactly what is meant by the term *command*.

Users coming from the DOS environment are probably familiar with the concept of commands that encompass core features of the operating system, such as DIR, COPY, and ATTRIB. These commands provided the basis on which more complicated actions could be built and from which sophisticated batch files could be written.

But in the DOS world, as in the world of many operating systems, the number of available commands is limited and generally static: Users don't add new commands.

In the Unix world, and by extension in Linux, the concept is different. A *command* is any executable file. That is, a command consists of any file that is designed to be run, as opposed to files containing data or configuration information. This means that any executable file added to a system becomes a new command on the system.

Executing a Linux Command

From the discussions of launching X Windows applications, you probably already have a sense of how to execute a command. From the command prompt, simply type the name of a command:

```
$ command
```

Or, if the command is not on your path, you type the complete path and name of the command, such as

```
$ /usr/bin/command
```

Using Paths in Linux

The concept of *paths* needs a little bit of explanation. Every user, when they log in, has a default path. Find your default path with the following command:

```
$ echo $PATH
```

The output should look something like this:

```
$ /usr/local/bin:/bin:/usr/bin:/usr/X11R6/bin:/home/mj/bin
```

The $PATH is a list of directories separated by colons. If a command is typed without a path, then all the directories in the default path are checked, in order, for the file associated with the command. In the above example, if there is a command named guess in both the /usr/local/bin and the /home/mj/bin directories, the one in the /usr/local/bin is executed. If you'd rather use the guess command in the /home/mj/bin directory, then you'll need to use the full path, i.e., type the /home/mj/bin/guess command. Chapter 16, "Understanding the Shell," provides complete details of how to set your path.

More complex ways of executing commands, including linking multiple commands together (called *piping*), are discussed in Chapter 16.

Common Linux Commands

The number of Linux commands that are available in a common Linux distribution such as Red Hat Linux 7.1 is quite large. But on a day-to-day basis, even an advanced user will take advantage of only a small selection of these commands.

This section presents some of the most frequently used Linux commands. These commands cover a range of tasks, from moving around your directories to finding out what is running on your system to finding that file you thought was lost. The commands discussed in this section are:

- su
- pwd, cd, and ls
- more and less
- find, locate, whereis, and grep
- tar and gzip
- man

su

The su command is one of the most basic and is useful in many different tasks. The su command is generally used to switch between different users. Consider an example: You are logged in as user1 and you need to switch to user2 to perform some work and then switch back to working as user1.

You could log out, log in as user2, do the work, log out again, and then log back in as user1, but that seems a bit time-consuming. Alternatively, you could log in as user1 in one virtual console and as user2 in another and switch back and forth. The problem with this is that you need to work with—and switch between—different screens.

A third option is to use the su command. If you are logged in as user1 and want to become user2, you simply type

```
$ su user2
```

and you are prompted for user2's password:

```
$ su user2
password:
```

When you finish working, enter the exit command to return to user1:

```
$ exit
```

Put together, a complete session should look like this:

```
[user1@localhost user1]$ su user2
```

```
Password:
[user2@localhost user1]$ some commands
[user2@localhost user1]$ exit
exit
[user1@localhost user1]$
```

A common use of the su command is when you need to become the root user, called the *superuser*, to perform many administrative tasks, including creating and managing user accounts, performing network configuration, and configuring printers.

If you issue the su command with no username, you are prompted for the root password and, once this is provided, you are switched to working as the root user:

```
[user1@localhost user1]$ su
Password:
[root@localhost user1]#
```

If you are logged in as the root user, you can use su to become any user on the system without a password (hence the importance of keeping your root password safe from prying eyes). This is particularly useful for the system administrator, who may need to become different users to debug problems but won't necessarily know other users' passwords. Note in the following example how using su to become user1 doesn't cause a password prompt to display when the root user issues the command:

```
[root@localhost /root]# su user1
[user1@localhost /root]$
```

The su command offers many other powerful features often used in advanced system administration tasks. You can learn about these from the su man page. See the section on the man command later in this chapter to learn how to read the su man page.

pwd, cd, and ls

When put together, the pwd, cd, and ls commands provide the basic tools you need to work with your directories and files.

The pwd command (which stands for present working directory) is the most basic of the three commands. By typing the command and pressing Enter, you will be informed of which directory you are currently in:

```
$ pwd
/home/armand
```

In this case, the pwd command returns /home/armand as its answer. This tells you that you are in the home directory of the user armand.

The cd command does more than simply look at the current state of things: It actually changes the state. The cd command allows you to change your current directory to any accessible directory on the system.

For instance, consider the previous example where the current directory is /home/armand. Using the cd command, you could change to a subdirectory of the armand home directory called wordfiles:

```
$ cd wordfiles
$ pwd
/home/armand/wordfiles
```

Typing the pwd command after you change directories confirms that you ended up where you wanted to be.

Similarly, you could change to the system's temporary directory, /tmp, with the following command:

```
$ cd /tmp
$ pwd
/tmp
```

The difference is in the forward slash (/) in front of the directory. The first command, cd wordfiles, did not have a forward slash, so the change is relative to the current directory. If you ran the same command from Mike's home directory, /home/mike, you would end up in the /home/mike/wordfiles directory.

The second command, cd /tmp, has a forward slash. You could run this second command from any directory and always end up in the same location.

Finally, the ls command can be used to view the contents of the current directory. For instance, if you use the ls command to view the contents of the armand home directory, the result looks like this:

```
$ ls
2341ch11a.doc                     dead.letter   scmp-jpc.bak
DISKCOPY.COM                      foo           svgalib-1.2.11-4.i386.rpm
DRWEBDEM.IMG                      foo.html      test.txt
Xconfigurator-3.26-1.i386.rpm     mail          wabi
Xrootenv                          nsmail        xserver-1.1-1.i386.rpm
armand                            scmp-jpc
```

Notice how the files or directory names are displayed in multiple columns and the width of the columns is determined by the width of the longest name.

In addition to listing the contents of the current directory, it is possible to list the contents of any accessible directory on the system. For instance, to list the contents of the directory /usr, you enter the command ls /usr:

```
$ ls /usr
X11         doc               i486-linuxaout    lib        sbin
X11R6       dt                ibase             libexec    share
X386        etc               include           local      spool
bin         games             info              man        src
dict        i486-linux-libc5  interbase         openwin    tmp
```

As mentioned above, notice how the number and width of columns in the listing depends on the length of the longest name being displayed.

Of course, you probably are wondering what use a list like this really is. There is no information to tell you which names indicate files and which names indicate subdirectories or what size the files are.

This information can be determined by using an extension of the ls command: ls -l. (To understand the command's structure, refer to the complete discussion of the ls command in Chapter 14, "Working with Files.") Used in the armand home directory, ls -l produces these results:

```
$ ls -l
total 1807
-rw-r--r--   1 armand   armand      52224 Apr 24 23:00 2341ch11a.doc
-rw-r--r--   1 armand   armand      24325 May  9 16:06 DISKCOPY.COM
-rw-r--r--   1 armand   armand    1474979 May  9 16:06 DRWEBDEM.IMG
-rw-r--r--   1 armand   armand      52313 Jan 21 18:04 Xconfigurator
➥-3.26-1.i386.rpm
-rw-r--r--   1 armand   armand        396 May 19 23:09 Xrootenv
drwx------   2 armand   armand       1024 May 17 09:55 armand
-rw-------   1 armand   armand      10572 May 18 22:29 dead.letter
-rw-------   1 armand   root         1455 Apr 24 21:38 foo
-rw-r--r--   1 armand   armand       2646 May  7 07:32 foo.html
drwx------   2 armand   armand       1024 Jun  4 07:12 mail
drwx------   2 armand   armand       1024 May 17 09:56 nsmail
-rw-r--r--   1 armand   armand       4288 May 14 22:17 scmp-jpc
-rw-r--r--   1 armand   armand       4289 May 14 22:12 scmp-jpc.bak
-rw-r--r--   1 armand   armand     195341 Mar 25 17:32 svgalib-1.2.11
➥-4.i386.rpm
```

```
-rw-rw-r--    1 armand    armand          94 May 17 11:44 test.txt
drwxr-xr-x    5 armand    armand        1024 May 19 23:07 wabi
-rw-r--r--    1 armand    armand        4493 Feb  4 15:31 xserver-wrapper-
➥1.1-1.i386.rpm
```

Note that each file contains reference information. The most important pieces of information are to the immediate left of each filename: the date of last modification of the file or directory and, in the case of files, the size of the file in bytes to the left of the date (so, for instance, a 1024-byte file is a 1KB file).

At the far left of each line, you will also notice that directories are indicated by the letter d while files are generally indicated with a simple hyphen (-). For instance, scmp-jpc is a file:

```
-rw-r--r--    1 armand    armand        4288 May 14 22:17 scmp-jpc
```

While mail is a directory:

```
drwx------    2 armand    armand        1024 Jun  4 07:12 mail
```

more and *less*

The more and less commands are closely related and provide similar functionality, and the great irony is that less provides more capabilities than more.

The basic purpose of both commands is to display long files or lists of text one screen or window at a time, allowing users to page down through the text and, in some cases, move back up through the text. Both also provide capabilities to search the text being displayed.

This is useful in many instances, including when you want to look quickly at a long text file without having to open it in an editor such as xedit and to view particularly long directory listings.

more

Let's start with the more command. The more command is fairly basic, allowing users to move forward a line or a screen at a time through a large body of text as well as search that text.

For instance, if you have a large text file called textfile, you could view it a page at a time with the following command:

```
$ more textfile
```

After pressing Enter, you see the first screen of the file with the text –More–(xy%) displayed on the last line of the screen, where xy represents the percentage of the file passed on the screen. Pressing the spacebar jumps you forward a full screen length, while pressing the Enter key moves you forward one line at a time. When you reach the end of the body of text, you are returned to the command prompt.

To search forward through the file, enter a slash (/) followed by the word or phrase you want to search for and then press Enter. The display jumps forward to the first occurrence of the word or phrase being searched for and displays the occurrence near the top of the screen. You can repeat the same search by entering **n** after the first search, avoiding the need to type the same word or phrase repeatedly.

In addition to using more to view the contents of a file, you can pass along the results of another command to more using piping (a technique discussed in detail in Chapter 16).

For instance, on my system, using ls -l to view the contents of the /tmp directory produces results 237 lines long—many more lines than my largest xterm window can display. In order to be able to view the results of my ls -l command a window at a time, I need to pass the results to more:

```
$ ls -l /tmp | more
```

This command connects the ls -l command to the more command with a vertical pipe (which usually corresponds to the double-vertical dashes above the backslash on most U.S. keyboards). The use of the pipe character is the source of the term *piping*. The result of this piping is that more is used to display the results of the ls -l command, which means you can move down a screen or line at a time or search the results, just as you did earlier with the contents of a file.

NOTE   Complete directions for using more are found in the more man page. Using a man page is discussed later in this chapter in the section on the man command.

---

less

For all intents and purposes, the less command is a vastly improved version of the more command. In addition to the basic functions described previously (moving forward a screen or line at a time and searching), the following are some of the other actions that can be performed on a body of text:

- Jumping directly to a line

- Jumping directly to the beginning or end of the file
- Moving backward through a file
- Searching backward through a file

To jump directly to a line in a file, type the line number followed by the letter **g**. If you don't specify a line number and simply enter **g**, you will be jumped to the first line in the file. Entering the uppercase **G** works in much the same way except that without a line number specified, entering **G** jumps you to the last line of the body of text.

It is easy to move backward through a file using less. The up arrow moves up one line of text at a time and the down arrow moves down one line at a time. You can use Ctrl+B to jump backward one screen at a time.

Finally, entering a slash (/) followed by a word or phrase and then pressing Enter will search forward through the text being displayed, and entering a question mark (?) followed by a word or phrase and then pressing Enter will search backward through the text.

As with the more command, you can look at the less man page for details on all the features of the command. Using the man pages is discussed later in this chapter in the section on the man command.

find, locate, whereis, and grep

The find, locate, whereis, and grep commands are powerful tools for searching for files. This section discusses only their most basic uses because it would be easy to devote a full chapter to using these commands. If you want a full discussion of the commands, check their man pages once you learn to use the man command later in this chapter.

While all these commands are used for searching, their purposes differ: find is used to search for files by any number of criteria, including name or date of creation, while grep is used to search the contents of files.

find

If you used computers prior to buying this book, then you have probably faced the situation where you know you have created a file but can't remember where you put it. The `find` command is the Unix answer to this dilemma.

The command can be used to search for files by name, date of creation or modification, owner (usually the user who created the file), size of the file, and even type of the file. This section describes the most frequent use: searching for files by name.

The basic structure of the `find` command is

```
$ find starting-directory parameters actions
```

The starting directory specifies where to begin searching. For instance, specifying /home means only subdirectories of /home will be searched (in other words, only the user's home directories will be searched), while specifying / means everything will be searched.

The parameters are where you specify the criteria by which to search. In this case, you use the command `switch and argument -name filename` to specify the file you are searching for.

The actions section indicates what action to take on found files. Generally, you will want to use the `-print` action, which indicates that the full name and path of the file should be displayed. Without this, the `find` command will perform the search indicated but will not display the results, which defeats the purpose.

Putting this together, if you want to search for all files named foo on your system, you could use the command

```
$ find / -name foo -print
```

In this case, the results look like this:

```
$ find / -name foo -print
/tmp/foo
/home/armand/foo
/home/tdanesh/foo
```

TIP   Notice that you attempted to search the entire system in the previous command. To do this effectively, you need to log in as the root user so that you can access all the directories on the system. If you don't, you will get `permission denied` errors every time `find` tries to search a directory for which you don't have permission.

It is also possible to search for partial filenames. For instance, if you know that the file you are looking for begins with fo, then you can use the expression fo* to indicate all files beginning with fo and ending with any combination:

```
$ find / -name 'fo*' -print
/tmp/foo
/var/lib/texmf/fonts
/usr/bin/font2c
/usr/bin/mh/folders
/usr/bin/mh/folder
/usr/bin/mh/forw
/usr/bin/formail
/usr/bin/fontexport
/usr/bin/fontimport
/usr/bin/fold
etc.
```

Notice the use of the single quotation marks around fo*. When you use the * character, it is important to place the single quotes around the entire expression. Otherwise, find will give you an error:

```
$ find / -name fo* -print -mount
find: paths must precede expression
Usage: find [path...] [expression]
```

If the results being produced by the find command are too numerous to fit in one screen, you can use piping and the more command just as you did earlier with the ls -l command:

```
$ find / -name 'fo*' -print | more
```

locate

If the find command takes too long, you may be able to use the alternative, the locate command. This command searches a database of files on your system, created nightly. It works slightly differently from the find command, since it returns every file and directory with your search string in its name. For example, the locate xauth command would give you these results:

```
$ locate xauth
/home/mj/.xauth
/home/mj/.xauth/refcount
/home/mj/.xauth/refcount/root
/home/mj/.xauth/refcount/root/testlinux
```

```
/lib/security/pam_xauth.so
/usr/X11R6/bin/mkxauth
/usr/X11R6/bin/xauth
/usr/X11R6/man/man1/mkxauth.1x.gz
/usr/X11R6/man/man1/xauth.1x.gz
/usr/share/doc/pam-0.72/txts/README.pam_xauth
/usr/share/man/man8/pam_xauth.8.gz
```

Observe how this command gives you the full path to all files and directories that include the text string "xauth," including the /home/mj/.xauth directory and the /usr/X11R6/bin/mkxauth and /usr/X11R6/bin/xauth commands.

This works a lot more quickly than the corresponding find command. The drawback is that locate works from a database file that is updated generally only once every 24 hours; therefore, the results may not reflect the current location or even the existence of a recently moved or created file.

whereis

If you're looking for a known command, you can use whereis to find the directory with the command, the source code, and the relevant man page. Unlike with find or locate, you need the exact spelling of the command. For example, the whereis fdisk command gives you the following results:

```
$ whereis fdisk
fdisk: /sbin/fdisk /usr/share/man/man8/fdisk.8.gz
```

This output specifies the location of the fdisk command (/sbin/fdisk), along with the location of its man page. Since the location of the fdisk source code is not shown, you can assume that it isn't installed.

The drawback to the whereis command is that since it looks through a specified set of directories, it may not find a new command or manual page that you just installed.

grep

Where find searches for a file by its name, type, or date, locate searches through a file database, and whereis identifies command locations, grep is used to look inside the contents of one or more files in an attempt to find the occurrence of a specific pattern of text inside the files.

Consider an example: You know that you created a text file that contains the word *radio* and stored it in your home directory. However, you have forgotten the name of the file and want to quickly check which files contain *radio*. This is where grep comes in handy.

Assuming you are in your home directory, the following command searches for the word *radio* in each file in your home directory and produces results as follows:

```
$ grep radio *
ab.txt:This is a test of searching for the word radio.
pop.txt:On another radio station, he found that
```

Notice how the grep command returns one line for each occurrence of the word *radio* in a file. The name of the file is shown followed by a colon, which is followed by the complete text of the line where the word appeared.

In general, the pattern for the grep command is

```
$ grep text-pattern file-list
```

The text pattern can be a simple word or phrase or a more complicated regular expression. (The use of regular expressions—a powerful method for searching for text patterns—with grep can be found in the grep man page.) The file list can take any form allowed by the shell. Consult Chapter 16 for a complete discussion of the types of expressions that constitute a file list.

Generally, though, you want to either check the contents of a single file, which takes the form

```
$ grep text-pattern file-name
```

or check the contents of all files in a directory using the command

```
$ grep text-pattern *
```

where the * is an expression indicating that all files in the current directory should be searched.

In its simplest form, the text pattern is a single word or part of a word containing no spaces. If you want to search for a phrase, such as "is a test," you need to enclose the text pattern in quotation marks, as in the following example:

```
$ grep "is a test" *
ab.txt:This is a test of searching for the word radio.
```

Just as it is sometimes useful to pipe the results of a command through the more or less commands, the same is true for grep. Consider the situation where you want a listing of all files in the current directory with the modification date of May 12. You can find this information by piping ls -l through a grep command:

```
$ ls -l | grep "May 12"
-rw-r--r--   1 root       root           19197 May 12 21:17 rfbprotoheader.pdf
-rw-r--r--   1 root       root          110778 May 12 21:20 rfprotoA.zip
-rw-r--r--   1 root       root           17692 May 12 23:03 svnc-0.1.tar.gz
-rw-r--r--   1 root       root           25222 May 12 19:58 vnc
➥-3.3.1_javasrc.tgz
drwxr-xr-x   2 root       root            1024 May 12 21:49 vncjava
```

Commands and Quotes

There are three different types of quotes that you can use with a command: a single quote ('), a double quote ("), and a back quote (`). The difference is in how they affect embedded commands such as date and variables such as $LOGNAME. Any pair of matched quotes sends the whole phrase to the command. For example, assume that $LOGNAME=mj and review the following commands:

```
echo Welcome $LOGNAME, the date is date
echo 'Welcome $LOGNAME, the date is date'
echo "Welcome $LOGNAME, the date is date"
echo "Welcome $LOGNAME, the date is `date`"
```

Linux may or may not run the date command or translate $LOGNAME, depending on the quotes. These commands include different combinations of quotes and result in the following:

```
Welcome mj, the date is date
Welcome $LOGNAME, the date is date
Welcome mj, the date is date
Welcome mj, the date is Mon June 14 10:45:20 EDT 2001
```

The first example has no quotes. $LOGNAME is translated as mj, but the date command is not run. The second example uses single quotes. $LOGNAME is not translated, and the date command is not run. The third example uses double quotes. While the result is the same as the first command, double quotes are useful with commands such as grep. The final example includes back quotes around date inside double quotes. As you can see, the back quotes make Linux run the subject command.

tar and *gzip*

Most users of other operating systems, including Windows 98/2000 and the Mac OS, are familiar with the concept of *compressed archives*. A compressed archive is a single file that contains one or more files in a compressed form.

Compressed archives are often used to distribute software on the Internet, as is the case with the Zip files common on the Internet. While Linux provides the unzip command to access the contents of Zip archives, in the Unix world, tar archives are generally used to distribute software. These archives are then compressed using the gzip compression program, which compresses individual files.

tar

The tar program was originally used to create system backups on tapes (or tape archives, hence the name *tar*). In its current form, it is widely used for creating archives of files for distribution.

Creating a tar archive is easy:

```
$ tar cvf tar-file-name file-list
```

This command creates a new archive specified by the filename tar-file-name (generally, tar files have a .tar extension) and then stores all the files from the file list in this archive. The file list can follow any valid expression as outlined in Chapter 16. It is important to remember that this process copies the files into the archive, so there is no danger that the original files will be deleted in the process.

Notice that the tar command is immediately followed by a series of options, in this case, cvf. Each of these options is used to control different aspects of the behavior of the tar command:

- c specifies that you are creating an archive, as opposed to viewing an existing archive or extracting files from the archive.

- v indicates that the command should be run in verbose mode, which means that each filename will be displayed as it is copied into the archive.

- f means that you are archiving to a file, as opposed to a tape drive.

For instance, if you want to archive all the .txt files in the current directory into an archive called text.tar, use the following command:

```
$ tar cvf text.tar *.txt
ab.txt
pop.txt
```

Notice how the filenames are listed as they are copied to the archive.

Sometimes you want to copy the entire contents of a directory into an archive. Luckily, tar copies all files and subdirectories in a directory into an archive if the directory is part of the file list. So, if you have a directory called vnc and you want the entire contents of that directory to be copied to a new archive called vnc.tar, you could use the command

```
$ tar cvf vnc.tar vnc
```

and get the following results:

```
$ tar cvf vnc.tar vnc
vnc/
vnc/LICENSE.TXT
vnc/README
vnc/README.vncserver
vnc/Xvnc
vnc/classes/
vnc/classes/DesCipher.class
vnc/classes/animatedMemoryImageSource.class
vnc/classes/authenticationPanel.class
vnc/classes/clipboardFrame.class
vnc/classes/optionsFrame.class
vnc/classes/rfbProto.class
vnc/classes/vncCanvas.class
vnc/classes/vncviewer.class
vnc/classes/vncviewer.jar
vnc/vncpasswd
vnc/vncserver
vnc/vncviewer
```

Notice that the first line indicates the creation of the vnc directory in the archive and then the copying of the files in that directory into the archive.

If you have an existing archive, you will generally want to either view a listing of the contents of a file or extract the contents of a file.

To view the contents of an archive, you replace the c option with a t. So, to view the list of files in the vnc.tar archive you just created, you could use the following command:

```
$ tar tvf vnc.tar
drwxr-xr-x root/root          0 2001-05-16 23:55 vnc/
-rw-r--r-- root/root      18000 2001-01-23 16:52 vnc/LICENCE.TXT
-rw-r--r-- root/root       6142 2001-01-23 16:53 vnc/README
-r--r--r-- root/root        601 2001-01-23 16:28 vnc/README.vncserver
-r-xr-xr-x root/root    1286834 2001-01-23 13:00 vnc/Xvnc
```

```
drwxr-sr-x root/root           0 2001-01-23 16:24 vnc/classes/
-r--r--r-- root/root        7143 2001-01-23 16:24 vnc/classes/DesCipher
➥.class
-r--r--r-- root/root        1329 2001-01-23 16:24 vnc/classes/
➥animatedMemoryImageSource.class
-r--r--r-- root/root        2068 2001-01-23 16:24 vnc/classes/
➥authenticationPanel.class
-r--r--r-- root/root        1761 2001-01-23 16:24 vnc/classes/
➥clipboardFrame.class
-r--r--r-- root/root        3210 2001-01-23 16:24 vnc/classes/
➥optionsFrame.class
-r--r--r-- root/root        8309 2001-01-23 16:24 vnc/classes/
➥rfbProto.class
-r--r--r-- root/root        7092 2001-01-23 16:24 vnc/classes/
➥vncCanvas.class
-r--r--r-- root/root        7100 2001-01-23 16:24 vnc/classes/
➥vncviewer.class
-r--r--r-- root/root       20564 2001-01-23 16:24 vnc/classes/
➥vncviewer.jar
-r-xr-xr-x root/root       11433 2001-01-23 13:00 vnc/vncpasswd
-r-xr-xr-x root/root       10795 2001-05-17 00:17 vnc/vncserver
-r-xr-xr-x root/root       49685 2001-01-23 13:00 vnc/vncviewer
```

Notice how the listing of files is in a complete form, similar to the way in which ls -l lists the contents of a directory.

To extract the contents of an archive into the current directory, replace the c or t with an x:

```
$ tar xvf vnc.tar
vnc/
vnc/LICENSE.TXT
vnc/README
vnc/README.vncserver
vnc/Xvnc
vnc/classes/
vnc/classes/DesCipher.class
vnc/classes/animatedMemoryImageSource.class
vnc/classes/authenticationPanel.class
vnc/classes/clipboardFrame.class
vnc/classes/optionsFrame.class
vnc/classes/rfbProto.class
vnc/classes/vncCanvas.class
vnc/classes/vncviewer.class
```

```
vnc/classes/vncviewer.jar
vnc/vncpasswd
vnc/vncserver
vnc/vncviewer
```

gzip

While tar is useful for archiving files, it doesn't perform any compression in the previous examples. Compression in Linux is generally achieved with the gzip command.

Unlike Windows Zip archives, which compress many files into a single compressed archive, gzip simply compresses individual files without compressing them into an archive.

For instance, if you have a particularly large file called test.pdf that you won't use for some time and you want to compress it to save disk space, use the gzip command:

```
$ gzip test.pdf
```

This command compresses the file and adds a .gz extension to the end of the filename, changing the name to test.pdf.gz.

Before compression, ls -l shows us that the file size is 110,778 bytes:

```
-rw-r--r--   1 root     root        110778 Jun  5 16:54 test.pdf
```

After compression, the size has dropped to 83,729 bytes:

```
-rw-r--r--   1 root     root         83729 Jun  5 16:54 test.pdf.gz
```

As with most commands described in this chapter, you can use any valid shell file expression to list more than one file. For instance,

```
$ gzip *
```

compresses all files in the current directory (but not those in subdirectories).

Uncompressing *gzip* Files   To uncompress a gzip file, you can use the gzip command with the -d option:

```
$ gzip -d test.pdf.gz
```

This uncompresses the file and removes the .gz extension, returning the file to its original uncompressed state with the name test.pdf.

An alternative command, gunzip, eliminates the need to use the -d option:

```
$ gunzip test.pdf.gz
```

Combining *gzip* and *tar* Because early versions of the tar command did not compress archives, this was typically done using gzip, as shown in the following example:

```
$ tar cvf text.tar *.txt
ab.txt
pop.txt
$ gzip text.tar
```

This produces a compressed archive called text.tar.gz.

To access the contents of this archive, uncompress the archive and then use tar:

```
$ gunzip text.tar.gz
$ tar tvf text.tar
-rw-r--r-- root/root          48 2001-06-05 16:13 ab.txt
-rw-r--r-- root/root           6 2001-06-05 16:13 pop.txt
```

Recent versions of the tar command, including those shipped with all current distributions, provide a method for directly accessing and creating gzip-compressed tar archives.

By simply adding a z option to any of the tar commands discussed earlier, you can create a compressed archive without the need for a second command. For instance,

```
$ tar czvf vnc.tar.gz vnc
vnc/
vnc/LICENSE.TXT
vnc/README
vnc/README.vncserver
vnc/Xvnc
vnc/classes/
vnc/classes/DesCipher.class
vnc/classes/animatedMemoryImageSource.class
vnc/classes/authenticationPanel.class
vnc/classes/clipboardFrame.class
vnc/classes/optionsFrame.class
vnc/classes/rfbProto.class
vnc/classes/vncCanvas.class
vnc/classes/vncviewer.class
vnc/classes/vncviewer.jar
vnc/vncpasswd
vnc/vncserver
vnc/vncviewer
```

creates a compressed version of the vnc.tar archive,

```
$ tar tzvf text.tar.gz
-rw-r--r-- root/root          48 2001-06-05 16:13 ab.txt
-rw-r--r-- root/root           6 2001-06-05 16:13 pop.txt
```

displays the contents of the compressed text.tar.gz archive, and

```
$ tar xzvf text.tar.gz
ab.txt
pop.txt
```

extracts the contents of the archive.

NOTE   Full details of the tar and gzip commands and their options can be found in the man pages for those commands.

---

man and *xman*

Throughout this chapter, you have seen references to *man pages*. These are manual pages that are provided in a standard format with most Linux software. Almost all the commands that ship with various Linux distributions include man pages.

Using the man command in its most basic form, you can read any existing man page:

```
$ man command-name
```

This displays the man page for the specified command and allows you to scroll through it and search it the same way as when you are using the less command to display text.

If the specified man page cannot be found, you get the following error:

```
$ man non-existent-man-page
No manual entry for non-existent-man-page
```

Since you already are familiar with X Windows, you have an alternative to using the man command to view man pages: the xman program.

To launch xman, use

```
$ xman &
```

or

```
$ /usr/X11R6/bin/xman &
```

This will display the initial xman window like the one in Figure 13.1.

FIGURE 13.1:

The initial *xman* window

From here, you can press the Manual Page button to display the main xman window, shown in Figure 13.2.

FIGURE 13.2:

The main *xman* window

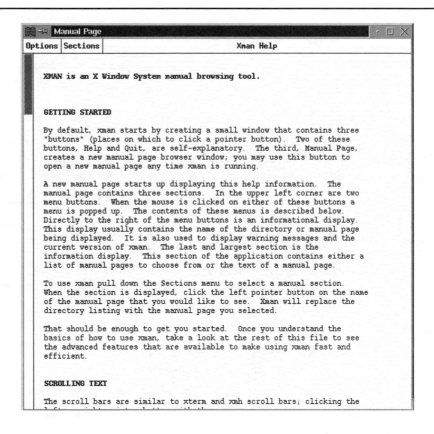

The main area of the window is used to display the text of the currently selected man page. Initially xman's help file is displayed. The window has two menus: Options and Sections.

The Options menu, shown in Figure 13.3, allows you to switch between listings of man pages (Display Directory) and the contents of the current man page (Display Manual Page), in addition to searching the contents of the current man page. The Help option displays the complete help file for xman, which provides detailed instructions on using xman. If you want to review a specific man page, select the Search option, then type the name of the command in the text box that appears.

FIGURE 13.3:

The Options menu

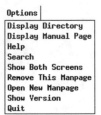

You are probably more interested in the Sections menu, shown in Figure 13.4, since this is where you begin the process of finding the man page you want to read.

FIGURE 13.4:

The Sections menu

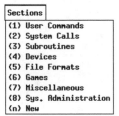

As you can see, the manual pages are divided into eight main categories, including User Commands, System Calls, and so on. Choosing one of these sections brings up a directory listing for the section like the one shown in Figure 13.5.

By double-clicking any of the command names, you can read the man page for that command.

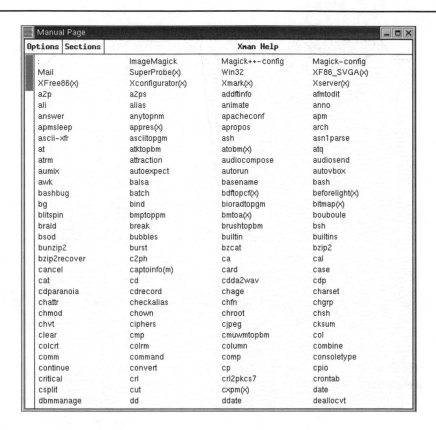

Looking Ahead

In this chapter, you've taken your first big step toward becoming a real Linux user by delving into the world of the command line.

Until now you have focused on X Windows and its capabilities, but the real heart of any Unix-like operating system lies in the command line.

In Chapter 14, "Working with Files," you will learn about the powerful commands provided by Linux for working with files and directories. You will build on the commands (such as ls) discussed in this chapter and explore creating directories and other advanced tasks.

CHAPTER
FOURTEEN

14

Working with Files

- Copying and Deleting Files

- Moving and Renaming Files

- Creating Files

- Creating Symbolic Links

- A Quick Introduction to Filename Expansion

In the last chapter, you got a glimpse of what's involved in using Linux. You saw how all commands are actually separate programs stored in separate files. You even began to learn how to manipulate files by seeing the various ways that the ls command can be used to display lists of files.

In this chapter, you are going to take a detailed look at the commands used to further manipulate files and directories, including copying, deleting, moving, renaming, and creating. This chapter wraps up with a quick look at filename expansion—that is, wildcards like the commonly used asterisks in DOS and Windows.

Copying and Deleting Files

Probably the two most common file-manipulation tasks are copying and moving files. You will regularly find yourself replicating files all over your disk drive or copying files to floppy disks, the latter for backup purposes or to "transmit" files using the cheapest of all networking methods: your feet. Similarly, the average PC user at some point will run short of disk space and will strike out in search of files to delete in order to free up precious disk space and avoid investing in a new hard drive.

Copying Files

Anyone with even brief experience using DOS or the DOS prompt in any version of Windows is probably aware that clicking, dragging, and dropping is not the only way to copy files. In fact, DOS's copy command offers additional features, such as wildcards, that can make it quicker, easier, and more powerful to use than File Manager or Windows Explorer.

Similarly, in the Linux world, the cp command (normally found at /bin/cp) is used for copying and provides a powerful tool for copy operations.

Basic Copying

Obviously, the most basic uses of the cp command are to copy a file from one place to another and to make a duplicate file in the same directory. For instance, if you want to copy a file (ThisFile) in the current directory to a second file (to be called ThisFile-Acopy) in the same directory, enter the following command:

```
$ cp ThisFile ThisFile-Acopy
```

Using ls -l to look at a directory listing of the files, you would find two files with identical sizes but different date stamps. The new file has a date stamp indicating when the copy operation took place. It is a new, separate file. Changes to ThisFile-Acopy do not affect the original ThisFile file.

Similarly, to make a copy of ThisFile in the /tmp directory (perhaps to share the file with another user), use the following command:

```
$ cp ThisFile /tmp
```

And if you want to copy ThisFile to /tmp but give the new file a different name, enter

```
$ cp ThisFile /tmp/NewFileName
```

Don't Overwrite That File

The scary thing about Linux distributions is that it is easy to accidentally overwrite a file by copying over an existing file. Consider the situation where ThisFile and NewFile both exist and you issue the command

```
$ cp ThisFile NewFile
```

Using this command, the contents of NewFile are overwritten by a copy of ThisFile and lost forever (unless you are disciplined about backing up your system).

To avoid this difficulty, you can use the -i flag of the cp command, which forces the system to confirm any file it will overwrite when copying. Then, you see a prompt like this when attempting to copy:

```
$ cp -i ThisFile NewFile
cp: overwrite `ThisFile'?
```

If you want to protect yourself, you can create an alias for the cp command. By issuing the command

```
$ alias cp='cp -i'
```

you are defining an alias so that any time you issue the cp command, you are in fact issuing the command cp -i. In this way, you are always prompted before overwriting a file while copying. As you will learn later in Chapter 16, "Understanding the Shell," you can

Continued on next page

configure the Bash shell using the `.bashrc` file to ensure that every time you log in, this alias is set. (The shell controls the command-line environment in which you work—but more about that later.)

Luckily, this alias is set by default in Red Hat Linux 7.1 when you log in as the superuser, or root. This is especially important because making a small mistake as the root user can have drastic consequences for the whole system. Using this default can help prevent major disasters.

Copying Multiple Files in One Command

One of the drawbacks of the DOS copy command is that it could copy only one file or file expression at a time. For instance, use the command

```
$ copy file /tmp
```

to copy a single file to /tmp, or enter the command

```
$ copy *.txt /tmp
```

to copy all text files in the current directory to /tmp. But if there are three separate files you want to copy, you need to use three commands; similarly, if you want to copy all text files and all executable files in the current directory, you need to use two commands.

The Linux cp command, however, makes this process a bit easier. The cp command can take more than the two arguments in the DOS version of the command. Instead, you can pass multiple arguments to the command, and the last argument is treated as the destination and all preceding files are copied to the destination.

Let's look at an example. Suppose you want to copy the files FileOne, FileTwo, and FileThree in the current directory to /tmp. Obviously, you could issue three commands:

```
$ cp FileOne /tmp
$ cp FileTwo /tmp
$ cp FileThree /tmp
```

However, you can bundle this all together into one command, making the process easier:

```
$ cp FileOne FileTwo FileThree /tmp
```

Similarly, you can add wildcards to the mix and copy large numbers of files in one command. For instance, the command

```
$ cp *.txt *.doc *.bak /tmp
```

copies all files with any of three extensions in one command.

When copying multiple files in this way, it is important to remember that the last argument must be a directory, since it is impossible to copy two or more files into a single file. If you forget to make the last argument a directory, then you will get an error message like this one:

```
cp: when copying multiple files, last argument must be a
directory. Try 'cp --help' for more information.
```

If you want to copy an entire directory and all its subdirectories, you can use the -R flag of the cp command. This command indicates that you want to recursively copy a directory. If a subdirectory called SomeDir exists in the current directory and you want to copy SomeDir in its entirety to a subdirectory in /tmp, then use the command

```
$ cp -R SomeDir /tmp
```

to create a directory /tmp/SomeDir as a copy of the SomeDir subdirectory in the current directory.

Advanced Copying

The cp command offers several advanced features that extend it beyond simple copying of files and directories. These capabilities include preserving the state of original files in their copies and alternate methods to protect existing files while copying.

Making Copies As Close to the Originals As Possible   Take a close look at the copies you make. Notice that certain characteristics of the copied files bear little resemblance to the original files. These characteristics include the file ownership, permissions, date stamps, and symbolic links. Let's consider these one by one.

When you copy a file, the resulting file is normally owned by the copier as opposed to the creator of the original file. Let's say that user1 has created a file called TheFile and put it in /tmp for user2 to copy to their home directory. If you look at the file listing, the file looks something like this:

```
-rw-r--r--  1 user1    users      16992 Apr  5 12:10 TheFile
```

After user2 copies the file with the command

```
$ cp /tmp/TheFile ~/NewFile
```

the resulting file has a new ownership, that of the copier (user2):

```
-rw-rw-r--   1 user2    users        16992 Apr  5 13:10 NewFile
```

Similarly, when a file is created in a directory, it has a set of default permissions assigned to it. When copying a file, the copy will have the permissions set to the default for the destination directory rather than retain the permissions of the original file. Notice in this example the change in permission between the original file and the new copy. The original file was only group readable but the copy is also group writable. A change has also occurred to the date of the copy, reflecting the date and time when the copy was made instead of the date stamp of the original file.

There are times, however, when you want to retain the original owner, date, and permissions of files when they are copied. Let's say, for example, that the root account is being used to copy a set of files to a removable hard disk for storage in a vault. Unlike a regular tape backup, which requires other tools, this type of backup can be done with the cp command. However, it is important that a backup like this match the original as closely as possible. Luckily, the cp command provides the -p flag, which preserves these attributes. Using the previous example, if the command used was

```
$ cp -p /tmp/TheFile
```

then the resulting file would match the original quite closely:

```
-rw-r--r--   1 user1    users        16992 Apr  5 12:10 TheFile
```

Another sticky problem in copying files is how to handle symbolic links. As you learned in the previous chapter, a symbolic link provides a pointer to a file from another location. In this way, you can pretend that a file is in more than one place at once. If you try to access the link, Linux actually accesses the file that the link points to.

Normally, when you copy a symbolic link, the resulting file is a copy of the file pointed to by the link instead of a new link to the same file. For instance, if TheFile had been a symbolic link as in this example

```
lrwxrwxrwx   1 user1    users        16992 Apr  5 12:10 TheFile
➥OtherFile
-rw-r--r--   1 user1    users            1 Apr  5 11:10 OtherFile
```

then issuing the following cp command

```
$ cp /tmp/TheFile ~/NewFile
```

results in a file that is a copy of OtherFile:

```
-rw-rw-r--   1 user2    users        16992 Apr  5 13:10 NewFile
```

But what if you want to copy the link instead of the file itself? What if you want the result to appear as follows:

```
lrwxrwxrwx  1 user2    users            2 Apr  5 13:10 NewFile
➥/tmp/OtherFile
```

Well, once again the cp command has a flag to address the situation: the -d flag, which preserves the link to the original file. Simply use the command

```
$ cp -d /tmp/TheFile ~/NewFile
```

to get the desired result.

Having said all this, it is time to put it all together. What if you want to use the cp command to create a useful backup copy of an existing directory and all its subdirectories? Using the combination of these two flags and a recursive copy, you can do this. For instance,

```
$ cp -pdR TheDirectory /backups
```

creates an exact copy of TheDirectory in the directory /backups/TheDirectory. But the cp command provides a simplified way to achieve this: the -a flag, which indicates that you want an archive of a directory. It is a quick way to indicate the three flags -pdR:

```
$ cp -a TheDirectory /backups
```

Preventing Mistakes   As you saw earlier, one way to prevent mistakes is to use the -i flag, which forces interactive prompting before overwriting occurs in the course of copying files or directories. Other methods are available to provide different degrees of protection.

One method is to use the -b or --backup flag to cause the cp command to create a backup copy of any file about to be overwritten. By default, the backup copy has the original filename with a tilde (~) after it. So, if you copy FileOne to FileTwo using the command

```
$ cp -b FileOne FileTwo
```

and FileTwo already exists, then a backup is made of the original FileTwo called FileTwo~.

It is possible to alter the way in which the cp command names the backup files with the -S flag. The -S flag allows you to change the character used in backup names from the default tilde to something else. For instance,

```
$ cp -b -S _ FileOne FileTwo
```

results in a backup filename FileTwo_.

Alternatively, you can specify one of three types of backup naming schemes with the --backup flag:

t or *numbered*   Create sequentially numbered backups. If an existing numbered backup file exists, then the new backup file created is numbered sequentially after the existing backup file; the resulting filenames look like FileTwo.~*Number*~ (for example, FileTwo.~2~ or FileTwo.~11~).

nil or *existing*   If a numbered backup file already exists, then create a numbered backup; otherwise, create a regular simple backup file.

never or *simple*   Create a simple backup file using the default tilde or alternative character indicated by the -S flag. This overwrites any previous backup with the same name.

For instance, to create a numbered backup in the example above, use the command

```
$ cp --backup=t FileOne FileTwo
```

or

```
$ cp --backup=numbered FileOne FileTwo
```

Similarly, both of the following commands create simple backup files:

```
$ cp --backup=never FileOne FileTwo
```

and

```
$ cp --backup=simple FileOne FileTwo
```

The -b switch does not work in Red Hat Linux 7.1 with these options.

NOTE   In Red Hat Linux 7.1, you can still use the -V switch to control backup naming schemes; however, you won't be able to use this switch in future releases of cp.

Alternative Flags

You may have noticed that this section covered a lot of flags for the cp command. Sometimes it is difficult to remember the flags. Fortunately, there are long forms for most of these flags that may make them easier to remember:

Short Form	Alternate Long Form
-I	--interactive
-R	--recursive
-p	--preserve
-d	--no-dereference
-a	--archive
-b	--backup
-S	--suffix

While the long forms may seem more intuitive at first, ultimately any regular Linux user will use the short forms. The long forms involve too much typing for frequent use. For instance, consider the following complex cp command:

```
$ cp -i -b -V simple -S _ -R ThisDir /tmp
```

If you use the long form of these flags, you end up with the following command:

```
$ cp --interactive --backup --version-control simple --suffix _
➥--recursive ThisDir /tmp
```

Sure, this command is more readable at first glance, but do you really want to type this simply to copy a directory?

Deleting Files

Just as it does for copying files, Linux provides a powerful command for deleting files: rm, found at /bin/rm.

In its simplest form, rm allows you to delete one or more files in the current directory. The command

```
$ rm ThisFile
```

deletes the file ThisFile in the current directory, and

```
$ rm *.txt
```

removes all files with the .txt extension in the current directory.

As with copying, it is possible to provide multiple arguments to the rm command, and all referenced files will be deleted. For instance,

```
$ rm ThisFile *.txt
```

performs the same action as the previous two commands combined.

Like the cp command, this can be extremely useful and potentially dangerous. After all, what happens if, wanting to delete a backup of a document, someone accidentally issues the command

```
$ rm thesis.doc
```

instead of

```
$ rm thesis.bak
```

This is a potential nightmare, and as unlikely as it sounds, it happens all the time, resulting in unnecessary work and headaches.

For this reason, it is wise to use the same -i flag for the rm command because it provides the prompts to avoid disastrous mistakes:

```
$ rm -i thesis.doc
rm: remove `thesis.doc'?
```

You can also create an alias for rm, making this the default behavior:

```
$ alias rm='rm-i'
```

Deleting Whole Directories

Users frequently want to delete entire directories. Consider, for instance, a directory created after unzipping a software archive downloaded from the Internet. After you have finished installing and testing the software, you will probably want to delete the entire directory. This is done using the -r flag. For instance, to remove a directory called TempInstall, you would use

```
$ rm -r TempInstall
```

Of course, if you have been following along in this chapter, you probably have an alias for the rm command, forcing it to prompt you for every deletion. This can become very tedious for big directories:

```
$ rm -r TempInstall
rm: descend directory `tempInstall'? y
rm: remove `TempInstall/File1'? y
rm: remove `TempInstall/File2'? y
...
rm: remove directory `TempInstall'? y
```

Just imagine if there were hundreds of files. Responding to prompts for each one would be impractical. In these instances, when you are absolutely certain that you want to delete a whole directory, you should use the -f flag of the rm command. This flag forces deletions, even when you have already indicated interactive operation with the -i flag in your alias:

```
$ rm -rf TempInstall
```

A Reminder...

Care needs to be taken when using the –f flag. While it is powerful, it can be extremely dangerous.

In Red Hat Linux 7.1, the superuser's account is configured so that the default alias for the rm command is rm -i. This is critically important, because even a seemingly small mistake can be disastrous. If the alias weren't being used, just consider what would happen if, in attempting to delete the /tmp directory, a space made its way in between the / and tmp:

```
$ rm -r / tmp
```

This would actually delete all the files and directories on the disk. This is why the alias for rm -i is so essential.

Similarly, using the –f flag requires great care when working as the superuser and underscores the need to limit your use of the superuser account to only essential tasks. After all,

```
$ rm -rf / tmp
```

would be just as dangerous if you did have the right alias in place.

Moving and Renaming Files

Moving files and renaming files are closely linked, and therefore they are treated together in this section. Unlike the DOS/Windows and Macintosh worlds, where renaming and moving are distinct actions, in the Linux environment renaming a file is just a special case of moving a file.

The Basic Move Operation

Let's start by considering the basic move operation:

```
$ mv FileOne /tmp
```

This command moves the file called FileOne from the current directory to the /tmp directory.

Moving and Renaming

Similarly, it is possible to move the file to the /tmp directory and change the name of the file using the following command:

```
$ mv FileOne /tmp/NewFileName
```

By using this concept, you can rename a file. Simply move a file from its existing name to a new name in the same directory:

```
$ mv FileOne NewFileName
```

See how moving and renaming are one and the same?

Moving More Than Just One File

As when copying files, it is possible to move multiple files in one step because the mv command can accept more than two arguments and the last argument serves as the destination directory of the move. (As with copying, you can't move multiple files to a file; the last argument must be a directory.) Consider the situation where you want to move all files in the current directory with the extension .bak, .tmp, or .old to /tmp. Use the command

```
$ mv *.bak *.tmp *.old /tmp
```

This simple command moves all the specified files to the destination (/tmp) in one operation.

It is also possible to move entire directories with the mv command without using any special flags. If there is a subdirectory named TheDir in the current directory and you want to move it so it becomes a subdirectory under /tmp, you would use the mv command just as you did earlier for files:

```
$ mv TheDir/ /tmp
```

Similarly, if you want TheDir to become a subdirectory under the directory called NewDir, you can use the following command:

```
$ mv TheDir/ /NewDir
```

> **NOTE**
> As with cp and rm, it is wise to set an alias for mv to mv -i to ensure that you don't accidentally overwrite files when moving. You can do this with $ alias mv=`mv -i`. In Red Hat Linux 7.1, this is set by default for the cp, rm, and mv commands for the superuser account.

Creating Files

You have already learned several ways to create files. After all, you create files when you copy files. You create files when you move files. Other obvious ways of creating files include creating a word processing document, saving an e-mail attachment, or making a screen capture.

However, there are cases where it is necessary to create a new file, even if the file is empty and has a length of zero. The most obvious instance of this would be in cases where a script needs to create a file to indicate a special state. The best example of this is a programming technique called *file locking*. If a script opens a file to make changes, it also creates a special file called a *lock file* that indicates to other programs and scripts that the current file is opened for editing and is therefore unavailable to be changed. Once the script closes the file, it deletes the lock file to make the file once again available.

In order to be able to create these lock files quickly and efficiently without exacting excessive disk space requirements, you need a shortcut method to signify an empty file of a specified name. This is achieved with the touch command. This command creates a file. For instance,

```
$ touch NewFile
```

creates a new file of zero length with the name NewFile:

```
-rw-rw-r--   1 armand    armand          0 Apr  6 21:06 NewFile
```

Another common use of the touch command is to change the modification date stamp of an existing file. Many programs depend on the date stamp of files they are working with to determine what action to take. The touch command lets you change the modification date of a file without opening and editing the file.

Creating Directories

One type of special file in Linux is the directory. A directory is just a special file that contains other files. You can set permissions for a directory that allow or prevent other users from seeing what is in that directory. Directories are as simple as the top-level root directory (/) or your personal home directory (e.g., /home/mj).

But you can't create a directory with the same commands as you might use to create a file. The key commands are mkdir and rmdir. If you wanted to create a directory of documents in your home directory, you might run the following command:

```
$ mkdir documents
```

But this would not work if you were not already in your home directory. To be sure, you can also specify the full desired path to that directory with a command such as

```
$ mkdir /home/mj/documents
```

Whether this command works or not depends on the privileges associated with your username and the permissions on the higher-level directory. For example, as a regular user, you probably wouldn't be able to create a new /golf directory, but as a root user, you could do this.

Of course, you can also remove directories. For example, the following command removes the directory created earlier:

```
$ rmdir /home/mj/documents
```

Whether this command works depends on the permissions in the /home/mj directory and whether this directory is empty. Of course, you could use the rm -r command discussed earlier in this chapter to delete a directory even if it is full of files.

Creating Symbolic Links

In addition to creating files, there are times when it is necessary to create symbolic links. *Symbolic links* (which are simply pointers to a real file in another location) are usually used by system administrators and application developers. Consider a programmer who has several versions of a program that is under development. The current version for testing may be prog5, prog8, or prog10, depending on how far along the development is. In order to ensure that the latest version is always being executed during testing, the programmer can create a symbolic link from prog to the latest version. By doing this, executing prog always executes the desired revision of the application.

There are two possible approaches to creating a symbolic link. The first is to use the ln command with the -s flag to indicate a symbolic link. This command takes two arguments: the file to be linked to and the location and name of the symbolic link to that file.

For instance, to create a link to /bin/cp in the current directory, MyCopy, you use the command

```
$ ln -s /bin/cp MyCopy
```

Using ls -l to see the listing of MyCopy shows us a symbolic link:

```
lrwxrwxrwx   1 armand   armand          7 Apr  6 22:50 MyCopy -> /bin/cp
```

Another, far less common way to create a symbolic link is to use the cp command with the -s flag:

```
$ cp -s /bin/cp MyCopy
```

A Quick Introduction to Filename Expansion

Before closing out this chapter, you need to take a quick look at an important sub-ject: *filename expansion*. Chapter 16 covers filename expansion in more detail when discussing the Unix shell, but since you have already seen examples of filename expansion in this chapter, this section will put it in context.

Filename expansion refers to a special syntax that can be used to expand a compact expression into a list of one or more file or directory names. The simple examples you have seen in this chapter involve the use of the asterisk (*) to rep-resent zero or more characters. For instance, the expression *.txt could match any of the following filenames:

- .txt
- a.txt
- file.txt
- txt.txt

The default Bash shell provides a rich syntax for filename expansion. This book will explore the Bash shell later, but two of the more useful symbols are outlined below:

?   Matches any single character, so file.? would match file.c but not file.txt.

[CharacterList]   Matches any single character in the character list, so file.[abc] would match file.a, file.b, and file.c but not file.d or file.txt. Alternatively, file.[x-z] would match file.x, file.y, and file.z.

Looking Ahead

You've come a long way. You now know how to use X Windows and have begun to delve into the real depths of Linux: the command line and the shell. You learned about some of the major programs available in the command-prompt environment and are able to manipulate files in sophisticated ways using concise and powerful commands.

The next step, which you will take in Chapter 15, "Using Linuxconf and Other Tools for System Configuration," is to learn to perform some important system configuration and management tasks using several Red Hat Linux tools, including Linuxconf. These functions include setting up printers for use in Linux, managing users, and more.

CHAPTER
FIFTEEN

15

Using Linuxconf and Other Tools for System Configuration

- Configuring Printers

- Launching Linuxconf

- Adding Modules

- Managing Users and Groups

- Configuring a Modem

- Setting the Time and Date

While avid Linux power users and system administrators will want to roll up their sleeves and get down to the business of hand-editing the files that control the behavior of their systems, the everyday computer user who wants to use Linux as a productivity tool may find this a daunting and overwhelming proposition.

In fact, the thought of having to hand-edit configuration files is so daunting that it may be one of the leading reasons why Linux is seen as user-unfriendly and Windows is perceived as user-friendly.

However, Red Hat, among others, has long strived to integrate tools into their distribution of Linux that help shield the user from dealing with the underlying configuration of a basic Linux workstation. A number of graphical configuration tools are available for managing users, printers, clocks, modems, networks, software packages, and more.

The most comprehensive of these tools is Linuxconf. This "all-in-one" utility provides facilities to perform the most common system-management tasks through easy-to-use graphical dialog boxes and windows. Linuxconf provides an alternative graphical interface for system management.

NOTE   Other Linux distributions also have graphical tools with similar functionality to Linuxconf, including Corel's Control Center, Caldera's WebMin, and S.u.S.E.'s YaST.

This chapter takes a close look at a couple of the Red Hat Linux 7.1 graphical tools, namely the Printconf utility and Linuxconf, and provides in-depth coverage of a few Linuxconf features.

Configuring Printers

Probably one of the more intimidating configuration tasks in Linux is trying to get a printer working—especially a PCL printer—by manually editing the necessary system configuration files.

Red Hat has done an admirable job of making this task manageable (if not exactly easy) using the Printconf utility. You can start this utility by selecting Programs ➤ System ➤ Printer Configuration from the GNOME main menu. You are prompted for the root user password, unless you're already logged in as the root user.

This calls up the Red Hat Linux Printer Configuration Tool shown in Figure 15.1.

FIGURE 15.1:

The Printer
Configuration Tool

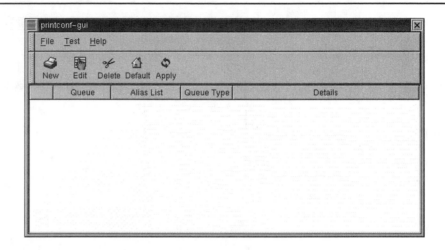

NOTE You can call up this same tool in KDE by selecting System ➤ Printer Configuration from the KDE main menu.

Printconf is the most convenient way yet to configure the /etc/printcap configuration file. In fact, with Printconf, you are no longer supposed to directly edit the /etc/printcap file. If you have printers that can only be configured manually, you can add their settings to the /etc/printcap.local file.

Setting up a new printer is a four-step process: First, you add a name. This can include aliases to make it easier to remember the name of your new printer. Next, you set up a queue. Queues can be local, or remote over a network. The queue you set up is also associated with a device. Third, you set up a driver to help Linux communicate with your printer. Finally, you need to save the changes and then restart the Line Printer Daemon, or lpd.

Adding a Printer

To start the process, click the New button in the Printconf toolbar. This opens the Edit Queue dialog box shown in Figure 15.2. In the Queue Name text box, enter a name for your printer. If you need more than one name, you can set up one or more aliases. Click the Add button, and enter the name of your choice. Repeat if additional aliases are desired. In Figure 15.2, the name of the printer is test, and it has an alias of hplj4.

FIGURE 15.2:

Selecting names and aliases

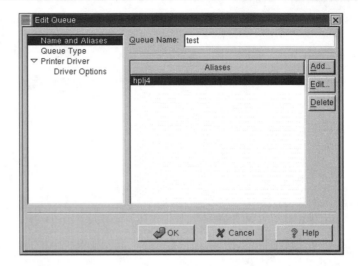

Setting Up a Queue

Now you'll set up the queue for your printer. In the Edit Queue dialog box, click Queue Type. As shown in Figure 15.3, there are two items to configure: the location of the printer and the assigned printer device.

FIGURE 15.3:

Selecting a queue and a device

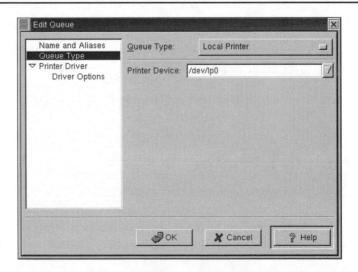

Five different types of queues are available. The simplest is Local Printer, where the printer is directly attached to your computer, through a parallel or USB port. When you click Local Printer, Printconf shows you all five Queue Type options. The other four options assume that your printer is connected through a network in one of the following ways:

UNIX Printer (lpd Queue)   If your target printer is connected to a Unix or another Linux computer through the network, and your computer uses the Network File System (NFS) protocol to communicate with it, then this option is for you. You'll need the name of the print server computer, as well as the queue name on that computer.

Windows Printer (SMB Share)   If your target printer is connected to a Microsoft Windows computer on the network, or the Linux and/or Unix computers on your network are connected using Samba, then you can set this queue type for connecting to that printer. You'll need the share name assigned to the printer and the IP address assigned to the computer with the printer. Depending on the type of network share, you may also need the name of the Windows workgroup, the username, and/or password required to access the printer.

TIP   The share name is the full path to the printer attached to the Microsoft Windows computer. For example, if the Windows computer name is `MSWin1`, and the printer share name is `HPLaserJ`, then the share name that you use is `//MSWin1/HPLaserJ`.

Novell Printer (NCP Queue)   If your network uses some Novell Network protocol to communicate, the NCP queue type may be for you. For a printer connected in this way, you'll need the name of the print server computer, the name of the queue on that computer, as well as the applicable username and password.

JetDirect Printer   The JetDirect Printer queue type is for HP and HP-compatible printers that connect directly to a network, without having any direct physical connection to any computer on that network. You'll need the IP address assigned to that printer, as well as the port number if different from the default of 9100.

After setting the printer queue, you can select the printer device. In Red Hat Linux 7.1, there are printer devices available for standard and USB printers, which include /dev/lp0, /dev/lp1, and /dev/lp2 for standard printers, and /dev/usb/lp0 through /dev/usb/lp15 for USB printers.

Configuring a Printer Driver

The next step is to configure a printer driver to help Linux communicate with your target printer. In the Edit Queue dialog box, click Printer Driver and select from four different kinds of printers, three of which are shown in Figure 15.4.

FIGURE 15.4:

Selecting a printer driver

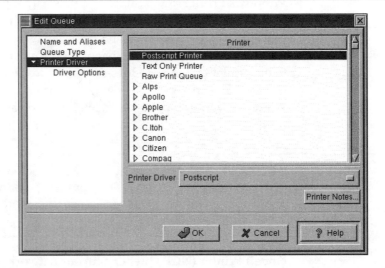

Postscript Printer In most cases, if you have a Postscript printer, the standard Postscript driver will work for you.

Text Only Printer If you need to print only text information from standard text files, or if your printer can handle only standard ASCII text codes, then select this option.

Raw Print Queue Raw print queues have no printer driver. If you have a program that already converts print output into data that your printer can use, this is a viable option.

Brand Specific   The Printconf utility includes a large number of printer drivers that are associated with an even larger number of printer models. If you do not have a Postscript printer, select the company and model associated with your printer.

A few printers are associated with more than one driver. In most cases, the default driver works fine. But if you suspect a problem, click the name of the actual printer driver to bring up a list of alternate drivers (if any) for your printer.

You can even set up the same printer with different drivers. For example, if you have a specific program that converts the print data into something that your printer can use, you don't need a driver and can set up a printer that uses the raw print queue. You can then set up the same printer with a driver to take care of the rest of your print needs. Just make sure to use different names, aliases, and or printer devices for each function.

Once you select a printer driver, then you can customize it with different driver options. For example, Figure 15.5 illustrates the driver options associated with the HP Laser Jet 4L printer.

FIGURE 15.5:

Printer driver options

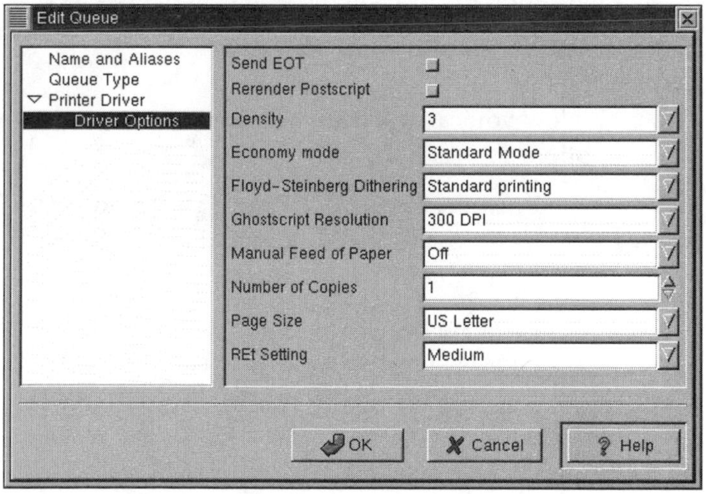

There are a wide variety of options available. The following are just the most common options for customizing your printer driver:

Send EOT EOT is short for "End of Transmission." If your printer is having trouble at the beginning or end of consecutive print jobs, you should enable this option.

Rerender Postscript This option resends your file as a Postscript file. Some printers require Postscript format in order to handle graphics. However, this option may not work for you, as some other printers cannot handle postscript data.

Page Size Set this option to the size of paper in your printer.

Other available options are generally printer-specific. For more information, consult your printer's documentation and/or the Linux printing documentation available at www.linuxprinting.org.

Once you've finished configuring, click OK to exit the Edit Queue dialog box.

Testing the Configuration

Before you test, you need to save what you configured in the /etc/printcap configuration file. Back in the Printconf main screen, select File ➢ Save Changes to save the changes to this file. Then select File ➢ Restart ➢ Lpd to make the Line Printer Daemon reread this file.

Now you can test the configuration. Under the Test menu, you have three options:

Print Postscript Test Page The standard Red Hat Postscript test page includes text, a color bar, and border lines 0.5 and 1.0 inches from the edge of an 8.5 × 11-inch printout.

Print A4 Postscript Test Page This is the standard Red Hat Postscript test page customized for the A4-sized paper more common in Europe.

Print ASCII Test Page This is a standard text printout, without graphics.

Managing Existing Printers

Once you've set up a printer, it is simple to edit its configuration. Highlight the desired printer and click Edit on the toolbar. This brings up the same dialog boxes discussed earlier.

Printconf Alternatives

There are two major alternatives to Printconf: PrintTool and Apsfilter. PrintTool is the utility that was used in Red Hat through version 7.0. Apsfilter is discussed in Chapter 18, "Using Peripherals." If you've used Red Hat Linux before, you may be more comfortable with PrintTool. To set up PrintTool, first uninstall Printconf. You can do this with the following rpm commands, in root user mode, in the following order:

```
# rpm -e printconf-gui
# rpm -e printconf
```

You can then install PrintTool from a Red Hat Linux 7.0 CD-ROM or by downloading it from a source such as www.rpmfind.net. The following two packages are required:

```
rhs-printfilters-1.81-1.i386.rpm
printtool-3.54-1.i386.rpm
```

If you downloaded these packages to the /tmp directory, you could then install them with the following rpm commands, in root user mode, in the following order:

```
# rpm -i /tmp/rhs-printfilters-1.81-1.i386.rpm
# rpm -i /tmp/printtool-3.54-1.i386.rpm
```

Launching Linuxconf

Starting with Red Hat Linux 7.1, Linuxconf is no longer installed by default. In fact, the associated rpm packages are not even included with the CD-ROM that comes with this book. However, if you have the full installation with two or more CD-ROMs, you can install the Linuxconf package, linuxconf-1.24r2-10.i386.rpm from the second Installation CD-ROM.

Depending on your configuration, the CD-ROM may already be mounted after you insert a CD into the drive. To check this, type the **mount** command. If you see something like the following line in the resulting list, the CD-ROM should already be mounted:

```
/dev/hdb on /mnt/cdrom type iso9660
```

Mount the CD-ROM if required on the /mnt/cdrom directory. Once mounted you can install Linuxconf with the following commands:

```
$ rpm -i /mnt/cdrom/RedHat/RPMS/linuxconf-1.24r2-10.i386.rpm
$ rpm -i /mnt/cdrom/RedHat/RPMS/gnome-linuxconf-0.64-1.i386.rpm
```

NOTE If you do not have the second Red Hat Linux 7.1 Installation CD-ROM, you can download these packages from another source such as ftp.redhat.com or www.rpmfind.net.

Once installed, Linuxconf can be launched from the command line by typing the following command at the command prompt in an xterm window:

```
$ linuxconf-auth
```

If you are not the root user, Red Hat Linux 7.1 prompts you for the root password before starting Linuxconf.

When Linuxconf launches, a window like the one in Figure 15.6 appears.

NOTE The first time you launch Linuxconf, you'll also see a welcome screen. As strange as it may sound, if you see this screen, click Quit to start Linuxconf.

Linuxconf can be used to control many different aspects of your Linux environment, including your network configuration and user and group management. These different sections of Linuxconf can be chosen from the expandable tree hierarchy in the center of the window. This expandable and collapsible tree works in much the same way as the tree for navigating files and directories in the Windows 98/Me and NT/2000 Explorer.

FIGURE 15.6:

The Linuxconf window

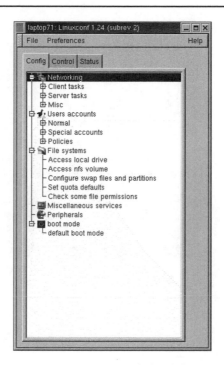

Adding Modules

When you first start Linuxconf, it may not have all of the tools that you need. Fortunately, it is easy to add modules. To review available modules, click the Control tab, and then select Control Files And Systems ➤ Configure Linuxconf Modules to open the List Of Modules tab shown in Figure 15.7.

You should select at least the modemconf modem configuration tool for the relevant discussion later in this chapter. To activate this tool, select modemconf and click the Accept button under the List Of Modules tab. Then in the toolbar, choose File ➤ Act/Changes and then choose File ➤ Quit. When you restart Linuxconf, the Modem option appears under Peripherals in the Config tab.

FIGURE 15.7:

The Linuxconf List Of Modules tab

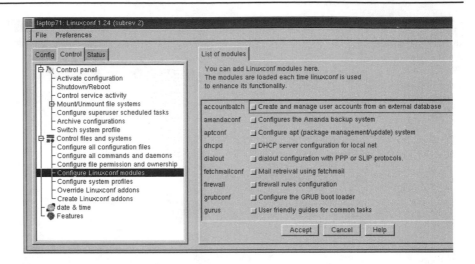

NOTE   There are two commands to exit from Linuxconf: File ➢ Quit and File ➢ Quit (no check). The second option cross-checks the configuration with the state of your Linux system. If there are differences, Linuxconf offers to update your system.

Managing Users and Groups

This section focuses on using Linuxconf to manage users and groups.

User and group management facilities can be found under the Config tab in the Users Accounts ➢ Normal section of the selection tree at the left side of the Linuxconf window.

Managing Users

To manage users, go to the Config tab in Linuxconf, then select Users Accounts ➢ Normal ➢ User Accounts. This opens the default user management screen shown in Figure 15.8. This screen lists details of existing users and includes a row of function buttons immediately below the list of users.

FIGURE 15.8:

Use the list of users and the row of function buttons to manage users.

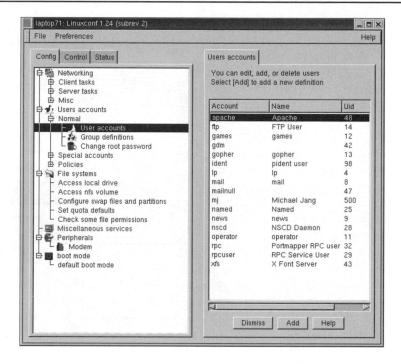

Using this screen, it is possible to

- Add new users
- Edit properties of existing users or view their current properties
- Lock and unlock users
- Permanently remove users from the system

Adding a New User

To add a new user, click the Add button. The User Account Creation screen shown in Figure 15.9 appears. Most of the information fields in the dialog box are empty, waiting for you to enter information about the new user. When you have finished entering the information as outlined here, click the Accept button to create the user.

FIGURE 15.9:

Adding a new user

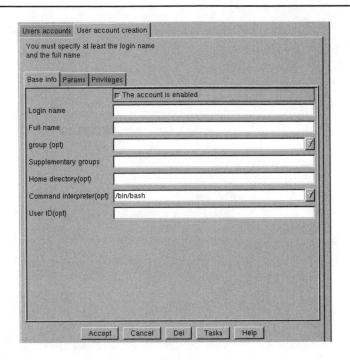

Login Name   The first field in the box is the Login Name field. In this field, enter the username of the user—the name the user types to log in to the system, not their complete name. These usernames should not contain spaces and should start with a letter or number.

For instance, for a user named Arman Danesh you might choose any of the following usernames because they all relate in some way to the name of the user:

- armand
- adanesh
- arman
- danesh
- arman_danesh
- ArmanDanesh

Full Name   The Full Name field is where you enter the full name of the user. The full name is used, for example, in constructing the From line of the user's e-mails, including both the e-mail address of the user, which is derived from the username, and the full name of the user. This field can contain blanks.

Group and Supplementary Groups   The Group field allows you to assign a user to a specific default group. If left blank, Red Hat Linux gives the user a unique group with a group ID number corresponding to that user's user ID number. Unless you know precisely what you are doing, you are probably best off using the preselected values that will be assigned by Linuxconf.

The Supplementary Groups field can be used to assign a new user to additional groups for security and access-control purposes. On most small systems and networks, this won't prove necessary.

Home Directory   The Home Directory field indicates the full path of the user's home directory. By default, on a Red Hat Linux system this is a subdirectory of the /home directory, and the directory name is the same as the username. In fact, once you enter the username in the Login Name field, Linuxconf automatically uses it to assign a default home directory under /home. You can override this default by providing an alternate directory path in the Home Directory field.

For example, the home directory for a user with the username armand would be /home/armand. Unless you have a large multiuser server or are implementing a custom scheme for placing home directories on your system, leave the default entry as is.

Command Interpreter   The Command Interpreter field is used to indicate the user's default shell, which governs the way in which the user's command-line environment functions. (To learn about different shells and their features, see Chapter 16, "Understanding the Shell.")

The default shell for all new users in most versions of Linux is the Bash shell. Clicking the drop-down menu next to the Command Interpreter field produces a list of alternate shells, including variations on Bash such as the Ash shell, or the C-Shell and the Enhanced C-Shell (/bin/tcsh). Normally, it is not necessary to change the default shell.

Creating the User   When you have finished providing the necessary information for a new user, click the Accept button to add the user. Once you click Accept, you are prompted twice for a password for the user (you are prompted twice because of the need to confirm the password). The password prompt looks like the one in Figure 15.10.

FIGURE 15.10:

The New UNIX Password prompt

Once you have entered the password twice and clicked Accept each time, the main user management screen shown previously in Figure 15.8 reappears and the new user now appears in the list of current users.

> **NOTE** If you use a dictionary word for your password, Linuxconf sends you an error message to that effect. If you still want to use the dictionary word as your password, click Accept, and then type the same password in the Retype New UNIX Password text box.

> **TIP** Good passwords contain a combination of letters and numbers. For example, a password like Itr29tmr is much more difficult to crack than any regular word. Such passwords need not be difficult to remember; Itr29tmr could stand for "I take route 29 to my restaurant."

Editing or Viewing a User

To view the details or change the information for a user, simply click their name in the list of users in the main user management screen. A screen box appears like the one in Figure 15.11. This screen box looks the same as the one you saw when you tried to add a new user, with one major difference: All the fields contain information relating to the user selected from the list. You can use this form to change any information about the user.

If you make changes to a user and want to commit those changes to the user list, simply click Accept. Otherwise, click Cancel to exit the dialog box without saving the changes.

Viewing and editing user information

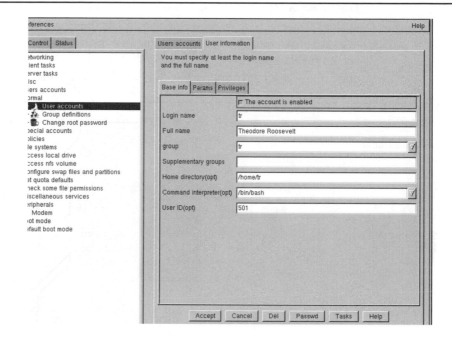

Enabling and Disabling Users

Enabling and disabling users is a useful concept. The idea behind disabling a user is to temporarily deactivate the user's account without permanently removing it from the system. This allows the user to be reinstated later. Examples of when this type of functionality is used might include an Internet service provider (ISP) who temporarily suspends access privileges when a user has not paid their access charges.

To disable a user's account, simply click the user in the user list and deselect The Account Is Enabled. When you accept the changes, the user's account is disabled.

Enabling a User   To enable a disabled user, simply click the user's name in the user list and select The Account Is Enabled in the edit screen for that user. Next, click Accept to commit the changes and enable the user's account.

Deleting a User   The final option in managing users is to delete a user from the system. Once you do so, you can bring a user back only by re-creating the user's account. To delete a user, click the user's name in the user list to open the edit screen for that user. Next, click the Del button at the bottom of the edit screen. A confirmation screen appears like the one in Figure 15.12.

FIGURE 15.12:

The Deleting Account
confirmation screen

On the Deleting Account confirmation screen, you have three options:

Archive The Account's Data   The data from the user's account (home directory, quotas, etc.) will be archived and compressed for later access in the /home/oldaccounts directory.

Delete The Account's Data   The data from the user's account will be permanently deleted.

Leave The Account's Data In Place   The data from the user's account will be left untouched even though the user account will no longer exist.

Select your desired option and click Accept to delete the user.

Managing Groups

The second aspect of managing users and groups is working with groups. To switch to group management, select the Config tab, and then select Users Accounts ➢ Normal ➢ Group Definitions in the left pane of the Linuxconf window. When managing groups, you work with a Group list and a row of function buttons like those in Figure 15.13. Groups are discussed in detail in Chapter 17, "General System Administration."

FIGURE 15.13:

Group management

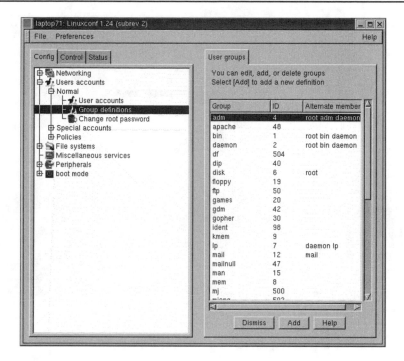

Adding Groups

To add a new group to the Group list, simply click Add. A screen like the one in Figure 15.14 appears.

This looks like a scaled-down version of the screen used for adding users to the system. Here you can

- Assign a group name

- Select a GID for the group if you don't like the default group provided by the system

- Assign alternate users as members of the group by entering a list of users in the Alternate Members field with a space between each user

FIGURE 15.14:

Adding a group

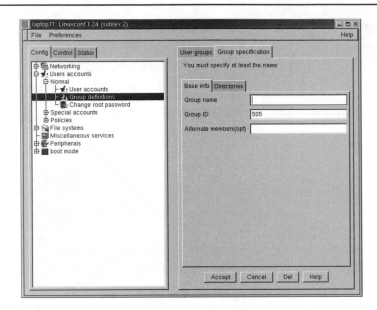

Editing and Viewing Groups

To edit or view a group's details, simply click the group in the Group list of the main group management screen to get a window like the one in Figure 15.15.

FIGURE 15.15:

Editing and viewing a group

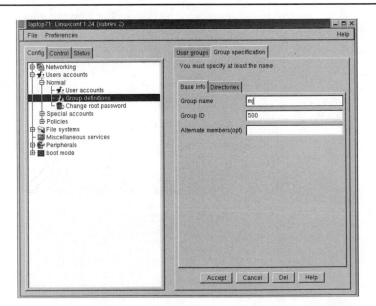

Notice that the screen box looks like it did when you added a group, except that here all the data is filled in. Although you can change the GID or user list for a group, don't do this, especially for administrative groups (with GID numbers lower than 100), unless you know exactly what you're doing.

Saving and Quitting

After finishing any configuration tasks with Linuxconf, it is necessary to activate your changes. To do so, choose File ➢ Act/Changes. If any additional changes are required, a confirmation screen similar to that shown in Figure 15.16 appears. This screen shows what needs to be done to record your changes in your Linux system files.

On the confirmation screen you can choose to

- Apply the changes you have made by clicking Do It, or

- Cancel the decision to quit from Linuxconf by clicking the Do Nothing button

Now you can choose File ➢ Quit to close Linuxconf.

FIGURE 15.16:

Activating Linuxconf
changes

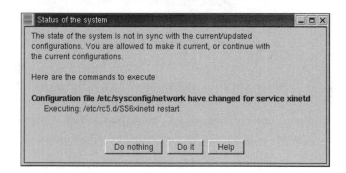

Configuring a Modem

You can also configure a modem through Linuxconf. Open up Linuxconf using the instructions discussed earlier in this chapter. If you added the modemconf module as discussed earlier, you should now be able to use Linuxconf to configure your modem. Under the Config tab, select Peripherals ≻ Modem, which calls up the Modem Configurator, as shown in Figure 15.17.

This window offers very little to choose from: You can select the port your modem is connected to or, in the case of an internal modem, configured to use. This creates the necessary link so that programs that expect the modem to be on the device /dev/modem can find your modem.

FIGURE 15.17:

The Modem Configurator

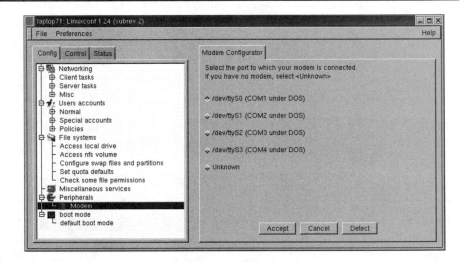

Alternatively, you can have Linuxconf detect the port to which your modem is connected. Connect your modem to a telephone line and then click Detect. If your modem is detected, you'll see a message to that effect, including the port; otherwise, you'll see a No Modem Detected message.

This process is independent of the configuration of programs that use the modem for accessing the Internet or faxing. These programs are discussed in later chapters such as Chapter 22, "Connecting Linux to the Internet."

TIP

If the Linuxconf Modem Configurator can't detect your modem, make sure it's connected to a phone line that has a dial tone. Alternatively, using the tools in Chapter 22 can help your Linux computer detect a modem.

Setting the Time and Date

You can also configure the date and time on your computer through Linuxconf. Open up Linuxconf using the instructions discussed earlier in this chapter. Under the Control tab, select Date & Time, which calls up the Workstation Date & Time Configurator, as shown in Figure 15.18.

FIGURE 15.18:

The Workstation Date & Time Configurator

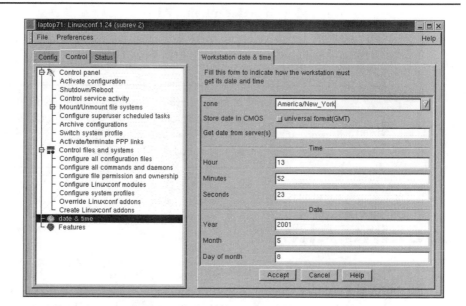

The time and date are displayed in the middle and bottom of the tab. You can select and change any part of the time or date (the hour, the minutes, the seconds, the month, the day, or the year).

Linux is set up to use Greenwich Mean Time (GMT). This makes it easier to synchronize Linux servers located in different time zones. To make this work with your computer, Linux needs to know your specific time zone, which you can select by clicking the drop-down menu next to the Zone field.

If Linux is the only operating system on your computer, select the Store Date In CMOS option. This stores the GMT version of the time that you set here on your computer's hardware clock. Otherwise, you'll need to change the Linux clock when the time changes in your time zone (e.g., for daylight saving time).

You can also use this tool to synchronize your computer's time with another server, which you can add to the Get Date From Server(s) text box. This is based on either the `netdate` command or the `xntp` time server. Neither of these utilities is included with Red Hat Linux 7.1.

When you have completed your desired changes, click Accept, and then activate your changes as discussed earlier in this chapter.

> **NOTE** If you have applications on different computers that need to be on the same time, the `ntpdate` utility can synchronize each of your computers with a time server. For more information, see the Web page for this utility, `http://www.eecis.udel.edu/~ntp/ntp_spool/html/ntpdate.htm`.

Looking Ahead

This chapter has given you a grounding in how to configure some of the most basic components of your system—components that you will use every day, such as printers, modems, users, and groups. Other related configuration tools are addressed in future chapters, including the Network Configurator, `netcfg`, which is discussed in Chapter 21, "Understanding Linux Networking," and the Firewall Configurator, `firewall-config`, which is addressed in Chapter 31, "Security and Red Hat Linux 7.1 As an Inexpensive Router."

With this knowledge and your basic grasp of Unix and managing Linux files, you are ready to delve into the world of the shell. The shell is the program that provides you with the powerful command-line environment that is loved by the Unix guru but feared by the Linux novice.

Chapter 16, "Understanding the Shell," will take a look at the role played by the shell, compare many of the available shells (including the ever-popular Bash and C shells), and then take a deeper look at Bash, the default shell of almost every Linux distribution.

CHAPTER
SIXTEEN

Understanding the Shell

- Comparing Shells

- Overview of the Bash Shell

Now that you have learned some basic Unix commands, it is important to understand the command-line environment you are using to enter them. This command-line environment is known as the *shell*—a command interpreter, similar to the DOS prompt in Windows 3.1 and Windows 98, that allows you to type commands, launch programs, and manipulate files.

Unlike the Windows world where the DOS prompt is a fixed environment with limited flexibility, Unix shells are small application programs that run as processes when you log in and provide a variety of command-line interface features and capabilities to suit different users and applications.

In the Unix world, and by extension in Linux, there are numerous shells to choose from. Each shell offers you a different set of features and capabilities and most offer their own scripting languages, which allow you to create sophisticated, self-executing programs similar to—but more powerful than—DOS batch files (with the familiar .BAT extension).

First, this chapter will give you an overview of the major Unix shells, including the Bourne Shell, the C Shell, and the Korn Shell, and then you will get an in-depth look at the Bourne Again Shell, known as Bash, which is the default shell installed with most Linux distributions.

Comparing Shells

The earliest Unix shell was very limited, with no history list, no command-line editing, and no job control. It was with the emergence of the Bourne Shell and the C Shell in the 1970s that shells began to garner serious attention in the Unix world. Today there is a plethora of shells available to Unix users, with a wide variety of unique features distinguishing them from each other.

There are two main classes of shell—those that derive their essential syntax and design from the Bourne Shell and those that base their model on the C Shell. Before taking a close look at the Bourne Again Shell—the default shell that ships with most Linux distributions—let's take a quick look at some of the major Unix shells.

TIP   If you want to keep track of the latest developments in the world of Unix shells, consider subscribing to the `comp.unix.shell` newsgroup.

Bourne Shell (*sh*)

The Bourne Shell (sh) is seen by many as the original Unix shell. In many ways it is rather limited, lacking features such as a history list and command-line editing. But since it is the original Unix shell, many features of the Bourne Shell, including its core command set, are found in many modern shells. It is rare, however, to find modern systems that use the Bourne Shell as their default shell. Instead, the Bourne Again Shell or the Enhanced C Shell is commonly found in most Linux distributions.

The Bourne Shell is well known for introducing many key shell concepts, such as the ability to test programs for success or failure status when they exit, which allows for sophisticated scripting. This concept is now standard in all Unix shells.

C Shell (*csh*)

The C Shell (csh) was an early Unix shell that was developed to provide a command set and scripting environment derived from the syntax of the popular C programming language. Like the early Bourne Shell, the C Shell lacked some important features, such as command-line editing. Still, the C Shell introduced many key ideas, including command aliases and command histories. An Enhanced C Shell (tcsh), which adds command-line editing and other features found in Bash, is usually shipped with most Linux distributions as an alternate shell.

The C Shell is generally hailed for introducing several key concepts that today are found even in shells based on the Bourne Shell. These include the idea that certain shell functions, such as arithmetic calculations and comparison testing, can be performed by the shell itself. In the case of the Bourne Shell, these tasks require calling external programs.

Bourne Again Shell (*bash*)

The Bourne Again Shell (bash) is the most common shell installed with Linux distributions. Known as Bash, this shell is based on the Bourne Shell (as the name implies) but provides a broad additional feature set including command-line editing, a history list, and filename completion. With Bash, it is possible to write sophisticated shell scripts using a Bourne Shell-like syntax. As the most common Linux shell, Bash is the focus of most of this chapter and is the default shell being used in all examples in this book.

Korn Shell (*ksh*)

The Korn Shell (ksh) is another of the family of shells that is derived from the original Bourne Shell. By some counts, the Korn Shell is the most popular Unix shell in use; however, it is generally not the default shell on most Linux systems. The Korn Shell was probably the first to introduce many of the popular features you now see in Bash, including command-line editing. The Korn Shell was also one of the first shells to bring many features introduced in the C Shell into the Bourne Shell world.

Other Shells

There are numerous other shells available, all of which provide their own unique command-line interfaces. None of these, however, is sufficiently popular or well known to be shipped with most Linux distributions. These shells include the Adventure Shell (ash), a subset of the Bourne Shell; the Extensible Shell (es), which provides a completely reprogrammable shell environment; the ERGO Shell (esh), a shell that aims to provide a more ergonomic, structured approach to a shell; and the Z Shell (zsh), which, like Bash, brings together features from several shells and is similar to the Korn Shell.

TIP   An excellent source of alternate shells for your Linux system is found at the SunSite Linux archive. In their Shells directory at `ftp://metalab.unc.edu/pub/Linux/system/shells/`, you will find all the shells listed here as well as a collection of less common shells such as `lsh`, `pash`, and `pdksh`.

Experimenting with Different Shells

At this point, you are probably wondering how you can try out these different shells without making them your default shell. You can do this by simply executing the shell as a program from within your default shell. For instance, the Enhanced C Shell comes preinstalled even though Bash is set up to be the default shell for all users. If you want to try out `tcsh`, you just need to enter the command

```
$ tcsh
```

This command assumes that tcsh is on your path; if not, you need to include the appropriate path to the shell, such as /bin/tcsh. Once you do this, the Enhanced C Shell executes and you are switched to that shell. Simply typing **exit** returns you to your default shell.

On most Linux systems, you will find a symbolic link from /bin/sh to /bin/tcsh, so using the command

```
$ csh
```

also launches the Enhanced C Shell.

If you plan to experiment with different shells, you can use this technique to try them all out before switching your default shell. In order to change the default shell that executes when you log in to your system, you need to change your entry in the Unix password file. You can do this using the chsh command.

Consider the user someuser whose default shell is currently /bin/bash (the Bourne Again Shell). Their current entry in the Unix password file might look like this:

```
someuser::790:103:Some User:/home/someuser:/bin/bash
```

In this password entry, the last section specifies the shell as /bin/bash. Running the command

```
$ chsh -s /bin/tcsh someuser
```

changes the shell for someuser to /bin/tcsh. The resulting entry for someuser in the Unix password file would be

```
someuser::790:103:Some User:/home/someuser:/bin/tcsh
```

and the next time they log in, the Enhanced C Shell would be their shell instead of the Bourne Again Shell.

Overview of the Bash Shell

Now let's take a closer look at Linux's most common shell, the Bash shell. As the first step to learning where the Bash shell fits into the Linux universe, it is important to understand the whole login process. When you log in at the Login: prompt, several things take place. The first of these is the launching of your shell (in this case, Bash), followed by the execution of any configuration file you may have created for your personal Bash environment.

In order to provide a personalized configuration to Bash, you need to create a file called .bashrc in your home directory. This is a simple text file that is executed by Bash whenever you launch the shell—generally, when you log in.

NOTE In Red Hat Linux 7.1, personalized configuration options are also included in the .bash_profile file, also in your home directory.

The .bashrc file can contain any legitimate combination of commands and Bash functions that you would type at the normal Bash prompt, as well as sophisticated scripting commands.

It is in the .bashrc file that you can configure the behavior of Bash, set environment variables such as your path, and launch any programs that you may want to launch every time you run the Bash shell. The following commands make up a simple .bashrc file that creates a customized prompt, sets a command alias called which, and assigns some environment variables:

```
PS1="[\u@\h \W]\\$ "
alias which="type -path"
export PATH=$PATH:.:~/bin
export EDITOR=emacs
```

There are several major features of the Bash shell at play in this seemingly small example, including the following:

- The setting of environment variables
- Command aliases
- Pattern expansion

All of these will be discussed in the rest of this chapter, along with the following major features of the Bash shell:

- Input and output redirection
- Filename completion
- Full command-line editing
- Command history list
- Job control

Setting Environment Variables in Bash

Each shell has its own syntax for the setting of environment variables. In Bash, this is generally done in two steps: setting the value of a variable and exporting the variable to the environment. For instance, if you want to assign emacs as your default text editor, you might set the EDITOR environment variable with the command

```
$ EDITOR=emacs
```

and export it with

```
$ export EDITOR
```

The two steps can also be combined into a single step where you assign a value to EDITOR and export EDITOR in one command:

```
$ export EDITOR=emacs
```

As you will learn in greater detail when pattern expansion is discussed, you can access the value of environment variables by adding a $ at the beginning of the name of the variable in a Bash command. In this way, you can add information to the current value of an environment variable. For instance, if the PATH variable currently contains

```
/bin:/usr/bin:/usr/X11R6/bin
```

you can add /usr/local/bin to the path by using the following command:

```
$ export PATH=$PATH:/usr/local/bin
```

Notice how this command uses $PATH to include the current value of the PATH variable in the new value of the PATH variable. The resulting value of the variable would be

```
/bin:/usr/bin:/usr/X11R6/bin:/usr/local/bin
```

Input and Output Redirection

One of the most useful concepts in the Unix world is that of standard input and standard output. Often, non-interactive programs receive their input data through the standard input—usually the keyboard. Similarly, they display their results to the standard output—usually the screen.

However, most shells provide the ability to redirect standard input and output, which allows you to build complex command combinations out of multiple commands and data files. As you saw in the last chapter, the use of the pipe (|) allows the redirection of standard output to standard input. For instance, in the command

```
$ ls -l | more
```

the output of the ls -l command is not displayed to standard output but is instead redirected to the standard input of the more command. The more command processes this redirected input and then displays the results to the standard output.

There is another way to redirect standard input and output in Bash: using the < and > redirection symbols. For instance, consider a situation where you want to save a directory listing to a file for later processing. You can use the > symbol to redirect the standard output:

```
$ ls -l > filelist
```

This command saves the output of the ls -l command in a file called filelist. Similarly, if you want to use the contents of a file as the standard input for a command, you use the < symbol:

```
$ mail user@juxta.com < filelist
```

This command causes the contents of the file filelist to be used as the input data for the mail command, effectively causing the contents of the file to be used as the body of the resulting e-mail message.

Filename Completion

Sometimes called word completion, filename completion is a simple but very useful concept. It works like this: If you type enough characters to uniquely identify a file, command, or directory name, Bash can complete the rest of the name. Consider if you typed

```
$ /usr/lo
```

On most systems, /usr/lo will uniquely identify the directory /usr/local/. If you simply press the Tab key, Bash attempts to complete the name. If only one file, command, or directory begins with /usr/lo, then Bash completes the name for you, in this case filling in the text to read /usr/local/.

Of course, there are going to be times when you don't provide enough information for Bash to know how to complete a name. In this situation, the shell is able to provide you with all possible alternatives to match the name you are trying to complete. For instance, if you type

`$ /usr/l`

`/usr/local/` and `/usr/lib/` would usually be matched. If you press Tab, then Bash is confused—it doesn't know which name to complete with, and so it cannot complete the name. If you press Tab a second time, Bash displays all the possible alternatives, as follows:

`lib        local`

You are free to type enough characters to uniquely identify the name you want and then press Tab again. In the example above, if you type an additional o and then press Tab, Bash completes the name as `/usr/local/`.

By now you are probably asking, "What happens if I want to type a filename in the local directory or somewhere else on my path without providing the complete path to the file? Can Bash complete filenames for me then?" Luckily, the answer is "yes." If you attempt to complete a file or directory name without providing a complete path, as in the case of

`$ gr`

Bash searches the path for names that match the entered characters. For most systems, the previous example will match only a few commands, including `grep` and `groff`, and Bash will present you with a list of possible alternatives:

`grep      groff      grotty`

If you want the command `grep`, all you would need to do is type **e** and then press Tab again, and Bash completes the command name for you.

Command Alias

Command aliasing is a powerful feature of the Bash shell that allows you to define your own custom commands. For instance, if you regularly check all running processes on your system, you might use a command like

`$ ps aux | more`

Rather than needing to type **ps aux | more** whenever you want to check all the processes running on your system, you can save yourself unnecessary keystrokes by defining an alias using Bash's built-in `alias` command.

In this example, let's say you want to create an alias called psa to use whenever you want to check all the running processes. You could define this alias using the following command:

```
$ alias psa="ps aux | more"
```

Once you do this, typing **psa** at the Bash prompt executes the command ps aux | more. The alias remains in place until the end of your current Bash session. When you log out and Bash exits, the aliases you have defined are lost.

If you want to create permanent command aliases, you should set the aliases in your .bashrc file using the same method you used earlier to make emacs the default text editor.

In addition to providing a way to create shortcuts to commonly used commands, command aliasing can be used to protect you from major mistakes. For instance, if you are logged in as the root user, normal use of the cp, mv, and rm commands can be quite dangerous. One mistake can overwrite or erase files, directories, or whole file systems without your realizing it. For this reason, the Bash shells of the root account are configured to have the following set of default aliases:

```
alias cp='cp -i'
alias mv='mv -i'
alias rm='rm -i'
```

In all these cases, the -i flag forces the command to interactively prompt the user for all actions it takes to overwrite or erase files. In order to cause the commands to run without prompting for each action, the user has to explicitly ask for this with the appropriate flags (for instance, rm -f).

Command-Line Editing

One feature of Bash that was missing in some earlier shells such as the Bourne Shell and the C Shell is the ability to edit a command line. Without this feature, once you type a sequence of characters on the command line, you are not free to go back to that sequence—your only choice is to delete all the characters back to the one you want to edit, fix the character, and then retype the rest of the line. For instance, if you had typed

```
$ /usr/kocal/bin/mycommand
```

and subsequently realized that kocal had to be local, you would have had to delete all the way back to the k, replace the k with an l, and then retype the rest of the line. Needless to say, this is a rather inefficient way to work.

For this reason, most modern shells, including Bash, provide full command-line editing. This allows you to use the arrow keys to move through the current line, delete and insert characters as needed, and press Enter to execute the command without moving the cursor to the end of the line. By default, Bash has insertion turned on, so if you type new characters, they are inserted at the cursor rather than overwriting existing characters.

Bash provides several useful key shortcuts to speed up editing, especially with long command lines. Table 16.1 highlights these shortcuts.

TABLE 16.1: Useful Command-Line Editing Key Shortcuts

Keystroke	Action
Ctrl+A	Jump to the start of the line.
Ctrl+E	Jump to the end of the line.
Ctrl+T	Transpose the character to the left of the cursor with the character at the current cursor position.
Esc, T	Transpose the word to the left of the cursor with the word at the current cursor position.
Esc, U	Uppercase the current word.
Esc, L	Lowercase the current word.
Esc, C	Capitalize the current word.
Ctrl+K	Delete from the current cursor position to the end of the line.

If you are familiar with the emacs editor, you will notice that many of the above keystrokes are the same as the ones you use in emacs. This is because the default editing mode of Bash is designed to use emacs-like commands. Alternatives include a vi-like mode, but since familiarity with vi and its more obscure style of editing is generally limited to programmers and advanced system administrators, this book won't discuss how to use the vi editing mode.

The list of commands in Table 16.1 represents only a small portion of all the editing commands available in Bash. It covers the core set of editing functions needed by most users to become efficient with Bash. If you want to delve more deeply into the editing functions of Bash, you should read the READLINE section of the bash man page, which you can find by typing **man bash** at the shell prompt.

Command History List

The idea behind the command history list is really rather simple. Every command you execute (by pressing Enter instead of Ctrl+C) is added to a history list buffer, which you can access in reverse order starting with the most recent command executed and ending with the oldest.

To access the history list, the simplest method is to press the up arrow key to cycle through the history list until you find the command you are looking for. The history list is most often used for two purposes: fixing mistakenly entered commands and repeating commands many times during a session.

Let's address the first application of the history list. Let's say you have just tried to view the contents of the file `testfile` by typing

```
$ moer testfile
```

When you press Enter, an error message is generated along the lines of

```
bash: moer: command not found.
```

To quickly correct and execute the command, you could simply hit the up arrow key to recall the last command, change `moer` to `more` using the command-line editing functions discussed above, and press Enter to view the file.

Similarly, let's consider the situation where you are experimenting with the configuration for a program you are installing. You might want to repeat the process of editing the configuration file and executing the program several times. You can do this by using the history list to repeatedly perform each step of this two-step process.

A quick method to access commands on the history list is to use the ! symbol. By typing ! followed by the first few letters of a command in the history list, the most recent command starting with the specified letters will be executed.

For instance, if you previously used the command

```
$ ps aux | grep httpd | more
```

and you want to execute the same command again, typing the command

```
$ !ps
```

executes the previous command as long as no other ps command had been used after ps aux | grep httpd | more was used. Using !ps executes the most recent command starting with ps in the history list.

As with command-line editing, there are some advanced key shortcuts to perform more advanced functions with the command history list. Table 16.2 outlines these keystrokes.

TABLE 16.2: Command History Key Shortcuts

Keystroke	Action
Ctrl+P	Move to the previous command in the history list.
Ctrl+N	Move to the next command in the history list.
Esc, <	Jump to the top of the history list (the least recent command).
Esc, >	Jump to the end of the history list (the most recent command).
Ctrl+R	Reverse-search through the history list.
Ctrl+O	Execute the current line and fetch the next line in the history list for editing and executing.

The most interesting of these is Ctrl+R, which allows you to search backwards through the history list in a dynamic, interactive fashion. As you start to type a command, Bash displays the most recent command that matches what you have typed so far. The more you type, the more you narrow down your search to the command you are looking for.

Let's say you want to execute a complicated find command that you have already executed once. You could use Ctrl+R to start a reverse search. When you do this, Bash presents an interactive search prompt:

```
(reverse-i-search)`':
```

As you type the letters in the find command, Bash finds the most recent command that has a match for the currently entered string. For instance, just typing **f** might bring up

```
(reverse-i-search)`f': pico info/.signature
```

and continuing on to typing **fi** might produce

```
(reverse-i-search)`fi': rm -rf StarOffice-3.1
```

until finally typing **fin** displays

```
(reverse-i-search)`fi': find / -name 'foo' -print
```

which is the command you are looking for. You can now press Enter to execute that command.

Job Control

The concept of job control is particularly useful in Linux given the multitasking nature of the operating system. Using job control, it is possible to use a single shell to execute and control multiple programs running simultaneously.

Normally, when you execute a command, it runs in the foreground. That is, the shell executes the command and the prompt doesn't return until the command is finished. In the case of interactive programs such as emacs, this means the program takes over the screen or window where the shell is running and only when you quit the program does the command prompt become available again. In the case of non-interactive programs such as find, the program runs and, even if it displays nothing on the screen, the command prompt is not returned until the program finishes.

Consider the following command:

```
$ find / -name '*.tmp' -print > templist
```

This command searches the entire directory structure of a Linux system for files with the .tmp extension and prints all of those filenames to the standard output. With the previous command, the output is redirected to a file called templist that can be used for later processing. This means that nothing is printed to the display—but you still won't be able to run other commands while find is running.

Such a limitation runs against the very notion of multitasking. There should be a way to start the find command and then continue with other work while find finishes running.

This is where the idea of running a program in the background comes into play. Rather than running it in the foreground, thus preventing the simultaneous execution of other commands, placing a job in the background allows the command to run while the user issues new commands at the command prompt.

The easiest way to place a job in the background is to add an ampersand (&) to the end of the command when you run it. This character tells Bash to run the command in the background and immediately gives you a new command prompt. To put the find command in the background, use the following command:

```
$ find / -name '*.tmp' -print > templist &
```

Once you press Enter to execute this command, you are immediately presented with a new command prompt; at the same time, find begins executing.

Using Bash's jobs command, it is possible to track the jobs that are running in the background. Using jobs might produce results like the following:

```
$ jobs
[1]+  Running                find / -name '*.tmp' -print >templist &
```

Here, the jobs command returns results telling us that there is one background (note the &) job running and that the first job running is find / -name '*.tmp' -print >templist &.

If you have several jobs running in the background, you might get results such as

```
[1]-  Running                find / -name '*.tmp' -print >templist &
[2]+  Running                ls -lR / >dirlist &
```

from the jobs command.

If you have already started a program in the foreground and want to put it in the background, you can do so. The key shortcut Ctrl+Z is interpreted by Bash as a request to temporarily suspend the current process. For instance, if the find command in the previous example is running in the foreground and you type Ctrl+Z, the process is temporarily stopped. Entering the jobs command at this point produces a result like this:

```
[1]+  Stopped                find / -name '*.tmp' -print >templist
```

Notice how the status of the job is Stopped instead of Running. You can then place the job in the background with the bg command

```
$ bg 1
```

where 1 specifies the number of the job. If there is only one stopped job, it is not necessary to specify the job number, and

```
$ bg
```

places the single stopped job in the background. Once a stopped job is placed in the background, typing **jobs** produces a result showing the job as Running.

Sometimes it is useful to temporarily suspend a job without placing it in the background. This is particularly true when you are using an interactive application such as emacs or another text editor and want to run one or more commands and then return to your editing. Instead of completely quitting from the editor, it is easier to use Ctrl+Z to stop the editor job, execute your desired commands, and then return the stopped job to the foreground. By their nature, though, interactive applications are not well suited to being run in the background, and they are best left stopped while they are not in use.

To send a stopped job (or a background job) to the foreground, you can use the fg command. For instance, if you were running emacs but stopped it with Ctrl+Z, executed some commands, and now you want to return to emacs, you can use

```
$ fg
```

If you have one or more stopped or background jobs, it is best to specify the job number when you enter the fg command. If your emacs command was job 2, then the command

```
$ fg 2
```

returns it to the foreground, and you could continue editing.

Finally, there may be times when you want to terminate or kill a stopped or background job. The kill command can be used to kill a command on the basis of a process ID (PID). Use the ps command to find out the process ID (check the ps man page for details) or to directly kill stopped and background jobs in Bash.

For instance, if you have two background jobs and the jobs command produces

```
[1]-  Running          find / -name '*.tmp' -print >templist &
[2]+  Running          ls -lR / >dirlist &
[3]+  Stopped          emacs somefile
```

then you can kill the ls command using the kill command, like this:

```
$ kill %2
```

Notice that, unlike killing a PID, killing a job requires that a percent sign (%) appear before the job number. Without the percent sign, kill would attempt to kill the process with the PID of 2 rather than job 2 in the current shell. This is an important distinction because the job number and the PID of a job are extremely unlikely ever to be the same.

Consider the following example: You already have a background process running in your shell and you start a new one as job 2. When you launch this new job, the system automatically assigns the job a PID from a list of PIDs. This number might be 100, 999, or 25,678. Generally, small PIDs (especially those below 100) are used up by all types of system processes that start when Linux boots and stay running until you shut the computer off. Therefore, it is unlikely that the PID of your job will match the job number.

Pattern Expansion

One of the strengths of many modern shells, including Bash, is the ability to use powerful patterns to specify one or more commands or files. Let's consider a simple example to illustrate the concept. Normally, if you use the command

```
$ ls -l
```

you get a full listing of all files in the current directory. Suppose you want to find a specific file and all you know is that the filename starts with the letter z. Then the command

```
$ ls -l z*
```

can be used. Here, you pass z* as an argument. The pattern z* says to list any file whose filename starts with z followed by zero or more characters. This is the same function of the * that any DOS or Windows user is probably familiar with. What really happens here is that Bash builds a list of all filenames starting with z and then replaces z* with this list, effectively passing all filenames as arguments to the ls -l command. Unlike DOS and the Windows DOS prompt, however, Bash offers a greater pattern of possibilities for the simple * symbol.

Pathname Expansion

One form of pattern expansion is *pathname expansion*. In addition to the *, you can use up to two other major special symbols to expand pathnames, as shown in Table 16.3.

TABLE 16.3:   Pathname Expansion in Bash

Symbol	Description
?	Match any single character.
[...]	Match one of the characters enclosed in the brackets.
[A-F]	Match any single character that falls between the first character and the second.
[^...] or [!...]	Match any single character other than those specified in the brackets.
[^A-F] or [!A-F]	Match any single character other than those that fall between the first character and the second.

Let's look at some examples. Suppose you want to list all files whose names are three letters long and start with a and end with z. You can use the command

```
$ ls -l a?z
```

Similarly, if you want to match any files whose names simply start with a and end with z, you can use the command

```
$ ls -l a*z
```

The difference is that the ? matches exactly one character in the first example, forcing the filename to be three characters long. In the second example, the * matches zero or more characters, meaning the filename could be two or more characters in length.

Next, consider the situation where you want to see a listing of all files starting with the letters a, b, c, or d. You can use the command

```
$ ls -l a* b* c* d*
```

but this is rather inefficient and becomes cumbersome when you want to see files starting with more letters. To make the process easier, you can use the command

```
$ ls -l [abcd]*
```

which tells you to list any file starting with one of a, b, c, or d followed by zero or more characters. However, because a, b, c, and d are a continuous sequence of letters, you can make the pattern even more concise by using the command

```
$ ls -l [a-d]*
```

Finally, you need to consider the case where you want to exclude a particular character or pattern and include all others. Consider situations where you are producing a compressed archive of all the home directories on a system for backup purposes. Let's say that, for whatever reason, you want to produce an archive of all home directories except those starting with the letter m. You can use the command

```
$ tar czvf home.tar.gz /home/[a-1]* /home/[n-z]*
```

However, you can make things easier with the command

```
$ tar czvf home.tar.gz /home/[!m]*
```

which indicates that all home directories starting with any letter except m should be processed by this command.

Taking things one step further, you can exclude all directories starting with the letters m, n, and o by using

```
$ tar czvf home.tar.gz /home/[^mno]*
```

or

```
$ tar czvf home.tar.gz /home/[!m-o]*
```

Brace Expansion

Closely related to the pathname expansion is *brace expansion*. Brace expansion provides a method by which it is possible to expand an expression regardless of whether the names being generated actually exist as files or directories at all. An example of a brace expression is the command

```
$ mkdir testdir{1,2,3,4}
```

which causes the directories testdir1, testdir2, testdir3, and testdir4 to be created.

Here each element in the braces is separated by a comma, and one by one these elements are used to produce the resulting names. Unlike the [...] expressions you saw earlier, the use of a comma means that the elements between the braces can be more than one character in length:

```
$ mkdir testdir{01,02,03,04}
```

It is important to keep in mind that a brace expression must contain at least one comma.

An interesting feature of both pathname expansion and brace expansion is that they can be used within another brace expression. This is possible because the first expansion to take place is brace expansion. Consider the following example:

```
$ mkdir newdir/{firstdir,firstdir/dir{01,02}}
```

This command creates the following directories:

```
firstdir
firstdir/dir01
firstdir/dir02
```

Here you used the brace expression {01,02} inside the outer brace expression.

Similarly, you can use any of the pathname expansion symbols inside a brace. The command

```
$ chmod 644 testfile.{tx?,bak,0[0-9]}
```

changes the permissions on a series of files including any file matching the expression `testfile.tx?`, `testfile.bak`, and `testfile0` through `testfile9`.

Command Substitution

Finally, let's take a look at *command substitution*, another form of pattern expansion. In some ways this is similar to piping commands together, but the difference is that in piping, the standard output of a command is passed to the standard input of another command. With command substitution, though, the standard output of one command becomes an argument or parameter to another command.

For instance, consider an example where you want to compress all files that have a `.bak` extension. You can get a list of all these files by using the following command:

```
$ find / -name '*.bak' -print
```

Using the exec flag of the `find` command, you can compress all the files in question:

```
$ find / -name '*.bak' -exec gzip {} \;
```

The other option is to use command substitution, as in the following command:

```
$ gzip `find / -name '*.bak' -print`
```

Here the `find` command is contained in backward single quotes. These quotes indicate that the results of the command should be used as part of the command line, in this case as arguments to the `gzip` command.

An alternative to the backward single quotes is the following form, which has the same meaning and gets the same result:

```
$ gzip $(find / -name \*.bak -print)
```

The main difference between these two forms is the meaning of the special character \. In the latter example, no characters have special meanings, while in the former example, the backslash retains special meaning except when followed by $, `, or \.

NOTE

In addition to the types of expansion described here, there are other types of expansion available in Bash. These are outlined in detail in the `bash` man page. However, the pattern expansion forms in this chapter provide a lot of power. If you find yourself needing more powerful pattern and expansion abilities, check out the man page using the command `man bash`.

Looking Ahead

Now that you are shell power users and can perform lots of nifty magic in the world of Bash, it is time to move on to working with real, productive applications in Linux.

In Chapter 17, "General System Administration," you are going to learn about the essential tasks of system administration. These include managing users and groups of users as well as scheduling tasks for automated execution and controlling the way in which a Linux system boots.

CHAPTER

SEVENTEEN

General System Administration

- Managing Users

- Managing Groups

- System Start-Up

- Scheduling Jobs with *crond*

- Managing Logs

This chapter describes some of the basic administrative tasks that are necessary for maintaining a working Linux system.

Fundamental to any Linux system, from a network server to a home computer shared by family members, is user management. This runs the gamut from creating new user accounts to changing user passwords to ensuring that a user's home directory is just the way you, as the system administrator, want it when the user's account is created.

On even a moderately sophisticated system, user access to system resources will be governed on both a per-user basis and a per-group basis, where a group consists of a number of users associated in a common organizational entity with a single name. Linux provides facilities to associate users in groups and to use these groups to manage access to system resources.

Another administrative essential—one that is crucial to taking full advantage of Linux—is the automation of tasks, both at start-up and on a scheduled basis. Linux's notion of run levels provides a powerful mechanism to specify what will occur at what point in the start-up process (and in the shutdown process as well). And the Cron scheduling daemon offers a mechanism to schedule one-time jobs as well as operations that are repeated daily, weekly, monthly, or yearly.

Finally, Linux provides sophisticated logging capabilities that make it possible to know exactly what is happening on your system. Of course, for logs to be of use, they need regular management. After all, if your log contains one year's worth of entries, it is probably too large to be useful for analysis or for quickly tracking down problems or potential problems.

Managing Users

Chapter 15, "Using Linuxconf and Other Tools for System Configuration," introduced you to user management when it described Red Hat Linux 7.1's version of the Linuxconf utility. However, Linuxconf is not universally available in all distributions of Linux, and to fully master the administration of Linux you must learn to manage users without this tool.

Creating Users

The creation of users in Linux is done through useradd (generally found in /usr/sbin/; the adduser command works in the same way). The version of useradd shipped with Red Hat Linux 7.1 is a highly complex tool that can make the creation of new user accounts exceptionally easy. Let's start with the simplest example and work up to more complicated cases. The simplest case is to create a user with all the default settings. For instance, to create a new user called testuser1, you simply type

```
# /usr/sbin/useradd testuser1
```

This command creates the user by performing the following actions:

- Creating an entry for the user in the /etc/passwd file without a password. In most Linux distributions, a password needs to be assigned before the user is able to log in.

- Assigning a user ID to the user. In Red Hat Linux 7.1, the default user ID is the smallest number greater than or equal to 500 that is greater than all other users' IDs.

- Adding the user to the appropriate group. Generally in Linux, this means creating a group for the user to which only that user belongs.

- Creating a home directory for the user (at /home/testuser1 on most Linux systems) and copying the contents of /etc/skel to the home directory. Skeleton directories are discussed in more detail in the section "Setting Up Default Home Directories," later in this chapter.

NOTE   On Red Hat Linux 7.1, the default options for creating new users are automatically specified in the /etc/login.defs and or the /etc/default/useradd configuration file.

Using the useradd command to add users leaves the system administrator free to assign a password for the user, utilizing the techniques described in the section "Changing Passwords."

What happens, though, if you want to override the system defaults for assignment of the user ID? Consider an organization where Red Hat Linux user IDs are based on the individual's corporate identification number. In this case, you will want to force the assignment of a particular ID, using the -u flag:

```
# useradd -u 10001 testuser1
```

This creates the account for testuser1 with the assigned user ID of 10001.

Similarly, what if you want to force the assignment of a particular group to the user as their default group? For instance, if testuser1 should be assigned to the collective group named users rather than to an individual group as is the default in Red Hat Linux, you could use the -g flag:

```
# useradd -g users testuser1
```

Let's go a step further and assume that testuser1 should belong to groups group1 and group2 in addition to the default group of users. You could create the user as indicated and then manually add it to the groups, as shown later in the section on managing groups. But useradd offers the -G flag, which allows you to specify additional groups to add the new user to when the account is created:

```
# useradd -g users -G group1,group2 testuser1
```

Finally, to specify an alternate home directory for a user, use the -d flag:

```
# useradd -d /other/home/directory testuser1
```

Changing *useradd* Defaults

There are some defaults used by useradd that you may want to override every time you create a user. For example, you may want all home directories to be created in /users instead of /home. Similarly, you may want all new users to belong to the default group users instead of their own private groups.

These defaults can be reset using the -D flag of the useradd command and several supplementary flags. The -D flag indicates that the command should not create a new user but should assign new defaults.

The -D flag is used in conjunction with supplementary flags. Here you will see how to use the -b and -g flags for resetting the default home directory path and default group, respectively.

To set the default home directory path to /users, use the command

```
# useradd -D -b /users
```

Similarly, to set the default group for all new users to users, use the command

```
# useradd -D -g users
```

These commands can be combined into one command:

```
# useradd -D -b /users -g users
```

You can check the current default values with the useradd -D command, without any supplementary flags.

Changing Passwords

Changing passwords is accomplished with the passwd command. Any user can change their password by simply typing the command at the prompt. They will be asked to enter their current password, followed by their new password twice for confirmation:

```
$ passwd
Changing password for test
(current) UNIX password:
New UNIX password:
Retype new UNIX password:
passwd: all authentication tokens updated successfully
```

In many versions of Linux, the passwd command checks to see if a password is too short, too simple, too similar to the username, or too similar to the previous password. An invalid password produces errors like these:

```
$ passwd
Changing password for test
(current) UNIX password:
New UNIX password:
BAD PASSWORD: it does not contain enough DIFFERENT characters
New UNIX password:
BAD PASSWORD: it is too short
New UNIX password:
BAD PASSWORD: is too simplistic/systematic
passwd: Authentication token manipulation error
```

WARNING   In earlier versions of Red Hat Linux, you could use a dictionary word as a password if you ignored the **BAD PASSWORD** warning. Starting with Red Hat Linux 7.1, this is no longer possible for non-root users.

The root user has the power to change any user's password by supplying the username as an argument to the `passwd` program. In this case, the only prompts are to enter the new password twice:

```
# passwd test
New UNIX password:
Retype new UNIX password:
passwd: all authentication tokens updated successfully
```

Setting Up Default Home Directories

You probably noticed a reference to skeleton directories earlier in the section "Creating Users." By default, every user is given a home directory, usually as a subdirectory of the /home directory. When the user's account is created, their home directory is created and populated with a default set of files. This default set of files is copied from the /etc/skel directory, which contains the skeleton directory for new home directories.

In order to include a file in every new home directory, simply create the file and place it in /etc/skel with the same name you would want it to have in users' home directories. All users added after you place the file there will find the file in their home directories when their accounts are created.

Removing Users

Deleting users is a parallel process to adding users: You use the `userdel` command. Fortunately, though, this command is far simpler to use than the `useradd` command. To delete a user's account and remove their entry from relevant system files such as /etc/passwd, simply provide the username as an argument:

```
# /usr/sbin/userdel username
```

The problem here is that the user's files are not deleted. To delete the user's home directory at the same time, provide the -r flag:

```
# /usr/sbin/userdel -r username
```

This leaves one other issue: What if the user owns files elsewhere on the system that need to be deleted? This can be achieved by using the `find` command after deleting the user. In order to do this, make note of the user's user ID from the /etc/passwd file before deleting the user, and then use the `find` command:

```
# find / -type f -uid 503 -print -exec rm {} \;
```

Let's break down the components of this command:

- The forward slash (/) indicates that the command should search the entire directory structure from the top level.

- `-type f` indicates that the command should find only files.

- `-uid 503` indicates that only files owned by the user with ID 503 should be returned. (This number should be substituted with the user ID of the user you are deleting.)

- `-print` indicates that the filenames should be printed as they are found so that you can track the progress of the command.

- `-exec rm {} \;` indicates that the command `rm` should be performed on every file found, effectively removing the files.

WARNING   Great care needs to be taken when using the `find` command described above. Because it runs as the root user, a mistake in typing the command or in the ownership of files on your system could cause critical data to be lost. Use the above `find` command only if the user is likely to own files outside their home directory.

Managing Groups

Managing groups—collections of associated users—is as simple as managing users and parallels the user management process. As with user management, Linux provides commands to automate the creation and modification of groups.

NOTE   On other Linux distributions, these commands may behave differently than described in this section, so you should check the documentation if you are not using the copy of Red Hat Linux 7.1 included with this book.

Creating Groups

You can add new groups to your system using the `groupadd` command (this command is called `addgroup` on some distributions). To create a group, simply provide the group name as an argument:

```
# /usr/sbin/groupadd groupname
```

The group is created and assigned a new user number based on the following rule from the Red Hat Linux 7.1 man page for `groupadd`: "The default is to use the smallest ID value greater than 500 and greater than every other group." Several other Linux distributions add new users to the users group (100) by default.

If you want to specify the group number, simply use the -g flag to indicate the number:

`# groupadd -g 503 groupname`

This should produce an entry similar to the following in /etc/group:

`groupname::503:`

This entry shows an empty group with the specified name and group ID.

TIP If you don't remember which group you want, existing group IDs are stored in the `/etc/group` file.

Adding Users to Groups

Unfortunately, there is no standard program available to easily add users to a group. In order to do this, the easiest thing is to directly edit the file /etc/group. Each line in this file represents the definition for a group and takes the form

`groupname::password:groupid:userlist`

The components of this line are as follows:

- The `groupname` entry is the name of the group.

- The `password` entry represents a password for the group; passwords generally are not applied to groups, so this entry is usually blank.

- The `groupid` is the numeric ID for the group and should be unique for the group.

- The `userlist` entry is a comma-separated list of users who belong to the group. For instance, if user1, user2, and user3 all belong to the group named group1 whose group ID is 505, the entry for the group would look like

  `group1::505:user1,user2,user3`

If you want to add users to an existing group, simply edit the file /etc/group with your favorite text editor and add the usernames to the end of the user list, separating each username with a comma.

Deleting Groups

Deleting groups is achieved with the groupdel command. This command is truly simple; no flags or options are available. Simply provide the group name to delete as an argument, and the group will be deleted, as follows:

```
# /usr/sbin/groupdel groupname
```

For all its simplicity, though, there are some caveats:

- Files belonging to the group won't be deleted or have their group changed.
- If the group serves as the primary group for a user (in other words, is indicated as the user's group in the password file), the group won't be deleted.

The first issue can be handled much as you dealt with deleting a user's files once the user had been deleted. First, you note the group ID of the group you are deleting (this can be found in the /etc/group file). Once the group is deleted with groupdel, you use the find command to change the group ownership of all files that belonged to the deleted group:

```
# find / -type f -gid 503 -print -exec chgrp newgroupname () \;
```

This find command will find all files belonging to the group whose ID is 503 and then use the chgrp command to change the group ownership of the file to the group named newgroupname.

System Start-Up

One area that is a mystery to many Linux users (as opposed to system administrators) is the boot sequence, when all those arcane messages flash by on the screen.

> **NOTE** Start-up messages are saved in the system log file /var/log/dmesg. Log files are discussed later in this chapter.

What Happens During Booting?

The boot cycle is really simpler than the boot-time messages suggest. Basically, there are two stages to the boot process:

1. Booting the kernel. During this phase, the kernel loads into memory and prints messages as it initializes each device driver.

2. Executing the program `init`. After the kernel finishes loading and initializing devices, the program `init` runs. Init handles the launching of all programs, including essential system daemons and other software that is specified to load at boot time.

The *init* Program

This section takes a closer look at the `init` program because it is here that you are able to easily customize which programs load during the boot cycle. Init has the job of launching new processes and restarting other processes when they exit. A perfect example of this is the set of processes that provide the virtual login consoles in Linux. On most Linux systems, six of these are initially loaded at boot time. When you log out of a console window, that process dies and `init` starts a new one so that six console windows are always available.

The rules that govern the operation of the `init` program are stored in the file /etc/inittab. Red Hat Linux 7.1's default /etc/inittab file looks like this:

```
#
# inittab      This file describes how the INIT process should set up
#              the system in a certain run-level.
#
# Author:      Miquel van Smoorenburg, <miquels@drinkel.nl.mugnet.org>
#              Modified for RHS Linux by Marc Ewing and Donnie Barnes
#

# Default runlevel. The runlevels used by RHS are:
#   0 - halt (Do NOT set initdefault to this)
#   1 - Single user mode
#   2 - Multiuser, without NFS (The same as 3, if you do not have
#   networking)
#   3 - Full multiuser mode
#   4 - unused
#   5 - X11
#   6 - reboot (Do NOT set initdefault to this)
#
```

```
id:3:initdefault:

# System initialization.
si::sysinit:/etc/rc.d/rc.sysinit

l0:0:wait:/etc/rc.d/rc 0
l1:1:wait:/etc/rc.d/rc 1
l2:2:wait:/etc/rc.d/rc 2
l3:3:wait:/etc/rc.d/rc 3
l4:4:wait:/etc/rc.d/rc 4
l5:5:wait:/etc/rc.d/rc 5
l6:6:wait:/etc/rc.d/rc 6

# Things to run in every runlevel.
ud::once:/sbin/update

# Trap CTRL-ALT-DELETE
ca::ctrlaltdel:/sbin/shutdown -t3 -r now

# When our UPS tells us power has failed, assume we have a few minutes
# of power left.  Schedule a shutdown for 2 minutes from now.
# This does, of course, assume you have powerd installed and your
# UPS connected and working correctly.
pf::powerfail:/sbin/shutdown -f -h +2 "Power Failure; System Shutting
    Down"

# If power was restored before the shutdown kicked in, cancel it.
pr:12345:powerokwait:/sbin/shutdown -c "Power Restored; Shutdown
    Cancelled"


# Run gettys in standard runlevels
1:2345:respawn:/sbin/mingetty tty1
2:2345:respawn:/sbin/mingetty tty2
3:2345:respawn:/sbin/mingetty tty3
4:2345:respawn:/sbin/mingetty tty4
5:2345:respawn:/sbin/mingetty tty5
6:2345:respawn:/sbin/mingetty tty6

# Run xdm in runlevel 5
# xdm is now a separate service
x:5:respawn:/usr/bin/X11/xdm -nodaemon
```

While it is not important to learn how to write your own inittab file, it is useful to understand what this file is telling us.

Linux has a system of *run levels*. A run level is a number that identifies the current state of the system and which processes init should run and keep running in that system state. In the inittab file, the first entry, id:3:initdefault, specifies the default run level that loads at boot time. In the previous example, it is a multi-user console mode, run level 3. Then, each entry in the inittab file specifies which run level it applies to in the second field of the entry (each field is separated by a colon). So, for run level 3, the following lines are relevant:

```
13:3:wait:/etc/rc.d/rc 3
1:2345:respawn:/sbin/mingetty tty1
2:2345:respawn:/sbin/mingetty tty2
3:2345:respawn:/sbin/mingetty tty3
4:2345:respawn:/sbin/mingetty tty4
5:2345:respawn:/sbin/mingetty tty5
6:2345:respawn:/sbin/mingetty tty6
```

The first line runs the start-up script /etc/rc.d/rc 3. This will run all the scripts contained in the directory /etc/rc.d/rc3.d. These scripts represent programs that need to start at system initialization, such as sendmail, PCMCIA services, the printer daemon, and crond. Generally, you will not want to edit these scripts or change them; they are the system defaults. The last six lines set up the six virtual consoles provided in Linux.

NOTE   Run levels and their scripts vary greatly by Linux distribution. Multiuser console mode is often associated with some number other than 3, and the directory with the multiuser console mode scripts can vary as well.

What is important to note is that the last script in the rc3.d directory to be executed will be the S99local script. This script is actually a link to the file /etc/rc.d/rc.local; it is here that you can put any custom start-up programs that you want to launch at boot time.

On other Linux systems, the structure of /etc/inittab may differ, as will the organization of the /etc/rc.d directory. In all systems, however, the file /etc/rc.d/rc.local represents the file in which you can add your own start-up commands.

Using the *rc.local* File

The default Red Hat Linux 7.1 `rc.local` file sets up the login prompt and does nothing else:

```
#!/bin/sh

# This script will be executed *after* all the other init scripts.
# You can put your own initialization stuff in here if you don't
# want to do the full Sys V style init stuff.

if [ -f /etc/redhat-release ]; then
    R=$(cat /etc/redhat-release)

    arch=$(uname -m)
    a="a"
    case "_$arch" in
       _a*) a="an";;
       _i*) a="an";;
    esac

    NUMPROC=`egrep -c "^cpu[0-9]+" /proc/stat`
    if [ "$NUMPROC" -gt "1" ]; then
        SMP="$NUMPROC-processor "
        if [ "$NUMPROC" = "8" -o "$NUMPROC" = "11" ]; then
            a="an"
    else
        a="a"
        fi
    fi
    # This will overwrite /etc/issue at every boot.  So, make any
    # changes you
    # want to make to /etc/issue here or you will lose them when you
    # reboot.
    echo "" > /etc/issue
    echo "$R" >> /etc/issue
    echo "Kernel $(uname -r) on $a $SMP$(uname -m)" >> /etc/issue

    cp -f /etc/issue /etc/issue.net
    echo >> /etc/issue
fi

touch /var/lock/subsys/local
```

This may look complicated, but it is actually quite simple. The steps here are as follows:

1. Identify the Red Hat Linux release being used.

2. Identify the hardware architecture (such as i386 for Intel or axp for Alpha).

3. Identify the number of processors, or CPUs, on your computer.

4. Store the contents of the login prompt in /etc/issue; this file is displayed at each console prompt.

Because the rc.local file is a standard shell script, you can do anything here that is legitimate in a shell script, including assigning environment variables and launching programs. For instance, on one system I manage, we launch a database daemon in our rc.local file with the following command:

```
# /usr/local/Minerva/bin/msqld &
```

Feel free to use the rc.local file to add any start-up programs that you want to run. For instance, if you want to receive an e-mail every time a particular machine on the network finishes booting, you can use the rc.local file on the machine in question to run the command

```
# /bin/mail -s "I have booted — machinename" username@some.domain
```

to send a quick mail message to *username@some.domain* with the subject line I have booted — *machinename*.

Shutting Down

Closely related to system start-up is system shutdown. In Linux, as in all other multitasking operating systems, it is essential to shut down your system cleanly in order to prevent corruption of data stored on attached hard disk drives. Generally, this is done by the root user with the shutdown command:

```
# shutdown -h now
```

The use of the now argument tells the program to shut down the system immediately. The -h flag tells the system to halt after shutting down. When you see the message System Halted, it is safe to power off your computer.

Closely related to the shutdown command is the reboot command, which cleanly shuts down the system and then reboots it. Hitting the key combination Ctrl+Alt+Delete invokes the reboot command, unless you disable it in the aforementioned /etc/inittab file.

TIP   It's a good idea to disable the Ctrl+Alt+Delete option in `/etc/inittab`. By default, Red Hat Linux 7.1 allows all users to run this key combination to reboot. You don't want one person's frustration to interrupt the work of every user who is accessing your Linux computer.

Scheduling Jobs with *crond*

One of the great strengths of a multiuser server-class operating system like Linux is that much can happen in an unattended manner. If you use Linux as a mail server, Web server, or FTP server, unattended activity occurs every time one of these applications answers incoming connections and requests for service. Similarly, individual users and the system administrator can configure Linux to perform prescheduled tasks in an unattended manner.

This activity is achieved through the facility of a daemon called `crond`. This daemon is standard and is generally installed to start every time the system boots.

How *crond* Works

The way in which `crond` works is amazingly simple. Once `crond` starts (generally at boot time), it wakes up every minute and checks whether any jobs have been scheduled to run during that minute. If so, the job is executed and the resulting output is sent by e-mail to the user who scheduled the job.

Because `crond` checks the date stamps on its configuration files every minute, any changes to schedules are noted without the necessity of restarting the `crond` process.

Scheduling Jobs

Scheduling jobs is an easy matter. All scheduled jobs are stored in an individual configuration file (known as a `crontab` file) for the user, with each line representing a job that has been scheduled.

Let's start by looking at the format of `crontab` file entries before moving on to how to edit the `crontab` file to create scheduled jobs.

Each entry takes the form

```
time-date command
```

The *time-date* entry consists of five numeric fields, each separated by spaces, which indicate when a job should be run. The five fields (in order) are:

- Minute: Possible values are 0–59.

- Hour: Possible values are 0–23.

- Day of month: Possible values are 0–31.

- Month: Possible values are 0–12.

- Day of week: Possible values are 0–7 where both 0 and 7 represent Sunday.

For all these fields, several rules provide flexibility:

- Ranges of numbers can be used. For instance, 1–3 in the hour field says to schedule the command for 1:00 A.M., 2:00 A.M., and 3:00 A.M. Similarly, 2–4 in the day of week field schedules the job for Tuesday, Wednesday, and Thursday.

- Ranges can be stepped through in increments greater than one. For instance, to run a command every other hour from midnight to midnight, use the range 0–23 and combine it with the step of 2, separating them with slashes: 0–23/2.

- An asterisk (*) indicates the entire range for a field from smallest value to largest value. Thus, * in the day of month field is the same as 0–31 and in the day of week field is the same as 0–7.

- The first three letters of the month or day's name can be substituted for the number in the applicable field.

Sample Times and Dates

Let's take a look at some example time-date fields:

`0 1 * * *`	This field indicates a job that should run every day at 1:00 A.M.
`30 14 * * 1`	This field indicates a job that should run every Monday at 2:30 P.M.

`0 12 1 * *`	This field indicates a job that should run at noon on the first day of every month.
`0 12 * 1 mon`	This field indicates a job that should run at noon on every Monday in January every year.
`0 12 2 feb *`	This field indicates a job that should run at noon on February 2 every year.

The Command Field

The `time-date` field is separated from the `command` field by one or more spaces and runs until the end of the line. The commands are processed by the `/bin/sh` shell.

For instance, the `crontab` entry

```
0 1 * * *      /usr/local/bin/backup
```

causes the program `/usr/local/bin/backup` to execute daily at 1:00 A.M.

Sometimes commands (such as the `mail` command) require information to be entered through the standard input. This is achieved using percent signs (%). The first percent sign marks the start of standard input, and each subsequent percent sign serves as a new line character in the standard input.

So the `crontab` entry

```
30 14 * * fri      /bin/mail -s "TGIF" armand@landegg.edu%Thank God It's
Friday%%Me.
```

sends the following e-mail message

```
Thank God It's Friday

Me.
```

to `armand@landegg.edu` each Friday at 2:30 P.M.

Editing the *crontab* File

You can edit your `crontab` file with the `crontab -e` command. Two approaches are available: Create a file containing all the entries desired in the `crontab` file and then load it with the `crontab` command, or edit the `crontab` file directly with the `crontab -e` command.

Loading Entries from a File   In order to load entries from a file, it is first necessary to create a file (using your favorite text editor) containing all the entries you wish to have appear in your crontab file. A sample file might contain two entries as follows:

```
0 1 * * *      /usr/local/bin/backup
30 14 * * fri    /bin/mail -s "TGIF" armand@landegg.edu%Thank God It's
Friday%%Me.
```

This file needs to be saved, under a suitable name such as cronjobs.

Once the file is created and saved, it can be loaded into a user's crontab file by issuing the command

```
$ crontab cronjobs
```

The contents of cronjobs overwrite any current entries in the crontab file for the user. Using this method, any user can manipulate their own crontab file.

The root user has special privileges that allow them to edit the crontab entries for any user. Using the -u flag, the root user can specify that another user's crontab file, rather than the root user's crontab file, should be altered. For instance, the command

```
# crontab -u username cronjobs
```

loads the file cronjobs as the crontab file for the user username.

Editing *crontab* Files Directly   Instead of creating a separate file and loading it into the crontab file, the crontab command provides the -e flag, which allows the user to edit the crontab file directly.

By default, crontab -e attempts to edit the crontab file using the vi editor. The vi editor is a powerful but hard-to-master editor popular among longtime Unix users. If you prefer to use another editor, such as xedit, you need to set the value of the EDITOR environment variable to this program:

```
$ export EDITOR=xedit
```

Then the command

```
$ crontab -e
```

opens the crontab file for editing using the specified editor, as shown in Figure 17.1.

FIGURE 17.1:

Editing the *crontab* file with *xedit*

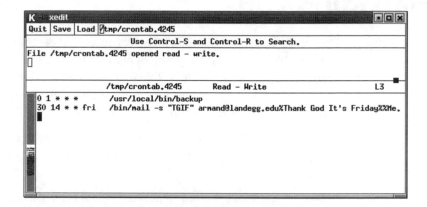

As when you load a file into the crontab file using the -u flag, the root user can directly edit another user's crontab file:

```
$ crontab -u username -e
```

Viewing the Contents of the *crontab* File   In order to view the contents of the crontab file, simply use the -l flag:

```
$ crontab -l
# DO NOT EDIT THIS FILE - edit the master and reinstall.
# (/tmp/crontab.555 installed on Mon Jul 13 00:07:05 2001)
# (Cron version -- $Id: crontab.c,v 2.13 1994/01/17 03:20:37 vixie Exp  $)
0 1 * * *        /usr/local/bin/backup
30 14 * * fri    /bin/mail -s "TGIF" armand@landegg.edu%Thank God It's
Friday%%Me
```

Notice that the crontab file has several comment lines at the beginning that start with the hash mark (#).

As with editing the crontab file, the root user can view the contents of any user's crontab file with the -u flag:

```
# crontab -u username -l
```

Removing the *crontab* File   In order to erase the contents of a user's crontab file, the user can use the -r flag:

```
$ crontab -r
```

Similarly, the root user can clear any user's crontab file with the -u flag:

```
# crontab -u username -r
```

Managing Logs

One of the benefits of Linux and all forms of Unix is that they provide standardized mechanisms for the logging of activity from the numerous daemons and programs running on the system. These logs can be used to debug system problems as well as track usage of the system, covering everything from possible security breaches to advanced warning of possible hardware failure.

For example, the following extract of the main Red Hat Linux 7.1 system log file (/var/log/messages) provides numerous pieces of information from a short period of time:

```
May  9 11:32:58 laptop71 network: Shutting down device eth0:   succeeded
May  9 11:33:00 laptop71 network: Bringing up device eth0:   succeeded
May  9 11:33:00 laptop71 kernel: eth0: flipped to 10baseT
May  9 11:33:01 laptop71 xinetd[3511]: Exiting...
May  9 11:33:02 laptop71 xinetd: xinetd shutdown succeeded
May  9 11:33:04 laptop71 xinetd[5598]: chargen disabled, removing
May  9 11:33:04 laptop71 xinetd[5598]: ftp disabled, removing
May  9 11:33:04 laptop71 xinetd[5598]: time disabled, removing
May  9 11:33:04 laptop71 xinetd[5598]: time disabled, removing
May  9 11:33:04 laptop71 xinetd[5598]: telnet disabled, removing
May  9 11:33:04 laptop71 xinetd[5598]: talk disabled, removing
May  9 11:33:04 laptop71 xinetd[5598]: rsync disabled, removing
May  9 11:33:04 laptop71 xinetd[5598]: shell disabled, removing
May  9 11:33:04 laptop71 xinetd[5598]: login disabled, removing
May  9 11:33:04 laptop71 xinetd[5598]: exec disabled, removing
May  9 11:33:04 laptop71 xinetd[5598]: ntalk disabled, removing
May  9 11:33:04 laptop71 xinetd[5598]: linuxconf disabled, removing
May  9 11:33:04 laptop71 xinetd[5598]: finger disabled, removing
May  9 11:33:04 laptop71 xinetd[5598]: echo-udp disabled, removing
May  9 11:33:04 laptop71 xinetd[5598]: echo disabled, removing
May  9 11:33:04 laptop71 xinetd[5598]: daytime-udp disabled, removing
May  9 11:33:04 laptop71 xinetd[5598]: daytime disabled, removing
May  9 11:33:04 laptop71 xinetd[5598]: chargen-udp disabled, removing
May  9 11:33:04 laptop71 xinetd[5598]: xinetd Version 2.1.8.9pre14
        started with
May  9 11:33:04 laptop71 xinetd[5598]: libwrap
May  9 11:33:04 laptop71 xinetd[5598]: options compiled in.
May  9 11:33:04 laptop71 xinetd[5598]: Started working: 0 available
        service
May  9 11:33:05 laptop71 xinetd: xinetd startup succeeded
May  9 11:33:21 laptop71 kernel: eth0: flipped to 10baseT
```

```
May  9 11:33:38 laptop71 kernel: smb_trans2_request: result=-104,
   setting invalid
May  9 11:33:39 laptop71 kernel: smb_retry: successful, new pid=2190,
   generation=8
```

What exactly do you learn here? The `network` program informs you that the network interface eth0 was shut down and restarted, in a 10baseT-type network, that xinetd disabled a number of services before restarting, and that there was an smb (Samba) file transfer with a PID of 2190.

What Gets Logged?

It is important to make a distinction between different types of logs in a Linux system. Basically, there are two types of logs: system logs and application logs. This section looks at system logs because all systems have them. Application-specific logs are dependent on the applications being run and how these applications are configured to generate their logs.

In the system logs, you are likely to find messages and warnings from the kernel that include information about modules that have loaded, data from the sendmail daemon that provides a trail of the messages that have been processed in the system, and messages about the success or failure of authentication (login) attempts.

System logs are generated by the syslogd daemon, which loads at boot time. The daemon accesses messages at eight levels of severity from various system processes such as the kernel, the mail system, user programs configured to use syslogd, and authentication programs such as the login program.

These levels of messages are, in order of increasing severity:

- debug

- info

- notice

- warning

- err

- crit

- alert

- emerg

These levels are used in the /etc/syslog.conf file to tell syslogd where to create logs for different types of information. The /etc/syslog.conf file contains multiple entries, one on each line, each containing two fields separated by one or more spaces: a facility-level list and a log file location.

The facility-level list is a semicolon-separated list of facility-level pairs. Facilities are indicated by facility names such as mail, kern (for the kernel), user (for user programs), and auth (for authentication programs). Sample facility-level pairs include the following:

- mail.err: errors generated by the mail daemon

- *.info: all information messages

- kern.emerg: emergency messages from the kernel

Let's look at the default /etc/syslog.conf file that is included with Red Hat Linux 7.1 to get a sense of how this works:

```
# Log all kernel messages to the console.
# Logging much else clutters up the screen.
#kern.*                                          /dev/console

# Log anything (except mail) of level info or higher.
# Don't log private authentication messages!
*.info;mail.none;news.none;authpriv.none         /var/log/messages
# The authpriv file has restricted access.
authpriv.*                                       /var/log/secure

# Log all the mail messages in one place.
mail.*                                           /var/log/maillog

# Log cron stuff
cron.*                                           /var/log/cron

# Everybody gets emergency messages, plus log them on another
# machine.
*.emerg                                          *

# Save mail and news errors of level err and higher in a
# special file.
uucp,news.crit                                   /var/log/spooler

# Save boot messages also to boot.log
local7.*                                         /var/log/boot.log
```

The first important line is

```
*.info;mail.none;news.none;authpriv.none        /var/log/messages
```

This line logs information messages from all facilities except mail, news, and authentication (hence, `mail.none;news.none;authpriv.none`) to the file `/var/log/messages`. This is followed by

```
authpriv.*                              /var/log/secure
```

which places all authentication messages in `/var/log/secure`.

Next you find the following line, which specifies that all mail log messages should be placed in `/var/log/maillog`:

```
mail.*                                  /var/log/maillog
```

This is followed a few lines later by

```
uucp,news.crit                          /var/log/spooler
```

which logs certain mail- and news-related messages to `/var/log/spooler`.

The first thing you will probably notice is that log messages are separated into different files. The goals behind this practice are to keep the size of each log manageable and to keep the information in each log related so that tracking down log messages is easy. If every message of every level from every facility ended up in a single log file, the information would be practically useless because the volume of information in the file would be unmanageable.

If you want to change your logging strategy by editing `/etc/syslog.conf`, you can do this by editing the `syslog.conf` file and then telling `syslogd` to reload the configuration with the command

```
# kill -HUP `cat /var/run/syslogd.pid`
```

Notice the use of the back quotes. These indicate that the command they contain should be executed and the resulting standard output should be provided as an argument to the `kill -HUP` command. The `-HUP` flag of the `kill` command indicates that the process should reread its configuration but keep running.

Rotating Logs

In order for logs to remain useful, they need to be rotated on a regular basis. This allows the size of the logs to be manageable and clears them of old information that is no longer of particular value. Also, because the size of logs will continue to grow, rotating them frees up the disk space they are using.

The simplest strategy for rotating logs is to remove them and restart `syslogd`. When `syslogd` restarts, it will create a new, empty log file to replace any that have been removed. For instance, the following commands

```
# rm /var/log/messages
# kill -HUP `cat /var/run/syslogd.pid`
```

remove the /var/log/messages file and restart `syslogd` to create a new, empty /var/log/messages file.

This strategy of removing files works well on a single-user or home system where historical logs may not serve a valuable purpose. On multiuser servers, however, historical information is of particular value, especially for tracking possible security breaches. In this case, the strategy may be slightly different. For instance, to keep one generation of historical logs, you can move the current logs to a new filename and then restart `syslogd` to create a new current log file:

```
# mv /var/log/messages /var/log/messages.1
# kill -HUP `cat /var/run/syslogd.pid`
```

Similarly, if you want to create two generations of historical log files, you need to move the first-generation files to the second-generation filename and then move the current logs to the first-generation filename:

```
# mv /var/log/messages.1 /var/log/messages.2
# mv /var/log/messages /var/log/messages.1
# kill -HUP `cat /var/run/syslogd.pid`
```

On most systems, you may want to automate this procedure, running it every week at a set time. To do this, you first need to create a script that performs the necessary actions to rotate your log files. For instance, on a Linux server where you keep one generation of logs, the script could look something like this:

```
#!/bin/sh

mv /var/log/messages /var/log/messages.1
mv /var/log/secure /var/log/secure.1
mv /var/log/maillog /var/log/maillog.1
mv /var/log/spooler /var/log/spooler.1
kill -HUP `cat /var/run/syslogd.pid`
```

This script file needs to be created with a text editor in a logical location (such as /usr/local/bin/newlogs) and then made into an executable file:

```
# chmod 755 /usr/local/bin/newlogs
```

Next, you need to edit the root user's `crontab` file, using the methods described earlier in this chapter, and add an appropriate entry. For instance, to run the script every Sunday at 12:01 A.M., you would use the entry

```
1 12 * * sun   /usr/local/bin/newlogs
```

| TIP | Red Hat Linux 7.1 automates the log rotation process, based on the `/etc/logrotate.conf` file. The first two commands in this file rotate logs each week, with four weeks of backlogs. For example, you may have five weeks of system logs: `/var/log/messages` and `/var/log/messages.1` through `/var/log/messages.4`. |

Looking Ahead

In this chapter, you have learned a handful of useful system administration tasks relating to users, scheduling, and logs.

Chapter 18, "Using Peripherals," describes how to configure and use two of the most popular PC peripherals: printers and modems.

You will learn how to configure both PostScript and PCL printers, and you will discover the mechanics of the Linux/Unix print spool systems.

Chapter 18 also discusses modem configuration, and you'll get to experiment with the `minicom` program to test and use your modems.

CHAPTER
EIGHTEEN

Using Peripherals

- Linux and Plug and Play

- Printers

- Modems

- Other "Modems"

- USB Mice/Keyboards

This chapter explains how to configure the two most common types of peripherals: printers and modems. You will get an understanding of how Linux ports work, take a look at the files that control the Linux printing system, and become acquainted with `minicom`, a standard Linux terminal emulator that you can use to access your modem. You will also examine the different systems required to configure USB mice and keyboards. But to understand how Linux device configuration works, you first need a basic understanding on how Linux works with Plug and Play.

Linux and Plug and Play

Linux is not a true Plug-and-Play (PnP) operating system. Yet it has programs that can detect hardware attached to your computer. This seeming contradiction requires some explanation.

Plug and Play is a system whereby the devices that you attach your computer are detected and automatically configured on various communication channels inside your computer. A fully PnP system includes four types of components: a PnP BIOS, a PnP motherboard, PnP devices, and a PnP operating system.

Most current BIOSes and devices are Plug and Play. Assuming you also have a PnP motherboard, the BIOS sets up the channels, ports, and addresses for devices such as your drives, keyboard, and mouse. This configuration is complete before the operating system is loaded. Linux can use these preset channels to detect your hardware with varying degrees of success. The success of Linux detection depends in part on the type of device in question.

Channels, Addresses, and Ports

Plug and Play sets up communication between devices and basic components such as your CPU and RAM. Computer devices communicate through various types of channels, addresses, or ports:

IRQ   Devices can use IRQ, or interrupt request, ports for getting service from your CPU.

I/O   Space is reserved in RAM for information exchange between different parts of your computer. This space is designated by I/O, or input/output, addresses.

DMA   Some devices can bypass your CPU with DMA, or Direct Memory Access, channels.

Different types of devices need different types of channels, addresses, or ports, depending on how they are attached to your computer. If you have a problem with a device such as a modem or a sound card, Linux may be looking for these devices on the wrong IRQ port, I/O address, or DMA channel.

ISA

Many peripheral devices installed inside older computers were built to some form of the Industry Standard Architecture (ISA).

Plug-and-Play ISA was introduced in 1993, so most ISA devices "conform" to PnP standards. Unfortunately, PnP ISA devices often do not get the channels that any operating system expects, so you may have to assign channels, ports, or addresses manually.

This is a somewhat common problem with network cards. Manual configuration of network cards is discussed in more detail in Chapter 28, "Configuring Red Hat Linux 7.1 for an Ethernet Network."

PCI

The Peripheral Component Interconnect, or PCI, bus was developed in part to overcome the limitations on ISA devices. The PCI bus is faster, and PCI devices can share some IRQ channels. Some PnP BIOS menus allow you to assign IRQ, I/O, and DMA channels directly to individual PCI devices.

NOTE   The Accelerated Graphics Card is a special type of PCI card optimized to handle graphics between the video card and the CPU.

External

External devices are often easier to configure, because they do not have independent channels. External devices such as modems or printers are usually connected to specific physical ports. These ports, which are usually serial or parallel connections, already have assigned channels. The attached devices use the same channels.

The exception to this principle for external devices is USB.

USB

The Universal Serial Bus (USB) is not just an external connection on your computer. Every USB root hub can theoretically handle up to 127 different peripherals. USB supports Plug and Play and "hot swapping," the ability to add and remove devices while the computer is running. The operating system is supposed to automatically recognize the new configuration.

Unfortunately, Linux does not currently support all USB devices. Although Red Hat Linux 7.1 supports a large number of USB devices, it does not support USB network cards. It does not work well with non-powered USB hubs, nor does it support booting from USB floppy drives. But there are a number of developers constantly working to improve Linux support for USB. For the latest information, review the Linux USB Web site at `http://www.linux-usb.org`.

Starting with Red Hat Linux 7.1, hot plugging is supported. But Linux won't recognize what you plug in or install if the needed drivers aren't in the `/lib/modules/2.4.2-2` databases. For more information, consult the Linux Hotplugging Web site at `http://linux-hotplug.sourceforge.net`.

WARNING   Linux USB documentation, as of this writing, is less than complete. As discussed on the first page of the Linux USB sub-system guide (`http://www.linux-usb.org/USB-guide/book1.html`), "Some [current Linux USB documentation] is outright guesswork, especially [for] the lesser known and more expensive devices."

Printers

In Chapter 15, "Using Linuxconf and Other Tools for System Configuration," you learned how to easily configure printers in Red Hat Linux 7.1 using the Printconf utility. There are two other options. This chapter will discuss the basics of configuring printers manually or with the help of the Apsfilter system. A good reference for this process is the Printing HOWTO at `http://www.linuxdoc.org/HOWTO/Printing-HOWTO/index.html`.

Which Printer to Use

Before discussing configuration of printers in Linux, let's take a quick look at which printers work with Linux and how to go about using them. Except as noted, most printers are supported as follows:

PostScript printers   Most Linux software generates PostScript output for printing, so your best choice is a PostScript printer. Of course, low-end laser printers and ink jet printers don't support PostScript.

Non-PostScript printers supported by Ghostscript   If your printer doesn't support PostScript but supports the Printer Control Language (PCL), it is probably supported by the Ghostscript application, a software-based Post-Script interpreter. To see if your printer is supported, check the Ghostscript home page at http://www.cs.wisc.edu/~ghost/. Table 18.1 contains a partial list of printers supported by Ghostscript.

TABLE 18.1:   Printers Supported by Ghostscript

Canon BubbleJet BJ10e	HP DeskJet 682C
Canon BubbleJet BJ200	HP DeskJet 683C
Canon BubbleJet BJC-210 (41)	HP DeskJet 693C
Canon BubbleJet BJC-240 (3.33, 43)	HP DeskJet 694C
Canon BubbleJet BJC-250 (5.10)	HP DeskJet 850
Canon BubbleJet BJC-70 (5.10)	HP DeskJet 855
Canon BubbleJet BJC-600	HP DeskJet 870Cse
Canon BubbleJet BJC-4000	HP DeskJet 870Cxi
Canon BubbleJet BJC-4100	HP DeskJet 890C
Canon BubbleJet BJC-4200	HP DeskJet 672C
Canon BubbleJet BJC-4300	HP DeskJet 680
Canon BubbleJet BJC-4550	HP DeskJet 1100C
Canon BJC-210	HP DeskJet 500C
Canon MultiPASS C2500 color printer/fax/copier	HP DeskJet 510
Canon BJC-240	HP DeskJet 520

Continued on next page

TABLE 18.1 CONTINUED: Printers Supported by Ghostscript

Canon BJC-70	HP LaserJet 5
Canon BubbleJet BJC-800	HP LaserJet 5L
Canon BubbleJet BJC-7000	HP LaserJet 6L
HP DeskJet	Oki OL410ex LED printer
HP DeskJet Plus	NEC SuperScript 860
HP DeskJet 500	HP PaintJet XL300
HP DeskJet Portable	HP DeskJet 1200C
HP DeskJet 400	HP DeskJet 1600C
HP DeskJet 500C	Ricoh 4081 laser printer
HP DeskJet 540C	Ricoh 6000 laser printer
HP DeskJet 690C	Epson Stylus Color
HP DeskJet 693C	Epson Stylus Color II
HP DeskJet 550C	Epson Stylus 500
HP DeskJet 560C	Epson Stylus 600
HP DeskJet 600	Epson Stylus 800
HP DeskJet 660C	

NOTE   Not all printers work with Linux. A few printers are set up to read information only through Microsoft Windows. Some USB printers are not yet supported. The Printer HOWTO, also available at `http://www.linuxprinting.org/`, includes tips on working with some of these troublesome printers. The same Web site also includes a more complete list of printers that work with Linux.

The *printcap* File

The printcap file is found in the /etc directory and is the core of Linux printer configuration. This file contains entries for each printer that is available to your

Linux system. When the Linux printer daemon, lpd, is loaded (generally at boot time), it looks at this file to learn about the printers it will be managing.

A basic entry in the printcap file is as follows:

```
# LOCAL
djet500lp|dj|deskjet:\
    :sd=/var/spool/lpd/dj:\
    :mx#0:\
    :lp=/dev/lp0:\
    :sh:
```

Each entry contains numerous fields separated by colons. If the entry needs to span more than one line, the backslash indicates that the entry continues on the next line.

This example has a printer with three possible names: djet500lp, dj, and deskjet. This printer has a spool directory at /var/spool/lpd/dj where lpd can store temporary files while they are waiting to be printed. The printer is connected to the first parallel port (/dev/lp0), and no header pages should be printed (sh). This all might seem very cryptic, and to a certain extent it is. The printcap file can take literally dozens of different fields. These are outlined in the printcap man page:

```
$ man printcap
```

If this information was all that was needed to get a printer to work, configuring your printers wouldn't be so bad. But lpd is essentially stupid. With an entry like the one above, whatever data is provided to lpd is sent directly to the printer. If the printer does not understand the data provided, you will get gibberish or nothing in return. Consider the following possible problems:

- An ASCII text file sent to a PostScript printer does not print.

- An ASCII text file sent to a PCL printer does not print with the correct formatting unless the control codes in the file are adjusted.

- A PostScript file sent to a PCL printer prints as a long list of PostScript commands instead of the actual page image defined by the commands.

These are just some of the problems encountered when printing using a barebones printcap entry like the one outlined above. They can be resolved by the use of print filters.

Print Filters

Print filters are special programs or scripts that process data before it is sent to the printer. For instance, if you have a PCL printer, you could write one script to process ASCII text before sending it to the printer so it will appear in correct format, and another script to send PostScript data through Ghostscript to generate correct PCL output. But if you do this manually, you need to have multiple printer entries in the printcap file, one for each type of filter you plan to make available:

```
# PCL Printer with ASCII filter
ascii-pcl:\
    :sd=/var/spool/lpd/ascii-pcl:\
    :mx#0:\
    :lp=/dev/lp0:\
    :sh:\
    :if=/var/spool/lpd/ascii-pcl/filter

# PCL Printer with PostScript filter
ps-pcl:\
    :sd=/var/spool/lpd/ps-pcl:\
    :mx#0:\
    :lp=/dev/lp0:\
    :sh:\
    :if=/var/spool/lpd/ps-pcl/filter

# PCL Printer with no filter
pcl:\
    :sd=/var/spool/lpd/pcl:\
    :mx#0:\
    :lp=/dev/lp0:\
    :sh:\
```

These filters would generate the correct output, but they would add complications to the printing process. Users would need to know what type of output is being generated by their application (plain text, PostScript, or PCL) and then select the correct printer accordingly. There might also be confusion because the filters suggest that there are three physical printers available when there is really only one.

These difficulties are addressed by *magic filters*. Magic filters, which are available for downloading from the Internet, handle all the printcap configuration for most supported printers, provide filters that can determine the type of data being sent to the printer, and perform the correct filtering on that basis.

The APS Print Filter System

The leading magic filter package is the APS Print Filter system. You can download the latest version of the APS Print Filter from http://www.apsfilter.org. At the time of this writing, the released version of the APS Print Filter is 6.1.1. The file you should download for this chapter is apsfilter-6.1.1.tar.gz. The operations discussed here may not be identical to those you need for other versions. If in doubt, read the README file after downloading and decompressing this file on your Linux system.

To install the software, use the tar command to uncompress and extract the archive in a logical location, such as /usr/local. You need to create a directory in which to store the uncompressed files. The following commands assume you have downloaded the original archive in /tmp:

NOTE   You need to perform these steps as the root user.

```
# cd /usr/local
# tar xzvf /tmp/apsfilter6.1.1.tar.gz
# cd apsfilter
```

To configure APS to work with your printer, the next step is to run the SETUP script that comes with the package:

```
# ./SETUP
```

The APS Print Filter works with the Ghostscript package. If you don't have a sufficiently up-to-date version of Ghostscript, the SETUP program lets you know. Despite the warning, the APS Print Filter 6.1.1 does work with the version of Ghostscript (5.5) included with Red Hat Linux 7.1.

NOTE   If you want the latest printer drivers, you should download the latest version of Ghostscript, which you can find at http://www.cs.wisc.edu/~ghost/. If you have used Ghostscript previously, note that the name has changed from Aladdin Ghostscript to APFL Ghostscript.

This brings up the welcome screen shown in Figure 18.1. Accept the terms of the GNU General Public License for the APS Print Filter by typing **y**, then press Enter. After going through the prompts about postal addresses, the SETUP program takes you to the Installation Program screen shown in Figure 18.2.

FIGURE 18.1:

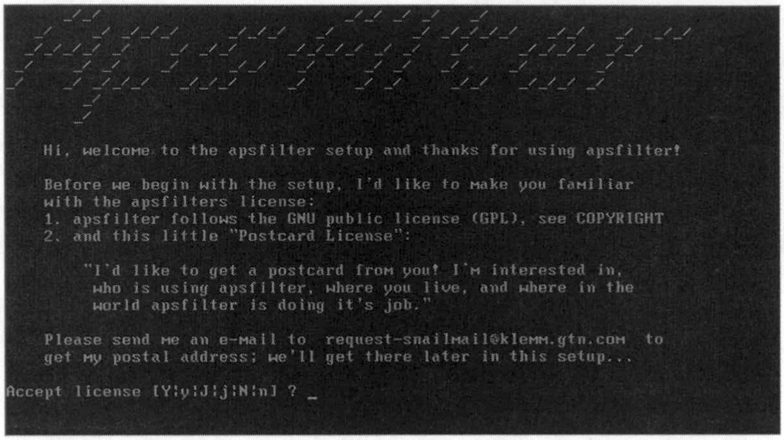

Starting the APS Print Filter utility

FIGURE 18.2:

Installing the APS Print Filter

Press Enter to continue. Read through the next screen, which describes the functions of the Apsfilter Setup script, then press Enter again to continue. The next step is to set up the configuration directory, where you want to keep the printer configuration files, as shown in Figure 18.3. While the /etc/apsfilter default option is most consistent with other Red Hat Linux 7.1 configuration files, the choice is up to you.

FIGURE 18.3:

Setting up the
configuration directory

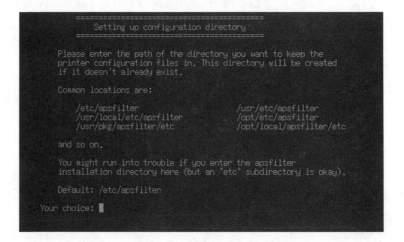

When you press Enter, follow the prompts. The script continues by checking the permissions of applicable directories and backing up your current printer configuration file in /etc/printcap.old.

Once you've made your selections, you are taken to the Apsfilter Setup Main Menu shown in Figure 18.4. To configure your printer, you need to address options 1 and 2. You can also set up a test page with options 3–5, which you can then run with the T option.

FIGURE 18.4:

The Apsfilter Setup
Main Menu

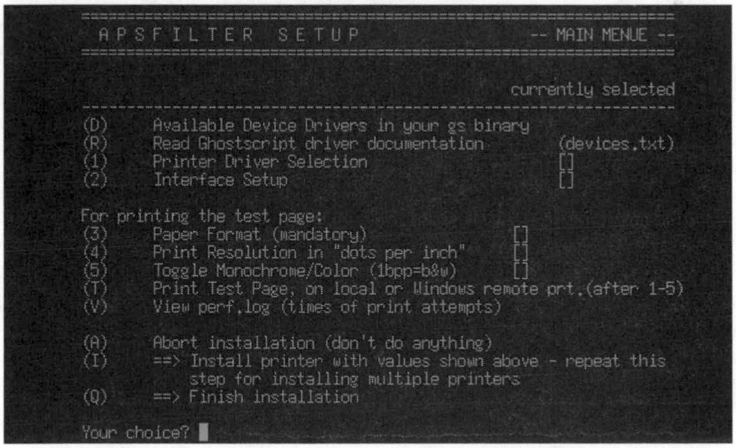

The first two menu options, D and R, list the available device drivers associated with your Ghostscript installation and page through your Ghostscript driver documentation. Options 1 and 2 configure your printer, as follows.

Printer Driver Selection

From the Main Menu, select option 1. The APS Print Filter utility includes eight different types of drivers, as shown in Figure 18.5. Modern printers are either true PostScript printers or they need some type of Ghostscript driver. If you are not sure about your printer, you may need to browse through several of these options. If your printer is not a true PostScript printer (see your printer's documentation), you'll probably see your printer listed in one of the other options.

NOTE   Three of the categories, gimp-print, pcl3, and IBM Omni, provide specialized Ghostscript support to their listed printers. If, after browsing through all of the categories, you still don't know which category is best for your printer, refer to the Printing HOWTO at `http://www.linuxdoc.org/HOWTO/Printing-HOWTO/index.html`.

FIGURE 18.5:

The APS Printer Driver Selection menu

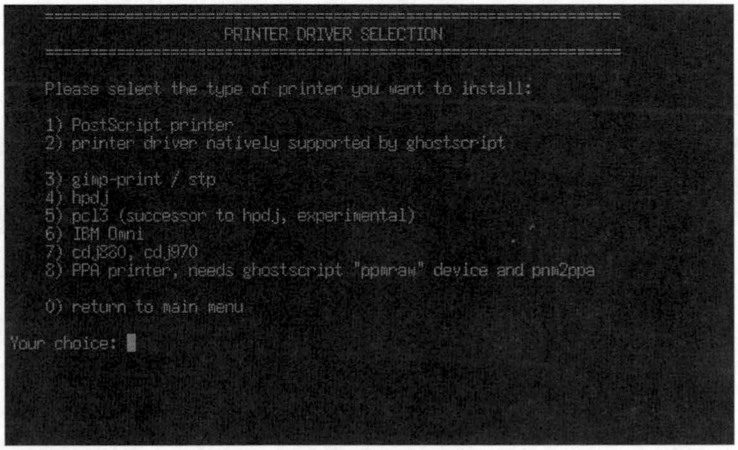

```
================================================================
                    PRINTER DRIVER SELECTION
================================================================

Please select the type of printer you want to install:

1) PostScript printer
2) printer driver natively supported by ghostscript

3) gimp-print / stp
4) hpdj
5) pcl3 (successor to hpdj, experimental)
6) IBM Omni
7) cdj880, cdj970
8) PPA printer, needs ghostscript "ppmraw" device and pnm2ppa

0) return to main menu

Your choice:
```

- Option 1 allows you to choose from different resolutions of true PostScript printers. Printer resolution is defined by the number of dots that printer can handle per square inch, or dpi. Red Hat Linux 7.1 includes PostScript drivers that can handle anything from 300dpi through 2880dpi.

- Option 2 allows you to choose from over 150 printers that are natively supported by Ghostscript.

- Option 3 is based on the gimp-print plug-in, which supports high-quality graphics on various Canon, Epson, Lexmark, and HP printers.

- Option 4 supports mainly HP DeskJet and DeskJet color printers.

- Option 5 is an alternative to Option 4. As it is "experimental," the output from this driver may be better, or it may not work at all.

- Option 6 is for over 250 printers supported through the IBM Omni printer driver.

- Option 7 is for some models of the HP DeskJet 800 and 900 series color printers.

- Option 8 is for some models of the HP DeskJet 700, 800, and 1000 series color printers.

Select the option that most closely matches your printer, and you will see a menu with options for navigating through a long list. When you press Enter, scroll through the list until you see the name of your printer. Record the number associated with that printer, and enter it when prompted. Alternatively, you can select 0 and press Enter to return to the Printer Driver Selection menu.

Once you confirm your selection, the script returns you to the Apsfilter Setup Main Menu, with your printer device added. As shown in Figure 18.6, the new printer device is [ljet4], which corresponds to the HP LaserJet 4L printer.

FIGURE 18.6:

The Apsfilter configuration menu

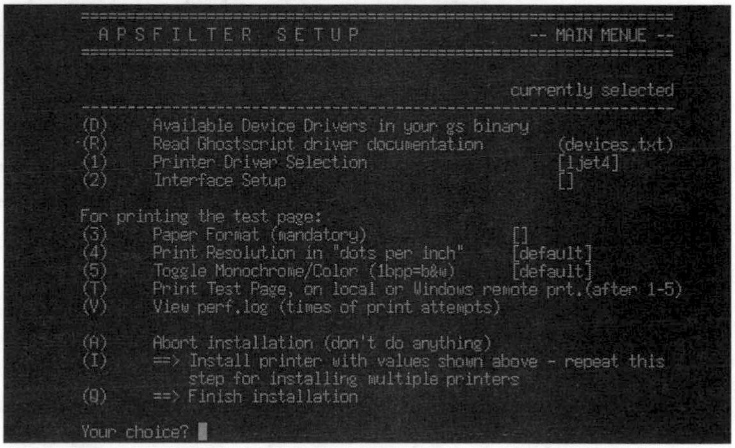

```
================================================
 A P S F I L T E R   S E T U P          -- MAIN MENUE --
================================================

                                        currently selected
------------------------------------------------
 (D)    Available Device Drivers in your gs binary
 (R)    Read Ghostscript driver documentation    (devices.txt)
 (1)    Printer Driver Selection                 [ljet4]
 (2)    Interface Setup                          []

 For printing the test page:
 (3)    Paper Format (mandatory)                 []
 (4)    Print Resolution in "dots per inch"      [default]
 (5)    Toggle Monochrome/Color (1bpp=b&w)       [default]
 (T)    Print Test Page, on local or Windows remote prt.(after 1-5)
 (V)    View perf.log (times of print attempts)

 (A)    Abort installation (don't do anything)
 (I)    ==> Install printer with values shown above - repeat this
             step for installing multiple printers
 (Q)    ==> Finish installation

 Your choice? █
```

NOTE   Many printers have more than one driver that you can use. For example, the HP LaserJet4L printer has both a Ghostscript and a gimp-print driver. Some trial and error may be required to find the driver that best suits your needs.

TIP   Check the resolution associated with your printer in this menu. If it is different from what is listed in your printer's documentation, you can reset it as described with the Apsfilter configuration menu, option 4, Print Resolution.

Interface Setup

You can define or change the interface associated with your printer. The next step is to configure the location of the printer. It could be attached to a local parallel or serial port. It could also be attached to a remote printer over various types of networks. To set up this configuration detail, select option 2 from the Apsfilter Setup Main Menu to get to the Apsfilter Interface Setup screen shown in Figure 18.7.

FIGURE 18.7:

The Apsfilter Interface Setup screen

```
A P S F I L T E R    S E T U P              -- Interface Setup --

The easiest way, to connect a printer to your computer is by
using the parallel interface, because it's usually *faster*,
more standardized and therefore much easier to configure.

When configuring a serial printer, the installation dialogue
asks you many questions about how to configure the serial
interface of your computer, so that it works well with your
printers current settings.

When using the serial interface, then you have to choose special
cables, depending on the communication protocol between computer
and printer (hardware/software handshaking). Many pitfalls here !

currently selected:                   Interface:  []
                                      Device:     []
configure local / remote printer
1) local parallel/USB          2) local serial
3) Unix/network printer (lpd)  4) Windows / NT (samba)
5) AppleTalk

Your choice? _
```

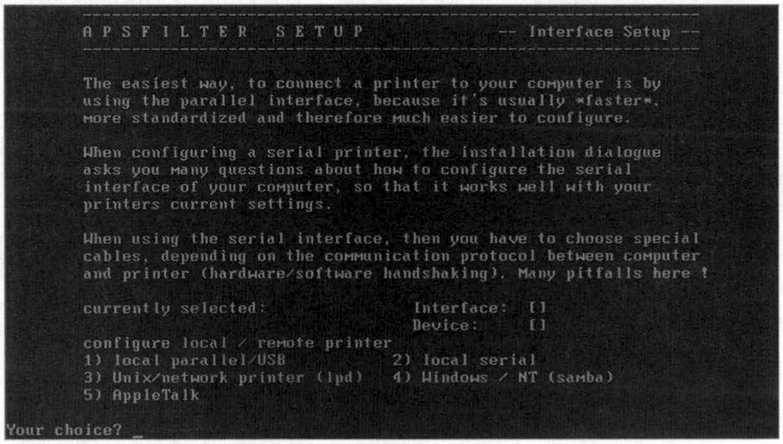

As you can see from the Interface Setup menu, there are five different categories of printer connections that you can configure:

Local Parallel/USB   The parallel port is generally associated with the 25-pin connection to your computer. Linux software associates this with devices such as /dev/lp0 and /dev/lp1, as explained earlier. Alternatively, if you have a USB printer, you can configure it in almost the same fashion.

NOTE

Some USB printers can be set up to use a Linux parallel port type device. While parallel ports are associated with devices such as /dev/1p0 and /dev/1p1, USB printer ports are associated with devices such as /dev/usb/1p0 and /dev/usb/1p1.

Local Serial The serial port is generally associated with the 9-pin connection to your computer. Linux software associates this with devices such as /dev/ttyS0 and /dev/ttyS1, as explained later in this chapter.

Unix/Network Printer Allows you to set up a connection to a printer connected to a different Linux or Unix computer on a local or other connected network.

Windows/NT (Samba) Allows you to set up a connection to a printer connected to a Microsoft Windows 95/98/Me/NT/2000 computer on a local or other connected network.

AppleTalk Allows you to set up a connection to a printer connected to an Apple computer on a local or other connected network.

Make a selection and press Enter to return to the Apsfilter Setup Main Menu.

Creating a Test Page

Before exiting from Apsfilter Setup, it is helpful to check your work with a test page. But before you can print out a test page, you need to configure the size or format of the paper, the resolution of the printer, and whether the printer is black and white or color.

To set the size of the paper, select option 3 from the Main Menu, Paper Format. It offers five choices:

- DIN A4 is a metric standard paper size, 8.27×11.69 (210×297 mm).

- DIN A3 is another metric standard paper size, 11.69×16.54 (297×420 mm).

- US Letter is the standard US letter paper size, 8.5×11 (215.9×279.4 mm).

- US Legal is the standard US legal paper size, 8.5×14 (215.9×355.6 mm).

- US Ledger is a larger size, 11×17 (279.4×431.8 mm)

Make the selection that most closely corresponds to the paper in your printer and press Enter.

When you see the Apsfilter Setup Main Menu again, select option 4, Print Resolution. If the default resolution was satisfactory when you selected a printer driver, no changes are required. Otherwise, this menu allows you to choose from a number of typical settings or to customize your own print resolution setting. Make an appropriate selection and press Enter.

If you're configuring a color printer, you may want to change the default color quality. To do so, select option 5, Toggle Monochrome/Color. The current version of this menu allows you to select anywhere from 1bpp (black and white) to 32bpp (true color). Make your selection and press Enter.

Testing the Configuration

Once you've completed the Apsfilter configuration and connected the necessary cables, you can test your work. From the Apsfilter Setup Main Menu, press **T** and follow the prompts. Setting up the test page can take some time, especially if you have a high-resolution or color printer. If successful, you'll see a page with a Screening Test and samples of a font at different sizes.

Once you're satisfied with your configuration, press **I** to install the settings that you created in the Apsfilter Setup Main Menu. After going through the prompts on default and "raw" printers, the settings are written to your /etc/printcap file. You can then quit by pressing **Q** from the Apsfilter Setup Main Menu.

After Configuration

After configuration, you should have a printcap file that looks something like this:

```
# /etc/printcap
#
# DO NOT EDIT! MANUAL CHANGES WILL BE LOST!
# This file is autogenerated by printconf-backend during lpd init.
#
# Hand edited changes can be put in /etc/printcap.local, and will be
# included.

##########################################################################
## Everything below here is included verbatim from /etc/printcap.local##
##########################################################################
#
# printcap.local
# This file is included by printconf's generated printcap,
# and can be used to specify custom hand edited printers.
```

```
# APS1_BEGIN:printer1
# - don't delete start label for apsfilter printer1
# - no other printer defines between BEGIN and END LABEL

lp|Printer1 auto:\
    :lp=/dev/lp0:\
    :if=/etc/apsfilter/basedir/bin/apsfilter:\
    :sd=/var/spool/lpd/lp:\
    :lf=/var/spool/lpd/lp/log:\
    :af=/var/spool/lpd/lp/acct:\
    :mx#0:\
    :sh:
raw1|Printer1 raw:\
    :lp=/dev/lp0:\
    :if=/etc/apsfilter/basedir/bin/apsfilter:\
    :sd=/var/spool/lpd/raw1:\
    :lf=/var/spool/lpd/raw1/log:\
    :af=/var/spool/lpd/raw1/acct:\
    :mx#0:\
    :sf:\
    :sh:
# APS1_END - don't delete this
```

WARNING   If you use Apsfilter, don't use the Printconf utility discussed in Chapter 15; otherwise, the settings you create with Apsfilter will be lost.

Regardless of the printer you configure for use with Linux, the Apsfilter system lets you create the following print queues:

lp | Printer1 auto   An automatic filter that will detect the file type and process it accordingly.

raw   An unfiltered print queue that can be used if the software you are using generates output in the native format required by your printer.

NOTE   The base Apsfilter configuration files, as discussed earlier, are saved in the directory you selected during installation. The default Apsfilter directory is /etc/apsfilter. If you want to run the Apsfilter configuration program again and used the default Apsfilter directory, run the /etc/apsfilter/basedir/SETUP command.

Printing

Now you are ready to print. You can do this with the `lpr` command. The `-P` flag specifies which printer queue to use. For instance, the command

```
$ lpr -Praw /etc/printcap
```

prints the `printcap` file out through the `raw` or plain-text print queue, while

```
$ lpr -Plp /etc/printcap
```

prints the same file through the automatic filter.

> **NOTE**
> There is no space between the `-P` and the name of the printer in the `lpr` commands shown above.

Modems

Modems are among the simplest types of peripherals to get working in Linux. In many cases, Linux uses the Plug-and-Play characteristics of a modem to configure it automatically. Generally, external modems can be plugged into an available serial port and be expected to work, while standard internal modems should be equally easy to get up and running under Linux.

> **NOTE**
> Not all internal modems are supported under Linux. If you have one, try it. If you are buying a new modem, it may be worth the extra cost to buy an external one, based on the configuration headaches that you could save. If you choose an internal modem, avoid software modems, sometimes known as *winmodems*, which uses specialized Windows software to implement flow control. But not all is lost even with these winmodems; there are drivers available for some winmodems at `http://www.linmodems.org`.

This section looks at the Red Hat Linux 7.1 hardware-detection tool, Kudzu. But if that tool does not detect your modem, you need to know how Linux handles ports in order to properly configure your modem. Finally, this section describes some simple ways to use your modem.

Modem Detection

Several Linux distributions include a hardware-detection tool. The one included with Red Hat Linux 7.1 is Kudzu, named after an East Asian vine that can grow over a foot a day. Go into root user mode to run Kudzu with the following command:

```
# /usr/sbin/kudzu
```

If everything is configured per the associated lists of installed hardware, Linux appears to stall for a while; after some time, you are returned to the command line. In fact, Kudzu is sending signals to your hardware based on the documented configuration. However, if you've made a recent hardware change, you should see the screen shown in Figure 18.8.

FIGURE 18.8:

The Kudzu welcome screen

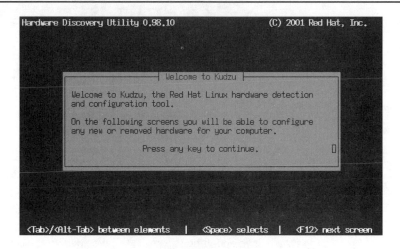

Press a key to see what Kudzu detected. An example is shown in Figure 18.9.

Since Kudzu detected the new hardware, in this case a modem, on a specific port, the only choice you need to make is whether to add it to your system.

When a tool such as Kudzu looks for new hardware, it checks it against a database of already-detected hardware, stored in the /etc/sysconfig/hwconf file. If this file hasn't yet been created, Kudzu checks detected hardware from your /etc/modules.conf, /etc/sysconfig/network-scripts, and /etc/X11/XF86Config or /etc/X11/XF86Config-4 configuration files.

FIGURE 18.9:

Kudzu detected
something new.

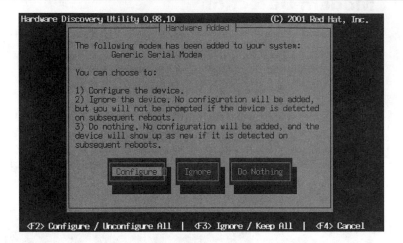

In many cases, you should be able to jump ahead to the Internet connection tools discussed in Chapter 22, "Connecting Linux to the Internet." However, Kudzu or the corresponding utility included with your distribution of Linux could have made a mistake. It may not be able to detect your new modem or other hardware, or it may set it up on the wrong port. In that case, you'll need the tools described in the following sections in order to work with Linux ports.

> **TIP** Kudzu runs automatically when you start or reboot Red Hat Linux 7.1. If it detects changes to your hardware configuration, you'll see a screen similar to Figure 18.8. You get 30 seconds to press a key to enter Kudzu to configure your new hardware. If you don't press a key in this time period, the Linux boot process continues. You can always start Kudzu after Linux finishes booting.

Understanding Linux Ports

In the Linux environment, every physical peripheral or connection port is associated with one or more files in the special directory /dev. This includes hard disk drives, CD-ROM drives, parallel ports, and serial ports.

The concept behind this is easy to understand. Let's look at hard drives as an example.

Each IDE hard drive or CD-ROM is named hd*x*, where *x* is a letter such as a for the first drive on the primary IDE bus, b for the second drive on the primary IDE bus, c for the first drive on the secondary IDE bus, and d for the second drive on the secondary IDE bus. Thus, the secondary master drive is associated with /dev/hdc.

NOTE   SCSI hard or CD-ROM drives are similarly named **sd*x***.

In addition, each partition on the drive is associated with a /dev entry. The second partition on the primary slave drive, for instance, is /dev/hdb2, while the first partition of the secondary master drive is /dev/hdc1.

Parallel Ports and Linux

So far, this is a simple concept. Let's now consider parallel ports. In the DOS and Windows world, parallel ports are referred to as LPT1:, LPT2:, LPT3:, and so on. On most PCs, there is generally only one parallel port, so you usually only have to deal with LPT1:.

In the Linux world, the parallel ports correspond to the device files lp*x*, where *x* is the number of the port. Here is where the crucial difference lies: Linux starts counting the ports at 0 instead of 1, so LPT1: is usually /dev/lp0 and LPT2: would then be /dev/lp1. There may be cases where you have only one port available in DOS and this is not LPT1:. In these cases, this port is mapped to /dev/lp0; /dev/lp0 is always the first available parallel port and /dev/lp1 the second available port.

Now, on to serial ports. You need to fully understand all of this to understand how to get your modems working.

Serial Ports and Linux

In Linux, serial ports are generally each associated with two device files: one for outgoing connections and one for incoming connections. Let's start with outgoing connections: These are ttyS*x*, where *x* is a number starting from 0. So DOS's COM1: maps to /dev/ttyS0 in Linux and COM2: to /dev/ttyS1. In some older versions of Linux, these ports may map to /dev/cua0 and /dev/cua1, respectively. These associations are shown in Table 18.2.

TABLE 18.2: DOS and Linux Serial Ports

DOS Name	Linux Device Files	Legacy Device Files
COM1:	/dev/ttyS0	/dev/cua0
COM2:	/dev/ttyS1	/dev/cua1
COM3:	/dev/ttyS2	/dev/cua2
COM4:	/dev/ttyS3	/dev/cua3

But these device drivers are difficult for most people to remember. Fortunately, when you configure your modem, most Linux distributions now establish a link between the /dev/modem file and the actual device. You can check this from the output of the ls -l /dev/modem command:

```
lrwxrwxrwx   1 root    root    10 Feb   3 19:21 /dev/modem -> /dev/ttyS0
```

> **NOTE**   Support for /dev/cua1, /dev/cua2, and so on is provided only for backward compatibility, and eventually these files will not be supported.

USB Ports and Linux

Theoretically, you should be able to connect up to 32 USB modems to your Linux computer. To use USB modems, you need to make sure the proper USB modules are included in your kernel, which will be covered in Chapter 20, "Recompiling the Linux Kernel." Some USB modules are already included with the latest distributions, including Red Hat Linux 7.1.

For USB modems, you'll also need the Communication Device Class Abstract Control Module, or acm.o. If it isn't already part of your kernel, you can incorporate it into your current configuration. In Red Hat Linux 7.1, you need to compile this module into your kernel. For more information on modifying your kernel refer to Chapter 20. Once this is complete, you can run the following command:

```
# /sbin/insmod /lib/modules/2.4.2-2/kernel/drivers/usb/acm.o
```

If your `insmod` or kernel versions are different, substitute accordingly. The actual directory on your Linux distribution may vary.

The appropriate devices should already exist in your /dev/usb directory. Check this with the `ls -l /dev/usb/ttyACM*` command. The output should look like the following:

```
crw-rw----   1 root   root   188,   0 Aug 24 09:00 /dev/usb/ttyACM0
crw-rw----   1 root   root   188,   0 Aug 24 09:00 /dev/usb/ttyACM1
crw-rw----   1 root   root   188,   0 Aug 24 09:00 /dev/usb/ttyACM2
crw-rw----   1 root   root   188,   0 Aug 24 09:00 /dev/usb/ttyACM3
```

If you don't get this type of output, run the following command:

```
mknod /dev/usb/ttyACM0 c 166 0
```

Repeat this command, substituting ttyACM1, ttyACM2, and so on for the USB modem ports that you may need.

Getting Your Modem Ready

In order for a modem to work properly, it must meet several criteria:

- It must be properly connected to the PC.

- It must be using a dedicated serial port.

- It must not have an IRQ or I/O address conflict with another device.

Connecting a Modem to Your PC

Connecting a modem is fairly simple. If you have an external modem, you need to connect it to a power supply as well as one of your existing serial ports. If you have no free ports, you need to consider purchasing a serial card; consult your PC or modem vendor about this. Generally, though, most PC users need only two external serial ports: one for their mouse and one for their modem. The usual practice is to connect your mouse to the first serial port (COM1:, /dev/ttyS0, /dev/cua0) and your modem to the second serial port (COM2:, /dev/ttyS1, /dev/cua1). Red Hat Linux 7.1 then typically links this to the /dev/modem file.

If you're using a single USB modem, link its device to the /dev/modem file. For example, if you're using /dev/usb/ttyACM0, run the `ln -s /dev/modem /dev/usb /ttyACM0` command.

Internal modems usually need to be placed into a free slot inside your PC. If you are wary about opening your PC, then you may want to consider getting a technician from the store where you purchased your PC or modem to install the modem.

Choosing a Serial Port

When installing an external modem, you select a serial port by simply choosing which physical port to connect the modem to. In doing this, it is important to make sure that you have not installed an internal device that is using the same serial port. If you haven't installed any hardware inside your PC, consult your PC's documentation to see if there are any preinstalled internal devices that are using the same serial port as one of your external connections. Generally, though, unless you already have an internal modem installed, you aren't likely to have an internal device conflicting with one of your available external serial ports.

Installing an internal modem requires a bit more work.

NOTE   Many older internal modems need to be configured to use a specific serial port in order to function. In some cases, you need to physically adjust DIP switches or jumpers on the modem card to specify a particular serial port. Consult your modem's documentation as required for instructions on how to do this.

As with external modems, you must make sure you don't choose a port that matches one already in use by an external device. For instance, you definitely wouldn't make your modem use the first serial port if you have a mouse connected to the external connector for this port. The third or fourth serial port is usually the best choice for an internal modem. Remember, the first serial port corresponds to /dev/ttyS0, the second to /dev/ttyS1, and so on. Read the next section for more guidance on selecting a serial port.

IRQs and I/O Addresses

Associated with each serial port are an interrupt request (IRQ) and an input/output (I/O) address. This numerically specified information ensures that your PC and operating system always know which physical device is providing data or information or is asking for the attention of the system.

Table 18.3 outlines the four common serial ports and their associated IRQs and I/O addresses.

TABLE 18.3:   Serial Port IRQs and I/O Addresses

DOS Name	Linux Device Files	IRQ	I/O Address
COM1:	/dev/ttyS0	4	0x3f8
COM2:	/dev/ttyS1	3	0x2f8
COM3:	/dev/ttyS2	4	0x3e8
COM4:	/dev/ttyS3	3	0x2e8

Notice that the first and third ports share the same IRQ and the second and fourth ports also share the same IRQ. This poses certain issues that have to be considered. The fact that port 1 and port 3 share the same IRQ but have different I/O addresses basically means that they cannot be used simultaneously. That is, you can't have devices on these two ports (or on ports 2 and 4) that will need to be in use at the same time.

This means, for example, that you can't have a mouse on the first port and put a modem on the third port unless you will never be using the mouse while the modem is in use. If you use X Windows, this is a highly improbable scenario. Therefore, when installing an internal modem, you also need to take care not to create an IRQ conflict. If you use a mouse on the first serial port, then you will probably want to put your internal modem on the fourth port to eliminate all possible conflicts with your mouse.

Finally, there is one more consideration: Internal modems often allow you to configure special IRQ and I/O addresses for the card that differ from the norms for the four serial ports. This should only be done if you have so many serial devices already on your system that you simply cannot make the modem work in any other way. In this situation, you will need to consult the serial devices HOWTO at http://www.linuxdoc.org/HOWTO/Serial-HOWTO.html to get a stronger sense of how to do this safely and correctly in Linux.

Plug-and-Play Modems

The introduction of Plug-and-Play motherboards and Microsoft operating systems starting with Windows 95 has caused some problems configuring internal cards with other operating systems. Many Plug-and-Play devices (modems included) are designed to work expressly with Windows and are configured using special Microsoft Windows operating system library software that is not available in Linux. If you have a card like this, you usually have four options:

- Configure the modem in Windows 95 or 98, then reboot to Linux. Some modems retain their configuration.

- You might be able to find a Linux driver for your modem. Some manufacturers include Linux drivers on a floppy disk, while others may have them on their Web sites.

- Some modem manufacturers include a configuration floppy disk that you can use (usually in MS-DOS mode) to set the IRQ, I/O, and DMA (if required) of the modem.

- If none of these options works (and your modem manufacturer offers no other alternatives), the modem will need to be configured every time the computer is power-cycled, and Windows will have to do this during the boot process. If such is the case, you need to start Linux from within Windows using `loadlin` to start Linux without rebooting the system. For more information about `loadlin`, refer to The Loadlin+Win95/98/ME mini-HOWTO, at `http://www.linuxdoc.org/HOWTO/mini/Loadlin+Win95-98-ME.html`.

If you still have problems configuring your modem, consider an external modem. It is easiest to configure because the port to which it is attached (usually /dev/ttyS0 or /dev/ttyS1) is already configured.

NOTE   If you have a winmodem, also known as a software modem, you have a modem that's designed to work with Microsoft Windows operating system software. Linux works with many winmodems, as described in `www.linmodems.org`.

Software for Working with Your Modem

There are numerous types of software in Linux that you will be using with your modem. These include the following:

minicom   A basic, text-based terminal emulation package

seyon   An X Windows-based terminal emulation package

pppd   A daemon used for establishing PPP connections to the Internet (see Chapter 22)

efax   A collection of programs used for sending and receiving faxes (see Chapter 25, "Faxing from Linux")

Some GUI utilities for setting up a dial-up Internet connection can also detect modems. These will be discussed in Chapter 22. The next section gives you a quick look at using minicom to make sure your modem is working properly.

Using *minicom* to Test Your Modem

The first step to using minicom is to create a global configuration file. This is done by running minicom as the root user with the -s flag:

```
# minicom -s
```

This command launches the minicom configuration environment, as illustrated in Figure 18.10.

FIGURE 18.10:

Configuring *minicom*

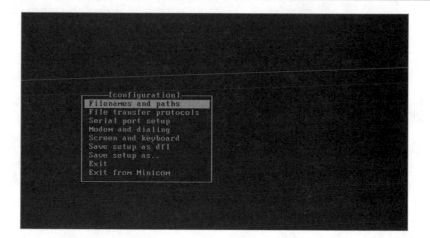

You can use the up and down arrow keys to move through the menu and the Enter key to select menu items.

The critical settings for testing your modem are under Serial Port Setup. Selecting this option displays the serial port setup screen, shown in Figure 18.11.

FIGURE 18.11:

Configuring your serial port

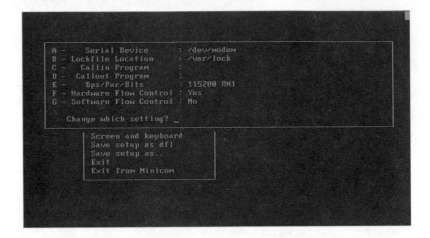

In order to change the values, select them by letter. First, you need to set your serial device. This is done with option A, Serial Device. You should change this location to the appropriate device file. For instance, if your modem is on the second serial port, you could set this to /dev/ttyS1 since you are using minicom for an outgoing connection.

TIP

If the serial port is already set to **/dev/modem**, like that shown in Figure 18.11, check its links with the **ls -1 /dev/modem** command. If it shows a link to a specific serial port, no changes should be required.

You also need to configure option E, Bps/Par/Bits, to match your modem's settings and the settings required by the system you will be connecting to (usually an Internet provider's system). Option E displays the communication parameters screen, shown in Figure 18.12.

FIGURE 18.12:

Configuring communication parameters

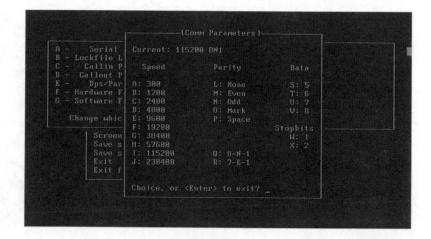

At the top of the screen, the current settings are shown. You can change the settings by selecting the appropriate letters.

For speed, you should choose your modem's top compressed connection speed. This is generally four times the speed of your modem. For instance, for a 14.4Kbps modem, this would be 57600bps; for a 28.8Kbps modem, this should be set to 115200bps. A 56Kbps modem can be set to 115200bps or 230400bps, if available.

For parity and data bit, the norm for most connections today is no parity, 8 data bits, and 1 stop bit (option Q). Confer with the administrator of the system you will be connecting to in order to determine the correct settings.

When you are finished, press the Enter key to return to the serial port setup screen. Pressing Enter at the serial port setup screen returns you to the main menu.

This information should be sufficient to allow you to test your modem. Select Save Setup As Dfl to save the configuration as the default setting, and then select Exit to exit the setup screen and use minicom with the settings you have selected. This brings up the minicom terminal emulator, as shown in Figure 18.13.

The main *minicom* screen

```
Welcome to minicom 1.83.1

OPTIONS: History Buffer, F-key Macros, Search History Buffer, I18n
Compiled on Aug 24 2000, 10:09:47.

Press CTRL-A Z for help on special keys

AT S7=45 S0=0 L1 V1 X4 &c1 E1 Q0
OK
_
```

```
CTRL-A Z for help |115200 8N1 | NOR | Minicom 1.83.1 | VT102 |        Offline
```

If you see an OK prompt, your modem should be configured correctly and work-ing. You can test this further by typing **AT** and pressing Enter. You should get back an OK message:

AT
OK

If this works, you can try dialing into a system to see if you can connect:

ATDT1234567

If this works, you may hear the sound of a connection and then should see a con-nection message and possibly some messages or prompts from the remote system:

ATDT1234567
CONNECT 115200

If you have problems with any of these stages, then your modem's physical connection or configuration may be incorrect. In this case, refer to the Modem HOWTO at http://www.linuxdoc.org/HOWTO/Modem-HOWTO.html for a detailed dis-cussion of getting a modem to work with Linux.

Issues with ISDN Adapters

ISDN adapters can be a little problematic with Linux. The difficulties stem from the fact that internal and external adapters function in fundamentally different ways, and among internal adapters there are distinctly different technological approaches. Standard ISDN connections are typically limited to 128 or 144Kbps, depending on your national telephone standards.

External ISDN adapters are your best choice for a Linux system because external adapters mimic the behavior of external modems, making their use generally transparent to Linux.

Internal adapters pose issues, though. Some internal adapters emulate standard serial modems and others emulate standard network cards, and both can be made to work with Linux. There are those known not to work, however. A good guide to addressing the problems of internal ISDN adapters is the isdn4linux FAQ, at `http://www.isdn4linux.de/faq/`. Several ISDN configuration utilities are available, including Red Hat's ISDN configuration tool, `isdn-config`. You can start this tool either directly from the command line or through the generic Red Hat `internet-config` tool. To start this tool in GNOME, click the Main Menu button, and then choose Programs ➢ System ➢ Internet-config. In the menu that appears, as shown in Figure 18.14, select ISDN as your dialup type and then click Next.

FIGURE 18.14:

Setting up an ISDN connection with internet-config

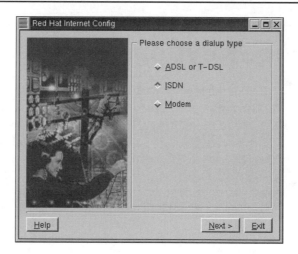

For a detailed discussion of Linux and ISDN, consult the ISDN Solutions for Linux page at `http://www.muc.de/~hm/linux/linux-isdn.html`.

Other "Modems"

There are a number of services faster than ISDN today. These are sometimes known as *broadband* services. You may already have a broadband connection through television cables, Digital Subscriber Lines (DSL) that use your telephone wires, connections through a satellite, or even high-speed wireless connections.

Many of the companies that provide these services also refer to their equipment as "modems." Names such as cable modems, DSL modems, and satellite modems are common today. Technically, this is wrong. You can't use `minicom`, `seyon`, `pppd`, `KPPP`, or Microsoft Dial-up Networking to connect to the Internet over these "modems." These devices are more properly known as *adapters*.

These adapters generally connect to your computer through network cards. If you want to configure one of these adapters, read through Part VI, "Using Linux in the Small Office/Home Office (SOHO)," especially Chapter 28, "Configuring Red Hat Linux 7.1 for an Ethernet Network."

USB Mice/Keyboards

Most of the newest Linux distributions support USB mice and keyboards. Much of this support was incorporated into various Linux distributions even before the release of Linux Kernel 2.4. Both are input devices, as described in Chapter 12, "Advanced X Windows Configuration." Both are also defined as USB Human Interface Devices, or HID.

> **NOTE**   Linux kernels starting with version 2.2.7 started incorporating USB devices. For reliable USB performance, you should have a kernel of 2.2.18 or 2.4.2 and above.

In most cases, the Red Hat Linux 7.1 installation program detects your USB mouse and or keyboard automatically. However, problems still do happen; therefore, you need some information about how USB supports mice and keyboards.

The first step is to check your kernel messages with the `dmesg | less` command. Scroll through the messages, looking for any that show USB or your USB equipment being loaded. If you can't find any relevant messages, next check for changes to the `/proc/bus/usb/devices` file. You can find the date and time of the most recent change with the `ls -l /proc/bus/usb/devices` command.

If you still don't see any response to your USB hardware, the necessary code is probably not part of your kernel. You can either compile it into your kernel or add the appropriate modules. For USB, you also need the USB device filesystem, which you can mount with the following command (as the root user):

```
# mount -t usbdevfs none /proc/bus/usb
```

For USB HID, you may need to recompile USB Human Interface Device support into the kernel, as well as mouse and keyboard support within the Input core support entry. Alternatively, you can add the input.o, hid.o, mousedev.o, and keybddev.o modules. You can add a module with the insmod command. For details on how to recompile, upgrade, or add modules to your kernel, read Chapter 20.

For more information on USB mice, keyboards, and more, refer to Brad Hards' document, "The Linux USB Sub-system," which is part of the Linux USB Project. You can read this document online at http://www.linux-usb.org/USB-guide/book1.html.

USB Mice

Once everything is properly installed, USB supports multiple mice. Linux can configure all USB mice on one mouse driver, /dev/input/mice. If your Linux distribution doesn't detect your USB mouse or mice with the steps listed earlier, make the necessary changes to your Linux kernel. If you want to do this by adding modules, make sure to use the mousedev.o module as well.

If the noted mouse driver doesn't exist, you'll need to create it. Create the /dev/input directory if required, then create a USB node device with the following command:

```
# mknod /dev/input/mice c 13 63
```

Assuming that you want to use your USB mouse or mice in the X Window, you'll also need to add configuration data for your USB mouse or mice to the relevant configuration file, XF86Config. The location and basic syntax are discussed in Chapter 12. For a standard USB mouse, you could add the following InputDevice section:

```
Section "InputDevice"

    Identifier  "USB Mice"
    Driver      "mouse"
```

```
        Option      "Protocol"    "IMPS/2"
        Option      "Device"      "/dev/input/mice"

    EndSection
```

And you also need to bind this new input device to your screen. As discussed in Chapter 12, this is done in the ServerLayout section of the XF86Config file. If this USB mouse is your only mouse, it is your core pointer, which you can add as a line to the ServerLayout section as follows:

```
InputDevice "USB Mice" "CorePointer"
```

If you're also using a regular (non-USB) mouse, this becomes a second Input-Device line as follows:

```
InputDevice "USB Mice" "SendCoreEvents"
```

Since this is based on XFree86 Version 4.0, the syntax of these additions may be different for your distribution and/or version of X Windows.

USB Keyboards

Many newer computers incorporate a USB root hub on the motherboard. The associated BIOS should normally support a USB keyboard. In this case, you probably don't need USB information to support your keyboard in your Linux kernel.

However, if you have another non-Unix/Linux operating system on your computer, a BIOS that does not configure USB, or special features on your keyboard, you need USB keyboard support. If you recompile your kernel to do this, avoid USB HIDBP Keyboard support, as this does not support most work in Linux.

WARNING   The Linux Loader, or LILO, is run before Linux has a chance to detect any USB keyboard. Therefore, unless USB support is built into your computer motherboard and detected by your BIOS, you can't use your keyboard for input at the LILO boot: prompt. To get around this issue, consider using other boot loaders such as Partition Magic or System Commander.

Looking Ahead

In Chapter 19, "Linux Multimedia," you will learn about an area that most users find important. You will see how to install and configure common multimedia peripherals such as sound cards, and you will take a quick tour through common Linux multimedia software.

CHAPTER
NINETEEN

Linux Multimedia

- Configuring Sound Cards

- Using XPlaycd

- Other Multimedia Applications

This chapter looks at an area of Linux that, unfortunately, is not as well developed as it is on competitive platforms such as Windows and the Mac OS: multimedia. It describes Red Hat Linux 7.1's built-in support for sound cards and discusses how to configure the cards. Next, it discusses a representative multimedia application, XPlaycd, and then reviews other available multimedia applications.

Unfortunately, fully mastering multimedia for Linux can be somewhat complicated. For hardware support, consult the Linux Sound HOWTO at `http://www.linuxdoc.org/HOWTO/Sound-HOWTO.html`. For multimedia application support, consult the Linux Sound Playing HOWTO at `http://www.linuxdoc.org/HOWTO/Sound-Playing-HOWTO.html` for detailed discussions of how to work with sound in Linux.

Configuring Sound Cards

Generally, Linux's support for sound cards has been sketchy. Strong support is provided for Sound Blaster cards and those cards that are compatible on a hardware-register level with genuine Sound Blaster cards. Other cards that are labeled "compatible" don't work with the standard Sound Blaster drivers.

A collection of other drivers for sound cards can be configured through the Red Hat Linux 7.1 `sndconfig` utility, but they all have their own quirks and unique ways of being configured, so this section will address only the Sound Blaster line of cards. The Linux Sound HOWTO mentioned above is a good reference if you find yourself facing another card on your Linux system.

Over time, the level of support for a broad range of sound cards has improved, and various modern Linux distributions, including Red Hat Linux 7.1, support a respectable selection of sound cards, although this support is by no means as complete as sound support in Windows 98.

Adding sound support may mean recompiling your kernel from source code. This is a difficult task discussed in Chapter 20, "Recompiling the Linux Kernel." Making the right decisions in compiling the kernel is tricky, and taking a wrong step can render your system non-bootable and difficult to return to a working state.

For this reason, Red Hat has developed the Sound Blaster driver into a loadable module, so it is possible to add Sound Blaster support to your Red Hat Linux 7.1 system without reconfiguring your kernel.

NOTE   In order to configure your card, you need to know all the relevant hardware settings of the card such as I/O port, IRQ, and DMA addresses. Consult your card's documentation for instructions on how to determine the settings of your card.

Using *sndconfig*

Red Hat includes the sndconfig program for configuring the Sound Blaster module. To run the sndconfig program, go into root mode, and then type the command

    # /sbin/sndconfig

at a command prompt in the console or an xterm window.

The initial screen, shown in Figure 19.1, states that sndconfig is about to probe your system for Plug-and-Play (PnP) sound cards. If it detects your card, its IRQ ports, I/O addresses, and DMA channels are recorded automatically. Otherwise, you're told that no cards were found. After you click OK, the next screen asks you to identify your sound card type, as shown in Figure 19.2.

FIGURE 19.1:

The *sndconfig* screen

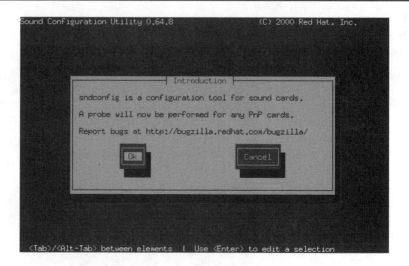

Selecting a Sound
Blaster card

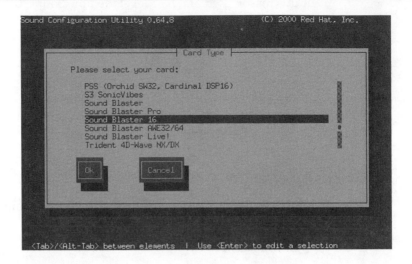

You can select from a list of standard supported cards. If you think you have a
proper hardware-compatible card, select the type of card it is supposed to be
compatible with.

The next screen that appears depends on the type of card you select. That screen
asks you to provide relevant hardware settings such as I/O port, IRQ, and DMA
addresses for your card. Figure 19.3 shows this screen for a regular Sound Blaster
16 card.

FIGURE 19.3:

Specifying hardware
settings for a Sound
Blaster 16 card

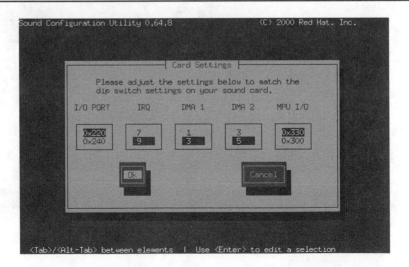

Once you specify and confirm these settings, `sndconfig` adds the entries to the `/etc/modules.conf` file (and backs up your original as `modules.conf.bak`). When you press OK, `sndconfig` sets up a test sound. After the next OK, it attempts to play a test sound (a conversational voice). The following screen asks you to confirm that you heard the sound.

> **NOTE**
>
> Older versions of Linux (before distributions such as Red Hat Linux 7.0) used the `/etc/conf.modules` file in place of the `/etc/modules.conf` file.

Next, `sndconfig` sets off a test MIDI sound (a stringed instrument) as shown in Figure 19.4.

FIGURE 19.4:

Testing a MIDI sound

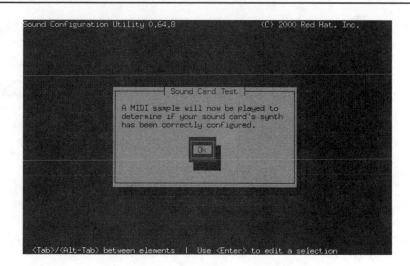

In Case of Silence

If `sndconfig` fails to play a sound, then one of several things may be wrong. First, check that your sound card is properly inserted in your PC and that your speakers are correctly plugged into the card and are turned on and have power.

If all these physical things are okay, then there are two likely sources of difficulty:

- You have chosen the wrong card type or have provided the wrong hardware settings. Check all these details and try running `sndconfig` again.

- Your card is not supported by any of the sound cards shown in the sndconfig utility. You need to consult the Linux Sound HOWTO for more details about Linux sound and building a new kernel with the correct driver for your card.

Using XPlaycd

One popular use of sound cards is to play audio CD-ROMs through the speakers of the sound card. You can do this with the XPlaycd program. This is an X Windows application that ships with Red Hat Linux 7.1 and provides a simple, graphical interface to your CD-ROM drive. You can access this from the GNOME Main Menu button by selecting Programs ➣ Multimedia ➣ XPlayCD.

As Figure 19.5 shows, XPlaycd should be familiar to anyone with an audio CD player as part of their stereo.

FIGURE 19.5:

The XPlaycd window

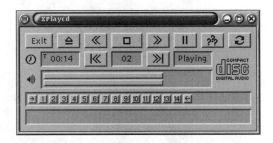

From left to right, the control buttons in the top row perform the following functions:

Exit   Quits XPlaycd.

Open/Close   Alternately ejects and closes the CD tray for drives that support software-controlled eject.

Rewind   Scans backward through the current track in two-second intervals.

Play/Stop   Alternately plays and stops the current track.

Fast Forward   Scans forward through the current track in two-second intervals.

Pause/Continue   Alternately pauses and resumes playing.

Shuffle/Resort   Alternately plays tracks in a random order and returns tracks to their physical order.

Repeat   Continuously repeats the playlist.

Immediately below the Rewind button is the Back Track button. Pressing the Back Track button once jumps to the start of the current track, and pressing it again moves back one track at a time. Immediately below the Fast Forward button is the Forward Track button, which jumps to the start of the next track.

The third row of controls is the volume control. You can control each channel separately or change both channels' values together. To change the setting of either volume bar, click to the left or the right of the current setting to move the bar one notch in the desired direction.

To move both bars in either direction, you need to click the desired side, but exactly between the two bars.

Finally, below the volume control is the playlist. The playlist shows a small icon for each track, initially in numerical order. The Start icon is represented by a right arrow and the End icon is marked with a left arrow.

The playlist is played from the Start icon to the End icon, playing each track between the two icons as it appears on the playlist in order from left to right. You can click and drag any icon to the right or left to change its place on the playlist. Figure 19.6 shows an altered playlist in which all tracks are played, but not in their original order.

FIGURE 19.6:

A reordered playlist

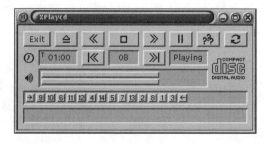

By moving the Start and End icons, it is possible to create a playlist that excludes some of the tracks, as shown in Figure 19.7.

FIGURE 19.7:

Adjusting the start and end of the playlist

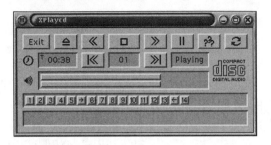

Other Multimedia Applications

While the availability of slick, fancy multimedia applications and games falls short of what is available on some other platforms, that hasn't prevented a healthy number of applications from being developed for Linux.

On the Linux Apps page at http://www.linuxapps.com, you can find a list of many available sound, movie, and other multimedia applications for Linux. This section takes a brief look at a small selection of multimedia applications.

The GNOME CD Player

GNOME, the default desktop manager in Red Hat Linux 7.1, includes an integrated CD player, shown in Figure 19.8. You can access this from the GNOME Main Menu button by selecting Programs ➢ Multimedia ➢ CD Player.

FIGURE 19.8:

The GNOME CD player

This CD player offers the standard functionality you might expect, centered around simple graphical control buttons similar to those in most PC-based CD players, as well as those in most physical CD players. Notably, this application contains a robust track editor to choose the order of tracks to play and offers other features such as keyboard controls that are missing in some Linux-based CD players.

MpegTV Player 1.0

This application, a U.S.$10 shareware application, is a real-time MPEG video/audio player for Linux and many other Unix platforms. It provides a simple, intuitive control panel that allows the user to control the playing of files, jump to any location in an open file, and adjust the volume. The software can be downloaded from http://www.mpegtv.com/.

Festival Speech Synthesis System

The Festival speech synthesis system is designed to offer a powerful, multilingual (currently English, Spanish, and Welsh) speech synthesis system that can be used to convert text to speech and provides the necessary tools for application developers to add speech to their own software. The current release of the package is available at http://www.cstr.ed.ac.uk/projects/festival/festival.html.

MiXViews

MiXViews is an X Windows-based digital sound editor that is freely distributable. Multiple files can be displayed and edited, allowing for cutting and pasting between files and for applying sound modifications to the data. The MiXViews home page is at http://www.create.ucsb.edu/~doug/htmls/MiXViews.html.

Grio and Krio

With the development of portable memory-based music players, the demand for MPEG encoders or recorders has increased. There are a substantial number of applications for managing input to systems such as the Rio player, including applications for the GNOME and KDE desktops. Not surprisingly, they are named grio and krio, respectively.

Both applications help you transfer data to and from the Rio player, erase files as needed, initialize the player, as well as rearrange the play order. You can download grio from `http://kipper.crk.umn.edu/~gerla/grio/`, or krio from `http://krio.sourceforge.net/index.php`.

RealPlayer

RealPlayer from RealNetworks is the popular player software for playing Real-Audio and RealVideo files in real time, streamed across the Internet. Many of the popular Web-based radio, television, and music sites use RealAudio and RealVideo technology, and RealPlayer is needed to view or listen to this content. Free and enhanced commercial versions of the player are available for download from `http://scopes.real.com/real/player/unix/unix.html?src=rpbform`.

FreePhone

FreePhone is an Internet audio-conferencing tool similar in concept to the Internet phone software that can be found for Windows and Macintosh systems. It is more than a one-to-one phone system; users can create unicast or multicast audio conferences. FreePhone supports a variety of popular audio compression systems and uses the Internet's multimedia backbone (Mbone). The software is online at `http://www.inria.fr/rodeo/fphone/obtain.html`.

Looking Ahead

This chapter looked at just the tip of the multimedia iceberg. Multimedia in the Linux environment can be technically demanding (as it can be in Windows), and a general book like this one can offer only a cursory look at the subject.

If you are using a supported card or a truly compatible one, you should now have it working with your Red Hat Linux system. You should have been able to download and test some multimedia applications and should feel at least comfortable with using multimedia applications in Linux.

Chapter 20, "Recompiling the Linux Kernel," discusses an important, but advanced, subject. Recompiling the kernel can be necessary for a number of reasons, including adding support for devices such as sound cards, adding support for less-common network protocols, or shrinking the size of the default kernel installed when you installed Linux. You will learn about the process of recompilation and review the major choices that you will need to make during recompilation.

CHAPTER
TWENTY

Recompiling the Linux Kernel

- Why Change the Kernel?

- Checking for Source Packages

- Backing Up the Old Kernel

- Getting a New Kernel

- Configuring the New Kernel

- Compiling and Running the New Kernel

Linux is one of the few operating systems where you can impact how your computer works at its core. Because Linux includes all of the source code to the kernel of the operating system, anything you can think of can be attempted in Linux. Of course, for most of us, that means reconfiguring the kernel with the tools provided, rather than modifying the C language source code files.

Nevertheless, hundreds of option settings are available as part of the standard kernel configuration utilities. This chapter describes how to use the kernel configuration tools to select options that you want included with your running Linux system and then shows how to recompile the kernel source code based on those options.

Why Change the Kernel?

If you're new to Linux, you may be asking yourself, "Why on Earth would I want to recompile the kernel?" You may also be thinking that it's a very difficult process.

Linux is much more user-friendly than it was two or three years ago; advancements in the installation process, graphical interfaces, and hardware support have all made Linux accessible to those of us who aren't computer science gurus. In fact, the process of recompiling the kernel, described here, uses a menu-driven configuration interface and a single (long) command line to remake the kernel.

Linux is highly "tunable"; you can refine its capabilities to meet your unique requirements. However, many of the features of Linux are not activated by default in the standard Linux kernel. This is true for several reasons.

The most important thing to understand is that every user makes trade-offs in their software. For example, when using a compression program, you can choose a faster compression time or choose a smaller compressed file.

In the same way, Linux kernels must make trade-offs. For example, you can have a smaller kernel or one that supports more hardware without additional configuration steps. Or you can have a system optimized for routing IP packets or for handling normal workstation tasks.

Programming Terms: Making, Building, and Compiling

As you read about working with the kernel, you'll see three terms used interchangeably: *remaking*, *rebuilding*, and *recompiling* the kernel. Although you can think of them as being synonymous, it's also helpful to understand what each of these terms really means.

When you develop software in Linux (and in many other operating systems), you use a configuration file for your programming project that describes how the pieces of source code and all libraries fit together. This information is stored in a file called `Makefile`, which is used by the utility `make`. (You'll use the `make` utility several times later in this chapter.)

The process of actually converting the source code of a project into something the computer can use (a binary) is called *compilation*. The standard C language compilers for Linux, `gcc` or `egcs`, are used to compile source code.

However, because a programming project generally has dozens of separate components, the `make` utility checks the dates and times on each component and recompiles only the components that have been updated since they were last compiled. This saves a great deal of time in creating a new version of a project when only part of the source code has been altered.

When you use the `make` utility, you can indicate that you want to recompile "from scratch" all of the components of your project. This is called a *build*.

So remaking the kernel, rebuilding the kernel, and recompiling the kernel all do similar things. And with several hundred thousand lines of source code, the process still takes a while to complete, no matter what you call it.

The kernel is configured to provide a good balance between kernel size, speed, and hardware support. This balance seeks to meet the needs of average users as the Linux vendor sees them. In this chapter, you will learn how to make your own decisions about which features are most important to your computing environment.

Learning about Modules

Kernel modules are a critical part of Linux. A kernel module allows you to add functionality to the core of Linux without recompiling the kernel source code. As you'll see later in this chapter, that's a great benefit.

For example, if you discover that you need to work with a special new SCSI interface card, you can load a kernel module to support it with a single command (the insmod command). Previously, Linux would have required you to rebuild the kernel to include support for that SCSI device.

As the number of hardware devices supported by Linux has increased, kernel modules have allowed the Linux kernel to remain relatively small, while still allowing users to easily add support for the hardware that they own.

> **TIP**
>
> A big difference between Linux and some other operating systems is the ability to load or remove support for hardware, file systems, languages, and so forth without ever rebooting the system.

Table 20.1 contains a summary of the commands used with kernel modules. You can view the man page for any of these commands to see more information.

TABLE 20.1:   Commands Used with Kernel Modules

Command	Description
lsmod	List all of the modules currently installed in the running kernel.
insmod	Insert a module into the running kernel. This command uses the module name and, optionally, additional parameters to define how the module behaves (for example, IRQ and address information for a hardware device).
rmmod	Remove a module from the running system. Be careful that you don't remove modules that are in use by other modules. (See the output of the lsmod command for details on dependencies of currently loaded modules.)
depmod	Create a dependencies file that can be used by the **modprobe** command to load a set of modules.
modprobe	Load the set of modules defined by the **depmod** command.

> **NOTE**
>
> All of the noted commands, except lsmod, require the user to be in root mode. In Red Hat Linux 7.1, these commands are in the /sbin directory, which is not on the path by default; therefore, you'll probably need to type the full path to these commands, e.g., /sbin/lsmod, /sbin/insmod, and so on.

Other information about the modules on your Linux system is available by reviewing certain system files.

Because kernel modules are inserted into the running source code, they are stored as object code (already compiled). Each module has the file extension .o.

Check the following files:

- /boot/module-info-2.4.2-2 contains per-module information that you can alter to reflect any specific settings of your hardware.

- /lib/modules/2.4.2-2/ contains several subdirectories that divide all of the available kernel modules on your system. For example, check the contents of the kernel/drivers/cdrom subdirectory to see all the modules available to support various CD-ROM drives.

NOTE
The kernel version associated with Red Hat Linux 7.1 is 2.4.2. If you are using a different version of Linux or have previously upgraded the kernel, substitute version numbers accordingly.

TIP
All Linux kernels have version numbers in a *major.minor.patch* format. The biggest changes are associated with a new major revision number. Changes to the minor revision number can be quite significant. When the minor revision is an even number, the kernel is considered to be stable. When it is an odd number, it is developmental and should not be used by novices or for production computers. As incremental changes are developed, the changes are incorporated into a patch revision.

Understanding Reasons to Recompile

If you're still wondering specifically why you would need to recompile your Linux kernel, the information in Table 20.2 should provide some insight. This table outlines some solutions to common problems you may encounter.

Of course, you may need to rebuild the kernel for only one of these reasons. But understanding why people work with the kernel will show you more about the flexibility of Linux.

TABLE 20.2:   Solutions to Problems Recompiling the Linux Kernel

Problem	Solution
You hear that your processor has a bug that could crash your system. Linux has a workaround, but you're using an older version.	Download the patch to the Linux kernel and remake the source code. In 20 minutes, the problem is solved.
You've purchased a new SCSI card that is supported in a Linux kernel module, but you can't boot the system from your SCSI hard disk unless the SCSI module is part of the default kernel.	Remake the kernel, indicating that the necessary SCSI support is built in rather than created as a module.
A security alert appears about problems with a Linux file system driver. A patch is available within hours.	Download the patch and remake your kernel to provide the most up-to-date security for your system.
A new network card driver is available for your system. You download the source code from the vendor's Web site.	Remake the kernel so that the source code version for all modules matches your new network card module.
You purchased a commercial Linux product that had a 2.2.16 Linux kernel, but now you'd like the latest revised kernel.	Download the kernel sources (they're fairly large) and remake the kernel so you have the latest version of the kernel.
Users on your system are complaining that they can't access certain file systems unless they use a bunch of strange commands first (such as `insmod`, for example).	Remake the kernel with the needed file system support built in so that file systems of that type can be mounted without explicitly adding a kernel module.

Finding Out about Kernel Updates

The Linux kernel can change literally every day. Fortunately, when you're running a stable system, you generally don't care to follow all of those changes. In fact, most of the changes to Linux occur in the development version of the kernel, which isn't something you want to run a production system on anyway.

To keep up-to-date on happenings with the Linux kernel and related topics, plan to visit the following Web sites regularly. These sites are updated several times a day with new information:

www.linuxhq.com   This site contains a large collection of information about the Linux kernel, with sections on the latest development and stable kernels, links to information resources, and many useful details about the Linux kernel.

www.freshmeat.net   This site is a clearinghouse for announcements about releases of open source software and related topics. This site includes a searchable archive of release information. The Freshmeat site is not focused on the Linux kernel per se, but it includes information about kernel releases.

www.linuxtoday.com   This site is a daily news digest about open source software and related topics. This site includes a searchable archive of release information. While the Linux Today site is not focused on the Linux kernel per se, new kernel release announcements are posted here.

Checking for Source Packages

In order to recompile your Linux kernel, you must have the source code to the kernel installed on your system. The kernel source code on Red Hat Linux 7.1 is located in a single `rpm` package installed by default. If it isn't installed, the package to check for is

```
kernel-source-2.4.2-2.i386.rpm
```

You can install this package using the `rpm` command after mounting the Red Hat 7.1 CD-ROM that comes with this book:

rpm –Uvh `kernel-source-2.4.2-2.i386.rpm`

NOTE   Red Hat includes the kernel source code in an `rpm` package that is not marked as a "source code package" with the file extension `.src.rpm`. The `.src.rpm` package is not what you need.

The kernel source package is not included on the Publisher's Edition of Red Hat Linux 7.1 that ships with this book, but it can be downloaded from `http://www.redhat.com`.

Checking for Tools

In addition to the source code itself, you must have a compiler available to rebuild the source code. The two tools you need are:

- The make utility

- The C language compiler, gcc or egcs

The exact versions of these utilities may vary from system to system. It's best if you have a recent version of the compiler, such as gcc 2.96 or egcs 1.1.2.

To check for these utilities on your Linux system, use the following commands (the output from a typical Red Hat installation is shown):

```
# rpm -q make
make-3.79.1-5
# rpm -q gcc
gcc-2.96-81
```

NOTE   The same commands should work on any Linux distribution that uses rpm for software package management.

If you don't see these tools installed on your system, you'll need to use rpm or a similar utility to install them from the Red Hat Linux 7.1 Publisher's Edition CD-ROM that comes with this book before proceeding with this chapter.

TIP   When you try to install gcc, you may see a `failed dependencies` message. This message lists other rpm packages that need to be installed first. In this case, the required additional packages are also available on the CD-ROM.

WARNING   If you don't already have a boot disk with your current kernel, you can create one in root user mode with the `/sbin/mkbootdisk -device /dev/fd0 2.4.2-2` command.

Backing Up the Old Kernel

Although the implication here is that rebuilding the Linux kernel is child's play, you should still take a few precautions before diving into the deep end of the pool. That means backing up your kernel and providing a method to reboot to the previous version of the kernel in case of problems.

Backing up the current kernel involves three steps:

1. Back up the source code tree for the kernel so you can re-create the current kernel if the configuration becomes corrupted.

2. Back up the kernel itself so you have a kernel to start your system with that you already know works.

3. Create a new boot loader entry so you can boot from the backup of your kernel.

Backing up the source code tree for your current kernel is simple. Just use a command such as the following cp command, which copies the entire kernel source code tree to a duplicate directory. (You can then copy it back to the original name if you need to use the backup.)

```
# cp -r /usr/src/linux-2.4.2 /usr/src/linux-2.4.2.sav
```

Backing up the kernel itself is almost as simple; use a command like the following cp command. (Change it to match the exact kernel version you're running.)

```
# cp /boot/vmlinuz-2.4.2-2 /boot/vmlinuz-2.4.2-2.orig
```

> **TIP**
>
> When you rebuild the kernel, the existing kernel is saved with the file extension .old. However, that old kernel version is not automatically accessible to boot your system, which is the purpose of these steps.

The LILO boot loader that normally launches Linux from your hard drive is configured by pointing to a kernel file in your root file system. For example, you may see a line like this in your /etc/lilo.conf file:

```
image = /boot/vmlinuz-2.4.2-2
```

This line indicates the path and filename of the kernel to start.

Once you have created a backup of the kernel itself (in the previous step), you should also create another entry in `lilo.conf` so that you can start your Linux system with the old (proven) kernel.

To do this, follow these steps:

1. Open the `/etc/lilo.conf` file in a text editor.

2. Find the section in the `/etc/lilo.conf` file that refers to your kernel image.

3. Make a copy of that entire section (usually about four or five lines of text).

4. In your copy, change two items:

    *   Change the name of the kernel to the name of your backed-up kernel (with the .orig ending in the example).

    *   Change the label field to something like `linux.original` or `linux-previous`.

5. If there is a line starting with `initrd`, change the name of this to an appropriate backup, such as `initrd-2.4.2-2.orig.img`. You'll create this file later, if required.

6. Save your changes to `/etc/lilo.conf`.

7. Run the command `/sbin/lilo` to add the new entry to your boot loader. As `lilo` runs, you see the different labels on screen as images are added to your boot loader.

The next time you reboot your system, you will see the new kernel entry appear in the graphical LILO boot prompt. If you are using a distribution that does not use a graphical LILO boot prompt, you may have to press Tab to see the additional image you defined as a precaution before rebuilding your kernel.

Getting a New Kernel

There are a number of ways to get a copy of a new kernel. Two major ways are through the Linux Kernel Archives at `http://www.kernel.org` or through your Linux distribution's Web site. If you're looking for an `rpm` version of the kernel, a central source is located at `http://www.rpmfind.net`. Downloading and installing `rpm` packages is already covered in previous chapters, so this section covers downloading kernels in the `tar.gz` format, in files such as `linux-2.4.4.tar.gz`.

WARNING   Make sure to back up the previous version of your kernel, as described earlier in this chapter.

Once you've downloaded the relevant kernel package, move it to the /usr/src/ directory. Remember, this section assumes that you've already backed up your current kernel as described earlier in this chapter.

To extract the kernel and associated files (over 8,000 in version 2.4.4), navigate to the /usr/src directory, then run the following command:

```
tar zxpvf linux-2.4.4.tar.gz
```

If your kernel package filename is different, substitute appropriately. Now you can use one of the utilities discussed in the following sections to configure your new kernel.

TIP   If you're upgrading a kernel, make sure that your software is advanced enough to accommodate the upgrade. For the kernel 2.4 series, review the /usr /src/linux-2.4.x/Documentation/Changes file for versions of critical software that you need.

Configuring the New Kernel

The interesting part of creating a new Linux kernel is setting up the new kernel configuration. This is the step in which you decide what the kernel will include, what it will not include, and so forth. You have a choice between configuring a kernel from new or existing sources. For example, if you're running Red Hat Linux 7.1, you could reconfigure the existing 2.4.2 kernel with new options. Alternatively, you could download and install the newer 2.4.4 kernel. While the detailed configuration options vary, the tools, utilities, and techniques remain the same.

Linux includes three separate configuration utilities. Each one is suited to different preferences:

A command-line interface   A command-line interface asks questions one at a time about what you want to include in the kernel. This interface is convenient for those who are very familiar with the kernel or who may have a script that processes the configuration information using this interface.

The command-line interface is also the choice for those who have very limited control over their screens and therefore can't use the menu-based interface. The greatest disadvantage of the command-line interface is that you can't return to a previous question and review it or change your selection.

A character-based menu interface   This interface uses several levels of menus that you can explore, selecting options as you go, and return to any area. This option is available for computers with some graphics capability, which you can access directly without having to configure or access an X Window interface.

A graphical, X-based interface   This interface is very similar to the character-based menu interface, but it is truly graphical. This is the most attractive interface, but it requires the installation of the X Windows system.

All three methods (command line, menus, and true graphical) create the same configuration file that the make utility uses during the compilation/rebuilding process. All three methods also include copious help information to answer your questions about specific options.

Understanding the Options

As you review the various options presented in any of the configuration methods (command line, menu, or graphical), you need to understand how each option can be applied to your Linux kernel.

The options are identified by different indicators, depending on which tool you use to configure the kernel, but the same options are available in each case. The configuration items fall in two groups:

- Module-capable

- Non-module-capable

If an option is not capable of being a loadable kernel module, then it must be either

- [*]   Part of the kernel, or

- [ ]   Not part of the kernel

The bracket indications above show how the selection of an option is shown in the menu-based configuration tool.

If an option is module-capable, you have these choices (again, these are shown as they would appear in the menu configuration tool; similar indications are shown in both of the other tools):

- < >   Not included, and not created as a module that can be loaded later.

- <*>   Included as part of the kernel, so that it doesn't have to be loaded later as a kernel; it's always part of the system.

- <M>   Included as a module, but not part of the kernel itself. Thus, this option can be added or removed from the running kernel at your discretion.

TIP   If you're having trouble changing an option, you may need to set another option first. For example, you must enable SCSI devices in general before you can select specific SCSI device support.

Once you have all the tools (make and gcc) and the source code installed, you are ready to start one of the configuration tools and configure your kernel.

Remember that you need to use only one of the three interfaces described in the following sections. Review each section briefly and decide which interface you want to use, based on the figures and descriptions given.

TIP   The first time you install and configure a freshly downloaded kernel, check every section. If there is anything remotely "special" about your computer (e.g., it has only one CPU, needs laptop PC Card support, requires USB support), you should change the kernel configuration. Also, keep the options that you activate to a minimum; fully loaded kernels can be so large that they slow down your system.

Starting the Command-Line Interface

To start the command-line interface, follow these steps:

1. Use the su command to obtain root access.

2. Change to the source code directory:

   ```
   # cd  /usr/src/linux-2.4.2
   ```

> **NOTE**   If you downloaded a different kernel to a different directory, substitute accordingly.

3. Execute the following make command:

    # **make config**

Almost immediately, you see the first configuration question. When you use the make config command, you are prompted to respond to a series of questions about the kernel. Figure 20.1 shows the first few questions.

FIGURE 20.1:

The most basic configuration option for the Linux kernel is *make config*, which asks you questions in a command-line format.

```
[root@linux71 linux-2.4.2]# make config
rm -f include/asm
( cd include ; ln -sf asm-i386 asm)
/bin/sh scripts/Configure arch/i386/config.in
#
# Using defaults found in arch/i386/defconfig
#
*
* Code maturity level options
*
Prompt for development and/or incomplete code/drivers (CONFIG_EXPERIMENTAL) [N/y
/?]
*
* Loadable module support
*
Enable loadable module support (CONFIG_MODULES) [Y/n/?]
  Set version information on all module symbols (CONFIG_MODVERSIONS) [Y/n/?]
  Kernel module loader (CONFIG_KMOD) [Y/n/?]
*
* Processor type and features
*
Processor family (386, 486, 586/K5/5x86/6x86/6x86MX, Pentium-Classic, Pentium-MM
X, Pentium-Pro/Celeron/Pentium-II, Pentium-III, Pentium-4, K6/K6-II/K6-III, Athl
on/Duron/K7, Crusoe, Winchip-C6, Winchip-2, Winchip-2A/Winchip-3) [Pentium-III]
  defined CONFIG_MPENTIUMIII
Toshiba Laptop support (CONFIG_TOSHIBA) [N/y/m/?] []
```

> **TIP**   The exact series of questions that you see depends on how you respond to questions as you go along.

If you want to select the default option for each question, simply press Enter. In each case, the default selection is shown as an uppercase letter. For example, you will see this question about networking:

```
Networking support (CONFIG_NET) [Y/n/?]
```

If you press Enter, the default of Y, for Yes, is selected. For those options that can be defined as built-in or as modules, the options appear as in this example:

```
Kernel support for ELF binaries (CONFIG_BINFMT_ELF) [Y/m/n/?]
```

Many of the device-related questions present only m/n options, for [Module] or [Don't include].

For each question you see, you can enter a question mark, ?, to see a screen of descriptive information. This information is usually very helpful in determining how to use the option.

Three disadvantages of using this configuration option are:

- You have to answer several hundred individual questions (depending on how you respond, the total number will vary).

- You can't go back and change a selection you've made without starting over.

- You can't easily see an overview of the options in various categories.

The advantages of using this configuration option include:

- Except for the Linux kernel source, you need only a very basic Linux installation to configure the kernel.

- You can create scripts to feed input to the configuration script for automated configurations.

The menu configuration option described in the next section provides an easier way for most people to review all of the kernel configuration parameters and create a kernel configuration file.

Starting the Character-Based Menu Interface

To start the character-based menu interface, follow these steps:

1. Use the su command to obtain root access.

2. Change to the source code directory:

   # **cd /usr/src/linux-2.4.2**

NOTE If you downloaded a different kernel to a different directory, substitute accordingly.

---

3. Execute the following make command:

   # **make menuconfig**

NOTE The menu-based configuration tool requires a package named **ncurses**. **Ncurses** is installed by default on most Linux systems, but if you see errors when you run the **make menuconfig** command, check that the **ncurses-devel** package is installed.

You'll see a collection of suspiciously confusing lines scroll down your screen as the make command compiles the menu-based configuration utility. You can ignore these lines; they are the output of the compiler and related programs. After a minute or two, you'll see the screen shown in Figure 20.2.

FIGURE 20.2:

You can configure the Linux kernel from this character-based menu interface.

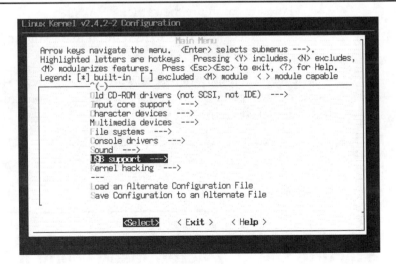

The menu configuration option starts with a list of the categories in which you can select kernel options. To navigate this interface, remember the following keystrokes:

- Use the up and down arrow keys to move among the options listed in the menus.

- Type **M** to select a kernel option as a module (when applicable).

- Use the Tab key to move between the buttons shown below the list of kernel options: Select, Exit, and Help.

- Press Enter to choose a selected item, such as the Help button.

The three buttons below the option list have the following functions:

Select   Displays the submenu of options associated with the high-lighted item.

Exit   Returns to the previous menu, finishing the configuration if selected from the highest-level menu.

Help   Displays a help screen full of information about the highlighted menu option.

A sample help screen is shown in Figure 20.3.

FIGURE 20.3:

Help information is available for every kernel option by choosing the Help button.

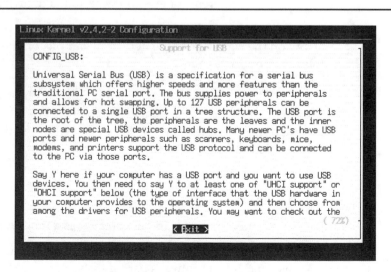

The kernel configuration tools described in this section are used to create a kernel configuration file that is used to rebuild the kernel. Once you have set up a kernel with all the options you prefer, you can save a copy of the configuration file for repeated use later.

This is done using the last two items on the main menu: Save Configuration To An Alternate File and Load An Alternate Configuration File. Use the down arrow or Page Down key to scroll down to these items.

These last two items on the main menu provide the capability to save your configuration settings or load an existing configuration file:

- Use the Save Configuration To An Alternate File option to create a second copy of the kernel configuration file to reuse yourself or to pass on to another person.

WARNING   Don't use the Save Configuration To An Alternate File option until you have completed the selection of all kernel options in the various menus.

- Use the Load An Alternate Configuration File option if you have a configuration file that someone has given you or that you have saved previously. Loading such a file sets all the options so that you don't have to select any of the menu items unless you want to make further changes.

Items in the menu list that have submenus of options are displayed with an arrow on the right side of the item; for example, on the main menu you see the following option:

```
USB Support  -->
```

When you view a menu item that actually sets a kernel option, you see the following options displayed to the left of the option, as described previously in this chapter (see also Figure 20.4):

- [*] Part of the kernel

- [ ] Not part of the kernel

- < > Not included, and not created as a module that can be loaded later.

- <*> Included as part of the kernel, so that it doesn't have to be loaded later as a module; it's always part of the system.

- <M>   Included as a module, but not part of the kernel itself. Thus, this option can be added or removed from the running kernel at your discretion. The relevant option highlighted in Figure 20.4, USB Modem, includes this module as part of your configuration. You can confirm this after the new or recompiled kernel is installed; just use the /sbin/lsmod command. Modules like this can be added and removed with the /sbin/insmod and /sbin/rmmod commands, respectively, as discussed earlier in this chapter.

FIGURE 20.4:

Individual options in the *menuconfig* tool are shown with selection brackets to the left of each item.

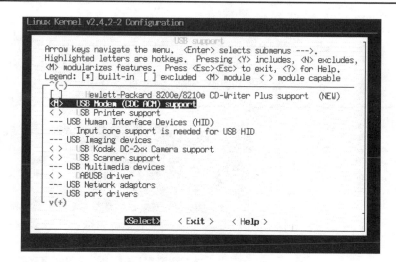

TIP

Depending on the screen on which you're viewing the menus, you should see a bold or different color character as part of each line. You can type that character to select that option rather than using the arrow keys and the Select button.

NOTE

Note how easy it is to configure options for USB support. Once they are configured, use the techniques discussed in Chapter 18, "Using Peripherals," to try to set up your USB peripherals.

The current state of each option is shown in the brackets to the left of that option. To change the selected option, type any of the following keys:

- **Y**   To include the feature in the kernel

- **M**   To create a module to support this feature (when a possibility)
- **N**   To not include the feature, nor make a module for it
- **?**   To display a help screen for the highlighted item

TIP   You can also press the spacebar repeatedly to toggle between the available options for the highlighted item.

When you have reviewed and set all of the kernel options that you want to check, choose the Exit item on the main menu. A configuration screen appears asking if you want to save the updated kernel configuration file based on your selections (see Figure 20.5). Choose Yes to create the configuration file.

FIGURE 20.5:

After choosing configuration options, be sure to save a new configuration file as you exit the menu-based configuration tool.

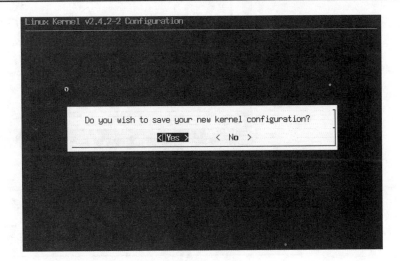

Starting the Graphical Interface

To start the graphical (X-based) kernel configuration interface, follow these steps:

1. Start the X Windows system (using any graphical environment or desktop that you prefer).

2. Open a terminal emulator (command-line) window.

3. Use the su command to obtain root access.

4. Change to the source code directory:

   ```
   # cd /usr/src/linux-2.4.2
   ```

NOTE If you downloaded a different kernel to a different directory, substitute accordingly.

5. Execute the following make command:

   ```
   # make xconfig
   ```

NOTE The X-based configuration tool requires a few X Windows system development packages. If you see errors when you run the `make xconfig` command, check that the appropriate development packages have been installed on your system.

As with the menu-based option, a series of lines scrolls down your screen as the make command compiles the X-based configuration utility. These lines are the output of the compiler and related programs. After a minute or two, you'll see the main window of the X-based configuration utility, as shown in Figure 20.6.

FIGURE 20.6:

The graphical kernel configuration tool provides menus and buttons for selecting kernel options.

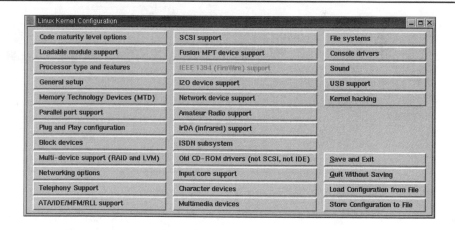

TIP
Any graphical program is likely to require more system resources than an equivalent character-based program. If your system is short on memory, the X-based kernel configuration tool may be sluggish. Try the menu-based configuration tool in the previous section.

Using the X-based `xconfig` tool is very similar to using the `menuconfig` tool. You choose categories for features that you want to select or deselect. For each category, a dialog box appears in which you can choose to have a feature built into the kernel, created as a loadable module, or not used at all. Figure 20.7 contains a sample of one of these dialog boxes.

FIGURE 20.7:

Dialog boxes similar to this one are used to select features in the X-based kernel configuration tool.

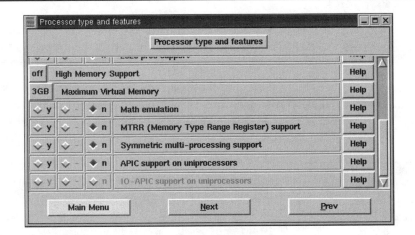

TIP
When you modify kernel 2.4.2 for Red Hat Linux, symmetric multiprocessing support is enabled by default. Change this setting to **n** unless you actually have more than one CPU on your computer.

As you review different features, you can always select the Help button to the right of an item to see a help screen about that feature. (See Figure 20.8.) The information provided in these screens is the same as what you would see in the command-line or menu-based configuration tools.

FIGURE 20.8:

Help information appears
in separate windows
when using the X-based
configuration tool.

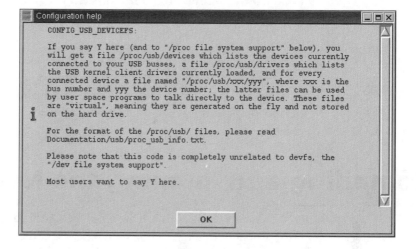

One great advantage of using the X-based configuration tool when you're first working with new kernel configurations is that the graphical interface shows you dependencies between various options. For example, in the Block Devices section, you must enable the Multiple Device Driver Support option before the RAID support options can be built in to your kernel.

The menuconfig tool shows a dependency by using indents on the menus, but the graphical tool disables the RAID options until you select the Multiple Device Driver Support option on which RAID depends. As a result, it is easier to understand relationships between modules and features by using the X-based configuration tool.

The options on the bottom of the X-based tool are similar to what you use in the menu-based tool:

Save And Exit   Create the kernel configuration file and close the configuration tool.

Quit Without Saving   Close the configuration tool, but don't create a kernel configuration file.

WARNING   If you don't create a kernel configuration file using one of the three tools described in this chapter, you can't rebuild the kernel.

Load Configuration From File   Load a previously saved configuration file (for use later on or to pass to a friend) that was stored under a name that you chose.

Store Configuration To File   Save a kernel configuration file (for use later on or to pass to a friend) under a name that you select. You must still use the Save And Exit option to create a kernel configuration file in the default location to be used immediately for kernel rebuilding.

Compiling and Running the New Kernel

Once your kernel reconfiguration is complete, check for a new configuration file (.config), probably in the /usr/src/linux-2.4.2 directory. Remember, to see hidden files, you need to use the ls -a command. If .config is there, you're ready to use the make command to rebuild your kernel.

The preferred commands vary slightly based on your Linux system but are straightforward in every case.

Return to a command line after configuring the kernel and make sure you can leave your system running for a while to let the compilation proceed.

Rebuilding the kernel can take from 15 minutes to several hours, depending on your processor, memory, and other factors. Because of this, most people prefer to combine all of the commands to rebuild the kernel on a single command line, separated by semicolons, so that they execute one after another. By doing this, you can simply return to your system after a while and find the whole process completed.

Starting the Rebuild Process

The commands given here create a new kernel and also rebuild all the kernel modules, placing them in the correct system directories to be accessible to your kernel using standard module commands.

To rebuild the system, use these commands:

```
# make dep; make clean; make bzImage; make modules; make
modules_install
```

You can also enter each `make` command separately, entering the next command after each one has finished. If you don't plan to use modules, you can omit the last two commands. Review the README file where you unpacked the new kernel (`/usr/src/linux-2.4.2` in this chapter) for more information.

When you enter these commands, you see lines of information scrolling slowly down your screen as the `make` program enters different directories, starts the `gcc` or `egcs` compiler for various source code files, and links together pieces of the code. Each of these commands may take a substantial number of minutes to complete.

If you have an `initrd` file in your `/etc/lilo.conf` file, you should create a new `initrd` file at this time. First, back up your current `initrd` file, which is `initrd-2.4.2-2.img` in Red Hat Linux 7.1. To do so, run the following commands:

```
# cp /boot/initrd-2.4.2-2.img /boot/initrd-2.4.2-2.orig.img
# /sbin/mkinitrd /boot/2.4.2-2.img 2.4.2-2
```

Now you're ready to make a boot disk from your new kernel with this command:

```
# make bzdisk
```

You'll need to insert a formatted floppy disk in the drive before running this command. Once the boot disk is ready, test it. Reboot your computer with the boot disk in the floppy drive.

Once the commands described previously have completed and you return to a command prompt, you have a new kernel on which you can run your system.

You need to move the newly created kernel to the standard location so it can be used. The command to do this is

```
# cp /usr/src/linux-2.4.2/arch/i386/boot/bzImage /boot/vmlinuz-2.4.2-2
```

Finally, to update the boot-loading map you must run the `lilo` command:

```
# /sbin/lilo
```

If the name of the copied kernel image has a different kernel version number (or even no number at all), substitute accordingly. Just make sure that it matches the appropriate filename given in your `/etc/lilo.conf` file, as discussed in the earlier section on backing up the kernel.

Testing the New Kernel

After you have moved your new kernel into the default position (as shown in the lilo.conf file), you can reboot your system to start the new kernel.

Once your Linux system has been rebooted, try the additional features that you specified in the kernel configuration. This might include things like the following:

- Comparing the size of the new kernel to the previous one. Also try the free command to see how much system memory is used.

- Mounting a file system or accessing a device without first loading a kernel module to support it (if you had built-in support for that service).

- Using a networking resource (such as IP aliases) that was not available in your original kernel.

You may also want to try the uname command to see the timestamp of your current kernel. This command verifies that the kernel you're running is the one that you rebuilt. Make sure that the date and time match when you rebuilt your kernel.

```
# uname  -v
#1 Tue Mar 9 13:27:39 EST 2001
```

NOTE   If the response from the uname command indicates that you are not running the new kernel, you may have a problem with your LILO boot loader. Check the information in the /etc/lilo.conf file to be sure that the correct kernel has been specified.

Looking Ahead

The next section of this book covers basic connectivity. The following chapters address a range of subjects related to connecting a stand-alone PC to the Internet, including the mechanics of establishing a PPP connection, browsing the World Wide Web with Linux, and sending and receiving e-mail with Linux.

In Chapter 21, "Understanding Linux Networking," you will start this journey with a review of basic networking concepts as they apply to Linux. This will include a quick overview of TCP/IP, the protocol that makes the Internet work and is the basis for most Unix- and Linux-based networks.

PART V

Basic Connectivity

CHAPTER

TWENTY-ONE

Understanding Linux Networking

- TCP/IP Fundamentals

- TCP/IP Ports

- Routing Concepts

This part of the book dives into a topic that is of interest to most computer users these days: networking.

This chapter starts by considering the basic Linux networking concepts, including TCP/IP networks and routing. You will discover the basic concepts behind TCP/IP and the components of a TCP/IP configuration, such as IP addresses, netmasks, ports, and gateways. Then you will look at the types of services that typically run on the TCP/IP connection of a standard Linux system.

TCP/IP Fundamentals

TCP/IP is the language of computer communication on the Internet. Because of the history of the Internet, TCP/IP was developed on Unix. Since Linux is derived from Unix, Linux is a great operating system for connecting to the Internet.

A language like TCP/IP is really a set, or suite, of protocols used for communication between computers. While these protocols communicate over physical media to other systems on the network, they are independent of the type of physical connection on which the network is built.

At a physical level, networks are built using a variety of technologies, including telephone wire, cable TV-sized copper cables, fiber optic cables, and more. You can run TCP/IP, or any other network protocol suite, on most any of these physical media.

What Is TCP/IP?

TCP/IP (Transmission Control Protocol/Internet Protocol) is a two-part name for a large number of protocols. Working together, these protocols can be used to communicate with almost every commercially available operating system today. That perhaps is the secret behind TCP/IP; its interoperability allows everyone to use it on their own network and their connection(s) to the Internet.

TCP/IP Configuration Essentials

In order to understand how TCP/IP is configured and networks are designed, it is important to understand some fundamental concepts:

- IP addresses

- Subnetworking and netmasks

- Broadcast addresses

- Gateway addresses

- Name servers

This information is based on IP version 4 (IPv4). Although we are currently in transition to IP version 6 (IPv6), this new version of IP addressing incorporates most of the important concepts in IPv4.

IP Addresses

In the world of TCP/IP, each computer is also known as a *host*. When connected to a TCP/IP network, each host gets a unique address known as an *IP address*.

An IP (IPv4) address is four numbers between 0 and 255, separated by dots. Each computer that directly connects to the Internet has a unique IP address. When you dial into the Internet through an Internet service provider (ISP), your ISP assigns a unique IP address to your computer while you're connected.

Computers communicate in binary code of 1s and 0s. An IP address such as 192.168.0.34, translated to binary code, is

```
11000000 10101000 00000000 00100010
```

Each of these 32 numbers is a binary digit, also known as a *bit*. As you can see, there are 32 bits in an IP address. The total number of unique combinations of 1s and 0s in a 32-bit number is 2^{32}, or 4,294,967,296. This may seem like a lot of addresses, but in fact, we have essentially run out of IP addresses on the current Internet.

IP version 6 (IPv6), discussed later, was developed to address this problem. In IPv6, IP addresses have 128 bits. The total number of unique combinations of 1s and 0s in a 128-bit address is 2^{128}, or 340,282,366,920,938,463,463,374,607,431,768,211,456 potential addresses.

As you might guess, over four billion addresses are not simply randomly used around the globe. Rather, they are assigned in chunks, known as *networks*, for use by organizations, ISPs, and other groups needing IP addresses for use on the Internet.

There are three types of TCP/IP networks available for regular networking: Class A, Class B, and Class C networks:

- In a Class A network, the network is identified by the first byte of the IP addresses while the remaining three bytes identify specific machines on the network, for a total of 16,777,214 available addresses. The first number in a Class A network is between 1 and 126. For example, in the Class A network starting with 98, the available IP addresses range from 98.0.0.1 through 98.255.255.254.

- In a Class B network, the network is identified by the first two bytes of the IP address while the remaining two bytes identify specific machines on the network, for a total of 65,534 available addresses. The first number in a Class B network is between 128 and 191. The second number can be anything between 0 and 255. For example, you could have a Class B network starting with 145.255. The available IP addresses on this network range from 145.255.0.1 through 145.255.255.254.

- In a Class C network, the network is identified by the first three bytes of the IP address while the remaining byte identifies specific machines on the network, for a total of 254 available addresses. The first number in a Class C network is between 192 and 223. The second and third numbers can each be anything between 0 and 255. For example, you could have a Class C network starting with 212.230.0. The available IP addresses on this network range from 212.230.0.1 through 212.230.0.254.

You might note that the first and last numbers (0 and 255) in the above ranges were left out. That is because the first address in a range is reserved as the network address, while the last address is reserved as the broadcast address. For example, the noted Class A network address is 98.0.0.0, and its broadcast address is 98.255.255.255.

You might also note that some first numbers in an IP address, including 0, 127, and 224–255 are not covered. There are also a number of addresses reserved for private use. For more information, refer to the documents listed in the note in the next section.

Subnetworking and Netmasks

It is not uncommon for organizations with large IP address needs to obtain a Class B network and then subdivide (subnetwork) it into 256 Class C-sized networks. A perfect example of this is a large ISP that needs to provide Class C-sized networks to its corporate clients and does this by dividing up a Class B network.

For example, if an ISP had a Class B network of 165.65, it could divide it up into 256 different networks, ranging from 165.65.0 through 165.65.255. Each of these subnetworks would have 254 available addresses, similar to the description of the Class C network in the last section.

There is a potential for confusion in this situation. How can a machine know what type of network it is on? If a machine has an IP address of 19.148.43.194, there is no immediately apparent way for it to know if it is on the Class A network 19, a Class B-size subnetwork 19.148, or a Class C-size subnetwork 19.148.43.

This situation is resolved by the use of a *network mask* (or *subnetwork mask*), also known as a *netmask* (or *subnetmask*). A netmask is another set of dot-separated one-byte integers that define which portion of the IP address identifies the network.

There are three generic netmasks: 255.0.0.0, 255.255.0.0, and 255.255.255.0. If you know the IP address and the netmask, you can define the network IP address and its range of available addresses.

Take the previous IP address, 19.148.43.194. If the netmask is 255.0.0.0, the network address is 19.0.0.0, and the range of possible addresses on that network is 19.0.0.1 through 19.255.255.254. If the netmask is 255.255.0.0, the network address is 19.148.0.0 and the range of possible addresses on that network is 19.148.0.1 through 19.148.255.254. If the netmask is 255.255.255.0, the network address is 19.148.43.0 and the range of possible addresses on that network is 19.148.43.1 through 19.148.43.254.

When a computer routes a message, it has a specific IP address. As discussed later, if it also has the network mask, it knows where to send that IP address.

NOTE   More sophisticated netmasks are available, but they are beyond the scope of this book. There are a number of other ways to subdivide (or even recombine) address blocks. For more information on this topic, refer to the IP Sub-networking mini-HOWTO at `http://www.linuxdoc.org/HOWTO/mini/IP-Subnetworking.html` or Chapter 2 in the *Linux Network Administrators Guide* at `http://www.linuxdoc.org/LDP/nag2/index.html`. If you're planning your own TCP/IP network, pay particular attention to discussions on private addresses.

IP Version 6 (IPv6)

We are currently in transition to IPv6, with its 2^{128} potential addresses. This transition won't happen all at once; network hardware and software are under development to use both IPv4 and IPv6 addresses simultaneously. Since there are so many IPv6 addresses, there is enough room to incorporate all IPv4 addresses. Your current IP addresses (IPv4) will still work in an IPv6 world.

In fact, the conventions developed for IPv6 make the difference seem simple; for example, the following IPv4 address

    192.168.33.54

is equivalent to the following IPv6 address

    ::192.168.33.54

When the transition is complete, we are supposed to think of IPv6 addresses in hexadecimal, or base 16 notation. In base 16, the numbers are 0, 1, 2, 3, 4, 5, 6, 7, 8, 9, a, b, c, d, e, and f. A typical IPv6 address in hexadecimal notation might look like

    3dfe:0b80:0a18:1def:0000:0000:0000:0287

Another IPv6 convention allows you to leave out leading zeros; the same IPv6 address can be written as

    3dfe:b80:a18:1def:0:0:0:287

You can convert the previously noted IPv4 address. To do so, first convert it to binary format; thus 192.168.33.54 becomes

    11000000 10101000 00100001 00111000

Converting this to hexadecimal notation, this becomes

    c0a8:2138

Therefore, the full corresponding IPv6 address is

    0000:0000:0000:0000:0000:0000:c0a8:2136

or alternatively

    0:0:0:0:0:0:c0a8:2136

or even

    ::192.168.33.54

Broadcast Addresses

The *broadcast address* is a special address that can be used when sending information to all hosts on the network. Instead of sending separate messages to each host, a single message can be sent to a broadcast address. All computers connected to that network receive that message. The best analogy to a broadcast message is a radio or a television signal, where every unit that is listening receives the message.

The broadcast address is based on the network address, with the host portions replaced by 255. So, for the Class B network 174.148, the broadcast address is 174.148.255.255, and for the Class C network 194.148.43, the broadcast address is 194.148.43.255.

Gateway Addresses

As you will see later in the section on routing, a computer configured for the local network or subnetwork has no knowledge of how to communicate with computers on external networks (for instance, on the Internet). It needs a gateway to an external network.

A *gateway* is a computer that provides a route to the outside world. It generally has at least two network interfaces: one connected to the local network and one to an outside network, often a corporate network or directly to the Internet. If a computer can't identify the destination address of a message on the local network, it sends the message to a gateway. The gateway reroutes the message to the external network.

If you want a host computer to connect to an external network, you need to identify the IP address of at least one gateway that is also connected to an outside network such as the Internet.

Name Servers

When you want to access the Sybex Web site, you could type 63.86.158.42 into the address text box in your browser. But it's easier to remember http://www.Sybex.com. Name servers provide the transition. Name servers, under the Domain Name System (DNS), are a database of domain names such as www.mommabears.com or www .Sybex.com and their corresponding IP addresses.

Any computer that is connected to the Internet or any other large network needs a name server. Therefore, when configuring TCP/IP on a host in a large network, you need a name server.

ISPs provide name servers for your connections to the Internet. In fact, you don't even need the IP address of a name server for most dial-up connections. It is automatically provided for you during your connection. Dial-up connections are discussed in more detail in Chapter 22, "Connecting Linux to the Internet."

TCP/IP Ports

When two machines wish to use TCP/IP to communicate with each other, they generally specify the destination by using a combination of the IP address and a port. For example, World Wide Web communication is done on port 80. To make this work, when you type http://www.mommabears.com, TCP/IP looks at www and automatically translates this to http://www.mommabears.com:80.

There are 65,536 (=2^{16}) available ports. The first 1,024 ports and a number of others are assigned to specific TCP/IP services such as www, FTP, and more. Widely used services such as TCP/IP, the Web, FTP, and e-mail all have assigned ports. Table 21.1 lists a few common TCP/IP port numbers.

TABLE 21.1: Common TCP/IP Port Numbers

Service Name	Port	Type	Description
FTP	21	TCP	File Transfer Protocol
Telnet	23	TCP	Telnet connections
SMTP	25	TCP	Simple Mail Transfer Protocol
Name	42	TCP	Domain Name System services
HTTP	80	TCP	Hypertext Transfer Protocol (World Wide Web)
POP3	110	TCP	Post Office Protocol 3 mail readers
IMAP	143	TCP	Internet Message Access Protocol mail readers

A more complete list of TCP and UDP ports can be found on the Internet at http://www.isi.edu/in-notes/iana/assignments/port-numbers. Web servers listen on port 80. When you try to reach Momma Bears' Bears with http://www.mommabears.com, the associated Web server hears the message and returns the Momma Bears' Web site as a message to your computer.

But the Momma Bears' Web server doesn't answer on port 80. If it did, it would clog up the channel (port 80), preventing others from reaching the Momma Bears' Web site. Fortunately, when you type in http://www.mommabears.com, TCP/IP also sends an unassigned port number to the Momma Bears' Web server. The server uses this port number to send the Web site back to the host, which leaves port 80 free for further incoming requests.

Routing Concepts

The discussion of gateways earlier in this chapter alluded to the notion of *routing*. Routing to the Internet is like zip or postal codes: It allows your message to find its destination.

After all, when you use Netscape or some other Web browser to connect to Yahoo's Web site, your machine knows nothing about the actual physical location of the Yahoo Web server. Your ISP translates www.yahoo.com into an IP address. And somehow, the request makes it to Yahoo, and Yahoo's response finds its way back to you.

Let's start with a simple example of routing. You are connected to a small corporate local area network (LAN) that has an Internet connection. The Internet connection is made through a router connected to the corporate LAN and your company's connection to its ISP. Each router acts as a gateway. As a gateway, it has a connection and an IP address on your LAN. It also has an IP address assigned by your ISP. Figure 21.1 illustrates this network layout.

FIGURE 21.1:

A LAN connected to the Internet

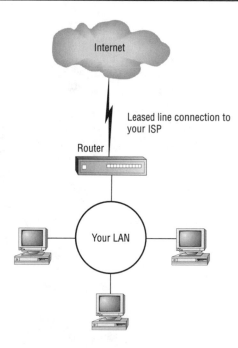

Because your LAN has only a single connection to the outside world through the router, routing is a simple matter. Each machine on the Internet is configured with a default gateway, which is the IP address of the router on your LAN. Whenever a host on the LAN wants to connect with a computer outside the local network, it sends the request to the gateway IP address, i.e., the router. The router is responsible for redirecting the information to your ISP.

In this way, the entire outside world is a black box: All outward-bound information is simply sent to the router as if the router encapsulated the entire network beyond the LAN.

Let's take things a step further and enlarge the black box to include the ISP's network and its connection to the Internet, as shown in Figure 21.2.

FIGURE 21.2:

The LAN and its ISP

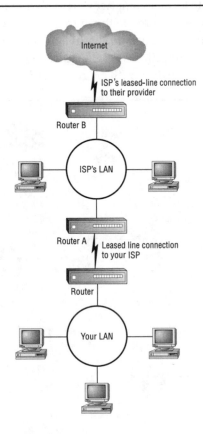

Now things get a bit more interesting. Consider the ISP's LAN. Here you see two routers: Router A, which connects the ISP's LAN to the connection to the local LAN, and Router B, which connects the ISP's LAN to the connection to the Internet.

Since each network needs a default gateway, Router B is the ISP's default gateway. When a host on the ISP's LAN is trying to connect to the Internet, it sends the information to Router B.

In other words, a message from a computer on your LAN is first sent to your default gateway, which is Router A. That router sends the message on to your ISP. Your ISP receives the message on Router A. The ISP checks the message's destination address. If the address is on the Internet, the ISP sends the message on to its default gateway, Router B.

Routing can become extremely complex in large organizations with multiple sites, multiple LANs, and multiple connections to the Internet. In these cases, routing has to be carefully designed to ensure the most efficient routing of information in the most secure manner possible. For instance, two remote locations may have a direct connection between them in addition to their own connections to the Internet. It wouldn't make sense to route packets between these sites through the public Internet. This is both inefficient and an unnecessary security hole.

Complex routing of large networks is beyond the scope of this book and belongs in tomes dedicated to networking. The discussion in this chapter should provide sufficient background for understanding the typical network routing environment in which most Linux users will find themselves.

Looking Ahead

In this chapter, you have learned some basic concepts of TCP/IP networking and routing.

Taking this theoretical knowledge into the realm of the practical, in Chapter 22, "Connecting Linux to the Internet," you will learn how to connect a Linux PC to the Internet through a dial-up PPP connection like those commonly offered by Internet service providers.

In the chapters that follow, you will learn how to use specific Internet services such as the World Wide Web and e-mail from Linux.

CHAPTER

TWENTY-TWO

22

Connecting Linux to the Internet

- What Is PPP?

- Required Hardware and Software

- Graphical PPP Connections

- Manual PPP Connections

- Automating Manual Internet Connections

The subject of connecting a Linux system (or any computer system, for that matter) to the Internet is a complex one and a subject that can require a thorough knowledge of that system's network environment.

Still, for many users, this process is simple enough that both X Windows and Linux work on the first attempt.

This chapter starts with a quick look at PPP and its role in the Internet world. It reviews the hardware and software requirements for connecting to the Internet and then walks you through the mechanics of manually making a PPP connection. Finally, this chapter wraps up by explaining how to automate these connections.

What Is PPP?

Most Internet users are probably familiar with the acronym PPP, simply because the type of account they have with their Internet service provider (ISP) is a PPP account. Many users, though, really don't understand what PPP is all about.

PPP stands for *Point-to-Point Protocol* and is designed to provide a method by which TCP/IP is extended across an analog modem connection. In this way, when you are connected to the Internet using PPP, you become part of your ISP's network, you are an actual host on the Internet, and you have an IP address.

Traditionally, dial-up Internet connections were done using terminal software and Unix shell accounts on central servers. In this environment, the terminal software on the client system merely acted as a display for the server, and only the server had an IP address on the Internet. This contrasts sharply with today's PPP connections, which bring the Internet right up to your modem.

The great flexibility of Internet connection technologies allows for a wide variety of PPP connection types. You can have PPP connections with fixed or dynamic IP addresses. Connections can use special authentication protocols such as PAP (Password Authentication Protocol) or CHAP (Challenge Handshake Authentication Protocol). They can even use standard clear-text-based prompt-and-response mechanisms. Connections can be made manually or can be made automatically as needed.

This chapter discusses the most common Internet connection scenario: connecting by modem to an ISP that offers PPP connections with dynamically assigned IP addresses.

NOTE   "PPP" and "ISP connections" are used interchangeably in this chapter. However, PPP connections are not limited to connections through ISPs. In fact, PPP is also a common way to connect to corporate or educational networks.

Required Hardware and Software

In order to make PPP work properly, some preparation is needed. Hardware and software needs to be in place and configured before you can get PPP to work properly. Three key components need to be considered:

- A modem needs to be installed, configured, and working.
- PPP support needs to be compiled into the Linux kernel.
- PPP software needs to be installed.

The Modem

Because PPP is designed for dial-up connections, a modem is an essential piece of the PPP puzzle.

Chapter 18, "Using Peripherals," discusses modems and how to install them, test them, and get them working. Refer to that chapter to get your modem up and running and to make a test connection to be sure everything is in order.

To configure PPP, you need to know the speed of your modem connection and which device it uses in Linux (probably /dev/modem or one of /dev/ttyS0 through /dev/ttyS3).

PPP in the Kernel

The Linux kernel is designed to be highly flexible. It can be compiled to include (or exclude) support for numerous technologies ranging from serial mice right up to networking facilities such as PPP.

In order to make a PPP connection with Linux, it is necessary for the kernel to include PPP support. You can check to see if support is there by watching the messages that scroll by while the operating system is booting. If you see a series of lines like these

```
PPP generic driver version 2.4.0
PPP Deflate Compression module registered
PPP BSD Compression module registered
```

then PPP is compiled into your kernel. If you find that the messages scroll by too quickly, you can use the dmesg command to see the part of the start-up messages that should include the PPP messages:

```
$ dmesg | less
```

> **NOTE**   If you find that you need to recompile your kernel to include PPP support, refer to Chapter 20, "Recompiling the Linux Kernel," which discusses the steps involved in recompiling your kernel.

Installing PPP Software

Red Hat Linux 7.1 installs PPP software with a complete or default installation.

Two programs are used to establish a PPP connection: /usr/sbin/pppd and /usr/sbin/chat. In Red Hat Linux 7.1, these are part of the ppp-2.4.0-2 package, and you can see if these are installed by using the rpm command:

```
$ rpm -q ppp
ppp-2.4.0-2
```

If you find that you are lacking either pppd or chat, you need to install a new set of PPP software before continuing. Mount the Red Hat CD-ROM at a suitable location (such as /mnt/cdrom) and then install the package ppp-2.4.0-2.i386.rpm:

```
$ rpm -i /mnt/cdrom/RedHat/RPMS/ppp-2.4.0-2.i386.rpm
```

Alternatively, you can download the latest sources for PPP from the pppd home page at the Samba download mirror site at ftp://ftp.samba.org/pub/ppp/. The current version of PPP is 2.4.1 and the filename is ppp-2.4.1.tar.gz.

You need to expand the archive in a suitable location such as /tmp with the command

```
$ tar xzvf ppp-2.4.1.tar.gz
```

and then read through the README.linux file carefully. Installing a new PPP package involves not only compiling the software but also upgrading your Linux kernel source files and recompiling the Linux kernel to match the version of the PPP software being installed.

Describing the details of this process would take up a whole chapter, so it is best left to the documentation.

TIP   Comprehensive sources for downloading Linux software can be found on numerous Web sites, including those for your distribution, as well as the Tucows Web site at http://www.tucows.com. If you prefer rpm packages, a comprehensive source of these packages is located at http://www.rpmfind.net.

Graphical PPP Connections

There are two major tools available to help you make a PPP connection, designed to help you get on the Internet with your Linux computer: RP3 for GNOME and KPPP for KDE. RP3 on Red Hat Linux 7.1 keeps the human interface as simple as possible. KPPP allows you to configure every part of your Internet connection.

The following sections assume a basic Internet connection where you need few special settings. However, some ISPs do require additional special settings. Both RP3 and KPPP can accommodate special settings as well as diagnostic checks. More information on these optional settings is available later in the sections on pppd and minicom.

RP3

RP3 is the Red Hat graphical PPP management tool. If you have an ISP that can handle Linux connections, you can be set up and connected to the Internet in three easy steps. You can make more sophisticated configuration changes later; you can even set up a terminal to troubleshoot any connection problems that you might have. But RP3 is easy to use. First, you configure it as the root user, and then any regular user on your system can connect to the Internet.

Configuring RP3

By default, access is configured right on the desktop. To start RP3, double-click the Dialup Configuration icon on your desktop or simply run the /usr/bin/rp3-config command from a terminal in the X Window.

Enter the root password if prompted. If this is the first time you're using RP3, then the Add New Internet Connection Wizard starts. Click Next to continue. If you do not yet have a modem configured, you will see a Select Modem dialog box. Plug your modem into a telephone line. Click Next to continue. As you can see in Figure 22.1, RP3 then checks every device that could be connected to a modem.

> **TIP**   If you do not see the Add New Internet Connection Wizard, but you see an Internet Connections dialog box, click the Add button. Otherwise, you may not have the RP3 package installed.

FIGURE 22.1:

Checking for modems

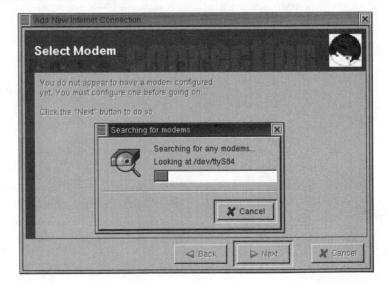

When RP3 finds a candidate device, it checks automatically for a dial tone. After it runs through each device file, it gives you a result like that shown in Figure 22.2.

FIGURE 22.2:

RP3 finds a modem.

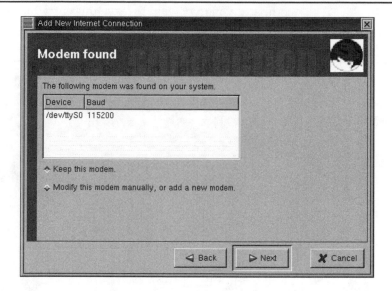

If it doesn't find a modem, the next window you'll see is shown in Figure 22.3. This screen allows you to edit the various settings shown to help Linux find and use your modem. Even if Linux found your modem, you can still access this window by selecting the Modify This Modem Manually... option shown back in Figure 22.2.

NOTE   The baud rate is not identical to the speed of your modem. It should typically be four times the speed of your modem, up to 115,200 baud. However, you can set a lower speed to reduce data loss from outside factors such as noise.

Once you have the modem configured, click Next. The next step is to set up the basics of your Internet connection, as shown in Figure 22.4:

- Account Name is the name of your ISP.

- Prefix is the number dialed on your telephone for outside access. You can leave this blank if no prefix is required.

- Area/Country Code is the numbers required to access the local telephone exchange of your ISP's access number. If you can reach the ISP through a local telephone call, depending on the rules set by your local telephone company, you may want to leave this entry blank as well.

- Phone Number is the local access number for your ISP.

FIGURE 22.3:

Manual modem configuration

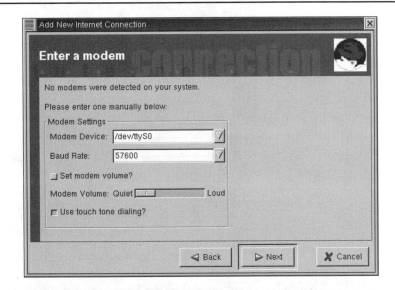

FIGURE 22.4:

Entering ISP access information

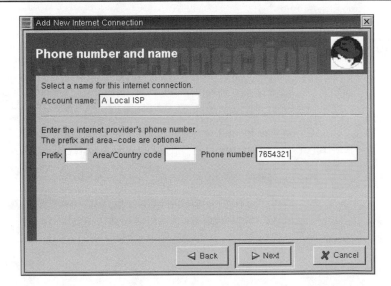

Click Next, enter the username and password that you use to log on to your ISP, and then click Next again. In the Other Options window, select Normal ISP or AT&T Global Network Services, and click Next. When you click Finish in the next window, you're ready to get connected.

Using RP3

Once a PPP connection is configured, any regular user on your system can run it. From the GNOME Main Menu button, choose Programs ➤ Internet ➤ RH PPP Dialer. The Choose window opens, as shown in Figure 22.5. Select the name you assigned to the ISP, click OK, and Linux connects to the Internet through your ISP.

FIGURE 22.5:

Selecting an ISP

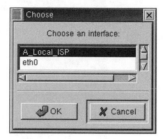

KPPP

The other major Linux GUI way to access the Internet is through KPPP, the KDE PPP dialer. If you're in the KDE desktop, click the KDE Main Menu button, then choose Internet ➤ Internet Dialer. In another desktop such as GNOME, open up a command-line window and enter the /usr/bin/kppp command. This brings up the KPPP window, shown in Figure 22.6.

FIGURE 22.6:

The KDE PPP configuration tool

Click Setup in this window. When you see the KPPP Configuration window, choose the Accounts tab if necessary, and then click New. This opens the Create A New Account... window, which is customized primarily for European ISPs. Unless you use an ISP in Europe or New Zealand, click Dialog Setup. This brings up the New Account window shown in Figure 22.7, where you can set up a connection to your ISP. In most cases, you need to set up only the items shown in Figure 22.7.

FIGURE 22.7:

Setting up an ISP

If you have trouble with your connection, come back to this window. You can configure a number of options under the other tabs shown in Figure 22.7:

Dial   Besides the phone number, you can configure the type of password authentication as well as the programs to execute at various points during your connection.

IP   If your ISP assigns you a static IP address, enter it here.

Gateway   If your ISP doesn't automatically set up a gateway on its network to the Internet for you, you can enter the associated gateway IP address here.

DNS   If your ISP doesn't automatically set up its DNS servers for your connection, you can enter the associated DNS IP addresses here.

Login Script   If your ISP requires the use of a login script, you can enter the associated commands here.

Execute   This allows you to set up programs or commands to run at different stages of the connection process.

Accounting   If you have to pay for local telephone access on a per-minute basis, you can enter the associated accounting rules here.

Once everything you need is configured, click OK to return to the KPPP Configuration window shown in Figure 22.8.

NOTE   U.S. readers need to understand that in many other countries, local calls are charged by the minute, which creates different requirements for Internet access.

FIGURE 22.8:

KPPP configuration options

If you have trouble with your modem setup, come back to this window. A number of helpful tools are available under the various tabs shown:

Accounts   Besides showing the name of your ISP account, this tab lets you get to the log files, which often contain useful messages to help you identify whatever problems may arise.

Device   Sets up the hardware parameters associated with your modem.

Modem   Allows you to test or monitor the modem in various ways.

Misc Determines the behavior of the PPP daemon when you connect, disconnect, or shut down the X Window.

If you need to enable access by regular users, you can set up suid permissions, which allow all regular users to run either program, without giving everyone full access. When you change the permissions on the /usr/sbin/kppp file as follows

```
# chmod u+s /usr/sbin/kppp
```

all regular users can then run the associated command, /usr/sbin/kppp, to access this utility.

Manual PPP Connections

The RP3 and KPPP utilities are enough for most users. But if you have problems or want to understand the inner workings of PPP connections in Linux, it is important to understand how the PPP daemon (pppd) and other connection utilities work.

In Linux, the PPP connection is made and maintained by pppd. But pppd assumes that a connection has already been made between your modem and your ISP's modem, that all the necessary logging in has taken place, and that the ISP's system is also trying to establish a PPP connection on top of the same modem connection.

This sounds like a lot of conditions, but it really isn't that bad. On almost every ISP, the connection process goes like this:

1. The modem connection is made.

2. The login process occurs.

3. Once the user is authenticated, the ISP begins to try to make a PPP connection by sending the IP address of the client to the client system.

The pppd program requires steps 1 and 2 to have occurred before step 3 gets under way.

Given this process, it is necessary to make a modem connection to the ISP before attempting to run pppd. Once the connection is made, the PPP connection can be established with pppd.

Making a PPP Connection

Fortunately, the pppd software is designed to bring things together and work with the chat program to handle the entire connection process. Before attempting to connect, you need to gather some information:

- Are you assigned an IP address each time you connect, or do you have a permanently assigned IP address? Because most ISPs work on the basis of assigning a dynamic IP address with each connection, you will also work on this basis.

- How do you log in to your ISP? One option uses plain-text prompt-and-response logins; another uses a special authentication protocol called PAP. A few use another authentication protocol known as CHAP. If you attempt to dial in to your ISP with minicom or other terminal software and are presented with a login prompt of some sort, then you are logging in with plain-text prompts. If you see random characters after connecting, or no characters at all, then you are probably using PAP or CHAP authentication.

NOTE   All the examples in this section assume that you are working as the root user on your machine. Because the process of connecting via PPP requires manipulation of interfaces and creation and deletion of network routes, the configuration programs involved need to be run by the root user.

TIP   Information on permanent IP addresses as well as authentication protocols can also help you configure RP3 or KPPP. Talk to your ISP if you aren't sure about or don't already have this information.

Connecting with Plain-Text Prompts

Let's start with plain-text prompts because they are a little easier to work with.

Because pppd by itself can take control of your modem device but cannot perform the actual dialing or logging in, you need a way to issue commands to the modem and provide the necessary login information. This is achieved with the chat program. The chat program allows you to create a conversational exchange.

For instance, the normal dialing process on a modem is to run a terminal editor and, in an empty terminal window, type a dial command such as **ATDT1234567**.

The response to this is usually a connect string such as CONNECT 115200, to which the user doesn't respond.

If you expect a response to an ATDT command, connect your modem. Substitute the number of an ISP or other server that can handle terminal connections for 1234567.

This exchange can be turned into a simple chat script:

```
"" ATDT1234567 CONNECT ""
```

This script is made up of two *expect-send pairs*: "" ATDT1234567 and CONNECT "". An expect-send pair contains two pieces of information separated by a space. In the first pair, chat is told to expect nothing (the first pair of double quotes) and in response to send back the string ATDT1234567. In other words, as soon as the script starts processing, the ATDT command dials the selected number. Next, the second pair is processed, and chat is told to expect the string CONNECT and in response to do nothing (the second pair of double quotes). If this were the complete script, chat would finish at this point and exit.

Of course, your chat script needs to be a bit longer. In order to complete your chat script, you need to find out exactly what your login session looks like. You can do this by logging in with regular terminal software such as minicom.

Login prompts at most ISPs generally take the form

```
Username:
Password:
```

or

```
Login:
Password:
```

or even

```
ogin:
ssword:
```

Consider the first case as the example in this chapter. If you find that your login prompts are different, substitute accordingly as you work through the section.

Instead of Login: and Password:, some ISPs are set up to send your computer ogin: or sername: and ssword: to accommodate different operating systems.

So, what is the next expect-send pair? After connecting, you are presented with a `Username:` prompt, in response to which you provide a username (let's say your username is `testuser`). The expect-send pair for this interaction would be `Username:` **testuser**.

Once a username is provided, you get a `Password:` prompt, to which you provide a password (let's assume this is `testpassword`). This produces the expect-send pair `Password:` **testpassword**.

For many ISPs this is sufficient, and PPP starts on the ISP's system after the correct password is entered. On a smaller number of systems, the ISP's computers present you with a command prompt at which you have to type a command to start PPP. In this case, you need to create an additional pair.

For this example, the complete chat script looks like this:

```
"" ATDT1234567 CONNECT "" Username: testuser Password: testpassword
```

To use this with the `chat` program (which is normally in `/usr/sbin`), you simply provide the script as an argument to `chat`:

```
/usr/sbin/chat "" ATDT1234567 CONNECT "" Username: testuser Password:
testpassword
```

Note, however, that you don't want to type this at the command line and press Enter. Without being integrated with `pppd` and provided access to the modem through that program, `chat` attempts to chat through the shell. You can use this to test your script, though. Simply type the command at the command prompt. When you see ATDT1234567, type **CONNECT** and then type **Username:**. You should see `testuser` in response. Follow this by typing **Password:** and you should see `testpassword` in response.

NOTE

If you need to work out problems with your **chat** script, try adding the –v flag to your **chat** command. This sends the output of the script to the system log, where you can analyze the results to find problems.

Once you have a working script, you need to integrate it with `pppd`. You are going to use a handful of `pppd` options to do this. (The `pppd` application takes many additional options, which can be found in the `pppd` man page.) The options you will use are the following:

> *connect*   This option is employed to specify a program or command used to establish a connection on the serial line being utilized. In this case, you use the `connect` option to specify the `chat` program and its script.

noipdefault   The default behavior of pppd is to determine the IP address of the local machine on the basis of its hostname. But if the ISP assigns a dynamic IP address, which is more common, then the `noipdefault` option is used to tell pppd to get the IP address from the remote machine to which it is connecting.

defaultroute   This option tells pppd to add a default route to the system's routing table, using the remote system (your ISP) as the default gateway. The entry is removed when the connection is broken.

The structure of the pppd command is

```
$ pppd device speed action chatcommands pppdoptions
```

If you are connecting with the device /dev/modem and the modem has a top compressed speed of 115200bps (in this case, a 56Kbps modem), then you use the following command to connect with the chat script:

```
$ pppd /dev/modem 115200 connect '/usr/sbin/chat "" ATDT1234567 CONNECT
    "" Username: testuser Password: testpassword' noipdefault defaultroute
```

When this command is issued, the modem should dial and, after connecting, it will authenticate and establish a PPP connection. If this process is successful, two things should happen.

First, issuing the command /sbin/ifconfig with no flags or arguments should return a list of interfaces including a PPP interface similar to this one:

```
ppp0      Link encap:Point-to-Point Protocol
          inet addr:194.209.60.101  P-t-P:194.209.60.97 Mask:255.255.255
          UP POINTOPOINT RUNNING  MTU:1500  Metric:1
          RX packets:10 errors:0 dropped:0 overruns:0
          TX packets:11 errors:0 dropped:0 overruns:0
```

Second, entries should be added to the routing table to create a default route through the remote machine (check for this using the /sbin/route command with no flags or arguments):

```
Kernel IP routing table
Destination Gateway       Genmask          Flags Metric Ref   Use Iface
du1.paus.ch *             255.255.255.255  UH    0      0       0 ppp0
default     du1.paus.ch 0                  UG    0      0       0 ppp0
```

In this example, du1.paus.ch is the remote machine in the PPP connection and is serving as the default gateway.

Connecting with PAP Authentication

Connecting with PAP authentication follows the same basic principles as the text-prompt example you just worked through, except that the method of providing the username and password differs.

The first major difference is that you don't provide the username and password on the command line as part of a PAP script. Instead, you create entries in a special `secrets` file that is used during the PAP authentication process. In Red Hat Linux 7.1, this file is `/etc/ppp/pap-secrets`. By default, the permissions on this file make it readable and writable only by the root user. Other users do not have read access to this file.

The format of entries in the `secrets` file is normally

```
username servername password
```

But since you connected to a server through a telephone modem, the second entry is not required. For instance, if you use the test username and password from the previous section, the entry might be

```
testuser * testpassword
```

The * indicates that this password can be used for connections on any interface.

Once your username and password are in the file, you need to write a new chat script. For most ISPs, as soon as the modem connection is established, PAP authentication can begin. Therefore, your chat script gets simpler:

```
"" ATDT12345678 CONNECT ""
```

This script dials the ISP and makes sure that a connect message is received before ending the chat program and proceeding on to authentication.

Finally, you need to introduce one more option for pppd: `user`. The user option indicates which PAP user from the `pap-secrets` file is to be authenticated. The end result is the following pppd command:

```
$ pppd /dev/modem 57600 connect '/usr/sbin/chat "" ATDT1234567 CONNECT'
    noipdefault defaultroute user testuser
```

As with the earlier text-login example, you can check that everything is in order using `ifconfig` and `route`.

Once You Have a Connection

Once you have an Internet connection, you need to make sure that you can fully connect to the Internet. To do this, you need to verify that your DNS services are properly configured to point to your ISP's nameserver.

This is done by editing two files: /etc/host.conf and /etc/resolv.conf. Both of these files are discussed more fully in Chapter 28, "Configuring Red Hat Linux 7.1 for an Ethernet Network." This section covers just the necessary basics of the files so that you can quickly get online.

The file /etc/host.conf should contain the following two lines:

```
order hosts,bind
multi on
```

Next, /etc/resolv.conf should contain at least two lines:

```
search
nameserver 100.100.100.100
```

In your case, replace the IP address 100.100.100.100 with the IP address of your ISP's DNS server, also known as a nameserver. Your ISP can provide this information. If your ISP provides you with more than one nameserver, create a separate line for each one as follows:

```
search
nameserver 100.100.100.100
nameserver 200.200.200.200
```

Once this is done, you should be able to resolve names and thus access the Internet. You should also be able to run Internet software such as Netscape and FTP. These programs are discussed in later chapters, such as Chapter 23, "Using the World Wide Web."

Hanging Up

When you have finished using the Internet, you should hang up to reduce phone costs and online charges. To do this, you need to kill the pppd process.

You can find out the process ID of the pppd program by using the ps command as the root user:

```
$ ps x | grep pppd
```

The entry for pppd should look something like this:

```
1316  ttyS0 S    0:00 /usr/sbin/pppd /dev/modem 115200 connect
   /usr/sbin/chat "" AT
```

The first number is the process ID. You can kill this process with the `kill` command, in this case

```
$ kill 1316
```

When pppd is killed, the modem should hang up.

Automating Manual Internet Connections

While it is great to be able to establish PPP connections to the Internet, if you have to type the long pppd and chat commands each time you connect, the practicality of using Linux to connect to the Internet will be limited.

To improve the situation, you can create two scripts: one for dialing and one for hanging up. These two scripts are going to be called dial and hangup (logical choices, yes?). You will want to place these files in a directory on your path such as /usr/local/bin.

Because you haven't learned about scripting yet, these two scripts are presented here with a brief discussion so that you can get right down to using them. These scripts can be created in any text editor. It is important to make sure that lines that appear as one line here stay as one line in your files.

For the dial script, let's assume that the PAP example earlier in the chapter is the way you want to connect to the Internet.

Once you have created the scripts, you will want to make them executable with the chmod command:

```
$ chmod 700 dial hangup
```

The permission 700 makes the script readable, writable, and executable by the root user and no one else. If you want to make the script usable by others in the same group as yours, substitute 750 for 700. If you want to make the script usable by anyone who accesses your Linux system, substitute 755 for 700.

TIP You don't have to create these scripts from scratch. If you have the **ppp rpm** package installed, preconfigured scripts are available in Red Hat Linux 7.1 in the `/usr/share/doc/ppp-2.4.0/scripts` directory. For example, you can set up the **ppp-on** and **ppp-off** scripts like the `dial` and `hangup` scripts described below.

The *dial* Script

The `dial` script should look something like this:

```
#!/bin/sh
/usr/sbin/pppd /dev/modem 115200 connect \
'/usr/sbin/chat "" ATDT1234567 CONNECT' \
noipdefault defaultroute user testuser
```

The first line tells Linux to process the script through the Bourne Shell, which is at /bin/sh. The other lines were covered earlier. Make sure to substitute the number of your ISP for 1234567. If necessary, substitute your modem device file for /dev/modem and speed for 115200.

Notice that the pppd command is split across three lines. It is still one command. The backslashes at the ends of the first and second lines of this command indicate that the line breaks shouldn't be treated as line breaks and that the command continues on the next line of the file. This is done to make the script more readable.

The *hangup* Script

The hangup script should look like this:

```
#!/bin/sh
kill `cat /var/run/ppp0.pid`
```

As with the `dial` script, you start by specifying that the script should be processed with the Bourne Shell. Next, you kill the process in a slightly different way than you learned before.

You are relying on the fact that the pppd process writes its process ID to a file that usually sits in /var/run on most modern Linux systems. The filename consists of the device name followed by a .pid extension. If you have only one modem and one PPP connection active at a time, you can assume that the device is ppp0 and type **/var/run/ppp0.pid** directly into your script.

The cat command simply displays the contents of the ppp0.pid file on the standard output. You put the cat command in back quotes to pass the result of the cat command (which is the process ID of the pppd process) to the kill command.

NOTE   You can find the back quote under the tilde (~) in the upper-left corner of a standard U.S. keyboard.

But what happens if you have multiple PPP interfaces and want to be able to specify which one to hang up? A quick modification of the hangup script makes this possible:

```
#!/bin/sh
kill `cat /var/run/$1.pid`
```

Here, you have replaced ppp0 with $1. The $1 indicates that the value of the first argument to the script should be placed in this location. Now you can pass the interface name to the script as an argument. The command

```
$ hangup ppp1
```

hangs up the modem that is being used for the ppp1 interface. Remember, the first modem is on ppp0, so you may need to run the hangup ppp0 command instead.

Looking Ahead

In this chapter, you took a big step. You brought your Linux system from the isolation of a lone computer on a desktop and connected it to the world with a PPP connection.

In Chapter 23, "Using the World Wide Web," you will take advantage of this new capability and learn how to use Netscape, the premier Web browser and Internet client for the Linux platform.

Following that, in Chapter 24, "Reading E-Mail," you will look at the rich variety of e-mail software available for Linux so that you can choose the one that best supports your style of using e-mail.

CHAPTER

TWENTY-THREE

Using the World Wide Web

- An Overview of Linux Browsers

- Installing and Using Netscape

- Configuring Netscape Mail

- Installing and Using Lynx

Now that you have your Linux system connected properly to the Internet, the first thing most of you will want to do is get out there and browse the World Wide Web.

This chapter takes a brief tour through the numerous Web browsers that are available for Linux and then takes a closer look at two browsers: Netscape 6 and Lynx.

Netscape 6 is the free Web browser and Internet client from Netscape. This full-featured package is available for Windows, Macintosh, and most Unix variants, including Linux.

NOTE   If a newer version is available when you explore the download section of the Netscape Web site, the instructions may be somewhat different from what you see in the rest of this chapter.

This chapter then continues with a look at mailboxes. Most home users of the Internet have remote mailboxes maintained on the servers of their Internet service provider (ISP). But when they read the mail using a mail reader such as Eudora or Netscape 6's built-in mail reader, they permanently copy their messages into a mailbox created locally by their mail software.

Another approach is to read mail online. In this way, the mailbox remains on the server and is simply manipulated by the mail software without permanently creating a local mailbox as new mail is read.

This chapter also looks at Lynx, the de facto standard in Unix/Linux text-based browsers. Lynx has a longer history than Netscape, going back to when Web technology was used to deliver small amounts of scientific information in a simple text-based hypertext system. Lynx has continued to evolve and ships with almost every distribution of Linux. While it lacks the fancy graphics and icon-driven interface of Netscape 6, for a quick way to go online, check some information, and go offline, nothing beats Lynx.

An Overview of Linux Browsers

There are several browsers available for the X Windows environment that work with Linux. These browsers range from the test platform Amaya, developed at the World Wide Web Consortium (W3C), to mainstream browsers such as Netscape.

This section takes a quick look at some of these browsers so that you have a sense of the breadth of available Web software for Linux.

Amaya

Amaya is a Web browser developed by the World Wide Web Consortium (W3C) as a test bed for new Web protocols and data formats. The W3C is the international organization founded by Tim Berners-Lee to help coordinate the development of the World Wide Web. As Berners-Lee is the person most often described as the inventor of the World Wide Web, it makes sense that the W3C should develop its own browser as part of developing new standards for this system.

Amaya is a combination Web browser and authoring tool that is supposed to support cascading style sheets and HTML, along with newer graphics formats such as PNG. Amaya also includes a powerful mathematical expression editor.

Although Amaya offers leading-edge features, it does not support all the features of the Web that are currently supported by commercial browsers such as Netscape.

Amaya is available for download through its home page at `http://www.w3.org/Amaya/`. The current version as of this writing is 4.3.2. Figure 23.1 contains a sample Amaya window.

FIGURE 23.1:

The Amaya Web browser

Lynx

Lynx is the de facto standard for text browsers for the World Wide Web and is available for different versions of Linux and Unix, as well as various versions of Windows 95 and above, MS-DOS, and OS/2. The Lynx home page is found at http://lynx.browser.org/.

You may be wondering what possible use a text browser could be. Unfortunately, not everyone has the hardware required to support a graphical browser. And not everyone has the data connections to support graphics. For example:

- Many public libraries use Lynx. All you need to access Lynx is a dumb terminal. Libraries with limited funds can inexpensively set up a group of terminals with Lynx, running from a single server.

- Many facilities in less-developed areas use Lynx. Because of its cost, Linux is popular in less-developed regions around the world. Cost also limits the power of the computers used in these areas. Other limitations include poor telephone service and slow modem connections. Since Lynx demands less power and lower modem speed than any graphical browser, it is well suited for these limitations.

Whatever the reason, Lynx has evolved into an ideal text browser with the means to cope with most of the advanced features of the Web today, including a way to view a site using frames. Figure 23.2 shows Lynx running in a command-line interface. Detailed coverage of Lynx is provided later in this chapter.

FIGURE 23.2:

The Lynx Web browser

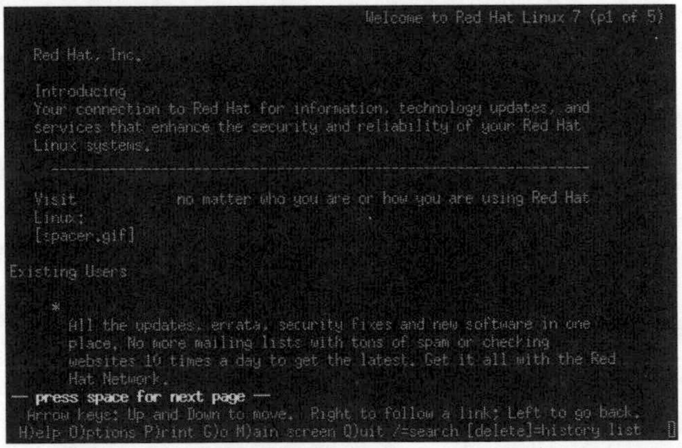

Opera

One of the most compact downloadable Linux browsers is Opera, shown in Figure 23.3. It was developed in the belief that "smaller is faster." On its features page, its developers state: "Opera is renowned for being the world's fastest browser." The current version, Opera 5, can be downloaded in a file less than a tenth the size of a comparable Netscape 6 download.

Despite its size, it still supports the major features of the larger browsers, including the following:

- Instant messaging to ICQ standards

- Cascading style sheet compatibility that can be developed into slide show-style presentations

- Wireless protocol (WAP) support, on an experimental basis

- Java

You can download Opera from its Web site at http://www.opera.com. As there are currently download servers only in Norway, download speeds to other countries may vary.

FIGURE 23.3:

The Opera Web browser

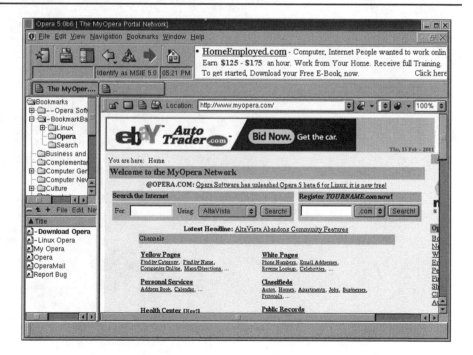

Mosaic

Mosaic was the first commercially available graphical Web browser. Developed by the National Center for Supercomputer Applications, Mosaic was a great upgrade to the text-based Gopher, the browser of the 1980s.

Early versions of Mosaic ran in the X Windows environment of popular Unix systems such as Sun's. Users of the then-fledgling World Wide Web were dazzled by Mosaic's pages of combined graphics and text and the new, easy-to-navigate, mouse-driven interface. One of the developers of Mosaic, Marc Andreesen, went on to develop Netscape based on the Mosaic Godzilla, or Mozilla, standard. The world has never been the same.

While Mosaic is no longer under active development, the last release (version 2.6 in the case of X Windows) is still available at the Mosaic Web page at the University of Illinois at Urbana-Champaign, `http://www.ncsa.uiuc.edu/SDG/Software/Mosaic/`. Figure 23.4 provides a sense of what the early pioneers of the Web used as their browser of choice.

FIGURE 23.4:

The last version of Mosaic for X Windows

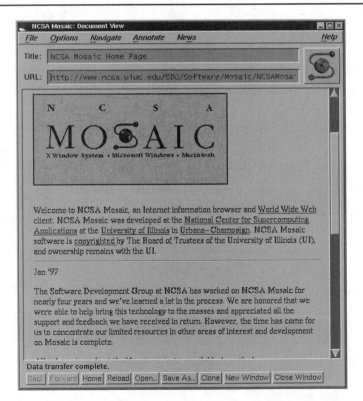

Netscape 6

Netscape 6, which includes the Navigator Web browser, can really be considered the flagship browser of the World Wide Web and has been the source of many browser features that you now consider standard. Although Netscape is no longer the browser market share leader, the release of its source code as well as its adaptation to Linux has won it a loyal following in the Linux community. As would be expected, Netscape 6 looks pretty much the same and behaves fairly consistently on all the platforms it is available for, including Linux. Figure 23.5 shows Netscape 6 for Linux. At first glance, it looks much the same as its Windows counterpart. Netscape 6 for Linux is discussed in detail later in this chapter.

FIGURE 23.5:

Netscape 6 for Linux

Installing and Using Netscape

Netscape Communicator version 4.76 is included on the CD-ROM that accompanies this book. You can download version 6 of Netscape from Netscape's Web site at http://home.netscape.com/. This section primarily focuses on Netscape 6.

This section takes a quick look at installing Netscape Communicator and Netscape 6 in Linux and then takes a brief introductory tour of the software. This tour is not intended to provide a comprehensive guide to Netscape, but rather to provide enough information so that you can use it to get online. Netscape 6 includes complete online help that has all the information needed to take full advantage of Netscape's features.

Installing from the CD-ROM

Netscape Communicator 4.76 is part of Red Hat Linux 7.1 and is likely to have been installed by default for most installations. If you find that Netscape is not on your system, you can install it from the CD-ROM that accompanies this book.

In order to install Communicator, you first must mount your CD-ROM to a logical location, such as /mnt/cdrom. Next, you want to use the rpm command to install the Netscape Communicator packages as follows:

```
$ rpm -i /mnt/cdrom/RedHat/RPMS/netscape-common-4.76-11.i386.rpm
$ rpm -i /mnt/cdrom/RedHat/RPMS/netscape-communicator-4.76-11.i386.rpm
```

These commands install the complete version of Netscape Communicator on your system.

Installing from the Web

If you decide to download a newer version of Netscape from the Netscape Web site, installation will be somewhat different. For example, you can download Netscape version 6.0 as a compressed tar archive called netscape-i686-pc-linux-gnu-sea_tar.gz.

TIP   This Netscape 6 download is nearly 30MB. If you don't want to download this much data, you could download a Netscape installer, which downloads and installs only the programs of your choice over the Internet. For this purpose, start by downloading the 64KB netscape-i686-pc-linux-gnu-installer.tar.gz file.

NOTE   The Netscape package, including the browser, mail manager, and Web page creator, was known as Netscape Communicator through version 4.76. When Netscape released their new package, they moved directly to version 6; there is no Netscape version 5.

You need to download this archive to a temporary location, such as /tmp/. Next, uncompress the archive with the command

```
$ tar xzvf /tmp/netscape-i686-pc-linux-gnu-sea_tar.gz
```

This command creates several files in the netscape-installer directory, including a README file and the netscape-installer script. Navigate to this directory with the cd /tmp/netscape-installer command, and then proceed to installation by running the installation script from an X Window terminal:

```
$ ./netscape-installer
```

From there, you are taken to a series of menus where you can select the packages that you want to install with Netscape.

NOTE   If you download a newer version of Netscape than 6.0, there is the chance that the installation procedure is different than outlined here. In this case, check the installation files for a README file or an INSTALL file and take a look at the instructions in the file using the more command. When in doubt, accept the default options for all questions asked during installation, as this is designed to ensure a smooth installation in a large majority of configurations.

Netscape Applications

There are five major applications included in the Netscape 6 package:

- Navigator, the Web browser

- Mail, the e-mail and news reader and message composer

- Instant Messenger, the America Online message utility

- Composer, an application for creating Web pages

- Address Book, used to store personal information about yourself and anyone that you communicate with

This chapter covers Web browsing and basic e-mail configuration. Chapter 24, "Reading E-Mail," covers the use of the Netscape Mail utility.

Accessing the World Wide Web

Accessing the Web with Netscape Version 6 requires no additional preparation. Simply connect to the Internet (as outlined in the previous chapter). Assuming you installed Netscape 6 in the default `/usr/local/netscape` directory, issue the following command

```
$ /usr/local/netscape/netscape
```

A window appears similar to the one in Figure 23.6.

From here, Netscape works pretty much in the same way as it does on Windows or Macintosh computers.

FIGURE 23.6:

The initial Netscape 6 window

Netscape Communicator browser window© 1999 Netscape Communications Corporation. Used with permission. Netscape Communications has not authorized, sponsored, endorsed, or approved this publication and is not responsible for its content.

> **NOTE** If you want just the Web browser, you could download the Netscape Navigator 4.76 package from `http://home.netscape.com`. However, this package is not included on the Publisher's Edition of Red Hat Linux 7.1 that ships with this book.

Access any of Netscape's five major components by clicking the associated icon in the lower-left corner of your current window. From left to right, they are Navigator (the Web browser), Mail, Instant Messenger, Composer, and Address Book.

Netscape Sidebars

A major new feature in Netscape 6 is the *sidebar*, which functions like a dedicated miniature browser. Default sidebars are included for more popular uses, from searches through news headlines.

If you want different sidebars, navigate to the My Sidebar Directory page at `http://search.netscape.com/mysidebar.tmpl`. You can adapt different sidebars from this page for your browser, or you can get more information about creating a custom sidebar for your group or organization.

Search Sidebar   The Netscape Search sidebar, shown in Figure 23.7, lets you access a standard Internet search engine without blocking what is currently in the main browser window. The default search engine used in Netscape 6 is Lycos; you can change this in the Preferences window. Choose Edit ➢ Preferences. In the Preferences window that opens, choose Navigator ➢ Internet Search. You can then select from several different search engines.

FIGURE 23.7:

The Netscape 6 Search sidebar

The example shown in Figure 23.7 illustrates a search for "Grateful Dead Bears." The Search Results list just the links from the search. When you click a link, Netscape navigates directly to the linked Web page.

What's Related Sidebar   The What's Related sidebar helps you find more information about your search. For example, if you want to find sites related to the Momma Bears' Bears Web site shown in Figure 23.8, this sidebar provides several options for related searches, based on applicable categories. For example, Momma Bears' Bears is a collectibles dealer. You can search for more dealers of this type by clicking Recreation: …: Dealers.

FIGURE 23.8:

The Netscape 6 What's Related sidebar

Buddy List Sidebar   If you use the AOL Instant Messenger (IM) service, you can communicate with other AOL IM users, or buddies, while they are online, in real time. You can set up a list of buddies in the Buddy List sidebar. If you haven't used Instant Messaging before on Netscape 6, this sidebar includes a wizard to help you set up and manage a buddy list.

Stocks Sidebar   The default Stocks sidebar includes the latest prices for the U.S. Dow Jones, NASDAQ, S&P 500, and AOL. If you want to add your stocks to this sidebar, click Edit and follow the instructions that appear.

News Sidebar   The default News sidebar includes a couple of the latest headlines in U.S. News, Sports, and Politics. Click the headline of your choice to link to the complete story.

Today's Tips Sidebar   This sidebar provides links to Netscape's Tips and Tricks, as well as additional preconfigured sidebars. For example, the sidebar shown in Figure 23.9 includes links to additional sidebars. If you clicked Health News or Home Improvement in this sidebar, Netscape would add these options as new sidebars on your browser.

FIGURE 23.9:

The Netscape 6 Today's Tips sidebar

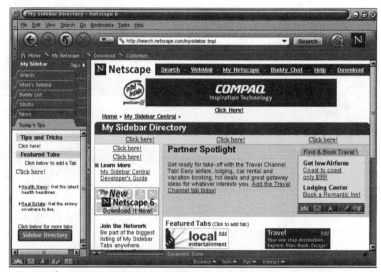

Netscape Communicator browser window© 1999 Netscape Communications Corporation. Used with permission. Netscape Communications has not authorized, sponsored, endorsed, or approved this publication and is not responsible for its content.

Opening a Web Page

Besides using the sidebar features, you can open a Web page in several other ways. The first is to type the URL of the desired page directly into the Search field of the main window, as shown in Figure 23.10. When you press Enter, Netscape 6 attempts to load the URL you have typed.

FIGURE 23.10:

The Search field

Another way to open a new page is to select Open Web Location from the File menu, as shown in Figure 23.11. This brings up the Open Web Location dialog box, like the one in Figure 23.12. Simply type the URL you want to open and select the window where you want to open the Web page.

FIGURE 23.11:

The File menu

FIGURE 23.12:

The Open Web Location
dialog box

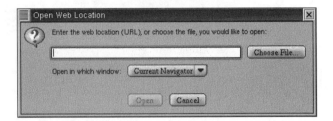

Returning to Previous Pages

Returning to the previously viewed page is as simple as clicking the Back button in the Netscape 6 toolbar. The toolbar is shown in Figure 23.13; the Back button is the left-facing arrow, which is the first button at the left.

FIGURE 23.13:

The Navigator toolbar

You can also return to the previous page by choosing Back from the Go menu, shown in Figure 23.14. The Go menu shows the history of documents you have viewed, and you can return to any displayed document by selecting it from the Go menu.

FIGURE 23.14:

The Go menu

Printing Pages

You can print Web pages from Netscape 6 as long as you have already installed and configured a printer as discussed in Chapter 15, "Using Linuxconf and Other Tools for System Configuration," and Chapter 18, "Using Peripherals."

To print a displayed page, select Print from the File menu, or simply click the Print button in the toolbar, located in the upper-right part of the browser. This brings up a dialog box like the one in Figure 23.15. You can use this dialog box to print to a file or print to a configured printer queue.

FIGURE 23.15:

The Print dialog box

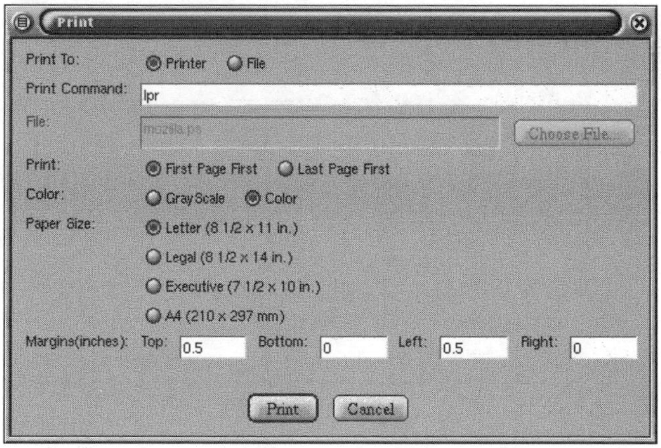

Printing to a File Printing to a file causes Netscape to generate a PostScript image of the page being printed. The resulting file can be viewed with a PostScript viewer such as GhostScript or can be used with software that can handle PostScript files (including word processors, graphics, and other applications) and sent directly to a printer at a later time.

To print to a file, return to the Print dialog box in Figure 23.15. Select File from the Print To options at the top of the box. This activates the File text box. You can then fill in the complete path and filename where you want Netscape to create the resulting file, similar to that shown in Figure 23.16.

FIGURE 23.16:

Printing to a file

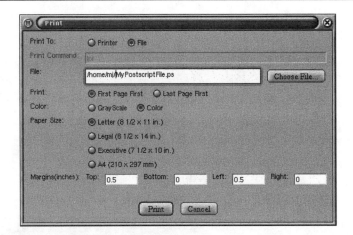

Printing to a Print Queue To print to a print queue, return to the Print dialog box shown in Figure 23.15. Next, enter the complete print command for your printer in the Print Command text box. For instance, if you want to print to a printer with a print queue called laserjet51, enter the print command **lpr -Plaserjet51**. Depending on your path, you may need to specify the full path of the lpr command, in which case your print command would be **/usr/bin/lpr -Plaserjet51**. The lpr command is covered in detail in Chapter 18.

NOTE Normally, Linux commands require a space between a switch such as -P and its option, laserjet51. The lpr command with the -P switch is one of the few cases where there is no space used between the switch and the option.

The choice of printing First Page First or Last Page First depends on the way in which pages come out of your printer. Generally, if they come out face down, choose First Page First; if they come out face up, select Last Page First.

Selecting the correct option of GrayScale or Color is important. If you have a black-and-white printer, you should select GrayScale; some black-and-white printers will produce unusable results if Color is selected, printing all colors as black and rendering documents unreadable. If you have a color printer, you can choose either option, depending on whether you want your final printout to be black and white or color.

Choose the correct paper size to match the paper in your printer. Finally, select the margins used for printing what is in your browser on your paper, and then click the Print button.

Using Help

Netscape 6 includes complete help for the software. Choose Help ➢ Help Contents to get to the Help menu, shown in Figure 23.17.

FIGURE 23.17:

The Help menu

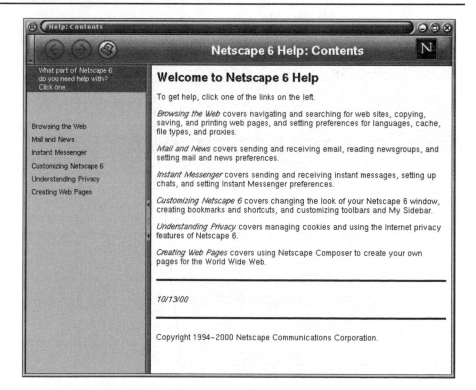

Netscape 6 help is divided into six major sections:

- Browsing The Web covers the basics of navigating through the Internet, manipulating Web files, using related language-translation services, and configuring proxies and security for your connection.

- Mail And News covers the basics of setting up mail and news servers, organizing address book lists, and sending and receiving e-mail and news messages.

- Instant Messenger helps you set up and use various features of the AOL Instant Messenger application through Netscape.

- Customizing Netscape 6 helps you configure the appearance of your browser, including its bookmarks, which allow you to navigate to the Web sites of your choice as a menu option.

- Understanding Privacy is a great introduction to security on the Internet, from managing cookies to password encryption to anonymous surfing.

- Creating Web Pages provides a basic introduction to Netscape Composer, which is a tool to help you create Web pages without having to learn HTML code.

As you can see in Figure 23.17, the six categories of Netscape help are organized in the left-hand pane of the window. Clicking one of these categories opens another window with a set of sub-options.

Configuring Netscape Mail

In addition to the Navigator Web browser, Netscape 6 includes an integrated mail package, Netscape Mail, which you can use to read mail stored on POP or IMAP servers. In order to use Netscape Mail, you need to configure it to know where to find your mail and how to send your mail. But first, you need to understand how POP and IMAP servers are actually local and remote mailboxes.

Local vs. Remote Mailboxes

The distinction between local and remote mailboxes may seem subtle and not a major issue, but this distinction is fundamental to understanding the various types of mail software in the Linux/Unix world.

In most Linux/Unix networks, users' mail is stored in local mailboxes in a format known as Berkeley Mail Folders (after the University of California at Berkeley where this type of folder originated). Linux/Unix mail systems such as Sendmail, which is responsible for routing incoming and outgoing mail, automatically store new messages in users' personal mailboxes in this standard format. Users can then use any of numerous standard Unix-based mail applications to read their mail, compose new messages, and organize their mailboxes.

All of this is available in the Linux world. All the common Unix mail tools are available for Linux, and, as you will see later in the book in the discussion of small business networks, the Berkeley Mail Folder with Sendmail and a Unix mail client is a common solution for providing users with e-mail capabilities.

But for a home user, mail generally sits in a mailbox on a remote server managed by their Internet service provider (ISP). There is no way for software to access these remote folders as if they were local Berkeley Mail Folders. Instead, it is necessary to use mail software that speaks either the POP3 or IMAP4 protocol. These protocols provide different ways to access remote mailboxes.

NOTE   POP is short for the Post Office Protocol. POP3 is actually the second major POP standard; POP2 was popular in the 1980s. IMAP is short for the Internet Message Access Protocol. IMAP4 was first released in 1995.

POP3 Mail Servers

Most users of Windows- or Macintosh-based mail software who access mail that sits on an ISP's mail server probably use the POP3 protocol.

In the POP3 model, users connect to the Internet, download new mail from their mailboxes, and then optionally delete the original copy from the mailboxes on the remote server. This effectively creates a local mailbox that can be read offline. The local mailbox contains a complete copy of the contents of the original mailbox on the server. Users can read their messages, compose replies and new messages, and organize their mail while offline, and then reconnect to send messages they have composed and check for new mail.

This is a simple protocol and is a familiar one to most users. It is an ideal solution when the cost of online time is expensive or the amount of available bandwidth is limited. Because it is designed for working offline, POP3 is well suited to users with limited network access. But the simplicity of the protocol creates some fundamental limitations.

For instance, consider the user who needs to access a remote mailbox from two or more locations. It is possible to leave copies of all downloaded messages on the remote server using POP3. This would allow all messages to be downloaded using mail software on two different PCs in two different locations. But there is no way to know whether a message has been answered from the other location, and if a message is deleted off the remote server for any reason before it is downloaded to both locations, then one location has an incomplete mailbox.

Consider this scenario of a user who uses two PCs, one at home and one on the road. Both PCs are used to read mail from the same mailbox using POP3 mail software. First thing in the morning, the home PC is used to download the day's mail. There are 50 messages, including 33 junk messages. The user immediately deletes the junk messages, responds to seven messages, and files 10 messages for later processing.

Later in the afternoon, this same user proceeds to access their mailbox using their portable system. They proceed to download their mail. The number of messages now numbers 58. This includes the 33 junk messages that were deleted on the home machine, the seven messages that have been replied to, and the 10 messages kept for later processing, in addition to eight new messages to be handled.

This situation, which is not uncommon, can lead to a lot of unnecessary repetition in trying to work with the same mail in two or more locations.

IMAP4 Mail Servers

One solution to this problem is an IMAP4 mail server. In the IMAP model, mailboxes exist on remote servers and remain there. Users then open and access these mailboxes using their client applications, but instead of copying the messages to a local mailbox, they are simply manipulating the remote mailbox without ever creating a local copy.

IMAP offers several benefits to address the problems found in POP3 systems. This includes the ability to work with, and maintain, a single mailbox from multiple locations and computers. This is achieved by the fact that the mail remains in a single remote mailbox instead of replicating into multiple local mailboxes. If a user deletes a message from the mailbox from one location and then accesses the mailbox from another, the message won't be there.

However, the very nature of IMAP4—manipulating a remote mailbox—makes it necessary to work online to read, reply to, and process mail. Thus, IMAP4 is best suited to situations where a network connection is either permanent or essentially free. For instance, in a location with flat-rate Internet costs and flat-rate local phone costs, POP3 and IMAP4 mail connections would cost the same. But if a user is paying per-minute Internet and phone call costs (a common situation outside the U.S.), then IMAP4 would prove much more expensive than POP3.

In addition, not many ISPs give users access to their mailboxes through IMAP4 servers. IMAP4 systems are far more common in corporations and allow users to access their mailboxes at work and from home without the difficulties introduced by POP3 systems.

Now that you understand the basic difference between POP3 and IMAP4 e-mail servers, you are ready to configure Netscape 6 for e-mail.

Configuring Netscape for E-Mail

First, open Netscape Mail. You can either choose Tasks ≻ Mail, or you can click the Mail icon in the lower-left corner. The first time you open Netscape Mail, you get the Account Wizard shown in Figure 23.18. With this wizard, you can set up four types of mail accounts: ISP Or Email Provider, Netscape WebMail, AOL Account, and Newsgroup Account.

NOTE   If you don't see the Account Wizard, you already have set up a mail account. In that case, in the Netscape Mail window, choose Edit ≻ Mail/News Account Settings. In the Account Settings window, click New Account to access the Account Wizard.

Most users want to select at least ISP Or Email Provider. The steps are similar for setting up a Newsgroup Account. If you have a Netscape WebMail or an AOL account, all you need is your e-mail address for that system. Select ISP Or Email Provider and click Next to continue.

In the next Account Wizard screen, enter your name and e-mail address, as shown in Figure 23.19. The name you enter is what is shown with your e-mail messages. The e-mail address that you enter here gets attached to your messages. Anyone who clicks Reply to your message will by default send the reply to that e-mail address.

NOTE   If you were setting up a Newsgroup Account, you would enter the name and e-mail address you want shown on your postings.

FIGURE 23.18:

Netscape Mail Account
Wizard

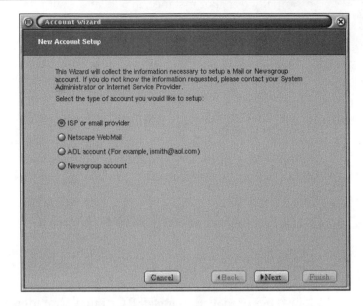

FIGURE 23.19:

Configuring your name and
e-mail address

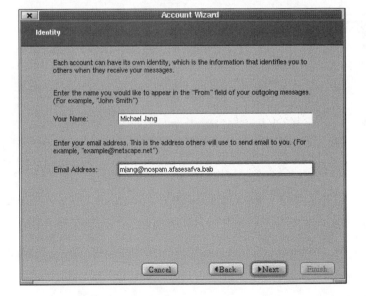

TIP

One common way to avoid unwanted e-mail such as sales pitches is to add **nospam** to your e-mail address. For example, if your e-mail address is **mike@mike.mke**, enter **mike@nospam.mike.mke**. Any computer that collects your e-mail address from your messages won't be able to send you unwanted e-mail. However, your friends and colleagues can still reach you by removing the **nospam** from the e-mail address that they see.

When you've entered the name and e-mail address of your choice, click Next. In the following screen, you can configure the servers associated with incoming and outgoing e-mail, like those shown in Figure 23.20.

FIGURE 23.20:

Configuring mail servers

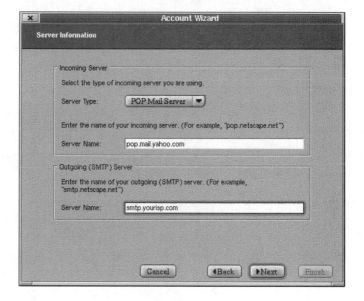

There are two main types of incoming mail servers: POP3 and IMAP4. As discussed earlier, POP3 servers are usually associated with ISPs and other Internet mail services. IMAP4 is a more versatile mail server that allows you to search through messages before downloading them to your computer. In either case, get the name associated with the incoming mail server from the company that set up your e-mail address. This should look something like pop.emailprovider.net.

Outgoing mail goes through your ISP's *SMTP server*, which manages all outgoing messages. Get the name of this server, which should look something like `smtp.yourISP.net`, from your ISP. Once you've entered the names of your incoming and outgoing mail servers, click Next to continue.

Enter the username given to you by your e-mail service provider. In many cases, this is the part of your e-mail address before the @ symbol. If you have forgotten your username, you can ask your e-mail service provider for it. Once you've entered it, click Next to continue.

The next screen, entitled Account Name, allows you to enter any name of your choice to represent this account. Once you've entered a name, click Next to continue.

The final screen, as shown in Figure 23.21, shows some of the data that you used to create this account. You can click Back to go back and change any information that you're not satisfied with. On the other hand, if you're satisfied, click Finish.

FIGURE 23.21:

The Account Wizard is finished.

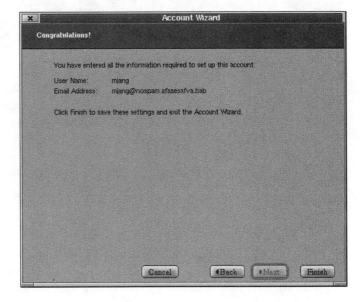

Reconfiguring Netscape Mail

It is easy to reconfigure any account that you've set up on Netscape Mail. When you have set up one e-mail address, five different configuration options are available. For each additional e-mail address, you get three additional configuration options to accommodate that extra address. To access the first of these screens, click Edit ➤ Mail/News Account Settings. This opens the Account Settings window shown in Figure 23.22.

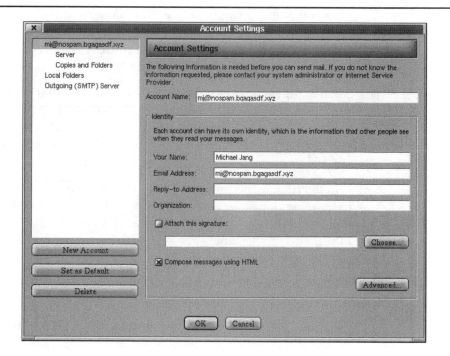

There are five options shown in Figure 23.22. Three of them are associated with a specific e-mail address. The e-mail address itself is the first setting, sometimes known as Account Settings. Server is the second setting. Copies And Folders is the third setting. The first two are configured when you set up your e-mail. The Copies And Folders setting includes the locations of your actual mail files and rarely needs to be changed. The information in each varies slightly depending on whether you're using a POP3 or IMAP4 server to receive your e-mail. The other panels provide configuration options that you may want to consider, but except for the name of the outgoing (SMTP) server, these are not essential to basic e-mail operation.

The Account Settings Panel

You use the Account Settings panel to configure the information (such as your e-mail address, name, and organization) that will appear on all e-mails you send. This panel is shown back on Figure 23.22.

The first entry is the only entry that must be accurate to receive e-mail. The Account Name must correspond to the actual e-mail address assigned by your e-mail provider.

The other important fields are Your Name, which should contain your full name as you would wish mail recipients to see it, and Email Address, which should contain your complete e-mail address as it needs to appear on the From line of your e-mails.

Fill in the Reply-To Address field if the address that people should use to reply to your messages is different than the From line of your outgoing e-mails. You can also fill in the Organization field. This information will be included in the header of all e-mails you send and will be displayed in some mail readers, including Netscape 6.

In the Attach This Signature field, you can specify a file containing a signature to be appended at the end of all the e-mails you send. A signature file is a text file that might include your name, address, and phone number or other identifying information. When you want to attach a signature, make sure to activate it by selecting the Attach This Signature check box.

The Advanced button allows you to change the outgoing (SMTP) mail server associated with the named account.

For this panel, the entries and options for a POP3 or an IMAP4 server are identical.

The Server Settings Panel

The Server Settings panel is used to tell Netscape Mail how to find your inbox and how to send mail you compose. If you have a POP3 account, it looks like Figure 23.23.

The Server Settings panel shares four basic characteristics whether you're using a POP3 or an IMAP4 account. First, the panel identifies the server by type (POP3 or IMAP4). Next, the Server Name is the fully qualified domain name of your ISP's SMTP server. Third, the User Name should correspond to the one that you use for your e-mail (which does not necessarily correspond to the name you use for your ISP). Finally, the Port is the communications channel used to send messages; by default, POP3 is 110 and IMAP4 is 143.

FIGURE 23.23:

The Server Settings panel

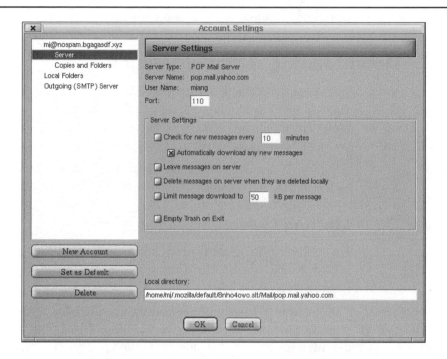

The other options in the Server Settings box are not critical to the operation of Netscape Mail and are not active unless you see a mark in the associated check box. The options you see depend on whether you're using a POP3 or an IMAP4 mail server. They are basically self-explanatory; some of the options depend on personal preferences or settings created by your ISP.

Installing and Using Lynx

The final browser this chapter discusses is Lynx, by far the most common text browser in use in the Unix and Linux worlds. Lynx is included in most Linux distributions, among them the Red Hat distribution bundled with this book.

You can check whether Lynx is installed with the command

```
$ rpm -q lynx
```

If you find that Lynx is not installed, use `rpm` to install `lynx-2.8.4-9.i386.rpm` from the RedHat/RPMS subdirectory of the CD-ROM:

```
$ rpm -i lynx-2.8.4-9.i386.rpm
```

Once it is installed, you can find Lynx at `/usr/bin/lynx`.

Downloading a Newer Version

The version of Lynx included with this book is version 2.8.4, which is the current developmental version at the time of this writing, also available on Red Hat Linux 7.1. By the time you read this, a newer version may be available through the Lynx home page at `http://lynx.browser.org/`.

You can download Lynx in the same `tar.gz` format used to download Netscape 6 earlier in this chapter, and it can be installed in a nearly identical fashion.

Starting Lynx

To use Lynx, you need to launch it in an `xterm` window or other similar window such as Konsole or GNOME terminal. You can even launch it at the command-line interface. With Lynx, you don't need an X Window to browse the Web.

If you launch Lynx without any arguments, Lynx attempts to load its default page. In the case of the binary version distributed with Red Hat Linux 7.1, this default page is an HTML documentation page that is installed with the operating system. If you compiled Lynx yourself, then this page is probably `http://lynx.browser.org/`.

Starting Lynx produces a screen like the one in Figure 23.24. This figure shows the local help file installed on Red Hat Linux 7.1.

If you want to directly access a specific page or file when you launch Lynx, simply provide the page URL or the filename as an argument to Lynx using the command

```
$ lynx http://www.yahoo.com/
```

or view an HTML document with the command

```
$ lynx /tmp/filename
```

Lynx also takes numerous flags that can alter its behavior. You can view the complete list with the `-help` argument:

```
$ lynx -help
```

Generally, however, you won't need to use any of these command-line arguments when browsing the Web with Lynx.

Opening a New Page

Notice that the bottom line of the Lynx screen displays the main key commands that you can use to browse the Web. To open a new page once Lynx is running, use the Go command by hitting the G key.

Lynx responds with the prompt

```
URL to Open:
```

Assuming that you're already connected to the Internet, simply enter a URL such as **www.mommabears.com** and press Enter to open the page.

Following Links

Links in a document show up in colored text when running in an xterm or a console window. The active link is shown in red; other links are shown in blue. Press Enter to follow the active link. You can activate other links by using the Tab key to move forward through the links or the up and down arrows to move backward and forward through the links.

Once you have selected a link to follow, press Enter or the right-arrow key to follow the link. You can return to the previously visited page by using the left-arrow key. A number of Lynx commands are shown in Table 23.1.

TABLE 23.1:   Lynx Commands

Command	Description
Enter	Follows the currently active link, shown in red.
Tab	Moves the active link forward.
Left arrow	Returns to the previously visited page.
Right arrow	Follows the currently active link, shown in red.
Up arrow	Moves the active link back.
Down arrow	Moves the active link forward.
H	Accesses Lynx help.
O	Opens a menu of Lynx configuration options.
P	Opens a menu of print options.
G	Opens an option where you can enter the Web site that you want to review, such as **www.sybex.com**.
M	Navigates to the currently configured home page.
Q	Exits Lynx.
/abc	Searches for the text string *abc*.
Delete	Shows the history of previously visited Web pages.

Viewing Images

If you are running Lynx in an xterm window, you can configure it so that you can view images embedded in pages in a separate window using a graphical viewer program such as gqview.

In order to do this, you need to configure Lynx so that it knows to use gqview to display images. You do this by editing the file /etc/lynx.cfg using your favorite text editor as the root user.

In this file, there are two lines that start with #XLOADIMAGE_COMMAND. One line appears under the header VMS and the other line appears under the header Unix.

You will work with the one under the header Unix. If you want to use gqview, change this line to read

```
XLOADIMAGE_COMMAND:/usr/bin/gqview %s &
```

Notice that the pound sign (#) at the start of the line has been removed. This uncomments the line so that Lynx will pay attention to it when Lynx loads.

Once you have done this, save the changed file and launch Lynx. Next, you need to turn on the Images-As-Links mode. The asterisk (*) command toggles the Images-As-Links mode. When you press the asterisk key, if you see the following message

```
Links will be included for all images! Reloading...
```

Lynx opens up image links in the program that you set up in the /etc/lynx.cfg file. Alternatively, if you see

```
Standard image handling restored! Reloading...
```

you won't be able to link to any embedded images.

Looking Ahead

Now that you've managed to get online and browse the Web using Linux, you are ready to look at the full range of options for the other major Internet function: e-mail.

You have already reviewed one of the popular mail-reading applications, Netscape 6. But Netscape is only one of many alternatives.

Linux offers a broad range of mail clients, both commercial and free. These range from powerful (but complicated) prompt-oriented systems to comprehensive and lightweight character-mode mail readers (such as the well-known pine and elm packages) to graphical mail readers (such as Xmail).

Chapter 24, "Reading E-Mail," will take a broad look at the mail readers available for Linux and then take a closer look at some of the more common mail readers available.

CHAPTER

TWENTY-FOUR

Reading E-Mail

- ■ Offline Mail Readers
- ■ Online Mail Programs

This chapter discusses the different approaches and programs available in Linux for reading, composing, and sending e-mail. It employs the Netscape 6 Mail utility to illustrate offline mail readers, using the POP3 incoming e-mail protocol. It continues with the Linux text-based `pine` e-mail reader as an example of an online mail program, using the IMAP4 incoming e-mail protocol. Both POP3 and IMAP4 were discussed in Chapter 23, "Using the World Wide Web."

Offline Mail Readers

For most users, accessing a remote mailbox with POP3 is the right solution. This can be done using any of numerous available mail applications for Linux, including Netscape Communicator, which is available on the enclosed CD-ROM, or Netscape 6, which is available for download from the `http://home.netscape.com/download` Web site.

> **NOTE**   The Netscape applications used in this chapter were downloaded from `ftp://ftp.netscape.com/pub/netscape6/english/6.0/unix/linux22/sea/`. When you read this, later versions may also be available for direct download through other directories on this site.

This section looks at Netscape 6 Mail because it is becoming one of the most popular graphical mail clients today and because users coming to Linux from the Windows and Macintosh platforms may already be familiar with Netscape's product. There are many other POP and IMAP mail readers available for Linux. You can check the Mail category at the Linux Applications Page at `http://www.linuxapps.com` for a list of alternative packages.

> **NOTE**   You can also use Netscape as an online mail reader if your mail server uses the IMAP incoming mail protocol.

Netscape 6

It is fairly simple to configure Netscape 6 to read your remote POP3 mailbox and to use it to compose messages offline and queue them. To launch Netscape 6, issue the command

```
$ /usr/local/netscape/netscape
```

from an xterm window, assuming that you installed Netscape in the default location (see the section about installing Netscape 6 in Chapter 23).

> **NOTE**   Netscape Messenger 4.76, which is included with Red Hat Linux 7.1, is not covered in this chapter. Although there are a number of detailed differences, the basic procedures for sending and receiving e-mail have not changed significantly.

Configuring Netscape 6 for E-Mail

Once Netscape 6 is launched, you can configure its mail reader from the Preferences dialog box by following the steps in the section "Configuring Netscape Mail" in Chapter 23.

Reading Mail with Netscape Mail

Once you have configured Netscape Mail to access your mailbox, you are ready to try reading messages. But before you are able to access your mailbox, you need to do two things:

1. Connect to the Internet (follow one of the methods discussed in Chapter 22, "Connecting Linux to the Internet").

2. Launch Netscape 6.

By default, Netscape 6 launches with a Web browser window open. You can open the mailbox window in two ways:

- Click the Mail icon in the lower-left corner. It's the envelope symbol, second from the left.

- Select Mail from the Tasks menu (or press Ctrl+2), as shown in Figure 24.1.

FIGURE 24.1:

The Tasks menu

The Netscape Mail window looks like the one in Figure 24.2.

FIGURE 24.2:

The Netscape Mail window

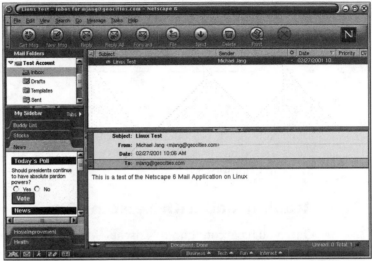

The Netscape Mail window is divided into four distinct areas, or panes. The Mail Folders pane, in the upper-left corner, displays the different mail folders associated with e-mail account. These folders include:

- Inbox, which collects mail that comes in through your incoming (POP3 or IMAP4) mail server.

- Drafts, where you can store messages for later editing and delivery.

- Templates, which includes different styles and backgrounds for the e-mail that you send.

- Sent, which collects the e-mail messages that you sent from this account.

- Trash, which collects messages that you deleted (and therefore can retrieve).

The List pane, in the upper-right corner, displays a list of the messages in the highlighted folder. In Figure 24.2, there is only one message in the Inbox.

The Message pane, in the lower-right corner, shows the contents of the message highlighted in the List pane. In Figure 24.2, the contents of the "Linux Test" message is shown in the Message pane.

Because Netscape Mail supports HTML mail, a mail message formatted using HTML is displayed in the Message pane just as if it were a Web page. Links are highlighted, as expected, and are clickable. Clicking a link opens the requested document in a browser window instead of in the mailbox window.

The My Sidebar pane, in the lower-left corner, by default includes all of the sidebars in Netscape Navigator, except Search and What's Related.

Composing Messages in Netscape Mail

The flip side of reading messages is being able to compose new messages. Composing new messages is actually quite simple. Simply click the New Msg button.

This brings up a message composition window like the one in Figure 24.3.

FIGURE 24.3:

The message composition window

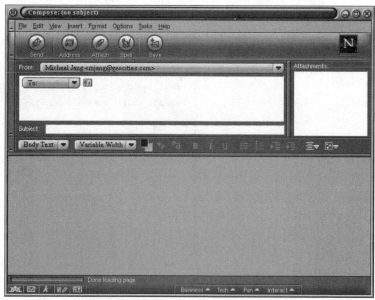

Netscape WebMail© 2000 Netscape Communications Corporation.

To address a message, simply fill in the address in the field next to the To field. Pressing the Enter key after typing in the address creates a new, blank To field on the next line so that you can address your message to multiple recipients. If you want some of the recipients to receive the message as a carbon copy (the Cc field) or blind carbon copy (the Bcc field), click the down arrow key next to the To field for the addressee you wish to change. This brings up an address field menu where you can specify the correct option.

To add an attachment to your message, click the Attach button on the toolbar.

This displays the Enter File To Attach window, as shown in Figure 24.4, which shows a listing of all files in your home directory. You can then navigate to any file on the system.

FIGURE 24.4:

The Enter File To Attach window

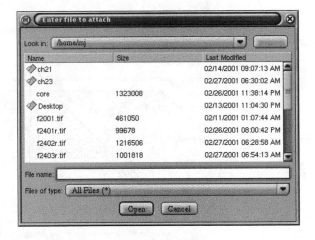

As shown in Figure 24.5, once you attach a file, the attached filename (in the example shown, it is f2401r.tif) is listed in the Attachments pane in the upper-right corner of your message.

FIGURE 24.5:

An attached file in the Attachments pane

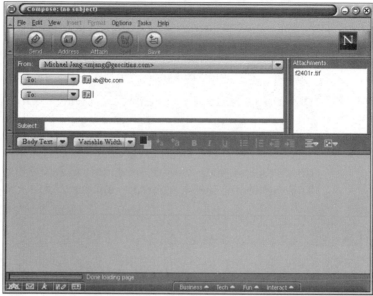

Netscape WebMail© 2000 Netscape Communications Corporation.

Type the subject of the message in the Subject field and the body of the message in the large text-editing area, as shown in the completed message in Figure 24.6.

FIGURE 24.6:

A completed message

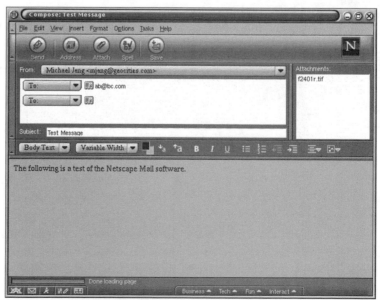

Netscape WebMail© 2000 Netscape Communications Corporation.

Finally, click the Send button to send the message (assuming you are connected to the Internet when you finish composing the message).

Queuing Messages   Usually, users with a POP3 mail connection to an Internet provider want to compose their messages while offline, queuing them for later delivery when they connect to their ISP. This is achieved quite easily. Once a message is composed, instead of clicking the Send button on the composition window's toolbar, simply select Send Later from the File menu shown in Figure 24.7. This queues the message for later delivery.

FIGURE 24.7:

The message composition
File menu

Once you have finished composing your messages, connect to the Internet, and from the main Netscape Mail window, select Send Unsent Messages from the File menu shown in Figure 24.8.

FIGURE 24.8:

Netscape Mail's File menu

Any unsent, queued messages are sent.

Replying to Messages and Forwarding Messages   Closely related to composing new messages are replying to messages and forwarding messages to other people.

Let's start with replying, since it is the more common activity for most people. To reply to a message, select the message in your mailbox and then click the Reply button on the toolbar.

This brings up a pre-addressed message composition window like the one in Figure 24.9. By default, Netscape Mail includes the contents of the original message in the Message pane.

Similarly, to forward a message, select the message and click the Forward button.

FIGURE 24.9:

Replying to a message

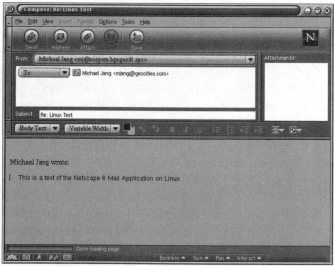

Netscape WebMail© 2000 Netscape Communications Corporation.

This brings up an unaddressed message composition window with the selected message attached to your message, as shown in Figure 24.10. Note that the Subject line indicates a forwarded message.

FIGURE 24.10:

Forwarding a message

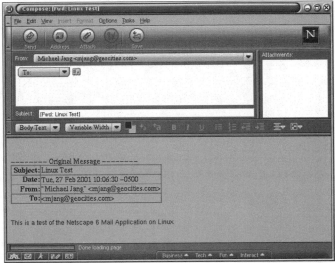

Netscape WebMail© 2000 Netscape Communications Corporation.

Online Mail Programs

This section describes those mail programs whose primary purpose is to read local Unix/Linux mailboxes; some mail programs can access IMAP4 servers as well. What distinguishes these from the offline software like Netscape 6 is that they assume a constant connection to a network such as the Internet.

pine and elm

In the Unix world, and by extension in the Linux world, the two most common mail programs are pine and elm. These programs are both designed to work in a character-based environment, so they can be used at the console or in an xterm window. They are both designed to read from local Berkeley Mail-style servers, and both are highly flexible with a large number of configurable options.

NOTE An interesting bit of history: `elm` predates `pine`. The idea behind `pine` was to make some aspects of `elm` easier for the average user to handle; `pine` is known to stand for "Pine Is Not Elm." While `pine` can read mail from IMAP servers, `elm` cannot.

Both `elm` and `pine` are commonly found in universities, where many students still have shell accounts to access e-mail. Because of space limitations, this section takes a close look at only one of these programs: `pine`. The choice of `pine` versus `elm` is a highly subjective one, and many diehard Linux and Unix users may argue that `elm` should be presented instead of `pine`. Unfortunately, `elm` is no longer well maintained. For example, although the latest release of `elm` is 2.5.5, the closest thing available to an `elm` home page, `http://www.math.fu-berlin.de/~guckes/elm/`, documents only the changes up to version 2.5.3.

The logic behind my choice is this: Both `elm` and `pine` are powerful packages, neither superior to the other. Most users are now likely to use graphical packages such as Netscape 6 to manage their mail, since today's average PC is more than capable of running processing-intensive graphical applications of that type. To give users a sense of these traditional (and still popular) Unix/Linux mail programs, I chose `pine` because it is somewhat more user-friendly for a newcomer to Linux. It is also easier to get up-to-date documentation for `pine`. And at the university where I worked as a system administrator, all users use `pine` as their mail application, and this has proven to be quite a successful choice.

Using *pine*

At first glance, `pine` may seem very complicated, but in reality it isn't. For the average user who wants to send and receive e-mail, `pine` is quite easy to use.

Most Linux systems will include `pine` already installed if the complete suite of networking applications was selected during the installation process. If yours doesn't, you can find `pine` at its home page, `http://www.washington.edu/pine/`. The version of `pine` included with Red Hat Linux 7.1 is version 4.33-8.

Simply type the command

```
$ pine
```

to launch the program. The default configuration on most Linux systems should work without any tweaking.

When it first launches, pine will present its default main menu, as shown in Figure 24.11.

FIGURE 24.11:

The *pine* main menu

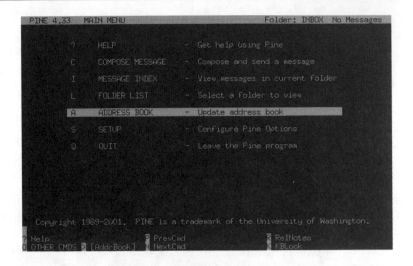

The pine screen contains four main areas:

- The top line presents the version number of pine that you are running, the name of the currently open folder (INBOX when pine first starts), and, if applicable, the current message being read, along with the total number of messages in the folder.

- The bottom two lines present the more common commands accessible from the current screen. These commands change as the context dictates.

- The rest of the screen represents the main work area.

From the main menu, there are four main options:

C (COMPOSE MESSAGE)   This option is used to compose and send a new message; it can also be accessed when viewing the contents of a mail folder.

I (MESSAGE INDEX)   This option is used to view the contents of the current folder (as displayed on the top line of the screen).

L (FOLDER LIST)   This option is used to view a list of available folders.

A (ADDRESS BOOK)   This option is used to access the address book.

Let's discuss two of these options, Folder List and Compose Message. All the options are documented fully in pine's online help, which is available from the main menu with the HELP command (press the **?** key).

Opening and Working in a Folder List   To open a folder list, use the up or down arrow keys to select the FOLDER LIST option and press the Enter key. Alternatively, type **L**. This opens a list of available folders, as shown in Figure 24.12.

FIGURE 24.12:

A list of current *pine* folders

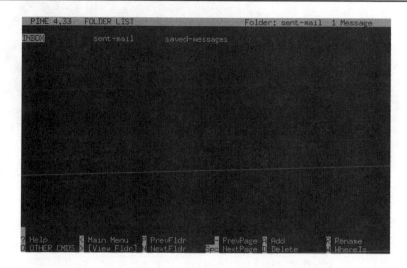

The folder list shows the currently available folders, in this case, INBOX, sent-mail, and saved-messages.

Opening and Working in a Message Index   From the folder list, highlight a desired folder and select it by pressing Enter. This takes you to a list of messages in the selected folder, like that shown in Figure 24.13. The top line of the display shows the currently selected message, the number of messages in the folder, and the status of the message (such as NEW for a new, unread message or ANS for an answered message).

Each message in the inbox is presented on a single line showing, from left to right, the status of the message (N for new, A for answered, D for deleted), the number of the message, the date the message was received, the sender of the message, the size of the message in bytes, and, finally, the subject line of the message.

FIGURE 24.13:

A list of messages in a
folder

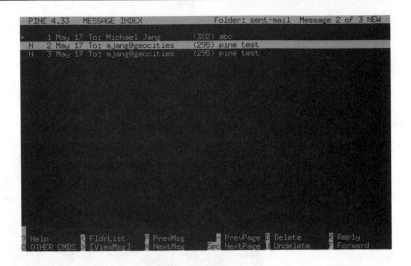

To select a message, use the up and down arrow keys until the desired message is highlighted. Alternatively, press the **P** key to move to the previous message or the **N** key to move to the next message.

To delete the currently selected message, type **D**. This marks the message for deletion and changes the status indication for that message to show that it has been marked for deletion. The message won't be deleted, however, until you quit pine. Until then, you can undelete the message by selecting it and typing **U**.

If you have a folder index that is longer than one screen, you can move through it quickly using the spacebar to jump down a page and the hyphen key to jump up a page. In addition, you can jump directly to a specific message using its message number. Type **J** and, when prompted, type the message number and press Enter.

To read a message in a folder, simply select the message and press Enter or type **V** to view the message. The message is displayed as shown in Figure 24.14.

While viewing a message, you can continue to type **P** and **N** to move through messages in the folder, and you can type **D** and **U** to delete and undelete messages.

If the message is more than one screen long, you can use the spacebar to move down a screen and the hyphen key to move up a screen, or use the up and down arrows to move up or down one line at a time.

To return to the main menu from the folder index or while viewing a message, simply type **M**.

FIGURE 24.14:

Viewing a message

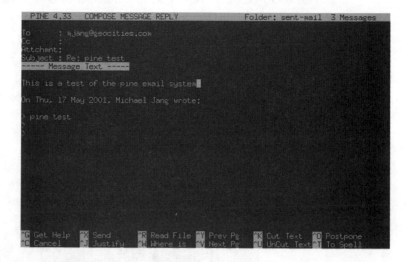

Composing a Message   You can start composing a message from the main menu or while viewing a folder index or a message. To do this, simply type **C** (from the main menu, you can also select the COMPOSE MESSAGE option and press Enter). A blank message form like the one in Figure 24.15 appears.

This screen is divided into two parts, one above the Message Text dividing line and one below. Above the dividing line, you can specify the recipients, the subject, and other details; below the line, you enter the message. You can move between sections and fields using the up and down arrow keys.

FIGURE 24.15:

The message composition screen

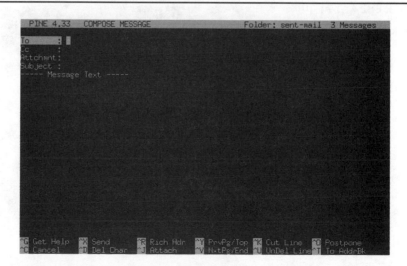

The To and Cc fields can take any number of e-mail addresses separated by commas. When the cursor leaves the field, the display refreshes to show each address on a separate line, as in Figure 24.16.

FIGURE 24.16:

Multiple message recipients

If you want to send a blind carbon copy, you can expand the available message header fields by pressing Ctrl+R while the cursor is in the header (not in the body of the message text). This calls up the rich headers feature, as shown in Figure 24.17.

FIGURE 24.17:

Rich headers

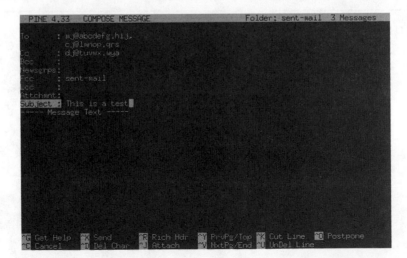

Here you will find a Bcc field for sending blind carbon copies of e-mail messages. The other fields provide more obscure functions such as specifying an alternate location for storing a copy of the outgoing message or copying the message to a newsgroup as a posting.

Below the Message Text divider, you can type the body of your message. Figure 24.18 shows a completed message.

Once you are finished, you have two choices: You can send the message or you can cancel it. To send the message, press Ctrl+X; you are prompted to confirm that you want to send the message, to which you can answer **y** for yes or **n** for no. To cancel the message, press Ctrl+C; again, you are prompted to confirm that you want to cancel the message. Once the message is canceled, you won't be able to recover its contents.

FIGURE 24.18:

A completed message

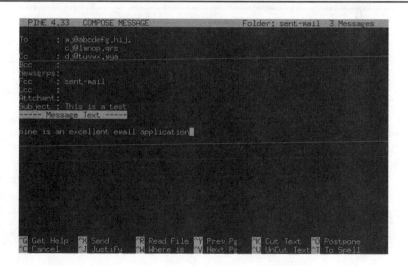

The *pico* Editor

When you are editing messages in pine, you are using its integrated text editor called pico. The following commands should help you use pico effectively:

- Ctrl+V: page down
- Ctrl+Y: page up

Continued on next page

- Ctrl+K: cut a line of text

- Ctrl+U: uncut (paste) cut text

- Ctrl+A: jump to the start of a line

- Ctrl+E: jump to the end of a line

- Ctrl+J: justify (adjust the layout of) the current paragraph

Cutting and pasting text requires some explanation. When you press Ctrl+K, a single line of text is cut and placed in a buffer in memory. If you press Ctrl+K to cut multiple lines in succession (these have to be continuous lines in the document), then all the lines are copied into the buffer. Ctrl+U, to uncut text, copies the entire contents of the buffer to the current cursor location but does not clear the contents of the buffer. In other words, you can paste multiple copies of cut text back into your messages.

Replying to and Forwarding Messages Replying to messages and forwarding them to other recipients is much the same as composing a new message. To reply to a message, select the message and type **R** (from the folder index or while viewing the message). You are prompted with one or two questions:

Include Original Message In Reply? If you answer affirmatively to this question, the entire contents of the message you are replying to will appear in your reply.

Reply To All Recipients? This question appears if there are multiple recipients of the original message (either in the To field or the Cc field). If you answer **Y** for Yes, then everyone who received the message will receive your response. If you answer **N** for No, then only the person who sent the message will receive your response.

Next, a message composition screen appears with the appropriate recipients, subject line, and any necessary body text already in place. An example of this is shown in Figure 24.19.

Just as you did when composing a new message, press Ctrl+X to send your reply and press Ctrl+C to cancel it.

Forwarding a message is similar to sending one: Select the message and type **F**. A message composition window appears like the one in Figure 24.20, with the text of the message in place and a subject line that indicates that this is a forwarded message.

FIGURE 24.19:

Replying to a message

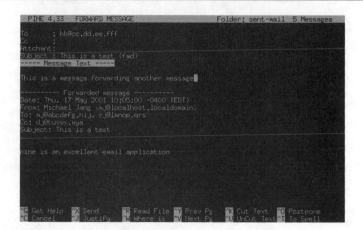

FIGURE 24.20:

Forwarding a message

Looking Ahead

You now know how to perform the two most common Internet operations: browsing the Web and sending and receiving e-mail. However, there is one more very popular use of modems to be discussed: faxing.

Chapter 25, "Faxing from Linux," will look at the software that allows you to send, receive, and print faxes on a Linux system. Among other tasks, you will learn how to send faxes in the same way that you print from your applications and how to set up an automated fax-reception system.

CHAPTER
TWENTY-FIVE

Faxing from Linux

- Linux Fax Software

- Efax for Linux

You've already learned about the use of modems to establish network connections, mostly with the goal of accessing the Internet and its myriad services. This chapter looks at the other popular use of modems: sending and receiving faxes.

There are several fax software packages available for Linux. As would be expected in the Linux and Unix world, at their heart these fax packages are powerful, fast command-line tools that make it possible to send a large variety of documents by fax and to build fax services into automated processes.

On top of this, it is possible with many fax packages for Linux to extend these command-line tools to allow faxing through the print features of some applications or to allow users to send faxes in the same way that they send e-mail.

In this chapter, you will take a broad look at Linux faxing and consider the major fax packages. Then you will learn in detail about efax, a common fax package that is found in several Linux distributions, including Red Hat Linux 7.1.

NOTE   The efax package is not included with the CD-ROM that comes with this book. If you have the standard distribution of Red Hat Linux 7.1, it is on the second installation CD. Otherwise, you can download the RPM from a site such as `http://www.redhat.com` or `http://www.rpmfind.net`.

Linux Fax Software

In the Linux world, and in the Unix world in general, there are only a few main software packages for sending and receiving faxes: efax, NetFax, mgetty+sendfax, and HylaFax.

Of all these, efax is generally considered the easiest to configure and install because it is ideally suited to a single-user system. For many home users of Linux, efax will suffice.

As a basic package, of course, efax doesn't have many of the sophisticated features that make HylaFax and NetFax well suited to multiuser network environments. Nonetheless, efax offers sufficient capabilities to meet the needs of all but the most demanding single and small office users.

Efax for Linux

Efax is almost the de facto standard fax software for Linux because it ships with many Linux distributions (including the standard distribution of Red Hat Linux 7.1). This chapter focuses on using efax for Linux.

TIP

If you are interested in other fax packages for Linux, see the listing at the Linux Applications Web site at `http://www.linuxapps.com/`. The discussion in this chapter assumes that you have a functioning fax modem installed in your system. Chapter 18, "Using Peripherals," discusses how to configure a modem for use with Linux, and you should follow those guidelines to make sure that your modem is properly configured.

NOTE

The efax program discussed in this chapter is not related to the applications of efax.com. It is, in fact, short for "Ed's fax program," based on the work of Ed Casas. You can get more information about efax by navigating to `http://www.cce.com/efax`.

Installing Efax in Linux

The first step in getting fax capabilities up and running on your system is to make sure you have the efax software installed on your system. If you have installed the version of Linux included with this book, you may already have the software installed. You can check this with the rpm command:

```
$ rpm -q efax
```

If efax is installed, then rpm informs you by displaying the name of the efax package, such as efax-0.9-8. If the package is not installed, then rpm will inform you with a message similar to this:

```
package efax is not installed.
```

If efax is not installed, then you have two choices:

- Install it from your distribution's installation CD. If you have the standard version of Red Hat Linux 7.1, it is on the second installation CD-ROM.

- Download and install it from the Internet.

Installing Efax from the Red Hat CD-ROM

If you have installed Red Hat Linux from the standard CD-ROM package (not the one accompanying this book) and want to install the version of efax that comes with the distribution, you need to mount the second Red Hat Linux 7.1 Installation CD-ROM at your standard location—typically at /mnt/cdrom—using the mount command. (This example assumes that the CD-ROM is the device /dev/cdrom):

```
$ mount /dev/cdrom /mnt/cdrom
```

Once the CD-ROM is mounted, you need to use rpm to install the package efax-0.9-8.i386.rpm:

```
$ rpm -i /mnt/cdrom/RedHat/RPMS/efax-0.9-8.i386.rpm
```

Downloading and Installing Efax from the Internet

If you want to install the latest version of efax, you can obtain it by FTP from ftp://metalab.unc.edu/pub/Linux/apps/serialcomm/fax/. At the time of this writing, the most recent version of the software is version 0.9 and the name of the file to be downloaded is efax-09.tar.gz.

Once you have downloaded the file, use the tar command to unarchive the files into a temporary location such as /tmp:

```
$ tar xzvf efax-09.tar.gz
```

Next, change your working directory to the temporary one where you unarchived the files (in this case, cd /tmp/efax-0.9) and, as the root user, issue the following command:

```
$ make
```

This causes the efax software to be compiled. Assuming that there are no errors during compilation (a safe assumption, since efax is a fairly simple program), you can install efax to its default location using the command

```
$ make install
```

For full instructions regarding the compilation and installation of the efax software, read the README file included with the distribution.

NOTE

For Red Hat Linux 7.1, you'll need to change the `Makefile` before using the `make install` command. Open the `Makefile` script in your favorite text editor. It's located in the same directory where you unarchived the `efax-09.tar.gz` file (`/tmp/efax-0.9`). Under the `install:` section, the second command in the original file reads `cp fax.1 efax.1 efix.1 $(MANDIR)/man1`. Make sure to change it to `cp fax.1 efax.1 efix.1 /usr/share/man/man1`, as shown in Figure 25.1.

FIGURE 25.1:

The edited efax *Makefile*

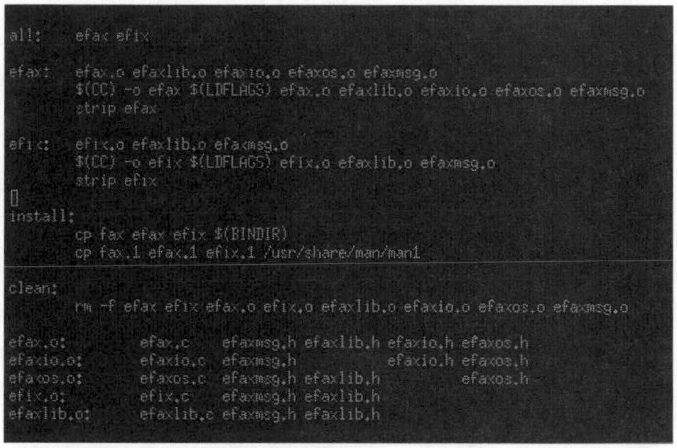

```
all:    efax efix

efax:   efax.o efaxlib.o efaxio.o efaxos.o efaxmsg.o
        $(CC) -o efax $(LDFLAGS) efax.o efaxlib.o efaxio.o efaxos.o efaxmsg.o
        strip efax

efix:   efix.o efaxlib.o efaxmsg.o
        $(CC) -o efix $(LDFLAGS) efix.o efaxlib.o efaxmsg.o
        strip efix

install:
        cp fax efax efix $(BINDIR)
        cp fax.1 efax.1 efix.1 /usr/share/man/man1

clean:
        rm -f efax efix efax.o efix.o efaxlib.o efaxio.o efaxos.o efaxmsg.o

efax.o:         efax.c    efaxmsg.h efaxlib.h efaxio.h efaxos.h
efaxio.o:       efaxio.c  efaxmsg.h           efaxio.h efaxos.h
efaxos.o:       efaxos.c  efaxmsg.h efaxlib.h          efaxos.h
efix.o:         efix.c    efaxmsg.h efaxlib.h
efaxlib.o:      efaxlib.c efaxmsg.h efaxlib.h
```

Configuring Efax for Linux

Before sending your first fax, you need to specify a few parameters that will allow efax to function properly. In order to do this, you need to edit the file `/usr/bin/fax` and set certain information:

- Find the line starting with `FROM` and set the value to your phone number (e.g., `FROM="+1 212 555 1212"`).
- Find the line starting with `PAGE` and set the default page size for your country (probably `PAGE=letter`, `PAGE=legal`, or `PAGE=a4`).
- Find the line starting with `DEV` and make sure the device corresponds to the device for your modem, such as `modem` or `ttyS0`. For more information on modem devices, refer to Chapter 18.
- Find the line starting with `NAME`, and change it to the name you want your recipients to see on the fax header.

When editing the file, note that lines starting with a hash mark (#) are comments and do not affect the configuration. You can comment out an existing line with a hash mark and add in your own variation on the line so that you can easily switch back to the default configuration.

TIP   If you're working outside of North America, search the **/usr/bin/fax** configuration file for the **TELCVT** variable, and make sure to uncomment only the **TELCVT** code line that applies to your national telephone service.

Preparing Directories

The final step before you can send or receive faxes is to prepare the spool, log, and lock directories, /var/spool/fax, /var/log/fax, and /var/lock, respectively.

First, check that the directory exists by using ls /var/spool and see if the fax subdirectory is there. The installation of efax should create this directory, so it should be there. Repeat the process for the /var/log directory.

Next, set the permissions on the directory as you did with KPPP in Chapter 22, "Connecting Linux to the Internet," so that any user can access the fax spool:

```
$ chmod u+s /var/spool/fax
```

Repeat the process on the fax log directory:

```
$ chmod u+s /var/log/fax
```

Finally, give all users access to the lock file directory, so that when they use fax, nobody else can use fax at the same time:

```
$ chmod 777 /var/lock
```

Sending Your First Fax

The efax package has three main components: efax, efix, and fax.

- The efax program is the core of the system. It sends and receives faxes to and from files in the standard fax file format: Group 3 compressed TIFF files. You can't use efax to send a text file or a PostScript file or any other type of file without first converting it to the necessary Group 3 compressed TIFF file format needed for faxing.

- The efix program is used for conversion purposes, providing the ability to convert files to and from text, bitmap, and the fax TIFF format. By combining efax and efix, it is possible to send many images and text files as faxes.

- The fax program provides an integrated layer from which it is possible to create, send, receive, view, and print faxes. This program integrates efax, efix, and other Linux components to provide fairly complete Linux faxing functionality.

In order to learn how to send and receive faxes with efax, let's focus on the fax program, since it brings together all the functionality you need.

Sending Faxes

The fax program makes it easy to send a fax from a text file or a PostScript file. For the purposes of sending, the syntax of the fax command is

```
$ fax send options number file
```

There are three available options that can be used when sending a fax:

-l   Use low resolution (96 dots per inch).

-v   Provide verbose messages and program status.

-m   Assume that the phone number has already been dialed (in which case the phone number should not be provided).

The phone number should be provided in the same form that you would use to dial it. For instance, if you want to dial the local phone number 555-1212, you could use 5551212 or 555-1212 as the phone number entry. If you need to dial 9 for an outside line, then use 95551212 or 9-5551212 or 9-555-1212.

Let's take a look at an example. Suppose you have a text file called textfile in the directory /tmp and you want to send it as a low-resolution fax to the number 123-4567, using 9 to access an outside line. To do this, you use the command

```
$ fax send -l 9-123-4567 /tmp/textfile
```

Given a text file containing the following text

```
FAX TRANSMISSION:

TO: Arman Danesh

FROM: Arman Danesh

NOTE:

This is a test of the efax package. Using the fax command, we can send
text files as faxes.
```

this produces a fax that looks like the one in Figure 25.2.

FIGURE 25.2:

A sample efax fax

```
FAX TRANSMISSION:

TO: Arman Danesh

FROM: Arman Danesh

NOTE:

This is a test of the efax package. Using the fax command, we can send
text files as faxes.
```

Sending Multiple Files As One Fax

In addition to sending a single file as a fax, you can use fax to send multiple files as a single fax. For instance, if you want to send the contents of /tmp/textfile followed by the contents of another text file called /tmp/textfile2, use the command

```
$ fax send 9-123-4567 /tmp/textfile /tmp/textfile2
```

to send the files in the specified order.

> **NOTE**   You can combine only multiple text files in this way. If you try to combine a PostScript file with text files or with another PostScript file, the process will not work.

But what if you want to send the pages out of order or send only some of the pages in a file? To do this, you need to first convert the file into a fax-formatted TIFF file. Each page of the fax is then placed in a separate file, and you can choose which pages to send by faxing only those files.

Here you utilize the fax program's ability to create fax-formatted files. For instance, if you have a PostScript file called /tmp/psfile that is three pages long, you can convert it into three fax-formatted TIFF files using the command

```
$ fax make /tmp/psfile
```

The resulting pages are contained in three separate files named /tmp/psfile.001, /tmp/psfile.002, and /tmp/psfile.003.

When you convert a file into fax format, the resulting pages retain the same name as the original file with three-digit, numerically ordered extensions. For instance, the file test.txt would create fax pages named test.txt.001, test.txt.002, and so on.

The only option available to you when using `fax make` is to choose low-resolution mode using the -1 option:

```
$ fax make -1 /tmp/psfile
```

Let's go back to the three-page document you converted earlier. If you want to send the third page followed by the first page and not send the second page, use the command

```
$ fax send /tmp/psfile.003 /tmp/psfile.001
```

Sending a Fax by Printing

While it is great to be able to send faxes using the `fax` command, this isn't very useful when it comes to printing from applications such as Netscape, WordPerfect, or ApplixWare Words.

> **NOTE**   Of course, if you have only one modem and are using this to browse the Internet with Netscape, you won't be able to send a fax from Netscape as long as the modem is being used to connect to the Internet.

For instance, consider the Netscape example. It is possible to print from Netscape to a file, generating a PostScript file as a result. But sending the page as a fax adds a second step to the process, requiring that the user switch to the command line to send the file as a fax.

Unfortunately, this isn't quite as simple as faxing from Windows or Macintosh applications, where faxing is generally as simple as printing.

Fortunately, it is possible to create a special printer device in Linux that uses efax to send the file being printed as a fax.

The process is fairly simple. The `lpd` printing system allows for input filters to be specified. If an input filter is specified for a printer queue, then the file being sent to the queue is sent to an input filter before being placed in the queue. If the filter doesn't return any data but instead faxes the file, the job is never sent to a printer.

There are three steps to setting up the necessary printer queue for printing to the fax modem:

1. Configure the printer queue.

2. Set up the faxlpr script.

3. Prepare the spool directory.

All of this preparation needs to be done as the root user on your system.

Configuring the Printer Queue

To set up the Printer Queue, you need to edit the /etc/printcap.local file. When you restart the Line Printer Daemon (lpd), this information gets incorporated into the standard /etc/printcap printer configuration file. Open up /etc/printcap.local in the text editor of your choice and add the following entry:

```
fax:\
        :sd=/var/spool/fax:\
        :mx#0:\
        :lp=/dev/null:\
        :if=/usr/bin/faxlpr:
```

This entry specifies the name of the queue as fax, sets the spool directory to /var/spool/fax, sets no limit on the job size with mx#0, sets the print device to /dev/null, and sets the input filter to /usr/bin/faxlpr.

> **NOTE** If you use only the Apsfilter utility described in Chapter 18, and will not use the Printconf utility described in Chapter 15, you can edit the /etc/printcap file directly.

Setting Up the *faxlpr* Script

The fax program is actually a highly flexible shell script. When the script is called by its regular name (fax), it assumes that the command is coming from the command line and behaves accordingly. If the script is called by an alternate name (faxlpr), the script assumes it is being asked to send a fax via an lpd printer queue.

In order to prepare for this, you need to create a link to your fax configuration file. For example, if it is .efaxrc in the /home/mj directory, use the following command:

```
$ ln /home/mj/.efaxrc /usr/bin/faxlpr
```

If you haven't set up an .efaxrc file in your home directory, you can link the fax command directly:

```
$ ln /usr/bin/fax /usr/bin/faxlpr
```

Finally, restart the lpd daemon. In Red Hat Linux 7.1, use the `/etc/rc.d/init.d/lpd restart` command. Other distributions may store the lpd daemon in a different directory.

Sending Faxes through the Print Queue

Once this is all done, you are ready to send your first fax using the lpd system. Just as you could print a file using the lpr command, now you can fax a text or PostScript file in the same way. The only new notion is that you use the -J argument of the lpr command to specify the phone number to send the fax to.

For instance, if you have a file called `/tmp/testfile` that you want to fax to 555-1212 using the print queue called fax, you could use the command

```
$ lpr -Pfax -J 5551212 /tmp/testfile
```

The lpd daemon passes the file over to the input filter (faxlpr), which attempts to fax the file. Following the attempt, faxlpr sends the user transmitting the fax an e-mail indicating the success or failure of the process.

You can print in this way from any program that allows you to specify options to the lpr command and that generates PostScript output (including, but not limited to, Netscape 6, WordPerfect for Linux, and StarOffice).

Receiving Faxes

Receiving faxes is a fairly straightforward process. There are three ways in which you can arrange to receive a fax: manually, automatically for a specific incoming call, or automatically for all incoming calls.

Manually Receiving a Fax

To manually receive a fax, you need to tell the modem to answer the telephone and receive the fax once the phone is ringing. This is done with the receive option of the fax command.

If the line is ringing and you know the call is an incoming fax, you simply need to issue the command

```
$ fax receive
```

to receive the fax.

With the `fax receive` command, you can specify a filename for the incoming fax. Each page of the fax is saved in a separate file with a sequentially numbered extension (001, 002, 003, etc.). For instance, if you receive a three-page fax with the command

```
$ fax receive testfax
```

the resulting fax is stored in three files named `testfax.001`, `testfax.002`, and `testfax.003`. To view the fax, use the `fax view` command, described later in this section.

If you don't specify a filename for the incoming fax, then the `fax` command builds a 10-digit filename derived from the date and time the fax is received. For instance, a fax received on December 24 at 9:52:35 P.M. will be saved in a series of files named `1224095235.001`, `1224095235.002`, `1224095235.003`, etc.

Faxes are stored in the default `/var/spool/fax` directory. You can view the contents of the fax spool directory with the `fax queue` command:

```
$ fax queue

Fax files in /var/spool/fax :

-rw-r--r--    1 root      root           247 Jul  2 17:49 0702174857.001
-rw-r--r--    1 root      root           247 Jul  2 17:59 0702175842.001
-rw-r--r--    1 root      root           247 Jul  4 17:14 0704171330.001
```

To view these faxes, use the `fax view` command while running X Windows:

```
$ fax view 0704171330.001
```

This command causes the fax to be filtered and displayed by the `xloadimage` program, as shown in Figure 25.3.

FIGURE 25.3:

A fax displayed in *xloadimage*

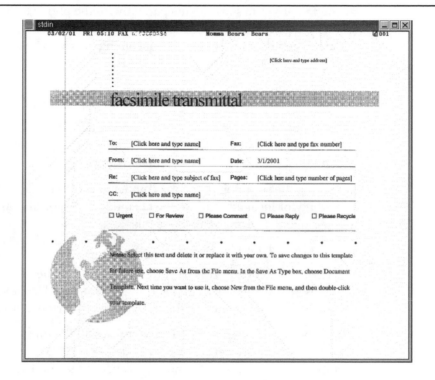

Advanced users can change the fax filter program by adjusting the VIEWCMD variable in the /usr/bin/fax script.

Printing is equally simple using the fax print command:

```
$ fax print 0704171330.001
```

This command prints the same fax to the default printer queue, usually called lp.

Automatically Receiving a Fax for a Specific Call

If you are expecting that the next phone call you receive will be an incoming fax, you can set things up so that the fax program will wait for the call, answer the phone, receive the fax, hang up, and then exit. To do this, you use the answer option of the fax command:

```
$ fax answer
```

The fax program starts, waits patiently for the phone to ring, and then answers after the second ring. As with fax receive, the incoming fax is stored using the date to generate a filename. The incoming fax can be viewed and printed using the fax view and fax print commands.

Automatically Receiving All Incoming Faxes

If your fax modem is connected to a dedicated phone line that you want to use for incoming faxes, you can make the efax program continually monitor the line for incoming faxes while still allowing outgoing calls.

Using the -w option of the fax command causes the program to run as a daemon waiting for incoming calls to the fax modem. A typical efax command on a dedicated phone line might look like this:

```
$ efax -d /dev/modem -w -iS0=5
```

The -d switch points efax to your modem device file /dev/modem. The -w switch makes efax wait for activity (a "ring" on standard U.S. telephones). The -iS0 switch makes efax wait, in this case for the fifth ring, before it becomes active.

If you want your system to answer faxes all the time, you can consider putting a command such as efax -d /dev/modem -w -iS0=5 in your /etc/rc.d/rc.local start-up file so that the daemon runs every time you launch Linux.

NOTE   The location of the rc.local start-up file often varies by Linux distribution.

If you need to stop the answering daemon, you can use the command

```
$ efax stop
```

to kill the daemon. Once you see a message that efax has disconnected, then all automatic answering ceases.

Looking Ahead

By now you should feel comfortable sending and receiving faxes using your Linux system.

The next section of the book moves into a whole new area: Linux in the small office/home office (SOHO) environment. You will learn how to install Linux in a network environment and how to examine basic network configuration. Then you will move on to a discussion of the types of services Linux can be used for in a SOHO environment, including mail server, intranet Web server, and file server for Unix, Windows, and Novell networks.

PART VI

Using Linux in the Small Office/Home Office (SOHO)

CHAPTER

TWENTY-SIX

26

Where to Use Linux in the SOHO

- Linux As a File Server

- Linux As a Print Server

- Linux As a Database Server

- Linux As an Intranet Server

- Linux As an Applications Server

- Linux As a Router

- Linux As a Workstation

At this point, the book is going to shift its focus. By now you have a firm grasp of using Linux on a stand-alone workstation, and perhaps even use Linux as your preferred operating system at home to access the Internet, surf the Web, compose e-mails and letters, and more.

Still, Linux's real home is in a networked world. Perhaps you run a small office at home with two PCs that you want networked. Linux makes a great file and print server in most networks. Perhaps in your business you are thinking about setting up an intranet. Linux provides an inexpensive way to move your business into an intranet environment by offering powerful Web and database servers.

If you want to connect a network of PCs to the Internet, Linux can be an excellent router. In many cases, it is far less costly to use a Linux computer as a router than to purchase a hardware router to connect your network to the world.

Finally, if you find that your current Windows-based desktops lack the performance or stability you would like to see on your home or office network, Linux as a workstation operating system may be the answer to your problems. It is possible to access both Windows and Unix applications from within Linux, network with other Unix, Windows, and Novell network systems, and easily share files and data with the rest of the world without worrying about bothersome crashes.

This chapter takes a quick look at these uses of the Linux operating system for small offices and home offices (commonly known as SOHO), where the cost of deploying expensive commercial solutions may be prohibitive.

Linux As a File Server

Perhaps the most fundamental need on a small network is a file server. File servers supply common places to store data, thus allowing shared files to be accessed by all users who need them and providing centralized locations for backing up files (thereby eliminating the need for daily data backups on each workstation on a network).

On a Windows or Novell network, this is generally done in one of two ways:

- Using dedicated file servers
- Using peer-to-peer networks

Dedicated File Servers

A *dedicated file server* is a system that is not used as a workstation but is set up as a central file server for the network. Users at different workstations or computers on the network can access directories on the file server as if these were directories or disk drives on their own computers.

Dedicated file servers offer the advantage of centralizing the management of shared data and the backup process, but they cost more than peer-to-peer networks. They also offer the benefit of being able to set up network access control policies for confidential, core, or shared data to ensure that unauthorized users don't have easy access to the information.

Linux is ideally suited to run as a low-cost file server for a small network. Linux can act as a file server to Unix/Linux, Windows, and Novell networks, making it an easily deployed universal file server for a network containing different types of computers and workstations. In addition, the stability and true multitasking capabilities of Linux make it a better choice than some other well-known options (such as Windows 95/98/Me) when a robust file-server solution is needed.

Chapter 29, "Integrating Red Hat Linux 7.1 in Windows and Novell Networks," discusses how to set up Linux as a file server.

Peer-to-Peer File Sharing

In a *peer-to-peer network,* there is no central file server. Instead, each user decides which directories and drives on their PC should be shared on the network and what level of access control to impose. In this way, each workstation or computer on the network becomes a small file server.

While there is flexibility in this approach, allowing users to decide what data to share and with whom, there are also drawbacks. These include no centralized management of file sharing and access control policies, no centralized location for the backing up of critical data, and a performance impact on a user's desktop when several other individuals on the network are accessing shared files on that user's PC.

Linux can act as a reasonable peer-to-peer file server because of its ability to share with multiple types of networks. In addition, the true multitasking abilities of Linux mitigate much of the impact on performance when multiple users access files on a PC being used for other work.

Ultimately, though, the low cost of setting up a Linux-based dedicated file server for a small network makes the dedicated file server approach more attractive because of the management and centralized backup benefits it provides.

Linux As a Print Server

In addition to file servers, print servers are another component of the network. Generally, a dedicated file server also plays the role of offering print services to the network, serving double duty.

It is not uncommon to find print services provided in both a centralized, dedicated fashion and the peer-to-peer method on the same network. Some users who use a printer heavily may warrant their own printers at their desks, while others who use the printers less frequently may share a printer located in a common area. Often, a user with a dedicated printer shares it on the network so that other users can print documents for that user's attention directly to the dedicated printer rather than to the common shared printer.

Linux, of course, can work in both environments. Linux supports a healthy range of printers, including most PostScript and HP-compatible PCL printers. In addition, its printer-sharing options include the ability to share printers on Unix/Linux, Windows, and Novell networks.

Chapter 29 also discusses how to set up Linux as a print server.

Linux As a Database Server

Like most Unix platforms, Linux has long had a wide selection of free database packages available for it, including PostgreSQL and mSQL.

Starting in 1998, though, major commercial database vendors gave Linux a boost in the database market by announcing and releasing Linux versions of their products. For example:

- Red Hat has just released as of this writing the Red Hat Database, which integrates PostgreSQL 7.1.2, optimized for Red Hat Linux 7.1. This database is targeted at mid-size businesses and independent corporate business units as an alternative to the large corporate database systems that seem to dominate the market.

- Oracle released in early 2001 its 9i suite of database/application server tools, optimized for the Linux 2.4 kernel. This promises to move a number of heavier business databases from higher-end Unix systems to Linux.

- Sybase PowerBuilder supports the SQL Anywhere database Studio application on Linux. They have documented examples where the total cost of this package is about half the cost of the equivalent Windows NT/2000-style solution.

- IBM has released its flagship DB2 Universal Database for Linux, which encourages users to move their databases from higher-end Unix as well as Windows NT/2000 systems.

Where Linux once provided only an attractive alternative for file servers and Web servers in an organization, Linux can now be deployed as a robust, scalable database platform for an organization using standard, widely-used relational database systems.

As we mention later, combining a Linux-powered database with a Linux-powered Web server allows Linux to serve as a complete intranet server solution.

Linux As an Intranet Server

If you follow the computing trends today, you have probably heard a lot about *intranets:* internal corporate networks that use Internet technology such as TCP/IP, Web browsers, and Internet-standard e-mail to share information and applications within an organization.

Many articles that discuss intranets and the hardware and software used to deploy them depict intranets as expensive endeavors suited only to large corporations and organizations. This couldn't be further from the truth.

Even in small offices, an intranet can provide a convenient way to publish information to be read by all employees through a Web browser. With a little forethought, you can eliminate some of the paperwork in your office by introducing electronic, online, Web-based forms for everything from leave requests to expense report submissions.

In addition, if you have small databases scattered across your organization, each used on a daily basis by different users, an intranet can provide a common means by which occasional users of the data can access the information in a database without needing full access to the database tools used to create, maintain, and update the data. By integrating the database with an intranet Web server, simple Web-based forms can be used to query the database.

Linux, which offers a wealth of powerful and flexible Web servers as well as fully functional relational database systems, can allow the creation of an intranet server without the cost involved in deploying Windows NT/2000, a commercial database such as Oracle, and an expensive Web database integration tool. There are even some free tools for Linux that make it relatively easy to produce intranet programs and applications that make use of your corporate databases.

Chapter 32, "Building Your Own Web Server," discusses the basics of getting a Linux-based intranet server up and running.

Linux As an Applications Server

Linux is by nature designed to act as both a file/print/intranet server and a full-fledged applications server. With an applications server, applications actually run on the server and are only displayed on a terminal or workstation, using the X Windows protocol or a terminal connection such as Telnet. In contrast, on many typical Windows networks, the applications run on the desktop and the data is stored on the server and accessed there.

For some types of applications and in some situations, centralizing the running of applications can bring both performance and management benefits. If you are running a Windows or Novell network, a Linux system can act as an applications server for several purposes:

- Running character-based programs such as powerful Unix/Linux mail software

- Running a custom-designed, character-based database interface to a centralized Linux database

- Accessing custom in-house applications, such as a corporate telephone book, designed to run in a Unix/Linux shell

If you install an X server on a Windows desktop, you can even deliver centrally managed X Windows applications to the desktop while running the applications on a Linux applications server.

Where budgets are low, Linux can create full-fledged GUI networks without the hardware or software expense of running Windows 95/98/Me or NT/2000. For instance, I have deployed a 10-desktop network running Linux exclusively. The desktops are all 486-class machines with 8MB of RAM. It would be exceptionally difficult to run Windows plus Microsoft Office on them, and the cost for the necessary software licenses would run over U.S.$300 per desktop.

But with Linux on their older hardware, these systems can act as simple X terminals, displaying applications that run on a single applications server. In this case, the applications server is a Pentium 200MHz system with just 96MB of RAM. With the development and free release of several Linux office suites, software-licensing costs are essentially down to zero.

A network like this can provide performance to the user that feels like a low-end Pentium system with 32MB of RAM running Windows 95/98/Me. All of the management of software, user accounts, backups, and system maintenance can be done centrally on one or two servers.

Of course, this type of solution takes a fundamental strategic decision: not to use popular Windows-based productivity applications. But where cost is of the essence or the availability of modern hardware is limited, Linux makes a strong candidate for an organization-wide computing platform.

Linux As a Router

The concept of a router is simple: Where two or more networks need to be connected, a router is the device that makes it possible to communicate between the networks.

Routers come in all shapes and sizes, from software-based routers running on Windows NT/2000 servers to hardware routers from well-known vendors such as Cisco. Routers can connect to networks in different ways, using technology ranging from regular modems to Ethernet cards to ISDN connections.

Let's consider an example: an office with a small network that is connected to the Internet by a high-speed connection such as DSL or a cable modem. That is, a small company has a single high-speed connection to the Internet but has a network of two or more computers that would like to share the connection.

A router for this situation offers a single Ethernet connection to the local network and a corresponding high-speed connection to the Internet. All computers on the network send all packets to the router. The router decides if the packet is destined for another location on the local network or for an outside address (in other words, somewhere on the Internet). Figure 26.1 contains a diagram of this network.

FIGURE 26.1:

A typical
Ethernet-to-Internet
routing diagram

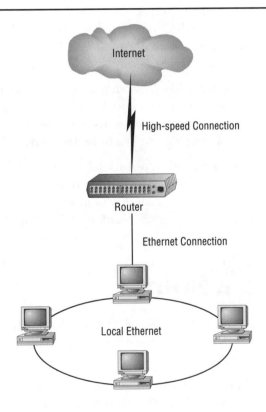

All local packets are sent by the router back out on the Ethernet connection to the local network. If a packet is destined for the outside world, it is sent through the high-speed connection. Since it is always connected, network packets do not have to wait for a modem connection to get to the Internet.

Similar routing situations include connecting two separate Ethernet networks through a router that has two or more Ethernet connections, as illustrated in Figure 26.2. The basic configuration of other high-speed networks such as Fast Ethernet (100Mbps), Gigabit Ethernet (1000Mbps), or Asynchronous Transfer Mode (155Mbps and up) is similar.

FIGURE 26.2:

Connecting two Ethernet networks with routers

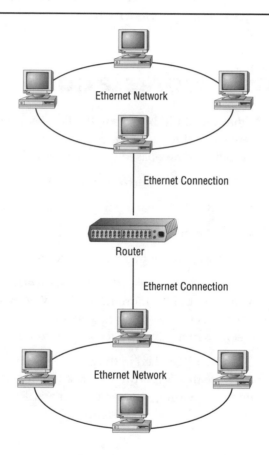

Linux has all the features needed to act as a router:

- Support for multiple Ethernet cards

- Support for regular modems and high-speed connections such as DSL and cable modems

- Support for IP forwarding (the means by which packets can be received, analyzed, and rerouted by the Linux-based router)

In fact, for small Ethernet-to-Ethernet interconnectivity or Ethernet-to-high-speed-connection Internet routing, a Linux-based solution can be far less expensive than dedicated hardware routers, and once it is properly configured can be very secure and reliable.

Chapter 31, "Security and Red Hat Linux 7.1 As an Inexpensive Router," discusses using Linux as a router.

Linux As a Workstation

A final use of Linux in a small office environment is as the actual desktop operating system. If the application base available in Linux is suitable to the work of the office, then Linux-based desktops provide the following advantages:

- Stability and performance

- Full remote management by the network administrator

- Full network backup capabilities

- Lower cost of ownership in comparison with Windows-based desktops

Where money is available, high-powered Linux workstations can offer speed rivaling that of the more expensive Windows-based systems. Linux also offers peer-to-peer networking that is more robust and offers better performance than is seen on many systems, especially those running Windows 95/98/Me.

Also, as mentioned in the previous section, Linux can enable low-end or old hardware that can't run the latest Windows software to become full-fledged X terminals, providing performance on obsolete desktop hardware that feels like that of a low-end Pentium system.

Looking Ahead

This chapter used broad brushstrokes to paint a picture of the ways in which Linux can be used in a small home or office network environment.

The following chapters cover this topic in more detail. First, you will learn to install Ethernet networking within Linux. Then, you'll learn about Linux as a server for files and for printers. After that, you'll consider Linux as a way to set up routers and intranet servers. Finally, you'll work with the advanced system administration techniques that can help you get the most out of Linux in a small network.

Chapter 27, "Installing Red Hat Linux 7.1 for the SOHO," looks at specific points of installing Linux in a networked environment.

CHAPTER

TWENTY-SEVEN

27

Installing Red Hat Linux 7.1 for the SOHO

- Choosing Packages for a LAN Installation

- Configuring Network Support During Installation

- Installing from a Network Source

In this chapter, you will move from considering principles that apply to Linux in the often-isolated context of a home workstation to examining another common role for Linux: as a desktop or server operating system in a local area network (LAN).

In fact, Linux has an increasingly important role to play in the small-office, home-office (SOHO) market, where Linux can deliver enterprise-class networking capabilities at a fraction of the cost of commercial Unix solutions.

Linux can easily be configured to work with most LANs and brings with it a wide range of tools, including Web servers, mail servers, and news servers—all essential components of successful intranet solutions.

Choosing Packages for a LAN Installation

An important piece of a network puzzle is consideration of which software packages to install on a networked Linux system.

If, as discussed in Chapter 4, "Installing Red Hat Linux 7.1," you find yourself unable to install all Linux components on your system, consider the guidelines listed in Table 27.1 when selecting packages to install on your network-enabled system.

TABLE 27.1:   Suggested Packages for Different Network Installations

Type of System	Packages to Install
Networked workstation	Mail/WWW/News tools Networked workstation NFS server (to connect to other Unix/Linux computers on your network) SMB (Samba) connectivity (to connect to Windows computers on your network)
Network management workstation	*Everything for a networked workstation plus:* IPX/NetWare connectivity (if you are connecting to a Novell network or a network that uses Novell protocols) Network management workstation

Continued on next page

TABLE 27.1 CONTINUED: Suggested Packages for Different Network Installations

Type of System	Packages to Install
Network server	*Everything for a network management workstation plus:* Anonymous FTP server Print server (assumes a printer is connected to this computer) News server (if you want to set up newsgroup-style messages on your network) Web server (if you want to serve Web pages from this computer), using Apache DNS nameserver (if you have a network of more than 10 computers) PostgreSQL server (if you need database support on your network)

The packages listed with each system are suggestions; for example, you do not need to install the NFS server package if this will be the only Unix/Linux computer on the local network. In fact, extra packages can be security holes; for example, if you do not use NFS but have it installed, someone outside your network may be able to use NFS as a way to break into your network.

Configuring Network Support During Installation

During the Linux installation process, you can configure LAN support for your Linux system. While Chapter 28, "Configuring Red Hat Linux 7.1 for an Ethernet Network," discusses how to configure an existing Linux system to communicate on a LAN, you can also do this during the installation process.

In order for LAN configuration to work, you need to have a network card already installed in your computer before you install Linux. This is important because the installation program tries to detect your card.

Regardless of what media you choose to install from (CD-ROM, hard disk partition, or network mount), you will have a chance to configure your network environment. Normally, you are given the option to configure your network following installation of the Linux files. Chapter 4 did not cover the options to configure LAN support. In Red Hat Linux 7.1, you can configure your computer to connect to a LAN during installation. If the installation program detects a network card, you will see the screen shown in Figure 27.1.

If you don't see this screen, either you haven't physically installed a network card or Linux can't find or detect that card in your computer. If this happened to you, refer to Chapter 28 for instructions on configuring your Linux computer for networking.

FIGURE 27.1:

Network configuration during Linux installation

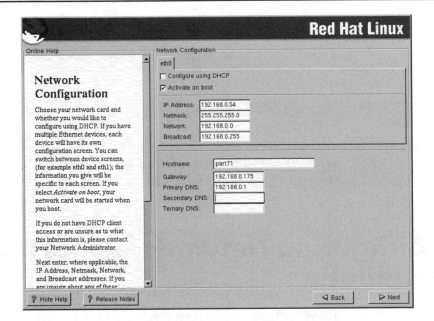

NOTE	Much of the information requested during the network configuration process is covered in Chapter 21, "Understanding Linux Networking," and Chapter 28, "Configuring Red Hat Linux 7.1 for an Ethernet Network." These discussions include definitions of such terms as IP address, network mask, and nameserver.

There are three areas in Figure 27.1, which correspond to the three basic steps for configuring a computer on a Linux network. Let's look at each area in detail.

Selecting a Network Card

Most current Linux distributions, including Red Hat Linux 7.1, detect most network cards. When Linux detects a network card, it assigns it a name, in this case, eth0. Figure 27.1 shows one network card. If you have more than one network card, you would see more than one tab in Figure 27.1, generally with names like eth1, eth2, etc.

Basic Network Configuration

When you set up network configuration, you have two basic choices: You can make all of the settings manually, or you can point your computer to a server that assigns each setting automatically.

If your network is already connected to a DHCP server, automatic configuration is easier. All you need to do in Figure 27.1 is select Configure Using DHCP. Linux will assign the selected network card, all necessary network settings, including its IP address as well as the IP address of the gateway, and DNS servers through DHCP.

Unless you know that you have a DHCP server, you'll need to set up your IP addresses manually, as described in the next section.

NOTE   Some Linux distributions have an option to configure using BOOTP. This protocol allows a DHCP server outside your network to assign network parameters to your computer.

Manual Network Address Configuration

There are two parts to a manual network configuration. First, you need to set up basic communication between your computer and other computers on your network. Then you can set up communication between your computer and outside networks.

The first part of a manual network configuration is the IP address. An IP address alone is not enough; you also need a network address and network mask to identify your network to computers outside your network. To allow your computer to recognize the other computers on your network, you also need a broadcast IP address. Based on Figure 27.1, this includes the following:

IP address   An IP address is four numbers between 0 and 255, separated by dots, such as 192.168.0.223.

Network mask   A network mask is a special IP address that typically (but does not always) includes 255s, such as 255.255.255.0.

Network (address)   A network address is how computers on outside connected networks identify your network. Since a network address can be determined from an IP address and a network mask, your Linux installation program may automatically fill in this entry for you.

Broadcast (address)   This is the IP address to use to send a message to all computers on a given network. Like the network address, the broadcast address can also be determined from an IP address and a network mask, and your Linux installation program may automatically fill in this entry for you.

If you don't know the correct values for these entries, consult your network administrator or ISP. You don't want to designate IP addresses that have already been assigned to someone else. For more information on IP addressing, refer to the sections in Chapter 21 related to IP addressing, specifically IP version 4 (IPv4).

Manual Networking Configuration

For any LAN connected to any other network, including the Internet, a default gateway and a primary nameserver are essential. For isolated networks, you may not need a gateway or a nameserver, so you may be able to leave these fields blank.

This secondary network configuration data includes the following, based again on Figure 27.1:

Hostname   This is the fully qualified name for your computer. For example, if you have set up the mommabears.com network, the computers on your network might have hostnames like `linux1.mommabears.com` and `windows1.mommabears.com`. If you don't have a domain, just a hostname such as `linux1` or `windows1` is sufficient during installation.

NOTE   Several Linux distributions also ask for a domain name during installation. Typical domain names include Sybex.com, linux.net, and mommabears.com. Don't use a standard Internet domain name unless you own the domain.

Gateway   The gateway IP address is the address of a computer on your network that is also connected to another network. If your network is not connected to any other network (including the Internet), you don't need a gateway address.

Primary DNS   A Domain Name Service (DNS) server includes a database that matches domain names such as mommabears.com to IP addresses such as 192.168.55.33. If you have a DNS server on your network, enter its IP address here. Alternatively, if you have an Internet connection from your network, you can enter your ISP's DNS address here.

Secondary and Ternary DNS   Many networks and systems connected to other networks including the Internet use more than one nameserver to ensure reliability of their domain name system. If you or your ISP uses multiple DNS servers, enter their IP addresses in these two fields.

NOTE   DNS servers are often known as *nameservers* in Linux.

This is the information you need to configure your computer on a network during Linux installation. But the situation is different if you access Linux installation files over a network, as described in the next section.

Installing from a Network Source

If your system is connected to a LAN during the installation process, then it is possible to install Linux from a source image located on a server on the network. You may be able to install Linux through an NFS network, an FTP server, or even a Web (HTTP) server.

In order to install from a network source, you need to use a different boot disk than you used in Chapter 4. You can create this boot disk from the bootnet.img disk image file, which is located in the images directory of the Red Hat Linux 7.1 Installation CD-ROM. Refer to Chapter 3, "Getting Ready to Install Linux," for a discussion of creating boot disks from the Linux CD-ROM. When you boot your computer from this bootnet.img disk, you'll come to different installation screens. For example, when you use the Red Hat Linux 7.1 bootnet.img disk and follow the installation prompts, you'll eventually get to the screen shown in Figure 27.2.

Other Linux distributions have similar disk image files on their installation CD-ROMs. Some Linux distributions don't even require this type of boot disk; network installation is a standard option when installing from their CD-ROMs.

FIGURE 27.2:

Installing from a network source

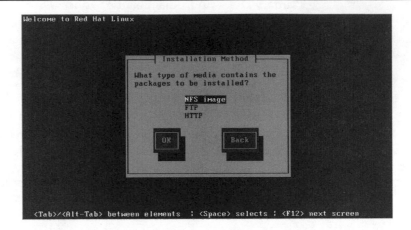

Installing from an NFS Source

In a network with only Unix and/or Linux computers, it is most common for the image to exist on a Network File System (NFS) server, which is the norm for sharing resources in Unix and Linux operating systems.

If you can access the Linux installation CD-ROM files from an NFS server on your network, you can use the network boot install disk to install from this source.

To set up installation from an NFS server, you'll need to set up your network address as discussed previously. You can do this automatically if you have a DHCP server for your network.

Once your computer is configured for your network, you need to identify the NFS server holding the Linux installation files that you need. The applicable Red Hat Linux 7.1 screen is shown in Figure 27.3. It requires two pieces of information: the IP address (or hostname) of the NFS server you want to use and the path on the server where the Red Hat Linux 7.1 installation source files are located.

For example, assume that your Red Hat Linux 7.1 installation files are on a remote CD-ROM, mounted on the NFS server at /mnt/cdrom. Also assume that the NFS server has the IP address 10.10.10.1. In that case, enter **10.10.10.1** as the NFS server name and **/mnt/cdrom** as the Red Hat directory.

FIGURE 27.3:

Installing from an NFS server

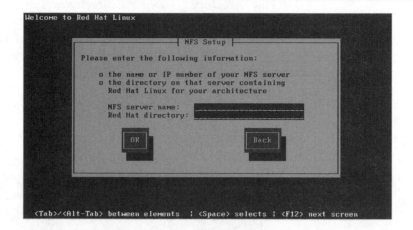

The rest of the installation procedure should then proceed with the same general steps as when you install from a local CD-ROM drive.

Installing from an FTP Source

Alternatively, you can install Linux from an FTP server. This server can be on a local network, or it can be from one of the many FTP servers with Linux installation files on the Internet.

> **NOTE** Unless you have a fast, dedicated Internet connection, installation from an Internet FTP server is not recommended. If you attempt this type of installation, it could take several days. Any interruptions to your Internet connection could mean that you would have to start over from the beginning.

If you want to use the FTP option, you need to select FTP in the installation screen shown back at Figure 27.2. Then you'll need to set up your network address as discussed previously. You can do this automatically if you have a DHCP server for your network.

Then the FTP Setup window appears, as shown in Figure 27.4. In this window, you can provide three pieces of information:

FTP Site Name   This is the name of the FTP server you plan to use. For example, if you want to install from the Red Hat FTP server, enter `ftp.redhat.com`.

Red Hat Directory This is the directory on the FTP server where the source files for your Linux distribution are located. For example, if the FTP server of your choice holds the Red Hat 7.1 installation files in its /pub/mirrors/redhat/i386/RedHat directory, use **/pub/mirrors/redhat/i386**. (Note the omission of the final "RedHat.")

Use Non-Anonymous FTP Select this option if you are required to log in to the FTP server you plan to use. If you select this option, you'll also need the account name and password used to log into the non-anonymous FTP server.

FIGURE 27.4:

Installing from an FTP server

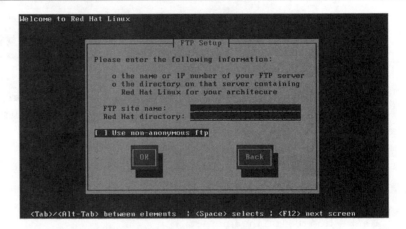

Installing from a Web Server

Some proxy servers do not allow access to FTP but allow access to Web servers using HTTP. Some users just find it easier to download information, even for Linux installation, from a Web server.

Unless you have a fast, dedicated Internet connection, installation from an Internet HTTP server is not recommended. If you try this type of installation, it could take several days. Any interruptions to your Internet connection could mean that you would have to start over again.

If you want to use the HTTP option, you need to select HTTP in the installation screen shown back at Figure 27.2. Then, you'll need to set up your network address as discussed previously. You can do this automatically if you have a DHCP server for your network.

Then the HTTP Setup window appears, as shown in Figure 27.5. In this window, you can provide the Web site from where you're downloading your Linux installation files and the applicable directory.

FIGURE 27.5:

Installing from a Web server

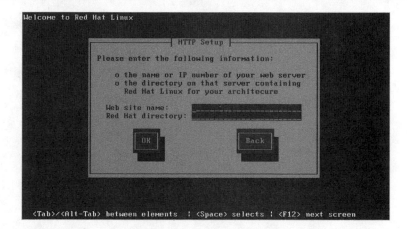

For example, assume that your Red Hat Linux 7.1 installation files are mounted on the HTTP server at /pub/mirrors/redhat/i386/RedHat. Also assume that the HTTP server is located at www.redhat.com. In that case, enter **www.redhat.com** as the Web Site Name and **/pub/mirrors/redhat/i386** as the Red Hat Directory.

The rest of the installation procedure should then proceed with the same general steps as when you install from a local CD-ROM drive.

Looking Ahead

Now that you have installed a networked Linux system, you are going to look at the details of Linux Ethernet configuration. This information will allow you to install existing non-networked Linux systems onto an Ethernet LAN or reconfigure existing network configurations as needed.

Once you have learned these details, you will spend much of the rest of the book looking at some of the roles that Linux can play in a small intranet, including the following:

- Serving as an inexpensive router or firewall

- Acting as an intranet Web server

- Handling e-mail services for your network

CHAPTER

TWENTY-EIGHT

Configuring Red Hat Linux 7.1 for an Ethernet Network

- Preparing and Configuring the Network

- Testing the Network

- Manual Network Configuration

- Sharing Files on a Linux/Unix Network

- Basic Network Security

In Chapter 27, "Installing Red Hat Linux 7.1 for the SOHO," you learned how to install Linux on a computer and connect it to a TCP/IP Ethernet network in the process. You also learned the basic steps to configure a network card during the installation of Linux.

In this chapter, you will learn how to configure an already-installed Linux system to connect to a Linux network. These steps including preparing your PC for a network, configuring the network, and testing the network. This chapter covers the entire process.

NOTE   Ethernet, more properly known as IEEE standards 802.2 and 802.3, is only the most popular of a wide range of network technologies. You can set up Linux to work with other network technologies, including Token Ring, ARCNet, Fast Ethernet, Gigabit Ethernet, and Asynchronous Transfer Mode (ATM). While the technologies are different, installation techniques are quite similar when using the command-line interface. More information is available, especially on various Ethernet options as well as ATM, in the second section of the Ethernet-HOWTO, accessible online at `http://www.linuxdoc.org/HOWTO/Ethernet-HOWTO-2.html`.

This chapter is based on traditional network commands associated with the Linux 2.2.*x* kernel, which are still used in Red Hat Linux 7.1. There are some new networking commands associated with the Linux 2.4 kernel; more information on this is available in the Linux 2.4 Networking HOWTO, currently available at `http://www.ds9a.nl/2.4Networking/HOWTO//cvs/2.4routing/output/2.4networking.html`.

Preparing and Configuring the Network

As you saw in the last chapter, there are two main steps that need to be taken to get your network working:

- Installing and setting up a network card

- Setting up your TCP/IP parameters

This chapter looks at how to configure these essentials after Linux has been installed. This process can be used to install new PCs onto the network or to change the configuration of current PCs.

Installing and Setting Up a Network Card

Installing and setting up a network card is highly dependent on the type of network card you plan to use. You should consult the discussion of network cards in Chapter 27 to decide what type of card to use and what information is needed to configure it properly with Linux. Having selected a card (part of this section assumes that you select a Novell-equivalent 2000-class card, which is a typical default option for many "no name" Ethernet cards), you need to first install the hardware according to the instructions that come with the card. In some cases, you'll need to restart your computer and let Red Hat Linux 7.1 load your new driver. In other cases, Red Hat Linux 7.1 detects, configures, and installs your card automatically. To see if your network card is active, go into root user mode and run the /sbin/ifconfig command. If you see something like the following result

```
eth0    Link encap:Ethernet  HWaddr 00:50:56:85:00:23
        inet addr:192.168.0.135  Bcast:192.168.0.255  Mask:255.255.255.0
        UP BROADCAST RUNNING MULTICAST  MTU:1500  Metric:1
        RX packets:50 errors:0 dropped:0 overruns:0 frame:0
        TX packets:0 errors:0 dropped:0 overruns:0 carrier:0
        collisions:0 txqueuelen:100
        Interrupt:9 Base address:0x1000

lo      Link encap:Local Loopback
        inet addr:127.0.0.1  Mask:255.0.0.0
        UP LOOPBACK RUNNING  MTU:16436  Metric:1
        RX packets:6 errors:0 dropped:0 overruns:0 frame:0
        TX packets:6 errors:0 dropped:0 overruns:0 carrier:0
        collisions:0 txqueuelen:0
```

then Linux has one Ethernet (eth0) network card (and the loopback device, lo) properly set up on your computer. If this corresponds to your hardware, you can read the rest of this chapter to examine the tools that help you maintain your network card.

However, if you have installed a network card and don't see an eth0 stanza, then Linux did not recognize your network card. Alternatively, if you have more than one network card and see only an eth0 stanza, Linux did not recognize your other network cards. You'll need to read the rest of this chapter to learn how to set up and configure your network card(s).

NOTE This assumes that you're using Ethernet network cards. Other types of network cards are represented differently; for example, the first ARCNet card on a computer would be arc0.

If Linux does not auto-detect your network card, you must manually instruct Linux to support your hardware. Begin by starting Linuxconf. You can launch Linuxconf from the command line by typing the following command at the command prompt in an xterm window:

```
$ linuxconf-auth
```

If you are not the root user, Red Hat Linux 7.1 prompts you for the root password before starting Linuxconf. If Linux didn't recognize this command, you'll probably have to install Linuxconf per the instructions shown in Chapter 15.

Once Linuxconf starts, navigate to Networking ➢ Client Tasks ➢ Host Name And IP Network Devices to get to the screen shown in Figure 28.1.

FIGURE 28.1:

Linuxconf network configuration

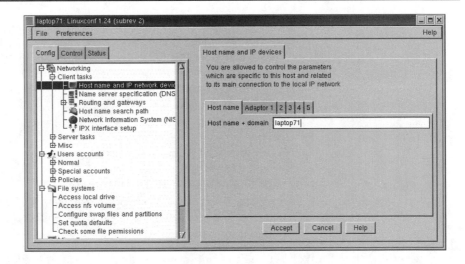

The Host Name And IP Devices section in this version of Linuxconf includes six tabs. The Host Name tab depicts the hostname associated with your computer. The other five tabs allow you to configure the network cards or adapters that you need.

One common problem is the detection of second network cards. When you're setting up a computer to connect to two different networks, you need two network cards. Click the Adaptor 1 tab. If Linux recognized your first network card, relevant configuration data is usually filled in under this tab. To configure your second card, click the Adapter 2 tab. Assume that it's blank, as shown in Figure 28.2.

FIGURE 28.2:

Adding a new network card

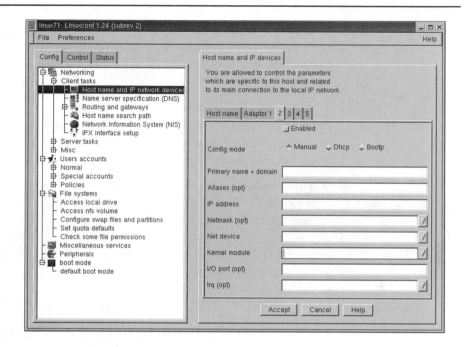

As you can see, there are a number of settings associated with each network card. Some are critical to network card configuration, while others are not:

Enabled   Select this option if you want to activate your card.

Config Mode   If you don't have a DHCP server for your network, select Manual. If you have a DHCP server on your local network, select Dhcp to allow that server to configure your network card. If you have a DHCP server on an adjacent network, select Bootp to allow that server to configure your card.

Primary Name + Domain   Enter the name of your computer and its domain. For example, if your computer is named linux71 on the mommabears.com network, enter **linux71.mommabears.com** here. Alternatively, you can leave this option blank and set this up later in your /etc/hosts file.

Aliases   If you have other names for your computer, enter them here. If you need more than one alias, just separate them with a space.

IP Address   As discussed in Chapter 21, "Understanding Linux Networking," an IP address is four numbers between 0 and 255, separated by dots. If your Config mode is Manual, enter the IP address for this network card here.

Netmask   Short for network mask. Despite the "opt" label, you need a network mask for each network card. As discussed in Chapter 21, network masks allow your computer to determine what other computers are connected into the local network. You can use the drop-down menu to review some typical network masks.

Net Device   The name Linux associates with your network card. If you have an Ethernet network, net device names are typically eth0, eth1, eth2, and so on. While this case describes a second Ethernet adapter (eth1), your situation may be different.

Kernel Module   This is the driver that you want to associate with your network card. The list shown in the drop-down menu is not comprehensive; if your card needs a different driver and it's installed in the /lib/modules/ 2.4.2-2/kernel/drivers/net directory (or one of its subdirectories), you can enter the module name here. Alternatively, you can leave this setting blank and use the insmod command described later.

TIP

If you cannot identify the kernel module associated with your network card, check the Ethernet-HOWTO at http://www.linuxdoc.org/HOWTO/Ethernet-HOWTO .html. Alternatively, look at driver disks and/or Web home pages for your network card. Some include Linux drivers and installation instructions.

I/O Port   The memory address associated with your network card. Red Hat Linux 7.1 normally assigns this automatically. If you have problems after the next steps, find the standard I/O port address associated with your network card and enter it here.

Irq   The Interrupt Request channel associated with your network card. Red Hat Linux 7.1 normally assigns this automatically. If you have problems after the next steps, find the standard IRQ channel associated with your network card and enter it here.

When you've filled out the appropriate text boxes, the next step is to test things out. Click Accept at the bottom of the tab, and then choose File ➤ Act/Changes in the upper-left corner of the Linuxconf window. When the Status Of The System dialog box appears, as shown in Figure 28.3, Linuxconf is telling you what it needs to do to implement your changes. In this case, it's suggesting that you restart your network daemon and reread your network configuration files. Click Do It to make it happen.

FIGURE 28.3:

Linuxconf activates
configuration changes

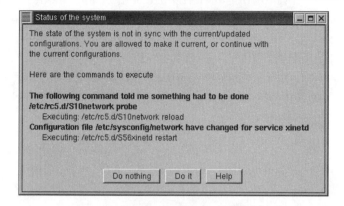

Rerun the /sbin/ifconfig command described earlier. If Linux now recognizes your network cards, you can read this chapter with a view toward maintaining your network.

Checking Whether the Module Loaded

If you were not able to set up your network card with Linuxconf, the next step is to verify the configuration, which is not the easiest task. Until you try to make the network work in the next section, there is no quick way to see if your Ethernet card is configured correctly. But you can check whether the module will load by manually using the insmod command to install a loadable kernel module.

In order to do this, either go to a console command line or open an xterm window as the root user. First, you need to change your current directory to the following:

```
$ cd /lib/modules/2.4.2-2/kernel/drivers/net/
```

This command assumes you have installed the Red Hat Linux 7.1 distribution that shipped with this book and have not upgraded the kernel. In this case, the kernel version is 2.4.2-2, which is reflected in the path of the directory.

Once you are in the correct directory, load your desired module (in this case, for the Novell series of cards) with the insmod command:

```
$ insmod ne.o
```

If Linux doesn't recognize your desired module, review the list of available modules in this directory (or its subdirectories). If you see the right module, check your spelling and try again. Notice that the filenames for the modules have a .o extension.

If successfully configured, your card loads and a series of messages is generated by the driver. They could be complex, as shown with this example of a 3c59x driver:

```
3c59x.c:v0.46C 10/14/97 Donald Becker
    http://cesdis.gsfc.nasa.gov/linux/drivers/vortex.html
loading device 'eth0'...
etho: 3Com 3c905 Boomerang 100baseTx at 0x1440, 00:60:08:71:ad:8c, IRQ
    111
  8k word-wide RAM 3:5 Rx:Tx split, autoselect/MII interface.
eth0: MII transceiver found at address 24.
eth0: Overriding PCI latency timer (CFLT) setting of 64, new value is
    248.
```

Or they could be as simple as this:

```
Using /lib/modules/2.4.2-2/kernel/drivers/net/pcnet32.o
```

If no errors appear, then the module has loaded successfully and your card should be configured just fine. If you continue to experience trouble configuring your network card, refer to the Ethernet-HOWTO at http://www.linuxdoc.org/ HOWTO/Ethernet-HOWTO.html.

Setting Up Your TCP/IP Parameters

The next step is to set up your TCP/IP parameters using the network configuration utility. To do so, start a terminal window, go into root user mode, and type the following command:

```
$ netcfg
```

This calls up the Red Hat Linux Network Configurator shown in Figure 28.4.

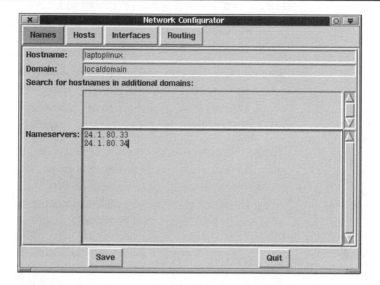

FIGURE 28.4:

The Network Configurator
dialog box

In this utility you specify critical information about your system in relation to the network it is connected to. This information includes the following:

- The name, domain, address, and DNS server for your computer

- The names and addresses of other computers on your network

- How each available network interface should be used

- How to correctly route traffic so that it reaches its destination

> **NOTE** If you are connecting to an existing network, much of the information needed for this section will come from your network administrator. If you plan to deploy your own network from scratch, it is a good idea to read up on the fundamentals of TCP/IP networking and network design. One good source for this is the Linux Network Administrator's Guide, available online at http://www.linuxdoc.org/LDP/nag2.

Setting Up Names

The first step is to configure your computer's name and nameserver. This is done in the Names panel, which is displayed by default when you open the Network Configurator dialog box. Figure 28.4, shown previously, shows this default panel.

You need to provide three main pieces of information in the Names panel:

Your hostname   This is the name that you assign to your computer. This name must be unique on your network.

The domain for your network   For example, if the fully qualified domain name for your computer is linux1.Sybex.com, then the domain for that network is Sybex.com. A domain name is not required, especially for computers on a local network that do not act as Internet servers such as Web servers.

Your DNSes or nameservers   This is a list, one per line, of computers that provide domain name services to your network. Domain name services translate the names of computers on internal and external networks to the IP addresses that computers can use to communicate with each other. DNSes are typically listed by their IP addresses.

Documenting Hosts

The next step involves the host table for your machine. Click the Hosts button. The host table, which actually is kept in the file /etc/hosts, is the simplest form of name lookup. If you use /etc/hosts on your network, every computer on that network should be set up with the identical /etc/hosts file. On smaller networks, it is less trouble to keep /etc/hosts files than setting up a DNS. Even if you have a DNS for your local network, every /etc/hosts file needs two entries:

- A local host entry

- An entry with the computer's name and IP address

To add an entry to the list, click the Add button. A dialog box appears like the one in Figure 28.5.

FIGURE 28.5:

Adding a host

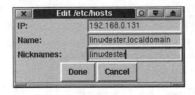

In this dialog box are three fields that you can fill in. At the very least, fill in the IP address and the complete name of the computer that you are configuring (such as linux1.mommabears.com). In the Nicknames field, you can enter alternative names for the machine separated by spaces. Frequently, system administrators place the hostname (in the case of linux1.mommabears.com, the hostname is linux1) in this field. When you are finished, click the Done button.

Editing entries in the host table is similar to adding new entries. Select an existing entry and then click the Edit button. A dialog box like that shown in Figure 28.5 appears, where you find the same three fields as when you were adding a new entry to the host table. Once you finish editing the contents of the entry, click the Done button to commit the changes to the host table. One possible result is shown in Figure 28.6.

FIGURE 28.6:

A typical host table

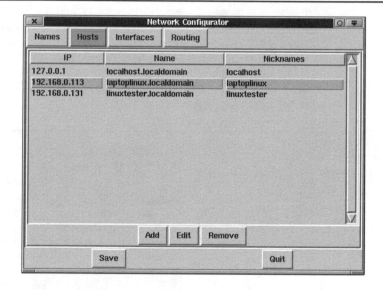

Managing Interfaces

The next panel is where you configure the network interfaces on your system. Click the Interfaces button. Interfaces can include modem-based connections, Ethernet connections through an Ethernet card, and even Token Ring connections. By default, this table should include at least one entry, called lo (this is the local loopback entry and is needed for Linux to work without a network present). Each interface is associated with an IP address.

The first step to adding a new interface (assuming yours isn't there) is to click the Add button. A dialog box appears like the one in Figure 28.7, where you can select the type of interface you are adding.

FIGURE 28.7:

The Interface Type
dialog box

In the case of a LAN, select the same type of device that you did earlier when setting up the module for your network card. This will probably be an Ethernet interface.

After you click OK, a dialog box appears, where you can configure the properties of the interface. In the case of an Ethernet interface, the dialog box looks like the one in Figure 28.8.

FIGURE 28.8:

Configuring an Ethernet
interface

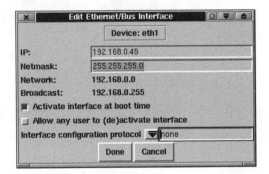

Unless your network includes a local or remote (via BOOTP) DHCP server (see the later note on the Interface Configuration Protocol), you need to provide the IP address of the interface and a netmask for the network. If you have only one network interface, then the IP address should be the same one you entered for the machine in the Names and Hosts panels. The other available options are these:

Activate Interface At Boot Time   Select this if you want the network to be enabled every time you boot your computer; if you don't select this, you will need to enable your network manually.

Allow Any User To (De)activate Interface   Normally, only the root user can activate or deactivate a network interface. Allowing any user to do so is particularly useful for dial-up interfaces where any user may want or need to dial out to establish a network connection. If you are dealing strictly with an Ethernet LAN connection and are activating the interface at boot time, then you probably won't need to enable this feature.

Interface Configuration Protocol   If your network has a local or remote (via BOOTP) DHCP server, you don't need to enter the IP address or netmask for this computer. If you don't have one of these DHCP servers, select None. Otherwise, select the type of DHCP server that matches the situation on your network.

Once you've set up the interface, click Done. In the Interfaces screen shown in Figure 28.9, you can immediately activate your interface by selecting it and then clicking the Activate button.

FIGURE 28.9:

Activating an Ethernet interface

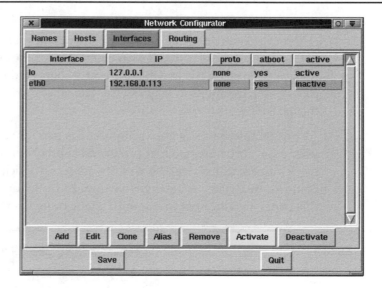

Setting Up Routes

The final piece of the network configuration puzzle is the setting of routes. Click the Routing button at the top of the window to display the Routing panel shown in Figure 28.10. The routing table is used to tell the computer how to direct data that is destined for different networks.

FIGURE 28.10:

The Routing panel

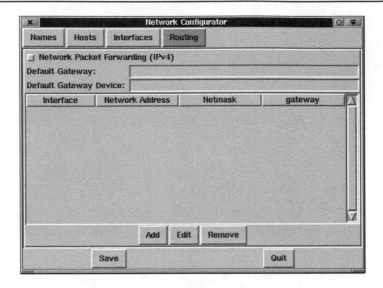

If your network has one default gateway computer, enter the IP address of the default gateway computer. If your computer has more than one network card, make sure to select the one that is directly connected to the gateway (e.g., eth0 or ppp0) as the Default Gateway Device. The other device becomes a static route to the local network.

For example, let's say your computer has two Ethernet cards, one attached to your main corporate network (eth0) and another connected to a small local network you are using to test some software (eth1). Click Add to bring up the Edit Static Route dialog box, shown in Figure 28.11. Set up the internal static route in this panel, making sure to assign the static route to eth1, and then click Done.

FIGURE 28.11:

Setting up a local static route

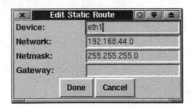

Your routing configuration includes a default gateway, at eth0, and a static route for your test network, at eth1, as shown in Figure 28.12. It is not uncommon to include a static route for the local Ethernet network you are connected to.

FIGURE 28.12:

Multiple routes

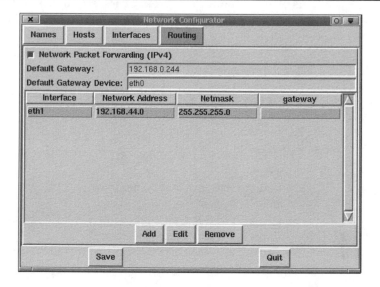

Testing the Network

The next step is to test your network connection to make sure everything is healthy. First, you need to test basic network connectivity. You can do this with the ping command, which allows you to send a query to a specific IP address to see if any machine is currently on and alive at the address. There are five basic ways to test your network with ping; you should perform these commands in order.

First, open a command window and enter the following command:

```
$ ping 127.0.0.1
```

This is the loopback address discussed earlier. If network software is properly installed, you should see a continuous stream of messages, such as these:

```
PING 127.0.0.1 (127.0.0.1) from 127.0.0.1 : 56(84) bytes of data.
64 bytes from localhost.localdomain (127.0.0.1): icmp_seq=0 ttl=255
    time=164 usec
64 bytes from localhost.localdomain (127.0.0.1): icmp_seq=1 ttl=255
    time=124 usec
64 bytes from localhost.localdomain (127.0.0.1): icmp_seq=2 ttl=255
    time=167 usec
```

This continues until you press Ctrl+C. If this doesn't work, you may need to reinstall networking, which is beyond the scope of this book.

The next command to try is

```
$ ping ipaddress
```

where *ipaddress* is the IP address for your computer. Substitute your computer's IP address in this command. The following output is based on an IP address of 192.168.4.65.

```
PING 192.168.4.65 (192.168.4.65) from 192.168.4.65 : 56(84) bytes of
    data.
64 bytes from localhost.localdomain (192.168.4.65): icmp_seq=0 ttl=255
    time=169 usec
64 bytes from localhost.localdomain (192.168.4.65): icmp_seq=1 ttl=255
    time=214 usec
64 bytes from localhost.localdomain (192.168.4.65): icmp_seq=2 ttl=255
    time=146 usec
```

Remember to press Ctrl+C. If this command works, you've successfully attached the right IP address to your network card. If it doesn't work, recheck the Interfaces section of netcfg.

Next, try the command

```
$ ping mycomputer
```

where *mycomputer* is the hostname for your computer. Substitute your actual computer's hostname in this command.

```
PING mycomputer (192.168.4.65) from 192.168.4.65 : 56(84) bytes of
data.
64 bytes from mycomputer.localdomain (192.168.4.65): icmp_seq=0 ttl=255
    time=163 usec
64 bytes from mycomputer.localdomain (192.168.4.65): icmp_seq=1 ttl=255
    time=124 usec
64 bytes from mycomputer.localdomain (192.168.4.65): icmp_seq=2 ttl=255
    time=216 usec
```

If this command works, you've successfully associated a hostname to your network card's IP address. If it doesn't work, recheck the Hosts section of netcfg or the /etc/hosts file.

Now that you know that networking on your local computer works, the next step is to check the connection to the gateway computer. For example, if the IP address of your gateway computer is 192.168.4.244, try this command:

```
$ ping 192.168.4.244
```

Substitute the actual gateway IP address for your network. If this works, the result is similar to that shown before. But you can't tell from this command whether the gateway computer actually works.

To test this, try the following ping command:

```
$ ping 63.86.158.42
```

This assumes that your gateway includes a connection to the Internet. This command pings the Sybex Web site, which has the aforementioned IP address. If this command works, the result you see is similar to what you saw before. You should also be able to ping other Internet Web sites with the same type of command.

Finally, to see if DNS is properly configured, try one last ping command:

```
$ ping www.sybex.com
```

This assumes that your gateway includes a connection to the Internet. If this command works, the result you see is similar to what you saw before, except the output uses the name and IP address of www.Sybex.com. You should also be able to ping other Internet Web sites with the same type of command.

The final step is to see if name lookups are working. To test this, you can use the nslookup command to try to look up a hostname using your default DNS server. For instance, you can try looking up www.yahoo.com:

```
$ nslookup www.yahoo.com
```

If successful, the nslookup command should produce results that look like this:

```
Server:   du1.paus.ch
Address:  194.209.60.97

Name:     www5.yahoo.com
Address:  204.71.177.70
Aliases:  www.yahoo.com
```

Notice that the name and address of the nameserver being used are displayed (you can use this to confirm that you have configured your DNS services correctly), and then the results of the name lookup are provided.

Assuming all of these steps work, then you probably have a fully functional network connection. If not, you may want to refer to the Networking-HOWTO document at http://www.linuxdoc.org/HOWTO/Networking-HOWTO.html.

Manual Network Configuration

This section describes an alternate series of steps that you can take to configure your network. These steps assume you have your Ethernet card's module loaded.

Setting Up the Interface

The first step is to activate the network interface you want to use. If you are trying to activate eth0 as IP address 100.100.100.10, then you can use the ifconfig command to activate the interface:

```
$ ifconfig eth0 100.100.100.10 netmask 255.255.255.0 up
```

This command tells the system to assign the IP address 100.100.100.10 and the netmask 255.255.255.0 to the eth0 interface, and then it activates the interface with the up argument.

To test whether the interface has been successfully activated, you can use the /sbin/ifconfig command discussed earlier to see a list of enabled interfaces like the one that follows:

```
eth0      Link encap: Ethernet  HWaddr 00:C0:F0:0D:76:5A
          inet addr:100.100.100.10  Bcast:100.100.100.255
          ➡Mask:255.255.255.0
          UP BROADCAST RUNNING MULTICAST  MTU:1500  Metric:1
          RX packets:11239889 errors:0 dropped:0 overruns:0
          TX packets:16384520 errors:3 dropped:0 overruns:0
          Interrupt:9 Base address:0x300

lo        Link encap:Local Loopback
          inet addr:127.0.0.1  Mask:255.0.0.0
          UP LOOPBACK RUNNING  MTU:3584  Metric:1
          RX packets:2142848 errors:0 dropped:0 overruns:0
          TX packets:2142848 errors:0 dropped:0 overruns:0
          collisions:0 txqueuelen:0
```

This list generally contains at least a loopback device (device lo) plus any network devices you have enabled. In this case, you are looking for the eth0 interface. Red Hat sets things up to configure a loopback device at boot time. To keep your system running happily, make sure you have a local loopback device configured. If lo is not set up on your system, you can configure and activate it with the following ifconfig command:

```
$ ifconfig lo 127.0.0.1 up
```

Setting Up a Nameserver (DNS)

The next step is to set up your nameserver, also known as a DNS server. In order to do this, you need to edit the file /etc/resolv.conf using your favorite text editor. This file tells the system everything it needs to know to go out and find the address for hostnames.

Generally, you want at least two lines in your resolv.conf file, such as

```
domain landegg.edu
nameserver 194.148.43.194
```

The domain line specifies the domain name of the local system. If your machine is being placed on a network whose domain is foo.bar, then this line should read domain foo.bar. The second line specifies the IP address of the primary nameserver that you will be using. This may be a machine on your local network, a server running at your Internet service provider (ISP), or a public nameserver on the Internet. Your network administrator can provide you with this information.

Many sites use multiple nameservers for redundancy. If one is down or not available for some reason, users should still be able to look up names using the alternate servers. You can specify multiple servers by including multiple nameserver lines in resolv.conf:

```
search landegg.edu
nameserver 194.148.43.194
nameserver 194.148.43.196
nameserver 194.148.8.10
nameserver 194.148.1.10
```

In a situation like this, the first listed server will be the first one tried when looking up a name. If this attempt fails, Linux moves on to the second machine on the list and so on. If all listed nameservers fail to respond to the query, then Linux gives up and the attempted name lookup fails.

Setting Up a Local Hosts File

While it is theoretically possible to use a DNS server to look up every name, including those of hosts on the local network, this is hugely inefficient. As an alternative to using a DNS server to look up the names of machines on moderately sized networks, you can use a local hosts file to perform these lookups.

A local hosts file sits on your system and contains a list that matches IP addresses with hostnames. To enable a local hosts file, you first need to edit the file /etc/host .conf with your favorite text editor. This file tells Linux how to go about looking up names and needs to contain the following two lines to enable a local hosts file:

```
order hosts,bind
multi on
```

The first line says that when a name is being looked up, first check the local hosts file (hosts) and then check the DNS (bind stands for the Linux daemon that runs DNS, the Berkeley Internet Name Daemon) by following the instructions in /etc/ resolv.conf.

Next, you need to create the local hosts file, which is called /etc/hosts. Edit this file with your favorite text editor and create a one-line entry for each host being listed. The entry should take the following form:

```
IP_Address hostname alias alias alias ...
```

Each section of the line (IP address, hostname, and alias) can be separated by one or more spaces. Comment lines begin with a hash mark (#) and can be used to structure and explain the entries in larger hosts files.

Let's consider an example. The following four entries are taken from a hosts file:

```
194.148.43.194      serv1.landegg.edu
194.148.43.195      apps.landegg.edu        apps
194.148.43.196      serv3.landegg.edu       serv3       www.landegg.edu
194.148.43.215      office15.landegg.edu    office15
```

Notice that all lines start with the IP address and then provide a hostname and any aliases for the host. Aliases are not required. In addition, notice that for many machines, the aliases include a short form of the hostname without the complete domain name. This is done so that you can access machines on the local network without having to type the complete hostname with domain name. In this example, apps.landegg.edu can be accessed locally as apps, and office15.landegg.edu as office15.

Setting Up Routes

The final step is to set up the necessary routes that allow you to talk to the network and the rest of the world. Basically, for each interface you need a routing entry that tells Linux what network is connected on that interface. In addition, you need an entry specifying a default gateway if your network is connected through a gateway to other non-local networks.

Let's start with the loopback device. Use the route command to specify that the local machine is accessed through the loopback device:

```
$ /sbin/route add -host 127.0.0.1 lo
```

This command says that the host 127.0.0.1 (the local host) should be accessed through the device lo.

Next, let's consider our eth0 device from earlier in this section. This device connects the PC to a network with the network address 100.100.100.0 and a netmask of 255.255.255.0. Use the route command again to tell Linux to send all information for the local network out on the eth0 interface:

```
$ /sbin/route add -net 100.100.100.0 netmask 255.255.255.0 eth0
```

Finally, use the route command once more to specify the default gateway that can be used to access remote networks. If your default gateway is at the IP address 100.100.100.1, use the following command:

```
$ /sbin/route add default gw 100.100.100.1 eth0
```

This indicates that the default gateway (gw) is at the address 100.100.100.1 and can be accessed by sending information destined for the gateway out through the eth0 interface.

Finally, check all your routing entries by using the route command with no parameters or arguments. This should return a routing table like this:

```
Kernel IP routing table
Destination     Gateway         Genmask         Flags Metric Ref Use Iface
100.100.100.0   *               255.255.255.0   U     0      0   317 eth0
127.0.0.1       *               255.0.0.0       U     0      0     6 lo
default         100.100.100.1   0               UG    0      0  2605 eth0
```

Automating Network Configuration at Boot Time

By now, you should have a fully functional network connection. However, it would be laborious to have to type all of those commands each time you start your Linux system.

Luckily, you can place all the needed ifconfig and route commands into one of the system's start-up scripts, such as /etc/rc.d/rc.local. In the case of the examples used here, you could add the following lines to your rc.local file using a text editor:

```
/sbin/ifconfig eth0 100.100.100.10 netmask 255.255.255.0 up
/sbin/ifconfig lo 127.0.0.1 up
/sbin/route add -host 127.0.0.1 lo
/sbin/route add -net 100.100.100.0 netmask 255.255.255.0 eth0
/sbin/route add default gw 100.100.100.1 eth0
```

Sharing Files on a Linux/Unix Network

Now that you have your Linux system talking with other machines on a local TCP/IP network, let's look at one of the most basic networking tasks: sharing files. In the Unix and Linux world, this is generally done using NFS, the Network File System.

Sharing takes place in two directions:

From other computers   Accessing shared directories and files from other hosts on the network

To other computers   Sharing files and directories from your PC on the local network

Sharing Directories on the Network

Before you can access a directory on a network, you need to share it. Exporting directories with NFS requires the use of two daemons, /usr/sbin/rpc.nfsd and /usr/sbin/rpc.mountd, plus one configuration file, /etc/exports. The files rpc.mountd and rpc.nfsd should be installed on most systems. If they're not on your system, you can install them from the enclosed Red Hat Linux 7.1 CD-ROM from the RPM file nfs-utils-0.3.1-5.i386.rpm.

NFS and Firewalls

If you installed the default firewall when you installed Red Hat Linux 7.1, it will prevent you from sharing directories through NFS. If your computer is inside a local area network and has no other connections to other networks, you can disable the firewall on the local computer. The only firewall you really need is on a computer that's also connected to an outside network (aka, your gateway computer).

You can disable most Linux firewalls with either the `/etc/rc.d/init.d/ipchains stop` or the `/etc/rc.d/init.d/iptables stop` command. But that disables the firewall only until you reboot. You can disable firewalls in the future through the **ntsysv** menu. Run the `/usr/sbin/ntsysv` command. When the Services menu appears, deselect the ipchains and iptables services shown in the following graphic.

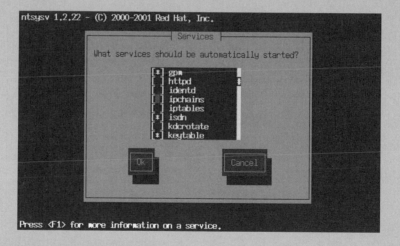

If the directories that you want to share are on your gateway computer, connected to your network and the Internet, you need a firewall. Even with a firewall, you probably shouldn't use NFS for security reasons. But if you still need to use NFS to share directories from that gateway computer, use the firewall configuration utility discussed in Chapter 31, "Security and Red Hat Linux 7.1 As an Inexpensive Router," to open up ports 111 and 2049. This opens up the channels of communication needed by the Network File System.

Then you can start sharing a directory on the network by editing /etc/exports using a text editor. Add one entry for each directory being shared. The entries take the form

```
/directory host (options)
```

In other words, when you share a directory, you share it not with specific users, but with specific computers. The following is a sample /etc/exports file from the man page for /etc/exports:

```
# sample /etc/exports file
/               master(rw) trusty(rw,no_root_squash)
/projects       proj*.local.domain(rw)
/usr            *.local.domain(ro)
/home/joe       pc001(rw,all_squash,anonuid=150,anongid=100)
/pub            (ro,insecure,all_squash)
/pub/private    (noaccess)
```

Let's break down this file line by line:

Line 1   This is a comment line, as indicated by a hash mark (#), and is ignored.

Line 2   Two computers (master, trusty) are being given different levels of access to the / directory: master with read and write permission (the rw option), and trusty with read and write permission enabled and permission for the root user to have full access to all the files and subdirectories being exported (the no_root_squash option). In other words, a root user on trusty has the same permissions as root on the local system.

Line 3   Any host whose name starts with proj and is part of the domain local.domain is given read and write access to the directory /projects.

Line 4   Any host in the domain local.domain has read-only (the ro option) access to /usr.

Line 5   The host pc001 is being given read and write access to the directory /home/joe. All users accessing this mount from pc001 are treated as the anonymous user (the all_squash option), and the anonymous user is considered to have a user ID of 150 and group ID of 150 (the anonuid=150 and anongid=150 options).

Line 6   The directory /pub is being made available to all hosts with access to the exporting system. Access is granted on a read-only basis, with all users treated as anonymous users. The insecure option allows clients that don't use a reserved TCP/IP port for NFS to access the mount.

Line 7   Access is denied (the noaccess option) to all hosts for the directory /pub/private.

Other options for the /etc/exports file can be found in the exports man page, which is accessed with the command

```
$ man exports
```

Once you have specified your exported directories in /etc/exports, you need to restart the rpc.nfsd and rpc.mountd processes (which usually run at boot time). First, use ps to check the process IDs of the two processes:

```
$ ps aux | grep rpc.nfsd
root 1103  0.2  0.8  872  508  ?  S  22:25  0:00 /usr/sbin/rpc.nfsd
$ ps aux | grep rpc.mountd
root 1105  0  0.7  836  500  ?  S  22:25  0:00 /usr/sbin/rpc.mountd
```

Next, kill and restart the processes:

```
$ kill 1103 1105; /usr/sbin/rpc.nfsd; /usr/sbin/rpc.mountd
```

WARNING   Run the ps aux commands shown above for yourself. The numbers that you see in the output from the ps aux commands shown above will probably be different from 1103 and 1105. Substitute accordingly.

Your new exports are made available on the network for remote users to access.

TIP   In several Linux distributions, to restart rpc.nfsd and rpc.mountd, you just need to restart the nfs daemon. For example, in Red Hat Linux 7.1, run the /etc/rc.d/init.d/nfs restart command as the root user.

Accessing Remote File Systems

Accessing remote files and directories is done using the mount command. The command takes the form

```
$ mount remote-directory-name local-directory
```

where the remote directory is specified with the form *hostname:/directory-name*, and the local directory is an existing directory, preferably empty, that becomes the location through which the remote directory is accessed.

Let's consider an example. Suppose you want to access the directory /test/dir on the machine foo.bar on your local network; the directory has been made available for remote mounting via NFS. You have an empty directory called /foo on your machine, which will be the mount point for the remote directory.

To assign this directory, you use the mount command:

```
$ mount foo.bar:/test/dir /foo
```

This command says to mount the directory /test/dir on machine foo.bar to the local directory /foo. Once this is done, you have access to the files and subdirectories in the remote directory on the basis of the file permissions assigned to the files. Listing the contents of /foo actually lists the contents of /test/dir on foo.bar.

WARNING There is one caveat to the NFS system. On your local system, the root user has godlike power to open, read, or erase a file anywhere on the system regardless of who created or owns the file. But in a remotely mounted directory, root has severe restrictions under the NFS model: It can access only files and directories for which explicit permission has been granted.

Mounting Remote Directories at Boot Time

If there are remote directories that you frequently use, you probably want them to mount automatically at boot time. To do this, you can use Linuxconf. Start Linuxconf with the linuxconf-auth command. Under the Config tab, select File Systems ➢ Access NFS Volume from the list of configuration screens. This screen contains a list of any current NFS mounts. Click the Add button to display the NFS Volume Specification screen shown in Figure 28.13.

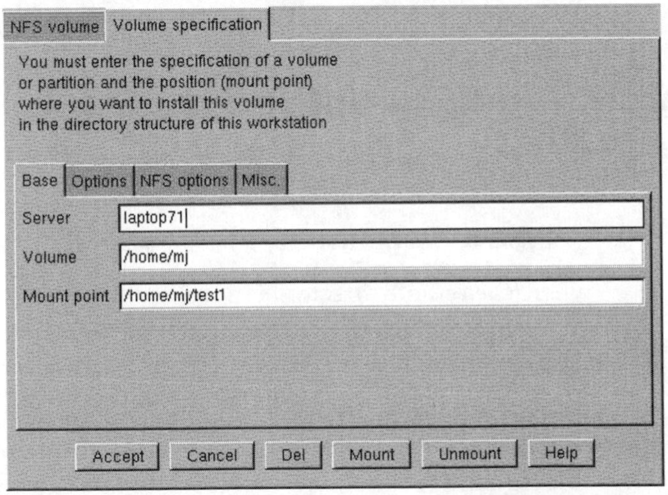

FIGURE 28.13:

The NFS Volume Specification screen

To use the remote mount example used above, enter **laptop71** for Server, **/home/mj** for Volume, and **/home/mj/test1** for Mount Point. If you want the mount to occur automatically at boot time, select the Options tab and make sure the Not Mount At Boot Time option is not selected. Finally, click the Accept button to complete configuration of the automatic mount.

This procedure adds an entry to the /etc/fstab file similar to the following:

```
linux71:/home/mj      /home/mj/test      nfs      exec,dev,ro      1 1
```

If you want to manually create an automatic mount to mount at boot time, you can add a similar entry to /etc/fstab on your system using a text editor.

Basic Network Security

While it is great to be able to connect to a network and access all of its resources, this does present a security risk. Luckily, Linux provides a basic mechanism that gives some control over which machines on the network can actually attempt to connect to services on your Linux system.

The basic security mechanism consists of two files: /etc/hosts.allow and /etc/hosts.deny. Together, these files are part of a three-part basic security chain:

1.   Allow access to any daemon-client combination in hosts.allow.

2.   Deny access to any daemon-client combination in hosts.deny.

3.   Grant access to everyone else.

By default, there are no entries in hosts.allow or hosts.deny, so the default is option 3: Anyone can attempt to connect to the system. Although you can still set up individual services such as Telnet and FTP to require further authentication, this doesn't prevent those initial probing attempts to connect that can be the start of many hackers' joyrides through unknown systems.

Creating entries for hosts.allow and hosts.deny is straightforward:

```
Daemon_List: Client_List
```

Any entry like this specifies which network daemons (e.g., ftpd, in.telnetd, in.rshd) should allow connections from which hosts (hosts.allow) or deny connections from which hosts (hosts.deny). Any network daemon can be listed. For instance, the entry

```
ftp: host1
```

in the file `hosts.allow` allows incoming FTP connections from the specified host, `host1`.

A few special keywords help make things easy, preventing the necessity of listing all daemons and clients individually. The `ALL` keyword can match any client or any daemon. For instance, the entry

```
ALL: ALL
```

in `hosts.allow` allows any type of access from any client, while the same entry in `hosts.deny` stops all access.

The `EXCEPT` keyword allows exceptions in a network that is otherwise thrown wide open by `ALL`. For instance, the entry

```
ALL EXCEPT ftpd: ALL
```

in `hosts.deny` denies access to all clients accessing any services except FTP services. Similarly,

```
ALL: .local.domain EXCEPT foo.local.domain
```

in `hosts.allow` allows access to all services to any machine in the domain `local.domain` (note the necessary "." in front of `local.domain`) except `foo.local.domain`.

Finally, the `LOCAL` keyword makes it easy to provide access to all machines in the local domain:

```
ALL: LOCAL
```

in `hosts.allow` allows any type of access from machines in the local domain.

The `hosts.allow` and `hosts.deny` files can take a very rich set of entries that provide more finely grained control than most users need. This is detailed in the man page for `hosts.allow`:

```
$ man hosts.allow
```

Looking Ahead

In this chapter, you learned the basics of connecting a Linux PC to an Ethernet network using TCP/IP. This allows Linux to communicate easily with other Unix systems on the network, including other Linux systems.

However, fully integrating your Linux system with Windows and Novell networks requires more work. In Chapter 29, "Integrating Red Hat Linux 7.1 in Windows and Novell Networks," you will take a look at the basics of integrating your Linux system with Windows and Novell.

CHAPTER

TWENTY-NINE

Integrating Red Hat Linux 7.1 in Windows and Novell Networks

- ■ Sharing Linux Files and Printers with Windows Networks

- ■ Accessing Windows Network Files and Printers from Linux Systems

- ■ Connecting Linux to a Novell Network

This chapter examines the capabilities of Linux that make it an attractive addition to many existing internal networks.

If your organization is running a standard Windows network, Linux is able to step in and play the role of an effective, efficient, and powerful file and print server. With a price-point far lower than Windows NT/2000 and stability that exceeds that of Windows 95/98/Me, Linux may be the ideal file and print server for budget-conscious offices that need to share files between Windows desktops on a network.

Working from the other direction, Linux can also access files on Windows file servers as if they are local hard disks on the Linux system. This serves any number of purposes. For instance, suppose you run a Linux-based Web server but your Web developer performs development on a Windows system. The Linux Web server could automatically connect to a pre-specified directory on the Windows development system and copy new files onto the Web server, preventing any need to manually update the Web server's content.

Next, this chapter looks at the integration of a Linux system into a Novell network. These tools are not as well developed and robust as those available for integration with Windows networks, but this chapter will discuss the Novell options and point you to sources of information on the subject.

Sharing Linux Files and Printers with Windows Networks

The most common method of Linux-Windows network integration is to make a Linux system act as a file and print server to Windows clients on the network. This is achieved through the use of Samba. Samba is a collection of software that makes Linux capable of the SMB (Server Message Block) protocol that is the basis of Windows network file and print sharing. Possible clients for a Linux-based SMB server include LAN Manager, Windows 95/98/Me, Windows NT/2000, OS/2, and other Linux systems.

Installing Samba

The full Samba package does not come with the CD for Red Hat Linux 7.1 that comes with this book. However, if you have the two-CD set, you may already have installed Samba when you installed Linux. You can check this using the `rpm` command:

```
$ rpm -q samba
$ rpm -q samba-client
$ rpm -q samba-common
```

If you find that Samba is not installed, you can install it from the appropriate Red Hat CD-ROM by mounting the CD-ROM to a logical location (such as /mnt/cdrom) and then using rpm to install the three Samba packages:

```
# rpm -i /mnt/cdrom/RedHat/RPMS/samba-2.0.7-36.i386.rpm
# rpm -i /mnt/cdrom/RedHat/RPMS/samba-client-2.0.7-36.i386.rpm
# rpm -i /mnt/cdrom/RedHat/RPMS/samba-common-2.0.7-36.i386.rpm
```

NOTE   Only the `samba-client` and `samba-common` packages are included on the Publisher's Edition CD-ROM that comes with this book. While this is enough to connect to shared resources from Microsoft Windows computers on a Local Area Network (see the `smbmount` command in a later section), it is not enough to share resources from your Linux computer with other Microsoft Windows computers on that same network.

Installing Samba from the Internet

If you want the latest version of Samba available, you can download the latest Samba source code or RPM. Follow the directions at the Samba Web site, `http://www.samba.org`, for finding the closest mirror site. In the U.S., one of the mirrors is located at `http://us1.samba.org/samba/ftp/`.

Once you download the required files, you need to extract the compressed archives and read the documentation for instructions about how to compile and install Samba from the source code. Because these procedures can change from version to version, they aren't included here.

Alternatively, if you are wary of compiling from the source code and don't have the two-CD set for Red Hat 7.1, the easiest approach is to download the RPM files from a source such as `ftp.redhat.com` or `www.rpmfind.net` and then install them with the appropriate rpm -i command.

What Gets Installed

When you install Samba, several files are installed, including the following:

/usr/sbin/smbd   The Samba server that handles connections from clients

/usr/sbin/nmbd   The NetBIOS server that allows clients to locate servers on a Windows network

/usr/bin/smbclient   A basic Samba client for accessing SMB servers

/etc/samba/smb.conf   The Samba configuration file

Configuring Samba

The entire Samba configuration is now contained in the file /etc/samba/smb .conf. The smb.conf file consists of multiple entries that contain a header followed by multiple parameters. For instance, the following entry shares the /tmp directory on the network:

```
[tmp]
    comment = Temporary file space
    path = /tmp
    read only = no
    public = yes
```

Notice that the header is contained in square brackets ([tmp]), that each parameter is on a separate line, and that the structure of parameters is *parameter = value*.

The *[global]* Section

Most smb.conf files start with a [global] section that defines some essential parameters that affect the overall behavior of Samba. Common parameters in the [global] section include these:

printing   Specifies the type of print system being used; unless you have an older distribution of Linux, this should be lprng.

printcap name   Specifies the location of the printcap file; generally, this is /etc/printcap.

load printers   Should be set to yes if you will be sharing printers.

guest account   Indicates which Linux user to use for attempted guest connections; most Linux administrators will make this nobody because of its extremely limited privileges.

workgroup   Indicates the Windows workgroup or domain to which the Samba server belongs.

security   Specifies how to authenticate users for access to system resources. There are four options: user, server, domain, and share.

user   Samba checks usernames and passwords from the local /etc/passwd file. This is the most common and easiest option available.

server   Samba authenticates from a Windows NT/2000 domain server specified by the `password server` parameter. Another Samba server can be set up to emulate a Windows NT/2000 domain server.

domain   Requires adding the NetBIOS name of the Samba server to the appropriate Windows domain controller. The NetBIOS name is typically the same as the hostname, if less than 15 characters.

share   For setting up Linux as part of a peer-to-peer network, characteristic of a Microsoft Windows-style workgroup. The NetBIOS name is typically the same as the hostname, if less than 15 characters.

Consider the following [global] section in the smb.conf file in a typical server:

```
[global]
    printing = lprng
    printcap name = /etc/printcap
    load printers = yes
    guest account = nobody
    workgroup = testgroup
    security = user
```

This section specifies the type of printing system, sets up the guest account to use the Linux user nobody, makes the server part of the testgroup Windows workgroup, and specifies that Samba should use the local /etc/passwd file for authentication.

The *[homes]* Section

The [homes] section is used to specify how to share users' home directories to the Windows network. Without this section, users' home directories need to be shared individually, as you will see later.

Consider the following [homes] section from an smb.conf file:

```
[homes]
    comment = Home Directories
    browseable = no
    read only = no
    preserve case = yes
    short preserve case = yes
    create mode = 0750
```

The comment parameter provides additional information about the section but doesn't affect its operation. The browseable parameter is used to indicate whether other users can browse the directory; setting it to no limits access to those users with permission. The read only parameter is set to no so that users can both read and write files in their home directories. The preserve case and short preserve case parameters ensure that case-insensitive Windows systems do not change the case of letters in filenames, because Linux is case-sensitive. Finally, the create mode parameter specifies what permission to give to files created by users connected through Samba; in this example, 0750 indicates that the files should be readable, writable, and executable by the owner, readable and executable by users in the same group as the owner, and off-limits to everyone else.

In order for a user to access their home directory from a Windows system, they must use their username for the share name. For instance, for the user username to access their home directory on smbserv, they would access the share \\smbserv \username.

The *[printers]* Section

As the [homes] section was used to share all users' home directories, the [printers] section is used to share all Linux printers to the Windows network.

Table 29.1 outlines common parameters in the [printers] section.

TABLE 29.1: Common *[printers]* Section Parameters

Parameter	Description
comment	Provides information about the section but does not affect its operation.
path	Specifies the spool path; you may want to create your own spool directory for Samba and point there. (For instance, Red Hat Linux creates /var/spool /samba and points there.)
browseable	As with the home directories, setting this parameter to **no** ensures that only users with permission can browse the printers.
printable	This should be set to **yes**, otherwise printing won't work. (How does one print to a non-printable printer?)
public	If set to **yes**, then the guest account can print; on many networks, it is wise to set this parameter to **no** to prevent excessive printing by guest users.
writable	Printers are not writable, so this parameter should be set to **no**.
create mode	This parameter specifies the permissions on spool files created during printing; this is often set to **0700**.

Put together, these parameters can be used to produce a fairly common [printers] section like the default Red Hat Linux one shown in the following example:

```
[printers]
    comment = All Printers
    path = /var/spool/samba
    browseable = no
    printable = yes
    public = no
    writable = no
    create mode = 0700
```

Accessing Linux printers from Windows works the same way as with directories. The share name is the Linux printer name in the printcap file. For instance, to access the printer printername on smbserv, Windows users should access \\smbserv\printername.

Sharing a Directory for Public Access

Sometimes it is necessary to create a publicly accessible directory that is accessible by all users and is read-only. The directory can be set up to share information centrally in a way that prevents users from altering the information.

Consider the following entry:

```
[public]
    path = /public/directory
    public = yes
    read only = yes
    printable = no
```

This entry creates a share named public that is accessible by all users (hence, public = yes) but is read-only (hence, read only = yes).

Consider another example: sharing /tmp as a publicly accessible temporary directory that can be read and written to by all users. This can be achieved with the following entry:

```
[tmp]
    path = /tmp
    read only = no
    public = yes
```

Sharing a Directory for Private Access

In addition to sharing directories for public access, it is sometimes necessary to create shared directories accessible by a limited number of users.

Consider a situation where you want to share the directory /private/directory as the share named private. Suppose, as well, that this directory is to be accessible by only three users: user1, user2, and user3. This could be achieved with an entry similar to the following:

```
[private]
    path = /private/directory
    valid users = user1 user2 user3
    public = no
    writable = yes
    printable = no
    create mask = 0765
```

Notice the use of a new parameter: valid users. This parameter takes as its value a list of users with permission to access the resource, with spaces separating the usernames.

Note, as well, that public is set to no to prevent unwanted prying eyes and writable is set to yes so that it is a fully writable resource.

Putting It All Together

Now, let's put this all together into a complete smb.conf file. There are two things to note here:

- Blank lines are ignored.

- Comment lines start with a semicolon or a hash mark (#) and continue to the end of the line.

Our completed file looks like this:

```
; Sample smb.conf

; Global Settings
[global]
    printing = bsd
    printcap name = /etc/printcap
    load printers = yes
; The guest user is nobody
```

```
    guest account = nobody
    workgroup = testgroup
    security = user

; Export All Home Directories to the Network
[homes]
    comment = Home Directories
    browseable = no
    read only = no
    preserve case = yes
    short preserve case = yes
    create mode = 0750

; Make All Printers Accessible on the Network
[printers]
    comment = All Printers
    path = /var/spool/samba
    browseable = no
    printable = yes
    public = no
    writable = no
    create mode = 0700

; Create Public read-only Directory
[public]
    path = /public/directory
    public = yes
    read only = yes
    printable = no

; Provide a Public Temporary Directory
[temp]
    path = /tmp
    read only = no
    public = yes

; Export a Private Workspace for user1, user2 and user3
[private]
    path = /private/directory
    valid users = user1 user2 user3
    public = no
    writable = yes
```

```
printable = no
create mask = 0765
```

Running Samba

If your network is running on TCP/IP, configuration is complete and you are ready to run Samba. However, if you have a NetBIOS network, you need to perform one more step. In the file /etc/services, look for the following lines (and if they aren't there, add them):

```
netbios-ns      137/tcp              # NETBIOS Name Service
netbios-ns      137/udp
netbios-dgm     138/tcp              # NETBIOS Datagram Service
netbios-dgm     138/udp
netbios-ssn     139/tcp              # NETBIOS session service
netbios-ssn     139/udp
```

Now that you have Samba configured, it is time to run the software. By default, the Red Hat Linux version of Samba is installed to start at boot time so that it is always available. In addition, the system script /etc/rc.d/init.d/smb can be used to manually start and stop Samba.

For example, you can start Samba with the command

```
# /etc/rc.d/init.d/smb start
```

and stop it with the command

```
# /etc/rc.d/init.d/smb stop
```

or start and stop both smbd and nmbd simultaneously with the command

```
# /etc/rc.d/init.d/smb restart
```

The following two commands can be used on the command line by the root user to manually start Samba:

```
/usr/sbin/smbd -D
/usr/sbin/nmbd -D
```

Accessing Windows Network Files and Printers from Linux Systems

The flip side of this procedure is for Linux to be able to access SMB shared files and printers. There are several ways in which this can be achieved. The simplest way involves use of two client programs that come with the Samba installation: smbclient and smbprint.

While this approach works, it is somewhat limited, particularly for file access. Smbclient provides an FTP-like way in which to access a remote share. Of course, this doesn't allow use of regular Linux/Unix commands such as cp and mv to manipulate files and thus prevents access to shares from other applications (unlike NFS-mounted remote file systems, which appear as local file systems to Linux applications).

This problem is effectively addressed using an alternative method: the smbfs package, which allows SMB shared file systems to be mounted on Linux, as NFS file systems and local file systems are.

Using *smbclient*

The smbclient program is normally installed in /usr/bin. The program can be used to move files to and from shared resources on an SMB server using an FTP-like interface.

The first step to using smbclient is to establish a connection to a resource on the SMB server. In its simplest form, the command looks like this:

```
$ smbclient //server/resourcename
```

Of course, things are rarely that simple. If you need to provide a password, for instance, to access a protected resource, your command gets somewhat more complicated:

```
$ smbclient //server/resourcename password
```

In addition to this, there are several flags that alter the way in which smbclient connects to the server. The major flags are outlined in Table 29.2.

TABLE 29.2: Common *smbclient* Flags

Flag	Effect
-L *host*	This flag displays a list of resources available on a server specified by host; when using this flag, a resource does not need to be specified.
-I *IP_address*	This flag is useful when you have the IP address but not the hostname for the named server; it forces smbclient to assume that the computer is at the specified IP address.
-N	This flag suppresses the password prompt. It is especially useful when a resource doesn't require a password; if this flag is not specified when a password is not required, the user is still prompted for a password and must press Enter to supply a null (blank) password.
-U *username*	Using this flag, you can specify the username to use to connect to a resource. Without this flag, the server uses the content of the USER or LOGNAME environment variable; if these are empty, no username is provided to the server. You can send a password along to the server by putting a percent sign (%) after the username and following it by the password: -U *username%password*.
-W *workgroup*	This flag specifies which workgroup is to be used when connecting to the server.
-T *tar options*	This flag allows you to move data into or out of a tar file on the local Linux system. For instance, -Tx backup.tar restores files from backup.tar to the remote share, while -Tc backup.tar creates a tar file called backup.tar that contains all files and directories in the remote share.

By way of example, let's build an smbclient command based on this information:

```
$ smbclient //server/resourcename -U username%password -W workgroup
```

This command attempts to connect to resourcename on server in the workgroup named workgroup, with the user username using the password password.

Available Operations for File Resources

Once a computer is connected to a file resource, there are a number of commands available for moving data back and forth. These are outlined in Table 29.3.

TABLE 29.3: File Operation Commands

Operation	Description
cd *directory*	Changes to another directory on the SMB shared resource.
del *file*	Deletes the specified file on the server. (You can also use the **rm** command).
dir	Displays the current directory listing from the server. (You can also use the **ls** command).
get *file*	Gets the specified file from the remote server and saves it with the same name in the current directory on the local system; optionally, you can specify a different name for the file on the local system: get *file localfilename*.
lcd *directory*	Changes to the specified directory on the local system.
mget *filemask*	Gets all files on the remote server matching the specified filemask.
mkdir *directory*	Makes the specified directory on the remote server. (You can also use the **md** command).
mput *filemask*	Puts all files in the local directory matching the specified filemask into the current directory on the remote server.
prompt	Toggles prompting on and off for multiple file operations (**mput** and **mget**). When on, users are prompted for each file copied.
put *file*	Copies the specified file in the current local directory to the current directory on the remote server and keeps the name of the file the same; the name of the file on the remote server can also be changed: put *file remotefilename*.
quit	Exits **smbclient**. (You can also use the **exit** command.)
recurse	Toggles directory recursion on and off for multiple file operations (**mput** and **mget**). When on, the commands search through all directories under the current directory when copying files.
rmdir *directory*	Removes the specified directory from the remote server. (You can also use the **rd** command).

Let's look at some examples:

- To change the local directory to the subdirectory foo, use the command lcd foo.

- To change the remote directory to the directory ../foo, use the command cd ../foo.

- To copy the file foo in the local directory to the remote share and give the copy the name newfoo, use the command put foo newfoo.

- To get all files ending in .txt from the remote share's current directory, use the command mget *.txt.

- To create a new directory on the remote share called foo, use the command mkdir foo.

Available Operations for Printer Resources

When you use smbclient to connect to a printer resource, the following commands are available for working with the printer:

print file   Prints the specified file using the current resource based on the mode specified by printmode.

printmode option   Sets the printer mode based on the specified option; possible options are graphics or text, where graphics mode indicates any binary data.

queue   Displays the current status of the remote print queue.

quit (or *exit*)   Exits smbclient.

Of course, this is a little cumbersome. If someone wants to print a text file, they can't simply print it from the application they used to create it the way they might normally do with a Unix print queue. Instead, they need to connect to the printer with smbclient and then issue the command printmode text, followed by print filename. Printing more complicated print formats gets even more difficult.

For instance, what if the remote printer is a PCL printer and the software being used generates only PostScript output (as is often the case in the Unix world)? In that case, the user needs to print to a file, pass this file through gs to convert it to PCL, connect the printer with smbclient, set the print mode, and then print the file. This is a lot of work.

Luckily, smbprint helps to solve this problem.

Using *smbprint*

The smbprint script is a tool that makes it possible to print using smbclient via a standard Linux/Unix print queue; smbprint makes printing to remote SMB printer resources virtually seamless for users.

With most Samba installations, you will find the script at /usr/bin/smbprint.

In order to use this script, you need to create a printcap entry for the remote printer and create a configuration file that indicates where the printer is.

First, let's look at the printcap entry:

```
queuename:\
        :sd=/var/spool/samba:\
        :af=/var/spool/samba/accountingfile:\
        :if=/usr/bin/smbprint:\
        :mx=0:\
        :lp=/dev/null:
```

Let's look at the important entries here:

sd=/var/spool/samba   Specifies the spool directory.

af=/var/spool/samba/accountingfile   Specifies the accounting file. This file should be in the same directory as the configuration file, probably in your spool directory.

if=/usr/bin/smbprint   Specifies that the input filter should be smbprint.

lp=/dev/null   Indicates that the printer is not physically connected to the machine where the printcap file exists.

Next, you need to create a configuration file called .config in the same directory as your accounting file. This file contains three entries and looks like this:

```
server=SERVERNAME
service=PRINTERNAME
password="password"
```

Substitute the name of the computer to which the printer is attached for *SERVERNAME* and the name of the printer for *PRINTERNAME*. Once this is done, most files should be printable using the lpr command:

```
$ lpr -P queuename filename
```

Because this is the way that applications like Netscape 6 handle printing, this configuration will work for many printers and applications.

Using *smbfs*

The smbfs package allows the direct mounting of SMB shares to Linux in the same way that NFS volumes are mounted by Linux. Usage of smbfs is fairly straightforward once it is installed. If you are using Red Hat Linux 7.1, then smbfs should be installed when you install the samba-2.0.7-36.i386.rpm package.

Using *smbmount*

At the core of the smbfs system is the smbmount program. The smbmount program is the tool you use to mount SMB shares to your Linux system.

At its most basic, smbmount takes the form

```
# smbmount //servername/resourcename mountpoint
```

As with the mount command, the mount point must be an existing directory (which should be empty) on your system. Forward slashes are used instead of back slashes in the specification of SMB shares to avoid problems using back slashes in some shells.

WARNING   There is one caveat here: smbmount doesn't use NetBIOS to look up the server name. Therefore, if the SMB server name is different than the TCP/IP hostname for the server, things won't work. In this situation, use the Linux/Unix hostname for the server in question.

Complete documentation for the smbmount command is in the smbmount man page (man smbmount).

Connecting Linux to a Novell Network

The world of NetWare-Linux integration is far less robust than Windows-Linux integration. For that reason, this section will discuss only the available options without going into the details of implementation.

NOTE   In the realm of freely available software, a fairly limited Novell NetWare client package called ncpfs is available, as is a still-beta NetWare server product called mars_nwe. Both of these products are limited as to the versions of NetWare they support and the types of NetWare products they can interact with. Both are included with Red Hat Linux 7.1. You may also need to install IPX on your computer. The IPX utilities package is available on the Red Hat Linux 7.1 CD-ROM that comes with this book, in the /RedHat/RPMS subdirectory, in ipxutils-2.2.0.18-3.i386.rpm.

Together, `ncpfs` and `mars_nwe` provide the closest thing to a complete free Linux NetWare solution. The `ncpfs` package is available from `ftp.gwdg.de/pub/linux/misc/ncpfs` and the `mars_nwe` package is available from `http://www.compu-art.de/download/mars_nwe.html`. While most of the documentation, especially for `mars_nwe`, is in German, good instructions are also available in the IPX-HOWTO, available online at `http://www.linuxdoc.org/HOWTO/IPX-HOWTO.html`.

Both products have limitations, however. For example:

- Both are only NetWare 3.*x* bindery-compatible, which means that you may be able to use NetWare 4.*x* and 5.*x* only in bindery-emulation mode.

- `ncpfs` is not backward compatible with NetWare 2.*x* servers.

- `ncpfs` does not work with some NetWare-compatible servers, such as Windows NT 3.51.

Looking Ahead

In this chapter, you learned how to integrate Linux into Windows intranets, enabling file sharing between Linux and Windows.

In Chapter 30, "Red Hat Linux 7.1 and DOS/Windows," you will take a look at an important topic in today's corporate world: the ability to run DOS and Windows software in Linux.

To a surprising extent, Linux is able to support DOS applications using its `dosemu` software. On top of that, efforts are under way, albeit still at an early stage, to write a Windows emulator called Wine that is capable of running 16-bit and 32-bit Windows applications. Although not ready for deployment as a tool for day-to-day work in a corporate environment, Wine can currently run Microsoft Word and other popular Windows applications. Chapter 30 discusses the features and uses of these two compatibility packages.

Chapter 30 also examines VMware, a commercial application that allows you to set up a virtual machine, where you can run the operating system of your choice, including just about any version of Microsoft Windows and Linux.

CHAPTER

THIRTY

Red Hat Linux 7.1 and DOS/Windows

- Running DOS Applications in Linux

- VMware

- Why Not Wine?

One of the biggest arguments against using Linux as a day-to-day operating system for productivity tasks such as word processing is that there is a lack of applications for Linux. Add to that the inability to run Windows applications (at least OS/2 can do that, right?) and Linux is just an oddity, a curious example of great technology with poor marketing.

The problem with this argument is that Linux alone *can* in fact run the majority of DOS applications and many Windows applications, and there is promise of even wider ranging Windows compatibility. Two commercial products that bring this promise to fruition are VMware and Win4Lin, both of which can run Microsoft Windows within Linux. While Win4Lin is limited to Microsoft Windows 95/98, VMware can run all versions of Microsoft Windows in Linux. VMware has a corresponding product that can also run all versions of Linux within Microsoft Windows NT/2000. This chapter will look at a basic installation of VMware Workstation for Linux.

DOS support has been available for Linux for some time, and numerous popular DOS applications can be run under Linux with little effort.

Also, several other efforts are currently under way to provide complete Windows compatibility within the Linux environment. Perhaps the leader in this effort is Wine. In true Linux spirit, a team of Linux developers has taken up the task of delivering Wine as a freely available, better-than-commercial Windows-compatibility package. With the help of interested commercial developers, Wine has blossomed into a suite of tools that software manufacturers can use to quickly port their Microsoft Windows applications to Linux.

Running DOS Applications in Linux

Support for DOS applications is the strongest compatibility offering in Linux and is included with most Linux distributions.

Under the DOSEmu environment, it is possible to install and run DOS, including versions such as DOS 6.2, or even the DOS that comes with Microsoft Windows 95/98, and then run most DOS applications. There are limitations, of course, including those that affect some graphics and font operations, but overall, things work well.

In addition, a DOS environment can run inside a separate window in X Windows, making it easy to run DOS applications next to Linux programs.

Among the features offered by DOSEmu are the following:

- The ability for multiple users to run DOS applications simultaneously

- The ability to mount Unix directories to specific drive letters in the DOS environment

- The ability to print to Unix printer spools

Installing DOSEmu

Since DOSEmu is not part of the standard Red Hat Linux 7.1 distribution, you need to download it. The latest distribution as of this writing, 1.0.1, is available in both compressed archive (tar.gz) and RPM formats from the DOSEmu home page at http://www.dosemu.org/stable.

If you are using Red Hat Linux 7.1 (or any other distribution that uses RPM packages), download DOSEmu and install it. For example, if you downloaded it to your /tmp directory, you could then install it in root user mode with the following command:

```
rpm -i /tmp/dosemu-1.0.1-1.i386.rpm
```

Configuring DOSEmu

There are numerous configurations that can be used to run DOSEmu in Linux. These include:

- Booting DOS from a floppy disk

- Booting DOS from a disk image

- Booting DOS from a separate partition

For the sake of simplicity, and to get a glimpse into how the software works, this chapter looks only at booting DOS from a disk image. Advanced configurations, including booting from other media, are well covered in the documentation. You can find this documentation after you install DOSEmu in the /usr/doc/dosemu/ directory.

In order to get DOS running, it is necessary to have a configuration file called `/etc/dosemu.conf`. This is a highly complex file that has extensive documentation.

The DOSEmu package makes things easy, coming with a preconfigured disk image file and a `dosemu.conf` file designed to boot from that disk image. The disk image itself is located at `/var/lib/dosemu/hdimage`. It provides many useful commands and utilities, including `fdisk`, `format`, `unix2dos`, and `lredir` (a utility for redirecting Linux directories to DOS drive letters). It also contains its own free variant of DOS, known as FreeDOS.

To get a sense of what is involved in configuring a typical DOSEmu environment, let's look at the contents of the default `dosemu.conf` file:

```
########################################################################
# This file is /etc/dosemu.conf, included by /var/lib/dosemu/global.conf
#
# Linux DOSEMU configuration for parser versions >= 3 (dosemu-0.97.1)
#
# ./doc/README.txt (chapter 2.) contains a description of the syntax
# and the usage of dosemu.conf.
#
#
# Access rights are defined in
#
#       /etc/dosemu.users
#
########################################################################


# Notes for editing this section:
#
#    In    $_xxx = (n)    n is a numerical or boolean value
#                  =      =
```

```
#   In    $_zzz = "s"    s is a string
#
# Please edit only between the brackets and quotes and keep the rest
intact.
#         ^^^^^^^^^^^^^^^^^^^^^^^^^^^^^^^^^^^^^^^^^^
^^^^^^^^^^^^^^^^^^^^^


$_debug = "-a"            # same format as -D commandline option
                          # (but without the -D in front)
$_features= ""            # list of temporary hacks, see release notes in
                          # the file ChangeLog. e.g "0:1 2:0", which means
                          # to set feature_0 to 1 and feature_2 to 0.
$_timint = (on)           # emulate INT08 type timer interrupts
$_mathco = (on)           # or off
$_cpu = (80386)           # CPU emulation, valid values:  80[345]86

$_rdtsc = (off)           # if possible use Pentium cycle counter
$_cpuspeed = (0)          # 0 = calibrated by dosemu, else given
                          ➥(e.g.166.666)

$_pci = (off)

$_xms = (1024)            # in Kbyte
$_ems = (1024)            # in Kbyte
$_ems_frame = (0xe000)
$_dpmi = (off)            # in Kbyte
$_dosmem = (640)          # in Kbyte, < 640
$_hardware_ram = ""       # list of segment values/ranges such as
                          # "0xc8000 range 0xcc000,0xcffff"

$_secure ="ngd"           # secure for: n (normal users), g (guest), d
                          ➥(dexe)
                          # empty string: depending on 'restricted'
                          # "0": always insecure (not recommended)
$_odd_hosts = ""          # black list such as "lucifer.hell.com
                          ➥billy.the.cat"
$_diskless_hosts=""       # black list such as "hacker1 newbee gateway1"

$_emusys = ""             # empty or 3 char., config.sys   -> config.XXX
$_emubat = ""             # empty or 3 char., autoexec.bat -> autoexec.XXX
$_emuini = ""             # empty or 3 char., system.ini   -> system.XXX

$_hogthreshold = (1)      # 0 == all CPU power to DOSEMU
```

```
$_irqpassing = ""        # list of IRQ number (2-15) to pass to DOS such
                         ➥as
                         # "3 8 10"
$_speaker = ""           # or "native" or "emulated"


$_term_char_set = ""     # Global code page and character set selection.
                         # "" == automatic, else: ibm, latin, latin1,
                         ➥latin2

$_term_color = (on)      # terminal with color support
$_term_updfreq = (4)     # time between refreshs (units: 20 == 1 second)
$_escchar = (30)         # 30 == Ctrl-^, special-sequence prefix

$_rawkeyboard = (0)      # bypass normal keyboard input, maybe dangerous
$_layout = "auto"        # one of: finnish(-latin1), de(-latin1), be, it,
                         ➥us
                         # uk, dk(-latin1), keyb-no, no-latin1, dvorak,
                         ➥po
                         # sg(-latin1), fr(-latin1), sf(-latin1),
                         ➥es(-latin1)
                         # sw, hu(-latin2), hu-cwi, keyb-user
                         # hr-cp852, hr-latin2, hu-cwi, keyb-user
                         # Or 'auto' (which tries to generate the table
                         # from the current Linux console settings)
$_keybint = (on)         # emulate PCish keyboard interrupt


$_X_updfreq = (5)        # time between refreshs (units: 20 == 1 second)
$_X_title = "DOS in a BOX"   # Title in the top bar of the window
$_X_icon_name = "xdos"   # Text for icon, when minimized
$_X_keycode = (auto)     # on == translate keybord via dosemu keytables
                         # or 'off' or 'auto'
$_X_blinkrate = (8)      # blink rate for the cursor
$_X_font = ""            # basename from /usr/X11R6/lib/X11/fonts/misc/*
                         # (without extension) e.g. "vga"
$_X_mitshm = (on)        # Use shared memory extensions
$_X_sharecmap = (off)    # share the colormap with other applications
$_X_fixed_aspect = (on)  # Set fixed aspect for resize the graphics
                         ➥window
$_X_aspect_43 = (on)     # Always use an aspect ratio of 4:3 for graphics
$_X_lin_filt = (off)     # Use linear filtering for >15 bpp interpolation
```

```
$_X_bilin_filt = (off)    # Use bi-linear filtering for >15 bpp
                          ➡interpolation
$_X_mode13fact = (2)      # initial size factor for video mode 0x13
                          ➡(320x200)
$_X_winsize = ""          # "x,y" of initial windows size (defaults to
                          ➡float)
$_X_gamma = (1.0)         # gamma correction
$_X_vgaemu_memsize = (1024)   # size (in Kbytes) of the frame buffer for
                              ➡ emulated vga
$_X_lfb = (on)            # use linear frame buffer in VESA modes
$_X_pm_interface = (on)   # use protected mode interface for VESA modes
$_X_mgrab_key = ""        # KeySym name to activate mouse grab, empty ==
                          ➡off
$_X_vesamode = ""         # "xres,yres ... xres,yres"
                          # List of vesamodes to add. The list has to
                          ➡contain
                          # SPACE separated "xres,yres" pairs


$_video = "vga"           # one of: plainvga, vga, ega, mda, mga, cga
$_console = (0)           # use 'console' video
$_graphics = (0)          # use the cards BIOS to set graphics
$_videoportaccess = (1)   # allow videoportaccess when 'graphics' enabled
$_vbios_seg = (0xc000)    # set the address of your VBIOS (e.g. 0xe000)
$_vbios_size = (0x10000)  # set the size of your BIOS (e.g. 0x8000)
$_vmemsize = (1024)       # size of regen buffer
$_chipset = ""            # one of: plainvga, trident, et4000, diamond,
                          ➡avance
                          # cirrus, matrox, wdvga, paradise, ati, s3, sis
$_dualmon = (0)           # if you have one vga _plus_ one hgc (2
                          ➡monitors)


$_vbootfloppy = ""        # if you want to boot from a virtual floppy:
                          # file name of the floppy image under
                          ➡/var/lib/dosemu
                          # e.g. "floppyimage" disables $_hdimage
                          #      "floppyimage +hd" does _not_ disable
                          ➡$_hdimage
$_floppy_a ="threeinch"   # or "fiveinch" or "atapi" or empty, if not
                          ➡existing
```

```
                                # optionally the device may be appended such as
                                # "threeinch:/dev/fd0"
          $_floppy_b = ""       # dito for B:

          $_hdimage = "hdimage.first" # list of hdimages under /var/lib/dosemu
                                # assigned in this order such as
                                # "hdimage_c hdimage_d hdimage_e"
                                # If the name begins with '/dev/', then partion
                                # access is done instead of virtual hdimage such
                                ⮕as
                                # "/dev/hda1" or "/dev/hda1:ro" for readonly
                                # Currently mounted devices and swap are
                                ⮕refused.
                                # Hdimages and devices may be mixed such as
                                # "hdimage_c /dev/hda1 /dev/hda3:ro"
                                # Note: 'wholedisk' is _not_ supported.
          $_hdimage_r = $_hdimage # hdimages for 'restricted access (if different)

          $_aspi = ""           # list of generic SCSI devices to make available
                                # for the builtin aspi driver (format of an
                                ⮕entry
                                # is 'device:type:mappedtarget' such as
                                # "sg2:WORM sg3:Sequential-Access:6 sg4:CD-ROM"
                                ⮕or
                                # "sg2:4 sg3:1:6 sg4:5" (which are equal)

          $_com1 = ""           # e.g. "/dev/mouse" or "/dev/cua0"
          $_com2 = ""           # e.g. "/dev/modem" or "/dev/cua1"
          $_com3 = ""           # dito                  "/dev/cua2"
          $_com4 = ""           # dito                  "/dev/cua3"
          $_ttylocks = ""       # Lock directory (e.g. "/var/lock")
                                # default ("") is /usr/spool/uucp

          $_mouse = ""          # one of: microsoft, mousesystems, logitech,
                                ⮕mmseries
                                # mouseman, hitachi, busmouse, ps2
          $_mouse_dev = ""      # one of: com1, com2, com3, com4 or /dev/mouse
          $_mouse_flags = ""    # list of none or one or more of:
                                # "emulate3buttons cleardtr"
          $_mouse_baud = (0)    # baudrate, 0 == don't set
```

```
$_printer = "lp"          # list of (/etc/printcap) printer names to
                          ➡appear as
                          # LPT1, LPT2, LPT3 (not all are needed, empty
                          ➡for none)
$_printer_timeout = (20)# idle time in seconds before spooling out

$_ports = ""              # list of portnumbers such as "0x1ce 0x1cf
                          ➡0x238"
                          # or "0x1ce range 0x280,0x29f 310"
                          # or "range 0x1a0,(0x1a0+15)"

$_ipxsupport = (off)      # or on
$_novell_hack = (off)
$_vnet = (off)            # 'on' for packet-multi (used by dosnet)

$_sound = (off)           # sound support on/off
$_sb_base = (0x220)
$_sb_irq = (5)
$_sb_dma = (1)
$_sb_dsp = "/dev/dsp"
$_sb_mixer = "/dev/mixer"
$_mpu_base = "0x330"
```

Fortunately, extensive reconfiguration is not required. With the current version of DOSEmu (1.0.1), you'll need to set up a hard disk image and a boot directory, and then copy some standard MS-DOS boot files to that new boot directory.

You can set up a hard disk image (hdimage.first) and a boot directory (/var/lib/dosemu/bootdir.first) with the following commands, which are located in the /var/lib/dosemu/ directory:

```
$ /var/lib/dosemu/setup-hdimage
$ /var/lib/dosemu/setup-bootdir
```

Unfortunately, FreeDOS doesn't support management of Linux files and directories from the DOS emulator. To make this happen, all you need are three basic DOS configuration files. For example, if you have just about any standard MS-DOS or PC-DOS boot disk, copy the COMMAND.COM, IO.SYS, and MSDOS.SYS files to the newly created /var/lib/dosemu/bootdir.first directory.

Let's assume these files are on an unmounted floppy disk in your /dev/fd0 device (aka the DOS A: drive). Since Linux is case-sensitive, you need to use the following commands to overwrite the FreeDOS versions of these files:

```
$ mcopy a:io.sys /var/lib/dosemu/bootdir.first/io.sys
$ mcopy a:command.com /var/lib/dosemu/bootdir.first/command.com
```

NOTE You can copy the aforementioned system files from any standard MS-DOS boot floppy, version 4.0.1 and above. This even works with some other versions of DOS, as well as the boot disks for Windows 95/98.

Finally, create or edit the .dosemurc configuration file in your home directory. This file needs just one line to point Linux to the appropriate DOS configuration files:

```
$_hdimage = "bootdir.first"
```

Launching DOS

The simplest way to run DOSEmu is using the dos command from the console or inside an xterm window. When you issue the command

$ dos

DOSEmu loads and boots from the specified boot device in /etc/dosemu.conf. By default, this means booting from the provided disk image file. Figure 30.1 shows the DOS prompt in an xterm window after the dos command has been issued.

FIGURE 30.1:

Running DOS in an *xterm* window

Despite the message, this result is based on DOSEmu 1.0.1. Once DOS is running, you can use standard DOS commands and syntax to run programs from floppy disks or, as you will see later in this chapter, to run applications contained in redirected directories.

Launching DOS in a Separate X Window

In addition to running DOS in the current window, DOS can be launched in its own window when running X Windows. You can do this by issuing the command

    $ **xdos**

The xdos command is actually a link to the main dos binary file. Running the program through the xdos link has the same effect as the command

    $ **dos -X**

Running DOS in its own X Window produces results like those in Figure 30.2.

FIGURE 30.2:

Running DOS in its own
X Window

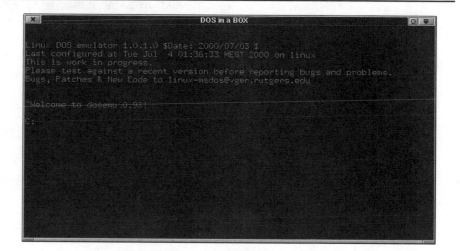

Useful DOSEmu Commands

The disk image that comes with DOSEmu contains several useful commands and utilities, including those outlined in the Table 30.1. These commands and many others can be found in the c:\bin and c:\dosemu directories when running DOSEmu using the default disk image.

TABLE 30.1: Selected DOSEmu Commands

Command	Description
eject.com	Ejects the CD-ROM drive.
emumouse.com	Tunes the DOSEmu mouse driver.
exitemu.com	Exits DOSEmu.
lredir.com	Redirects a Unix directory to a DOS drive letter.
unix.com	Executes a Linux command from within DOSEmu.

Mounting Directories with *lredir*

For DOSEmu to be useful, it needs to do more than work with disk images or floppy disks. It must be able to access parts of the Linux directory structure as if they were DOS disk drives. This ability allows your DOS environment to access data and applications that are stored on any existing DOS or Linux partitions or hard drives on your system.

The first step of the process takes place before the DOSEmu environment is launched: You need to make sure that the partitions you want to access are mounted at a logical location in your Linux directory structure. For instance, if you have an existing DOS partition, you could mount it at /dos.

Once all the directories and partitions you want to make available are accessible in Linux, you can start your DOS environment with

   $ **dos**

or

   $ **xdos**

Once DOS is running, use the lredir command to redirect Linux directories to DOS drive letters. The basic syntax of the lredir command is

   $ **lredir** *driveletter***: linux\fs/***linuxdirectory*

This command causes the specified Linux directory to be made available in DOS using the specified drive letter. For instance, to make a DOS partition mounted as /dos in Linux available in your DOSEmu environment as D:, use the command

   $ **lredir D: linux\fs/dos**

NOTE   By default, `lredir` is in the `c:\dosemu` directory. If this directory is not on your path, either use the complete path for the command (`c:\dosemu\lredir`) or make `c:\dosemu` your current directory.

Another useful application of `lredir` is to make users' home directories available to them on a pre-specified DOS drive letter. To do this, use the following variation on the `lredir` command you just saw:

```
$ lredir E: linux\fs\${HOME}
```

In this command, a user's home directory is obtained from the Linux environment variable `HOME`, where Red Hat stores the current user's home directory.

Finally, if you are booting initially from the provided disk image but want all booting from the loading of the `config.sys` file onward to occur from another location (such as a mounted DOS partition), you can use a simple two-step trick:

1. Edit the `config.sys` file on the initial disk image that is used to boot the DOSEmu environment. In the aforementioned example, it is located in the `/var/lib/dosemu/bootdir.first` directory. Make the following line the first line of the file (assuming the DOS partition is mounted under Linux at /dos):

   ```
   install=c:\dosemu\lredir.exe c: linux\fs/dos
   ```

2. Make sure the `config.sys` files on the disk image and the DOS partition are identical. This means including the line from step 1 in the `config.sys` file on your DOS partition.

Now, before executing the rest of `config.sys` and then `autoexec.bat`, the disk image is unmounted and the DOS partition is redirected to `C:` in the DOS environment.

VMware

VMware (www.vmware.com) is a virtual machine technology. What it does is create a virtual computer that uses all of your existing PC's resources to provide a complete virtual computer running inside of a window into which you can install practically any operating system that would normally run directly on your PC's hardware.

The version of VMware Workstation available as of this writing can run DOS, Windows 3.1, Windows 95/98, Windows NT/2000, plus popular Unix distributions for PCs, such as FreeBSD and Linux. Work is also under way to support Windows XP. Because you are installing and running the real operating system in what appears to be a full-blown hardware PC (the "virtual machine"), compatibility is almost never an issue. This provides a powerful way to run multiple operating systems on your Linux system for development, testing, and compatibility purposes. You can even run multiple instances of VMware at the same time, each running a different operating system.

Of course, powerful hardware is an issue. To get reasonable performance, you need fast Pentium II, Pentium III, or higher CPUs and a lot of memory since Linux and any client operating systems you run with VMware will have to share the available memory. While 96MB is the minimum to run VMware on Linux, large amounts of memory, even 256MB and more, are useful when running this kind of virtual machine.

Getting VMware

VMware is commercial software, not covered under the GNU General Public License. Nevertheless, you can still try the standard versions of VMware for 30 days for free. You can download VMware from the corporate Web site, `http://www.vmware.com`.

As of this writing, there are two consumer versions of VMware available. VMware Workstation allows you to run any of the listed operating systems within its virtual machine. VMware Express allows you to run only Windows 95/98 on Linux. Depending on the desktop version of VMware you want, and whether you're buying it for commercial use, the cost of a license ranges from $59 to $329. This chapter assumes that you will download and install VMware Workstation 2.0.4 (build 1142) for Linux. If you have a different version of VMware, the steps you take may be different.

Installing VMware

You can download VMware in `tar.gz` or RPM format. Based on the versions of VMware available of this writing, the general installation instructions are the same. If you have a version of VMware other than 2.0.4, the commands that you use may vary from those shown below. Check the documentation section of the `http://www.vmware.com` Web page for the latest instructions.

For example, if you downloaded the `tar.gz` file in the `/tmp` directory, you'll need to extract the file, change to the newly created installation directory, and then run the installation script in root user mode with the following commands:

```
$ tar xzvf VMvmware-2.0.4-1142.tar.gz
$ cd vmware-distrib
$ ./vmware-install.pl
```

Alternatively, if you downloaded the RPM file in the `/tmp` directory, you'll need to extract the file, change to the newly created installation directory, and then run the installation script in root user mode with the following commands:

```
$ rpm -i vmware-2.0.3-799.i386.rpm
$ /usr/bin/vmware-config.pl
```

After unpacking the basic software from the `tar.gz` or RPM file, the basic installation instructions are the same. Generally, you'll be able to accept most of the prompts. However, if you already have Samba installed, as discussed in Chapter 29, "Integrating Red Hat Linux 7.1 in Windows and Novell Networks," answer "no" to the following question:

```
Do you want this script to automatically configure your system to allow
your virtual machines to access the host file system?
```

Otherwise, VMware would then configure Samba for you, potentially in ways that you do not want.

> **NOTE**
>
> If you are installing the evaluation version of VMware, apply for an evaluation license from `http://www.vmware.com`. Follow the instructions that you get from VMware by e-mail about installing the evaluation license on your computer.

Installing an Operating System on VMware

You need to run VMware in an X Window. Open up a command-line interface such as GNOME terminal or Konsole in GNOME or KDE. Start VMware Workstation with the following command:

```
$ /usr/bin/vmware
```

When VMware starts, you are taken to a menu with three basic options, as shown in Figure 30.3. The simplest way to install an operating system on VMware is to select Run The Configuration Wizard and then click OK.

FIGURE 30.3:

Starting VMware

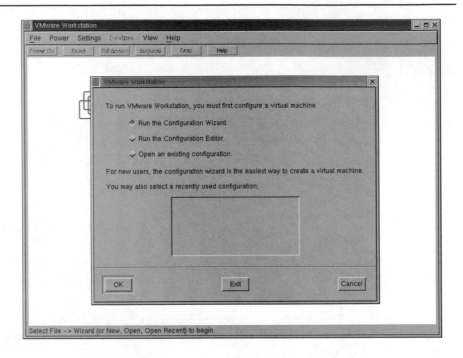

VMware then takes you through a series of options, where you select the following:

Operating System   In VMware Workstation, you can install Windows 3.1, 95, 98, NT 4.0, 2000, Linux, or another major Unix clone known as FreeBSD.

Disk Type Setting   You can set up your new operating system in a new virtual disk or an existing physical disk.

New Virtual Disk   Allows you to create a virtual disk in a Linux file. This file can be quite large; the default maximum file size is 2000MB.

Existing Physical Disk   If you've already installed another operating system on the same computer, you can set up access through VMware. This section assumes that you're setting up a new virtual disk.

CD-ROM Access   You can set up the virtual machine to access your existing CD-ROM drive.

Floppy Access   You can set up the virtual machine to access your existing floppy drive.

Networking   You have two basic networking options. If your computer has a working Ethernet adapter, you can choose Bridged Networking, which gives your computer equal access to your current local area network. Choosing Host-only Networking lets you set up a two-computer network between your computer and the operating system on your virtual machine.

When you've finished, VMware confirms the settings that you created. For example, Figure 30.4 shows typical settings for setting up the installation of Windows 2000 on a Linux computer.

FIGURE 30.4:

Configuring VMware

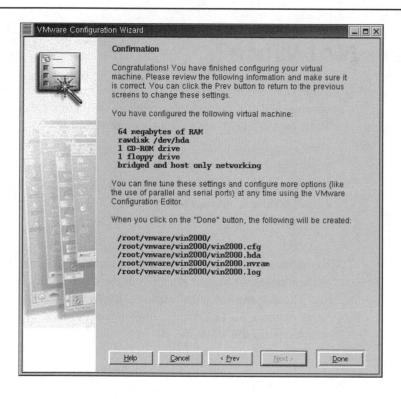

After confirming your selections, you have essentially created a computer inside your computer. When you click the Power On button on the empty VMware screen, you are powering up that computer for the first time. You can then run setup or installation disks in the floppy or CD-ROM drives, as appropriate.

TIP   Since Red Hat Linux 7.1 includes Linux kernel 2.4.2, it won't work with any versions of VMware before 2.0.4.

Another commercial option for running Microsoft Windows 95/98 within Linux is Win4Lin, available from NeTraverse at http://www.netraverse.com.

Why Not Wine?

Wine is a completely different product than VMware for two reasons: It is not commercial and it aims to provide a completely free environment in which to run Windows applications on Linux systems.

The latter point is especially significant. While current development versions of Wine still rely on an existing Windows installation for some of the Windows system files, the goal of the project is to provide a complete alternative: If you install Wine on your Linux system, you won't need to install any version of Windows to run Windows applications.

As is typical of many open-source Linux applications, Wine is under constant development and revision and is considered pre-release software. In fact, the release notes for Wine indicate that the software is considered development code and should be used with caution. The Wine home page is at http://www.winehq .org; new releases of Wine come out frequently and you can always get the latest version from this Web site.

The compilation, configuration, and installation of Wine reflect this early development phase. Even so, it is possible to get some heavy-duty Windows applications, including Word 6, to run under Wine (25 percent of an earlier edition of this book was written this way).

The Future of Wine

The Wine team has a lot of plans for the Wine project that make it significant. These plans include:

- Being able to run Windows 3.1, 95, 98, NT, and 2000 software on major PC Unix platforms, including Linux, FreeBSD, OpenBSD, and Solaris.

- Being able to run Windows applications without having an installed, licensed version of Windows available. Wine plans to provide a complete alternative set of system DLLs that are free of Microsoft code. You can still use your original Windows system DLLs if you have them, but they won't be required when Wine is finished. Planned support includes the following:

  - Partial DirectX support for Windows games

  - Full GDI support

  - Support for native Windows 16-bit printer drivers

  - Support for Winsock networking

  - Support for scanners

  - Limited support for Unicode

  - Support for multiple languages

Wine is officially alpha developers-only code and is not yet suitable for general use. Nevertheless, many people find it useful to run many different Windows applications in Linux, with some versions of Wine supporting a surprising range of Windows applications.

Many users have tested thousands of Microsoft Windows-based applications on Wine, with varying degrees of success. To see reviews of applications that interest you, use the following Web page to search through the Wine database: http://www.winehq.com/Apps/query.cgi.

Wine Success Stories

Even though it is incomplete, Wine is still a success. Other software manufacturers have used Wine tools to "port" their products from Windows to Linux. In other words, they use Wine to enable their software to work in Linux, without rewriting code.

Corel, the company behind the WordPerfect suite of office products, started working with Wine in 1998. They developed their own versions of Wine tools in support of their production releases of WordPerfect for Linux, starting with version 7 and continuing through the current version, WordPerfect Office 2000 for Linux. They have also ported their CorelDraw Graphics Suite using Wine.

Although Corel has developed Wine tools separately from the people behind the Wine project, they have subsequently shared their work, in keeping with the GNU General Public License.

Deneba, one of the leaders in graphic and computer-aided design, wanted to port its high-performance Canvas application to Linux. They were able to use Wine tools to port Canvas to Linux within six months. In fact, most of the work (pre-beta) was complete with only minor modifications to Wine libraries within two months.

These applications stand on their own. No emulator such as VMware is required. This functionality forms the basis for what Wine stands for: Wine Is Not an Emulator.

Looking Ahead

In this chapter, you learned about several available paths for running your existing Windows and DOS applications in Linux. With each passing week, support for Windows and DOS applications under Linux improves, and it may not be too long before most off-the-shelf Windows applications can be run fairly successfully on a well-configured Linux system.

Chapter 31, "Security and Red Hat Linux 7.1 As an Inexpensive Router," will look at an interesting topic. As a robust networking operating system, Linux is ideally suited to act as a router for a small network, connecting it to the Internet through a regular modem or ISDN connection or connecting to another LAN as an inter-LAN router.

Specifically, you will consider a typical example for many small offices: connecting an entire LAN to the Internet on a dial-up connection that provides only one real IP address.

CHAPTER

THIRTY-ONE

Security and Red Hat Linux 7.1 As an Inexpensive Router

- Basic Security Issues

- Configuring Firewall Support During Installation

- Configuring Firewall Support After Installation

- Creating a Linux-Based Router

This chapter addresses two related topics: security and connecting networks to the Internet.

You will learn about Linux security at several levels, first considering how to keep individual Linux systems secured and then exploring the broader issue of keeping a LAN secure when it is connected to the Internet. You'll also learn about creating firewalls to secure your system during and after installation.

In addition, you will take a look at the Linux Router Project, which allows you to use a single floppy disk containing a special distribution of Linux to create a Linux-based router that can act as a gateway between your network and your existing Internet connection.

Basic Security Issues

The area of computer security is a huge one that cannot be addressed adequately in a single chapter of a book. In fact, entire books are devoted to only small areas of computer and network security.

Given the scope of the subject, this section discusses computer security in general and points out the basic concepts that you can consider applying to your specific circumstances.

Securing a Stand-Alone System

If you have a stand-alone Linux system, your security needs are the most basic. Because the system is not connected to a LAN and, assuming that you connect to the Internet through a modem, is not left connected permanently or for long periods of time, your security concerns are relatively minor.

Still, there are some fundamental security issues that you should address:

- Make sure your passwords are sufficiently complex that they can't be guessed or cracked easily. This includes combining letters and numbers and other characters into non-word passwords. Passwords should also be changed frequently. It is especially important that your root password be a non-word, complex password that is changed regularly.

NOTE   There are a number of programs available specifically designed to decipher passwords. While a password based on a dictionary word can be found in minutes with the power of a current PC, a password of mixed numbers and upper- and lowercase letters can take weeks for the same PC to crack. One easy way to set up complex passwords is based on a favorite sentence; for example, a complex password like OM15IftP could be created from "On March 15, I'm flying to Paris."

- Make sure your computer is kept physically secure. If it contains important data, don't leave your office unlocked while you go to lunch. Similarly, don't walk out of the office and leave the system logged in, especially if you have logged in as the root user at the console or in a terminal window.

- Do not create unnecessary user accounts. If only two people use the system on a regular basis, create accounts only for those users and not for anyone else. This makes it easier to keep track of who is using the system and where any security violations originate.

- Most important of all, do not share passwords (user or root), even with people who are authorized to use the system on a regular basis. Especially keep the root password secure. All it takes is the wrong user obtaining the root password and you could find all the data on your system erased one day.

- Because no system can be completely secure, consider encrypting important data. There are many tools for doing this, including PGP encryption. A HOWTO that includes coverage of PGP is available online at `http://www` `.linuxdoc.org/HOWTO/Mutt-GnuPG-PGP-HOWTO.html`. An older step-by-step guide to PGP encryption can also be found on the Internet at the Linux Focus Web site at `http://www.linuxfocus.org/English/November1997/` `article7.html`.

Securing a Linux System on a LAN

The instant you connect your Linux system to a LAN, new security issues appear. After all, even if you follow all the rules outlined previously for a stand-alone system (which you should also follow when the system is on a LAN), it is still possible for the intent hacker to gain access to your Linux system by exploiting any number of security weaknesses via the network.

Two simple policies can help minimize this problem:

- Do not run unnecessary network services. For example, if you do not need to allow users to telnet into your system, make sure the Telnet daemon (/usr/sbin/in.telnetd) is not installed and there is no entry for the daemon in the /etc/xinetd.d directory. Similarly, if your machine does not act as a mail server, deactivate the sendmail daemon. The same rules go for most network services: FTP, finger, news, DNS, and many others. Run only those network service daemons that are necessary to connect to the network and perform the tasks that you are using your Linux system for.

TIP   If you use the /etc/inetd.conf file common in other versions of Linux (including Red Hat Linux 6.x), you can convert it to Red Hat 7.1's xinetd format with the /usr/sbin/inetdconvert command.

If you use another version of Linux that does not have an /etc/xinetd.conf file, make sure there is no entry for the daemon in question in the /etc/inetd.conf file (you can also comment out the entry by adding a hash mark [#] in front of the line with the daemon).

- Make effective use of /etc/hosts.allow and /etc/hosts.deny, which are discussed in Chapter 28, "Configuring Red Hat Linux 7.1 for an Ethernet Network." Not only should you deny access from all IP addresses to all the services you chose not to run in the previous point, but you should also be sure you are allowing incoming access only to services that you are running to hosts with permission to use those services. For instance, if you are running an FTP server to allow incoming FTP access by only two users, allow just their computers to have access to the FTP service instead of allowing any user on your LAN to make an FTP connection.

xinetd

Red Hat has incorporated the extended Internet services daemon, or xinetd, as a replacement for inted, starting with Red Hat Linux 7.0. The inetd "super server" regulated Internet access to Unix/Linux computers by port. To allow less-experienced users to quickly start services such as Telnet, FTP, POP e-mail, and more, inetd is by default set up with a number of open ports. As described above, you can then use the hosts.allow and hosts.deny files to regulate access to your computer. Unfortunately, if you want to allow one computer access just for FTP downloads, you allow access for all services on your computer.

The xinetd daemon lets you regulate access by service. In other words, if you need to let someone access your FTP server, you don't have to let them access other services, like Telnet or NFS. If someone breaks into their computer, the only risk is through the FTP service that you opened.

Another advantage of xinetd is protection from Denial of Service (DoS) attacks. DoS is a process in which someone sends a constant stream of messages to your server, perhaps as simple as a ping, which keeps others from accessing your servers.

For more information on xinetd, navigate to their Web site at http://www .xinetd.org. This site includes documentation and examples of the configuration files that you need.

Keeping Your Network Secure

Even if you keep your Linux system fairly secure on your LAN, if your LAN is connected to the Internet, the rest of your network is open to a wide range of possible security threats and attacks.

Keeping a network secure is a large job and requires detailed knowledge of network security. Fundamentally, though, there are two main techniques (and many variations on them) for ensuring at least minimal network security.

Remember that your network will be connected to the Internet through some type of router that has the job of moving data on and off the LAN as appropriate. Generally, a router can provide some level of security to ensure that the most malicious attacks cannot infiltrate your LAN.

Router-level protection is usually provided in one of two ways:

Using a packet-filtering firewall   *Packet filtering* is a process that every router is capable of performing. Whenever a packet of information from the Internet is received by the router and is destined for a system on the LAN, the originating IP address, the destination IP address, and the port of the connection are examined and compared to a table to determine whether the packet is allowed into the LAN, or is dropped from the network. In this way, connections from specific hosts, to specific hosts, or for specific ports (or any combination of these) can be allowed or denied.

Using a proxy firewall A *proxy firewall* is a different approach because it prevents direct connections between the machines inside the firewall and those on the Internet. If a host on your LAN makes a connection to a host on the Internet, it actually connects to the proxy system and then the proxy system makes the actual connection to the system on the Internet, serving as the relay for all data traveling back and forth. Similarly, if you allow any incoming connections to your LAN, the proxy plays the same role of middleman. In addition to keeping the LAN and the Internet totally separate, the proxy firewall has capabilities similar to a packet-filtering firewall. It can be configured to allow only certain types of traffic through the firewall in either direction or to deny connections on the basis of several variables, including originating IP address, destination IP address, and port being used.

To really understand the fundamentals of network security, you should read the Linux Security-HOWTO at `http://www.linuxdoc.org/HOWTO/Security-HOWTO.html`.

A Linux system can easily be configured to act as a router between your LAN and the Internet, providing connections over standard analog phone modems, ISDN lines, or faster connections such as cable modems or DSL adapters. This router can also be configured to act as a packet-filtering or proxy firewall as well. Setting up a Linux-based router generally costs less than buying complete hardware router solutions and offers more security options than do many hardware-based routers.

Configuring Firewall Support During Installation

If you never connect your computer to another network, and you never connect to the Internet, you do not need a firewall. If you connect to the Internet for short periods of time, the risk and thus the need for a firewall are relatively small. However, if your computer is on a network that frequently connects to the Internet, you could be exposed to all kinds of attacks. If your computer is directly connected to the Internet with an "always on" connection such as DSL or a cable modem, you may have the highest risk of all.

During the Red Hat Linux 7.1 installation process, you can configure firewall support for your Linux system, as shown in Figure 31.1. Later, you'll see how you can use the `lokkit` utility to set up a new firewall configuration. Finally, you'll get to analyze a simple firewall and get a small idea of the power behind it.

FIGURE 31.1:

Firewall configuration during Linux installation

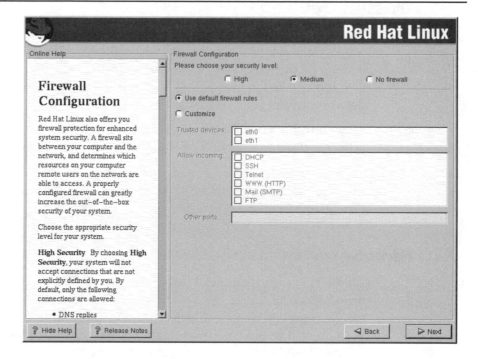

Generally, a firewall works by blocking all traffic, with exceptions. The exceptions are like customized gates that allow certain kinds of traffic in and or out through a specific port or channel.

In TCP/IP, the language of the Internet, there are 65,536 ports. Each of these ports is like a door for certain kinds of data transfer. Your computers need some open doors for basic communication. The Red Hat Linux 7.1 installation program allows you to set up high- or medium-security firewalls, where you can customize the ports that you leave open.

NOTE   The 65,536 TCP/IP ports are divided into three categories. The Well Known Ports, 0 through 1023, are for services such as Web pages, e-mail, and Internet chat lines. The Registered Ports, 1024 through 49,151, include other services such as Internet phones and NFS. You may be able to use the other ports (49,152 through 65,535) on an "ad hoc" basis. The official list is available through the Internet Assigned Numbers Authority at `www.iana.org/assignments/port-numbers`. Many of these ports are listed in your `/etc/services` file.

Trusted Devices

All detected network cards are listed in the Firewall Configuration screen. Figure 31.1 shows two network cards, eth0 and eth1. Assume that this computer is a router between two networks; eth0 is connected to a Local Area Network, and eth1 is connected to the Internet. If you enable one of these cards as a trusted device, you're turning off the firewall on that device.

If you trust all of the users of all of the computers on your Local Area Network, select the Customize option. This allows you to enable eth0 as a trusted device.

On the other hand, you should not trust any connection to the Internet, so in this case choose eth1. Otherwise, your firewall won't protect you from attacks through the Internet.

High Security

The highest-security firewall has no connection at all to outside networks. Since most users want at least a connection to the Internet, this is generally not practical. The next best thing would be a one-way firewall: Traffic would go out, but your firewall would block traffic from coming in. A great idea in theory, but such a firewall would keep you from navigating the Internet.

Besides the things you ask for, such as Web pages, the default Red Hat Linux 7.1 high-security firewall lets in two kinds of traffic: computer address information from DNS servers and configuration information from DHCP servers.

DNS   As discussed in Chapter 21, "Understanding Linux Networking," a nameserver, also known as the Domain Name Service (DNS), is a database of Web site domain names such as www.Sybex.com and their corresponding IP addresses such as 192.168.0.131. Your computer needs that IP address in order to tell the Internet where to look for the Web site you want. If you've included the IP addresses of any DNS servers during the installation process (check your /etc/resolv.conf file), the firewall utility keeps port 53 open for you.

DHCP   As discussed in Chapter 4, "Installing Red Hat Linux 7.1," a Dynamic Host Configuration Protocol (DHCP) server configures IP address information for you on a Local Area Network. If you are using a DHCP server outside your network, you need to let that server talk to your computers through the firewall. If you've enabled DHCP in the Allow Incoming section of Figure 31.1, the firewall utility keeps ports 67 and 68 open for you.

A high-security firewall lets in no other traffic. You won't be able to use common Internet utilities such as RealAudio or most chat programs. You won't even be able to share NFS files through such a firewall. And if you have a Web server on your computer, nobody will be able to find your Web pages.

Medium Security

Medium security sets up more open doors in your firewall. It closes off the Well Known Ports (0 through 1023), as well as the ports for NFS (2049), the X Server (6000-6009), and X Fonts (7100). It opens the ports required to use DNS and DHCP as described in the previous section. In other words, medium security leaves most Registered Ports open, which automatically allows you to receive a lot of specialized services such as RealAudio broadcasts.

If you are concerned about some of the ports being left open under a medium-security firewall, select high security, and then read the next section about customized settings. If you know the services that you want, you can then use customized settings to open just the ports that you need.

Customized Settings

If either the high- or the medium-security firewall is too restrictive, you can set up exceptions on the ports of your choice. In the screen shown in Figure 31.1, select the Customize option. This allows you to open doors in your firewall for the data that you need. The Allow Incoming list includes the typical traffic that you might need on an Internet connection. The Other Ports text box allows you to open up the other ports of your choice.

Incoming Traffic

There are six typical ports shown in the Allow Incoming list. These ports relate to data that you may need when you connect to the Internet, or when others connect to your computer as a Web, e-mail, or FTP server, as follows:

DHCP   Enabled by default during Red Hat Linux installation. The purpose, as discussed earlier, is to allow DHCP servers outside your network to configure computers on your network.

SSH Short for Secure Shell. When you use SSH, the entire login session is encrypted. If you want to use the Secure Shell package to administer your computer from a remote site, you'll need to connect through the firewall that you're setting up. Enabling SSH opens up port 22, which allows for Secure Shell logins. To use SSH, you'll need the `openssh-server-2.5.2p2-5.i386.rpm` package.

Telnet Telnet is the unsecure way to log in and enter commands on remote computers. Once you've connected to a remote computer by Telnet, you can use the command line just as if you were connected locally. Since Telnet communications are not encrypted, any user who has the tool to listen in on your network (this tool is also known as a *sniffer*) can record any password or other information that you use.

WWW (HTTP) If you're setting up a Web server on your computer, you need to enable this option. Otherwise, people who try to get Web pages from your computer will find nothing. This option isn't required in order to get Web pages from the Internet.

Mail (SMTP) If you have a mail server on your computer, you need to enable this option. People who are trying to send e-mail send their messages to their mail server. If the Mail port (25) is not open, the e-mails won't get past the firewall.

FTP If you have certain types of FTP servers on your computer, you should enable this option. A common FTP server package is `wu-ftpd-2.6.1-16.i386.rpm`, available on the CD-ROM that comes with this book.

Customized Port Traffic

The ports listed in the Allow Incoming section are not enough for all users. For example, if you want to share directories with other Linux and Unix computers through your firewall, you need to open both the portmap and NFS doors, which correspond to ports 111 and 2049.

The next step is to review the kinds of traffic that go through each port. Open the `/etc/services` file or the previously cited Web page. The relevant information is as follows:

```
sunrpc          111/tcp     portmapper      #RPC 4.0 portmapper TCP
sunrpc          111/udp     portmapper      #RPC 4.0 portmapper UDP

nfs             2049/tcp    nfsd
nfs             2049/udp    nfsd
```

Based on this information, you can open up the relevant doors in the Firewall Configuration screen shown in Figure 31.1. Click Customize, and then type the following in the Other Ports text box:

```
111:tcp,111:udp,2049:tcp,2049:udp
```

This opens up ports 111 and 2049, which are both used in sharing through NFS, to TCP and UDP traffic. You can add other ports in the same way. Just remember to separate the ports by a comma, and don't use any spaces between entries.

Configuring Firewall Support After Installation

After installing Red Hat Linux 7.1, you can reconfigure your firewall with the `lokkit` utility. If required, mount your installation CD-ROM on the `/mnt/cdrom` directory and then use the following command to install this package:

```
# rpm -i /mnt/cdrom/RedHat/RPMS/lokkit-0.43-6.i386.rpm
```

Once it is installed, you can start `lokkit` with the following in a command-line interface screen:

```
# /usr/sbin/lokkit
```

When `lokkit` is open, you'll see the Firewall Configuration screen shown in Figure 31.2, which allows you to set up high or medium security or no firewall at all on your computer. In `lokkit`, you can navigate between options with the Tab key and make a selection by pressing the spacebar.

Select the High or Medium security level and click Customize to continue. You'll see something like the Firewall Configuration - Customize menu shown in Figure 31.3.

In this menu, you see the same customization options as you had in the Firewall Configuration menu shown during the Red Hat installation. In this case, the network card options include an infrared device (`irlan0`) and a regular Ethernet adapter (`eth0`). Make your selections using the methods described earlier, and then select OK. This returns you to the original screen shown in Figure 31.2. Then you can click OK, and `lokkit` documents your new firewall in the `/etc/sysconfig/ipchains` file.

FIGURE 31.2:

The *lokkit* Firewall
Configuration screen

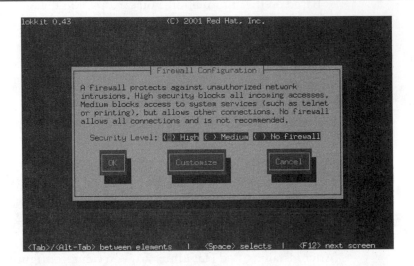

FIGURE 31.3:

Customizing the firewall

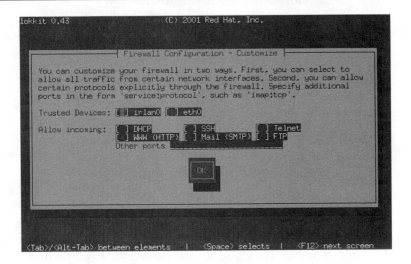

NOTE When you use `lokkit` after installation, the default high- and medium-security firewalls do not open the DHCP port.

NOTE   The default firewall command for Red Hat Linux 7.1 is `ipchains`. The new firewall command for the 2.4.*x* kernel is `iptables`. You can disable `ipchains`, and then `iptables` will be automatically usable in your firewall. However, the `lokkit` utility does not support configuration of `iptables`. The documentation for `iptables` isn't yet final; the current HOWTO can be found at `http://va.samba.org/netfilter/unreliable-guides/packet-filtering-HOWTO/index.html`. When it's ready, look for it on the `www.linuxdoc.org` Web site.

NOTE   A second firewall configuration utility, `/usr/sbin/firewall-config`, is also available. It is somewhat more difficult to use than `lokkit`.

You can customize the ports that you open by IP address. In other words, only a computer with a specific IP address will have the key to open the door to send you specific kinds of data. The techniques for setting this up are beyond the scope of this book. For more information on firewalls and network configuration, refer to *Linux Firewalls*, written by Robert Ziegler (New Riders, 1999).

In the next section, you'll create a firewall with a version of Linux based on a floppy disk. It includes information on masquerading, which you could also use in conjunction with a `lokkit`-based firewall. Masquerading hides the addresses of computers inside your network.

Creating a Linux-Based Router

This section walks you through the steps for creating a Linux-based router using the Linux Router Project's distribution of Linux.

Designed as a minimalist Linux installation, the Linux Router Project's distribution of Linux can fit on a single 1.44MB floppy disk for most sites and provides all the components needed to route between two Ethernet LANs or between an Ethernet LAN and the Internet via PPP. With add-on modules, support is available for additional hardware for WAN connections. Other features such as SNMP management are also available.

The benefit of setting up a router using the Linux Router Project's Linux distribution instead of full-scale versions of Linux such as Red Hat is that all the hard work has been done for you. You won't need to make the effort to identify what needs to be installed to get routing to work. In addition, the software includes a simple, menu-driven configuration system that allows you to check that everything that needs configuration is done.

The Linux Router Project software can be downloaded from their Web site at `http://www.linuxrouter.org/`.

The following sections provide an excellent example on how to configure a router between secure and insecure networks. Unfortunately, production Linux Router Project (LRP) software is based on Linux kernel 2.0 and 2.2. The LRP software for kernel 2.0 includes the obsolete `ipfwadm` command, which has security holes. The LRP software for kernel 2.2 includes `ipchains`, which is more secure. As of yet, there is not full production-level support for the `iptables` command associated with Linux kernel 2.4.

What You Will Create

You will use the Linux Router Project software to create a router that serves as a firewall, protecting the private areas of your LAN from the Internet. This procedure that you will follow makes two assumptions:

- You have an existing Internet connection, most likely through a cable modem or DSL adapter and an existing router, or through an ISDN connection and an ISDN router.

- You want to allow some incoming access to servers on your network. For instance, you may have a Web server that the public should be able to access, but you don't want any incoming access to the sensitive file, application, and database servers on the rest of your network.

NOTE   Many providers of cable modem, DSL, or ISDN service do not allow their customers to run public Web, FTP, or other types of servers on their lines. If in doubt, consult your provider for more information.

Given these assumptions, your network arrangement will resemble Figure 31.4. The internal router that you will create sits between your secure internal network and your unsecure accessible network.

FIGURE 31.4:

A typical firewall-protected
network

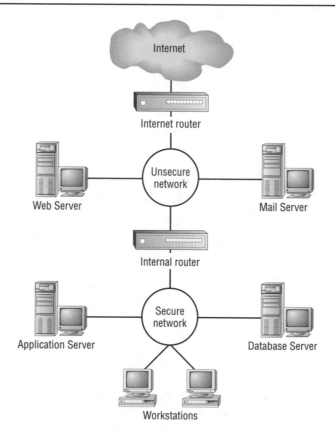

Notice that the router connecting you to the outside world provides looser
protection than does the router between your unsecure and secure networks.
This means that, at the worst, only the systems sitting on your unsecure network are directly open to possible attacks from outside. Because your second
router, between the unsecure and secure LANs, does not allow incoming connections into the secure network, your systems are—as far as this is possible in
a networked environment—safe from outside attack. It is this second router,
between the unsecure and secure LANs, that you will implement using the
Linux Router Project software.

Getting Ready

The following instructions allow you to create a Linux Router Project floppy disk from an existing Linux system. As of this writing, you can download these files from one of the sites listed on the http://www.linuxrouter.org/download.shtml Web page.

1. Download the Linux "idiot-image" file and save it in a convenient location, for instance, /tmp/. As of this writing, the most current "idiot-image" file is idiot-image_1440KB_FAT_2.9.8_Linux_2.2.gz.

2. Change your current directory to the directory containing the downloaded file with a command such as cd /tmp.

3. Decompress the archive. The image comes in gzip format, which can be decompressed with the following command:

   gunzip idiot-image_1440KB_FAT_2.9.8_Linux_2.2.gz

4. Copy the disk image file to your floppy disk. This erases any data currently on that disk. Use a dd command such as:

   dd if=idiot-image_1440KB_FAT_2.9.8_Linux_2.2 of=/dev/fd0

Once this is done, you have a boot floppy disk for the Linux Router Project distribution. But this is not enough. You also need network card drivers using the same kernel version, in this case, 2.2.16-1.

Repeat the basic process with the 2.2.16-1.tar.gz file, available from the same download site. Copy this file to the /tmp directory. Unzip and unarchive this file with the tar xzvf 2.2.16-1.tar.gz command. Copy the network modules from the unarchived /tmp/2.2.16-1/modules/net subdirectory to the second floppy disk. Save both floppy disks for later use.

NOTE   As of this writing, Linux Router Project version 2.9.8 is "beta quality." In other words, until it is final, it is not recommended for use in a production computer.

Be sure you have sufficient hardware to run the router. While a 386SX with 8MB of RAM can function as a router and a 486DX2 66MHz with 12MB of RAM will be respectable, these days you really want to run a Pentium 100MHz or faster system with at least 16MB of RAM. No hard drive is needed, just a floppy drive to boot from. If you want to add many add-ons to your Linux Router Project configuration, then the software may exceed the size of your floppy disk, in which case consider booting from a hard disk or a bootable Zip drive and increasing your RAM to 32MB. Details of how to boot from other media can be found on the Linux Router Project home page.

WARNING   If you are using an Intel type 386- or 486-based computer, the best available option is the "idiot-images" with the obsolete ipfwadm commands based on the 2.0.36 kernel. Follow the same steps above, using the `idiot-image_ 1440KB_FAT_2.9.8_Linux2.0.gz` image file and the `2.0.36pre15-1.tar.gz` kernel module file.

NOTE   Slackware has a variant of their Linux distribution that is designed to fit on a Zip drive. For more information, look at `http://www.Slackware.com/zipslack`.

The PC needs to have two Ethernet cards. One will be used to connect to the unsecure network and the other will connect to the secure network.

The Operating Environment

Before starting the Linux router software, let's define the environment in which the router will run so that the configuration you perform later makes sense.

First, you need to determine IP addresses. Your unsecure network will use the addresses 200.200.200.0 through 200.200.200.255 with the netmask 255.255.255.0. The router connecting the network to the outside world is at 200.200.200.1, and the router you will build has the IP address 200.200.200.254 on the unsecure side of the router. These are genuine IP addresses in that the rest of the Internet knows they exist and they are unique on the Internet. If your router to the external world allows it, machines on the Internet can communicate directly with any host on the unsecure LAN.

Your secure network will use the addresses 10.10.10.0 through 10.10.10.255 with the netmask 255.255.255.0. The router connecting the secure and unsecure LANs will use the IP address 10.10.10.1 on the secure side of the router. These are private, or non-routable, IP addresses. The rest of the world doesn't know about the existence of hosts on the internal network, and no direct communication is possible with hosts on the internal network; your router, in its firewall role, hides the existence of the secure network from the rest of the world (including your unsecure network).

In the router you are building, the device eth0 will be connected to the unsecure LAN (with IP address 200.200.200.254) and the device eth1 will be connected to the secure LAN (with the IP address 10.10.10.1).

You will allow only outgoing connections from the secure LAN—no incoming connections. What's more, you will use a feature of the Linux kernel known as *IP masquerading* in order to implement a security feature known as *network address translation*. Under network address translation, the router not only handles the work of routing data into and out of the secure LAN but, when a machine inside the secure LAN makes a connection through the router, it also hides the IP address of that machine and translates it into an address on the unsecure LAN. In this way, the connection cannot be traced back to the real IP address of the host, thus helping to hide the existence of hosts on the secure network from the rest of the world.

Because the secure network uses non-routable IP addresses, the hosts on your unsecure network do not know about the existence of hosts on that network and cannot attempt to communicate with them. Similarly, the router connecting the unsecure network to the Internet doesn't know about the existence of the internal, secure network and so will never route packets directly to hosts on the internal network.

Starting the Linux Router

To boot your computer as a Linux-based router, simply insert the floppy boot disk you created earlier and restart your computer. Your computer should boot from the floppy disk.

The Linux Router Project software then creates a RAM disk and loads the contents of the boot disk into the RAM disk. Then the entire router runs from RAM. Any configuration changes you make can be saved back to the boot disk so that the next time you boot, your configuration is retained.

After you boot, you are prompted to log in. Log in as the root user with no password and the Linux router software starts, presenting you with a configuration menu, shown in Figure 31.5. Let's walk through the steps to get a minimal network running as described previously:

1. Network card modules: Take the second floppy disk that you created. Assuming that you mount that floppy on the /mnt/floppy directory, copy the module that you need for each of your two installed network cards from the /mnt/floppy directory to the /lib/modules directory.

2. Basic settings: Configure the IP addresses, network masks, and routes of the two Ethernet cards.

3. Basic security: Configure the network security needed to implement network address translation.

4. Further configuration: Configure additional network parameters, such as nameservers (DNS) and host tables.

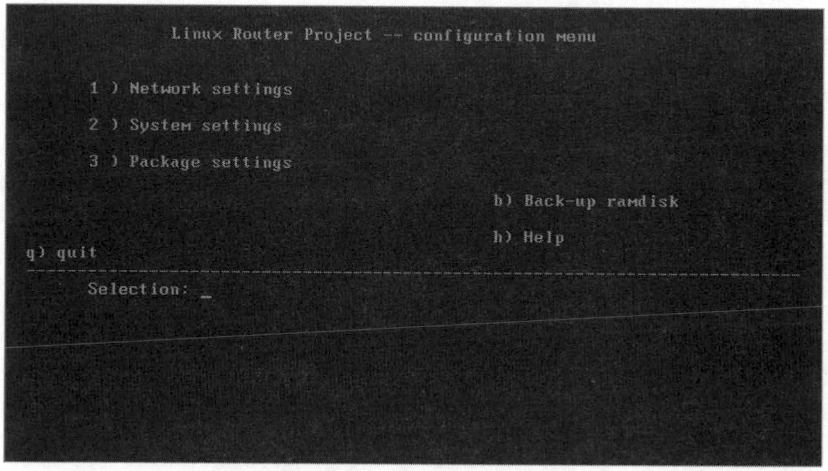

FIGURE 31.5:

The Linux Router Project main menu

The menus are entirely numeric and are accessed by typing the number of a selection and pressing Enter. For instance, typing **1** for Network Settings on the main configuration menu causes the network settings submenu to be displayed. Selecting an entry on a submenu opens the file for editing (for configuration purposes) in a simple editor. To use the editor effectively, you really only need to know how to save (press Ctrl+W and then press Enter to confirm the filename) and quit (press Ctrl+C). If you don't remember these commands, press F1 while in the editor, and you'll see a list of commands.

Installing Network Card Modules

The Linux Router Project boot disk, the first one that you created, does not include any network card modules. They are part of the second floppy disk that you created. In the following steps, you copy the modules that you need from the second floppy to the RAM disk on the computer that you booted with the Linux Router Project boot disk.

From the Linux Router Project configuration menu, take the following steps:

1. Press **Q** to exit the Linux Router Project menu.

2. Insert and mount the second floppy (with the network card modules) with the `mount /dev/fd0 /mnt` command.

3. Copy the modules that you need to the `/lib/modules` directory on the RAM disk. For example, if you have cards that require the ne2000 and pcnet32 drivers, run the `cp /mnt/ne.o /lib/modules` and `cp /mnt/pcnet32.o /lib/modules` commands.

4. Return to the Linux Router Project configuration menu with the `/usr/sbin/lrcfg` command.

5. Configure the `/etc/modules` file to incorporate the network card drivers. To access this file, select 3 from the first menu, 2 from the second menu, and 1 from the third menu. Add the name of the module, such as `pcnet32` and `ne` as required, including necessary ports and addresses such as `irq=10` and `io=0x300`. Press F1 for a list of commands to use in the default editor.

6. Set up IP masquerading for the modules that you need. For example, if you want to set up FTP access through your router, delete the hash mark (#) in front of `ip_masq_ftp`.

7. Write the file with the Alt+S command. Exit this editor with the Alt+Q command. Return to the main menu with two Q commands.

8. Finally, to check your configuration, reboot the system. Keep the Linux Router Project boot disk in the floppy drive. The computer should now detect the installed network cards.

Configuring Basic Network Settings

The next thing to do is configure your basic network settings: Tell your router who you are, which interface is connected to which network, and so on.

To do this, you need to edit the main network settings file, option 1 on the network settings submenu (accessed by selecting option 1 on the main configuration menu). The main network settings file opens in the editor.

The router that you're setting up will forward messages from network to network. Therefore, you need to set up IP Forwarding, which means that you need to change the following lines from NO to YES.

```
IPFWDING_KERNEL=YES
IPFWDING_FW=YES
```

Next, make sure that you can assign a hostname to the router by changing the following line from NO to YES.

```
CONFIG_HOSTNAME=YES
```

Now you can assign IP addresses and network masks to your Ethernet cards. Find the lines

```
#IF0_IFNAME=eth0
IF0_IPADDR=dhcp
IF0_NETMASK=255.255.255.255
IF0_BROADCAST=255.255.255.255
IF0_IP_SPOOF=YES
```

Change them to the correct settings for eth0 and activate the interface by removing the # from the first line:

```
IF0_IFNAME=eth0
IF0_IPADDR=200.200.200.254
IF0_NETMASK=255.255.255.0
IF0_BROADCAST=200.200.200.255
IF0_IP_SPOOF=YES
```

Next, find the lines

```
#IF1_IFNAME=eth1
IF1_IPADDR=192.168.0.20
IF1_NETMASK=255.255.255.0
IF1_BROADCAST=192.168.0.255
IF1_IP_SPOOF=YES
```

and likewise change them to the correct settings for eth1 (your internal, secure network) and remove the hash mark:

```
IF1_IFNAME=eth1
IF1_IPADDR=10.10.10.1
IF1_NETMASK=255.255.255.0
IF1_BROADCAST=10.10.10.255
IF1_IP_SPOOF=YES
```

These steps configure the respective Ethernet cards in the router to communicate with their assigned networks. (Make sure the Ethernet cards are physically connected to the correct networks.)

Next, comment out the host information. Add hash marks to the front of all host-related lines. Since this computer is serving only as a router, in general, you don't need to assign host information.

```
#HOST0_IPADDR=192.168.7.123
#HOST0_GATEWAY_IF=default
#HOST0_GATEWAY_IP=192.168.1.200
#HOST0_IPMASQ=NO
#HOST0_IPMASQ_IF=default
```

Now make sure to properly assign the network addresses for the internal and external networks. The default file includes just the following lines for one network:

```
#NET0_NETADDR=192.168.0.0
NET0_NETMASK=$IF1_NETMASK
NET0_GATEWAY_IF=$IF1_IFNAME
NET0_GATEWAY_IP=default
NET0_IPMASQ=YES
NET0_IPMASQ_IF=$IF0_IFNAME
```

Make sure to change this to reflect the configuration of both the secure and unsecure network:

```
NET0_NETADDR=200.200.200.0
NET0_NETMASK=$IF0_NETMASK
NET0_GATEWAY_IF=$IF0_IFNAME
NET0_GATEWAY_IP=default
NET0_IPMASQ=NO               # No need to masquerade real IP addresses
NET0_IPMASQ_IF=$IF0_IFNAME

NET1_NETADDR=10.10.10.0
NET1_NETMASK=$IF1_NETMASK
NET1_GATEWAY_IF=$IF1_IFNAME
NET1_GATEWAY_IP=default
NET1_IPMASQ=YES              # You must masquerade private IP addresses
NET1_IPMASQ_IF=$IF1_IFNAME
```

Finally, configure the Gateway, which is the default route from your network to the Internet.

```
GW0_IPADDR=200.200.200.1
GW0_IFNAME=$IF0_IFNAME
GW0_METRIC=1
```

Other sections of the configuration file set up default routes without requiring additional configuration. You should assign a hostname to your router. Change the following line to give your router a hostname of your choice:

```
HOSTNAME=tourettes
```

Now save this file. Press Ctrl+W and press Enter to save, and then press Ctrl+C to return to the network configuration menu. Press 2 in this menu to enter the /etc/network_direct.conf file, where you can set up basic security.

Setting Up Basic Security

Add the following line to the /etc/network_direct.conf file:

```
[ "IF$" ] && ipfwadm -F -a -m -S "$NETWORK1"/24 -D 0.0.0.0/0
```

Without going into the syntax of ipfwadm (which you can find at http://www .dreamwvr.com/ipfwadm/ipfwadm-faq.html), note that this command does the following:

- Enables IP forwarding for outgoing connections from the secure network to the outside world.

- Enables IP masquerading so that the source address of all outbound connections is the external IP address of the router, rather than the original host address on the secure network. Since those on the outside don't see the IP addresses inside your secure network, they cannot easily use these addresses to break into your system.

- Handles all return connections to make sure that data in response to an outgoing connection is returned to the correct host inside your secure network.

Now you can save the file (Ctrl+W) and quit the editor (Ctrl+C).

NOTE   Basic security for the more up-to-date ipchains is beyond the scope of this book. For more information, refer to the security links in the Linux Router Project documentation Web site, lrp.c0wz.com. One good example of these scripts is the "Seattle Firewall," available at seawall.sourceforge.net.

Further Network Configuration

Further network configuration should not be necessary. For example, look at the hosts.allow and hosts.deny files. These files are designed to protect the router itself from unwanted attack by denying attempts to log in to the router remotely across the network. In other words, the router needs to be configured at the console rather than through a network login. It is probably wise to leave these files unchanged.

Saving Your Changes

Once you have configured the router, it is necessary to save your changes back to the boot floppy. You can do this by choosing b from the main configuration menu. You are backing up the etc module because you have changed files in the /etc directory only. You can do this by selecting 2 from the backup menu.

After writing the changes back to the boot floppy, you are ready to reboot your system to enable your new configuration. Now you should have a functioning router serving as a basic firewall.

Going Further

Using these basic principles, it is possible to work with the Linux Router Project distribution to implement (among other things) more advanced routers that support high-speed Internet connections, ISDN connections, and dial-up PPP users. These all require additional combinations of modules and system-specific configuration. More information is available on the Linux Router Project Web site at http://www.linuxrouter.org.

Looking Ahead

In this chapter, you saw how flexible Linux is, allowing you to turn a PC into not just a powerful workstation or network server, but also a router and a security firewall.

In Chapter 32, "Building Your Own Web Server," you will continue your look at Linux in a networked environment with a detailed discussion of how to use Linux as an intranet Web server. Linux is an increasingly popular platform for Internet and intranet Web servers because of the availability of high-performance, industry-standard Web server software that can be run on inexpensive hardware.

In fact, the reliability and speed of Linux Web servers makes them popular in many circumstances where high-cost, commercial Web server solutions could have been used.

If you don't have a background in Web development or design, the chapter still provides the basic knowledge you need to begin setting up your own Web server in your organization.

PART VII

Using Red Hat Linux 7.1 As a Web and E-Mail Server

CHAPTER
THIRTY-TWO

Building Your Own Web Server

- ■ What Is a Web Server?

- ■ Linux Web Servers

- ■ Installing Apache

- ■ Configuring Apache

- ■ Managing Your Web Server

- ■ Building a Web Site

You've come a long way in your study of Linux and you are now ready to look at one of the most popular applications of Linux: using the operating system as the basis for small and medium-sized Web servers.

In fact, Linux is widely used for deploying Web servers for a number of reasons:

- It provides the flexibility and manageability of Unix.

- It costs little or nothing to set up and run.

- It provides a wide breadth of tools for building fairly sophisticated Web sites.

This chapter covers the basics of turning a Linux PC into a Web server for an intranet or Internet site. It starts with an overview of the job played by a Web server and then examines some of the major Web servers available for Linux.

It then provides detailed information about installing, configuring, and managing the Apache Web server, arguably the most popular Web server on the Internet and the one that currently ships with Red Hat Linux 7.1.

This chapter closes by taking a guided tour through the building of a simple Web site using Apache. By the end of the chapter, you should be in a position to create your own Web site using Linux and Apache and feel confident enough to experiment with other Web servers available for Linux.

What Is a Web Server?

If you have used the Web at all, you have probably heard the term "Web server" bandied about, but you may not have a clear picture of what a Web server does.

While it is often the case that a term serves a dual purpose, referring to physical machines as well as the software they run, "Web server" correctly refers to the software that can be run to answer requests from Web clients such as Web browsers.

Web server software is designed to serve a simple purpose: to answer requests from clients, using the Hypertext Transfer Protocol (HTTP), for documents available from the Web site being handled by that software.

What happens is this: The client requests a document using a URL; the Web server receives the request, maps the URL to a physical file on the system (which could be an HTML file or any one of numerous other file types), and then, after making sure that the client has permission to retrieve the file, returns the file to the client. In addition, the Web server generally keeps logs of who has requested which documents and how many times requests were made, allowing for the production of statistics used to determine how popular Web sites are.

More Than Just Retrieving Files

The description above is overly simplistic, but that explanation serves to describe the work done by the majority of Web servers most of the time.

Of course, as you browse the Web, you quickly become aware that the Web is more than simply a set of static documents that a Web server sends to Web browsers on request. Forms can be used to request information from the server or provide information to the organization running the server. Products can be ordered, credit cards can be verified, and many other types of transactions can take place.

In order for all this interactivity to occur, modern Web servers must do more than simply answer HTTP requests. Web servers generally provide two mechanisms for interactions:

- The Common Gateway Interface (CGI)
- Server application program interfaces (APIs)

The Common Gateway Interface

CGI is the most widely deployed method for adding interactivity to a Web server. Under the CGI model, a very simple extension is added to the HTTP for requesting static files.

CGI provides a standardized method for causing a program to be run on the server and for data from a form to be passed to the program for processing. These programs can be written in almost any programming or scripting language—C, Perl, and Java are commonly used.

When a user requests a CGI program—possibly by submitting a form or by clicking a link to the program—the Web server passes the user's data to the CGI program and waits for the program to return data. Any data returned by the program is passed straight back to the client in the same way that the contents of a static file are returned to a browser. It is the program's job to produce valid content to be returned to the browser and to handle all contingencies so that valid content is returned to the client.

Overall, the CGI concept has worked quite well. The simplicity of the way data is passed from the server to the CGI program, and the way in which the program needs to build the data it returns to the server, means that simple CGI programs can be written with little programming experience.

In addition, it is easy to change and test CGI programs, since popular scripting languages such as Perl can be used to write them.

The standard nature of the CGI interface also means that a CGI script or program written for one Linux Web server will likely function without alteration on any other Linux Web server—and possibly on any other Unix server—if it is written using a language commonly found in all operating systems.

Still, for all its advantages, CGI suffers from some serious drawbacks that make it unattractive for some Web sites. Its two main weaknesses pertain to security and speed.

Since the emergence of the Web, significant security holes in the CGI interface have been discovered that, if a script is poorly written, can allow a system running a Web server to be completely accessible to a knowledgeable hacker. This makes CGI less than desirable where the security of the data on the Web server is paramount, as it would be on most corporate Internet and intranet servers—and especially on sites offering online financial transactions and credit card sales.

In addition, the CGI interface is not very efficient. The Web server runs one or more processes that answer client requests. The browser then starts child processes for the CGI program, passing data to this new process and waiting for it to finish. On a busy site, this can lead to large numbers of new processes needing to start in short periods of time, especially where CGI scripts are being heavily used. Each request for a CGI program leads to a separate process for each request.

This is a highly inefficient way to process large amounts of data and requests, and it's the reason why many leading Web servers have implemented their own APIs for writing server-side programs.

Application Program Interfaces

APIs provide a way to write programs that integrate tightly into the Web server and generally don't require new processes for each request. APIs have enabled the development of Web-based applications that are capable of handling large numbers of requests as compared to similar CGI-based solutions. In addition, API-based solutions have been the subject of less criticism with regard to security.

API-based programs can generally do the same jobs as CGI programs do, such as processing information provided in forms, accessing data in databases, and verifying credit cards.

The biggest disadvantage of server APIs is that they commit an application to a particular Web server. Moving an application to a new server can require significant reprogramming, and with a large application this can be impractical.

Just remember that a server needs to be well tested with regard to security, performance, and flexibility before you deploy a large application on it using the server's built-in API.

Linux Web Servers

Since the framework for the Internet was developed by many of the same people who developed Unix, it isn't surprising that Unix and Linux platforms enjoy the broadest choice of available Web servers.

As with most things in the Unix world, this same range of Web servers is available for Linux. The majority of Linux Web servers are free. The best-known Linux Web servers are these:

- NCSA httpd
- Apache
- AOLserver
- Boa
- WN
- W3C/Cern

In addition to these free servers, there are several commercial alternatives available for Linux, including the following:

- FastTrack/iPlanet
- Java Web Server
- Stronghold
- Zeus

Apache

By some counts, Apache is the most widely used Web server software. Standing for "A Patchy Server," Apache grew out of efforts to patch NCSA httpd, one of the original Web servers, to fix some problems and add functionality.

Since then, Apache has emerged as the non-commercial server of choice for Unix systems. More recently, it has been ported to Windows and can be used as a Web server on Windows NT/2000 systems.

Apache offers numerous features that make it attractive for Unix/Linux system administrators. Besides using a configuration based on the original NCSA httpd configuration files, Apache is available in full source code and is collectively developed, like many other popular applications for the Linux environment.

Apache offers its own API, which can be used as an alternative to CGI (which is also supported by Apache). In addition, the API can be used to produce plug-in modules that serve numerous purposes. Among the available modules are the following:

- Alternative authentication systems, including authentication from NIS authentication servers or from LDAP (Lightweight Directory Access Protocol) databases.

- Server-side scripting environments that serve the same function as Microsoft Active Server Pages or Netscape LiveWire, including PHP/FI and HeiTML.

- Modules designed to improve the performance of traditional CGI. For instance, the FastCGI module uses shortcuts to minimize the time it takes to execute a CGI program and return the results. The Perl module allows Perl scripts to run in a single process and to be compiled on first execution only, making Perl-based CGI perform almost as fast as compiled CGI programs and some API-based Web applications.

The original source code for the latest version of Apache is available from httpd.apache.org, along with precompiled binaries for many different systems including Linux. Apache is included as the default Web server installed with Red Hat Linux 7.1.

NCSA httpd

NCSA httpd is one of the two original Web servers (along with the Cern Web server) upon which the Web was first built. NCSA httpd comes out of the National Center for Supercomputer Applications at the University of Illinois at

Urbana-Champaign, which is also the home of Mosaic, the original graphical Web browser that launched the Web onto the road to widespread popularity.

NCSA httpd offers a core set of functions designed to meet the needs of all but the most demanding of Web sites. These features include built-in support for multiple hosts, Basic and Digest authentication, directory-level access controls, server-side includes, and full CGI support.

While NCSA httpd is no longer under active development, it does provide the background for the current structure of Apache. The original source code and precompiled binaries for NCSA httpd are available from hoohoo.ncsa.uiuc.edu.

W3C/Jigsaw

The Jigsaw Web server is the Java-based successor to Cern, which was one of the first Web servers powering the Internet. As a completely Java-based server, it is designed to run on any operating system that supports this language, including Unix/Linux and Microsoft Windows.

Jigsaw is set up with several different types of Java objects, including:

Resources   What is seen on the Web page. This includes static objects such as text or image files, and dynamic objects such as scripts.

Frames   What actually handles the resource. A frame includes all of the necessary information to serve a specific resource; for example, an HTTPframe object serves an HTTP resource.

Filters   A way to dynamically modify a resource. For example, if a Web site doesn't see that a user has logged in, it can "filter" in a login page.

Indexer   The way to classify resources. The two main indexes are directories (to group files) and extensions (for common files such as TXT or INI).

The stable version available at the time of this writing is Jigsaw 2.2.0. Jigsaw version numbers parallel Linux kernel versions; for example, if you see a Jigsaw version in the future with an odd middle number, such as Jigsaw 2.3.4, that version is unstable. The W3C maintains a page about the server at www.w3.org/Jigsaw.

NOTE   The former W3C server, Cern, was one of the original Web servers on the Internet. Unfortunately, it is no longer supported.

WN

This chapter's survey of free servers is now moving toward less-commonly used servers. Still, these niche market servers help you to see the diversity possible in Web server technology and features.

WN is another freely available server with unique features that set it apart from other Web servers. For instance, WN allows full-text searching of what the developer refers to as a *logical HTML document*: a document that consists of multiple linked files. In addition, users can search files on the server and easily obtain matching documents. Users can also download a single logical document made up of multiple linked documents, making it easy for them to print files that are structured as a series of small documents.

Another unique feature of the WN server is its ability to serve up conditional documents. That is, it is possible to create a single document with definitions that cause the correct version to be sent to a client on the basis of such variables as the IP address of the client or the browser version of the client.

The security model of the WN server as well as its relatively small size also set it apart from the likes of Apache and the NCSA httpd Web server. In the latter servers, the default action is to serve a file unless permission is specifically denied. With WN, no file is served unless permission is specifically granted for the file. This potentially makes the server more secure and provides finer-grained control over access to files. You can get a copy of WN at `hopf.math.nwu.edu`.

Boa

The last free Web server in our survey is the Boa server. This is a little-known server that is still in a pre-1 release as of the writing of this book.

Boa is included here to show that servers can be small, simple, and basic and still serve a useful role. Boa offers very basic functionality and less fine-grained access control than Apache or WN.

But Boa is designed in a way that makes it potentially faster than almost any other available Web server for Linux. In fact, the creators of Boa claim that the server is significantly faster than Apache, although more real-world testing on large Web sites is needed to prove this claim.

Boa achieves this performance gain through a single-tasking design. Where traditional Web servers create multiple processes to listen for requests and then create a process to handle each request, the Boa server runs as a single process and handles all the processing and juggling of multiple requests internally rather than allowing the operating system's multitasking mechanism to do so. Boa spawns a child process only when a CGI request is made. You can learn more about Boa at `www.boa.org`.

Stronghold

Stronghold is probably one of the best-known commercial Web servers for Linux. Stronghold is a commercially available version of Apache that offers an extremely secure and fully supported software package.

Stronghold provides all the tools you need to set up a secure server, including Certificate Authority tools. With a Certificate Authority you can, if necessary, issue digital certificates approved by a third-party certificate authority such as VeriSign. Other Stronghold security features include support for hardware cryptographical acceleration, as well as 128-bit data encryption for additional security.

In addition, since Stronghold comes with full source code, you can use it for everything you use Apache for, including compiling in Apache modules and writing your own modules. Stronghold is now distributed by Red Hat at `http://www.c2.net/products/sh3/index.php3`.

FastTrack/iPlanet

FastTrack is one of Netscape's well-known families of Web servers. Unfortunately, until its recent decision to release its browser and browser source code into the public domain, Netscape had no interest in developing Web servers for noncommercial operating systems such as Linux.

With the advent of the alliance between AOL/Netscape and Sun, interest in FastTrack has revived. It is now a part of the iPlanet family of Web and application servers. FastTrack is now a Java-based free version of the iPlanet Web server. The Enterprise version of this server is a commercial product.

FastTrack is an easy-to-manage Web server. All configuration and administration is done through Web-based forms. These forms allow a Webmaster to do everything from creating users to controlling access to files at the directory level.

FastTrack provides support for server-side includes, CGI, and Netscape's own API for developing applications. In addition, FastTrack can support Netscape's server-side JavaScript development environment, LiveWire.

The server is also capable of being used as a secure server with SSL technology. For more information on FastTrack, navigate to `http://home.netscape.com/fasttrack/v3.0/index.html`.

AOLserver

AOLserver has an interesting history, moving from a commercial offering in 1995 to one of the most full-featured free servers currently available.

AOLserver started its life as NaviPress, one of the first commercial servers available. In late 1995, AOL acquired the company producing NaviPress and began to use the server internally. In early 1997, AOL released the server as a free product for distribution on the Internet.

At the time of this writing, the latest release (3.4) of AOLserver includes the following features:

- Built-in full-text indexing for offering a search function on a Web site

- A built-in API that is accessible from the C programming and the Tcl scripting languages

- Full CGI (optional) and server-side include support

- Server-side dynamic page functionality similar to Microsoft's Active Server Pages

- Database connectivity for building database-driven dynamic applications without third-party Web-database integration tools

As of this writing, AOLserver is still being supported, despite the efforts of the alliance between AOL/Netscape and Sun on the iPlanet series of servers. You can download AOLserver from the AOLserver Web site at `www.aolserver.com`.

Java Web Server

The Java Web Server from Sun's JavaSoft division is a unique Web server on this list. Like the W3C/Jigsaw server, the Java Web Server is developed fully in Java and can theoretically run on any platform with a Java Virtual Machine.

The Java Web Server offers numerous features that make it a competitive commercial offering, including a server applet framework for writing applications without falling back on CGI and full support for SSL so that the server can be used in secure applications such as online storefronts.

To help improve performance, it is possible to produce compiled pages that contain both HTML and program code. For statistical purposes, user sessions can be tracked in programs using a built-in server-tracking mechanism.

Unfortunately, with growth of the alliance between AOL/Netscape and Sun, they have had three Web servers to support. As of this writing, the decision was made to stop development on this product in early 2001. Nevertheless, this is still a popular commercial option for Web servers. If you ever need to administer or support the Java Web Server, you can read its specifications at the Java Web Server home page at `http://www.sun.com/software/jwebserver/index.html`.

Zeus

The final Web server discussed in this survey is the Zeus Web server. The latest version of Zeus, 3.3.8, is a Web server for Unix/Linux and the Macintosh OS X. It offers built-in clustering support, which clearly positions it as a potential choice for high-volume sites. With clustering, it is possible to serve a single Web address from multiple Web servers. This allows the load of requests to be distributed over a group of servers, and it means that more simultaneous hits can be handled.

This functionality has helped Zeus become the Web server of choice for some of the most-heavily used Web sites, including eBay and British Telecom. Developments related to the Linux 2.4 kernel suggest that the capacity of the Zeus Web server will grow. In a recent article, the IBM Linux Technology Center found that Zeus performance on Linux 2.4 kernel-based servers was nearly double that on Linux 2.2 kernel-based servers.

In addition, Zeus offers support for ISAPI, the API from Microsoft's Internet Information Server, and offers this support on Unix as well as Windows NT/2000. Zeus also supports Java servlets like those used in the Java Web Server and offers integrated database connectivity using the JDBC standard for accessing databases.

Perhaps most interesting is that Zeus offers SSL with full 128-bit encryption worldwide. Because the U.S. government limits the export of 128-bit encryption technology, the majority of secure products being exported by U.S. companies have offered only watered-down 56-bit encryption. Most reported occurrences of people cracking the encryption of products such as Netscape have involved the 56-bit encryption versions of products. Zeus information is available at `www.zeus.co.uk`.

Installing Apache

The rest of this chapter takes a detailed look at the Apache Web server, for two reasons:

1. The Apache server is the default Web server that ships with most Linux distributions (including Red Hat Linux 7.1 on the CD-ROM accompanying this book).

2. Since Apache is the most popular Web server currently on the Internet, it will most likely be the Web server you want to use.

If you performed a reasonably complete installation when you set up your Linux system, in all likelihood you already have Apache installed. There are several ways you can check this. For example, you can use the rpm command:

```
$ rpm -q apache
```

If you have Apache installed, you should get back a result like this:

```
apache-1.3.19-5
```

If you get back an indication that Apache is installed, you can skip forward to the section titled "Configuring Apache."

Installing Apache from the Red Hat CD-ROM

The simplest way to install Apache is from the Red Hat CD-ROM that comes with this book. In order to do this, simply mount the CD-ROM (normally at /mnt/cdrom) and then use the cd /mnt/cdrom/RedHat/RPMS command. (If you mounted your CD-ROM somewhere other than /mnt/cdrom, you need to change to the appropriate directory based on your mount point.) This directory contains all the RPM files for the complete Red Hat Linux distribution. Here you simply use rpm to install the package:

```
$ rpm -i apache-1.3.19-5.i386.rpm
```

Downloading the Latest Version of Apache

If you plan to run a mission-critical or high-volume Web server, you may want to download the latest version of Apache from httpd.apache.org (see Figure 32.1). By using the latest version, you can be sure that small bugs that wouldn't affect the average site won't come to plague your more complex or heavily used site.

FIGURE 32.1:

The Apache Web site

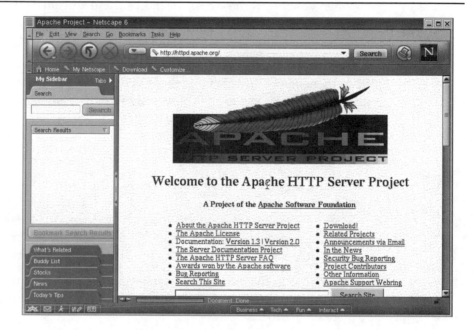

All discussion of configuration and management of Apache assumes that you are using the version of Apache on the Red Hat CD-ROM included with this book. Generally, new versions of Apache are backward-compatible. That is, the configuration files you look at in this chapter should work with newer versions of Apache.

When downloading Apache from the Apache Web site, you have the option to download either the original source code or precompiled binary files for Linux. While there are compelling reasons to use the source code version, especially if you plan to develop programs using the Apache API or you want to build extra modules into your server, you should download the precompiled binaries to set up a Web site with the basic Apache feature set. This book won't discuss compiling your own copy of Apache, since this requires a much deeper discussion of Web servers than can be provided in a single chapter.

If you want to obtain the latest binary distribution from Apache, point your browser to the Apache Web site (httpd.apache.org) and select the Download link there. This leads to a directory of files. Sometimes the latest release can be found in this directory. If not, follow the httpd and binaries links, and then select your operating system (in our case, Linux). Here you will find a list of available files.

When you review these files, the most current version depends on your processor. For example, the i586 and i686 designations indicate that the package has been compiled with optimizations for either Pentium- or Pentium II-class processors.

The README files in any download directory are text files; it is a good idea to read them before downloading. The GZ files are compressed using the gzip utility. The ASC files include a PGP security signature. Once you have your chosen a package to download, expand the file in a temporary location. You can use the command

```
$ tar xzvf apache_file-name
```

to expand the archive into a subdirectory of the current directory. In this case, the subdirectory is called apache_1.3.20, but this may be different depending on the version of Apache that is available when you download the binaries. Inside this directory is the complete source code for the version you have downloaded, along with sample configuration files and full documentation in HTML format.

In order to install the binaries you have downloaded, you need to run the install-bindist.sh installation script from the top-level directory of the expanded archive:

```
$ install-bindist.sh
```

By default, this command installs the Apache server, configuration files, and Web documents in /usr/local/apache. This differs from Red Hat, which places the Apache server in /usr/sbin and the configuration files in /etc/httpd/conf and makes /var/www/html the root directory for Web documents. This chapter assumes the Red Hat defaults since this is what you will find if you install Apache from the CD-ROM included with the book.

NOTE   If you're using a different version of Apache, the directories may vary. Use the find or locate commands to get the applicable directories for you.

The binary Apache distributions include complete instructions for compiling the application from the included source code, so if you find that the binaries you have downloaded are not working as expected (perhaps because of problems such as incompatible libraries in your version of Linux), you may want to follow those instructions and try building your own Apache binaries.

Configuring Apache

Prior to version 1.3.6, Apache was configured using three main configuration files: `httpd.conf`, `srm.conf`, and `access.conf`. In the standard Red Hat installation of Apache, these files are found at `/etc/httpd/conf/`, although this location can easily be changed (as you will see later when this chapter discusses starting the Apache Web server). From version 1.3.6, these three files are combined into a single file: `httpd.conf`. This file includes the purposes of all three files and the content is essentially the same as the original three files combined.

The roles of these three configuration files are not very clearly defined and there is some overlap, but essentially they are used as follows:

httpd.conf This file is used to set general settings such as the port number used by the server as well as to load modules into the server when it starts. This file also indicates the location of the `srm.conf` and `access.conf` files.

srm.conf This file sets other general settings such as the root document tree of the server and the rules related to CGI programs.

access.conf This file can be used to set access control restrictions for the server or for specific directories.

Let's discuss the handful of major settings that any Webmaster should consider before running Apache on an open Web server. In these examples, you will use the Apache 1.3.19 server that was included with Red Hat Linux 7.1. This version of Apache uses the single `/etc/httpd/conf/httpd.conf` configuration file.

With the parameters in this file, you can specify the behavior of the Apache server as a whole, how the main server responds to HTTP requests, and the response of any virtual hosts, which looks like distinct individual Web sites to anyone with just a Web browser.

Apache Configuration File

While the `/etc/httpd/conf` subdirectory includes all three original configuration files, the only one that must be configured is the `httpd.conf` file. The remaining CONF files are for backward compatibility. The structure of the `httpd.conf` file is fairly straightforward. Below is the default `httpd.conf` file:

```
##
## httpd.conf - Apache HTTP server configuration file
##
```

```
#
# Based upon the NCSA server configuration files originally by Rob McCool.
#
# This is the main Apache server configuration file.  It contains the
# configuration directives that give the server its instructions.
# See <URL:http://www.apache.org/docs/> for detailed information about
# the directives.
#
# Do NOT simply read the instructions in here without understanding
# what they do.  They're here only as hints or reminders.  If you are unsure
# consult the online docs. You have been warned.
#
# After this file is processed, the server will look for and process
# /usr/conf/srm.conf and then /usr/conf/access.conf
# unless you have overridden these with ResourceConfig and/or
# AccessConfig directives here.
#
# The configuration directives are grouped into three basic sections:
#  1. Directives that control the operation of the Apache server process as a
#     whole (the 'global environment').
#  2. Directives that define the parameters of the 'main' or 'default' server,
#     which responds to requests that aren't handled by a virtual host.
#     These directives also provide default values for the settings
#     of all virtual hosts.
#  3. Settings for virtual hosts, which allow Web requests to be sent to
#     different IP addresses or hostnames and have them handled by the
#     same Apache server process.
#
# Configuration and logfile names: If the filenames you specify for many
# of the server's control files begin with "/" (or "drive:/" for Win32), the
# server will use that explicit path.  If the filenames do *not* begin
# with "/", the value of ServerRoot is prepended - so "logs/foo.log"
# with ServerRoot set to "/usr/local/apache" will be interpreted by the
# server as "/usr/local/apache/logs/foo.log".
#


### Section 1: Global Environment
#
# The directives in this section affect the overall operation of Apache,
# such as the number of concurrent requests it can handle or where it
# can find its configuration files.
#
```

```
#
# ServerType is either inetd, or standalone.  Inetd mode is only supported on
# Unix platforms.
#
ServerType standalone

#
# ServerRoot: The top of the directory tree under which the server's
# configuration, error, and log files are kept.
#
# NOTE!  If you intend to place this on an NFS (or otherwise network)
# mounted filesystem then please read the LockFile documentation
# (available at <URL:http://www.apache.org/docs/mod/core.html#lockfile>);
# you will save yourself a lot of trouble.
#
# Do NOT add a slash at the end of the directory path.
#
ServerRoot "/etc/httpd"

#
# The LockFile directive sets the path to the lockfile used when Apache
# is compiled with either USE_FCNTL_SERIALIZED_ACCEPT or
# USE_FLOCK_SERIALIZED_ACCEPT. This directive should normally be left at
# its default value. The main reason for changing it is if the logs
# directory is NFS mounted, since the lockfile MUST BE STORED ON A LOCAL
# DISK. The PID of the main server process is automatically appended to
# the filename.
#
LockFile /var/lock/httpd.lock

#
# PidFile: The file in which the server should record its process
# identification number when it starts.
#
PidFile /var/run/httpd.pid

#
# ScoreBoardFile: File used to store internal server process information.
# Not all architectures require this.  But if yours does (you'll know because
# this file will be  created when you run Apache) then you *must* ensure that
# no two invocations of Apache share the same scoreboard file.
#
ScoreBoardFile /var/run/httpd.scoreboard
```

```
#
# In the standard configuration, the server will process this file,
# srm.conf, and access.conf in that order.  The latter two files are
# now distributed empty, as it is recommended that all directives
# be kept in a single file for simplicity.  The commented-out values
# below are the built-in defaults.  You can have the server ignore
# these files altogether by using "/dev/null" (for Unix) or
# "nul" (for Win32) for the arguments to the directives.
#
#ResourceConfig conf/srm.conf
#AccessConfig conf/access.conf


#
# Timeout: The number of seconds before receives and sends time out.
#
Timeout 300


#
# KeepAlive: Whether or not to allow persistent connections (more than
# one request per connection). Set to "Off" to deactivate.
#
KeepAlive On


#
# MaxKeepAliveRequests: The maximum number of requests to allow
# during a persistent connection. Set to 0 to allow an unlimited amount.
# We recommend you leave this number high, for maximum performance.
#
MaxKeepAliveRequests 100


#
# KeepAliveTimeout: Number of seconds to wait for the next request from the
# same client on the same connection.
#
KeepAliveTimeout 15


#
# Server-pool size regulation.  Rather than making you guess how many
# server processes you need, Apache dynamically adapts to the load it
# sees -- that is, it tries to maintain enough server processes to
# handle the current load, plus a few spare servers to handle transient
# load spikes (e.g., multiple simultaneous requests from a single
# Netscape browser).
#
```

```
# It does this by periodically checking how many servers are waiting
# for a request.  If there are fewer than MinSpareServers, it creates
# a new spare.  If there are more than MaxSpareServers, some of the
# spares die off.  The default values are probably OK for most sites.
#
MinSpareServers 5
MaxSpareServers 20


#
# Number of servers to start initially -- should be a reasonable ballpark
# figure.
#
StartServers 8


#
# Limit on total number of servers running, i.e., limit on the number
# of clients who can simultaneously connect -- if this limit is ever
# reached, clients will be LOCKED OUT, so it should NOT BE SET TOO LOW.
# It is intended mainly as a brake to keep a runaway server from taking
# the system with it as it spirals down...
#
MaxClients 150


#
# MaxRequestsPerChild: the number of requests each child process is
# allowed to process before the child dies.  The child will exit so
# as to avoid problems after prolonged use when Apache (and maybe the
# libraries it uses) leak memory or other resources.  On most systems, this
# isn't really needed, but a few (such as Solaris) do have notable leaks
# in the libraries. For these platforms, set to something like 10000
# or so; a setting of 0 means unlimited.
#
# NOTE: This value does not include keepalive requests after the initial
#       request per connection. For example, if a child process handles
#       an initial request and 10 subsequent "keptalive" requests, it
#       would only count as 1 request towards this limit.
#
MaxRequestsPerChild 100


#
# Listen: Allows you to bind Apache to specific IP addresses and/or
# ports, in addition to the default. See also the <VirtualHost>
```

```
# directive.
#
#Listen 3000
#Listen 12.34.56.78:80
Listen 80


#
# BindAddress: You can support virtual hosts with this option. This directive
# is used to tell the server which IP address to listen to. It can either
# contain "*", an IP address, or a fully qualified Internet domain name.
# See also the <VirtualHost> and Listen directives.
#
#BindAddress *


#
# Dynamic Shared Object (DSO) Support
#
# To be able to use the functionality of a module which was built as a DSO you
# have to place corresponding `LoadModule' lines at this location so the
# directives contained in it are actually available _before_ they are used.
# Please read the file README.DSO in the Apache 1.3 distribution for more
# details about the DSO mechanism and run `httpd -l' for the list of already
# built-in (statically linked and thus always available) modules in your httpd
# binary.
#
# Note: The order is which modules are loaded is important.  Don't change
# the order below without expert advice.
#
# Example:
# LoadModule foo_module modules/mod_foo.so

#LoadModule mmap_static_module modules/mod_mmap_static.so
LoadModule vhost_alias_module modules/mod_vhost_alias.so
LoadModule env_module          modules/mod_env.so
LoadModule config_log_module   modules/mod_log_config.so
LoadModule agent_log_module    modules/mod_log_agent.so
LoadModule referer_log_module  modules/mod_log_referer.so
#LoadModule mime_magic_module   modules/mod_mime_magic.so
LoadModule mime_module         modules/mod_mime.so
LoadModule negotiation_module  modules/mod_negotiation.so
LoadModule status_module       modules/mod_status.so
LoadModule info_module         modules/mod_info.so
```

```
LoadModule includes_module      modules/mod_include.so
LoadModule autoindex_module     modules/mod_autoindex.so
LoadModule dir_module           modules/mod_dir.so
LoadModule cgi_module           modules/mod_cgi.so
LoadModule asis_module          modules/mod_asis.so
LoadModule imap_module          modules/mod_imap.so
LoadModule action_module        modules/mod_actions.so
#LoadModule speling_module       modules/mod_speling.so
LoadModule userdir_module       modules/mod_userdir.so
LoadModule alias_module         modules/mod_alias.so
LoadModule rewrite_module       modules/mod_rewrite.so
LoadModule access_module        modules/mod_access.so
LoadModule auth_module          modules/mod_auth.so
LoadModule anon_auth_module     modules/mod_auth_anon.so
LoadModule db_auth_module       modules/mod_auth_db.so
#LoadModule digest_module        modules/mod_digest.so
#LoadModule proxy_module         modules/libproxy.so
#LoadModule cern_meta_module     modules/mod_cern_meta.so
LoadModule expires_module       modules/mod_expires.so
LoadModule headers_module       modules/mod_headers.so
#LoadModule usertrack_module     modules/mod_usertrack.so
#LoadModule example_module       modules/mod_example.so
#LoadModule unique_id_module     modules/mod_unique_id.so
LoadModule setenvif_module      modules/mod_setenvif.so
#LoadModule bandwidth_module     modules/mod_bandwidth.so
#LoadModule put_module               modules/mod_put.so
<IfDefine HAVE_PERL>
LoadModule perl_module          modules/libperl.so
</IfDefine>
<IfDefine HAVE_PHP>
LoadModule php_module           modules/mod_php.so
</IfDefine>
<IfDefine HAVE_PHP3>
LoadModule php3_module          modules/libphp3.so
</IfDefine>
<IfDefine HAVE_PHP4>
LoadModule php4_module          modules/libphp4.so
</IfDefine>
<IfDefine HAVE_DAV>
LoadModule dav_module           modules/libdav.so
</IfDefine>
<IfDefine HAVE_ROAMING>
```

```
LoadModule roaming_module      modules/mod_roaming.so
</IfDefine>
<IfDefine HAVE_SSL>
LoadModule ssl_module          modules/libssl.so
</IfDefine>

#   Reconstruction of the complete module list from all available modules
#   (static and shared ones) to achieve correct module execution order.
#   [WHENEVER YOU CHANGE THE LOADMODULE SECTION ABOVE UPDATE THIS, TOO]
ClearModuleList
#AddModule mod_mmap_static.c
AddModule mod_vhost_alias.c
AddModule mod_env.c
AddModule mod_log_config.c
AddModule mod_log_agent.c
AddModule mod_log_referer.c
#AddModule mod_mime_magic.c
AddModule mod_mime.c
AddModule mod_negotiation.c
AddModule mod_status.c
AddModule mod_info.c
AddModule mod_include.c
AddModule mod_autoindex.c
AddModule mod_dir.c
AddModule mod_cgi.c
AddModule mod_asis.c
AddModule mod_imap.c
AddModule mod_actions.c
#AddModule mod_speling.c
AddModule mod_userdir.c
AddModule mod_alias.c
AddModule mod_rewrite.c
AddModule mod_access.c
AddModule mod_auth.c
AddModule mod_auth_anon.c
AddModule mod_auth_db.c
#AddModule mod_digest.c
#AddModule mod_proxy.c
#AddModule mod_cern_meta.c
AddModule mod_expires.c
AddModule mod_headers.c
#AddModule mod_usertrack.c
#AddModule mod_example.c
```

```
#AddModule mod_unique_id.c
AddModule mod_so.c
AddModule mod_setenvif.c
#AddModule mod_bandwidth.c
#AddModule mod_put.c
<IfDefine HAVE_PERL>
AddModule mod_perl.c
</IfDefine>
<IfDefine HAVE_PHP>
AddModule mod_php.c
</IfDefine>
<IfDefine HAVE_PHP3>
AddModule mod_php3.c
</IfDefine>
<IfDefine HAVE_PHP4>
AddModule mod_php4.c
</IfDefine>
<IfDefine HAVE_DAV>
AddModule mod_dav.c
</IfDefine>
<IfDefine HAVE_ROAMING>
AddModule mod_roaming.c
</IfDefine>
<IfDefine HAVE_SSL>
AddModule mod_ssl.c
</IfDefine>


#
# ExtendedStatus: controls whether Apache will generate "full" status
# information (ExtendedStatus On) or just basic information (ExtendedStatus
# Off) when the "server-status" handler is called. The default is Off.
#
#ExtendedStatus On


### Section 2: 'Main' server configuration
#
# The directives in this section set up the values used by the 'main'
# server, which responds to any requests that aren't handled by a
# <VirtualHost> definition.  These values also provide defaults for
# any <VirtualHost> containers you may define later in the file.
#
# All of these directives may appear inside <VirtualHost> containers,
# in which case these default settings will be overridden for the
```

```
# virtual host being defined.
#


#
# If your ServerType directive (set earlier in the 'Global Environment'
# section) is set to "inetd", the next few directives don't have any
# effect since their settings are defined by the inetd configuration.
# Skip ahead to the ServerAdmin directive.
#


#
# Port: The port to which the standalone server listens. For
# ports < 1023, you will need httpd to be run as root initially.
#
Port 80


#
# If you wish httpd to run as a different user or group, you must run
# httpd as root initially and it will switch.
#
# User/Group: The name (or #number) of the user/group to run httpd as.
#  . On SCO (ODT 3) use "User nouser" and "Group nogroup".
#  . On HPUX you may not be able to use shared memory as nobody, and the
#    suggested workaround is to create a user www and use that user.
#  NOTE that some kernels refuse to setgid(Group) or semctl(IPC_SET)
#  when the value of (unsigned)Group is above 60000;
#  don't use Group nobody on these systems!
#
User apache
Group apache


#
# ServerAdmin: Your address, where problems with the server should be
# e-mailed.  This address appears on some server-generated pages, such
# as error documents.
#
ServerAdmin root@localhost


#
# ServerName: allows you to set a host name which is sent back to clients for
# your server if it's different than the one the program would get (i.e., use
# "www" instead of the host's real name).
#
```

```
# Note: You cannot just invent host names and hope they work. The name you
# define here must be a valid DNS name for your host. If you don't understand
# this, ask your network administrator.
# If your host doesn't have a registered DNS name, enter its IP address here.
# You will have to access it by its address (e.g., http://123.45.67.89/)
# anyway, and this will make redirections work in a sensible way.
#
#ServerName localhost

#
# DocumentRoot: The directory out of which you will serve your
# documents. By default, all requests are taken from this directory, but
# symbolic links and aliases may be used to point to other locations.
#
DocumentRoot "/var/www/html"

#
# Each directory to which Apache has access, can be configured with respect
# to which services and features are allowed and/or disabled in that
# directory (and its subdirectories).
#
# First, we configure the "default" to be a very restrictive set of
# permissions.
#
<Directory />
    Options FollowSymLinks
    AllowOverride None
</Directory>

#
# Note that from this point forward you must specifically allow
# particular features to be enabled - so if something's not working as
# you might expect, make sure that you have specifically enabled it
# below.
#

#
# This should be changed to whatever you set DocumentRoot to.
#
<Directory "/var/www/html">
```

```
#
# This may also be "None", "All", or any combination of "Indexes",
# "Includes", "FollowSymLinks", "ExecCGI", or "MultiViews".
#
# Note that "MultiViews" must be named *explicitly* -- "Options All"
# doesn't give it to you.
#

    Options Indexes Includes FollowSymLinks


#
# This controls which options the .htaccess files in directories can
# override. Can also be "All", or any combination of "Options", "FileInfo",
# "AuthConfig", and "Limit"
#

    AllowOverride None


#
# Controls who can get stuff from this server.
#
    Order allow,deny
    Allow from all
</Directory>


#
# UserDir: The name of the directory which is appended onto a user's home
# directory if a ~user request is received.
#
UserDir public_html


#
# Control access to UserDir directories.  The following is an example
# for a site where these directories are restricted to read-only.
#
#<Directory /home/*/public_html>
#    AllowOverride FileInfo AuthConfig Limit
#    Options MultiViews Indexes SymLinksIfOwnerMatch IncludesNoExec
#    <Limit GET POST OPTIONS PROPFIND>
#        Order allow,deny
#        Allow from all
#    </Limit>
#    <Limit PUT DELETE PATCH PROPPATCH MKCOL COPY MOVE LOCK UNLOCK>
#        Order deny,allow
#        Deny from all
```

```
#    </Limit>
#</Directory>

#
# DirectoryIndex: Name of the file or files to use as a pre-written HTML
# directory index.  Separate multiple entries with spaces.
#
DirectoryIndex index.html index.htm index.shtml index.php index.php4 index
➥.php3 index.cgi

#
# AccessFileName: The name of the file to look for in each directory
# for access control information.
#
AccessFileName .htaccess

#
# The following lines prevent .htaccess files from being viewed by
# Web clients.  Since .htaccess files often contain authorization
# information, access is disallowed for security reasons.  Comment
# these lines out if you want Web visitors to see the contents of
# .htaccess files.  If you change the AccessFileName directive above,
# be sure to make the corresponding changes here.
#
# Also, folks tend to use names such as .htpasswd for password
# files, so this will protect those as well.
#
<Files ~ "^\.ht">
    Order allow,deny
    Deny from all
</Files>

#
# CacheNegotiatedDocs: By default, Apache sends "Pragma: no-cache" with each
# document that was negotiated on the basis of content. This asks proxy
# servers not to cache the document. Uncommenting the following line disables
# this behavior, and proxies will be allowed to cache the documents.
#
#CacheNegotiatedDocs

#
# UseCanonicalName:  (new for 1.3)  With this setting turned on, whenever
```

```
# Apache needs to construct a self-referencing URL (a URL that refers back
# to the server the response is coming from) it will use ServerName and
# Port to form a "canonical" name.  With this setting off, Apache will
# use the hostname:port that the client supplied, when possible.  This
# also affects SERVER_NAME and SERVER_PORT in CGI scripts.
#
UseCanonicalName On


#
# TypesConfig describes where the mime.types file (or equivalent) is
# to be found.
#
TypesConfig /etc/mime.types


#
# DefaultType is the default MIME type the server will use for a document
# if it cannot otherwise determine one, such as from filename extensions.
# If your server contains mostly text or HTML documents, "text/plain" is
# a good value.  If most of your content is binary, such as applications
# or images, you may want to use "application/octet-stream" instead to
# keep browsers from trying to display binary files as though they are
# text.
#
DefaultType text/plain


#
# The mod_mime_magic module allows the server to use various hints from the
# contents of the file itself to determine its type.  The MIMEMagicFile
# directive tells the module where the hint definitions are located.
# mod_mime_magic is not part of the default server (you have to add
# it yourself with a LoadModule [see the DSO paragraph in the 'Global
# Environment' section], or recompile the server and include mod_mime_magic
# as part of the configuration), so it's enclosed in an <IfModule> container.
# This means that the MIMEMagicFile directive will only be processed if the
# module is part of the server.
#
<IfModule mod_mime_magic.c>
    MIMEMagicFile /usr/share/magic
</IfModule>


#
# HostnameLookups: Log the names of clients or just their IP addresses
# e.g., www.apache.org (on) or 204.62.129.132 (off).
```

```
# The default is off because it'd be overall better for the net if people
# had to knowingly turn this feature on, since enabling it means that
# each client request will result in AT LEAST one lookup request to the
# nameserver.
#
HostnameLookups Off


#
# ErrorLog: The location of the error log file.
# If you do not specify an ErrorLog directive within a <VirtualHost>
# container, error messages relating to that virtual host will be
# logged here.  If you *do* define an error logfile for a <VirtualHost>
# container, that host's errors will be logged there and not here.
#
ErrorLog /var/log/httpd/error_log


#
# LogLevel: Control the number of messages logged to the error_log.
# Possible values include: debug, info, notice, warn, error, crit,
# alert, emerg.
#
LogLevel warn


#
# The following directives define some format nicknames for use with
# a CustomLog directive (see below).
#
LogFormat "%h %l %u %t \"%r\" %>s %b \"%{Referer}i\" \"%{User-Agent}i\""
➥combined
LogFormat "%h %l %u %t \"%r\" %>s %b" common
LogFormat "%{Referer}i -> %U" referer
LogFormat "%{User-agent}i" agent


#
# The location and format of the access logfile (Common Logfile Format).
# If you do not define any access logfiles within a <VirtualHost>
# container, they will be logged here.  Contrariwise, if you *do*
# define per-<VirtualHost> access logfiles, transactions will be
# logged therein and *not* in this file.
#
CustomLog /var/log/httpd/access_log common
```

```
#
# If you would like to have agent and referer logfiles, uncomment the
# following directives.
#
#CustomLog /var/log/httpd/referer_log referer
#CustomLog /var/log/httpd/agent_log agent


#
# If you prefer a single logfile with access, agent, and referer information
# (Combined Logfile Format) you can use the following directive.
#
#CustomLog /var/log/httpd/access_log combined


#
# Optionally add a line containing the server version and virtual host
# name to server-generated pages (error documents, FTP directory listings,
# mod_status and mod_info output etc., but not CGI generated documents).
# Set to "EMail" to also include a mailto: link to the ServerAdmin.
# Set to one of:  On | Off | EMail
#
ServerSignature On


#
# Aliases: Add here as many aliases as you need (with no limit). The format is
# Alias fakename realname
#
# Note that if you include a trailing / on fakename then the server will
# require it to be present in the URL.  So "/icons" isn't aliased in this
# example, only "/icons/"..
#
Alias /icons/ "/var/www/icons/"

<Directory "/var/www/icons">
    Options Indexes MultiViews
    AllowOverride None
    Order allow,deny
    Allow from all
</Directory>


#
# ScriptAlias: This controls which directories contain server scripts.
# ScriptAliases are essentially the same as Aliases, except that
# documents in the realname directory are treated as applications and
# run by the server when requested rather than as documents sent to the client.
```

```
# The same rules about trailing "/" apply to ScriptAlias directives as to
# Alias.
#
ScriptAlias /cgi-bin/ "/var/www/cgi-bin/"

#
# "/var/www/cgi-bin" should be changed to whatever your ScriptAliased
# CGI directory exists, if you have that configured.
#
<Directory "/var/www/cgi-bin">
    AllowOverride None
    Options ExecCGI
    Order allow,deny
    Allow from all
</Directory>

#
# Redirect allows you to tell clients about documents which used to exist in
# your server's namespace, but do not anymore. This allows you to tell the
# clients where to look for the relocated document.
# Format: Redirect old-URI new-URL
#

#
# Directives controlling the display of server-generated directory listings.
#

#
# FancyIndexing: whether you want fancy directory indexing or standard
#
IndexOptions FancyIndexing

#
# AddIcon* directives tell the server which icon to show for different
# files or filename extensions.  These are only displayed for
# FancyIndexed directories.
#
AddIconByEncoding (CMP,/icons/compressed.gif) x-compress x-gzip

AddIconByType (TXT,/icons/text.gif) text/*
AddIconByType (IMG,/icons/image2.gif) image/*
AddIconByType (SND,/icons/sound2.gif) audio/*
AddIconByType (VID,/icons/movie.gif) video/*
```

```
AddIcon /icons/binary.gif .bin .exe
AddIcon /icons/binhex.gif .hqx
AddIcon /icons/tar.gif .tar
AddIcon /icons/world2.gif .wrl .wrl.gz .vrml .vrm .iv
AddIcon /icons/compressed.gif .Z .z .tgz .gz .zip
AddIcon /icons/a.gif .ps .ai .eps
AddIcon /icons/layout.gif .html .shtml .htm .pdf
AddIcon /icons/text.gif .txt
AddIcon /icons/c.gif .c
AddIcon /icons/p.gif .pl .py
AddIcon /icons/f.gif .for
AddIcon /icons/dvi.gif .dvi
AddIcon /icons/uuencoded.gif .uu
AddIcon /icons/script.gif .conf .sh .shar .csh .ksh .tcl
AddIcon /icons/tex.gif .tex
AddIcon /icons/bomb.gif core

AddIcon /icons/back.gif ..
AddIcon /icons/hand.right.gif README
AddIcon /icons/folder.gif ^^DIRECTORY^^
AddIcon /icons/blank.gif ^^BLANKICON^^

#
# DefaultIcon: which icon to show for files which do not have an icon
# explicitly set.
#
DefaultIcon /icons/unknown.gif

#
# AddDescription: allows you to place a short description after a file in
# server-generated indexes.  These are only displayed for FancyIndexed
# directories.
# Format: AddDescription "description" filename
#
#AddDescription "GZIP compressed document" .gz
#AddDescription "tar archive" .tar
#AddDescription "GZIP compressed tar archive" .tgz

#
# ReadmeName: the name of the README file the server will look for by
# default, and append to directory listings.
#
```

```
# HeaderName: the name of a file which should be prepended to
# directory indexes.
#
# The server will first look for name.html and include it if found.
# If name.html doesn't exist, the server will then look for name.txt
# and include it as plaintext if found.
#
ReadmeName README
HeaderName HEADER


#
# IndexIgnore: a set of filenames which directory indexing should ignore
# and not include in the listing.  Shell-style wildcarding is permitted.
#
IndexIgnore .??* *~ *# HEADER* README* RCS CVS *,v *,t


#
# AddEncoding: allows you to have certain browsers (Mosaic/X 2.1+) uncompress
# information on the fly. Note: Not all browsers support this.
# Despite the name similarity, the following Add* directives have nothing
# to do with the FancyIndexing customization directives above.
#
AddEncoding x-compress Z
AddEncoding x-gzip gz tgz


#
# AddLanguage: allows you to specify the language of a document. You can
# then use content negotiation to give a browser a file in a language
# it can understand.  Note that the suffix does not have to be the same
# as the language keyword -- those with documents in Polish (whose
# net-standard language code is pl) may wish to use "AddLanguage pl .po"
# to avoid the ambiguity with the common suffix for perl scripts.
#
AddLanguage en .en
AddLanguage fr .fr
AddLanguage de .de
AddLanguage da .da
AddLanguage el .el
AddLanguage it .it
```

```
#
# LanguagePriority: allows you to give precedence to some languages
# in case of a tie during content negotiation.
# Just list the languages in decreasing order of preference.
#
LanguagePriority en fr de


#
# AddType: allows you to tweak mime.types without actually editing it, or to
# make certain files to be certain types.
#
# The following is for PHP4 (conficts with PHP/FI, below):
<IfModule mod_php4.c>
  AddType application/x-httpd-php .php4 .php3 .phtml .php
  AddType application/x-httpd-php-source .phps
</IfModule>

# The following is for PHP3:
<IfModule mod_php3.c>
  AddType application/x-httpd-php3 .php3
  AddType application/x-httpd-php3-source .phps
</IfModule>

# The following is for PHP/FI (PHP2):
<IfModule mod_php.c>
  AddType application/x-httpd-php .phtml
</IfModule>


AddType application/x-tar .tgz


#
# AddHandler: allows you to map certain file extensions to "handlers",
# actions unrelated to filetype. These can be either built into the server
# or added with the Action command (see below)
#
# If you want to use server side includes, or CGI outside
# ScriptAliased directories, uncomment the following lines.
#
# To use CGI scripts:
#
#AddHandler cgi-script .cgi
```

```
#
# To use server-parsed HTML files
#
AddType text/html .shtml
AddHandler server-parsed .shtml

#
# Uncomment the following line to enable Apache's send-asis HTTP file
# feature
#
#AddHandler send-as-is asis

#
# If you wish to use server-parsed imagemap files, use
#
AddHandler imap-file map

#
# To enable type maps, you might want to use
#
#AddHandler type-map var

#
# Action: lets you define media types that will execute a script whenever
# a matching file is called. This eliminates the need for repeated URL
# pathnames for oft-used CGI file processors.
# Format: Action media/type /cgi-script/location
# Format: Action handler-name /cgi-script/location
#

#
# MetaDir: specifies the name of the directory in which Apache can find
# meta information files. These files contain additional HTTP headers
# to include when sending the document
#
#MetaDir .web

#
# MetaSuffix: specifies the file name suffix for the file containing the
# meta information.
#
#MetaSuffix .meta
```

```
#
# Customizable error response (Apache style)
#  these come in three flavors
#
#    1) plain text
#ErrorDocument 500 "The server made a boo boo.
#  n.b.  the (") marks it as text, it does not get output
#
#    2) local redirects
#ErrorDocument 404 /missing.html
#  to redirect to local URL /missing.html
#ErrorDocument 404 /cgi-bin/missing_handler.pl
#  N.B.: You can redirect to a script or a document using server-side-includes.
#
#    3) external redirects
#ErrorDocument 402 http://some.other_server.com/subscription_info.html
#  N.B.: Many of the environment variables associated with the original
#  request will *not* be available to such a script.


#
# The following directives modify normal HTTP response behavior.
# The first directive disables keepalive for Netscape 2.x and browsers that
# spoof it. There are known problems with these browser implementations.
# The second directive is for Microsoft Internet Explorer 4.0b2
# which has a broken HTTP/1.1 implementation and does not properly
# support keepalive when it is used on 301 or 302 (redirect) responses.
#
BrowserMatch "Mozilla/2" nokeepalive
BrowserMatch "MSIE 4\.0b2;" nokeepalive downgrade-1.0 force-response-1.0


#
# The following directive disables HTTP/1.1 responses to browsers which
# are in violation of the HTTP/1.0 spec by not being able to grok a
# basic 1.1 response.
#
BrowserMatch "RealPlayer 4\.0" force-response-1.0
BrowserMatch "Java/1\.0" force-response-1.0
BrowserMatch "JDK/1\.0" force-response-1.0


# If the perl module is installed, this will be enabled.
<IfModule mod_perl.c>
```

```
   Alias /perl/ /var/www/perl/
   <Location /perl>
     SetHandler perl-script
     PerlHandler Apache::Registry
     Options +ExecCGI
   </Location>
</IfModule>

#
# Allow http put (such as Netscape Gold's publish feature)
# Use htpasswd to generate /etc/httpd/conf/passwd.
# You must unremark these two lines at the top of this file as well:
#LoadModule put_module               modules/mod_put.so
#AddModule mod_put.c
#
#Alias /upload /tmp
#<Location /upload>
#     EnablePut On
#     AuthType Basic
#     AuthName Temporary
#     AuthUserFile /etc/httpd/conf/passwd
#     EnableDelete Off
#     umask 007
#     <Limit PUT>
#      require valid-user
#     </Limit>
#</Location>

#
# Allow server status reports, with the URL of http://servername/server-status
# Change the ".your_domain.com" to match your domain to enable.
#
#<Location /server-status>
#     SetHandler server-status
#     Order deny,allow
#     Deny from all
#     Allow from .your_domain.com
#</Location>

#
# Allow remote server configuration reports, with the URL of
#  http://servername/server-info (requires that mod_info.c be loaded).
```

```
# Change the ".your_domain.com" to match your domain to enable.
#
#<Location /server-info>
#    SetHandler server-info
#    Order deny,allow
#    Deny from all
#    Allow from .your_domain.com
#</Location>

# Allow access to local system documentation from localhost
Alias /doc/ /usr/share/doc/
<Location /doc>
  order deny,allow
  deny from all
  allow from localhost
  Options Indexes FollowSymLinks
</Location>

#
# There have been reports of people trying to abuse an old bug from pre-1.1
# days.  This bug involved a CGI script distributed as a part of Apache.
# By uncommenting these lines you can redirect these attacks to a logging
# script on phf.apache.org.  Or, you can record them yourself, using the script
# support/phf_abuse_log.cgi.
#
#<Location /cgi-bin/phf*>
#    Deny from all
#    ErrorDocument 403 http://phf.apache.org/phf_abuse_log.cgi
#</Location>

#
# Proxy Server directives. Uncomment the following lines to
# enable the proxy server:
#
#<IfModule mod_proxy.c>
#ProxyRequests On
#
#<Directory proxy:*>
#    Order deny,allow
#    Deny from all
#    Allow from .your_domain.com
```

```
#</Directory>

#
# Enable/disable the handling of HTTP/1.1 "Via:" headers.
# ("Full" adds the server version; "Block" removes all outgoing Via: headers)
# Set to one of: Off | On | Full | Block
#
#ProxyVia On

#
# To enable the cache as well, edit and uncomment the following lines:
# (no cacheing without CacheRoot)
#
#CacheRoot "/var/cache/httpd"
#CacheSize 5
#CacheGcInterval 4
#CacheMaxExpire 24
#CacheLastModifiedFactor 0.1
#CacheDefaultExpire 1
#NoCache a_domain.com another_domain.edu joes.garage_sale.com

#</IfModule>
# End of proxy directives.

### Section 3: Virtual Hosts
#
# VirtualHost: If you want to maintain multiple domains/hostnames on your
# machine you can setup VirtualHost containers for them.
# Please see the documentation at <URL:http://www.apache.org/docs/vhosts/>
# for further details before you try to setup virtual hosts.
# You may use the command line option '-S' to verify your virtual host
# configuration.

#
# If you want to use name-based virtual hosts you need to define at
# least one IP address (and port number) for them.
#
#NameVirtualHost 12.34.56.78:80
#NameVirtualHost 12.34.56.78
```

```
#
# VirtualHost example:
# Almost any Apache directive may go into a VirtualHost container.
#
#<VirtualHost ip.address.of.host.some_domain.com>
#     ServerAdmin webmaster@host.some_domain.com
#     DocumentRoot /www/docs/host.some_domain.com
#     ServerName host.some_domain.com
#     ErrorLog logs/host.some_domain.com-error_log
#     CustomLog logs/host.some_domain.com-access_log common
#</VirtualHost>

#<VirtualHost _default_:*>
#</VirtualHost>

<IfDefine HAVE_SSL>
##
## SSL Virtual Host Context
##

# Apache will only listen on port 80 by default.  Defining the virtual server
#  (below) won't make it automatically listen on the virtual server's port.
Listen 443

<VirtualHost _default_:443>

# General setup for the virtual host
DocumentRoot "/var/www/html"

#   SSL Engine Switch:
#   Enable/Disable SSL for this virtual host.
SSLEngine on

#   SSL Cipher Suite:
#   List the ciphers that the client is permitted to negotiate.
#   See the mod_ssl documentation for a complete list.
#SSLCipherSuite ALL:!ADH:RC4+RSA:+HIGH:+MEDIUM:+LOW:+SSLv2:+EXP:+eNULL

#   Server Certificate:
#   Point SSLCertificateFile at a PEM encoded certificate.  If
#   the certificate is encrypted, then you will be prompted for a
#   pass phrase.  Note that a kill -HUP will prompt again. A test
#   certificate can be generated with `make certificate' under
```

```
#   built time. Keep in mind that if you've both a RSA and a DSA
#   certificate you can configure both in parallel (to also allow
#   the use of DSA ciphers, etc.)
SSLCertificateFile /etc/httpd/conf/ssl.crt/server.crt
#SSLCertificateFile /etc/httpd/conf/ssl.crt/server-dsa.crt

#   Server Private Key:
#   If the key is not combined with the certificate, use this
#   directive to point at the key file.  Keep in mind that if
#   you've both a RSA and a DSA private key you can configure
#   both in parallel (to also allow the use of DSA ciphers, etc.)
SSLCertificateKeyFile /etc/httpd/conf/ssl.key/server.key
#SSLCertificateKeyFile /etc/httpd/conf/ssl.key/server-dsa.key

#   Server Certificate Chain:
#   Point SSLCertificateChainFile at a file containing the
#   concatenation of PEM encoded CA certificates which form the
#   certificate chain for the server certificate. Alternatively
#   the referenced file can be the same as SSLCertificateFile
#   when the CA certificates are directly appended to the server
#   certificate for convinience.
#SSLCertificateChainFile /etc/httpd/conf/ssl.crt/ca.crt

#   Certificate Authority (CA):
#   Set the CA certificate verification path where to find CA
#   certificates for client authentication or alternatively one
#   huge file containing all of them (file must be PEM encoded)
#   Note: Inside SSLCACertificatePath you need hash symlinks
#         to point to the certificate files. Use the provided
#         Makefile to update the hash symlinks after changes.
#SSLCACertificatePath /etc/httpd/conf/ssl.crt
#SSLCACertificateFile /etc/httpd/conf/ssl.crt/ca-bundle.crt

#   Certificate Revocation Lists (CRL):
#   Set the CA revocation path where to find CA CRLs for client
#   authentication or alternatively one huge file containing all
#   of them (file must be PEM encoded)
#   Note: Inside SSLCARevocationPath you need hash symlinks
#         to point to the certificate files. Use the provided
#         Makefile to update the hash symlinks after changes.
#SSLCARevocationPath /etc/httpd/conf/ssl.crl
#SSLCARevocationFile /etc/httpd/conf/ssl.crl/ca-bundle.crl
```

```
#    Client Authentication (Type):
#    Client certificate verification type and depth.  Types are
#    none, optional, require and optional_no_ca.  Depth is a
#    number which specifies how deeply to verify the certificate
#    issuer chain before deciding the certificate is not valid.
#SSLVerifyClient require
#SSLVerifyDepth  10


#    Access Control:
#    With SSLRequire you can do per-directory access control based
#    on arbitrary complex boolean expressions containing server
#    variable checks and other lookup directives.  The syntax is a
#    mixture between C and Perl.  See the mod_ssl documentation
#    for more details.
#<Location />
#SSLRequire (    %{SSL_CIPHER} !~ m/^(EXP|NULL)-/ \
#            and %{SSL_CLIENT_S_DN_O} eq "Snake Oil, Ltd." \
#            and %{SSL_CLIENT_S_DN_OU} in {"Staff", "CA", "Dev"} \
#            and %{TIME_WDAY} >= 1 and %{TIME_WDAY} <= 5 \
#            and %{TIME_HOUR} >= 8 and %{TIME_HOUR} <= 20       ) \
#            or %{REMOTE_ADDR} =~ m/^192\.76\.162\.[0-9]+$/
#</Location>
#    SSL Engine Options:
#    Set various options for the SSL engine.
#    o FakeBasicAuth:
#      Translate the client X.509 into a Basic Authorisation.  This means that
#      the standard Auth/DBMAuth methods can be used for access control.  The
#      user name is the `one line' version of the client's X.509 certificate.
#      Note that no password is obtained from the user. Every entry in the user
#      file needs this password: `xxj31ZMTZzkVA'.
#    o ExportCertData:
#      This exports two additional environment variables: SSL_CLIENT_CERT and
#      SSL_SERVER_CERT. These contain the PEM-encoded certificates of the
#      server (always existing) and the client (only existing when client
#      authentication is used). This can be used to import the certificates
#      into CGI scripts.
#    o StdEnvVars:
#      This exports the standard SSL/TLS related `SSL_*' environment variables.
#      Per default this exportation is switched off for performance reasons,
#      because the extraction step is an expensive operation and is usually
#      useless for serving static content. So one usually enables the
#      exportation for CGI and SSI requests only.
```

```
#      o CompatEnvVars:
#         This exports obsolete environment variables for backward compatibility
#         to Apache-SSL 1.x, mod_ssl 2.0.x, Sioux 1.0 and Stronghold 2.x. Use this
#         to provide compatibility to existing CGI scripts.
#      o StrictRequire:
#         This denies access when "SSLRequireSSL" or "SSLRequire" applied even
#         under a "Satisfy any" situation, i.e. when it applies access is denied
#         and no other module can change it.
#      o OptRenegotiate:
#         This enables optimized SSL connection renegotiation handling when SSL
#         directives are used in per-directory context.
#SSLOptions +FakeBasicAuth +ExportCertData +CompatEnvVars +StrictRequire
<Files ~ "\.(cgi|shtml)$">
    SSLOptions +StdEnvVars
</Files>
<Directory "/var/www/cgi-bin">
    SSLOptions +StdEnvVars
</Directory>

#      Notice: Most problems of broken clients are also related to the HTTP
#      keep-alive facility, so you usually additionally want to disable
#      keep-alive for those clients, too. Use variable "nokeepalive" for this.
SetEnvIf User-Agent ".*MSIE.*" nokeepalive ssl-unclean-shutdown

#      Per-Server Logging:
#      The home of a custom SSL log file. Use this when you want a
#      compact non-error SSL logfile on a virtual host basis.
CustomLog /var/log/httpd/ssl_request_log \
          "%t %h %{SSL_PROTOCOL}x %{SSL_CIPHER}x \"%r\" %b"

</VirtualHost>

</IfDefine>
```

The first thing you should notice is that this file consists of comments and actual configuration entries. Comments are preceded by the hash mark (#). Configuration entries consist of an entry name followed by an entry value.

There are three main sections in the httpd.conf file: Global Environment, Main Server Configuration, and Virtual Hosts. Let's look at each section in detail.

Global Environment

Directives and modules in this section control the operation of Apache server processes as a whole. What you see here applies to all Apache hosts, whether they are the main server or any virtual hosts as discussed in later sections.

ServerType

The first directive you will learn about is `ServerType`. The Apache server can run in two ways: in `standalone` mode with its own processes listening for connections or in `inetd` mode, which you saw in the section on networking. In `inetd` mode, `inetd` listens for connections and then starts an Apache process when a connection comes. If this is your first time running a Web server, you are best off running Apache in `standalone` mode unless you are familiar with `inetd`, are using a Unix server, and have compelling reasons for running the server in this way.

ServerRoot

`ServerRoot` is used to indicate the base directory where configuration files and logs for the server can be found. Red Hat sets this up in the directory `/etc/httpd`. Inside this directory is a `conf` directory containing the three configuration files plus a `logs` directory as a link to `/var/log/httpd`.

You are free to move the directory anywhere on your system to match the style of management you are using. However, it is usually easiest to keep things where your distribution of Linux puts them.

Loading Modules

The first main section consists of a series of `LoadModule` directives followed by a series of `AddModule` directives. Apache's functionality is created and extended through the use of modules. In earlier versions of Apache, these modules were combined into the executable Apache `httpd` file. Starting with version 1.3 of Apache, it is now possible to create modules that load at the time the server starts.

Because most of these modules are configured through directives, it is important that all relevant modules are loaded before any other directives occur in the `httpd.conf` file.

For most basic installations, the default module list is fine and you won't need to change it. If you need to extend or change the functionality of your Web server, consult the online Apache documentation at httpd.apache.org for more information on adding loadable modules and using the LoadModule and AddModule directives.

Main Server Configuration

You can set up any number of virtual hosts on an Apache server. But every Apache server needs a main host. The directives in the main server section determine default parameters for the main host, as well as any directives not specified in any virtual host.

Port

The next important entry is the Port entry. By default, a Web server is supposed to run on port 80. When a browser requests a URL without a port, it assumes that the URL is being requested from a server on port 80. If you're running a high- or medium-security firewall, just make sure that it's customized to allow incoming WWW data, as discussed in Chapter 31, "Security and Red Hat Linux 7.1 As an Inexpensive Router."

Because of the vulnerability of processes running below port 1024, if you are running a Web server that is not being made publicly available on the Internet and want to avoid the risks associated with these ports, you can try running the server on a port above 1024. Common ports for these types of Web servers are 8000 and 8080, but you can choose any free port. If you're running a high-security firewall, make sure to let in WWW data for the port you select. When you customize your firewall with the lokkit utility described in Chapter 31, if you're going to use port 8080, enter **8080:udp,8080:tcp** in the Other Ports text box in the Customization section.

User and Group

The User and Group entries are critical entries because they affect the very security of your system. Normally, the httpd process is fired by the root account, but this process does not listen for connections. Rather, this process launches one or more child processes as the user and group (which are specified by name or ID number) indicated with these configuration directives.

This is done because all processes fired by the Web server, including CGI programs, would otherwise be run as root. This would pose a huge security risk, especially if a poorly written CGI script leaves a large security hole. By running the Web server and its related children as a user with limited power, it is possible to limit these security holes.

The normal operation is to run the Web server as apache with a group of apache or #-1. I generally use user apache and group apache, since they are easily identifiable when reading the configuration file. This user has limited privileges on the system, and potential hackers can wreak only limited havoc if a CGI script lets them into the system.

ServerAdmin

This directive indicates the e-mail address of the administrator of the Web site. When the server generates an automated error message, such as one indicating that a page is not found, then this e-mail address is usually added to the page indicating whom to contact to report the problem. Make sure that this is a valid address and that the address is the correct one for the server's administrator.

ServerName

The ServerName configuration directive identifies the hostname returned to clients with the pages they request. This is one of the legitimate names for your Web server as identified in a DNS record or host table on your network. In an intranet environment, you can define a hostname in host tables using NIS or in the DNS server for your site. For an Internet Web server, you should make sure that the name you indicate here is a valid name in your domain's DNS record. If you aren't sure, consult with your domain name records manager.

In the case of the example file, ServerName is localhost. If you own the domain, you can change this to a regular Internet domain name such as mommabears.com.

DocumentRoot

The DocumentRoot configuration entry specifies where the root directory for HTML files is located. In the case of Red Hat Linux 7.1, the default is usually set to /var/www/html. If ServerName is set to mommabears.com, someone with a browser should be able to access the file /var/www/html/file.html using the URL http://www.mommabears.com/file.html.

Enabling the HTML Directory

The code below is the section of the sample `httpd.conf` file dealing with the HTML document root directory, without any comments.

```
<Directory /var/www/html>
Options Indexes Includes FollowSymLinks
AllowOverride None
order allow,deny
allow from all
</Directory>
```

The structure of the entry is to enclose the necessary directives inside opening and closing `<Directory>` and `</Directory>` tags. The opening tag specifies the directory that all directives between the tags should apply to, in this case /var/www/html.

Inside the `<Directory>` and `</Directory>` tags, notice four directives: The `Options` directive is used to indicate what special actions can be taken on the files contained in the directory and its subdirectories. Possible values include `None`, `All`, `Indexes`, `Includes`, `FollowSymLinks`, `ExecCGI`, and `MultiViews`. Commonly used values for HTML directories are `None` when only normal HTML files and images appear on a site and `Includes` when you plan to enable server-parsed HTML files. (Some server-parsed HTML files offer the capability to include other files in the contents of a file, and this value allows this action to occur.)

The next directive is the `AllowOverride` entry, which indicates how much power a local `.htaccess` file has to override entries in the global `httpd.conf` file. Possible values include `None`, `All`, `Options`, `FileInfo`, `AuthConfig`, and `Limit`. For instance, the `Options` value limits the `.htaccess` file to overriding the `Options` directive. On servers where the Webmaster has good control over all content, it is usually easiest to allow full right to override. When you run a server with multiple users controlling their own directories' content, it may be wise to limit the power of these users to override global access configuration.

Finally, the `order` and `allow` directives go together to control who has access to pages in the directory. Here, `order allow,deny` indicates that first the `allow` directive should be used, and if that directive doesn't allow the user to obtain the file in question, then any `deny` directive should be applied.

Normally, when you are not applying access control you will want to use `order allow,deny`. When you are attempting to implement access controls, `order deny,allow` is the best entry (as you will see later when you build your small sample Web site with access control).

Following the order directive is the allow directive, which indicates that all users should be allowed access. If you want to fully understand how to deny users, you should read the Apache documentation available online at http:// httpd.apache.org.

UserDir

UserDir is a directive that is useful when a Webmaster wants to enable each user on the system to have their own personal Web site that they manage through a subdirectory in their home directory. This directive indicates the name of the subdirectory in their home directory that should be considered as their Web directory.

The norm is to use public_html. So, if the user testuser has a directory /home/testuser/public_html, then this directory can be accessed via the Web using the URL http://servername/~testuser.

DirectoryIndex

DirectoryIndex is an important directive in that it indicates which files should be considered default files. This is how it is possible for a URL such as http:// www.mommabears.com to access the correct file.

For instance, in the sample httpd.conf file above, there are seven entries given for the Directory Index: index.html, index.htm, index.shtml, index.php, index .php4, index.php3, and index.cgi. This means that for any URL that doesn't specify a filename and gives only a directory, the server will first try to return index .html from the specified directory. If that file is missing, index.htm is returned; if that file is missing, index.shtml is sent back to the client. If no file match is found, the server returns either a directory listing or an error message based on other configuration options.

AccessFileName

AccessFileName is used to specify the filename that contains access control information for a given directory. It is possible to store access control information in the httpd.conf file or in .htaccess configuration files in each home directory.

The sample file indicates that if a file named .htaccess exists in a directory, then that file contains access control information for the directory.

ScriptAlias

It is important to set the ScriptAlias directive so that you can set up a directory to store CGI programs and scripts. ScriptAlias specifies which directory is used for CGI scripts and what the URL is for that directory. Unless other permissions are given to run CGI programs on the basis of file extensions (as you will see in the next section's discussion of the AddHandler directive), files in this directory are automatically treated as CGI programs.

For instance, the sample file used the following directive:

```
ScriptAlias /cgi-bin/ "/var/www/cgi-bin"
```

This line indicates that the URL http://www.mommabears.com/cgi-bin/ points to /var/www/cgi-bin/. In this directory, files are considered CGI scripts, and the server attempts to execute the files instead of returning them directly to the requesting client.

Enabling the CGI Directory

When compared to the HTML directory entry described earlier, things look a little bit different with the CGI directory entry:

```
<Directory /var/www/cgi-bin>
AllowOverride None
Options ExecCGI
Order allow,deny
Allow from all
</Directory>
```

Notice that all overrides have been disallowed. This is generally a wise idea, since CGI is a security hole even on a well-configured system and it is prudent to prevent all possible security mistakes with CGI directories.

AddHandler and *AddType*

The AddHandler and AddType directives really need to be considered together. AddHandler allows files with a specified extension to be mapped to a particular action, which can be a built-in action in the server (such as running CGI programs) or an external action that generally invokes a special program outside the server and passes the file in question through that program.

`AddType` creates a new MIME type for a specific extension. MIME types are important in informing the client how to handle a file. For instance, if a file is passed with MIME type `text/plain` to the browser, the browser won't attempt to interpret the file for any HTML code it contains, while a MIME type of `text/html` causes the browser to process the file it receives as an HTML file.

Two of the main uses of these directives are to allow the execution of CGI scripts outside the specified CGI script directory and to enable server-parsed HTML, which allows special tags embedded in an HTML file to be processed by the server before it returns the page to the client.

Enabling CGI Scripts   You can use the `AddHandler` directive to enable CGI processing outside the specified CGI directory by adding the directive

```
AddHandler cgi-script .cgi
```

to the `httpd.conf` file. This indicates that any file with the extension `.cgi` that is found outside the specified CGI directory should be treated as a CGI program and handled in that way. Without this directive, a CGI script found outside the CGI directory is not processed as a CGI program; instead, the contents of the file are simply returned to the client. Generally, this means that the user sees the actual program code of a script rather than the results of running a script.

Enabling Server-Parsed HTML   Both the `AddHandler` and `AddType` directives are used to enable server-parsed HTML. The normal usage for Apache is

```
AddType text/html .shtml
AddHandler server-parsed .shtml
```

Here `AddType` ensures that the results of a server-parsed HTML file (those with the extension `.shtml`) are viewed as HTML by the client browser and are displayed as such.

The `AddHandler` line indicates that files with the extension `.shtml` should be handled by the `server-parsed` action of the server. This effectively enables server-parsed HTML for SHTML files.

Managing Your Web Server

In addition to being able to start and stop your Web server, once you have your Web server up and running there are a few tasks that you will need to do occasionally to make sure your server continues to run without incident. These steps include creating and deleting users and groups, protecting directories by using access control, and maintaining the server logs so that they continue to be useful.

Starting and Stopping Apache

If you installed Apache when you installed Red Hat, then your start-up files have been set up to start Apache at boot time. This occurs in the file /etc/rc.d/init.d/ httpd. This file is an executable script that takes two possible arguments: start and stop. If you are planning to use the version of Apache included with your Red Hat installation and don't plan to move the location of the configuration files, then you can start and stop your Web server manually, using the command

```
# /etc/rc.d/init.d/httpd start
```

to start the server and using the command

```
# /etc/rc.d/init.d/httpd stop
```

to stop the server.

NOTE   All starting and stopping of your Web server needs to be done by the root user so that the main server process can change users to launch child processes to listen for connections.

However, if you want to install your own binaries or compile new binaries from source code, or if you wish to change the location of the configuration files, you will need to know how to invoke the httpd command by hand.

Usually, httpd is found in /usr/sbin/. Two flags are available:

- -f specifies an alternate location for the httpd.conf file.
- -d specifies the server root, overriding the configuration file.

Usually, using -f is sufficient since ServerRoot is specified in httpd.conf. For instance, if you keep your configuration files in /etc/httpd/conf, then you can issue the command

```
# /usr/sbin/httpd -f /etc/httpd/conf/httpd.conf
```

to start the server.

If you want to stop your server manually and you started it yourself without using /etc/rc.d/init.d/httpd, then you need to know the correct process ID (PID) for the server. You can determine the PID of the server by using the ps command:

```
# ps -aux | grep httpd
```

This command produces a list of processes similar to the one shown here:

```
apache    545  0.1  3.8  1104  572  ?  S  17:52  0:00 [httpd]
apache    546  0.0  3.8  1104  572  ?  S  17:52  0:00 [httpd]
apache    547  0.2  3.8  1104  572  ?  S  17:52  0:00 [httpd]
apache    548  0.1  3.8  1104  572  ?  S  17:52  0:00 [httpd]
apache    549  0.0  3.8  1104  572  ?  S  17:52  0:00 [httpd]
apache    550  0.3  3.8  1104  572  ?  S  17:52  0:00 [httpd]
root      544  0.5  4    1104  592  ?  S  17:52  0:00 /usr/sbin/httpd
```

Notice that all the processes are owned by apache, except for one owned by root. This is the parent process of all the httpd processes, and this is the one that needs to be stopped, in this case with the command

```
# kill 544
```

Managing Apache Users and Groups

As you will see in the next section on protecting directories, one main method of protection is by username and password, restricting access to a specified list of users who must correctly provide their username and password to gain access to a protected directory.

Creating users is straightforward and is done using the command htpasswd, which, in the default installation of Apache that comes with Red Hat Linux, is found at /usr/bin/htpasswd. This program is used both to create a password file and to create individual users. The password file serves as the repository for usernames and encrypted passwords, which can then be used by Apache for access control.

You create the password file the first time you create a user, using the command

```
# htpasswd -c filename username
```

With this command, the file specified by filename is created and the first user is added to the file. The -c flag indicates that the file needs to be created. You can store your password file anywhere that is accessible by the Apache Web server. A good place to store it is with your configuration files. For instance, the command

```
# htpasswd -c /etc/httpd/conf/users user1
```

creates a users file in the same directory as the other Apache configuration files and creates the user user1.

When you issue the previous command, you are prompted to enter the password for the user twice to make sure it has been entered correctly. Then the password is encrypted and stored in /etc/httpd/conf/users. The entry looks like this:

```
user1:N31mVAxFtivO
```

The format of the entry is the username followed by a colon followed by the encrypted password. Each user entry is on a separate line.

While it looks like the passwords in the system password file (/etc/passwd) and the Apache password file are encrypted in the same way, the encryption process used by htpasswd is different, and you can't simply copy encrypted passwords from /etc/passwd to create your Apache password file.

To add additional users once the file is created, simply use the htpasswd command without the -c flag:

```
$ htpasswd /etc/httpd/conf/users user2
```

This command adds the user user2, again evoking two prompts for the password. The resulting password file would contain two entries:

```
user1:N31mVAxFtivO.
user2:WROTrbH6.3pPk
```

In addition to creating users, you usually want to create groups. Groups associate multiple users together under a single name, making it easier to address related users when configuring access control for directories.

To create groups, make a groups file by simply editing the file using a text editor such as vi or emacs. You should probably place the groups file in the same directory as your users file, such as /etc/httpd/conf/groups. This file contains one or more entries, each on a separate line, with the format

```
groupname: username1 username2 username3 ...
```

For instance, to create a group called authors with the two users you created previously as members, use the entry

```
authors: user1 user2
```

Protecting Directories with Access Control

As noted previously in the section "Enabling the HTML Directory," it is possible to configure access control on a directory-by-directory basis. Normally, this is done by creating a file called .htaccess in the directory you want to protect and then placing the necessary configuration directives in the file.

The main directives used in this file for access control purposes are as follows:

- AuthUserFile
- AuthGroupFile
- AuthName
- AuthType
- require
- order
- deny
- allow

AuthUserFile and *AuthGroupFile*

These directives are used to specify the location of the users and group files you learned how to create in the last section. In the sample, these directives would read

```
AuthUserFile /etc/httpd/conf/users
AuthGroupFile /etc/httpd/conf/groups
```

These directives are important because without them, the server won't know where to look for the users and their passwords.

AuthName

AuthName is used to specify the domain of the authentication. Ultimately, this is a prompt that is displayed to the users so they know which username and password to provide. For instance,

```
AuthName Authors Only
```

displays an Authors Only prompt to the user when asking for username and password.

AuthType

AuthType is used to specify the authentication type used to access Web pages on the listed directories. As the only currently available AuthType option is basic, this directive affects little in current versions of Apache.

require

The require directive is used in limiting access for users and groups. The directive can be used to restrict access to all users in the password file, to a list of specific users, or to a list of specific groups.

To restrict access to any existing user, use the directive

```
require valid-user
```

To restrict access to specific users, use the format

```
require user username1 username2 username3 ...
```

Finally, to restrict access to a group, use the entry

```
require group groupname1 groupname2 groupname3 ...
```

order

The order directive is used in conjunction with the deny and allow entries to control access based on host rather than user. Using order, deny, and allow, it is possible to permit access only to specified hosts by IP address or hostname.

The order directive specifies the order in which the deny and allow directives should be applied. For instance,

```
order allow,deny
```

says that the allow directive should be applied first, and if the client host does not fall within those users specified by the directive, then the deny directive should be applied.

Similarly,

```
order deny,allow
```

reverses the order, testing the deny directive first.

deny

The deny directive specifies which hosts should be denied access to a directory. Possible values include all, a partial hostname, and a partial or full IP address. For instance,

```
deny from all
```

means that all hosts are denied. Similarly,

```
deny from .juxta.com
```

denies access to all hosts in the juxta.com domain. With IP addresses, the format is the same:

```
deny from 194.148.43.195
```

The directive denies access to the specified host.

allow

The allow directive is the opposite of the deny directive, specifying which hosts should be allowed access to the directory in question. It takes the same possible values as the deny directive.

Putting It All Together

Let's consider now how this all fits together with two examples: enabling access by group and allowing access by domain name.

Enabling Access by Group The following sample .htaccess file enables access to the specific directory only for users in the group authors:

```
AuthName Authors Only
AuthUserFile /etc/httpd/conf/users
AuthGroupFile /etc/httpd/conf/groups
require group authors
```

Notice that this sample specifies an AuthName for the prompt, identifies the password and group file, and then indicates that a user must be part of the group authors in order to access the directory.

Enabling Access by Domain Name The following sample .htaccess file enables access to the specific directory only to users accessing the Web site from hosts in the juxta.com domain:

```
order allow,deny
```

```
allow from .juxta.com
deny from all
```

In this sample, notice the order of `allow` and `deny`. The logic works like this: When a host accesses a directory, the host's domain is first compared to the domain juxta.com. If the host falls within the specified domain, access is granted. If the host does not, the `deny` directive is looked at and, because it indicates that all hosts should be denied access, the host in question is denied access.

Maintaining Logs

The final management function to consider is log management. Apache produces two important logs: an access log and an error log. Together, these provide information vital for several functions, including debugging buggy CGI scripts and producing statistical access reports with detailed information about usage patterns for your Web site.

However, left on their own, these log files will continue to grow, reaching an extremely large size. As their size grows, their value decreases as it becomes more difficult to process the volumes of data they contain.

For this reason, it is wise to establish a schedule for rotating your logs. Rotating logs means saving the existing version to an archive and starting afresh with a new, empty log. Depending on how many hits you receive, the ideal frequency for rotating logs can be anything from monthly to weekly to daily.

Red Hat Linux 7.1 incorporates Apache logs into the `/var/log/httpd` directory. They are rotated along with other logs in `/var/log`, as a daily task as defined in the `/etc/cron.daily/logrotate` script.

Alternatively, if you've installed the downloaded version of Apache, you can use the `rotatelogs` utility to automate rotating your logs. By default, Red Hat Linux installs this at `/usr/sbin/rotatelogs`. In order to use the program, you need to add an entry to `httpd.conf`:

```
TransferLog "|/usr/sbin/rotatelogs /some/location/file time"
```

The entry `/some/location/file` provides a base filename for the rotated logs. A number indicating the system time at which the log starts is appended to the filename. The `time` parameter specifies in seconds how often to rotate the logs.

Building a Web Site

Now that you have your Web site configured and running smoothly, let's create a small sample Web site that shows how to deploy content for the Web.

The site that you are going to build will be the information for a small publishing company you will call On The Web Publishers. This site will offer a list of new titles, general information about the publisher, a contact form, and a password-protected section exclusively for the use of authors who have contracts with the publisher.

All together, this will let you create a site that includes HTML and images, uses CGI programming, and implements access control for the password-protected section of the site. First, you need to identify the structure of your site, as we see in Figure 32.2.

FIGURE 32.2:

The structure of your Web site

Having done this, you need to create the necessary files to implement this structure. Assuming the configuration used in the sections earlier in this chapter, the root document tree for HTML files is at /var/www/html and the CGI directory is at /var/www/cgi-bin. Therefore, your directory and file tree for the site might include the following files:

```
/var/www/html/index.html
/var/www/html/about/index.html
/var/www/html/books/index.html
/var/www/html/contact/index.html
```

```
/var/www/html/authors/index.html
/var/www/cgi-bin/formmail
```

With the exception of the last file, which will be discussed shortly, all these files are HTML files. Any supporting images that are used by the HTML files can be placed in the same directory as the HTML files, but to keep things clean, many Webmasters prefer to place all their images in another directory. In your case, that directory could be

```
/var/www/html/images/
```

Since you aren't learning HTML in this chapter, let's just look at two of the HTML files as examples of how they might be written. Let's start with the main home page at /var/www/html/index.html. In your example, the source code for this file would be

```
<HTML>

    <HEAD>
    <TITLE>On the Web Publishers</TITLE>
    </HEAD>

    <BODY BGCOLOR=lightcyan TEXT=midnightblue>

    <DIV ALIGN=CENTER>
        <A HREF="/"><IMG SRC="/images/logo.gif" BORDER=0></A>
        <TABLE BORDER=0 CELLPADDING=5 CELLSPACING=5
            BGCOLOR=lightpink>
        <TR>
            <TD ALIGN=CENTER><A HREF="about">ABOUT
                US</A></TD>
            <TD ALIGN=CENTER><A HREF="books">OUR
                BOOKS</A></TD>
            <TD ALIGN=CENTER><A HREF="contact">CONTACT
                US</A></TD>
            <TD ALIGN=CENTER><A HREF="authors">JUST FOR
                AUTHORS</A></TD>
        </TR>
        </TABLE>
    </DIV>

    <FONT SIZE=5>W</F>elcome to <STRONG>On the Web
    Publishers</STRONG>. We offer the finest in
```

```
on-line electronic books at reasonable prices.
Check out what we have to offer ...

<UL>
<LI><A HREF="about">Learn about what we do</A>
<LI><A HREF="books">See what books we offer</A>
<LI><A HREF="contact">Contact us</A>
</UL>

</BODY>

</HTML>
```

This file would produce results like those in Figure 32.3.

FIGURE 32.3:

The main home page

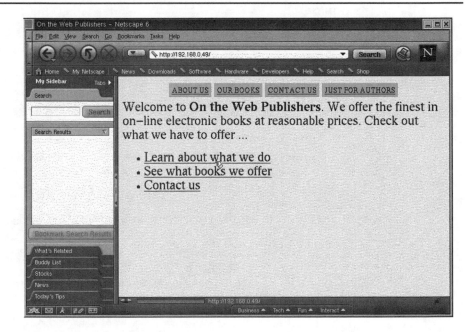

The other pages would have similar-looking source code, with the exception of the contact form at /var/www/html/contact/index.html. This page would look like Figure 32.4, which is produced by the following source code:

```
<HTML>

<HEAD>
```

```
<TITLE>On the Web Publishers</TITLE>
</HEAD>

<BODY BGCOLOR=lightcyan TEXT=midnightblue>

<DIV ALIGN=CENTER>
    <A HREF="/"><IMG SRC="/images/logo.gif" BORDER=0></A>
    <TABLE BORDER=0 CELLPADDING=5 CELLSPACING=5
        BGCOLOR=lightpink>
    <TR>
        <TD ALIGN=CENTER><A HREF="/about">ABOUT
            US</A></TD>
        <TD ALIGN=CENTER><A HREF="/books">OUR
            BOOKS</A></TD>
        <TD ALIGN=CENTER BGCOLOR=yellow>CONTACT
            US</TD>
        <TD ALIGN=CENTER><A HREF="/authors">JUST FOR
            AUTHORS</A></TD>
    </TR>
    </TABLE>

    <H1>Drop Us A Line ...</H1>
</DIV>

<TABLE ALIGN=CENTER><TR><TD>
<FORM METHOD=POST ACTION="/cgi-bin/formmail">
<INPUT TYPE=TEXT WIDTH=30 NAME=name> Name<BR>
<INPUT TYPE=TEXT WIDTH=30 NAME=address> Address<BR>
<INPUT TYPE=TEXT WIDTH=30 NAME=city> City<BR>
<INPUT TYPE=TEXT WIDTH=30 NAME=state> State<BR>
<INPUT TYPE=TEXT WIDTH=30 NAME=zip> Zip/Post Code<BR>
<INPUT TYPE=TEXT WIDTH=30 NAME=country> Country<BR>
<INPUT TYPE=TEXT WIDTH=30 NAME=email> E-mail<BR>
Comments:<BR>
<TEXTAREA ROWS=10 COLS=30 NAME=comments
    WRAP=HARD></TEXTAREA><BR>
<INPUT TYPE=SUBMIT VALUE="Send Comments">
</FORM>
</TD></TR></TABLE>

</BODY>

</HTML>
```

FIGURE 32.4:

The contact form

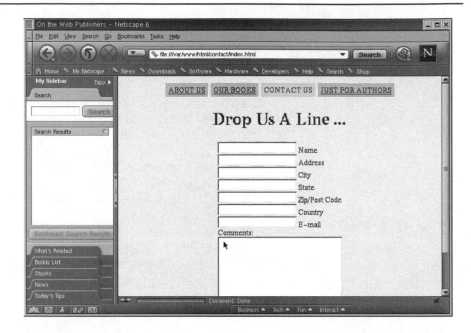

What makes this page special is that it includes a form and a reference to a CGI program that processes the data in the form. The program you are using in this case is called `formmail`, a freely available CGI script written in Perl, which takes the contents of a form and mails them to a predefined mail address. In this way, the contact information from the form can be e-mailed to the bookstore's main e-mail address.

`Formmail` is written by Matthew M. Wright and is available at `http://www .worldwidemart.com/scripts/formmail.shtml`. Even though this chapter doesn't discuss Perl or CGI programming, the source code is presented here so you can see how simple it is to create basic CGI programs with little effort:

```perl
#!/usr/bin/perl
##########################################################################
# FormMail                     Version 1.6                              #
# Copyright 1995-1997 Matt Wright mattw@worldwidemart.com               #
# Created 06/09/95             Last Modified 05/02/97                   #
# Matt's Script Archive, Inc.:  http://www.worldwidemart.com/scripts/   #
##########################################################################
```

```
# COPYRIGHT NOTICE                                                        #
# Copyright 1995-1997 Matthew M. Wright  All Rights Reserved.             #
#                                                                         #
# FormMail may be used and modified free of charge by anyone so long as this #
# copyright notice and the comments above remain intact.  By using this   #
# code you agree to indemnify Matthew M. Wright from any liability that    #
# might arise from its use.                                                #
#                                                                         #
# Selling the code for this program without prior written consent is       #
# expressly forbidden.  In other words, please ask first before you try and #
# make money off of my program.                                            #
#                                                                         #
# Obtain permission before redistributing this software over the Internet or #
# in any other medium.  In all cases copyright and header must remain intact #
###########################################################################
# Define Variables                                                        #
#    Detailed Information Found In README File.                            #

# $mailprog defines the location of your sendmail program on your unix     #
# system.                                                                  #

$mailprog = '/usr/lib/sendmail';

# @referers allows forms to be located only on servers which are defined   #
# in this field.  This security fix from the last version which allowed    #
# anyone on any server to use your FormMail script on their web site.      #

@referers = ('linux.juxta.com');

# Done                                                                     #
###########################################################################

# Check Referring URL
&check_url;

# Retrieve Date
&get_date;

# Parse Form Contents
&parse_form;
```

```perl
# Check Required Fields
&check_required;

# Return HTML Page or Redirect User
&return_html;

# Send E-Mail
&send_mail;

sub check_url {

    # Localize the check_referer flag which determines if user is valid.   #
    local($check_referer) = 0;

    # If a referring URL was specified, for each valid referer, make sure   #
    # that a valid referring URL was passed to FormMail.                     #

    if ($ENV{'HTTP_REFERER'}) {
        foreach $referer (@referers) {
            if ($ENV{'HTTP_REFERER'} =~ m|https?://([^/]*)$referer|i) {
                $check_referer = 1;
                last;
            }
        }
    }
    else {
        $check_referer = 1;
    }

    # If the HTTP_REFERER was invalid, send back an error.                   #
    if ($check_referer != 1) { &error('bad_referer') }
}

sub get_date {

    # Define arrays for the day of the week and month of the year.          #
    @days   = ('Sunday','Monday','Tuesday','Wednesday',
               'Thursday','Friday','Saturday');
    @months = ('January','February','March','April','May','June','July',
               'August','September','October','November','December');
```

```perl
    # Get the current time and format the hour, minutes and seconds.  Add     #
    # 1900 to the year to get the full 4 digit year.                          #
    ($sec,$min,$hour,$mday,$mon,$year,$wday) = (localtime(time))[0,1,2,3,4,5,6];
    $time = sprintf("%02d:%02d:%02d",$hour,$min,$sec);
    $year += 1900;

    # Format the date.                                                        #
    $date = "$days[$wday], $months[$mon] $mday, $year at $time";

}

sub parse_form {

    # Define the configuration associative array.                            #
    %Config = ('recipient','',          'subject','',
               'email','',              'realname','',
               'redirect','',           'bgcolor','',
               'background','',          'link_color','',
               'vlink_color','',         'text_color','',
               'alink_color','',         'title','',
               'sort','',               'print_config','',
               'required','',           'env_report','',
               'return_link_title','',  'return_link_url','',
               'print_blank_fields','', 'missing_fields_redirect','');

    # Determine the form's REQUEST_METHOD (GET or POST) and split the form    #
    # fields up into their name-value pairs.  If the REQUEST_METHOD was       #
    # not GET or POST, send an error.                                         #
    if ($ENV{'REQUEST_METHOD'} eq 'GET') {
        # Split the name-value pairs
        @pairs = split(/&/, $ENV{'QUERY_STRING'});
    }
    elsif ($ENV{'REQUEST_METHOD'} eq 'POST') {
        # Get the input
        read(STDIN, $buffer, $ENV{'CONTENT_LENGTH'});

        # Split the name-value pairs
        @pairs = split(/&/, $buffer);
    }
    else {
```

```perl
        &error('request_method');
    }

# For each name-value pair:                                                  #
foreach $pair (@pairs) {

    # Split the pair up into individual variables.                           #
    local($name, $value) = split(/=/, $pair);

    # Decode the form encoding on the name and value variables.              #
    $name =~ tr/+/ /;
    $name =~ s/%([a-fA-F0-9][a-fA-F0-9])/pack("C", hex($1))/eg;

    $value =~ tr/+/ /;
    $value =~ s/%([a-fA-F0-9][a-fA-F0-9])/pack("C", hex($1))/eg;

    # If they try to include server side includes, erase them, so they
    # aren't a security risk if the html gets returned.  Another
    # security hole plugged up.
    $value =~ s/<!--(.|\n)*-->//g;

    # If the field name has been specified in the %Config array, it will #
    # return a 1 for defined($Config{$name}) and we should associate     #
    # this value with the appropriate configuration variable.  If this   #
    # is not a configuration form field, put it into the associative     #
    # array %Form, appending the value with a ', ' if there is already a #
    # value present.  We also save the order of the form fields in the   #
    # @Field_Order array so we can use this order for the generic sort.  #
    if (defined($Config{$name})) {
        $Config{$name} = $value;
    }
    else {
        if ($Form{$name} && $value) {
            $Form{$name} = "$Form{$name}, $value";
        }
        elsif ($value) {
            push(@Field_Order,$name);
            $Form{$name} = $value;
        }
    }
}
```

```
    # The next six lines remove any extra spaces or new lines from the      #
    # configuration variables, which may have been caused if your editor     #
    # wraps lines after a certain length or if you used spaces between field #
    # names or environment variables.                                        #
    $Config{'required'} =~ s/(\s+|\n)?,(\s+|\n)?/,/g;
    $Config{'required'} =~ s/(\s+)?\n+(\s+)?//g;
    $Config{'env_report'} =~ s/(\s+|\n)?,(\s+|\n)?/,/g;
    $Config{'env_report'} =~ s/(\s+)?\n+(\s+)?//g;
    $Config{'print_config'} =~ s/(\s+|\n)?,(\s+|\n)?/,/g;
    $Config{'print_config'} =~ s/(\s+)?\n+(\s+)?//g;

    # Split the configuration variables into individual field names.         #
    @Required = split(/,/,$Config{'required'});
    @Env_Report = split(/,/,$Config{'env_report'});
    @Print_Config = split(/,/,$Config{'print_config'});
}

sub check_required {

    # Localize the variables used in this subroutine.                        #
    local($require, @error);

    if (!$Config{'recipient'}) {
        if (!defined(%Form)) { &error('bad_referer') }
        else                 { &error('no_recipient') }
    }

    # For each require field defined in the form:                            #
    foreach $require (@Required) {

        # If the required field is the email field, the syntax of the email  #
        # address if checked to make sure it passes a valid syntax.          #
        if ($require eq 'email' && !&check_email($Config{$require})) {
            push(@error,$require);
        }

        # Otherwise, if the required field is a configuration field and it    #
        # has no value or has been filled in with a space, send an error.    #
        elsif (defined($Config{$require})) {
            if (!$Config{$require}) {
```

```
                push(@error,$require);
           }
       }

       # If it is a regular form field which has not been filled in or     #
       # filled in with a space, flag it as an error field.                #
       elsif (!$Form{$require}) {
           push(@error,$require);
       }
   }

   # If any error fields have been found, send error message to the user.  #
   if (@error) { &error('missing_fields', @error) }
}

sub return_html {
   # Local variables used in this subroutine initialized.                 #
   local($key,$sort_order,$sorted_field);

   # If redirect option is used, print the redirectional location header.  #
   if ($Config{'redirect'}) {
       print "Location: $Config{'redirect'}\n\n";
   }

   # Otherwise, begin printing the response page.                         #
   else {

       # Print HTTP header and opening HTML tags.                         #
       print "Content-type: text/html\n\n";
       print "<html>\n <head>\n";

       # Print out title of page                                         #
       if ($Config{'title'}) { print "  <title>$Config{'title'}</title>\n" }
       else                  { print "  <title>Thank You</title>\n"        }

       print " </head>\n <body";

       # Get Body Tag Attributes                                         #
       &body_attributes;
```

```
# Close Body Tag                                          #
print ">\n  <center>\n";

# Print custom or generic title.                          #
if ($Config{'title'}) { print "   <h1>$Config{'title'}</h1>\n" }
else { print "   <h1>Thank You For Filling Out This Form</h1>\n" }

print "</center>\n";

print "Below is what you submitted to $Config{'recipient'} on ";
print "$date<p><hr size=1 width=75\%><p>\n";

# Sort alphabetically if specified:                       #
if ($Config{'sort'} eq 'alphabetic') {
    foreach $field (sort keys %Form) {

        # If the field has a value or the print blank fields option  #
        # is turned on, print out the form field and value.          #
        if ($Config{'print_blank_fields'} || $Form{$field}) {
            print "<b>$field:</b> $Form{$field}<p>\n";
        }
    }
}

# If a sort order is specified, sort the form fields based on that.  #
elsif ($Config{'sort'} =~ /^order:.*,.*/) {

    # Set the temporary $sort_order variable to the sorting order,   #
    # remove extraneous line breaks and spaces, remove the order:    #
    # directive and split the sort fields into an array.             #
    $sort_order = $Config{'sort'};
    $sort_order =~ s/(\s+|\n)?,(\s+|\n)?/,/g;
    $sort_order =~ s/(\s+)?\n+(\s+)?//g;
    $sort_order =~ s/order://;
    @sorted_fields = split(/,/, $sort_order);

    # For each sorted field, if it has a value or the print blank    #
    # fields option is turned on print the form field and value.     #
    foreach $sorted_field (@sorted_fields) {
        if ($Config{'print_blank_fields'} || $Form{$sorted_field}) {
            print "<b>$sorted_field:</b> $Form{$sorted_field}<p>\n";
```

```
                }
            }
        }

        # Otherwise, default to the order in which the fields were sent.    #
        else {

            # For each form field, if it has a value or the print blank     #
            # fields option is turned on print the form field and value.     #
            foreach $field (@Field_Order) {
                if ($Config{'print_blank_fields'} || $Form{$field}) {
                    print "<b>$field:</b> $Form{$field}<p>\n";
                }
            }
        }

        print "<p><hr size=1 width=75%><p>\n";

        # Check for a Return Link and print one if found.                    #
        if ($Config{'return_link_url'} && $Config{'return_link_title'}) {
            print "<ul>\n";
            print "<li><a href=\"$Config{'return_link_url'}\">$Config{'return_
            ➡link_title'}</a>\n";
            print "</ul>\n";
        }

        # Print the page footer.                                             #
        print <<"(END HTML FOOTER)";
<hr size=1 width=75%><p>
<center><font size=-1><a href="http://www.worldwidemart.com/scripts/
➡formmail.shtml">FormMail</a> V1.6 &copy; 1995 -1997  Matt Wright<br>
A Free Product of <a href="http://www.worldwidemart.com/scripts/">Matt's
➡Script Archive, Inc.</a></font></center>
        </body>
        </html>
(END HTML FOOTER)
    }
}
```

```perl
sub send_mail {
    # Localize variables used in this subroutine.                          #
    local($print_config,$key,$sort_order,$sorted_field,$env_report);

    # Open The Mail Program
    open(MAIL,"|$mailprog -t");

    print MAIL "To: $Config{'recipient'}\n";
    print MAIL "From: $Config{'email'} ($Config{'realname'})\n";

    # Check for Message Subject
    if ($Config{'subject'}) { print MAIL "Subject: $Config{'subject'}\n\n" }
    else                    { print MAIL "Subject: WWW Form Submission\n\n" }

    print MAIL "Below is the result of your feedback form.  It was submitted
➥by\n";
    print MAIL "$Config{'realname'} ($Config{'email'}) on $date\n";
    print MAIL "-" x 75 . "\n\n";

    if (@Print_Config) {
        foreach $print_config (@Print_Config) {
            if ($Config{$print_config}) {
                print MAIL "$print_config: $Config{$print_config}\n\n";
            }
        }
    }

    # Sort alphabetically if specified:                                     #
    if ($Config{'sort'} eq 'alphabetic') {
        foreach $field (sort keys %Form) {

            # If the field has a value or the print blank fields option     #
            # is turned on, print out the form field and value.            #
            if ($Config{'print_blank_fields'} || $Form{$field} ||
                $Form{$field} eq '0') {
                print MAIL "$field: $Form{$field}\n\n";
            }
        }
    }
```

```perl
# If a sort order is specified, sort the form fields based on that.    #
elsif ($Config{'sort'} =~ /^order:.*,.*/) {

    # Remove extraneous line breaks and spaces, remove the order:       #
    # directive and split the sort fields into an array.                #
    $Config{'sort'} =~ s/(\s+|\n)?,(\s+|\n)?/,/g;
    $Config{'sort'} =~ s/(\s+)?\n+(\s+)?//g;
    $Config{'sort'} =~ s/order://;
    @sorted_fields = split(/,/, $Config{'sort'});

    # For each sorted field, if it has a value or the print blank        #
    # fields option is turned on print the form field and value.         #
    foreach $sorted_field (@sorted_fields) {
        if ($Config{'print_blank_fields'} || $Form{$sorted_field} ||
            $Form{$sorted_field} eq '0') {
            print MAIL "$sorted_field: $Form{$sorted_field}\n\n";
        }
    }
}

# Otherwise, default to the order in which the fields were sent.         #
else {

    # For each form field, if it has a value or the print blank          #
    # fields option is turned on print the form field and value.         #
    foreach $field (@Field_Order) {
        if ($Config{'print_blank_fields'} || $Form{$field} ||
            $Form{$field} eq '0') {
            print MAIL "$field: $Form{$field}\n\n";
        }
    }
}

print MAIL "-" x 75 . "\n\n";

# Send any specified Environment Variables to recipient.                #
foreach $env_report (@Env_Report) {
    if ($ENV{$env_report}) {
        print MAIL "$env_report: $ENV{$env_report}\n";
    }
}
```

```
        close (MAIL);
    }

sub check_email {
    # Initialize local email variable with input to subroutine.        #
    $email = $_[0];

    # If the e-mail address contains:                                  #
    if ($email =~ /(@.*@)|(\.\.)|(@\.)|(\.@)|(^\.)/ ||

        # the e-mail address contains an invalid syntax.  Or, if the   #
        # syntax does not match the following regular expression pattern #
        # it fails basic syntax verification.                          #

        $email !~ /^.+\@(\[?)[a-zA-Z0-9\-\.]+\.([a-zA-Z]{2,3}|[0-9]{1,3})(\]?)
        ➡$/) {

            # Basic syntax requires:  one or more characters before the @ sign, #
            # followed by an optional '[', then any number of letters, numbers, #
            # dashes or periods (valid domain/IP characters) ending in a period #
            # and then 2 or 3 letters (for domain suffixes) or 1 to 3 numbers #
            # (for IP addresses).  An ending bracket is also allowed as it is #
            # valid syntax to have an email address like: user@[255.255.255] #

            # Return a false value, since the e-mail address did not pass valid #
            # syntax.                                                   #
            return 0;
    }

    else {

            # Return a true value, e-mail verification passed.         #
            return 1;
    }
}

sub body_attributes {
    # Check for Background Color
    if ($Config{'bgcolor'}) { print " bgcolor=\"$Config{'bgcolor'}\"" }
```

```perl
    # Check for Background Image
    if ($Config{'background'}) { print "  ➢  background=\"$Config{'background'}\
➥"" }

    # Check for Link Color
    if ($Config{'link_color'}) { print " link=\"$Config{'link_color'}\"" }

    # Check for Visited Link Color
    if ($Config{'vlink_color'}) { print " vlink=\"$Config{'vlink_color'}\"" }

    # Check for Active Link Color
    if ($Config{'alink_color'}) { print " alink=\"$Config{'alink_color'}\"" }

    # Check for Body Text Color
    if ($Config{'text_color'}) { print " text=\"$Config{'text_color'}\"" }
}

sub error {
    # Localize variables and assign subroutine input.                          #
    local($error,@error_fields) = @_;
    local($host,$missing_field,$missing_field_list);

    if ($error eq 'bad_referer') {
        if ($ENV{'HTTP_REFERER'} =~ m|^https?://([\w\.]+)|i) {
            $host = $1;
            print <<"(END ERROR HTML)";
Content-type: text/html

<html>
 <head>
  <title>Bad Referrer - Access Denied</title>
 </head>
 <body bgcolor=#FFFFFF text=#000000>
  <center>
   <table border=0 width=600 bgcolor=#9C9C9C>
    <tr><th><font size=+2>Bad Referrer - Access Denied</font></th></tr>
   </table>
   <table border=0 width=600 bgcolor=#CFCFCF>
    <tr><td>The form attempting to use
     <a href="http://www.worldwidemart.com/scripts/formmail.shtml">FormMail</a>
```

```
      resides at <tt>$ENV{'HTTP_REFERER'}</tt>, which is not allowed to access
      this cgi script.<p>

      If you are attempting to configure FormMail to run with this form, you
      ➡ need
      to add the following to \@referers, explained in detail in the README
      ➡file.<p>

      Add <tt>'$host'</tt> to your <tt><b>\@referers</b></tt> array.<hr size=1>
      <center><font size=-1>
       <a href="http://www.worldwidemart.com/scripts/formmail.shtml">FormMail
       ➡</a> V1.6 &copy; 1995 - 1997  Matt Wright<br>
       A Free Product of <a href="http://www.worldwidemart.com/scripts/">Matt's
       ➡Script Archive, Inc.</a>
      </font></center>
     </td></tr>
    </table>
   </center>
 </body>
</html>
(END ERROR HTML)
        }
        else {
            print <<"(END ERROR HTML)";
Content-type: text/html

<html>
 <head>
  <title>FormMail v1.6</title>
 </head>
 <body bgcolor=#FFFFFF text=#000000>
  <center>
   <table border=0 width=600 bgcolor=#9C9C9C>
    <tr><th><font size=+2>FormMail</font></th></tr>
   </table>
   <table border=0 width=600 bgcolor=#CFCFCF>
    <tr><th><tt><font size=+1>Copyright 1995 - 1997 Matt Wright<br>
        Version 1.6 - Released May 02, 1997<br>
        A Free Product of <a href="http://www.worldwidemart.com/scripts/">
        ➡Matt's Script Archive,
        Inc.</a></font></tt></th></tr>
```

```
      </table>
     </center>
    </body>
   </html>
   (END ERROR HTML)
           }
       }

      elsif ($error eq 'request_method') {
              print <<"(END ERROR HTML)";
   Content-type: text/html

   <html>
    <head>
     <title>Error: Request Method</title>
    </head>
    <body bgcolor=#FFFFFF text=#000000>
     <center>
      <table border=0 width=600 bgcolor=#9C9C9C>
       <tr><th><font size=+2>Error: Request Method</font></th></tr>
      </table>
      <table border=0 width=600 bgcolor=#CFCFCF>
       <tr><td>The Request Method of the Form you submitted did not match
         either <tt>GET</tt> or <tt>POST</tt>.  Please check the form and make
         ➡sure the
         <tt>method=</tt> statement is in upper case and matches <tt>GET</tt> or
         ➡<tt>POST</tt>.<p>

         <center><font size=-1>
          <a href="http://www.worldwidemart.com/scripts/formmail.shtml">ForMail
          ➡</a> V1.6 &copy; 1995 - 1997  Matt Wright<br>
          A Free Product of <a href="http://www.worldwidemart.com/scripts/">Matt's
          ➡Script Archive, Inc.</a>
         </font></center>
       </td></tr>
      </table>
     </center>
    </body>
   </html>
   (END ERROR HTML)
       }
```

```
        elsif ($error eq 'no_recipient') {
                print <<"(END ERROR HTML)";
Content-type: text/html

<html>
 <head>
  <title>Error: No Recipient</title>
 </head>
 <body bgcolor=#FFFFFF text=#000000>
  <center>
   <table border=0 width=600 bgcolor=#9C9C9C>
    <tr><th><font size=+2>Error: No Recipient</font></th></tr>
   </table>
   <table border=0 width=600 bgcolor=#CFCFCF>
    <tr><td>No Recipient was specified in the data sent to FormMail.  Please
     make sure you have filled in the 'recipient' form field with an e-mail
     address.  More information on filling in recipient form fields can be
     found in the README file.<hr size=1>

     <center><font size=-1>
      <a href="http://www.worldwidemart.com/scripts/formmail.shtml">FormMail
     ➥</a> V1.6 &copy; 1995 - 1997  Matt Wright<br>
      A Free Product of <a href="http://www.worldwidemart.com/scripts/">Matt's
     ➥Script Archive, Inc.</a>
     </font></center>
    </td></tr>
   </table>
  </center>
 </body>
</html>
(END ERROR HTML)
        }

    elsif ($error eq 'missing_fields') {
        if ($Config{'missing_fields_redirect'}) {
            print "Location: $Config{'missing_fields_redirect'}\n\n";
        }
        else {
            foreach $missing_field (@error_fields) {
                $missing_field_list .= "        <li>$missing_field\n";
            }
```

```
            print <<"(END ERROR HTML)";
Content-type: text/html

<html>
 <head>
  <title>Error: Blank Fields</title>
 </head>
  <center>
   <table border=0 width=600 bgcolor=#9C9C9C>
    <tr><th><font size=+2>Error: Blank Fields</font></th></tr>
   </table>
   <table border=0 width=600 bgcolor=#CFCFCF>
    <tr><td>The following fields were left blank in your submission form:<p>
     <ul>
$missing_field_list
     </ul><br>

     These fields must be filled in before you can successfully submit the
     ➥form.<p>
     Please use your browser's back button to return to the form and try
     ➥again.<hr size=1>
     <center><font size=-1>
      <a href="http://www.worldwidemart.com/scripts/formmail.shtml">FormMail
      ➥</a> V1.6 &copy; 1995 - 1997  Matt Wright<br>
      A Free Product of <a href="http://www.worldwidemart.com/scripts/">Matt's
      ➥Script Archive, Inc.</a>
     </font></center>
    </td></tr>
   </table>
  </center>
 </body>
</html>
(END ERROR HTML)
        }
     }
     exit;
}
```

What is important to note is that this program is designed to return an HTML page to the user, indicating that the contact information in the form has been processed or indicating an error, if there was one. This is an important component of all CGI programs: Either they should return valid data to the browser (such as HTML or the contents of an image file) or they should redirect the browser to a valid URL.

The `formmail` program offers many other features, such as the ability to set the subject line of e-mails and ensure that the script is not abused by users on other Web sites. Full details are available at the Web site for the program.

The last important piece of your Web site is to create access restrictions for the directory /var/www/html/authors/ so that only authorized users have access to the files in this directory. To do this requires a three-step process. First, you need to create a users file with the necessary users in it, as you did in the last section on protecting directories with access control. You create access restrictions for all users you wish to give access to the directory.

Second, you want to create a group—let's call it authors—to make the job of managing access to the directory easier. You create this group by adding an entry for the group to your Web server's group file that looks like this:

```
authors: author1 author2 author3
```

This entry assumes that there are three users being given access to the directory.

Finally, you need to create a .htaccess file called /var/www/html/authors/ ("Auth" in these directives refers to authentication, not to our authors group):

```
AuthName Just For Authors
AuthType Basic
AuthUserFile /etc/httpd/conf/users
AuthGroupFile /etc/httpd/conf/groups
require group authors
```

The contents of this file are fairly straightforward. AuthName specifies the prompt presented to the user. AuthUserFile tells the server where to find the list of valid usernames and passwords, just as AuthGroupFile tells the server where the list of valid groups is. Finally, the require directive indicates that only members of the group authors should be given access to the directory.

Now, when a user tries to access the directory in question for the first time in a session, they see an authentication dialog box displayed by their browser, like the one in Figure 32.5 produced by Netscape.

FIGURE 32.5:

An authentication dialog
box in Netscape

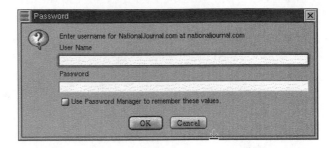

By default, if a user fails to authenticate properly, they receive a generic error page that states that authentication is required. In order to provide a customized page indicating failure, you can edit the httpd.conf file to indicate a custom error message by adding the following entry to the file:

```
ErrorDocument 401 /error.html
```

This entry indicates that when error 401 (Authorization Required) occurs, the server should return the indicated URL instead of the default message. Now when a user fails to authenticate, they will receive your customized message, which could tell them to sign up for your services.

Looking Ahead

This chapter showed you how the Linux operating system provides a flexible tool as a network server, in this case a Web server.

Chapter 33, "Linux As a Mail Server: The Power of Sendmail," examines another important role that Linux can play: the job of a mail server. A mail server handles the processing of all the incoming and outgoing mail for a network, deciding which messages are destined for internal users and directing these messages to the users' mailboxes, and directing messages bound for external networks onto the Internet for delivery.

Setting up a mail server can be a daunting task in a Unix environment, especially using the Sendmail program, which is the dominant Linux mail server. Still, for many networks the job is manageable and, once it is done, a Linux mail server can be relied on to deliver high volumes of messages with little day-to-day administration.

CHAPTER

THIRTY-THREE

Linux As a Mail Server: The Power of Sendmail

- The Concept of a Mail Transport Agent

- Sendmail As the Foremost MTA

- Configuring Sendmail with M4

In this chapter, you are going to learn how to turn Linux into an organizational mail server using the Sendmail mail transport agent.

The need for a mail server arises when you begin to connect together multiple desktops on a network and want to provide e-mail services to them. Using Sendmail, it is possible to configure a Linux system to act as the mail server for internal messages as well as for outgoing and incoming messages to and from the Internet.

This chapter first considers the concept of a mail transport agent (MTA) and then takes a quick look at Sendmail, the foremost MTA in the Unix world, and some alternative MTAs. Finally, it gets down to the business of configuring Sendmail.

The Concept of a Mail Transport Agent

Normally, when users think of e-mail systems, they think of the software they use to read, compose, and send messages. This may be Netscape's mail module, Eudora, Pegasus Mail, or pine, but in all cases these programs are simply an interface to the back-end systems that really do the work of routing and delivering mail.

In none of these cases does the user's software actually handle delivery of outgoing mail or receipt of incoming mail. These programs are mail user agents (MUAs). There are numerous MUAs, and their job is to provide the user interface to the world of e-mail.

Behind these MUAs are the mail transport agents. MTAs handle the job of delivering, receiving, and routing mail messages. Generally, they all adhere to certain standard protocols (such as the Simple Mail Transport Protocol, known as SMTP) that make up the Internet's e-mail system (and the e-mail system of almost every Unix-based network).

This distinction between an MUA and an MTA is an important one. In order to set up a mail server for an organization or any other network of computers, it is necessary to work with mail transport agents.

More information on various MTAs is available in the Linux Electronic Mail Administrator-HOWTO, available online at http://www.linuxdoc.org/HOWTO/ Mail-Administrator-HOWTO.html.

Sendmail as the Foremost MTA

There is little doubt that in the Unix world the foremost MTA is the Sendmail program. This program defines the mail system you are familiar with on the Internet, providing the addressing structure you all know (`username@some.domain`) and the features you have come to expect (such as automatic mail-forwarding).

In its dominance, Sendmail has grown to be the most powerful and complex Unix MTA available. In fact, configuration and management of a Sendmail system can be so complex in a large organization that several books are dedicated to the subject of designing a Sendmail system, configuring it, and keeping it running happily.

This chapter focuses its attention on the configuration and use of Sendmail, since this is the default MTA included with Red Hat Linux and since it is so common on Unix networks.

> **TIP**   This chapter gives only a cursory look at Sendmail and how to configure it. To gain deeper insight into the subject, visit the Web site `www.sendmail.org`.

First, though, let's take a brief survey of some of the alternative MTAs available for Linux.

Smail

Sendmail may be the dominant Unix mail transport agent, but in the Linux world, smail is widely used as an MTA. Its configuration can be easier than Sendmail's (though not always), and it offers similar features, including SMTP support and UUCP support, that make it well-suited to an online mail server configuration.

Red Hat Linux 7.1 uses Sendmail as its default MTA and doesn't include the smail package. You can download the latest version of smail from `ftp://ftp.planix.com/pub/Smail/` or by searching for the latest RPM at `http://www.rpmfind.net`.

Qmail

Qmail is an alternative to Sendmail with several features that make it a strong contender in the MTA arena.

The author of qmail has made security a stated priority for the package. Over the years, Sendmail has had a number of security bugs exposed, though they have always been closed subsequently. The qmail philosophy is to do everything possible to avoid hidden holes because mail is a perpetually running service and therefore constantly open to hacking attempts.

Qmail also tries to make the delivery process as reliable as possible, with an inbox format that is safer than most from corruption should a system crash occur while a message is being delivered to the inbox.

To top it off, qmail brings together features that are kept in separate applications in traditional MTAs: forwarding, aliasing, mailing lists, load management, and more.

The qmail home page is at `http://www.qmail.org`. The qmail home page lists a number of commercial enterprises where you can purchase support.

Configuring Sendmail with M4

As mentioned earlier, configuration of Sendmail can be a daunting task for even an experienced Unix system administrator. Mastering the intricacies of the system can take years.

Sendmail's configuration is stored in `/etc/sendmail.cf`, and just a look at the default configuration file that ships with Red Hat Linux 7.1 shows the complexity of the configuration.

If you look through this file, notice that it contains a large number of extremely cryptic rules that define the behavior of Sendmail. To expect anyone other than an expert in Sendmail to configure a basic system would be unreasonable if it were necessary to manually create and edit this type of configuration file.

Luckily, Sendmail provides a facility for creating a configuration file: a program called m4. M4 allows you to produce much simpler configuration files. M4 then processes these files and converts them into full-fledged Sendmail configuration files. All but the most knowledgeable users should create their Sendmail configurations in this manner.

NOTE You can find a discussion of m4 Sendmail configuration at `http://www.sendmail.org/m4/readme.html`. For examples of how to configure Sendmail using m4, see `http://www.sendmail.org/m4/intro.html`.

This section starts by installing the necessary Sendmail configuration files for m4 to work and then looks at the configuration of an online mail server.

Installing the Sendmail Files

As of this writing, Sendmail is divided into three different RPM packages. They are for the software itself, for the configuration utilities, and for the documentation. If this is your first time using and/or configuring Sendmail, you'll want to install all three packages. You can install the following package from the CD-ROM included with this book:

```
$ rpm -i /mnt/cdrom/RedHat/RPMS/sendmail-8.11.2-14.i386.rpm
```

Only some of the Sendmail configuration files are installed by default when you install Red Hat Linux 7.1. Installing the packages is easy. Mount the Red Hat CD-ROM that comes with this book, and use the `rpm` command to install two of the packages:

```
$ rpm -i /mnt/cdrom/RedHat/RPMS/sendmail-8.11.2-14.i386.rpm
$ rpm -i /mnt/cdrom/RedHat/RPMS/sendmail-cf-8.11.2-14.i386.rpm
```

The Sendmail documentation files are not installed by default when you install Red Hat Linux 7.1. Unless you have the second Red Hat CD-ROM (not included with this book), you'll have to download the `sendmail-8.11.2-14.i386.rpm` package from a site such as `ftp.redhat.com` or `www.rpmfind.net`. Assuming you downloaded to the /tmp directory, you can then install them with the following command:

```
$ rpm -i /tmp/sendmail-doc-8.11.2-14.i386.rpm
```

Creating an Online Mail Server

Now you can look at the configuration file for an online mail server. You do this because online mail servers are a little bit easier to configure and understand than offline servers.

NOTE Even though the m4 system eases Sendmail configuration, the number of options is still immense. Only those options that appear in the configuration files are discussed in this chapter. There are a substantial number of sample configuration files in the subdirectories of the `/usr/share/sendmail-cf` directory. When you finally create a Sendmail configuration file, it belongs in the `/usr/share/sendmail-cf/cf` directory.

An online mail server is a mail server for a network that is fully connected to the Internet by a dedicated line. When someone outside the network directs a mail message to a user on the local network, it can be delivered directly, and when a user on the network sends a message, it is sent immediately.

In your case, you need to configure Sendmail to direct incoming messages to users' mailboxes and to immediately attempt to deliver messages sent by users. Messages are queued for later delivery only if there is a problem delivering a message, such as a failure in the Internet connection while attempting to deliver the message.

Our m4 configuration file looks something like this:

```
include(`../m4/cf.m4')
OSTYPE(`linux')
undefine(`UUCP_RELAY')dnl
undefine(`BITNET_RELAY')dnl
FEATURE(redirect)dnl
FEATURE(always_add_domain)dnl
MAILER(local)dnl
MAILER(smtp)
```

NOTE Watch the quote marks carefully in m4 configuration files. The first quote mark is always a back quote mark (`), which is above the Tab key on U.S. keyboards. The second quote mark (') is a regular single quote mark.

Let's break this down line by line.

Line 1: *include(`../m4/cf.m4')*   These are the generic configuration files needed to build a Sendmail configuration file.

Line 2: *OSTYPE(`linux')*   Your operating system type is defined as Linux so that the appropriate defaults are set.

Line 3: *undefine(`UUCP_RELAY')*   By not defining a UUCP relay, you are indicating that there is no host to receive UUCP-directed mail and that UUCP recipients must be directly connected. Given that UUCP mail was designed for the era when most networks were not directly connected, most sites will leave UUCP_RELAY undefined.

Line 4: *undefine(`BITNET_RELAY')*   Because you are not connected to the Bitnet network, leave this undefined; addresses using the Bitnet format will not work.

Line 5: *FEATURE(redirect)*   If set, any mail addressed to address.REDIRECT is rejected with a message indicating the user's new address. In this way, when a user leaves, their new address can be aliased to their old address with .REDIRECT appended.

Line 6: *FEATURE(always_add_domain)*   This feature ensures that the From line always contains the local domain so that messages can be replied to by the recipients.

Line 7: *MAILER(local)*   Local mailer support allows Sendmail to deliver mail to local Unix mailboxes.

Line 8: *MAILER(smtp)*   SMTP mailer support allows Sendmail to send messages directly to recipient mail servers. This works in a system where the server is connected to the Internet and DNS services are available.

NOTE   The dnl at the end of several of these sendmail lines stands for "delete through newline," which usually minimizes blank lines in the .cf output file discussed below.

To create your Sendmail configuration file from the m4 configuration file, you need to create the m4 file in the directory /usr/lib/sendmail-cf/cf. In this case, let's call the file online.mc. The extension .mc is the generally accepted one for m4 configuration files.

NOTE   If you're unfamiliar with Sendmail, there are a number of sample configuration files in this directory, including generic-linux.mc and redhat.mc, that you could copy to online.mc.

Next, change the directory to /usr/lib/sendmail-cf/cf and issue this command:

```
$ m4 online.mc > online.cf
```

This command processes the file using m4 and generates a Sendmail configuration file called online.cf.

The next step is to make a backup of your existing sendmail.cf file and then replace it with the one you just created. This needs to be done by the root user:

```
# cp /etc/sendmail.cf /etc/sendmail.cf.keep
# cp online.cf /etc/sendmail.cf
```

The last and final step is to restart the Sendmail daemon:

```
# /etc/rc.d/init.d/sendmail restart
```

The daemon control utilities may be in slightly different directory locations if you're using a distribution other than Red Hat Linux.

When the Sendmail daemon starts at boot time, it will now load your new configuration file. If you want to load Sendmail manually, use the command

```
# /usr/sbin/sendmail -bd
```

By default, the Sendmail daemon loads at boot time in most distributions of Linux unless you choose to disable it. You can use the /usr/sbin/sendmail -bd command in your rc.local file if you need to add Sendmail to your boot cycle.

TIP   If you plan to run a large Sendmail site, then the book *Sendmail* by Costales and Allman from O'Reilly & Associates (2nd ed., 1997) is the definitive reference.

Looking Ahead

This chapter wraps up the main body of this book by covering the basics of setting up your own mail server using Linux. With this knowledge in hand, plus the experience you now have in using, configuring, and managing Linux systems, you should be able to perform every computing task you need to do using Linux.

The rest of this book consists of several appendices, many of which you will find helpful in your daily use of Linux. In particular, "Linux Command Reference" (Appendix C) provides a quick guide to the syntax of major Linux commands, many of which you will find yourself using on a regular basis.

In addition, refer to Appendix B, "Sources of Linux Information," for useful resources for expanding your Linux knowledge and skills. Linux is a vast terrain that cannot be mastered quickly. Even the most adept Linux experts find themselves learning new tricks, secrets, and skills on an almost-daily basis. Don't be afraid to do the same. More important, don't be afraid to ask questions in the Linux newsgroups or of the authors of popular Linux applications. As long as you have read the basic documentation such as the HOWTOs at `http://www` `.linuxdoc.org`, the authors or other expert users are usually more than happy to provide guidance, insight, and advice to fledgling Linux users. After all, it is in the interest of Linux developers and users to foster knowledge, awareness, and skill among the growing community of Linux users.

APPENDIX

A

Linux around the World (Non-English Linux Distributions)

- Linux in Croatian

- Linux in French

- Linux in German

- Linux in Japanese

- Linux in Portuguese

- Linux in Russian

- Linux in Spanish

- Linux in Swedish

- Linux in Turkish

- Linux in Multiple Languages

A

Linux is and has always been an international phenomenon. With a kernel from Finland, a GUI from Germany, and an unconventional license from the U.S. that encourages free distribution, Linux has caught on worldwide. In some countries, developers have translated Linux into their own local language(s). Many of the groups behind the major distributions have done their own translations.

As this book is written by English-language authors, it makes no claim as to the quality of the following non-English distributions.

Linux in Croatian

MicroLinux

MicroLinux is a small Croatian-language distribution that is designed to sit on a DOS partition. This makes it convenient for users who can't repartition their Windows 95/98/Me systems and need to run both Windows (or DOS) and Linux.

HULK - Hrvatska udruga Linux korisnika

WWW: `http://linux.hr/`

Linux in French

MNIS Linux

MNIS produces a French distribution of Linux known as MNIS Linux. MNIS Linux is billed as a PC-based X workstation and includes unique features such as the K Desktop Environment. They also have a commercial X-Win32 package that runs Windows 95/NT/2000 applications directly on their distribution.

MNIS

57, rue d'Amsterdam

75008 Paris

France

E-mail: mnis@mnis.fr

WWW: http://www.mnis.fr/

Linux in German

EasyLinux

EasyLinux is a German-based Linux distribution designed for non-Linux users. They have included a number of graphical configuration utilities for most of the Linux configuration files that you need.

easy Information Technology GmbH

Am Seerhein 8

78467 Konstanz

Germany

WWW: http://www.easyLinux.com/

Icepack Linux

Icepack Linux is a German-based Linux distribution designed for non-Linux users. Even though it uses many of the same packages, such as GNOME and KDE, it was developed independently of other Linux distributions.

Icepack Linux

E-mail: support@icepack-linux.com

WWW: http://www.icepack-linux.com/

Linux in Japanese

Laser5 Linux

Laser5 Linux is a Japanese distribution based on Red Hat Linux. They also have Linux workstation, server, and clustering systems.

LASER5 Co., Ltd.

NOV Building, 3F, 3-10-7 Yushima

Bunkyo-ku

Tokyo

Japan

113-0034

E-mail: `info@laser5.co.jp`

WWW: `http://www.laser5.co.jp/`

Vine Linux

Vine Linux is another Japanese distribution. The latest version as of this writing, Vine Linux 2.1, is based on Red Hat Linux 6.2. Vine Linux includes a number of Japanese fonts and applications. It is sold by Red Hat Linux on their Japanese Web site.

Vine Linux

WWW: `http://www.vinelinux.org/`

Linux in Portuguese

Conectiva Linux

Conectiva Linux is a Portuguese version of Red Hat Linux produced by Conectiva Informática in Brazil. At the time of this writing, the current distribution of Conectiva Linux is version 6, which includes KDE version 2 and XFree version 4.0.1.

Conectiva Informática

Rua Tocantins, 89 – Cristo Rei

Zip: 80050-430

Curitiba(PR)

Brazil

E-mail: info@conectiva.com.br

WWW: http://www.conectiva.com.br/

Linux in Russian

Open Kernel: Linux

Open Kernel: Linux from UrbanSoft is a Russian distribution based on Red Hat Linux, which offers Russian console fonts, a Russian X Windows environment, and additional Russian packages that are not part of the standard Red Hat environment. The current version is derived from Red Hat 6.2.

UrbanSoft

E-mail: info@usoft.spb.ru

WWW: http://www.usoft.spb.ru/

Linux in Spanish

Eurielec Linux

Eurielec Linux is yet another non-English Linux distribution based on Red Hat Linux, this time in Spanish. The current version of Eurielec Linux is based on Red Hat Linux 6.2.

Escuela Técnica Superior Ingenieros de Telecomunicación

Avda. Complutense s/n - 28040

Madrid

Spain

E-mail: linux@eurielec.etsit.upm.es

WWW: http://www.eurielec.etsit.upm.es/linux/

ESware Linux

ESware Linux is a non-English Linux distribution with all material in Spanish (Castellano), including installation, command lines, documentation, and user manual.

ESWARE LINUX

Proción 1-3

Edif. Oficor

28023 La Florida

Madrid

Spain

WWW: http://www.esware.com/

Linux in Swedish

Blue Linux

Blue Linux is a Swedish distribution based on Debian Linux 2.2. According to Linux Online, it does not have to be installed on a hard disk.

Blue Linux

WWW: http://blue.swt.nu/

Linux in Turkish

Gelecek Linux

Gelecek Linux is yet another non-English Linux distribution based on Red Hat Linux, this time in Turkish.

Gelecek Bilisim ve Iletisim A.S

Perpa Ticaret Merkezi

B Blok Kat: 11 No: 1932

Sisli, Istanbul

Turkey

E-mail: info@gelecek.com.tr

WWW: http://www.gelecek.com.tr/

Linux in Multiple Languages

A number of the major distributions have versions or at least installation programs in several different languages. This list includes several Linux distributions that are available in more than one language (other than English).

Best Linux

Best Linux is an independent, Finnish-based distribution. Their current product, Best Linux 2000, is designed to install straight into a "graphical Windows-like KDE desktop which includes almost all of the software that you use daily." Best Linux includes support for Finnish, Swedish, English, Russian, Estonian, French, German, and Spanish. It also includes partial support in 14 other European languages.

SOT Finnish Software Engineering Ltd.

Hermiankatu 8 E

Fin-33720 Tampere

Finland

E-mail: finland@bestlinux.net

WWW: http://www.bestlinux.net/

Caldera Linux

Caldera has developed versions of its distributions in a number of major languages. According to its Web site, Caldera provides OpenLinux technical support in several different languages, including German, French, Italian, Japanese, and Korean.

Caldera Systems, Inc.

240 West Center Street

Orem, Utah 84057

U.S.A.

E-mail: info@calderasystems.com

WWW: http://www.caldera.com/

Debian Linux

Debian Linux is developed by volunteers. Many of these volunteers are working to translate Debian Linux into other languages. As of this writing, varying degrees of documentation and support are available in 17 different languages. As it is developed by volunteers, there is no one support center for this distribution.

E-mail: debian-project@lists.debian.org

WWW: http://www.Debian.org/

Mandrake Linux

Mandrake Linux (also known as Linux-Mandrake) is developed from Red Hat Linux, extended to support additional features, including additional languages.

MandrakeSoft Inc.

2400 N. Lincoln Ave.

Altadena, CA 91001

U.S.A.

E-mail: sales@mandrakesoft.com

WWW: http://www.linux-mandrake.com/

Red Hat Linux

Red Hat has developed versions of its distributions in a number of major languages. The Linux documentation CD-ROM that comes with the full version of Red Hat Linux 7.1 includes documentation in French, English, German, Italian, and Spanish. The Red Hat Linux 7.1 installation program allows you to install Linux in 19 different European languages, and Japanese.

Red Hat, Inc.

2600 Meridian Parkway

Durham, NC 27713

U.S.A.

E-mail: See `http://www.redhat.com/about/contact/directory.html` for a list of e-mail contacts.

WWW: `http://www.redhat.com/`

S.u.S.E Linux

As they are based in Germany, S.u.S.E. may be the Linux leader in the international arena. Their support database is available in French, English, German, Italian, and Spanish. Their installation program includes support in a large number of European languages.

> S.u.S.E.
>
> Schanzackerstraße 10
>
> 90443 Nürmberg
>
> Germany
>
> E-mail: `suse@suse.de`
>
> WWW: `http://www.suse.de/`

or

> S.u.S.E.
>
> 580 Second Street Suite 210
>
> Oakland, CA 94607
>
> U.S.A.
>
> E-mail: `info@suse.com`
>
> WWW: `http://www.suse.com/`

TurboLinux

TurboLinux is available in Japanese and Chinese. Each language specific version of TurboLinux includes language-customized tools such as the browser and desktop.

TurboLinux

8000 Marina Boulevard

Suite 300

Brisbane, CA 94005

E-mail: support@turbolinux.com

WWW: http://www.turbolinux.com/

APPENDIX
B

Sources of Linux Information

This appendix lists Internet resources where you can find additional Linux-related information, download or purchase Linux distributions, and ask for help. By no means is this intended to reflect a complete list of Linux resources on the Internet; it is more a record of the sites I have found useful around the Internet in my years of using Linux.

General Information

Just Linux	`http://www.justlinux.com/`
Linux Administrator's Security Guide	`http://www.linuxdoc.org/LDP/lasg/`
Linux Documentation Project	`http://www.linuxdoc.org/`
Linux Frequently Asked Questions with Answers	`http://www.mainmatter.com/linux-faq/toc.html`
Linux Hardware	`http://www.linuxhardware.net/`
Linux Installation and Getting Started	`http://www.linuxdoc.org/LDP/gs/gs.html`
Linux International	`http://www.li.org/`
Linux Journal	`http://www.linuxjournal.com/`
Linux NOW!	`http://www.linuxnow.com/`
Linux Online	`http://www.linux.org/`
Linux System Administrators' Guide	`http://www.linuxdoc.org/LDP/sag/index.html`
Linux Today	`http://www.linuxtoday.com/`
Linux User Group Registry	`http://www.linux.org/users/index.html`
The Linux Web Ring	`http://linuxwebring.org/`
Slashdot	`http://www.slashdot.org/`

The Network Administrators' Guide   `http://www.linuxdoc.org/LDP/`
                                         `nag2/index.html`

Woven Goods for Linux   `http://www.fokus.gmd.de/linux/`

Linux Professional Certifications

Digital Metrics   `http://www.digitalmetrics.com/`

Linux Professional Institute   `http://www.lpi.org/`

Red Hat Certified Engineer   `http://www.redhat.com/`
                                         `training/rhce/courses/`

Sair GNU/Linux   `http://www.linuxcertification`
                                         `.org/`

Linux Distributions

Best Linux   `http://www.bestlinux.net/`

Black Cat Linux   `http://www.blackcatlinux.com/`

Blue Linux   `http://blue.swt.nu/`

Caldera OpenLinux   `http://www.calderasystems.com/`

Conectiva Linux (Brazilian Portuguese)   `http://www.conectiva.com.br/`

Corel Linux   `http://linux.corel.com/`

Debian/GNU Linux   `http://www.debian.org/`

DLX Linux   `http://www.wu-wien.ac.at/usr/`
                                         `h93/h9301726/dlx.html`

EasyLinux   `http://www.easylinux.com/`

ESware Linux   `http://www.esware.com/`

Eurielec Linux (Spanish)   `http://www.eurielec.etsit`
                                         `.upm.es/linux/`

Gelecek Linux	`http://www.gelecek.com.tr/`
Icepack Linux	`http://www.icepack-linux.com/`
Laser5 Linux	`http://www.laser5.co.jp/`
Linux Mandrake	`http://www.linux-mandrake.com/`
LinuxPPC (for PowerPC chips)	`http://www.linuxppc.org/`
LinuxWare	`http://www.trans-am.com/` `linux.htm`
MkLinux (for the Power Macintosh)	`http://www.mklinux.org/`
MNIS Linux (French)	`http://www.mnis.fr/`
Red Hat Linux	`http://www.redhat.com/`
Slackware Linux	`http://www.slackware.com/`
Stampede Linux	`http://www.stampede.org/`
S.u.S.E. Linux (German and English)	`http://www.suse.com/`
TurboLinux	`http://www.turbolinux.com/`
Vine Linux	`http://www.vinelinux.org/`

Mailing Lists and Newsgroups

alt.os.linux.best	`news:alt.os.linux.best`
alt.os.linux.caldera	`news:alt.os.linux.caldera`
alt.os.linux.corel	`news:alt.os.linux.corel`
alt.os.linux.dial-up	`news:alt.os.linux.dial-up`
alt.os.linux.mandrake	`news:alt.os.linux.mandrake`
alt.os.linux.redhat	`news:alt.os.linux.redhat`
alt.os.linux.slackware	`news:alt.os.linux.slackware`

alt.os.linux.storm	`news:alt.os.linux.storm`
alt.os.linux.suse	`news:alt.os.linux.suse`
alt.os.linux.turbolinux	`news:alt.os.linux.turbolinux`
comp.os.linux.admin	`news:comp.os.linux.admin`
comp.os.linux.advocacy	`news:comp.os.linux.advocacy`
comp.os.linux.alpha	`news:comp.os.linux.alpha`
comp.os.linux.announce	`news:comp.os.linux.announce`
comp.os.linux.development.apps	`news:comp.os.linux` `.development.apps`
comp.os.linux.development.system	`news:comp.os.linux` `.development.system`
comp.os.linux.embedded	`news:comp.os.linux.embedded`
comp.os.linux.hardware	`news:comp.os.linux.hardware`
comp.os.linux.help	`news:comp.os.linux.help`
comp.os.linux.m68k	`news:comp.os.linux.m68k`
comp.os.linux.misc	`news:comp.os.linux.misc`
comp.os.linux.networking	`news:comp.os.linux.networking`
comp.os.linux.portable	`news:comp.os.linux.portable`
comp.os.linux.powerpc	`news:comp.os.linux.powerpc`
comp.os.linux.questions	`news:comp.os.linux.questions`
comp.os.linux.redhat	`news:comp.os.linux.redhat`
comp.os.linux.security	`news:comp.os.linux.security`
comp.os.linux.setup	`news:comp.os.linux.setup`
comp.os.linux.x	`news:comp.os.linux.x`
Linux Mailing Lists	`http://www.linuxlookup.com/` `html/main/mailinglists.html`

Non-Intel Platforms

Linux Alpha FTP Archive	http://gatekeeper.dec.com/pub/DEC/Linux-Alpha/
Linux for BeBox	http://www.sowerbutts.com/belinux/introduction.html
Linux for Sparc Processors	http://www.ultralinux.org/
Linux/m68k for Macintosh	http://www.mac.linux-m68k.org/
The Linux/m68k Home Pages	http://www.linux-m68k.org/
MK Linux Archive	http://ftp.sunet.se/pub/os/Linux/mklinux/mklinux/
SGI-Linux	http://linus.linux.sgi.com/

Non-English Sites

EPC Home Page (Spanish)	http://www.arrakis.es/~epujol/linux/
Linux (Czech)	http://www.linux.cz/
Linux - Viel Unix für wenig Geld (German)	http://www.uni-tuebingen.de/zdv/projekte/linux/
Linux Indonesia (Indonesian)	http://www.linux.or.id/

Places to Purchase Linux CD-ROMs

CD-ROM Shop	http://www.cdromshop.com/
CheapBytes	http://www.cheapbytes.com/
InfoMagic	http://www.infomagic.com/
Linux Central	http://linuxcentral.com/
Linux Mall	http://www.linuxmall.com/

Places to Download Linux and Linux Files

BLINUX's FTP Site	`ftp://leb.net/pub/blinux/`
Caldera's FTP Site	`ftp://ftp.caldera.com/pub/`
Debian's FTP Site	`ftp://ftp.debian.org/`
Freshmeat.net	`http://www.freshmeat.net/`
Georgia Tech's Linux Archive	`ftp://ftp.cc.gatech.edu/pub/linux/`
Linux Applications	`http://www.linuxapps.com/`
Linux Kernel Archives	`ftp://ftp.kernel.org/`
Linux Software Map	`http://www.execpc.com/lsm/`
Red Hat's FTP Site	`ftp://ftp.redhat.com/pub/`
Tucows Linux	`http://linux.tucows.com/`
UNC's Linux Archive	`http://www.ibiblio.org/pub/Linux/`
Woven Goods for Linux's Software Page	`http://www.fokus.gmd.de/linux/linux-softw.html`

X Windows

MetroLink	`http://www.metrolink.com/`
XFree86 Project	`http://www.xfree86.org/`
Xi Graphics	`http://www.xinside.com/`

Linux Command Reference

This appendix provides a guide to using the common Linux commands and utilities found in the following directories in most Red Hat Linux installations:

- /bin

- /sbin

- /usr/bin

- /usr/sbin

The approach taken here is to provide a quick reference to the syntax and common options for many major Linux commands. More details about these commands and about commands not listed here are generally found in the man pages for the commands (accessed by typing man *command*).

By no means should this appendix be considered a complete guide to all options, flags, and arguments for every Linux command. Instead, it is designed to get you started using common and important commands in their most common forms. In all cases, you can consult the relevant man page of a command to learn further details about that command.

This appendix presents the overall syntax of commands using the style found in standard Linux man pages, and then provides a description of the command followed by a description of major flags and arguments.

In order to keep this appendix to a reasonable size, most interactive programs, daemons, and Red Hat–specific commands have been excluded. Even so, there are almost 200 commands covered in this appendix.

Commands appear in alphabetical order.

Commands Covered in This Appendix

The following commands are covered in this reference:

arch	atrm	biff	chgrp
at	badblocks	cal	chkconfig
atd	batch	cat	chmod
atq	bc	checkalias	chown

clear	grep	listalias	mkdir
compress	groupadd	ln	mkdosfs
cp	groupdel	loadkeys	mke2fs
crontab	groupmod	logger	mkfs
cryptdir	groups	login	mkpasswd
date	grpck	logname	mkswap
dc	gunzip	logrotate	mlabel
decryptdir	gzexe	lpd	mmd
depmod	gzip	lpq	mmove
df	halt	lpr	modprobe
dir	head	lprm	more
dmesg	hostname	ls	mount
dnsdomainname	id	lsdev	mrd
dnsquery	ifconfig	lsmod	mren
domainname	ifdown	mail	mtype
du	ifport	mailq	mv
e2fsck	ifup	mailto	netstat
echo	insmod	man	newgrp
egrep	kbd_mode	mattrib	newusers
false	kbdrate	mbadblocks	nisdomainname
fdisk	kill	mcd	nslookup
fgrep	killall	mcopy	passwd
file	ksyms	mdel	paste
find	last	mdeltree	pathchk
finger	ldd	mdir	pidof
free	less	messages	ping
gpasswd	lilo	mformat	pppstats

ps	route	tar	uudecode
pwck	rsh	timeconfig	uuencode
pwconv	runlevel	timed	vipw
pwd	rup	timedc	vmstat
pwunconv	rusers	top	w
quota	rwho	touch	wc
quotacheck	rwhod	traceroute	whereis
quotaoff	setclock	true	which
quotaon	setkeycodes	umount	whoami
rcp	showkey	uname	ypdomainname
rdate	showmount	uncompress	zcat
rdist	shutdown	unzip	zgrep
repquota	sort	uptime	zip
rlogin	statserial	useradd	zipgrep
rm	su	userdel	zipinfo
rmdir	sync	usermod	zmore
rmmod	tail	users	znew

arch

Description	Displays the architecture of the machine on which Linux is running. For instance, i586 represents a Pentium-based system, i486 represents an 80486-based computer, and axp represents Linux running on an Alpha-based computer.
Syntax	arch
Important Flags and Options	None

at

Description	Schedules commands to be executed at a specific time. User is prompted for the commands, or the commands can be provided from a file. Each job is added to a schedule queue and is provided a job number.
Syntax	at [-q *queue*] [-f *filename*] [-1] [-m] [-d *job* [*job* ...]] TIME
Important Flags and Options	

- -d *job*: Deletes a job specified by job number.

- -f *filename*: Reads commands to be scheduled from the specified file rather than prompting for the commands.

- -1: Displays commands in the schedule queue (the TIME argument is ignored).

- -m: E-mails the user who scheduled the job once the job is finished, and includes any generated output in the body of the message.

- -q *queue*: Specifies the queue to operate on. Queues are specified with a single letter (a-z or A-Z). By default, the a queue is used for at and related commands.

Notes	Specifying times: Several options exist for specifying time, including these:

- HH:MM specifies the hour and minutes, such as 11:15 or 22:30. AM and PM suffixes are allowed, as in 11:15AM or 11:30PM.

- midnight (24:00 or 12:00PM), noon (12:00), and teatime (16:00) are reserved words specifying the times indicated.

- MMDDYY, MM/DD/YY, or DD.MM.YY can be used to indicate specific dates, as in 022598 or 25.02.98.

- now specifies the current time.

- tomorrow specifies the next day.

- Using a + can specify offsets in minutes, hours, days, or weeks from a specified time. For instance, to schedule a command for noon two days from the current day, you could use noon + 2 days.

atd

Description	Daemon that runs jobs scheduled for later execution by programs such as at and batch.
Syntax	atd [-1 *load*] [-b *interval*]
Important Flags and Options	

- -b *interval*: Indicates the minimum interval in seconds between the start of two batch jobs. By default, this is 60 seconds.

- -1 *load*: Specifies a load limit over which scheduled batch jobs will not be run. By default, this load is 0.8.

atq

Description	Displays jobs scheduled by the command **at** that are in the schedule queue. This is the same as **at -l**.
Syntax	`atq [-q queue]`
Important Flags and Options	`-q queue`: Specifies the queue to operate on. Queues are specified with a single letter (a-z or A-Z). By default, the **a** queue is used for **at** and related commands.

atrm

Description	Removes specified jobs from the **at** schedule queue. This is the same as **at -d**.
Syntax	`atrm job [job ...]`
Important Flags and Options	None

badblocks

Description	Checks a device (usually a hard disk) for bad blocks.
Syntax	`badblocks [-o filename] [-w] device blocks-count`
Important Flags and Options	• `-o filename`: Specifies a file where results should be written instead of displaying them on the standard output.
	• `-w`: Uses a write test, instead of a read-only test, in which data is written to each block of the device and then reread from the block.
Notes	You should specify the device using the full Linux device path, such as **/dev/hda2** or **/dev/sdb3**. The number of blocks on the device is essential (this information can be determined using **fdisk**).
Warnings	Do not use the **-w** flag on devices that contain important data. Data stored on devices that are checked with the **-w** flag will get erased during the checking process.

batch

Description	Schedules commands to be executed at a specified time as long as system load levels permit. User is prompted for the commands, or the commands can be provided from a file. Each job is added to a schedule queue and is provided a job number.
Syntax	`batch [-q queue] [-f filename] [-m] TIME`

Important Flags and Options	• -f *filename*: Reads commands to be scheduled from the specified file rather than prompting for the commands.

• -m: E-mails the user who scheduled the job once the job is finished and includes any generated output in the body of the message.

• -q *queue*: Specifies the queue to operate on. Queues are specified with a single letter (a-z or A-Z). By default, the b queue is used for batch.

Notes   Specifying times: Several options exist for specifying time, including these:

• *HH:MM* specifies the hour and minutes, such as 11:15 or 22:30. AM and PM suffixes are allowed, as in 11:15AM or 11:30PM.

• midnight (24:00 or 12:00PM), noon (12:00), and teatime (16:00) are reserved words specifying the times indicated.

• *MMDDYY*, *MM/DD/YY*, or *DD.MM.YY* can be used to indicate specific dates, as in 022598 or 25.02.98.

• now specifies the current time.

• tomorrow specifies the next day.

• Using a + can specify offsets in minutes, hours, days, or weeks from a specified time. For instance, to schedule a command for noon two days from the current day, you could use noon + 2 days.

bc

Description   An interactive, arbitrary-precision calculator. Processes all expressions in specified files as well as prompting user to provide expressions for evaluation.

Syntax   bc [*file* ...]

Important Flags and Options   None

Notes   The syntax of expressions used by bc is largely based on the C programming language. Refer to the bc man page for details.

Expressions in files provided as arguments are processed before presenting a prompt to the user for entering additional expressions to be processed.

biff

Description   Notifies users when new mail arrives and indicates who sent the message.

Syntax   biff [ny]

Important Flags and Options

• n: Disables mail arrival notification when it is enabled.

• y: Enables mail arrival notification when it is disabled.

cal

Description	Displays a calendar for a month or an entire year. If no month or year is specified, the current month's calendar is displayed.
Syntax	`cal [-j] [-y] [month [year]]`
Important Flags and Options	• `-j`: Specifies that Julian dates should be used instead of Gregorian dates.
	• `-y`: Displays a yearly calendar instead of a monthly calendar.
Notes	A single numeric argument specifies a year between the year 1 and the year 9999 (years must be complete--e.g., 1998, not 98). With two arguments, the first specifies the month numerically from 1 to 12 and the second specifies the year from 1 to 9999.

cat

Description	Combines one or more files and displays them on the standard output. If no files are given, then the standard input is written to the standard output.
Syntax	`cat [--benstvAET] [--number] [--number-nonblank] [--squeeze-blank]` `➥[--show-nonprinting] [--show-ends] [--show-tabs] [--show-all]` `➥[file ...]`
Important Flags and Options	• `-A/--show-all`: Displays a $ at the end of each line, tab characters as ^I, and control characters preceded by a ^. This is the same as the combination of -v, -T, and -E.
	• `-b/--number-nonblank`: Causes all non-blank lines to appear numbered. Numbering starts at 1.
	• `-e`: Displays a $ at the end of each line and control characters preceded by a ^. This is the same as the combination of -v and -E.
	• `-E/--show-ends`: Displays a $ at the end of each line.
	• `-n/--number`: Causes all lines to appear numbered. Numbering starts at 1.
	• `-s/--squeeze-blank`: Replaces sequences of multiple blank lines with single blank lines when displayed.
	• `-t`: Displays tab characters as ^I and control characters preceded by a ^. This is the same as the combination of -v and -T.
	• `-T/--show-tabs`: Displays tab characters as ^I.
	• `-v/--show-nonprinting`: Displays control characters preceded by a ^.

checkalias

Description	Checks the user's file and then the system alias file in order to see if a specified alias is defined.
Syntax	checkalias *alias*[, *alias*,...]
Important Flags and Options	None

chgrp

Description	Changes the group ownership of one or more files or directories.
Syntax	chgrp [-Rcfv] [--recursive] [--changes] [--silent] [--quiet] ➥[--verbose] *group filename* ...
Important Flags and Options	• -c/--changes: Displays the names of only those files whose ownership is being changed.
	• -f/--silent/--quiet: Suppresses display of error messages when a file's ownership cannot be changed.
	• -R/--recursive: Recursively changes the ownership of all files in all subdirectories of any directory that has its ownership changed.
	• -v/--verbose: Displays the results of all ownership changes.
Notes	The group can be specified either by name or by group ID.

chkconfig

Description	Manipulates or displays settings for system run levels.
Syntax	chkconfig –list [*name*]
	chkconfig –add *name*
	chkconfig –del *name*
	chkconfig <on | off | reset> [--level *levels*]
	chkconfig [--level *levels*] name
Important Flags and Options	• --add *name*: Adds a new service for management by chkconfig and checks that the necessary start and kill entries exist. If entries are missing, they are created.
	• --del *name*: Deletes the named service from management; any links to it are also deleted.

- --level [*levels*]: Specifies numerically which run level a named service should belong to.

- --list *name*: Lists all services that chkconfig knows about and any relevant information about them. If a named service is specified, only information about that service is displayed.

- off: When specified after the service name, the service's status for the specified run level is changed to a stopped state. If no run level is specified, then this option affects run levels 3, 4, and 5.

- on: When specified after the service name, the service's status for the specified run level is changed to a started state. If no run level is specified, then this option affects run levels 3, 4, and 5.

- reset: When specified after the service name, the service's status for the specified run level is set to the default status indicated by the init script. If no run level is specified, then this option affects all run levels.

chmod

Description	Changes the access permissions of one or more files or directories.
Syntax	chmod [-Rcfv] [--recursive] [--changes] [--silent] [--quiet] ➥[--verbose] *mode file* ...
Important Flags and Options	

- -c/--changes: Displays the names of only those files whose permissions are being changed.

- -f/--silent/--quiet: Suppresses display of error messages when a file's permissions cannot be changed.

- -R/--recursive: Recursively changes the permissions of all files in all subdirectories of any directory that has its permissions changed.

- -v/--verbose: Displays the results of all permission changes.

Notes	Modes can be specified in two ways: symbolically and numerically. When done symbolically, modes take the form [ugoa][[+-=][rwxXstugo ...]. The first element ([ugoa]) represents the users whose permissions are being affected (u=user who owns the file or directory, g=all members of the group that owns the file or directory, o=anyone who is not the owner or in the owner group, a=all users). The + symbol means that the specified modes should be added to already specified permissions, the - symbol means the specified modes should be removed from existing permissions, and the = symbol means that the specified modes should replace existing permissions. There are many different permissions that can be specified in the third element of the mode, including r for read permissions, w for write permissions, and x for execute permissions.

Full details of symbolic and numeric modes appear in the **chmod** man page.

chown

Description	Changes the user and/or group ownership of one or more files or directories.
Syntax	`chown [-Rcfv] [--recursive] [--changes] [--silent] [--quiet]` ➡`[--verbose] [user][:.][group] file ...`

Important Flags and Options

- `-c/--changes`: Displays the names of only those files whose ownership is being changed.

- `-f/--silent/--quiet`: Suppresses display of error messages when a file's ownership cannot be changed.

- `-R/--recursive`: Recursively changes the ownership of all files in all subdirectories of any directory that has its ownership changed.

- `-v/--verbose`: Displays the results of all ownership changes.

Notes

The user and group can be specified either by name or by IDs. User and group can be combined in several ways:

- The user followed by a dot or colon followed by a group changes both the user and group ownerships to those specified.

- The user followed by a dot or colon and no group changes the user ownership as specified and changes the group ownership to the specified user's login group.

- If the colon or dot and group are specified without a user, then only group ownership is changed. This is the same as `chgrp`.

- If the user is not followed by a dot or colon, then only the user ownership is changed.

clear

Description	Clears the terminal screen and resets the prompt and cursor location to the first line of the screen.
Syntax	`clear`
Important Flags and Options	None

compress

Description	Compresses files or the standard input using Lempel-Ziv compression.
Syntax	`compress [-f] [-v] [-c] [-r] [file ...]`

Important Flags and Options

- -c: Returns compressed data on standard output rather than to a file as is the default when compressing a file.

- -f: Forces compression of hard-linked files, which are ignored by default.

- -r: Operates recursively. If a directory is specified as an argument, then compresses all files within that directory and in its subdirectories.

- -v: Displays the percentage reduction in size for each file compressed.

Notes

When compressing files, the compress command replaces the original file with a file whose name has a .Z prefix but otherwise remains unchanged. This behavior is overridden by the -c flag. If no files are specified, the standard input is compressed and the results are returned through standard output.

cp

Description

Copies files and directories.

Syntax

```
cp [-a] [--archive] [-b] [--backup] [-d] [--no-dereference] [-f]
➥[--force] [-i] [--interactive] [1] [--link] [-p] [--preserve]
➥[-R] [--recursive] [-s] [--symbolic-link] [-u] [--update] source
destination

cp [options] source ... destination
```

Important Flags and Options

- -a/--archive: Copies files and directories recursively, maintaining symbolic links as links and preserving ownership and permissions of the original files. This is the same as -dpR.

- -b/--backup: Makes backup copies of files before the original files are overwritten.

- -d/--no-dereference: Copies links as links rather than copying the files to which the links point.

- -f/--force: Forces removal of existing destination files that need to be overwritten.

- -i/--interactive: Prompts before overwriting existing destination files.

- -l/--link: Makes hard links instead of copying files. This applies only to files, not to directories.

- -p/--preserve: Preserves the ownership and permissions of the original files.

- -R/--recursive: Recursively copies directories. That is, for every source directory specified, every file in the directory and all its subdirectories are copied while retaining the matching directory structure.

- -s/--symbolic-link: Makes symbolic links instead of copying files. Source files must be specified with full paths.

- -u/--update: Replaces only those destination files that have older modification times than the corresponding source files.

Warnings

Care needs to be taken with the -f flag when working as the root user. Making a mistake can cause important system files to be overwritten because the root user generally has write permission for all files and directories.

crontab

Description	Displays or alters a user's Cron table (`crontab`). The Cron table specifies scheduled actions that are executed by the Cron daemon.
Syntax	`crontab [-u user] file`
	`crontab [-u user] { -l|-r| -e }`
Important Flags and Options	• `-e`: Edits the `crontab` file of the user executing the command or the user specified by the `-u` flag. The editor invoked is specified by the `EDITOR` environment variable.
	• `-l`: Displays the contents of the `crontab` file of the user executing the command or the user specified by the `-u` flag.
	• `-r`: Deletes the `crontab` file of the user executing the command or the user specified by the `-u` flag.
	• `-u user`: Specifies which user's `crontab` file to work with if it is not the same user as the one executing the command. This flag can only be used by the root user.
Notes	The format of entries in `crontab` files is discussed in Chapter 17, "General System Administration."

cryptdir

Description	Encrypts all files in a specified directory. If no directory is specified, then all files in the current directory are encrypted.
Syntax	`cryptdir [directory]`
Important Flags and Options	None
Notes	When encrypting files, you will be prompted twice for a password. This password is needed to decrypt files. Encrypted files will have the `.crypt` extensions added to their names. Use `decryptdir` to decrypt the files.

date

Description	Displays or sets the current system date and time.
Syntax	`date [-u] [--universal] [MMDDhhmm[[CC]YY][.ss]]`
Important Flags and Options	`-u/--universal`: Displays the time in Greenwich Mean Time (also known as Coordinated Universal Time).

Notes

If a date and time are provided as an argument, this is done entirely with numbers where the two-digit elements shown previously represent the following values:

- *MM*: month
- *DD*: day of the month
- *hh*: hour
- *mm*: minute
- *CC*: century (first two digits of the year)
- *YY*: last two digits of the year
- *ss*: seconds

Keep in mind that only the root user can set the system clock.

dc

Description

An interactive, arbitrary-precision, reverse-polish notation calculator. Processes all expressions in specified files as well as prompting user to provide expressions for evaluation.

Syntax

`dc [file ...]`

Important Flags and Options

None

Notes

Detailed syntax of expressions used by **dc** is documented in the **dc** man page. Expressions in files provided as arguments are processed before presenting a prompt to the user for entering additional expressions to be processed.

decryptdir

Description

Decrypts all files in a specified directory. If no directory is specified, then all files in the current directory are encrypted. Files must have been encrypted with the `encryptdir` command.

Syntax

`cryptdir [directory]`

Important Flags and Options

None

Notes

You will be prompted for a password when decrypting files. You need to provide the same password that was used when encrypting the files, or the process will fail.

depmod

Description	Returns module dependencies on the standard output. These can be stored in a file and then used by **modprobe** for installing loadable modules.
Syntax	depmod *module1.o module2.o* ...
Important Flags and Options	None

df

Description	Displays free space on one or more mounted disks or partitions. If no files (or directories) are specified, then the free space on all mounted file systems is displayed. If filenames are specified, then the free space for the file system containing each file is displayed.
Syntax	df [-T] [-t *fstype*] [-x *fstype*] [--all] [--inodes] [--type=*fstype*] ➥[--exclude-type=*fstype*] [--print-type] [*filename* ...]
Important Flags and Options	• -t/--type=*fstype*: Displays information only for file systems of the specified type.
	• -T/--print-type: Displays the file system type for each file system reported.
	• -x/--exclude-type=*fstype*: Does not report information for file systems of the specified type.

dir

Description	Displays a listing of the files in a specified directory, in alphabetical order unless otherwise specified. By default, displays the contents of the current directory unless another directory is specified.
Syntax	dir [-acCGlnrRStuU] [--all] [--no-group] [--numeric-uid-gid] ➥[--reverse] [--recursive] [file ...]
Important Flags and Options	• -a/--all: Shows all entries, including those whose names start with ".".
	• -c: Sorts by the creation time of the file and, when displaying complete file information (with the -l flag), displays the creation time.
	• -C: Displays entries in columns.
	• -G/--no-group: Prevents display of group information.
	• -l: Displays files with long listing format.
	• -n/--numeric-uid-gid: Lists user IDs and group IDs (UIDs and GIDs) instead of names.
	• -r/--reverse: Reverses order of entries when sorting.

- -R/--recursive: Recursively lists contents of subdirectories.
- -S: Sorts files by size.
- -t: Sorts by the modification time of the file and, when displaying complete file information (with the -1 flag), displays the modification time.
- -u: Sorts by the last access time of the file and, when displaying complete file information (with the -1 flag), displays the last access time.
- -U: Displays entries in their directory order rather than sorted.

dmesg

Description	Displays or manipulates the kernel ring buffer. This is where many bootup messages are kept.
Syntax	dmesg [-c]
Important Flags and Options	-c: Clears the ring buffer after displaying the contents.

dnsdomainname

Description	Displays the system's DNS domain name based on its fully qualified domain name.
Syntax	Domainname [-f *filename*] [--file *filename*]
Important Flags and Options	-f/--file *filename*: Specifies a file from which to read the host name.

dnsquery

Description	Queries DNS servers to look up information about a specified host.
Syntax	dnsquery [-n *nameserver*] [-t *type*] [-c *class*] [-r *retry*] ➥[-p *retryperiod*] host
Important Flags and Options	• -c *class*: Specifies the class of records being searched for.
	• -n *nameserver*: Specifies the name server to use for the query. If not specified, then uses the default name server.
	• -p *retryperiod*: Specifies how long to wait before assuming the server is not responding.
	• -r *retry*: Specifies the number of times to retry the query if the server is not responding.
	• -t *type*: Specifies the type of query to make.

<table>
<tr><td>Notes</td><td>When specifying the type of query, possible types include:</td></tr>
</table>

Notes   When specifying the type of query, possible types include:

- **A**: Looks up the address only.
- **NS**: Finds the name server for the host.
- **CNAME**: Finds the canonical name for the host.
- **PTR**: Finds the domain name pointer.
- **SOA**: Finds the start of the authority record for the host.
- **MX**: Finds the mail exchanges for the domain.
- **ANY**: Finds anything and everything that can be found (this is the default behavior).

When specifying classes of information, possible classes include:

- **IN**: Internet (This is the default and you probably won't want to change it.)
- **HS**: Hesiod
- **CHAOS**: Chaos
- **ANY**: Any

domainname

Description   Displays or sets the system's NIS domain name. Without arguments or flags, the default behavior is to display the current NIS domain name.

Syntax   `domainname [-F file] [--file file] [name]`

Important Flags and Options   `-F/--file file`: Indicates that the domain name should be set based on the contents of the specified file instead of expecting it as an argument on the command line.

du

Description   Displays a report of disk space usage for each specified file or directory as well as all subdirectories of specified directories. By default, displays information for all files and directories in the current directory.

Syntax   `du [-abcksx] [--all] [--bytes] [--total] [--kilobytes] [--summarize]`
`➥[--one-file-system] [file ...]`

Important Flags and Options

- `-a/--all`: Displays usage information for files and directories.
- `-b/--bytes`: Displays usage information in bytes.

- -c/--total: Displays a total usage figure for all.

- -k/--kilobytes: Displays usage information in kilobytes.

- -s/--summarize: Displays a total for each argument and does not display individual information for each file or subdirectory inside a directory.

- -x/--one-file-system: Skips directories that are not part of the current file system.

e2fsck

Description	Checks the state of a Linux second extended file system. This is the default file system used for Linux partitions.
Syntax	`e2fsck [-cfnpy] [-B blocksize] device`
Important Flags and Options	• -B blocksize: Specifies a specific block size to use in searching for the superblock. By default, the program will search at various different block sizes until it finds the superblock.
	• -c: Causes the **badblocks** program to be run and marks any bad blocks accordingly.
	• -f: Forces checking of file systems that outwardly seem clean.
	• -n: Opens the file system in a read-only state and answers "no" to all prompts to take action.
	• -p: Forces automatic repairing without prompts.
	• -y: Assumes an answer of "yes" to all questions.
Notes	The device to be checked should be specified using the complete Linux device path, such as **/dev/hda1** or **/dev/sdb3**. It is advisable that the file system not be mounted or, if you need to check the root file system or a file system that must be mounted, that this be done in single-user mode.

echo

Description	Displays a line of text, optionally without a trailing new line (a new line is included by default).
Syntax	`echo [-ne] [string ...]`
Important Flags and Options	• -e: Enables interpretation of backslashed special characters in the string.
	• -n: Disables output of a trailing new line.

Notes

Backslashed special characters include:

- \b: backspace
- \f: form feed
- \n: new line
- \r: carriage return
- \t: horizontal tab
- \\: backslash

egrep

Description

Searches files for lines matching a specified pattern and displays the lines. The pattern is interpreted as an extended regular expression.

Syntax

egrep [-bCciLlnvwx] [-number] [-e pattern] [-f file] [--byte-offset]
➥[--context] [--count] [--regexp=pattern] [--file=file] [--ignore=case]
➥[--files-without-match] [--files-with-match] [--line-number]
➥[--revert-match] [--word-regexp] [--line-regexp] [pattern] file
➥[file ...]

Important Flags and Options

- -number: Displays matching lines with the specified number of lines of leading and trailing context.

- -b/--byte-offset: Prints the byte offset of the match before each line.

- -c/--count: Instead of displaying matching lines, simply outputs a count of the total number of lines matching the expressions (when combined with -v, displays the total count of non-matching lines).

- -C/--context: Displays matching lines with two lines of leading and trailing context (this is the same as -2).

- -e pattern/--regexp=pattern: Uses the specified regular expression rather than one provided as an argument.

- -f file/--file=file: Uses the regular expression found in the specified file rather than one supplied as an argument.

- -i/--ignore=case: Ignores case in both the pattern and the files being searched.

- -l/--files-with-matches: Instead of displaying each matched line, simply displays the name of each file that contains at least one match for the regular expression.

- -L/--files-without-match: Instead of displaying each matched line, simply displays the name of each file that contains no matches for the regular expressions.

- -n/--line-number: Prefixes each output line with its line number in the file.

- -v/--revert-match: Displays non-matching lines instead of matching lines.

- -w/--word-regexp: Displays only those lines with matches for the regular expression that are complete words.

- -x/--line-regexp: Displays only those lines with matches for the regular expression that are complete lines.

Notes	The syntax of regular expressions used by **egrep** can be found in the **egrep** man page.

false

Description	Does nothing and returns a failure exit status.
Syntax	`false`
Important Flags and Options	None

fdisk

Description	Provides tools for manipulating partition tables. By default, **fdisk** starts ready to work with the current device unless a different device is specified as an argument.
Syntax	`fdisk [-l] [-s partition] [device]`
Important Flags and Options	

- -l: Lists the partition tables for **/dev/hda**, **/dev/hdb**, and **/dev/sda** through **/dev/sdh** and then exits.

- -s partition: Returns the size of the specified partition on the standard output and exits.

fgrep

Description	Searches files for lines matching a specified pattern and displays the lines. The pattern is interpreted as a list of fixed strings as opposed to regular expressions. Strings are separated by new lines and any of the strings can be matched.

Syntax	`fgrep [-bCciLlnvwx] [-number] [-e pattern] [-f file] [--byte-offset]`
	`➡[--context] [--count] [--regexp=pattern] [--file=file] [--ignore=case]`
	`➡[--files-without-match] [--files-with-match] [--line-number]`
	`➡[--revert-match] [--word-regexp] [--line-regexp] [pattern] file`
	`➡[file ...]`

Important Flags and Options	

- -number: Displays matching lines with the specified number of lines of leading and trailing context.

- -b/--byte-offset: Prints the byte offset of the match before each line.

- -c/--count: Instead of displaying matching lines, simply outputs a count of the total number of lines matching the expressions (when combined with -v, displays the total count of non-matching lines).

- -C/--context: Displays matching lines with two lines of leading and trailing context (this is the same as -2).

- -e pattern/--regexp=*pattern*: Uses the specified pattern rather than one provided as an argument.

- -f file/--file=*file*: Uses the pattern found in the specified file rather than one supplied as an argument.

- -i/--ignore=*case*: Ignores case in both the pattern and the files being searched.

- -l/--files-with-matches: Instead of displaying each matched line, simply displays the name of each file that contains at least one match for the pattern.

- -L/--files-without-match: Instead of displaying each matched line, simply displays the name of each file that contains no matches for the pattern.

- -n/--line-number: Prefixes each output line with its line number in the file.

- -v/--revert-match: Displays non-matching lines instead of matching lines.

- -w/--word-regexp: Displays only those lines with matches for the pattern that are complete words.

- -x/--line-regexp: Displays only those lines with matches for the pattern that are complete lines.

file

Description	Determines and displays the type of files.
Syntax	`file [-zL] [-f file] file ...`
Important Flags and Options	

- -f *file*: Reads the list of files to be checked from the specified file. These will be checked before checking files provided as arguments.

- -L: Causes symbolic links to be followed.

- -z: Attempts to look at the type of files inside compressed files.

find

Description	Looks for files below the specified paths that match all the criteria indicated by the command-line options and takes any action indicated by those options. If no paths are specified, the search takes place below the current directory.

Syntax	`find [path ...] [options]`
Important Flags and Options	• `-amin minutes`: Looks for files last accessed the specified number of minutes ago.

• `-anewer file`: Looks for files that were accessed more recently than the specified file was modified.

• `-atime days`: Looks for files last accessed the specified number of 24-hour periods ago.

• `-cmin minutes`: Looks for files whose status was last changed the specified number of minutes ago.

• `-cnewer file`: Looks for files whose status was last changed more recently than the specified file was modified.

• `-ctime days`: Looks for files whose status was changed the specified number of 24-hour periods ago.

• `-empty`: Looks for empty files or directories.

• `-exec command \;`: Executes the specified command. The string { } is replaced by the currently found filename and the command is repeated for each found filename.

• `-gid gid`: Looks for files with the specified numeric GID.

• `-group group`: Looks for files belonging to the named group.

• `-ilname pattern`: Looks for symbolic links whose names match the specified pattern in a case-insensitive manner.

• `-iname pattern`: Looks for files whose names match the specified pattern in a case-insensitive manner.

• `-ipath pattern`: Looks for files whose path matches the specified pattern in a case-insensitive manner.

• `-lname pattern`: Looks for symbolic links whose names match the specified pattern in a case-sensitive manner.

• `-maxdepth levels`: Descends at most the specified numbers of levels below the specified paths.

• `-mindepth levels`: Descends at least the specified number of levels below the specified paths before starting testing.

• `-mmin minutes`: Looks for files that were last modified the specified number of minutes ago.

• `-mount`: Does not descend any directories that are on other file systems than the current one.

• `-mtime days`: Looks for files that were last modified the specified number of 24-hour periods previously.

• `-name pattern`: Looks for files whose names match the specified pattern in a case-sensitive manner.

• `-newer file`: Looks for files modified more recently than the specified file.

- **-nogroup**: Looks for files whose numeric GID does not correspond to any existing group.

- **-nouser**: Looks for files whose numeric UID does not correspond to any existing user.

- **-ok** *command* **\;**: Executes the specified command for each file found after prompting the user. The string { } is replaced by the currently replaced filename.

- **-path**: Looks for files whose path matches the specified pattern in a case-sensitive manner.

- **-perm** *mode*: Looks for files whose permissions exactly match the specified mode. If +*mode* is used, then matches any of the specified permission bits; if –*mode* is used, then matches all of the specified permission bits.

- **-print**: Prints the full filename of all found files.

- **-regex** *pattern*: Looks for files whose names match the specified regular expression.

- **-size** *size*[bckw]: Looks for files of the specified size in the specified units. Units include **b** (512-byte blocks), **c** (bytes), **k** (kilobytes), and **w** (2-byte words).

- **-type** *type*: Looks for files that match the specified type. Types include **d** (directories), **f** (regular files), and **l** (symbolic links).

- **-uid** *uid*: Looks for files with the specified UID.

- **-user** *username*: Looks for files owned by the specified username or UID.

Notes

When providing numeric time information such as minutes and days, normally the match must be exact. Preceding the number with a + matches any value greater than the specified number and preceding a value with a – matches any value less than the number.

finger

Description

Looks up specified information about a user on the local system or remote systems. Users are specified on local systems by their username or their first or last name and on remote systems as *username@host*. With no users specified for the local system, all users logged in to the current system are listed. If a host with no username is provided in the form *@host*, then a list of all users logged into the remote system is displayed.

Syntax

`finger [user ...]`

Important Flags and Options

None

free

Description	Displays a report of free and used memory.
Syntax	`free [-b|-k|-m] [-s delay] [-t]`
Important Flags and Options	

- `-b`: Displays the amount of memory in bytes.

- `-k`: Displays the amount of memory in kilobytes (this is the default).

- `-m`: Displays the amount of memory in megabytes.

- `-s delay`: Displays continued reports separated by the specified delay in seconds.

- `-t`: Displays an extra line containing totals.

gpasswd

Description	Administers the `/etc/group` file. Without flags, **gpasswd** allows changing of the specified group's password.
Syntax	**gpasswd** *group*
	gpasswd -a *user group*
	gpasswd -d *user group*
	gpasswd -R *group*
	gpasswd -r *group*
	gpasswd [-M *user,...***]** *group*
Important Flags and Options	

- `-a user`: Adds a user to the group.

- `-d user:` Removes a user from the group.

- `-M user,...:` Specifies one or more users who are members of the group.

- `-r`: Removes the group password.

- `-R`: Disables access to the group through the **newgrp** command.

grep

Description	Searches files for lines matching a specified pattern and displays the lines.

Syntax	`grep [-bCcEFGiLlnvwx] [-number] [-e pattern] [-f file] [--basic-` `➥regexp] [--byte-offset} [--extended-regexp] [--fixed-strings]` `➥[--byte-offset] [--context] [--count] [--regexp=pattern]` `➥[--file=file] [--ignore=case] [--files-without-match]` `➥[--files-with-match] [--line-number] [--revert-match]` `➥[--word-regexp] [--line-regexp] [pattern] file [file ...]`
Important Flags and Options	• `-number`: Displays matching lines with the specified number of lines of leading and trailing context.
	• `-b/--byte`-offset: Prints the byte offset of the match before each line.
	• `-c/--count`: Instead of displaying matching lines, simply outputs a count of the total number of lines matching the expressions (when combined with `-v`, displays the total count of non-matching lines).
	• `-C/--context`: Displays matching lines with two lines of leading and trailing context (this is the same as `-2`).
	• `-e pattern/--regexp=pattern`: Uses the specified pattern rather than one provided as an argument.
	• `-E/--extended-regexp`: Treats the pattern as an extended regular expression (similar to `egrep`).
	• `-f file/--file=file`: Uses the pattern found in the specified file rather than one supplied as an argument.
	• `-F/--fixed-strings`: Treats the pattern as a list of new line separated strings, one of which must match. This is the same as `fgrep`.
	• `-G/--basic-regexp`: Treats the pattern as a basic regular expression.
	• `-i/--ignore=case`: Ignores case in both the pattern and the files being searched.
	• `-l/--files-with-matches`: Instead of displaying each matched line, simply displays the name of each file that contains at least one match for the patterns.
	• `-L/--files-without-match`: Instead of displaying each matched line, simply displays the name of each file that contains no matches for the patterns.
	• `-n/--line-number`: Prefixes each output line with its line number in the file.
	• `-v/--revert-match`: Displays non-matching lines instead of matching lines.
	• `-w/--word-regexp`: Displays only those lines with matches for the patterns that are complete words.
	• `-x/--line-regexp`: Displays only those lines with matches for the patterns that are complete lines.
Notes	The syntax of regular expressions used by `grep` can be found in the `grep` man page.

groupadd

Description	Creates a new group.
Syntax	`groupadd [-g gid [-o]] [-r] [-f] group`
Important Flags and Options	

- `-f`: Prevents the program from exiting when trying to add a group that already exists. In this case, the group won't be altered.

- `-g gid`: Uses the specified GID for the group instead of automatically assigning a value.

- `-o`: Indicates that group IDs do not need to be unique.

- `-r`: Adds a system account with a group ID lower than 499.

groupdel

Description	Deletes a group.
Syntax	`groupdel group`
Important Flags and Options	None

groupmod

Description	Modifies an existing group.
Syntax	`groupmod [-g gid [-o]] [-n groupname] group`
Important Flags and Options	

- `-g gid`: Changes the group ID of the specified group to the new GID. This value must be unique unless `-o` is specified.

- `-n groupname`: Changes the group name of the specified group to the new group name.

- `-o`: Indicates that group IDs do not need to be unique.

groups

Description	Prints the groups that one or more users belongs to. If no user is specified, then displays the groups that the user running the command belongs to.
Syntax	`groups [username ...]`
Important Flags and Options	None

grpck

Description	Checks the integrity of a group file such as /etc/group or /etc/gshadow. If no files are specified, then the default files are checked.
Syntax	grpck [-r] [*group shadow*]
Important Flags and Options	-r: Operates in read-only mode, not allowing any alterations to be made to the files.

gunzip

Description	Decompresses files compressed with the gzip command (as well as the compress command and the zip command).
Syntax	gunzip [-cflrt] [--stdout] [--to-stdout] [--force] [--list] ↪[--recursive] [--test] [*name* ...]
Important Flags and Options	

- -c/--stdout/--to-stdout: Writes output to standard output, keeping original file unchanged. By default, gunzip replaces the original compressed files with the uncompressed versions of the files.

- -f/--force: Forces decompression even when a corresponding file already exists and will be overwritten by the decompressed file.

- -l/--list: Lists files in the compressed file without decompressing.

- -r/--recursive: Decompresses recursively, descending the directory structure and decompressing all files in subdirectories of directories named on the command line as arguments.

- -t/--test: Tests the integrity of compressed files.

gzexe

Description	Creates an executable compressed file. If you compress a binary file or script with gzexe, then you can run it as if it were uncompressed. The file will simply uncompress into memory and execute, leaving the compressed version on your hard drive.
Syntax	gzexe [-d] [*name* ...]
Important Flags and Options	-d: Uncompresses the specified file or files rather than compressing them.
Notes	When you compress a file named *filename*, the original, uncompressed file will be copied to *filename~* and the compressed file will retain the name *filename*. Once you have tested the compressed executable to see that it works, you can then delete the uncompressed copy.

gzip

Description	Compresses files using Lempel-Ziv encoding. The resulting file generally replaces the original, uncompressed file and will have a `.gz` extension.
Syntax	`gzip [-cdflrt] [--decompress] [--uncompress] [--stdout] [--to-stdout]` ➥`[--force] [--list] [--recursive] [--test] [name ...]`
Important Flags and Options	• `-c/--stdout/--to-stdout`: Writes output to standard output, keeping original file unchanged. By default, `gzip` replaces the original, uncompressed files with the compressed versions of the files.
	• `-d/--decompress/--uncompress`: Decompresses the specified files, like `gunzip`, rather than compressing them.
	• `-f/--force`: Forces compression even when a corresponding file already exists and will be overwritten by the compressed file.
	• `-l/--list`: Lists files in a compressed file.
	• `-r/--recursive`: Compresses recursively, descending the directory structure and compressing all files in subdirectories of directories named on the command line as arguments.
	• `-t/--test`: Tests the integrity of compressed files.

halt

Description	Halts the system. If the system is not in run level 0 or 6, this is done by calling the `shutdown` program.
Syntax	`halt [-n] [-w] [-d] [-f] [-i]`
Important Flags and Options	• `-d`: Doesn't log the halt to `/var/log/wtmp`. By default, the halt is noted in this file.
	• `-f`: Forces a halt or reboot without calling `shutdown`.
	• `-i`: Shuts down network interfaces before halting.
	• `-n`: Doesn't sync the file systems before halting.
	• `-w`: Writes a record of a halt to `/var/log/wtmp` but doesn't actually halt the system.
Warnings	Care needs to be taken with this command. The `-n` flag, halting the system without syncing the disks, is of special concern because failing to sync the file systems before unmounting them can corrupt the data stored on them.

head

Description

Displays the first part of one or more files. By default, unless otherwise specified, the first 10 lines of each file are displayed. If no filenames are provided, then reads data from the standard input and displays the first section of the data, following the same rules as for files.

Syntax

`head [-c number[bkm]] [-n number] [-qv] [--bytes number[bkm]]`
`➡ [--lines number] [--quiet] [--silent] [file ...]`

Important Flags and Options

- `-c/--bytes number`: Displays the specified number of bytes from the start of each file. Optionally, the number can be followed by b for 512-byte blocks, k for kilobytes, and m for megabytes.

- `-n/--lines number`: Displays the specified number of lines from the start of each file.

- `-q/--quiet/--silent`: Prevents printing of filename headers when multiple files are being processed.

hostname

Description

Displays or sets the system's host name. If no flags or arguments are given, then the host name of the system is displayed.

Syntax

`hostname [-a] [--alias] [-d] [--domain] [-f] [--fqdn] [-i]`
`➡ [--ip-address][--long] [-s] [--short] [-y] [--yp] [--nis]`

Important Flags and Options

- `-a/--alias`: Displays the alias name of the host if available.

- `-d/--domain`: Displays the DNS domain name of the host.

- `-f/--fqdn/--long`: Displays the fully qualified domain name of the host.

- `-i/--ip-address`: Displays the IP address of the host.

- `-s/--short`: Displays the host name without the domain name.

- `-y/--yp/--nis`: Displays the NIS domain name of the system.

id

Description

Displays real and effective user and group ID information for a specified user. If no user is specified, then prints the information for the user running `id`.

Syntax

`id [-gnruG] [--group] [--name] [--real] [--user] [--groups] [username]`

Important Flags and Options

- **-g/--group**: Prints only the group ID.

- **-G/--groups**: Prints only the supplementary groups.

- **-n/--name**: Prints the user or group name instead of the ID number. Used in conjunction with **-u**, **-g**, or **-G**.

- **-r/--real**: Prints the real user or group ID instead of the effective ones. Used in conjunction with **-u**, **-g**, or **-G**.

- **-u/--user**: Prints only the user ID.

ifconfig

Description

Configures a network interface, or displays its status if no options are provided. If no arguments are provided, the current state of all interfaces is displayed.

Syntax

ifconfig *interface options address*

Important Flags and Options

- *interface*: Specifies the name of the network interface (e.g., **eth0** or **eth1**).

- **up**: Activates the specified interface.

- **down**: Deactivates the specified interface.

- **netmask** *address*: Sets the network mask for the interface.

- **broadcast** *address*: Sets the broadcast address for the interface.

- **pointtopoint** *address*: Enables point-to-point mode for an interface, implying a direct link between two machines. Also sets the address for the other end of the link.

- *address*: Specifies the host name or IP address for the interface. This is required.

ifdown

Description

Disables a specified interface, such as **eth0** or **eth1**.

Syntax

ifdown *interface*

Important Flags and Options

None

ifport

Description	Sets the transceiver type for a specified network interface.
Syntax	ifport *interface type*
Important Flags and Options	*type*: Specifies transceiver type. Possible types include: **auto** (automatic selection); **10baseT** (twisted-pair Ethernet); **10base2** (coaxial-cable Ethernet); **aui** (AUI interface Ethernet); **100baseT** (twisted-pair Fast Ethernet).

ifup

Description	Enables a specified interface, such as **eth0** or **eth1**.
Syntax	ifup *interface*
Important Flags and Options	None

insmod

Description	Installs a loadable module into the current kernel.
Syntax	insmod [-fpsxX] [-o *module_name*] *object_file* [symbol=*value* ...]
Important Flags and Options	• -f: Tries to load the module even if the version of the kernel and the expected kernel version do not match.
	• -o *module*: Explicitly names the module instead of basing the name on the object file for the module.
	• -p: Probes the module to make sure it is loaded.
	• -s: Logs activity to the system log daemon rather than standard output.
	• -x: Doesn't export the module's external symbols.
	• -X: Exports the module's external symbols (this is the default).

kbd_mode

Description	Displays or sets the keyboard mode.
Syntax	kbd_mode [-a|-u|-k|-s]

Important Flags and Options

- -a: Sets the keyboard to ASCII (XLATE) mode.
- -k: Sets the keyboard to keycode (MEDIUMRAW) mode.
- -s: Sets the keyboard to scanmode (RAW) mode.
- -u: Sets the keyboard to UTF-8 (UNICODE) mode.

kbdrate

Description

Sets the repeat rate and delay time for the keyboard.

Syntax

kbdrate [-r rate] [-d milliseconds]

Important Flags and Options

- -d milliseconds: Sets the delay (before repeating) to the specified number of milliseconds.
- -r cps: Sets the repeat rate to the specified number of characters per second. Not all values are possible. You should select from the following values: 2.0, 2.1, 2.3, 2.5, 2.7, 3.0, 3.3, 3.7, 4.0, 4.3, 4.6, 5.0, 5.5, 6.0, 6.7, 7.5, 8.0, 8.6, 9.2, 10.0, 10.9, 12.0, 13.3, 15.0, 16.0, 17.1, 18.5, 20.0, 21.8, 24.0, 26.7, 30.0.

kill

Description

Sends a kill signal to one or more running processes.

Syntax

kill [-s signal|-p] pid ...

kill -l

Important Flags and Options

- -l: Displays a list of signal names.
- -p: Prints the process ID of a specified process rather than sending it a signal.
- -s signal: Sends the specified signal to the specified processes.
- pid: Specifies either the ID of a process or its name. When specifying processes by name, all processes with the specified name will receive the signal.

killall

Description

Sends a signal to all processes sharing a common process name.

Syntax

killall [-eiw] [-signal] process ...

killall -l

Important Flags and Options
- -e: Forces the program to send the signal to only exact matches for process names longer than 15 characters.
- -i: Asks for confirmation before sending the signal to each process.
- -l: Displays a list of signal names.
- -w: Waits for all killed processes to die. This means `killall` may wait indefinitely if a process fails to die.

ksyms

Description   Displays information about exported kernel symbols, including the address, name, and defining module.

Syntax   `ksyms [-a] [-m]`

Important Flags and Options
- -a: Displays all symbols, including those from the actual kernel.
- -m: Displays module information, including the address and size of the module.

last

Description   Displays a history of user logins and logouts based on the contents of `/var/log/wtmp`. If a specific tty such as `tty0` or `tty1` is specified, then only logins to that tty are displayed.

Syntax   `last [-R] [-number] [-n number] [-adx] [name ...] [tty ...]`

Important Flags and Options
- -a: Forces the host name to be displayed in the last column.
- -d: In the case of remote logins, displays all IP addresses as host names.
- -n number/-number: Indicates how many lines of history to display.
- -R: Suppresses the display of the host name in the report.
- -x: Causes system shutdown and run level changes to be displayed along with logins and logouts.

ldd

Description   Displays shared library dependencies for one or more programs.

Syntax   `ldd [-dr] program ...`

Important Flags and Options	• -d: Reports missing functions after performing relocations.
	• -r: Reports missing data objects and functions after performing relocations.

less

Description	Displays a text file one screen at a time while allowing searching and backward scrolling.
Syntax	`less [-aeEGiINrsS] file ...`
Important Flags and Options	• -a: Causes searching to start after the last line on the screen. By default, searches include visible text.
	• -e: Causes `less` to exit the second time it encounters the end of a file. Otherwise, users must quit with the "q" command.
	• -E: Causes `less` to exit the first time it encounters the end of a file.
	• -G: Suppresses highlighting of strings found by a search.
	• -i: Causes searches to be case insensitive. This is ignored if the search pattern includes uppercase letters.
	• -I: Causes searches to be case insensitive even when the search pattern contains uppercase letters.
	• -N: Causes a line number to be displayed at the beginning of each line.
	• -r: Causes raw control characters to be displayed using caret notation (e.g., Ctrl+A is ^A).
	• -s: Squeezes consecutive blank lines into a single blank line.
	• -S: Chops lines wider than the screen rather than wrapping them to the next line.

lilo

Description	Installs the Linux boot loader.
Syntax	`lilo [C file] [-d deciseconds] [-q] [-D label] [-u device]`
Important Flags and Options	• -C file: Specifies a specific configuration file to use in loading the boot loader. The default configuration file is `/etc/lilo.conf`.
	• -d deciseconds: Indicates the number of deciseconds to wait at the LILO prompt during booting before loading the default kernel.
	• -D label: Uses the kernel with the specified label as the default kernel rather than the first kernel in the configuration file.

- -q: Displays the currently mapped files listing the kernels to be booted.
- -u *device*: Uninstalls the boot loader for the specified device.

listalias

Description	Displays user and system aliases. If a regular expression is provided, then only aliases that match the expression are displayed.
Syntax	listalias [-s|-u] [*regular-expression*]
Important Flags and Options	• -s: Displays only system aliases.
	• -u: Displays only user aliases.

ln

Description	Makes links between files. When the last argument is a directory, then each of the other source files specified is linked into a file with the same name in the specified directory.
Syntax	ln [-bis] [--backup] [--interactive] [--symbolic] *source* [*destination*]
	ln [-bis] [--backup] [--interactive] [--symbolic] *source* ... *directory*
Important Flags and Options	• -b/--backup: Makes backups of files that are being removed.
	• -i/--interactive: Prompts when it is necessary to remove a destination file.
	• -s/--symbolic: Makes symbolic links instead of hard links.

loadkeys

Description	Loads compose key translation tables from one or more specified files. If no files are specified, the information is read from the standard input.
Syntax	loadkeys [-c --clearcompose] [-d --default] [-m --mktable] ➥[-s --clearstrings] [*file* ...]
Important Flags and Options	• -c/--clearcompose: Clears the current accent table before loading new entries. If no entries are found, the table will be empty.
	• -d/--default: Loads the default keymap.
	• -m/--mktable: Prints a table on standard output of the current mappings.
	• -s/--clearstring: Clears the kernel string table.

logger

Description	Places entries in the system log. If no messages are specified and no input file is provided, then the standard input is logged to the system log.
Syntax	`logger [-is] [-f file] [-p priority] [-t tag] [message ...]`
Important Flags and Options	• `-f file`: Logs the specified file to the system log.
	• `-i`: Places the process ID of the process making the entry with each line in the log file.
	• `-p priority`: Indicates the priority of the log entry.
	• `-s`: Logs the message to standard error in addition to the system log.
	• `-t tag`: Marks every line in the log entry with the specified tag.

login

Description	Log in to the system.
Syntax	`login username`
Important Flags and Options	None

logname

Description	Displays a user's username.
Syntax	`logname`
Important Flags and Options	None

logrotate

Description	Rotates log files, mailing the current file and then compressing it for archiving.
Syntax	`logrotate [-s|--state file] configfile`
Important Flags and Options	• `-s/--state file`: Uses the specified state file instead of the default `/var/lib/logrotate.status`.

lpd

Description   Runs the line printer spooler daemon to control printing to attached and remote printers. If a port number is specified, it overrides the default port to listen to for incoming requests.

Syntax   `lpr [-1] [port]`

Important Flags and Options   -1: Logs valid network requests.

lpq

Description   Examines and displays the current status of a printer spool queue. If no printer is specified, then the default printer is queried. Normally, all jobs for the queried printer are displayed unless specific job numbers are given. If users are specified, only these users' print jobs will be displayed for the queried printer.

Syntax   `lpq [-1] [-Pprinter] [job, ...] [user, ...]`

Important Flags and Options   • -1: Prints all information about the files composing the job entry instead of just what will fit on one line.

                               • -Pprinter: Queries the specified printer.

lpr

Description   Prints one or more files to the specified printer spool. If no files are indicated, then the standard input is sent to the printer spool. If no printer is specified, data will be sent to the default printer.

Syntax   `lpr [-Pprinter] [-#number] [-C class] [-J job] [-i [numcols]]`
                               ➥`[-hlmrs] [file ...]`

Important Flags and Options   • -#number: Specifies the number of copies to print of each file. The default is one copy.

                               • -C class: Prints the specified class name instead of the host name on the header page.

                               • -h: Suppresses the printing of a header page.

                               • -i [numcols]: Indicates that output should be indented by the number of blanks specified, or by 8 characters if no number is indicated.

                               • -J job: Prints the specified job name instead of the filename on the header page.

- -1: Allows control characters to be printed while suppressing page breaks.

- -m: Sends an e-mail to the user when the print job is finished.

- -Pprinter: Prints to the specified printer.

- -r: Removes files after printing them.

- -s: Creates a symbolic link to the file being printed rather than copying the file to the spool directory. This is useful when printing extremely large files.

lprm

Description	Deletes one or more jobs from a specified print queue. If no printer is specified, it attempts to remove the jobs from the default print queue. If a username is specified, all jobs owned by the user are removed, unless specific jobs are indicated.
Syntax	lprm [-Pprinter] [*job* ...] [*user* ...]
Important Flags and Options	-Pprinter: Deletes jobs from the specified printer spool queue.

ls

Description

Displays a listing of files and directories. If no file or directory is specified, then the current directory's contents are displayed. By default, contents are sorted alphabetically.

Syntax

ls [-acdlrRsStuX] [--all] [--time=ctime] [--time=status] [--directory]
➥[--format=long] [--format=verbose] [--reverse] [--recursive] [--size]
➥[--sort-size] [--sort=time] [--time=atime] [--time=access]
➥[--time=use][--sort=extension] [*file*|*directory* ...]

Important Flags and Options

- -a/--all: Lists all files in the directory, including those that start with ".".

- -c/--time=ctime,--time=status: Sorts entries by the change time of the files.

- -d/--directory: Lists directory names only, without showing directory contents. By default, directory contents are listed.

- -l/--format=long/--format=verbose: Lists files in long format, including file type, permissions, owner, and size.

- -r/--reverse: Displays files in reverse order.

- -R/--recursive: Lists the content of all subdirectories recursively.

- -s/--size: Displays the size of files, in kilobytes.

- -S/--sort=size: Sorts entries by file size starting with the largest file.

- -t/--sort=time: Sorts entries by timestamp starting with the newest files.

- -u/--time=atime/--time=access/--time=use: Sorts entries by the last access time.
- -X/--sort=extension: Sorts files by file extension in alphabetical order.

lsdev

Description	Displays information about installed hardware.
Syntax	lsdev
Important Flags and Options	None

lsmod

Description	Displays a list of loaded modules.
Syntax	lsmod
Important Flags and Options	None

mail

Description

Sends and receives e-mails. The user will be prompted for the text of the message unless it is provided through the standard input. Also, other information such as the subject can be provided as a flag when sending messages, or the program can prompt for the information. If no options or arguments are specified, the current user's mailbox is opened for reading.

Syntax

mail [-s *subject*] [-c *address*,...] [-b *address*,...] *address*

mail -f [*mailbox*]

mail -u [*user*]

Important Flags and Options

- -b *address*,...: Indicates a list of addresses that should receive blind carbon copies of outgoing messages.
- -c *address*,...: Indicates a list of addresses that should receive a carbon copy of outgoing messages.
- -f [*mailbox*]: Reads mail from your inbox or the mailbox specified.
- -s *subject*: Specifies the subject line of outgoing messages.
- -u *user*: Opens the specified user's inbox for reading.

Notes

The mechanics of using mail to read messages is discussed in the mail man page.

mailq

Description	Displays the contents of the outgoing mail queue.
Syntax	`mailq`
Important Flags and Options	None

mailto

Description	Sends an e-mail to one or more recipients. If no recipients are indicated on the command line, the user will be prompted for the recipients. If no standard input is provided, then the user is prompted for the content of the message.
Syntax	`mailto [-a character-set] [-c address,...] [-s subject]` ➥`[recipient ...]`
Important Flags and Options	• `-a character-set`: Specifies an alternate character set, such as ISO-8859-8. The default is US-ASCII.
	• `-c address,...`: Specifies carbon-copy addresses.
	• `-s subject`: Specifies the subject line of the message. If the subject is more than one word, enclose it in quotation marks.
Notes	To finish composing a message, use Ctrl+D or type **a** . alone on a blank line.

man

Description	Displays the manual page for a specified command.
Syntax	`Man command`
Important Flags and Options	`command`: Specifies the command whose manual page is to be displayed.

mattrib

Description	Changes the attributes of a file on an MS-DOS file system such as a DOS floppy disk. This is similar to the DOS **ATTRIB** command.
Syntax	`mattrib [-a|+a] [-h|+h] [-r|+r] [-s|+s] msdosfile [msdosfile ...]`
Important Flags and Options	• `+a|-a`: Sets or unsets the archive bit.
	• `+h|-h`: Sets or unsets the hidden bit.

- +r|-r: Sets or unsets the read-only bit.

- +s|-s: Sets or unsets the system bit.

Notes   Use the + before an option to set a bit and the - to unset a bit.

mbadblocks

Description   Tests a DOS floppy disk for bad blocks. If any are found, they are marked in the disk's FAT.

Syntax   mbadblocks *drive:*

Important Flags and Options   None

mcd

Description   Changes the directory on an MS-DOS file system such as a floppy disk. If no argument is provided, then the current device and directory are displayed. Similar to the DOS **CD** command.

Syntax   mcd [*msdosdirectory*]

Important Flags and Options   None

mcopy

Description   Copies files in both directions between Unix and MS-DOS file systems such as floppy disks. Multiple files can be copied to a single directory when the directory is the last argument. Using a DOS drive designator such as a: implies a DOS file; otherwise a Unix file system is assumed. With only a single DOS file as an argument, this file will be copied to the current Unix directory. Similar to the DOS **COPY** command.

Syntax   mcopy [-tnm] *sourcefile targetfile*

                            mcopy [-tnm] *sourcefile [sourcefile ...] targetdirectory*

                            mcopy [-tnm] *MSDOSsourcefile*

Important Flags and Options   - -m: Preserves file modification times when copying.

                            - -n: Does not ask for confirmation when overwriting Unix files.

                            - -t: Converts text files between Unix and DOS text files while copying.

mdel

Description	Deletes files on an MS-DOS floppy disk. Similar to the DOS **DEL** command.
Syntax	mdel *msdosfile* [*msdosfile* ...]
Important Flags and Options	None

mdeltree

Description	Deletes one or more MS-DOS directories. Similar to the DOS **DELTREE** command.
Syntax	mdeltree *msdosdirectory* [*msdosdirectory* ...]
Important Flags and Options	None

mdir

Description	Displays the contents of a directory on an MS-DOS file system such as a floppy disk. If specific files are indicated, then only those files are listed. Similar to the DOS **DIR** command.
Syntax	mdir [-w] *msdosdirectory*
	mdir [-a] [-f] [-w] *msdosfile* [*msdosfile* ...]
Important Flags and Options	• -a: Lists hidden files as well as regular files.
	• -f: Displays files without listing total free space at the end of the listing.
	• -w: Displays files in wide output.

messages

Description	Displays a count of the number of messages in the user's inbox or, if named, in a specific mail folder.
Syntax	messages [*folder*]
Important Flags and Options	None

mformat

Description	Formats an MS-DOS floppy disk. Similar to the DOS **FORMAT** command.
Syntax	mformat *drive:*
Important Flags and Options	None

mkdir

Description	Creates one or more directories.
Syntax	mkdir [-p] [-m *mode*] [--parents] [--mode=*mode*] *directory* ...
Important Flags and Options	• -m/--mode *mode*: Sets the mode for the created directory using the same symbolic notation as the **chmod** command. If this is not specified, the default mode is assigned to the directory.
	• -p/--parents: Ensures that the parents of the specified directory exist and creates any missing parent directories needed.

mkdosfs

Description	Formats an MS-DOS file system on a specified device.
Syntax	mkdosfs [-c] [-F *fatsize*] [-n *name*] *device*
Important Flags and Options	• -c: Checks for bad blocks before formatting.
	• -F *fatsize*: Indicates the type of file allocation to create. This can be either **12** for a 12-bit FAT or **16** for a 16-bit FAT. The program will select the best option for you, usually **16**.
	• -n *name*: Sets the volume label to the specified name. The name can be up to 11 characters long. With no name, the volume label will not be set.

mke2fs

Description	Formats a Linux second extended file system.
Syntax	mke2fs [-c] [-m *percentage*] [-L *label*] *device*
Important Flags and Options	• -c: Checks for bad blocks before formatting.

- -L *label*: Sets the volume label as specified.

- -m *percentage*: Specifies the percentage of blocks to reserve for the superuser. This is set to 5 percent by default.

mkfs

Description	Creates a file system (similar to formatting a drive in DOS). Optionally, the number of blocks for the file system can be specified.
Syntax	mkfs [-t *fstype*] [-c] [-l *file*] *device* [*blocks*]
Important Flags and Options	

- -c: Checks the device for bad blocks before formatting.

- -l *file*: Reads the bad block list for the device from the specified file.

- -t *fstype*: Specifies the type of file system that should be created. The default file system type is minix if no other alternative can be found for the device in /etc/fstab.

mkpasswd

Description	Generates a random password and optionally assigns it to a user.
Syntax	mkpasswd [-2] [-l *number*] [-d *number*] [-c *number*] [-C *number*] ➥[-p *file*] [*user*]
Important Flags and Options	

- -2: Forces characters to alternate between the right and left hand when typing on a standard U.S. keyboard.

- -c *number*: Specifies the minimum number of lowercase letters in the password.

- -C *number*: Specifies the minimum number of uppercase letters in the password.

- -d *number*: Specifies the minimum number of digits in the password.

- -l *number*: Specifies the number of characters in the password.

- -p *file*: Specifies the program to use to set the password. By default, this is /etc/yppasswwd, or, if that is missing, /bin/passwd.

Notes	The use of the –2 flag makes it harder for the casual observer to see what is being typed by a user. But this can make it easier for a password-guessing program to guess the password.

mkswap

Description	Sets up a device as a swap area. The size of the file system can be specified in blocks if desired.
Syntax	`mkswap [-c] device [blocks]`
Important Flags and Options	`-c`: Checks the device for bad blocks before creating the swap file system.
Notes	It is also possible to create swap files instead of swap partitions. Consult the `mkswap` man page for more information.

mlabel

Description	Labels an MS-DOS file system such as a floppy disk. If the label is not provided, the user is prompted for the label.
Syntax	`mlabel [-cs] drive:label`
Important Flags and Options	• `-c`: Clears the current label without any prompt to the user. • `-s`: Displays the current label.

mmd

Description	Makes one or more directories on an MS-DOS file system such as a floppy disk.
Syntax	`mmd msdosdirectory [msdosdirectory ...]`
Important Flags and Options	None

mmove

Description	Moves (also renames) MS-DOS files or directories. If the last argument is a directory, then all source files are moved into the target directory.
Syntax	`mmove sourcefile targetfile` `mmove sourcefile [sourcefile ...] targetdirectory`
Important Flags and Options	None

modprobe

Description	Loads one or more loadable modules, based on a pattern or a specified module object file.
Syntax	modprobe *module*.o [symbol=*value* ...]
	modprobe -t *tag pattern*
	modprobe -a -t *tag pattern*
	modprobe -l [-t *tag*] *pattern*
	modprobe -r *module*
	modprobe -c
Important Flags and Options	• -a: Loads all modules rather than the first module that loads successfully.
	• -c: Displays configuration information.
	• -l: Lists all modules of a specified type.
	• -r *module*: Unloads the specified module stack.
	• -t *tag*: Loads only modules marked with the specified tag.

more

Description	Displays one or more files screen-by-screen and allows for searching and jumping to an arbitrary location in the file.
Syntax	more [-dlfs] [-*number*] [+*number*] [*file* ...]
Important Flags and Options	• -*number*: Sets the number of lines per screen.
	• +*number*: Specifies the line to start on when displaying.
	• -d: Prompts the user at the end of each screen.
	• -f: Causes long lines not to be folded and to be counted as a single line.
	• -l: Prevents Ctrl+L from being treated as a form feed.
	• -s: Squeezes multiple blank lines into a single blank line.
Notes	For details of the commands that can be used when viewing files, consult the **more** man page.

mount

Description	Mounts a file system to a specified directory.
Syntax	`mount -a [-rw] [-t vfstype]`
	`mount [-rw] [-o options [,...]] device|dir`
	`mount [-rw] [-t vfstype] [-o options] device dir`
Important Flags and Options	• `-a`: Mounts all file systems in `/etc/fstab`. If a type is specified with `-t`, then only the file systems in `/etc/fstab` of the specified type will be loaded.
	• `-o`: See Note below.
	• `-r`: Mounts the file system in read-only mode. This is the same as `-o ro`.
	• `-t fstype`: Indicates the file system type.
	• `-w`: Mounts the file system in read-write mode. This is the same as `-o rw`.
Notes	Possible file system types for the `-t` flag include:

`Minix`	`vfat`	`ufs`
`ext`	`proc`	`romfs`
`ext2`	`nfs`	`sysv`
`xiafs`	`iso9660`	`xenix`
`hpfs`	`smbfs`	`coherent`
`msdos`	`ncpfs`	
`umsdos`	`affs`	

For a list of options for the `-o` flag, consult the **mount** man page, which provides detailed descriptions of the various options available.

mrd

Description	Removes one or more MS-DOS directories.
Syntax	`mrd msdosdirectory [msdosdirectory ...]`
Important Flags and Options	None

mren

Description	Renames an MS-DOS file. Similar to the DOS **REN** command, except that it can rename directories as well.
Syntax	mren *oldname newname*
Important Flags and Options	None

mtype

Description	Displays the contents of one or more MS-DOS files. Similar to the DOS **TYPE** command.
Syntax	mtype [-ts] *msdosfile* [*msdosfile ...*]
Important Flags and Options	• -s: Removes the high bit from data.
	• -t: Translates DOS text files to Unix text files before displaying them.

mv

Description	Renames and moves files. When a directory is the last argument, move all other specified files into that directory.
Syntax	mv [-bfiu] [--backup] [--force] [--interactive] [--update] ↪{*source destination*|*source ... directory*}
Important Flags and Options	• -b/--backup: Makes a backup of files that are being moved.
	• -f/--force: Removes existing files that are about to be overwritten by the move without prompting.
	• -i/--interactive: Prompts before overwriting any existing files.
	• -u/--update: Does not overwrite an existing file if it has the same or newer modification time.

netstat

Description	Displays network status information, including connections, routing tables, and interface statistics. When no options are provided, a list of active sockets will be displayed.

Syntax	`netstat [-Mnrs] [-c] [-i interface] [--interface interface]` ➥`[--masquerade] [--route] [--statistics]`
Important Flags and Options	• `-c`: Displays the select information every second until Ctrl+C interrupts it.
	• `-i [interface]/--interface [interface]`: Displays information about a specified interface, or all interfaces if none is specified.
	• `-M/--masquerade`: Displays a list of masqueraded sessions.
	• `-n`: Shows numerical addresses instead of their host, port, or user names.
	• `-r/--route`: Displays the kernel routing tables.
	• `-s/--statistics`: Displays network statistics.

newgrp

Description	Logs the user into a new group, changing the user's group ID. If no group is specified, the group ID is changed to the user's login group ID.
Syntax	`newgrp [group]`
Important Flags and Options	None

newusers

Description	Reads a file containing a list of new users and creates the users. If no file is specified, the user information should be provided from standard input.
Syntax	`newusers [file]`
Important Flags and Options	None
Notes	The format of the file read by the **newusers** command is the same as the `/etc/passwd` file with the following exceptions:

• Passwords should not be encrypted. They will be encrypted when the user's account is created.

• If the group specified does not exist, the new group will be created.

• If the user's home directory doesn't exist, a new one will be created; if a directory with that name already exists, the ownership will be changed to that of the new user.

• Because this file will contain decrypted passwords, it is essential that it be kept secure at all times.

nisdomainname

Description	Displays the current NIS domain name.
Syntax	`nisdomainname`
Important Flags and Options	None

nslookup

Description	Queries a DNS name server. Can be run in interactive mode. If no host name is provided, then the program enters interactive mode. By default, the DNS server specified in `/etc/resolv.conf` is used unless another is specified. If you want to specify a server but not look up a specified host, you must provide a – in place of the host.
Syntax	`nslookup [host|-[server]]`
Important Flags and Options	None
Notes	For instructions on the commands available in interactive mode, see the `nslookup` man page.

passwd

Description	Changes a user's password. When run by the root user, it can be used to change a specific user's password by providing the username as an argument.
Syntax	`passwd [username]`
Important Flags and Options	None

paste

Description	Merges corresponding lines from one or more files. Prints sequentially corresponding lines on the same line, separated by a tab with a new line ending the line. If no filenames are provided, input is taken from the standard input.
Syntax	`paste [-s] [-d delim-list] [--serial] [--delimiters list] [file ...]`
Important Flags and Options	• `-d/--delimiters list`: Specifies a delimiter to use instead of the default tab character. If more than one character is in the list, then the characters will be used consecutively, returning to the first character in the list after the final character has been used.
	• `-s/--serial`: Pastes the lines of one file followed by the lines from the next file, rather than one line from each file.

pathchk

Description	Checks the validity and portability of filenames. Specifically, checks that all directories in the path of the file have appropriate execute permission and that the length of each component of the path and filename is no larger than the maximum length for a filename component.
Syntax	`pathchk [-p] [--portability] file ...`
Important Flags and Options	`-p/--portability`: Tests the length of each filename against POSIX.1 standards instead of the length limitations of the actual file system. Checks are also made for the portability of the characters used in the filename.

pidof

Description	Finds the process IDs of one or more named programs and displays the PIDs.
Syntax	`pidof [-s] [-x] [-o pid] [-o pid ...] program [program ...]`
Important Flags and Options	• `-o pid`: Omits the specified process ID from the list returned.
	• `-s`: Returns only a single PID.
	• `-x`: Returns the PIDs of shells running named scripts as well as named programs.

ping

Description	Sends echo request packets to a network host to see if it is accessible on the network.
Syntax	`ping [-R] [-c number] [-d] [-i seconds] host`
Important Flags and Options	• `-c number`: Stops sending packets after the specified number of packets have been sent.
	• `-d`: Outputs packets as fast as they come back or 100 times per second. The greater number will be generated. This option can only be used by the root user because it can generate extremely high volumes of network traffic. Care should be taken when using this option.
	• `-i seconds`: Specifies the number of seconds to wait between sending each packet. The default is one second. This option cannot be used along with the `-f` option.
	• `-R`: Records the route the packet takes and displays the route buffer of packets that have returned.

pppstats

Description	Displays statistics of PPP activities.
Syntax	`pppstats [-a] [-v] [-r] [-z] [-c count] [-w secs] [interface]`
Important Flags and Options	None

ps

Description

Displays status reports for currently running processes. Given a specific process ID as an argument, **ps** displays information about that particular process. Without options or arguments, **ps** displays the current user's processes.

Syntax

`ps [lumaxwrf] [txx] [pid ...]`

Important Flags and Options

- **a**: Shows processes owned by other users in addition to the current user's processes.

- **f**: Displays processes in a tree showing which processes are children of which other processes.

- **l**: Displays information in long format.

- **m**: Displays memory information in the report.

- **r**: Displays only processes that are running.

- **txx**: Displays only those processes controlled by the tty specified by **xx**.

- **u**: Displays information in user format that includes the user name and start time of the format.

- **w**: Displays information in wide output mode, which prevents the truncation of commands to fit them on one line. For each **w** included as an option, an additional line is provided for displaying commands. Up to 100 **w** options may be used.

- **x**: Shows processes without a controlling terminal (this is useful for seeing daemons that were launched during the boot process and are still running.

pwck

Description

Checks the password file for errors and problems. The format of all entries is checked to be sure that valid information appears in each field. In addition, duplicate entries are found and the user is given the chance to delete poorly formatted or duplicate entries. If no password or shadow files are specified, the default `/etc/passwd` and `/etc/shadow` are used.

Syntax	`pwck [-r] [passwordfile shadowfile]`
Important Flags and Options	• `-r`: Executes in read-only mode so that no changes are made to the password file but the checks are done.

pwconv

Description	Copies entries from a password file to a shadow file, merging them with the existing shadow file. The new password file will be called **npasswd** and the new shadow file will be called **nshadow**.
Syntax	**pwconv**
Important Flags and Options	None

pwd

Description	Displays the name of the current directory.
Syntax	**pwd**
Important Flags and Options	None

pwunconv

Description	Restores a password from a shadow password file. The new password file will be called **npasswd**.
Syntax	**pwunconv**
Important Flags and Options	None

quota

Description	Displays a user's disk usage quota information. The root user can indicate specific users and groups and get reports about them. Non-root users can only view information about their own account and the groups to which they belong.
Syntax	`quota [-guv] [user|group]`

Important Flags and Options
- -g: Prints group quota for the groups that the user belongs to.
- -u: This is the default flag, causing the display of quota information for the user.
- -v: Displays quotas for file systems where no storage is allocated.

quotacheck

Description
Scans a file system for disk usage by a user or group and outputs the results to two quota files: **quota.*user*** and **quota.*group***.

Syntax
quotacheck [-g] [-u] [-a|*filesystem*]

Important Flags and Options
- -a: Checks all file systems in the **/etc/fstab** file.
- -g: Checks for the files and directories used by a particular group ID.
- -u: Checks for the files and directory used by a particular user ID.

quotaoff

Description
Disables disk usage quotas for one or more file systems.

Syntax
quotaoff [-g] [-u] [-a|*filesystem* ...]

Important Flags and Options
- -a: Disables quotas for all file systems in **/etc/fstab**.
- -g: Disables group quotas for the specified file systems.
- -u: Disables user quotas for the specified file systems.

quotaon

Description
Enables disk usage quotas for one or more file systems.

Syntax
quotaon [-g] [-u] [-a|*filesystem* ...]

Important Flags and Options
- -a: Enables quotas for all file systems in **/etc/fstab**.
- -g: Enables group quotas for the specified file systems.
- -u: Enables user quotas for the specified file systems.

rcp

Description	Remote-copies one or more files between two systems. If the final argument is a directory, all other file arguments are copied to that directory.
Syntax	`rcp [-px] file ...`
Important Flags and Options	• `-p`: Preserves modification times and modes of the source file whenever possible.
	• `-x`: Turns on DES encryption for all copies.
Notes	Remote files and directories are specified with the form `remoteuser@remote-host:/path/to/file`.

rdate

Description	Retrieves the current time from one or more hosts on the network and displays the returned time.
Syntax	`rdate [-p] [-s] host ...`
Important Flags and Options	• `-p`: Displays the time returned from the remote system (this is the default behavior).
	• `-s`: Sets the local system's time based on the time retrieved from the network. This can only be used by the root user.

rdist

Description	Remotely distributes files in order to maintain identical copies on several hosts, preserving ownership, mode, and modification time wherever possible. If no destination directory is specified on the remote host, then the source files will be placed in the same location on the remote system.
Syntax	`rdist -c file|directory ... [login@]host[:directory]`
Important Flags and Options	`-c`: Specifies a list of files to distribute to the remote system.
Notes	`Rdist` allows for controlling distribution from configuration files. This enables many more flags and options to be used. Consult the `rdist` man page for a complete description of this tool.

repquota

Description	Displays a summary of disk usage quotas for one or more file systems.
Syntax	`repquota [-gu] [-a|filesystem ...]`
Important Flags and Options	• `-a`: Displays reports for all file systems in `/etc/fstab`.
	• `-g`: Displays a report of group usage quotas for the specified file systems.
	• `-u`: Displays a report of user usage quotas for the specified file systems.

rlogin

Description	Logs in to a remote host.
Syntax	`rlogin [-Kx] [-l username] host`
Important Flags and Options	• `-K`: Turns off all Kerberos authentication.
	• `-l username`: Indicates that the connection should be logged in under the specified username rather than the user running `rlogin`.
	• `-x`: Turns on DES encryption for all data sent while logged in to the remote system.

rm

Description	Deletes one or more files or directories.
Syntax	`rm [-firR] [--force] [--interactive] [--recursive] file|directory ...`
Important Flags and Options	• `-f/--force`: Does not prompt the user for permission to delete files. This is dangerous if used as the root user.
	• `-i/--interactive`: Always prompts the user before deleting each file.
	• `-r/-R/--recursive`: Recursively removes the content of directories.

rmdir

Description	Deletes empty directories.
Syntax	`rmdir [-p] [--parents] directory ...`
Important Flags and Options	• `-p/--parents`: Removes the directory as well as all parents explicitly indicated on the command line as long as deleting the directory causes the parent to become empty.

rmmod

Description	Unloads one or more loaded modules.
Syntax	`rmmod [-as] module ...`
Important Flags and Options	• `-a`: Removes all unused modules.
	• `-s`: Sends all output to the system log instead of the display.

route

Description	Displays or alters the IP routing table. When no options are provided, the routing table is displayed.
Syntax	`route add [-net|-host] targetaddress [netmask Nm] [gw Gw] [[dev] If]`
	`route del [-net|-host] targetaddress [gw Gw] [netmask Nm] [[dev] If]`
Important Flags and Options	• `add`: Indicates that a route is being added.
	• `del`: Indicates that a route is being deleted.
	• `[dev] If`: Forces the route to be connected to the specified interface.
	• `gw Gw`: Specifies the gateway for the route.
	• `-host`: Indicates the target is a host.
	• `-net`: Indicates the target is a network.
	• `netmask Nm`: Specifies the netmask for the route.

rsh

Description	Opens a shell on a remote system. If a command is provided, the command is executed on the remote host, the results are returned, and the connection is terminated.
Syntax	`rsh [-Kx] [-1 username] hostname [command]`
Important Flags and Options	• `-K`: Disables Kerberos authentication.
	• `-1 username`: Attempts to connect to the remote host as a different user than the one running `rsh`.
	• `-x`: Enables DES encryption for all data sent between the two hosts.

runlevel

Description	Displays the current and previous run level of the system.
Syntax	`runlevel`
Important Flags and Options	None

rup

Description	Displays the status of one or more remote systems. If no host is specified, then the status of all machines on the local network is displayed.
Syntax	`rup [-dhlt] [host ...]`
Important Flags and Options	• `-d`: Displays the local time on each host.
	• `-h`: Sorts the entries by host name.
	• `-l`: Sorts the entries by load average.
	• `-t`: Sorts the entries by up time.

rusers

Description	Displays who is logged on to one or more machines on the local network. If no host is indicated, then all users logged in to all machines on the local network are displayed.
Syntax	`rusers [-l] [hostname ...]`
Important Flags and Options	`-l`: Displays results in a long format, including username, host name, tty being used by the user, and the time of login, among other information.

rwho

Description	Displays a list of users logged into all machines on the local network.
Syntax	`rwho`
Important Flags and Options	None

rwhod

Description	Answers incoming requests from the **rwho** client.
Syntax	**rwhod**
Important Flags and Options	None

setclock

Description	Sets the computer's hardware clock to the value of the current system clock.
Syntax	**setclock**
Important Flags and Options	None

setkeycodes

Description	Loads key mappings into the scancode-to-keycode mapping table. Arguments are provided in pairs with the first argument being the scancode for a key and the second being the keycode to be associated with it.
Syntax	**setkeycodes** *scancode keycode* **...**
Important Flags and Options	None
Notes	To understand how to specify scancodes and keycodes, consult the **setkeycodes** man page.

showkey

Description	Displays scancodes and keycodes generated by the keyboard. The program remains active for 10 seconds after the last key is pressed.
Syntax	**showkey [-sk --scancodes --keycodes]**
Important Flags and Options	• **-k/--keycodes**: Displays keycodes. • **-s/--scancodes**: Displays scancodes.

showmount

Description	Shows the current state of mounts from an NFS server. If a host is specified, then only mounts from the particular host are displayed.
Syntax	`showmount [-ade] [--all] [--directories] [--exports] [host]`
Important Flags and Options	• `-a/--all`: Displays both the client's host name and the mounted directory using `host:directory` format.
	• `-d/--directories`: Displays only directories.
	• `-e/--exports`: Displays the server's list of exported directories.

shutdown

Description	Shuts down the system, stopping logins and possibly delaying before shutting down and issuing an optional warning message. When a time is specified, the shutdown will occur at the specified time; otherwise it occurs immediately.
Syntax	`shutdown [-rkhc] time [warning]`
Important Flags and Options	• `-c`: Cancels a running shutdown.
	• `-h`: Halts after shutting down.
	• `-k`: Sends the warning message but doesn't actually shut down the system.
	• `-r`: Reboots after shutting down.
Notes	The time can be specified as an absolute time in the form *HH:MM* or as a number of minutes to wait before shutting down in the form `+minutes`.

sort

Description	Sorts the lines contained in one or more text files and displays the results. If no files are indicated, data is taken from the standard input and sorted. The resulting sorted data is displayed to the standard output.
Syntax	`sort [-cu] [-t separator] [-o file] [-T tempdir] [-bdfMnr]` ➡ `[+POS1 [-POS2]] [-k POS1[,POS2]] [file ...]`
Important Flags and Options	• `-b`: Ignores leading blanks in lines when trying to find sort keys.
	• `-c`: Checks whether the input data is sorted and prints an error message if it isn't. No sorting actually takes place.

- -d: Ignores all characters except letters, digits, and blanks in the sorting process.

- -f: Converts lowercase letters to uppercase letters during the sorting process.

- -k *POS1*[,*POS2*]: Specifies the field to use as the sorting key. The field will start at *POS1* and run up until *POS2* or the end of the line. Fields and character positions are specified starting at zero.

- -M: Sorts months. That is, any strings that starts with zero or more blanks followed by three letters are converted to uppercase and sorted as if they were abbreviated month names.

- -n: Compares strings numerically, which assumes that strings start with zero or more blanks followed by an optional sign and then a number.

- -o *file*: Outputs the results to the specified file instead of the standard output.

- +*POS1* [-*POS2*]: Specifies the field to use as the sorting key. The field will start at *POS1* and run up until *POS2* or the end of the line. Fields and character positions are specified starting at zero.

- -r: Reverses the sort order.

- -t *separator*: Indicates that the specified separator should serve as the field separator for finding sort keys on each line.

- -u: When two lines compare as equal, only outputs the first.

statserial

Description	Shows the status of a serial port by displaying the signals on the pins of the port and the status of the handshaking line. If no device is specified, the default will be the value of the MODEM environment variable, or /dev/cua1 if the variable isn't set. The program will loop continuously, providing an updated status every second until Ctrl+C is pressed.
Syntax	statserial [-n|-d|-x] [*device*]
Important Flags and Options	

- -d: Displays the status of the port as a decimal number.

- -n: Disables looping and only displays a single status.

- -x: Displays the status of the port as a hexadecimal number.

su

Description	Runs a new shell under different user and group IDs. If no user is specified, the new shell will run as the root user.

Syntax	`su [-flmp] [-c command] [-s shell] [--login] [--fast] [--preserve-`➥`environment] [--command=command] [--shell=shell] [-] [user]`
Important Flags and Options	• `-c command/--command=command`: Passes the specified command as a single command line to the shell instead of running the shell in an interactive mode.
	• `-f/--fast`: Passes the `-f` option to the shell, which in the case of the C Shell and the Extended C Shell disables filename pattern expansion.
	• `-/-l/--login`: Forces the new shell to be a login shell. This means new environment variables will be set, the path will change, and the current directory will switch to the user's home directory.
	• `-m/-p/--preserve-environment`: Prevents the HOME, USER, LOGNAME, and SHELL environment variables from changing.
	• `-s shell/--shell=shell`: Runs the specified shell instead of the default shell included in the password file.

sync

Description	Saves the disk cache to the physical disks. This forces any changed information to be saved to the disk.
Syntax	`sync`
Important Flags and Options	None

tail

Description	Displays the last part of one or more files. By default, unless otherwise specified, the last 10 lines of each file are displayed. If no filenames are provided, then reads data from the standard input and displays the last section of the data following the same rules as for files.
Syntax	`tail [-c number[bkm]] [-n number] [-q] [--bytes number[bkm]]`➥`[--lines number] [--quiet] [--silent] [file ...]`
Important Flags and Options	• `-c/--bytes number`: Displays the specified number of bytes from the end of each file. Optionally, the number can be followed by b for 512-byte blocks, k for kilobytes, or m for megabytes.
	• `-n/--lines number`: Displays the specified number of lines from the end of each file.
	• `-q/--quiet/--silent`: Prevents printing of filename headers when multiple files are being processed.

tar

Description   Creates an archive file of one or more files or directories.

Syntax   `tar [-crtuxz] [-f tarfile] [--file tarfile] [--create] [--delete]`
➡️ `[--preserve] [--append] [--same-owner] [--list] [--update]`
➡️ `[--extract] [--get] [--gzip] [--gunzip] [file|directory ...]`

Important Flags and Options
- `-c/--create`: Creates a new archive.
- `--delete`: Deletes files from an existing archive.
- `-f tarfile/--file tarfile`: Specifies the name of the archive file being created or read from.
- `--preserve`: Keeps permissions and order of files the same in the archive.
- `-r/--append`: Adds files to an existing archive.
- `--same-owner`: Signifies that extracted files keep their original owners.
- `-t/--list`: Displays a list of an archive's contents.
- `-u/--update`: Only adds files to an existing archive that are newer than the copy in the archive.
- `-x/--extract/--get`: Extracts files from an existing archive.
- `-z/--gzip/--ungzip`: Filters the archive through `gzip` when archiving and unarchiving.

timeconfig

Description   Configures time parameters. If a time zone is specified, then the system time zone is changed to the specified time zone. Otherwise, displays a list of available time zones.

Syntax   `timeconfig [--utc] [timezone]`

Important Flags and Options
- `--utc`: Assumes the system clock is running in Universal/Greenwich Mean Time.

timed

Description   Runs the time server daemon, which can synchronize the time with time on other machines on the local network.

Syntax   `timed [-M] [-i network] [-n network]`

Important Flags and Options

- -i *network*: Specifies which network the server belongs to, overriding any default choice made by **timed**.

- -M: Prepares to take on the job of the master time server if the master server crashes.

- -n *network*: Adds the specified network to the list of valid networks.

timedc

Description

Controls the **timed** daemon.

Syntax

timedc [clockdiff *host* ...|msite [*host* ...]|election *host*]

Important Flags and Options

- clockdiff *host* ...: Computes the difference between the system's clock and the time on the specified hosts.

- election *host*: Resets the election timer and ensures that a time master has been elected from among the slaves.

- msite [*host* ...]: Shows the master timeserver for the specified host or hosts. If no hosts are specified, shows the master for the current system.

top

Description

Displays a regularly updated report of processes running on the system.

Syntax

top [d *delay*] [q] [c] [S] [s]

Important Flags and Options

- c: Displays the complete command line of a process instead of just the command name.

- d *delay*: Specifies the delay between updates, in seconds.

- q: Causes updates to occur without any delays. If the root user runs **top** with this option, **top** will run with the highest possible priority.

- s: Runs in a secure mode that prevents the use of dangerous interactive commands.

- S: Statistics should be displayed in a cumulative manner. That is, CPU time should be reported for a process and its dead children as a total.

Notes

For a list of commands that can be used while **top** is running and for a description of the various fields in the reports, read the **top** man page.

touch

Description	Changes the timestamp of files without changing their contents. If a file doesn't exist, it will be created with a size of zero. By default, it uses the current time as the new timestamp.
Syntax	touch [-acm] [-t *MMDDhhmm*[[*CC*]*YY*][.*ss*]] [--time=*atime*] [--time=*access*] ➥[--time=*use*] [--time=*mtime*] [--time=*modify*] [--no-create] *file* ...
Important Flags and Options	• -a/--time=*atime*/--time=*access*/--time=*use*: Changes only the access time.
	• -c/--no-create: Will not create files that don't exist.
	• -m/--time=*mtime*/--time=*modify*: Changes only the modification time.
	• -t *MMDDhhmm*[[*CC*]*YY*][.*ss*]: Sets the timestamp to the specified month, day, hour, and minutes plus, optionally, the specified century, year, or seconds. This overrides the default of using the current time.

traceroute

Description	Displays the route a packet travels to reach a remote host on the network.
Syntax	traceroute [-ir] *host*
Important Flags and Options	• -i: Specifies a network interface for outgoing packets. This is useful in systems with more than one network interface.
	• -r: Bypasses normal routing tables and attempts to send directly to an attached host.

true

Description	Does nothing and returns a successful exit status.
Syntax	true
Important Flags and Options	None

umount

Description	Unmounts a mounted file system. The file system is specified by either its device name, its directory name, or its network path.

Syntax	`umount -r device|directory|path ...`
Important Flags and Options	`-r`: If unmounting fails, tries to remount the file system in read-only mode.

uname

Description	Displays selected system information. When no options are provided, the operating system name is displayed. When multiple pieces of information are requested, the display order is always: operating system, network host name, operating system release, operating system version, and machine type.
Syntax	`uname [-snrvma] [--sysname] [--nodename] [--release] [--machine] [--all]`

Important Flags and Options

- `-a/--all`: Displays all information.

- `-m/--machine`: Displays the machine's type (that is, its hardware type).

- `-n/--nodename`: Displays the machine's network host name.

- `-r/--release`: Displays the operating system release.

- `-s/--sysname`: Displays the operating system name. This is the default action when no options are specified.

- `-v`: Displays the operating system's version.

uncompress

Description	Uncompresses files compressed with the `compress` program. If no files are specified, the standard input will be decompressed.
Syntax	`uncompress [-c] [file ...]`
Important Flags and Options	`-c`: Sends the uncompressed data to the standard output instead of overwriting the old compressed file.

unzip

Description	Manipulates and extracts ZIP archives.
Syntax	`unzip [-cflptuz] [-d exdir] file[.zip]`

Important Flags and Options

- `-c`: Extracts files to the standard output, printing the name of each file as it is extracted.

- -d *exdir*: Uncompresses the archive to the specified directory instead of the current directory.

- -f: Extracts only those files that are newer than already-existing versions of the files.

- -l: Displays the contents of the archive without extracting.

- -p: Extracts files to the standard output without sending any other data such as filenames.

- -t: Tests the integrity of files in the archive.

- -u: Extracts files that are newer than already-existing versions of files as well as files that do not already exist in the extract directory.

- -z: Displays the archive comment.

Notes

This is a powerful program that supports many modifiers. See the unzip man page for details.

uptime

Description

Displays the length of time the system has been running.

Syntax

uptime

Important Flags and Options

None

useradd

Description

Adds a user to the system. Alternately, the default values for new users can be changed. If no options are provided, the program will display the current default values for new users.

Syntax

useradd [-d *home_dir*] [-e *expire_date*] [-f *inactive_time*]
➥[-g *initial_group*] [-G *group*[,...]] [-s *shell*] [-u *uid* [-o]]
➥*username*

useradd –D [-g *default_group*] [-b *default_home*] [-f *default_inactive*]
➥[-e *default_expiration*] [-s *default_shell*]

Important Flags and Options

- -b *default_home*: Sets the default home directory prefix to the specified path. Only to be used when –D is used.

- -d *home_dir*: Uses the specified home directory for the user instead of the default home directory.

- -D: Indicates that default values for new users should be changed rather than that a new user should be created.

- -e *expire_date*: Specifies the expiration date for the account. The data is provided in MM/DD/YY format. When –D is used, –e will be used to set the default expiration for all new passwords as a number of days instead of in a date format.

- -f *inactive_time*: Indicates that once a password expires, the specified amount of time should elapse before permanently disabling the password. When –D is used, –f will be used to set the default amount of time before passwords will be disabled after expiring.

- -g *initial_group*: Specifies the default login group for the user. When used with –D, –g will specify the default group for all new users.

- -G *group*[,...]: Specifies other groups the user should belong to.

- -s *shell*: Specifies the default shell for the user. If not provided, the default shell for new users will be used. When used with –D, –s will specify the default shell for all new users.

- -u *uid* [-o]: Specifies a user ID for the user rather than automatically assigning one. The value must be unique unless the –o flag is used.

userdel

Description	Deletes a user's account.
Syntax	userdel [-r] *user*
Important Flags and Options	-r: Deletes the user's home directory when deleting the account.
Notes	If you choose to delete the user's home directory, keep in mind that any other files the user owns that are outside their home directory are not deleted when their account is deleted. These have to be deleted manually. Such files might include the user's mail inbox, for example.

usermod

Description	Modifies the settings for an existing user's account.
Syntax	usermod [-d *home_dir* [-m]] [-e *expire_date*] [-f *inactive_time*] ➥[-g *initial_group*] [-G *group*[,...]] [-l *login_name*] [-s *shell*] ➥[-u *uid* [-o]] *login*
Important Flags and Options	• -d *home_dir* [-m]: Changes the user's home directory as specified and, if the –m option is used, moves the current home directory to the new location. • -e *expire_date*: Sets a new expiration date for the account after which it will be disabled. The date should be in the form MM/DD/YY.

- -f *inactive_days*: Provides a new setting for the number of days after a password expires when it will be permanently disabled.

- -g *initial_group*: Defines a new login group for the user.

- -G *group*[,...]: Indicates which other groups a user should be a member of. If the user is currently a member of a group that is not on this list, they will be removed from the group.

- -l *login_name*: Changes the user's login name.

- -s *shell*: Changes the user's default shell as specified.

- -u *uid*: Changes the user's ID as specified.

users

Description	Displays the user names of current users on the system. This is normally found by looking at the contents of **/etc/utmp**. If a file is specified, the program will look in that file for the information.
Syntax	**users [*file*]**
Important Flags and Options	None

uudecode

Description	Decodes ASCII files created by **uudecode**, to recreate the original binary files. By default, the name of the decoded file will be the original name of the encoded file. If no files to decode are provided, then the standard input is decoded.
Syntax	**uudecode [-o *outputfile*] [*file* ...]**
Important Flags and Options	-o *outputfile*: Specifies an alternate name for the resulting decoded file.

uuencode

Description	Encodes a binary file into a form that can be used where binary files cannot (such as with some mail software). If no file is provided, the standard input is encoded.
Syntax	**uuencode [*file*]**
Important Flags and Options	None

vipw

Description	Edits the system password file using the editor specified in the **EDITOR** environment variable.
Syntax	`vipw`
Important Flags and Options	None

vmstat

Description	Reports statistics about virtual memory.
Syntax	`vmstat [delay [count]]`
Important Flags and Options	• *count*: Indicates the number of times to repeat the report. If not specified, the report will repeat continuously until interrupted with Ctrl+C.
	• *delay*: Indicates how often to repeat the report, in seconds. If not specified, then only one report is provided.
Notes	For details of the report generated by **vmstat**, read the **vmstat** man page.

w

Description	Displays a list of current users and the tasks they are running. If a user is specified, then only that user's tasks are displayed.
Syntax	`w [user]`
Important Flags and Options	None

wc

Description	Prints the number of bytes (characters), words, and lines in one or more documents. When multiple filenames are provided, each file will be counted and displayed separately and then a cumulative total will be displayed. If no files are specified, then the standard input is counted.
Syntax	`wc [-clw] [--bytes] [--chars] [--lines] [--words] [file ...]`
Important Flags and Options	• `-c/--bytes/--chars`: Displays only the number of bytes.

- -1/--lines: Displays only the number of lines.
- -w/--words: Displays only the number of words.

Notes

The results are displayed in this order: characters, words, lines. The values are separated by spaces.

whereis

Description

Attempts to locate the binary, source code, and man page files for one or more commands.

Syntax

whereis [-bms] [-BMS *directory* ... -f] *file* ...

Important Flags and Options

- -b: Searches only for binary files.
- -B *directory* ... -f: Searches only the specified directories for binary files. The -f flag is necessary to delineate the end of the directory list and the start of the file argument list.
- -m: Searches only for man pages.
- -M *directory* -f: Searches only the specified directories for man pages. The -f flag is necessary to delineate the end of the directory list and the start of the file argument list.
- -s: Searches only for source code.
- -S *directory* ... -f: Searches only the specified directories for source code. The -f flag is necessary to delineate the end of the directory list and the start of the file argument list.

Notes

The whereis command will search, at a minimum, the following directories for the programs it is trying to locate:

/bin

/usr/bin

/etc

/usr/etc

/sbin

/usr/sbin

/usr/games

/usr/games/bin

/usr/emacs/etc

/usr/lib/emacs/19.22/etc

```
/usr/lib/emacs/19.23/etc
/usr/lib/emacs/19.24/etc
/usr/lib/emacs/19.25/etc
/usr/lib/emacs/19.26/etc
/usr/lib/emacs/19.27/etc
/usr/lib/emacs/19.28/etc
/usr/lib/emacs/19.29/etc
/usr/lib/emacs/19.30/etc
/usr/TeX/bin
/usr/tex/bin
/usr/interviews/bin/LINUX
/usr/bin/X11
/usr/X11/bin
/usr/X11R5/bin
/usr/X11R6/bin
/usr/X386/bin
/usr/local/bin
/usr/local/etc
/usr/local/sbin
/usr/local/games
/usr/local/games/bin
/usr/local/emacs/etc
/usr/local/TeX/bin
/usr/local/tex/bin
/usr/local/bin/X11
/usr/contrib
/usr/hosts
/usr/include
/usr/g++-include
```

which

Description	Displays the full pathname of one or more programs. Only programs that are on the path as specified by the PATH environment variable will be displayed.
Syntax	which *program* ...
Important Flags and Options	None

whoami

Description	Displays the current effective user ID.
Syntax	whoami
Important Flags and Options	None

ypdomainname

Description	Displays the system's NIS domain name.
Syntax	ypdomainname
Important Flags and Options	None

zcat

Description	Uncompresses one or more compressed files and displays the results to the standard output. If no files are specified, then the standard input is uncompressed and displayed.
Syntax	zcat [-f] [*file* ...]
Important Flags and Options	• -f/--force: Forces uncompression even when a corresponding file already exists and will be overwritten by the uncompressed file.

zgrep

Description	Searches one or more compressed files for a specified pattern.
Syntax	zgrep [*options*] *pattern file* ...

Important Flags and Options	None
Notes	For a list of possible entries and a discussion of pattern syntax, refer to the `grep` command.

zip

Description	Creates a ZIP archive from one or more files and directories.
Syntax	`zip [-efFgmrSu@] [zipfile [file1 file2 ...]]`
Important Flags and Options	

- `-@`: Accepts the list of files to be archived from the standard input.

- `-e`: Encrypts the archive after prompting for a password. The password will be necessary to extract files from the archive.

- `-f`: Replaces entries in an existing archive only if the file is newer than the file currently in the archive.

- `-F`: Tries to fix a damaged archive.

- `-g`: Adds files to an existing archive.

- `-m`: Moves files into the archive, deleting them from their original location once they are in the archive.

- `-r`: Recursively works with directories, adding all files in subdirectories to the archive.

- `-S`: Includes system and hidden files in the archive.

- `-u`: Replaces entries in an existing archive if a file is newer than the file currently in the archive or if the file does not already exist in the archive.

Notes	The `zip` command offers many other options that have subtle, sometimes useful, impact on the behavior of the program. Consult the `zip` man page for more details.

zipgrep

Description	Searches for a pattern in one or more files in a ZIP archive using **egrep**. If no files in the archive are specified, then all files in the archive are searched.
Syntax	`zipgrep [egrepoptions] pattern zipfile file ...`
Important Flags and Options	None
Notes	For a complete discussion of **egrep**'s and **zipgrep**'s pattern syntax, refer to the **egrep** command.

zipinfo

Description	Displays details about ZIP archives, including encryption status, compression type, operating system used to create the archive, and more. By default, information about each file in the archive is also listed on separate lines. If no ZIP files are specified, the standard input will be processed.
Syntax	`zipinfo [-121M] zipfile[.zip] [file ...]`
Important Flags and Options	<ul><li>`-1`: Lists only filenames, each on a separate line.</li><li>`-2`: Lists only filenames, including headers, trailers and comments.</li><li>`-1`: Lists information in long format (similar to `ls -1`).</li><li>`-M`: Displays information one page at a time in a fashion similar to `more`.</li></ul>

zmore

Description	Displays the contents of compressed text files, one screen at a time, allowing searching in much the same way as the `more` command. If no files are specified, the standard input will be used.
Syntax	`zmore [file ...]`
Important Flags and Options	None
Notes	See the `zmore` man page for a complete list of commands that can be used while viewing a file.

znew

Description	Converts files compressed with `compress` (`.Z` files) into the format used by `gzip` (`.gz` files). If no files are specified, then the standard input is processed.
Syntax	`znew [-ft9K] [file.Z ...]`
Important Flags and Options	<ul><li>`-9`: Uses the best, but slowest, compression method.</li><li>`-f`: Forces compression even when a `.gz` file already exists.</li><li>`-K`: Keeps a `.Z` file if it will be smaller than the new `.gz` file.</li><li>`-t`: Tests the new `.gz` file before deleting the original `.Z` file.</li></ul>

APPENDIX

D

GNU General Public License

Version 2, June 1991

Copyright (C) 1989, 1991 Free Software Foundation, Inc.

675 Mass Ave, Cambridge, MA 02139, USA

Preamble

The licenses for most software are designed to take away your freedom to share and change it. By contrast, the GNU General Public License is intended to guarantee your freedom to share and change free software—to make sure the software is free for all its users. This General Public License applies to most of the Free Software Foundation's software and to any other program whose authors commit to using it. (Some other Free Software Foundation software is covered by the GNU Library General Public License instead.) You can apply it to your programs, too.

When we speak of free software, we are referring to freedom, not price. Our General Public Licenses are designed to make sure that you have the freedom to distribute copies of free software (and charge for this service if you wish), that you receive source code or can get it if you want it, that you can change the software or use pieces of it in new free programs; and that you know you can do these things.

To protect your rights, we need to make restrictions that forbid anyone to deny you these rights or to ask you to surrender the rights. These restrictions translate to certain responsibilities for you if you distribute copies of the software, or if you modify it.

For example, if you distribute copies of such a program, whether gratis or for a fee, you must give the recipients all the rights that you have. You must make sure that they, too, receive or can get the source code. And you must show them these terms so they know their rights.

We protect your rights with two steps: (1) copyright the software, and (2) offer you this license which gives you legal permission to copy, distribute and/or modify the software.

Also, for each author's protection and ours, we want to make certain that everyone understands that there is no warranty for this free software. If the software is modified by someone else and passed on, we want its recipients to know that what they have is not the original, so that any problems introduced by others will not reflect on the original authors' reputations.

Finally, any free program is threatened constantly by software patents. We wish to avoid the danger that redistributors of a free program will individually obtain patent licenses, in effect making the program proprietary. To prevent this, we have made it clear that any patent must be licensed for everyone's free use or not licensed at all.

The precise terms and conditions for copying, distribution and modification follow.

Terms and Conditions for Copying, Distribution, and Modification

0. This License applies to any program or other work which contains a notice placed by the copyright holder saying it may be distributed under the terms of this General Public License. The "Program", below, refers to any such program or work, and a "work based on the Program" means either the Program or any derivative work under copyright law: that is to say, a work containing the Program or a portion of it, either verbatim or with modifications and/or translated into another language. (Hereinafter, translation is included without limitation in the term "modification".) Each licensee is addressed as "you".

Activities other than copying, distribution and modification are not covered by this License; they are outside its scope. The act of running the Program is not restricted, and the output from the Program is covered only if its contents constitute a work based on the Program (independent of having been made by running the Program). Whether that is true depends on what the Program does.

1. You may copy and distribute verbatim copies of the Program's source code as you receive it, in any medium, provided that you conspicuously and appropriately publish on each copy an appropriate copyright notice and disclaimer of warranty; keep intact all the notices that refer to this License and to the absence of any warranty; and give any other recipients of the Program a copy of this License along with the Program.

You may charge a fee for the physical act of transferring a copy, and you may at your option offer warranty protection in exchange for a fee.

2. You may modify your copy or copies of the Program or any portion of it, thus forming a work based on the Program, and copy and distribute such

modifications or work under the terms of Section 1 above, provided that you also meet all of these conditions:

a) You must cause the modified files to carry prominent notices stating that you changed the files and the date of any change.

b) You must cause any work that you distribute or publish, that in whole or in part contains or is derived from the Program or any part thereof, to be licensed as a whole at no charge to all third parties under the terms of this License.

c) If the modified program normally reads commands interactively when run, you must cause it, when started running for such interactive use in the most ordinary way, to print or display an announcement including an appropriate copyright notice and a notice that there is no warranty (or else, saying that you provide a warranty) and that users may redistribute the program under these conditions, and telling the user how to view a copy of this License. (Exception: if the Program itself is interactive but does not normally print such an announcement, your work based on the Program is not required to print an announcement.)

These requirements apply to the modified work as a whole. If identifiable sections of that work are not derived from the Program, and can be reasonably considered independent and separate works in themselves, then this License, and its terms, do not apply to those sections when you distribute them as separate works. But when you distribute the same sections as part of a whole which is a work based on the Program, the distribution of the whole must be on the terms of this License, whose permissions for other licensees extend to the entire whole, and thus to each and every part regardless of who wrote it.

Thus, it is not the intent of this section to claim rights or contest your rights to work written entirely by you; rather, the intent is to exercise the right to control the distribution of derivative or collective works based on the Program.

In addition, mere aggregation of another work not based on the Program with the Program (or with a work based on the Program) on a volume of a storage or distribution medium does not bring the other work under the scope of this License.

3. You may copy and distribute the Program (or a work based on it, under Section 2) in object code or executable form under the terms of Sections 1 and 2 above provided that you also do one of the following:

   a) Accompany it with the complete corresponding machine-readable source code, which must be distributed under the terms of Sections 1 and 2 above on a medium customarily used for software interchange; or,

   b) Accompany it with a written offer, valid for at least three years, to give any third party, for a charge no more than your cost of physically performing source distribution, a complete machine-readable copy of the corresponding source code, to be distributed under the terms of Sections 1 and 2 above on a medium customarily used for software interchange; or,

   c) Accompany it with the information you received as to the offer to distribute corresponding source code. (This alternative is allowed only for noncommercial distribution and only if you received the program in object code or executable form with such an offer, in accord with Subsection b above.)

The source code for a work means the preferred form of the work for making modifications to it. For an executable work, complete source code means all the source code for all modules it contains, plus any associated interface definition files, plus the scripts used to control compilation and installation of the executable. However, as a special exception, the source code distributed need not include anything that is normally distributed (in either source or binary form) with the major components (compiler, kernel, and so on) of the operating system on which the executable runs, unless that component itself accompanies the executable.

If distribution of executable or object code is made by offering access to copy from a designated place, then offering equivalent access to copy the source code from the same place counts as distribution of the source code, even though third parties are not compelled to copy the source along with the object code.

4. You may not copy, modify, sublicense, or distribute the Program except as expressly provided under this License. Any attempt otherwise to copy, modify, sublicense or distribute the Program is void, and will automatically terminate your rights under this License. However, parties who have

received copies, or rights, from you under this License will not have their licenses terminated so long as such parties remain in full compliance.

5. You are not required to accept this License, since you have not signed it. However, nothing else grants you permission to modify or distribute the Program or its derivative works. These actions are prohibited by law if you do not accept this License. Therefore, by modifying or distributing the Program (or any work based on the Program), you indicate your acceptance of this License to do so, and all its terms and conditions for copying, distributing or modifying the Program or works based on it.

6. Each time you redistribute the Program (or any work based on the Program), the recipient automatically receives a license from the original licensor to copy, distribute or modify the Program subject to these terms and conditions. You may not impose any further restrictions on the recipients' exercise of the rights granted herein. You are not responsible for enforcing compliance by third parties to this License.

7. If, as a consequence of a court judgment or allegation of patent infringement or for any other reason (not limited to patent issues), conditions are imposed on you (whether by court order, agreement or otherwise) that contradict the conditions of this License, they do not excuse you from the conditions of this License. If you cannot distribute so as to satisfy simultaneously your obligations under this License and any other pertinent obligations, then as a consequence you may not distribute the Program at all. For example, if a patent license would not permit royalty-free redistribution of the Program by all those who receive copies directly or indirectly through you, then the only way you could satisfy both it and this License would be to refrain entirely from distribution of the Program.

    If any portion of this section is held invalid or unenforceable under any particular circumstance, the balance of the section is intended to apply and the section as a whole is intended to apply in other circumstances.

    It is not the purpose of this section to induce you to infringe any patents or other property right claims or to contest validity of any such claims; this section has the sole purpose of protecting the integrity of the free software distribution system, which is implemented by public license practices. Many people have made generous contributions to the wide range of software distributed through that system in reliance on consistent application of that system; it is up to the author/donor to decide if he or she is willing to distribute software through any other system and a licensee cannot impose that choice.

This section is intended to make thoroughly clear what is believed to be a consequence of the rest of this License.

8. If the distribution and/or use of the Program is restricted in certain countries either by patents or by copyrighted interfaces, the original copyright holder who places the Program under this License may add an explicit geographical distribution limitation excluding those countries, so that distribution is permitted only in or among countries not thus excluded. In such case, this License incorporates the limitation as if written in the body of this License.

9. The Free Software Foundation may publish revised and/or new versions of the General Public License from time to time. Such new versions will be similar in spirit to the present version, but may differ in detail to address new problems or concerns.

    Each version is given a distinguishing version number. If the Program specifies a version number of this License which applies to it and "any later version", you have the option of following the terms and conditions either of that version or of any later version published by the Free Software Foundation. If the Program does not specify a version number of this License, you may choose any version ever published by the Free Software Foundation.

10. If you wish to incorporate parts of the Program into other free programs whose distribution conditions are different, write to the author to ask for permission. For software which is copyrighted by the Free Software Foundation, write to the Free Software Foundation; we sometimes make exceptions for this. Our decision will be guided by the two goals of preserving the free status of all derivatives of our free software and of promoting the sharing and reuse of software generally.

No Warranty

11. BECAUSE THE PROGRAM IS LICENSED FREE OF CHARGE, THERE IS NO WARRANTY FOR THE PROGRAM, TO THE EXTENT PERMITTED BY APPLICABLE LAW. EXCEPT WHEN OTHERWISE STATED IN WRITING THE COPYRIGHT HOLDERS AND/OR OTHER PARTIES PROVIDE

THE PROGRAM "AS IS" WITHOUT WARRANTY OF ANY KIND, EITHER EXPRESSED OR IMPLIED, INCLUDING, BUT NOT LIMITED TO, THE IMPLIED WARRANTIES OF MERCHANTABILITY AND FITNESS FOR A PARTICULAR PURPOSE. THE ENTIRE RISK AS TO THE QUALITY AND PERFORMANCE OF THE PROGRAM IS WITH YOU. SHOULD THE PRO-GRAM PROVE DEFECTIVE, YOU ASSUME THE COST OF ALL NECES-SARY SERVICING, REPAIR OR CORRECTION.

12. IN NO EVENT UNLESS REQUIRED BY APPLICABLE LAW OR AGREED TO IN WRITING WILL ANY COPYRIGHT HOLDER, OR ANY OTHER PARTY WHO MAY MODIFY AND/OR REDISTRIBUTE THE PROGRAM AS PERMITTED ABOVE, BE LIABLE TO YOU FOR DAMAGES, INCLUD-ING ANY GENERAL, SPECIAL, INCIDENTAL OR CONSEQUENTIAL DAMAGES ARISING OUT OF THE USE OR INABILITY TO USE THE PROGRAM (INCLUDING BUT NOT LIMITED TO LOSS OF DATA OR DATA BEING RENDERED INACCURATE OR LOSSES SUSTAINED BY YOU OR THIRD PARTIES OR A FAILURE OF THE PROGRAM TO OPER-ATE WITH ANY OTHER PROGRAMS), EVEN IF SUCH HOLDER OR OTHER PARTY HAS BEEN ADVISED OF THE POSSIBILITY OF SUCH DAMAGES.

END OF TERMS AND CONDITIONS

Appendix: How to Apply These Terms to Your New Programs

If you develop a new program, and you want it to be of the greatest possible use to the public, the best way to achieve this is to make it free software which every-one can redistribute and change under these terms.

To do so, attach the following notices to the program. It is safest to attach them to the start of each source file to most effectively convey the exclusion of warranty; and each file should have at least the "copyright" line and a pointer to where the full notice is found.

```
<one line to give the program's name and a brief idea of what it does.>
Copyright (C) 19yy <name of author>
This program is free software; you can redistribute it and/or modify
```

```
it under the terms of the GNU General Public License as published by
the Free Software Foundation; either version 2 of the License, or
(at your option) any later version.
This program is distributed in the hope that it will be useful,
but WITHOUT ANY WARRANTY; without even the implied warranty of
MERCHANTABILITY or FITNESS FOR A PARTICULAR PURPOSE. See the
GNU General Public License for more details.
You should have received a copy of the GNU General Public License
along with this program; if not, write to the Free Software
Foundation, Inc., 675 Mass Ave, Cambridge, MA 02139, USA.
```

Also add information on how to contact you by electronic and paper mail.

If the program is interactive, make it output a short notice like this when it starts in an interactive mode:

```
Gnomovision version 69, Copyright (C) 19yy name of author
Gnomovision comes with ABSOLUTELY NO WARRANTY; for details type `show
w'.
This is free software, and you are welcome to redistribute it
under certain conditions; type `show c' for details.
```

The hypothetical commands "show w" and "show c" should show the appropriate parts of the General Public License. Of course, the commands you use may be called something other than "show w" and "show c"; they could even be mouse-clicks or menu items—whatever suits your program.

You should also get your employer (if you work as a programmer) or your school, if any, to sign a "copyright disclaimer" for the program, if necessary. Here is a sample; alter the names:

```
Yoyodyne, Inc., hereby disclaims all copyright interest in the program
`Gnomovision' (which makes passes at compilers) written by James
Hacker.
<signature of Ty Coon>, 1 April 1989
Ty Coon, President of Vice
```

This General Public License does not permit incorporating your program into proprietary programs. If your program is a subroutine library, you may consider it more useful to permit linking proprietary applications with the library. If this is what you want to do, use the GNU Library General Public License instead of this License.

APPENDIX

E

Linux on Non-Intel Hardware

Linux is available for numerous hardware platforms other than the Intel *x*86 and Pentium microprocessors. This appendix serves as a quick overview of some of the major, interesting non-Intel versions of Linux that are available. For a comprehensive list of Linux ports that are available, consult Linux Online's list of hardware port projects at `http://www.linux.org/projects/ports.html`.

Linux for the Compaq Alpha Processor

Compaq's Alpha CPU is widely hailed as an exemplary RISC CPU, offering one of the fastest processors on the market.

Linux for the Alpha CPU is perhaps among the most robust, stable, and highly tested versions of Linux for non-Intel hardware currently available. Everything from X Windows to networks to Web browsers works well, and emulation is even available to run many programs designed for the Intel *x*86 version of Linux. See `http://www.alphalinux.org` for more information about Linux for the Alpha CPU.

Linux for Alpha runs on numerous Compaq Alpha-based systems ranging from low-end Universal Desktop Boxes to high-end 64-bit CPU systems.

Red Hat offers a version of Red Hat Linux for the Alpha processor.

Embedded Linux

The ELKS (Embedded Linux Kernel Subset) project is aiming to create a version of Linux for embedded systems such as older 8086- and 80286-class PCs, palmtop computers, and embedded control systems. The current version of Linux available from the project runs on PCs and requires around 400 to 512K of RAM for a full system.

The current version is far from complete, offering only the ability to boot, use virtual consoles, access floppy disks, and run a collection of small programs. Work in progress includes microwindows, which is supposed to bring features of modern graphical user interfaces to smaller devices.

This is a development system, but it highlights the flexibility that enables Linux to run under a variety of hardware constraints. The ELKS project is online at `http://www.elks.ecs.soton.ac.uk/`.

Linux for Motorola 680x0 Processors

Linux/m68k is a port of Linux designed to run on Motorola 68020 through 68060 CPUs, such as those found in many Amiga, Atari, and Macintosh computers.

Robust, stable releases of Linux/m68k are currently available to run on Amiga, Atari, Macintosh, and NeXT computers, including the following systems:

- Amiga A2500
- Amiga A3000
- Amiga A3000T
- Amiga A4000/040
- Amiga A4000T/040
- Amiga A4000T/060
- Amiga DraCo (clone)
- Amiga BoXeR (clone)
- Atari Falcon
- Atari Falcon with AfterBurner 040
- Atari TT
- Atari Medusa (clone)
- Atari Hades (clone)
- HP 9000/300 workstations
- Macintosh II (several models)
- Macintosh SE/30
- Macintosh LC (several models)
- Macintosh Performa (several models)
- Macintosh Quadra (several models)
- Macintosh Centris (several models)
- NeXT workstations
- Q40 (Sinclair derivative)
- Sun 3 workstations (3/50, 3/60, 3/160)

Linux for MIPS Processors

Linux/MIPS is a port of Linux designed to run on most systems sporting MIPS processors, including the following:

- Acer PICA-61

- Compaq DECStation 5000/2x, 5000/100, and 3100

- MIPS Magnum 4000PC

- Olivetti M700-10

The current release is considered stable and includes networking and NFS support, with some shortcomings in support for on-board peripherals in some machines. While not quite up-to-date (the current version is based on Linux kernel 2.1.73), you can still put together a complete distribution from the software on the project's Web site. Linux/MIPS is on the Web at `http://lena.fnet.fr/`.

Linux for the Power Macintosh

MkLinux is an attempt to run Linux on the Open Group Mach microkernel running natively on the Power Macintosh line of computers. Microkernel architecture is designed to ease porting of the operating system, with the focus on porting the microkernel itself.

Apple Computer fully supports the MkLinux project, which has a Web site at `http://www.mklinux.org`. A complete distribution is currently available online or on CD-ROM.

Other projects aimed at porting Linux to the Power Macintosh include the PowerPC Linux distribution (which is discussed in the section on the PowerPC processor later in this appendix) and Powermac/Linux (`http://www.cs.wisc.edu/~tesch/linux_info/`). Both of these projects are versions of Linux that are native to the PowerPC processor (which is at the heart of Power Mac systems) instead of being layered on a microkernel. This design provides better performance but less portability to other hardware. The Powermac/Linux code, once a distinct project, has now been merged with the LinuxPPC source code developed by PowerPC Linux to produce one version of Linux for the PowerPC.

Apple has extended this version of Linux, known as Darwin, to its latest Mac OS X operating system. While the Mac OS X kernel is based on two other Unix clones (Carnegie-Mellon's Mach 3.0 and the Berkeley Standard Distribution version 4.4-lite), it still includes a substantial amount of Linux software.

Linux for PowerPC Processors

Great strides have been made in supporting Linux on the PowerPC processor family. The LinuxPPC project (http://www.linuxppc.org/) is managed and developed by PowerPC Linux. It offers a stable and complete distribution that runs a wide range of Power Macintosh computers, Amiga's Power-UP systems, the BeBox from Be Inc., PowerPC-based RS/6000, PReP, and CHRP systems from IBM, and workstations from Umax.

Supported applications and features include the following:

- PCI-bus systems
- SCSI and IDE hard disk drives
- Multimedia support
- Web browsers such as Netscape
- X Windows and a wide range of window managers
- Java JDK 1.2.2

A project is also under way to develop an emulator of the Mac OS to run inside Linux on the PowerPC, just as Wine is an attempt to develop a Windows emulator for Linux on the Intel x86 CPU. Part of the result is the recently released Mac OS X.

Linux for SPARC Processors

UltraLinux (http://www.ultralinux.org/), formerly known as S/Linux, is a project to port Linux to Sun's SPARC and UltraSPARC processors. Currently, the port is quite stable, and it even supports the newest 64-bit UltraSPARC-based workstations. As of this writing, Slackware and Debian have SPARC versions of their most recent distributions.

INDEX

Note to the Reader: Throughout this index **boldfaced** page numbers indicate primary discussions of a topic. *Italicized* page numbers indicate illustrations.

(

D

E

F

G

H

I

J

K

M

0

P

V

Y

Z

What's on the CD-ROM?

This book includes a CD-ROM. The disc contains the Publisher's Edition of Red Hat Linux 7.1 from Red Hat, Inc., which you may use in accordance with the license agreements accompanying the software.

Due to space constraints, certain components present in the official Red Hat Linux are not available in the Red Hat Linux Publisher's Edition. The Official Red Hat Linux, which you may purchase from Red Hat, includes the complete Official Red Hat Linux distribution, Red Hat's documentation, and may include technical support for Official Red Hat Linux. You also may purchase technical support from Red Hat. You may purchase Official Red Hat Linux and technical support from Red Hat through the company's Web site (www.redhat.com) or its toll-free number 1.888.REDHAT1.

System Requirements

- Pentium II CPU or equivalent or higher (While Red Hat Linux 7.1 will run on a 486 or Pentium/K5 system, the performance may not be worthwhile.)

- 32MB of RAM or more (You will notice a significant performance gain with 64MB or more of memory.)

- At least 1GB of hard disk space; 1.5GB for the Workstation or Laptop configurations (3GB or more will greatly enhance your freedom to experiment with Linux.)

- CD-ROM recommended (preferably a bootable ATAPI/IDE or SCSI drive)

- Red Hat Linux supports most modern Intel-compatible PC hardware. If you have questions about hardware compatibility with Red Hat Linux 7.1, check the hardware compatibility list at hardware.redhat.com.

- A backup of your current system in case of emergency

- A supported video card and monitor. See Red Hat's hardware compatibility list.

- A keyboard and mouse

Software Support

Components of the supplemental Software and any offers associated with them may be supported by the specific Owner(s) of that material but they are not supported by SYBEX. Information regarding any available support may be obtained from the Owner(s) using the information provided in the appropriate README files or listed elsewhere on the media.

Should the manufacturer(s) or other Owner(s) cease to offer support or decline to honor any offer, SYBEX bears no responsibility. This notice concerning support for the Software is provided for your information only. SYBEX is not the agent or principal of the Owner(s), and SYBEX is in no way responsible for providing any support for the Software, nor is it liable or responsible for any support provided, or not provided, by the Owner(s).